The Supporting Players
of
Television

1959-1983
Illustrated

by

JACK WARD

Lakeshore West Publishing Company

Cover Design by Susan Coman.

Printed by Walsworth Publishing Company, Marceline, Missouri

Cataloging-in-Publication Data

920   Ward, W. Jack, 1930
WAR   The Supporting players of television 1959-1983 / by Jack
         Ward : illustrated with over 500 photos. - Cleveland,
         Okla.; Lakeshore West Publishing, @ 1996.

            400 p.; ill.; cm.
            Includes bibliography (p.387)

          Summary: Profiles 500 television performers from shows
         aired between 1959 and 1983. Each profile contains a photo-
         graph, brief biography, career hightlights and a comprehensive
         list of guest credits of the period.

            ISBN 0-9653481-0-5

            1. Television actors and actresses - United States - Biography
         2. Television personalities - United States - Biography.
          I. Title

         PN1992.4   791.45'092 [B]-dc20

            Provided in cooperation with Unique Books, Inc.

            LCCN 96-094626

Manufactured in the United States of America

                         Lakeshore West Publishing Company
                                Post Office Box 314
                                Cleveland, OK 74020

Dedication

This book is dedicated to the deceased players in this book, those who have left this life but have given us a continuing legacy of carefully crafted interpretations of roles, large and small. Through syndicated reruns they live, and their wonderful work will remain for us to enjoy for decades.

During their lifetimes their work was viewed by tens of millions, and with worldwide distribution, by hundreds of millions of television viewers and movie goers. Even the least-known had roles that evoked laughter, tears, fear, anger and approval.

The intimacy of television made us feel that they were friends, invited guests in our homes, and we feel sorrow when we hear of their passing. It is the mark of the true artist who leaves a lasting legacy, whether it be a beautiful painting, a touching poem, a lovely piece of music or skilled acting that lingers in our memories for years.

Because of the period covered herein, 1959-1983, so many performers are deceased, and others are in frail health. Rarely a month passes that another familiar and respected name passes into eternity. Hopefullly, the following pages will help to keep their memories fresh in the mind of the reader.

Photo Credits

The photographs in this book, and on it's covers, are from my personal collection. Some of them were originally issued to publicize or promote television series or films made or distributed by the following companies to whom I offer grateful acknowledgement: ABC-TV, CBS Television, Columbia Pictures Corporation, Metro-Goldwyn Mayer, Inc., Metromedia Producer's Corporation, MGM-TV, NBC-TV, Paramount Pictures Corporation, United Artists Corporation, Universal City Studios, Inc., Universal-International, Universal Pictures and Universal Television. Individual photos by Maurice Manson and Cliff Riddle.

Cover photos of Pilar Seurat and Jason Evers are by courtesy of The Academy of Motion Picture Arts and Sciences.

Numerous photos were produced by agencies representing the artists for publicity purposes and for use in employment of the performers. Some were utilized in various issues of *The Academy Players Directories* to assist in matching performers with casting directors and studio employment personnel.

ON THE FRONT COVER

Upper left: Nancy Kovack (a.k.a. Nancy Mehta); upper right: Gregory Walcott; lower left: Harry Townes; lower right: Pilar Seurat; at right: Charles Aidman.

ON THE BACK COVER

Left row, from top: Ken Curtis, Karen Steele, and Jason Evers. Right row, from top: Susan Oliver, Ron Hayes, and Billy Mumy.

Contents

Dedication III

Photo Credits V

Introduction 1

Introduction

This book is a continuation, and affirmation, of a nearly lifelong appreciation of the contributions made to television (and films) by supporting players. It recognizes men and women whose faces and work are virtually forgotten unless you are fortunate enough to see them on syndicated reruns. Thankfully, cable provides daily and nightly reruns of the better television series of earlier years as an alternative to so much of the vulgarity being presented by major networks today.

Chronicled in *The Supporting Players of Television* are episode and telefilm credits, and biographies, of 500 of the more talented individuals who graced the small screen during the years 1959-83, a quarter of a century of wonderfully entertaining television. There is a photograph of each player to jog your memories, for some have been absent the medium for decades.

There are large numbers who were in television from it's infancy and worked well into the era covered by the book, and numerous others who came to television during the seventies and who continue to work today. Younger readers will remember many of the players from childhood viewing, while some will be familiar with their work only from seeing these talented individuals on today's reruns. It is my hope that this book does provide a continuing recognition of their talents.

Some may wonder, if I cover 25 years, why not start at something like 1960 and run until 1985? A fair question, but an easy one for me. The 1959-1983 period is a time frame in which I watched the most episodic television, and the period with which I am most familiar with TV series and actors. I am simply not knowledgeable of many actors who have come on the scene in more recent years.

The book covers dramatic series only, and does not include credits for sitcoms. Sixties and seventies sitcoms provided so many pleasant hours of viewing for my family, and for me, but the book would be unwieldy if they were included in actors' individual credits. And those credits are widely available, for virtually every popular series of that period has one or more books available detailing every facet, every episode and providing guest credits in a comprehensive manner.

This is the second book that I have written on supporting players. The first, *Television Guest Stars* (McFarland and Co., Inc-1993), covered a period from 1960-1979, incorporating the chronologies of actors with 15 or more guest credits during the inclusive period. A majority were career-long supporting or character players, but some became major TV and film stars. Actors like Telly Savalas, Charles Bronson, Robert Duvall and Gene Hackman did numerous TV guest shots early in their careers and qualified for inclusion in the book.

658 actors were chronicled in the previous book (with over 500 photographs), and to hold it's size to one volume, I excluded the western TV series genre, with the exception of *Gunsmoke* and a few "modern" westerns. If you are western TV series buffs you will see virtually every significant player of that genre who provided support to the series stars, in this book. **The criteria for inclusion in this book is 12 guest credits during 1959-1981, inclusive**.

Regarding the individual actors' chronicles, some general concepts of format should be provided. I have endeavored to give as comprehensive as possible biographical information: birthdates, birthplaces, dates of death, education and acting training/experience. Where possible I have indicated when stage, film and television debuts took place, for they are important milestones in the lives of each performer. To add career "flavor" I have listed prominent film credits, especially for character actors whose work might not be as familiar to some.

Each performer's television series regular credits are indicated in the text of their bios., and important soap opera stints are listed, for they contribute significantly to the body of work for many actors. Since this book chronicles guest credits for the period 1959 to 1983, inclusive, significant credits for the period preceding this coverage are provided by series name only, generally without air dates, simply to give an idea of early work, as appropriate. For more contemporary actors, the same concept is applied for post-1983 guest work going into the late eighties. Multiple appearances on a series or program are indicated within parentheses. Inasmuch as sitcom credits are not detailed, actor's bios. may have sitcom credits, by series name only—if, in my opinion, they were an important part of the body of work.

Each of the 500 performers in this book have their 1959-83 guest credits chronicled by television series, episode names, and original air dates. I have endeavored to be as comprehensive and accurate in these credits as possible, utilizing micofilm of back-dated issues of *TV Guide* and several other reference sources. I have gleaned countless credits for small roles by watching the closing credits on syndicated reruns, for they are not listed in any sources.

And a couple of brief notes of explanation would be appropriate at this point. When I use the term "actor", in some cases it includes men and women, for use of the term actress if fading from today's vocabularies, and "actor" often has no implied gender. Secondly, the term "supporting" actor in my definition herein refers to members of guest casts on episodic television or members of large casts of TV anthologies. Some of the players in this book were generally described as "leading men" or "leading women" for much of their careers and the "support" designation is not intended to derogate. For purposes of this book, the numerous "character" players are also considered as "supporting" actors.

Approximately 36 of the 500 actors in this book were "carryovers" from *Televison Guest Stars*, primarily to incorporate, and chronicle, their large number of TV western series credits that did not appear in my previous book. The two books of mine, combined, chronicle over 1,100 players and I hope that you see all your favorites in one of my works. But it's likely that some will say "But I didn't see anything on ....". Some series stars are not chronicled in either of my two books, but I have endeavored to incorporate photographs in which many of them appeared, in order to commerate their contributions to the era. Some who come to mind are James Arness, Richard Boone, Mike Connors, William Conrad, Buddy Ebsen and Barbara Stanwyck.

I'd like to add some personal reasons for having such a continuing interest in supporting players. I'm from a generation that greatly anticipated Saturday matinees, a weekly event that totally immersed us for entire afternoons. For a dime or a quarter we could see an episode of a cliff-hanger serial and a "B" western double feature—enough action to satiate us for another week.

Early on, I became intrigued with learning the names of the heavies, the adversaries of Roy Rogers, Gene Autry, Charles Starrett and all the others who wore the white hats. Most of the heavies were not listed on the lobby cards, so I had to watch the cast lists in the hope I could identify some of the performers with whom I was particularly impressed. Four of my favorite "bad guys" from the forties are pictured below:

Roy Barcroft   **Kenne Duncan**

George J. Lewis   **Ken Terrell**

This book, and the one that preceded it, are direct outgrowths of this early fascination with the actors who always got their lumps from the heroes, but were back week after week, practicing their particular style of villainy.

As a youngster I had an opportunity to meet Gene Autry, a very nice man, but the highlight of my young years was a Saturday afternoon visit to the old Republic Studios in North Hollywood. There, during a break between shots on a western set, a familiar husky figure came striding up to me, shook my hand and said "Hi, I'm Roy Barcroft". I shall never forget his response to my question, "Do you really like acting?" His reply, "It beats the heck out of working for a living", really didn't describe his acting career, for he had hundreds of film and television credits, and he worked steadily until his death in 1967. My chat with Roy cemented my feeling about supporting players and I have since met many like him: down-to-earth, hard working and without the ego problems of some of today's film and TV stars.

During the late fifties, after college and military service, I became a much more frequent television viewer. And I found my fascination with learning the names of supporting players hadn't abated. But the dozens of weekly TV episodes, with hundreds of guest players, created a bit of a blur for a time.

But cream rises to the top, and I began to identity many of those players whose superb work I saw repeated often, and began to watch for their names in opening credits, or if not there, to look for their faces during the episodes, and hopefully verify their names in closing credits. That process surely enhanced my enjoyment of television for many years, during countless episodes of my most watched shows.

Which brings me to a current time frame; by the time I wrote my first book, in 1992, I had mentally catalogued hundreds of performers that had enriched my television years. I was determined to bring those names and faces to the reading public, for existing reference books on television actors skipped over many of my favorite performers. And there were also pictorial books on supporting actors of the thirties, forties and fifties, but very little on performers of recent years. So I feel my books definitely fill a void in recognition of so many talented people.

And I believe that constantly increasing availability , and viewing, of reruns makes my books especially relevant today, for the actors chronicled appeared often in syndicated series from the 1959-83 period.

I have also included all telefilm (also known as Movie-of-the-Week, and MMTV, Movies Made for Television) credits for actors herein. Telefilm credits are from the 1964 inception of the telefilm form through the inclusive 1983 period. Miniseries credits were excluded, inasmuch as there were at least three episodes; many of the actors appeared in only one or two of them, and it was impossible to verify dates and episodes that they appeared in.

Telefilms, especially in the early years, added a great deal to TV viewing enjoyment. Many were quite memorable, and I well remember some that I haven't seen for over 20 years. Some that I regard as particularly memorable were: *The Borgia Stick* (1967), *Night Gallery* (1969), *Silent Night, Lonely Night* (1969), *Duel* (1971), *Brian's Song* (1971), *Evil Roy Slade* (1972), *The Night Stalker* (1972), *Haunts of the Very Rich* (1972), *Death Be Not Proud* (1975), *The Dark Secret of Harvest Home* (1978) and *Bill* (1981). They were full of drama, love, adventure, suspense and comedy—so well written and acted.   These come to mind, but there were dozens of offerings from some of the best writers in Hollywood that I'm sure most of you remember well as excellent entertainment. And the telefilms provided a great deal of work for the fine actors of the era.

It probably sounds like I am on a great nostalgia kick, often because I am like millions of Americans who find in reruns the values that so many are desperately seeking to restore in our society: respect for others, civility, apprehension and punishment of violent criminals, virtue appreciated and respected, personal responsibility taught and reinforced early in life, with marriage and families the glue that holds the whole fabric together. A steadily increasing number of viewers, sickened by the vulgarity and negative values of today's TV, are turning to reruns of an earlier time. And they are appreciating what they see!

It is my hope, and intent, that this book will enhance your enjoyment of those much loved and appreciated series of a very special era in television.

5

The Supporting Players of Television
1959-1983

Rodolpho Acosta
(born 1920, Mexico; died 1974)

Rodolpho came to the U.S. from his native Mexico at age 3 and later attended L.A. City College and U.C.L.A. During World War II he served in the Intelligence Branch of the U.S. Navy. After a 1947 film debut he was often cast as banditos and appeared in some significant films: *One Eyed Jacks, The Second Time Around, How the West Was Won, The Sons of Katie Elder* and *Return of the Seven.* Following numerous TV guest roles, Rudolpho received a series regular role on *High Chaparral* (1967-1971). He last appeared on television in 1973.

GUEST CREDITS

1959 *Rawhide* "Incident of the Power and the Plow" 2-13; *Have Gun-Will Travel* 4-25; *Rebel* episode 10-18; **1961** *One Step Beyond* "Persons Unknown" 2-7; *Have Gun-Will Travel* "Fandango" 3-4; **1962** *Maverick* "Poker Face" 1-7; **1963** *Virginian* "The Mountain of the Sun" 4-17; **1964** *Rawhide* "Incident at Gila Flats 1-30; *Bob Hope Chrysler Theater* "Turncoat" 10-23; **1965** *Big Valley* "The Way to Kill a Killer" 11-24; *Daniel Boone* "The Thanksgiving Story" 11-25; **1966** *Daniel Boone* "Grizzly" 10-6; *Iron Horse* "Cougar Man" 10-24; *Fugitive* "Wine Is a Traitor" 11-1; 1968 *Bonanza* "Yonder Man" 12-8; **1969** *Mission: Impossible* "The Vault" 4-6; **1970** *Bonanza* "El Jefe" 11-15; **1971** *Bold Ones: The Lawyers* "The Search for Leslie Gray" 1-10; *Cade's County* "Crisscross" 10-10; *O'Hara, U.S. Treasury* "Operation: Heroin" 10-29; **1973** *Ironside* "The Helping Hand" 11-1.

TELEFILMS

1967 *Strangers on the Run* 10-31 NBC; **1970** *Run Simon Run* 12-1 ABC.

Wesley Addy
(born August 4, 1913, Omaha, Nebraska)

Wesley Addy made his stage debut in 1935 and came to the screen in 1951. Among his numerous films were *Whatever Happened to Baby Jane?, Hush...Hush, Sweet Charlotte, Mister Buddwing,*

Tora! Tora! Tora! and *Network*. In 1961 Wesley was
wed to famed actress Celeste Holm.

He began working in television in 1950 and
appeared in countless live dramas from New York.
Addy worked on the soap *The Edge of Night* during
1958-59 and followed with guest work through much
of the sixties and into the seventies. He became a
regular on the soap *Ryan's Hope* during 1977-78, but
his best known TV work came when he joined the
cast of the soap *Loving* as Cabot Alden in 1983, a
role he continued until 1991.

GUEST CREDITS

1961 *Armstrong Circle Theater* "The Spy Next
Door" 2-15; **1962** *Perry Mason* "The Case of the
Weary Watchdog" 11-29; **1965** *Outer Limits* "The
Brain of Colonel Barham" 1-2; *Fugitive* "Conspiracy
of Silence" 10-12; *The FBI* "All the Streets Are
Silent" 11-28; **1966** *Perry Mason* "The Case of the
Tsarina's Tiara" 3-20; *I Spy* "Crusade to Limbo" 3-
23; *The FBI* "The Plunderers" 4-24; *12 O'Clock
High* "Burden of Guilt" 12-2; **1967** *Invaders*
"Doomsday Minus One" 2-28; **1969** *The FBI* "The
Fraud" 1-12; *The FBI* "Silent Partners" 10-12; **1970**
Ironside "Goodwill Tour" 3-26; **1973** *Medical
Center* "No Margin for Error" 2-7; **1977** *Andros
Targets* "In the Event of My Death" 2-12; *Rockford
Files* "Dirty Money, Black Light" 4-1.

TELEFILMS

1977 *Love Boat II* 1-21 ABC; *Tail Gunner Joe* 2-6
NBC; **1983** *Rage of Angels* 2-20, 2-21 NBC.

Charles Aidman

(born January 31, 1925, Frankfort, Indiana; died
November 7, 1993)

The son of a physician, Charles Aidman was
like many other boys of his era-very preoccupied
with sports. He became a fine athlete and earned a
football scholarship to Indiana University. A broken
arm suffered on the gridiron ended his playing days
and he concentrated on drama courses. He felt
acting would compensate for an innate shyness.

Charles served in the U.S. Navy from 1946-48,
earning the rank of Lieutenant.

Following military service his growing acting
talent led him to turn down a teaching position at
Indiana University and move to New York City's
Neighborhood Playhouse where he studied with
Sanford Meisner. During his struggling days he sold
toys at Bloomingdale's to help make ends meet. He
played Marc Anthony in the first New York
Shakespear Festival production of *Julius Caesar*, in
1956. His stage career begain in 1957, playing the
lead in *Career*; he continued to do stage work
throughout his life.

His incredibly prolific television career began
with a 1954 role on *The Web*, followed by fifties
work on *Star Tonight*, *Kraft Television Theatre*, *Big
Story*, *Matinee Theatre*, *Have Gun-Will Travel* and
Gunsmoke. When he came to Hollywood, he helped
found Theater West (with Curt Conway and Joyce
Van Patten) and was instrumental in developing the
free-verse poems of Edgar Lee Masters into a play,
writing lyrics himself and directing it. The play,
Spoon River Anthology, was originally performed by
the theater group at U.C.L.A. and then moved to
Broadway in 1969.

Aidman guested on virtually every significant
television series from 1959 until 1983. He played
every type of role, but the ones that suited him best
were those requiring a quiet strength, sincerity and

humility, Gary Cooper-like qualities that he conveyed so well. He was never a TV series regular, but did have a recurring role on *Wild Wild West*, filling in admirably while series co-star Ross Martin was recuperating from a heart attack. Later, his voice was heard as narrator on the *New Twilight Zone* series (1985-86). His calm and soothing voice made him a sough-after talent for numerous television commercials: U.S. Air, Toyota, Minolta, American Airlines and banking associations.

Perhaps Charles' finest role of a distinguished career came in 1964-65 in a touring company of Arthur Miller's *After the Fall*, playing the lead role of Quentin. He was on stage the entire three hours, involved in every scene. The reviews convey a sense of his wonderful work: *St. Louis Dispatch* "Aidman is magnificent!"; *San Francisco Examiner* "Aidman gives a moving, appealing superb portrayal"; *Oakland Tribune* "Aidman gives a masterful portrayal…Theatrical magic!"; *Variety* "Aidman is a forceful actor and shows dramatic power".

Charles was married from February 9, 1969 to actress-choreographer Betty Hyatt Linton. Their happy union was ended on November 7, 1993 when Charles succumbed to cancer. A stepson, Chuck, also survived. To those who were fortunate to see him work his magic onstage, and to the countless millions who saw him in hundreds of television roles, he left a legacy of beautifully crafted interpretations.

GUEST CREDITS

1959 *Californians* "Crimps' Meat 1-27; *Wanted: Dead or Alive* "Competition" 1-31; *Trackdown* "The Samaritan" 2-18; *One Step Beyond* "Epilogue" 2-24; *Richard Diamond* "Private Detective" 4-19; *Colt .45* "The Confession" 4-26; *Black Saddle* "Client Neal Adams" 5-9; *Millionaire* "Millionaire Lorraine Daggett" 9-30; *Wanted: Dead or Alive* "Estralita" 10-3; *Zane Grey Theater* "Confession" 10-15; *Richard Diamond* "The Runaway" 11-2; *Twilight Zone* "And When the Sky Was Opened" 12-11; **1960** *Wichita Town* "Ruby Dawes" 1-16; *Have Gun-Will Travel* "Return to Fort Benjamin" 1-30; *Perry Mason* "The Case of the Gallant Grafter" 2-6; *Gunsmoke* "Unwanted Deputy" 3-5; *Rawhide*

"Incident at Sulphur Creek" 3-11; *Wagon Train* "The Amos Gibbon Story" 4-20; *Peter Gunn* "Witness in the Window" 5-2; *Johnny Ringo* "The Stranger" 5-19; *Have Gun-Will Travel* "The Search" 6-18; *M Squad* "The Bad Apple" 6-28; *Outlaws* "Ballad for a Badman" 10-6; *Thriller* "Knock Three-One-Two" 12-13; *Wagon Train* "The River Crossing" 12-14; *One Step Beyond* "The Legacy of Love" 12-20; **1961** *Americans* "The Rebellious Rose" 2-13; *Gunsmoke* "About Chester" 2-25; *Law and Mr. Jones* "Mea Culpa"4-7; *Bonanza* "The Rival" 4-15; *Thriller* "Terror in Teakwood" 5-16; *Rebel* "Ben White" 5-28; *Wagon Train* "The Janet Hale Story" 5-31; *Adventures in Paradise* "Nightmare in the Sun" 6-19; *Michael Shayne* "Murder 'Round My Wrist" 7-7; *New Breed* "No Fat Cops" 10-3; *Tall Man* "Shadow of the Past" 10-7; *Detectives* "A Piece of Tomorrow" 11-10; *Rawhide* "The Blue Sky" 12-8; *Target: The Corruptors* "Prison Empire" 12-15; *Laramie* "The Jailbreakers" 12-19; **1962** *87th Precinct* "King's Ransom" 2-19; *Twilight Zone* "Little Girl Lost" 3-16; *Dr. Kildare* "One for the Road" 4-12; *Wide Country* "Who Killed Eddie Gannon?" 10-11;

Virginian "The Devil's Children" 12-5; **1963** *Defenders* "Poltergeist" 1-26; *G.E. True* "Security Risk" 3-3; *Nurses* "Security Risk" 4-11; *Kraft Suspense Theatre* "The Case Against Paul Ryker" 10-10; **1964** *Arrest and Trial* "Modus Operandi" 3-15; *DuPont Show of the Week* "Don't Go Upstairs" 5-17; *Nurses* "A Postcard from Yucatan" 5-28; *Slattery's People* "Question: Do the Ignorant Sleep in Pure White Beds?" 11-30; **1965** *Fugitive* "Trial by Fire" 10-5; *Man Called Shenandoah* "The Siege" 12-13; **1966** *Run for Your Life* "Night of Terror" 1-31; *12 O'Clock High* "Day of Reckoning" 3-28; *Voyage to the Bottom of the Sea* "Werewolf" 9-25; *Felony Squad* "A Date with Terror" 10-10; *Bob Hope Chrylser Theater* "Crazier Than Cotton "10-12; **1967** *Run for Your Life* "Cry Hard, Cry Fast" 11-22, 11-29; **1968** *Felony Squad* "Bed of Strangers" 1-1; *Invaders* "The Pit" 1-16; *High Chaparral* "Champion of the Western World" 2-4; *The FBI* "The Tunnel" 4-21; *Mission: Impossible* "Heir Apparent" 9-19; *Ironside* "Shell Game" 9-19; *Wild Wild West* "The Night of the Camera" 11-29; *Wild Wild West* "The Night of Miguelito's Revenge" 12-13; *Outcasts* "The Bounty Children" 12-23; *Wild Wild West* "The Night of the Pelicans" 12-27; *Gunsmoke* "The Money Store" 12-30; **1969** *Wild Wild West* "The Night of the Janus" 2-14; *Gunsmoke* "The Intruders" 3-3; *Bold Ones: The Lawyers* "Rockford Riddle" 11-16; **1970** *Hawaii Five-0* "Nightmare Road" 2-18; *Virginian* "No War for the Warrior" 2-18; *Mod Squad* "The Loser" 4-7; *Medical Center* "The Clash" 10-14; *San Francisco International Airport* "Crisis" 11-18; *Interns* "An Act of God" 11-20; **1971** *Mannix* "A Gathering of Ghosts" 2-6; *Name of the Game* "The Broken Puzzle" 3-12; **1972** *Man and the City* "Diagnosis: Corruption" 1-5; *Mannix* "Moving Target" 1-9; *Ghost Story* "Alter-Ego" 10-27; *Rookies* "Rabbits on the Runway" 12-25; **1973** *Emergency* episode 1-24; *Wide World of Mystery* "The Picture of Dorian Grey" 4-23; **1974** *Hec Ramsey* "Scar Tissue" 3-10; *Hec Ramsey* "Only Birds and Fools" 4-7; *Kolchak: The Night Stalker*" The Zombie 9-20; *Barnaby Jones* "The Challenge" 9-24; *Nakia* "A Matter of Choice" 12-7; **1975** *Kung Fu* "The Last Raid" 4-26; *Blue Knight* "Odds Against Tomorrow" 12-31; **1976** *Cannon* "Madman" 3-3; *S.W.A.T.* "Any Second Now" 3-13; *Spencer's Pilots* "The Crop Duster" 10-

8; **1977** *Six Million Dollar Man* "Fires of Hell" 1-30; *Little House on the Prairie* "The Election" 3-21; *Rockford Files* "The Mayor's Committee from Deer Lick Falls" 11-25; **1978** *Kojak* "Justice for All" 1-7; *Police Woman* "Shadow on the Sea" 3-8; **1979** *Quincy,M.E.* "Walk Softly Through the Night" 2-1; *Quincy, M.E.* "Nowhere to Run" 11-8; *Lou Grant* "Andrew" 12-10; **1980** *Quincy, M.E.* "The Hope of Elkwood" 12-3; **1981** *Quincy,M.E.* "D.U.I." 12-2; **1982** *Magnum, P.I.* "Computer Date" 1-14; *Today's FBI* "Blue Collar" 2-21; *Quincy, M. E.* "Sleeping Dogs" 11-17; **1983** *Dallas* episodes 11-11, 11-18.

TELEFILMS

1968 *The Sound of Anger* 12-10 NBC; **1973** *Deliver Us from Evil* 9-11 ABC; **1974** *The Red Badge of Courage* 12-3 NBC; **1975** *Barbary Coast* 5-4 ABC; **1976** *Amelia Earhart* 10-25 NBC; **1980** *Alcatraz: The Whole Shocking Story* 11-5, 11-6 NBC; **1982** *Marian Rose White* 1-9 CBS; *Prime Suspect* 1-20 CBS.

Claude Akins

(born May 25, 1918, Nelson, Georgia; died January 27, 1994)

After attending Northwestern University in Evanston, Illinois, Claude worked as a salesman in Indiana before joining Barter Theatre for a season. He then spent several years traveling with touring companies.

Moving to California, he made his film debut in 1953 and appeared in *From Here to Eternity* later in the year. The following year he had a nice role in *The Caine Mutiny*; his later films included *Rio Bravo, Inherit the Wind, How the West Was Won, Return of the Seven* and *Battle for the Planet of the Apes.*

In television from 1954, he made an appearance on *Gunsmoke* in 1956 and went to work in 70 TV western series episodes. Other mid-fifties work included guest appearances on *Perry Mason, Alfred Hitchcock Presents* (2), *I Love Lucy, The Millionaire, Richard Diamond* and *General Electric Theater.*

Although the bulk of his guest work was on western series, he branched out to shows like *The Twilight Zone, The Fugitive, Combat* (2), *Mission: Impossible, Love, American Style* and *Hallmark Hall of Fame*. In 1974 he gained his first series regular role, co-starring in *Movin' On*, a series that ran until 1976. He was heavily involved in seventies telefilms, appearing in a total of sixteen.

A character that he played while performing as a regular on *B. J. and the Bear*, Sheriff Elroy P. Lobo, was spun off into a starring series for Akins, variously called *The Misadventures of Sheriff Lobo* and simply, *Lobo* (1979-81). He was slated for a series regular slot on *Murder, She Wrote* (appearing in four 1984 fall episodes), but he decided against the grind of another series. He returned to guest roles during the mid-eighties, in shows like *Hotel* (2), *The Love Boat* (2), *Crazy Like a Fox* and *The New Mike Hammer*.

During the early nineties Claude became a television and radio pitchman for AAMCO Transmissions and other national products and services. Stricken with cancer, he died on January 27, 1994, leaving the memory of a very unique and powerful personna. He was survived by his wife, two daughters and a son.

GUEST CREDITS

1959 *Loretta Young Show* "Sister Ann" 1-11; *77 Sunset Strip* "Lovely Alibi" 2-20; *Restless Gun* "Melany" 3-2; *Yancy Derringer* "Collector's Item" 3-26; *Loretta Young Show* "Trouble in Fenton Valley" 5-10; *Bat Masterson* "The Death of Bat Masterson" 5-20; *Riverboat* "Escape to Memphis" 10-25; *Texan* "Border Incident" 12-7; **1960**

Rawhide "Incident of the Druid Curse" 1-8; *Laramie* "Death Wind" 2-2; *Bonanza* "Desert Justice" 2-20; *Law of the Plainsman* "A Question of Courage" 2-25; *Untouchables* "The Unhired Assassin" 2-25, 3-3; *Twilight Zone* "The Monsters Are Due on Maple Street" 3-4; *Overland Trail* "Fire in the Hole" 4-17; *Wanted: Dead or Alive* "Prison Trail" 5-14; *Alaskans* "The Silent Land" 5-15; *Rifleman* "Meeting at Midnight" 5-17; *Laramie* "Queen of Diamonds" 9-20; *Bonanza* "The Mill" 10-1; *Rebel* "The Waiting" 10-9; *Rifleman* "Strange Town" 10-25; *Tall Man* "Wagon Train to Tularosa" 11-5; *Zane Grey Theater* "Ransom" 11-12; *Klondike* "Swoger's Mules" 11-21; *Surfside 6* "The International Set" 12-5; *Riverboat* "Duel on the River" 12-12; *Wagon Train* "The Roger Bigelow Story" 12-21; **1961** *Tales of Wells Fargo* "The Hand That Shook the Hand" 2-6; *Shirley Temple Theater* "The Peg Leg

Pirate of Sulu" 3-12; *Rawhide* "Incident of the Lost Idol" 4-28; *Bonanza* "Sam Hill" 6-3; *Deputy* "Lorinda Belle" 6-24; *Route 66* "Blue Murder" 9-29; *Rawhide* "The Sendoff" 10-6; *Tales of Wells Fargo* "The Dodger" 10-7; *Surfside 6* "A Matter of Seconds" 11-27; *Roaring 20's* "So's Your Old Man" 12-2; **1962** *Frontier Circus* "The Balloon Girl" 1-11; *Bus Stop* "The Stubborn Stumbos" 1-21; *Gunsmoke* "He Learned About Women" 2-24; *Outlaws* "Charge!" 3-22; *Twilight Zone* "The Little People" 3-30; *Untouchables* "The Monkey Wrench" 7-5; *Laramie* "Among the Missing" 9-25; *Empire* "Ride to a Fall" 10-16; *Hawaiian Eye* "There'll Be Some Changes Made" 10-16; *Bonanza* "The Deserter" 10-21; *Wide Country* "Straightjacket foran Indian" 10-25; *Rawhide* "Incident of the Four Horsemen" 10-26; *Alfred Hitchcock* Presents "Day of Reckoning" 11-22; *Virginian* "West" 11-28; *Gunsmoke* "The Way It Was" 12-1; *Rawhide* "Incident at Quivera" 12-14; **1963** *Alcoa Premiere* "The Hat of Sgt. Martin" 2-7; *Untouchables* "The Spoilers" 3-23; *Dick Powell Show* "Epilogue" 4-2; *Dakotas* "The Chooser of the Slain" 4-22; *Empire* "65 Miles Is a Long, Long Way" 4-23; *Laramie* "Trapped" 5-14; **1964** *Rawhide* "Incident of the Rusty Shotgun" 1-9; *Destry* "The Solid Gold Girl" 2-14; *Fugitive* "Never Stop Running" 3-31; *Kraft Suspense Theatre* "Operation Greif" 10-8; *Mr. Novak* "One Monday Afternoon" 10-27; *Gunsmoke* "Innocence" 12-12; **1965** *Branded* "The Vindicator" 1-31; *Daniel Boone* "The Place of 1000 Spirits" 2-4; *Slattery's People* "How Do We Hang the Good Samaritan?" 2-19; *Gunsmoke* "Gilt Built" 5-1; *Rawhide* "Walk Into Terror" 10-5; *Man Called Shenandoah* "Obion-1866" 10-22; *Virginian* "The Laramie Road" 12-8; *The FBI* "How to Murder an Iron Horse" 12-12; *Big Valley* "The Brawlers" 12-15; *Man from UNCLE* "The Very Important Zombie Affair" 12-31; **1966** *Legend of Jesse James* "The Colt" 1-17; *Laredo* "Limit of Law Larkin" 1-27; *Combat* "Ask Me No Questions" 2-8; *Laredo* "The Treasure of San Diablo" 2-17; *Gunsmoke* "Snap Decision" 9-17; *Monroes* "Ride with Terror" 9-21; *Combat* "Ollie Joe" 9-27; **1967** *Laredo* "Hey Diddle Diddle" 2-24; *Combat* "Nightmare on the Red Ball Run" 2-28; *Laredo* "A Question of Guilt" 3-10; *Gunsmoke* "Ladies from St. Louis" 3-25; *Laredo* "Walk Softly" 3-31; *Guns of Will Sonnett* episode 9-

8; *Hondo* "Hondo and the Gladiators" 12-15; *Judd, for the Defense* "Everyone Loved Harlow But His Wife" 12-29; **1968** *Garrison's Gorillas* "Ride with Terror" 1-30; *Outsider* "Along Came a Spider" 10-2; **1972** *McMillan and Wife* "The Face of Murder" 1-5; *Longstreet* "Eye of the Storm" 1-20; *Gunsmoke* "The Predators" 1-31; *The FBI* "Dark Journey" 3-12; **1973** *Hec Ramsey* "The Mystery of the Yellow Rose" 1-28; *Mission: Impossible* "Speed" 2-16; *Barnaby Jones* "Murder-Go-Round" 2-18; *Medical Center* "Time of Darkness" 9-17; *Rookies* "Margin for Error" 9-17; *Cannon* "Target in the Mirror" 10-3; *Police Story* "The Ten Year Honeymoon" 10-23; *Marcus Welby, M.D.* "A Cry in the Night" 12-11; **1974** *Streets of San Francisco* "A String of Puppets" 2-7; *McCloud* "The Colorado Cattle Caper" 2-24; *Mannix* "Mask for a Charade" 3-3; *Toma* "The Accused" 5-10; **1975** *Hallmark Hall of Fame* "Eric" 11-10; **1976** *Police Story* "The Long Ball" 2-13; **1977** *Oregon Trail* "Trapper'sRendezvous" 10-12; **1981** *Darkroom* "Uncle George" 12-4.

TELEFILMS

1971 *Lock, Stock and Barrel* 9-24 NBC; *River of Mystery* 10-1 NBC; **1972** *The Night Stalker* ABC; **1973** *The Norliss Tapes* 2-21 NBC; **1974** *The Death Squad* 1-8 ABC; *In Tandem* 5-8 NBC; **1975** *Medical Story* 9-4 NBC; **1976** *Kiss Me, Kill Me* 5-8 ABC; **1977** *Yesterday's Child* 2-3 NBC; **1977** *Killer on Board* 10-10 NBC; *Tarantulas: The Deadly Cargo* 12-28 CBS; **1978** *Little Mo* 9-5 NBC; *B. J. and the Bear* 10-4 NBC; **1979** *Murder in Music City* 1-6 NBC; *Ebony, Ivory and Jade* 8-3 CBS; *Concrete Cowboys* 10-17 CBS.

Marc Alaimo

(born May 5, Milwaukee, Wisconsin)

Educated at Marquette University, Marc developed an early enthuiasm for theater. He spent nine years in classical repertory theatre, with numerous Shakespearean roles: Cassius in *Julius Caesar*, Iago in *Othello* and Laertes in *Hamlet*.

He came to Hollywood during the early seventies and gained a role on the soap *Somerset*. He

Hunter "The Hit" 3-11; *Kingston: Confidential* "The Rage at Hannibal" 6-8; Six Million Dollar Man "Sharks" 9-11, 9-18; *Bionic Woman* "African Connection" 10-29; **1978** *CHiPs* "Vintage '54" 1-26; *Kojak* "In Full Command" 3-18; *American Girls* "Torch" 10-14; *Incredible Hulk* "Alice in Disco Land" 11-3; **1979** *Kaz* "A Piece of Cake" 3-7; *Wonder Woman* "The Phantom of the Roller Coaster" 9-14, 9-11; *Incredible Hulk* "The Slam" 10-19; **1980** *Quincy, M.E.* "Raid!" 1-31; *Incredible Hulk* "Nine Hours" 4-4; **1981** *CHiPs* "Diamond in the Rough" 11-22; **1982** *McClain's Law* "Takeover" 3-6; *Greatest American Hero* "There's Just No Accounting…" 3-24; *Phoenix* "One of Them" 4-2; *Knight Rider* "Slammin' Stanley's Stunt Spectacular" 10-22.

TELEFILMS

1974 *Cage Without a Key* 3-14 CBS; **1975** *Matt Helm* 5-7 ABC; *The Blue Knight* 5-9 CBS; **1976** *Helter Skelter* 4-1, 4-2 CBS; **1977** *The 3,000 Mile Chase* 6-16 NBC; **1979** *High Midnight* 11-27 CBS; **1981** *The Archer: Fugitive from Empire* 4-12 ABC; *Broken Promise* 5-5 CBS; **1982** *The Ambush Murders* 1-5 CBS.

began guesting on TV series in 1974, appearing often in crime series like *Police Story* (4), *Rockford Files* and *Kojak*. Tall and slender, Marc was ideal in villainous roles, adopting a malevolent mien.

Marc was busy during the eighties in telefilms and continuing guest roles, including 8 episodes of *Hill Street Blues*. He appeared in contemporary hit films like *Total Recall*, *Tango and Cash*, and a featured role in *The Dead Pool*. Currently he has a recurring role as Dakat, the Cardassian on *Star Trek: Deep Space Nine*. *Star Trek: The Next Generation* used his talents in four episodes.

Uniquely, Marc shares a May 5 birthdate with both a son and a daughter.

GUEST CREDITS

1974 *Police Story* "Country Boy" 2-19; *Toma* "Indictment" 4-26; *Police Story* "A Dangerous Age" 9-10; *Rockford Files* "The Dark and Bloody Ground" 9-20; *Gunsmoke* "The Iron Man" Oct. 21; **1976** *Blue Knight* "The Candy Man" 2-4; *Police Story* "Open City" 3-12; *Baretta* "Aggie" 3-24; *Police Story* "Three Days to Thirty" 11-9; **1977**

Chris Alcaide

(born 1928)

One of the busiest actors of the TV western series dominated era of the latefifties/early sixties, Chris played dozens of bad guys on the top series of the era. He was a special favorite on The *Rifleman*, with 8 guest appearances. He worked often in television from 1955 (including several fifties *Gunsmoke* episodes) through 1967.

GUEST CREDITS

1959 *Perry Mason* "The Case of the Shattered Dream" 1-3; *Have Gun-Will Travel* "The Scorched Feather" 2-4; *Rawhide* "Incident of the Dry Drive" 4-22; *Texan* "Image of Guilt" 5-25; *Wanted: Dead or Alive* "Estralita" 10-3; *Black Saddle* "The Long Rider" 10-16; *Rifleman* "Obituary" 10-20; *Law of the Plainsman* "Blood Trails" 11-5; *Wanted: Dead or Alive* "Chain Gang" 12-12; *Lawman* "The Shelter" 12-27; *Law of the Plainsman* "Calculated Risk" 12-31; **1960** *Richard Diamond* "Popskull" 1-4; *Rifleman* "A Case of Identity" 1-19; *Tales of Wells Fargo* "Forty Four-Four" 2-29; *Bonanza* "Escape to the Ponderosa" 3-5; *Rifleman* "A Time for Singing" 3-8; *Texan* "Presentation Gun" 4-4; *Law of the Plainsman* "Amnesty" 4-7; *Rawhide* "Incident of the Arana Scar" 4-22; *Rifleman* "Meeting at Midnight" 5-17; *Rifleman* "Dead Cold Cash" 11-22; **1961** *Rifleman* "Wyoming Story" 2-7, 2-14; *Klondike* "The Hostages" 2-13; *Gunsmoke* "Big Man" 3-25; *Lawman* "Cold Fear" 6-1; *Tall Man* "The Liberty Bell" 9-16; *Rifleman* "The Journey Back" 10-30; *Rawhide* "Incident of the Inside Man" 11-3; **1962** "*Have Gun-Will Travel* "Justice in Hell" 1-6; *Cheyenne* "The Quick and the Deadly" 10-22; *Laramie* "The Sunday Shoot" 11-13; *Rifleman* "Squeeze Play" 12-3; *Perry Mason* "The Case of the Lurid Letter" 12-6; **1963** *Dakotas* "Thunder in Pleasant Valley" 2-4; *Have Gun-Will Travel* "The Eve of St. Elmo" 3-23; *Bonanza* "Five into the Wind" 4-21; **1964** *Daniel Boone* "Tekaurha McLeod" 10-1; **1965** *Fugitive* "Trial by Fire" 10-5; *Man Called Shenandoah* "The Locket" 11-22; **1966** *Daniel Boone* "The Prisoners" 2-10; *Big Valley* "Legend of a General" 9-19; 9-26; *Big Valley* "Hide the Children" 12-19; **1967** *Dragnet* "The Big Bank Jobs" 10-5; *Big Valley* "Lady Killer" 10-16; *Hondo* "The Ghost of Ed Dow" 11-24.

Mario Alcalde
(born 1926, died April 22, 1971)

Primarily a stage and television actor, Mario made the first of only five films in 1956. During the sixties he was one of more visible guest actors in television episodes. He also wrote screenplays for series like *The Fugitive*. Mario died of cancer on April 22, 1971 at age 44, survived by his wife, three sons and his parents.

GUEST CREDITS

1960 *One Step Beyond* "House of the Dead" 6-7; *Islanders* "The Phantom Captain" 11-13; **1961** *Roaring 20's* "The Maestro" 1-7; *Adventures in Paradise* "Treasure Hunt" 1-9; *Investigators* "De Luca" 11-23; **1962** *New Breed* "Cave Is No Cure" 1-23; *New Breed* "The Man with the Other Face" 4-10; *77 Sunset Strip* "Flight from Escondito" 5-18; *Lloyd Bridges Show* "El Medico" 9-18; **1963** *Eleventh Hour* "A Medicine Man in This Day and Age?" 5-1; **1964** *Great Adventure* "The Testing of Sam Houston" 1-31; *Ben Casey* "Make Me the First American" 4-1; *Voyage to the Bottom of the Sea* "The Magnus Beam" 11-23; **1965** *Daniel Boone* 4-15; *Run for Your Life* "Make the Angels Weep" 12-13; **1967** *Run for Your Life* "The List of Alice McKenna" 1-13;

Gunsmoke "Fandango" 2-11; *Wild Wild West* "The Night of the Jack O' Diamonds" 10-6; *The FBI* "Flood Verdict" 10-8; *Man from UNCLE* "The Man from Thrush Affair" 12-4; **1968** *It Takes a Thief* "When Thieves Fall In" 2-27; *The FBI* "Southwind" 3-3; *It Takes a Thief* "Hands Across the Border" 11-11, 11-19; **1970** *Immortal* "Legacy" 10-15; **1971** *Ironside* "From Hruska, with Love" 1-21.

TELEFILMS

1967 *The Outsider* 11-21 NBC*;* **1970** *McCloud: Who Killed Miss U. S. A.?* 2-17 NBC.

Jed Allan
(born 1937, New York City)

Best known for his outstanding work on soap operas, Jed has also done a number of guest appearances on TV series. He was host of *Celebrity Bowling* from 1971 to 1978, was a regular on *Lassie* (1968-70), and was a repertory player on *Love, American Style* (1973-74).

His soap roles included *Love of Life* (1964), *The Secret Storm* (1964-65), an Emmy-Nominated long-running role on *Days of Our Lives* (1975-85) and a featured role on *Santa Barbara* (1987-92).

GUEST CREDITS

1968 *Mannix* "To the Swiftest, Death" 10-19; **1970** *Adam-12* "Log 144-Bank Robbery" 4-11; *Mod Squad* "The Song of Willie" 10-20; **1971** *Adam-12* "Log 155-I.A.D." 1-21; **1972** *Adam-12* "Sub-Station" 2-16; *Mod Squad* "Kristie" 12-14; **1973** *Adam-12* "Anatomy of a 415" 3-7; *New Perry Mason* "The Case of the Ominous Oath" 9-30; *Marcus Welby, M.D.* "A Question of Fault" 10-16; *Chase* "The Scene Stealers" 10-23; **1974** *Kojak* "Dead on His Feet" 3-6; *Marcus Welby, M.D.* "The 266 Days" 12-10; **1977** *McMillan* "Affair of the Heart" 3-20; *Streets of San Francisco* "Interlude" 4-28; **1978** *CHiPs* "Vintage '54" 1-26; **1979** *Eischied* "Friday's Child".

TELEFILMS

1971 *Ransom for a Dead Man* 3-1 NBC; **1973** *Incident on a Dark Street* 1-13 NBC; **1974** *Thursday's Game* 4-14 ABC; **1975** *The Specialists* 1-6 NBC; *Conspiracy of Terror* 12-29 NBC; **1976** *Brenda Starr* 5-8 ABC; **1979** *Fast Friends* 3-19 NBC.

Phillip R. Allen
(born March 26, 1939, Pittsburgh, Pa.)

A familiar seventies television actor, Phillip R. Allen often played characters with flippant, casual or sarcastic attitudes. He was in a memorable episode of *The Bob Newhart Show*, playing a playboy pschologist.

Allen was a regular on *The Hardy Boys Mysteries* (1978-79), *Bad News Bears* (1979-80) and *Alice* (1981-82).

GUEST CREDITS

1974 *Get Christie Love!* "Downbeat for a Dead Man" 11-13; **1975** *Joe Forrester* "Powder Blue" 11-

18; **1976** *Most Wanted* "The Two Dollar Kidnappers" 11-6; *Quincy, M.E.* "A Star Is Dead" 11-28; **1977** *Streets of San Francisco* "Monkey Is Back" 1-13; *Lou Grant* "Psych-Out 11-22; *Kojak* "The Summer of '69" 12-3, 12-10; **1978** *Baretta* "The Stone Company 2-23; *Quincy, M.E.* "Speed Trap" 10-12; **1979** *240 Robert* "Out of Sight" 10-15; **1980** *Lou Grant* "Scandal" 3-24; **1981** *Lou Grant* "Stroke" 5-4; **1982** *Cassie and Company* "The Golden Silence" 1-29.

TELEFILMS

1974 *Trapped Beneath the Sea* 10-22 ABC; **1976** *The Lindbergh Kidnapping* 2-26 NBC; *Helter Skelter* 4-1, 4-2 CBS; **1977** *Mary Jane Harper Cried Last Night* 10-5 CBS; **1978** *A Family Upside Down* 4-9 NBC; *More Than Friends* 10-20 ABC; **1979** *The Child Stealer* 3-9 ABC; *Friendly Fire* 4-22 ABC; **1980** *A Rumor of War* 9-24, 9-25 CBS; *Blinded by the Light* 12-16 CBS; **1982** *Honey Boy* 10-17 NBC; **1983** *An Uncommon Love* 11-30 CBS.

Merry Anders

(born Mary Anderson, May 22, 1932, Chicago, Illinois)

Merry signed a contract with 20th Century Fox in 1952, with her first significant acting job as a regular

on *The Stu Erwin Show* during it's final season (1954-55). She moved into a sitcom version of *How to Marry a Millionaire* called *It's Always Jan* (1955-56). A year later, she was featured in another version, this time titled *How to Marry a Millionaire*, which ran from 1957 until 1959. Thereafter, she worked in guest roles until her career wound down in the early seventies.

GUEST CREDITS

1960 *Maverick* "The People's Friend" 2-7; *Hawaiian Eye* "Hong Kong Passage" 2-10; *Bonanza* "Bitter Water" 4-9; *Cheyenne* "The Long Rope" 10-3; *Maverick* "The Town That Wasn't There" 11-12; *Maverick* "Destination: Devil's Flat" 12-25; **1961** *Loretta Young Show* "Enter at Your Own Risk" 1-8; *Surfside 6* "Yesterday's Hero" 1-23; *77 Sunset Strip* "A Face in the Window" 2-24; *77 Sunset Strip* "Tiger by the Tail" 3-3; *Perry Mason* "The Case of the Blind Man's Bluff" 3-11; *Hawaiian Eye* "Don't Kiss Me Goodbye" 3-29; *Michael Shayne* "Dead Air" 5-19; *77 Sunset Strip* "The Lady Has the Answers" 10-20; *Hawaiian Eye* "Pill in a Box" 11-1; **1962** *Perry Mason* "The Case of the Glamorous

Ghost" 2-3; *Straightaway* "Tiger by the Tail" 2-21; *Hawaiian Eye* "Koko Kate" 6-13; *77 Sunset Strip* "Odds on Odette" 12-21; **1964** *Arrest and Trial* "The Best There Is" 2-16; **1967** *Dragnet* "The Big Candy Store" 3-9; *Dragnet* "The Big Fur Robbery" 3-16; *Dragnet* "Juvenile-DR-05" 9-26; **1971** *Gunsmoke* "Waste" 9-27, 10-4.

John Anderson

(born October 20, 1922, Clayton, Illinois; died August 9, 1992)

John Anderson spent his childhood years in Missouri, Oklahoma, Arkansas and Indiana before graduating from high school in Quincy, Illinois. While in high school, he announced and wrote commercials for a local radio station, and acted in little theater. Shortly after graduation he began his acting career on the Mississippi River showboat *Golden Rod*, a job he enjoyed for over three years.

When World War II broke out John enlisted in The Coast Guard, becoming a sonar operator on a destroyer escort that operated in the North Atlantic and in the Mediterranean. Following his military discharge he came home and married his high school sweetheart, Patricia Carson.

John enrolled at The University of Iowa on the GI Bill as a speech and drama major. He obtained a Master's Degree in Drama, then took a job at the

Cleveland Playhouse, followed by a stint in stock at Buffalo, New York. Next came a season in Atlanta, doing musicals like *Guys and Dolls* and *Call Me Madam*.

Moving to New York, he did off-Broadway work and had some small roles on shows like *Studio One* and *Kraft Television Theatre*. He began having significant TV roles in 1955 and came to Hollywood in 1957.

In early 1958 he guested in a *Gunsmoke* episode that earned him rave notices; the lengthy brawl between John and series star James Arness served for years as a classic for college students learning film editing.

That episode, and a couple of early *Have Gun-Will Travel* episodes, resulted in a career emphasizing western TV series guest roles, some 92 in all. His remarkable contributions in the genre, primarily in TV, but also in films, resulted in him being presented the prestigious Western Heritage Award at TheNationalCowboy Hall of Fame in 1967.

His stern, no-nonsense personna often created castings as peace officers or upright citizens. His versatility provided many non-western series guest shots from The *Twilight Zone* (4) to *Quincy, M.E.* (3). John worked well into the late eighties on shows like *Matt Houston* (2), *MacGyver* (3) and *Dallas* (3).

On February 18, 1989, John lost Patricia, his beloved wife of over forty years. A heart attack took John on August 9, 1992. He was survived by daughter Kelsey, son Jeff and five grandchildren.

GUEST CREDITS

1959 *Zane Grey Theater* "Hang the Heart High" 1-15; *Rifleman* "The Retired Gun" 1-20; *Texan* "Return to Friendly" 2-2; *Rifleman* "The Shivaree" 2-3; *Rough Riders* "End of Track" 3-5; *Alcoa Theater* "Man of the House" 3-9; *Peter Gunn* "Breakout" 3-30; *Rifleman* "The Hawk" 4-14; *Steve Canyon* "The Bomb" 4-14; *Perry Mason* "The Case of the Calendar Girl" 4-18; *Richard Diamond* episode 5-3; *Yancy Derringer* "Outlaw at Liberty" 5-7; *Trackdown* "Toss-Up" 5-20; *Rough Riders* "Ransom for Rita Renee" 6-11; *Have Gun-Will Travel* "First Catch a Tiger" 9-21; *Rifleman* "The

John Anderson (left), Chuck Connors and Paul Fix appear in a 1963 episode of *The Rifleman*, "Incident at Line Shack Six" (ABC).

Rifleman "Face of Yesterday" 1-31; *Twilight Zone* "The Odyssey of Flight 33" 2-4; *Lawman* "Hassayampa" 2-12; *Adventures in Paradise* "Captain Butcher" 2-20; *Wyatt Earp* "Wyatt Earp's Brothers Join Up" 6-16; *Wyatt Earp* "Just Before the Battle" 6-13; *Wyatt Earp* "Gunfight at O.K. Corral" 6-20; *Wyatt Earp* "The Outlaws Cry Murder" 6-27; *87th Precinct* "The Modus Man" 10-16; *Rifleman* "The Journey Back" 10-31; *Cheyenne* "Retaliation" 11-13; *Bonanza* "The Countess" 11-19; *Alfred Hitchcock*

Patsy" 9-29; *Colt .45* "Queen of Dixie" 10-4; *Gunsmoke* "Tail to the Wind" 10-24; *Law of the Plainsman* "Appointment in Santa Fe" 11-19; *Perry Mason* "The Case of the Battered Bikini" 12-5; **1960** *Rifleman* "Day of the Hunter" 1-5; *Detectives* "Karate" 1-8; *Rifleman* "Mail Order Groom" 1-12; *Law of the Plainsman* "Endurance" 1-14; *Bonanza* "A House Divided" 1-16; *Black Saddle* "The Indian Tree" 2-19; *Detectives* "Anatomy of Fear" 2-26; *Lawman* "Left Hand of the Law" 3-27; *Rifleman* "Shotgun Man" 4-12; *Law of the Plainsman* "Jeb's Daughter" 4-14; *Bronco* "Legacy of Twisted Creek" 4-19; *Detectives* "The Prowler" 4-22; *Wanted: Dead or Alive* "The Inheritance" 4-30; *Rebel* "Paint a Horse with Scarlet" 5-15; *Johnny Ringo* "The Derelict" 5-26; *Man from Blackhawk* "The Money Machine" 6-10; *Westerner* "School Days" 10-7; *Laramie* "The Long Riders" 10-25; *Wyatt Earp* "Big Brother" 11-1; *Untouchables* "A Seat on the Fence" 11-24; *Wyatt Earp* "Winning Streak" 12-27; **1961** *Bat Masterson* "The Court-Martial of Mayor Mars" 1-12;

Presents "The Old Pro" 11-28; **1962** *Laramie* "The Perfect Gift" 1-2; *Tales of Wells Fargo* "Reward for Genie" 1-20; *Laramie* "A Grave for Cully Brown" 2-13; *Tall Man* "Night of the Hawk" 3-3; *Thriller* "Innocent Bystanders" 4-9; *Sam Benedict* "Nor Practice Makes Perfect" 9-29; *Virginian* "Throw a Long Rope" 10-3; *Dr. Kildare* "The Visitors" 10-11; *Eleventh Hour* "I Don't Belong in a White-Painted House" 10-24; *Stoney Burke* "Spin a Golden Web" 11-26; *Alfred Hitchcock Hour* "Ride the Nightmare" 11-29; *Laramie* "Bad Blood" 12-4; **1963** *Rifleman* "Incident at Line Shack Six" 1-7; *Gunsmoke* "The Cousin" 2-2; *Route 66* "Shall Forfeit His Dog and Six Shillings to the King" 2-22; *Alcoa Premiere* "Blow Hard, Blow Clear" 2-14; *Laramie* "The Violent Ones" 3-5; *Stoney Burke* "To Catch the Kaiser" 3-11; *Rifleman* "Old Man Running" 3-18; *Twilight Zone* "Of Late I Think of Cliffordville" 4-11; *Perry Mason* "The Case of the Greek Goddess" 4-18; *Untouchables* "The Torpedo" 5-7; *Kraft Mystery Theatre* "Shadow of a Man" 6-19; *Dr.*

Kildare "The Good Samaritan" 10-3; *Bonanza* "Rain from Heaven" 10-6; *Great Adventure* "The Story of Nathan Hale" 10-25; *Ben Casey* "Little Drops of Water, Little Grains of Sand" 10-30; *Twilight Zone* "The Old Man in the Cave" 11-8; *Redigo* "Home of Hate" 11-19; *Outer Limits* "Nightmare" 12-2; **1964** *Lieutenant* "Gone the Sun" 1-18; *Fugitive* "Come Watch Me Die" 1-21; *Rawhide* "Incident at Hourglass" 3-12; *Ben Casey* "But Who Shall Beat the Drum?" 9-28; *Ben Casey* "You Fish Or You Can Bait" 10-12; **1965** *Fugitive* "Scapegoat" 2-2; *Voyage to the Bottom of the Sea* "Cradle of the Deep" 3-1; *Kraft Suspense Theatre* "Won't It Ever Be Morning?" 3-18; *Rawhide* "The Retreat" 3-26; *Alfred Hitchcock Hour* "The Second Wife" 4-26; *Man Called Shenandoah* "Survival" 9-20; *Virginian* "Day of the Scorpion" 9-22; *Big Valley* "Boots with My Father's Name" 9-29; *Big Valley* "The Guilt of Matt Bertell" 12-8; *Gunsmoke* "Gold Mine" 12-25; **1966** *The FBI* "Forests of the Night" 1-2; *Gunsmoke* "The Raid" 1-22, 1-29; *Branded* "Nice Day for a Hanging" 2-6; *Virginian* "Harvest of Strangers" 2-16; *Legend of Jesse James* "The Hunted and the Hunters" 4-11; *Virginian* "An Echo of Thunder" 10-5; *Rat Patrol* "The Last Harbor Raid" 12-19, 12-26; **1967** *Felony Squad* "The Deadly Panther" 1-9; *Tarzan* "The Day the Earth Trembled" 1-13; *Gunsmoke* "Mail Drop" 1-28; *Road West* "Road to Glory" 2-20; *Iron Horse* "Five Days to Washtiba" 10-7; *Cimarron Strip* "Whitey" 10-19; *Virginian* "Bitter Autumn 11-1; *Dundee and the Culhane* "Death of a Warrior Brief" 11-15; *Mannix* "Then the Drink Takes the Man" 12-30; **1968** *Rat Patrol* "The Pipeline to Disaster" 1-1; *Lancer* "Blood Rock" 10-1; *Bonanza* "The Fence" 4-27; **1969** *Gunsmoke* "A Matter of Honor" 11-17; *Virginian* "Home to Methuselah" 11-26; *Gunsmoke* "Roots of Fear" 12-15; *Bonanza* "The Fence" 12-28; **1970** *Mission: Impossible* "Hunted" 11-21; **1971** *Gunsmoke* "Mirage" 1-11; *Cade's County* "Violent Echo" 10-24; *MacMillan and Wife* "Death Is a Seven Point Favorite" 12-8; *Bearcats* episode 12-30; **1972** *Sixth Sense* "Through the Flame, Darkly" 11-4; *The FBI* "The Loner" 11-19; **1973** *Kung Fu* "Blood Brother" 1-18; *Gunsmoke* "Kimbrough" 2-12; *Hec Ramsey* "Mystery of Chalk Hill" 2-18; *Cannon* "Deadly Heritage" 3-21; *Kung Fu* "The Third Man" 4-26; **1974** *Kung Fu* "Cross-Ties" 3-21; *Petrocelli* "A

Life for a Life" 10-9; *Born Free* "The White Rhino" 11-25' **1975** *Emergency* episode 1-11; *Barnaby Jones* "Jeopardy for Two" 4-1; *Little House on the Prairie* "Haunted House" 9-24; *Bronc* "Deception" 12-7; **1976** *The Quest* "Shanklin" 10-13; *Rockford Files* "Coulter City Wildcat" 11-12; **1977** *Tales of the Unexpected* "The Force of Evil" 3-13; *Hallmark Hall of Fame* "The Last Hurrah" 11-16; *Lou Grant* "Take Over" 12-6; *Quincy, M.E.* "Last of the Dinosaurs" 12-16; **1978** *Quincy, M.E.* "Last Six Hours" 9-21; **1979** *Incredible Hulk* "Wild Fire" 1-17; *Project UFO* "Sighting 4025: The Spaceship Incident" 7-5; **1980** *Tenspeed and Brownshoe* "This One's Gonna Kill Ya" 6-6; **1981** *Greatest American Hero* "Operation Spoil Sport" 11-11; *Hart to Hart* "Hart of Darkness" 12-8; **1982** *Quincy, M.E.* "Sleeping Dogs" 11-17; *Voyagers* "The Day the Rebs Took Lincoln" 11-21; **1983** *Fall Guy* "Happy Trails" 1-12.

TELEFILMS

1966 *Scalplock* 4-10 ABC; **1973** *Set This Town on Fire* 1-8 NBC; *Call to Danger* 2-27 CBS; *Brock's Last Case* 3-5 NBC; **1974** *Heat Wave* 1-26 ABC; *Smile Jenny, You're Dead* 2-3 ABC; *The Manhunter* 2-26 CBS; **1975** *Log of the Black Pearl* 1-4 NBC; *Dead Man on the Run* 4-2 CBS; *Death Among Friends* 5-20 NBC; **1976** *The Dark Side of Innocence* 5-20 NBC; *Bridger* 9-10 NBC; **1977** *Tail Gunner Joe* 2-6 NBC; *Peter Lundy and the Medicine Hat Stallion* 11-6 NBC; **1978** *Donner Pass: The Road to Survival* 10-24 CBS; *The Deerslayer* 12-18 NBC; **1982** *The First Time* 11-8 ABC; *Missing Children: A Mother's Story* 12-1 CBS.

E. J. Andre

(born 1908, Detroit, Michigan; died September 6, 1984)

E. J. made his screen debut in 1933, but his film roles were rather infrequent. He did appear in the *Ten Commandments, The Shakiest Gun in the West, Papillon,* and *The Duchess and the Dirtwater Fox.*

He made a much significant impact on television, frequently cast as tough oldsters on western

and crime series. He is remembered for his work on *Dallas* as Eugene Bullock (1982-83).

GUEST CREDITS

1963 *Virginian* "The Man Who Couldn't Die" 1-30; **1964** *Wagon Train* "The Geneva Balfour Story" 1-20; *Perry Mason* "The Case of the Tragic Trophy" 11-19; **1965** *Alfred Hitchcock Hour* "Where the Woodbine Twineth" 1-11; *Virginian* "A Slight Case of Charity" 2-10; *Alfred Hitchcock Hour* "An Unlocked Window" 2-15; *Wild Wild West* "The Night of the Howling Light" 12-17; **1966** *Daniel Boone* "The Accused" 3-24; *Blue Light* "Jet Trail" 4-6; *Shane* "The Great Invasion" 12-17, 12-24; *1967* *Green Hornet* "Seek, Stalk and Destroy" 1-6; *Road West* "Long Journey to Leavenworth" 10-17; *Invaders* "Labyrinth" 11-21; **1968** *Gunsmoke* "A Noose for Dobie Price" 3-4; **1969** *Mannix* "A Pittance of Faith" 1-11; *Lancer* "Devil's Blessing" 4-22; **1970** *Bonanza* "The Trouble with Trouble" 10-25; *Night Gallery* "The Little Black Bag" 12-30; **1971** *Adam-12* "Log 106-Post Time" 3-18; *Cannon* "Dead Pigeon" 11-9; **1972** *Delphi Bureau* "The White Plague Project" 11-16; **1974** *Harry O* "Accounts Balanced" 12-26; **1975** *Waltons* "The Shivaree" 1-30; *Starsky and Hutch* "Death Ride" 9-24; **1976** *Little House on the Prairie* "His Father's Son" 1-7; *Switch* "Quicker Than the Eye" 11-9; **1977** *Little House on the*

Prairie "Gold Country" 4-4; *Charlie's Angels* "Magic Fire" 11-30.

TELEFILMS

1974 *The Day the Earth Moved* 9-18 ABC; **1975** *Miles to Go Before I Sleep* 1-8 CBS; **1982** *Mysterious Two* 5-31 NBC.

Jim Antonio
(born Oklahoma City)

The brother of actor-director Lou Antonio, Jim made his film debut in 1962. He began working extensively on television in 1974 and appeared in 14 telefilms and 2 miniseries during the decade. Jim appeared in an additional 5 telefilms in 1980-81.

GUEST CREDITS

1971 *Mannix* "Voices in the Dark" 2-20; *Mannix* "Woman in the Shadows" 10-13; *Owen Marshall, Counselor at Law* "Nothing Personal" 11-11; *Alias Smith and Jones* "Shootout at Diablo Station" 12-2; **1972** *Sixth Sense* "The House That Cried Murder" 2-5; **1973** *Streets of San Francisco* "The Albatross" 3-15; **1974** *Griff* "Fugitive from Fear" 1-5; *McMillan and Wife* "Downshift to Danger" 9-29; *Rockford Files* "In Pursuit of Carol Thorne 11-8; *Mannix* "A

Small Favor for an Old Friend" 11-10; **1975** *The Law* "Special Circumstances" 4-16; *PetrocelliI* "Terror on Wheels" 11-5; *Doctor's Hospital* episode 11-12; **1976** *Police Story* "Firebird" 2-6; **1977** *Hardy Boys/ Nancy Drew Mysteries* "The Mystery at the Haunted House" 1-30; **1978** *Quincy, M.E.* "Passing" 1-27; *Eddie Capra Mysteries* "Where There's Smoke" 9-22; **1980** *Little House on the Prairie* "Portrait of Love" 10-27; **1981** *Quincy, M.E.* "Who Speaks for the Children?" 2-25; *Lou Grant* "Stroke" 5-4; *Fall Guy* "Colt's Angels" 12-2; **1982** *Quincy, M.E.* "Deadly Protection" 5-5.

TELEFILMS

1972 *Playmates* 10-3 ABC; *Visions* 10-10 CBS; **1974** *Planet Earth* 4-23 ABC ; *Hurricane* 9-10 ABC; *Savages* 9-11 ABC; **1975** *Returning Home* 4-29 ABC; **1976** *Lannigan's Rabbi* 6-17 NBC; **1977** *The Amazing Howard Hughes* 4-13, 4-14 CBS; *Delta County, U. S. A.* 5-20 ABC; **1978** *A Question of Guilt* 2-21 CBS; *The Critical List* 9-11, 9-12 NBC; **1979** *Silent Victory: The Kitty O'Neil Story* 2-24 CBS; *Breaking Up Is Hard to Do* 9-5, 9-7 ABC; **1980** *Homeward Bound* 11-19 CBS; **1981** *Terror Among Us* 1-12 CBS; *The Killing of Randy Webster* 3-11 CBS; *The Star Maker* 5-11, 5-12 NBC; **1982** *Terror at Alcatraz* 7-4 NBC.

Luke Askew

(born 1937)

Luke went to Hollywood after working as a television announcer and as manager of a waste-paper plant; his first acting experiences were in off-Broadway roles. Tall and sober-looking, he naturally gravitated to villainous roles. He made his film debut in 1967 in *Hurry Sundown*, with subsequent roles in *Cool Hand Luke, Will Penny, The Green Berets, Easy Riders* and *The Culpepper Cattle Company*.

His first television appearance was on an episode of *Mission: Impossible* and he continued his villainy in guest roles well into the eighties.

GUEST CREDITS

1968 *Mission: Impossible* "The Execution" 11-10; **1969** *High Chaparrel* "Shadow of the Wind" 1-10; **1971** *Bonanza* "Kingdom of Fear" 4-4; *1972 Longstreet* "The Sound of Money Talking" 3-2; **1973** *Mission: Impossible* "The Fountain" 1-26; **1975** *Police Story* "Headhunter" 1-14; *S.W.A.T.* "Murder by Fire" 12-6; **1976** *Police Story* "Eamon Kinsella Royce" 2-20; *Jigsaw John* "Eclipse" 3-29; *Switch* "The Twelfth Commandment" 9-28; *Rockford Files* "Feeding Frenzy" 10-15; **1977** *Streets of San Francisco* "Hang Tough" 2-17; *Rockford Files* "New Life, Old Dragons" 2-25; *Quincy, M.E.* "Let Me Light the Way" 5-27; **1978** *Six Million Dollar Man* "Date with Danger" 2-20, 2-27; **1980** *Hart to Hart* "This Lady Is Murder" 11-25; **1981** *B. J. and the Bear* "Who Is B. J.?" 4-25; *Quincy, M.E.* "For Want of a Horse" 12-9; **1983** *Knight Rider* "A Nice, Indecent Little Town" 2-18; *A-Team* "The Rabbit Who Ate Las Vegas" 3-1; *T. J. Hooker* episodes 10-22, 10-29; *Matt Houston* episode 10-28.

TELEFILMS

1972 *Truman Capote's "The Glass House"* 2-4 CBS; **1974** *Manhunter* 2-26 CBS; *Night Games* 3-16 NBC; *This Was the West That Was* 12-17 NBC; **1975** *Attack on Terror: The FBI versus the Ku Klux Klan* 2-20, 2-21 CBS; **1976** *The Invasion of Johnson County* 7-31 NBC; *A Matter of Wife...and Death* 4-10 NBC; *The Quest* 5-13 NBC.

Rene Auberjonois
(born June 1, 1940, New York City)

Educated at Carnegie-Mellon University, Rene became a highly successful stage actor, winning a Tony Award for his role in *Coco* (1970). He began appearing in TV guest roles and telefilms in 1971. His best known work came in his series role as the sarcastic and overbearing governor's aid in *Benson* (1980-86).

Rene taught drama at the college level while continuing an acting career. Eighties guest credits included *The Love Boat*, *Blacke's Magic* and *Murder, She Wrote* (2). He also provided voices for Saturday morning cartoons like *Scooby and Scrappy-Doo Show*, *The New Jetsons*, *Challenge of the Gobots* and *Wildfire*.

GUEST CREDITS

1971 *Night Gallery* "Camera Obscure" 12-8; **1975** *Harry O* "Anatomy of a Frame" 9-11; *Ellery Queen* "The Adventure of Colonel Niven's Memoirs" 10-23; *Rookies* "Voice of Thunder" 12-9; **1976** *Delvecchio* "The Avenger" 9-26; *Black Sheep Squadron* "Devil in the Shoot" 9-28; *Charlie's Angels* "The Seance" 12-15; **1977** *Bionic Woman* "The Dejon Caper" 3-16; *Rosetti and Ryan* "Is There a Lawyer in the House?" 10-20; *Man from Atlantis* "Crystal Water, Sudden Death" 11-22; *1978 Richie Brockelman, Private Eye* "A Title on the Door, and a Carpet on the Floor" 3-31; *Starsky and Hutch* "Dandruff" 11-14; **1979** *Rockford Files* "With the French Heel Back, Can the Nehru Jacket Be Far Behind?" 1-5; *Wonder Woman* "Spaced Out" 1-26; *Mrs. Columbo* "Word Games" 2-26; *Family* "Ballerina" 3-15; *Hart to Hart* "Max in Love" 11-13; *Charlie's Angels* "Angels on Skates" 11-21; *Kates Loves a Mystery* "Feelings Can Be Murder" 12-6; **1980** *Tenspeed and Brownshoe* episode 6-13.

TELEFILMS

1971 *Once Upon a Dead Man* 9-11 NBC; *The Birdman* 9-18 NBC; **1973** *Shirts/Skins* 10-9 ABC; **1979** *The Wild Wild West Revisited* 5-9 CBS; *More Wild Wild West* 10-7, 10-8 CBS; **1982** *The Kid from Nowhere* 1-4 NBC.

Skye Aubrey
(born 1945)

The lovely daughter of actress Phyllis Thaxter and one-time MGM president James Aubrey, Skye was seen often on television following her 1967 debut on multiple episodes of *Batman*. She did numerous seventies telefilms and dramatic series guest shots and also appeared on a couple of episodes of *Love, American Style*. Retiring from acting after marriage to producer Alexander Salkind, Skye returned in 1989 for an episode of the syndicated *Superboy*.

GUEST CREDITS

1970 *Marcus Welby, M.D.* "The Merely Syndrome" 3-3; *Interns* "Some Things Don't Change" 10-2; **1971** *Most Deadly Game* "The Classical Burial Position" 1-2; *Marcus Welby, M.D.* "A Yellow Bird" 11-23; **1972** *Emergency* episode 10-7; *Assignment: Vienna* "Hot Potato" 10-19; *Jigsaw* "The Bradley Affair" 11-2; *Owen Marshall, Counselor at Law* "Who Saw Him Die?" 11-2; *Banyon* "The Murder Game" 12-15; **1973** *Jigsaw* "Girl on the Run" 2-24; *Ironside* "Another Shell Game" 3-1; *Toma* "Stake-Out" 10-25; **1974** *Chopper One* "Chopper One" 1-17; **1977** *Switch* "Lady of the Deep" 12-19.

TELEFILMS

1971 *Vanished* 3-8, 3-9 NBC; *The City* 5-17 ABC; *Ellery Queen: Don't Look Behind You* 11-19 NBC; **1972** *A Very Missing Person* 3-4 ABC; *The Longest Night* 9-12 ABC; **1974** *The Phantom of Hollywood* 2-12 CBS; *In the Steps of a Dead Man* 5-27 ABC.

Phyllis Avery

(born Novelmber 14, 1924, New York City)

A fifties/sixties performer, Phyllis was a regular on *The Ray Milland Show* (1953-55), played the wife of George Gobel on his show (1958-59) and was also a regular on *Mr. Novak* (1964-65). She also did a stint on the soap *Clear Horizon* (1960-62). Fifties guest credits included work on *Schlitz Playhouse of Stars* (3), *Zane Grey Theater*, *General Electric Theater*, *Playhouse 90*, *Studio One* and *Perry Mason*.

Following retirement from acting, Phyllis became a real estate agent in Los Angeles. She was marriedto actor-director Don Taylor for years.

GUEST CREDITS

1959 *Rawhide* "Incident in No Man's Land" 6-12; *Millionaire* "Millionaire Jim Hayes" 10-28; *Riflelman* "The Baby Sitter" 12-15; **1960** *Laramie* "Ride into Darkness" 1-12; *Deputy* "Queen Bea" 2-20; *Peter Gunn* "Send a Thief" 5-16; *Tate* "The Reckoning" 8-24; **1961** *Perry Mason* "The Case of the Brazen Request" 12-2; **1962** *Adventures in Paradise* "The Beach at Belle Anse" 3-4; *Have Gun-Will Travel* "The Man Who Struck Moonshine" 3-24; *Alcoa Premiere* "Guest in the House" 10-11;

Sam Benedict "The View from the Ivory Tower" 10-11; **1963** *Laramie* "The Fugitives" 2-12; *Virginian* "If You Have Tears" 2-13; *Eleventh Hour* "The Wings of Morning" 3-20; *Kraft Suspense Theatre* "Are There Any More Out There Like You?" 11-7; *Dr. Kildare* "Four Feet in the Morning (Part 1)" 11-21; *Eleventh Hour* "Four Feet in the Morning (Part 2)" 11-27; **1964** *Greatest Show on Earth* "Man in a Hole" 2-18; **1966** *Bob Hope Chrysler Theater* "Massacre at Fort Phil Kearney" 10-26; **1967** *Daniel Boone* "The Renegade" 9-28; **1977** *Charlie's Angels* "Angel Trap" 1-5.

TELEFILM

1971 *The Last Child* 10-15 ABC.

Tol Avery

(born 1915, died 1973)

Onscreen from 1952, heavy-set character actor Tol Avery was on television often from 1955. His was a regular on *The Thin Man* in 1957-58, playing a police lieutenant. He later guested in a variety of TV series genres, including sitcoms like *The Andy Griffith Show*, *Gomer Pyle, U.S.M.C.*, *My Three Sons*, *F Troop* and *Batman*. Tol also had a promi-

nent role on *Slattery's People* in 1964-65.

GUEST CREDITS

1959 *Maverick* "Yellow River" 2-8; *Lawman* "The Posse" 3-8; *Colt .45* "Queen of Dixies" 10-14; *Maverick* "Maverick Springs" 12-6; **1960** *Bourbon Street Beat* "Key to the City 2-1; *Cheyenne* "Outcast of Cripple Creek" 3-29; *Maverick* "Last Wire from Stop Gap" 10-16; **1961** *Hawaiian Eye* "Talk and You're Dead" 1-18; **1962** *Maverick* "Poker Face" 1-7; *Bus Stop* "How Does Charlie Feel?" 2-4; *77 Sunset Strip* "The Bel Aire Hermit" 2-23; *Ben Casey* "Preferably the Less Used Arm" 4-30; *Bonanza* "The Miracle Worker" 5-20; *Ben Casey* "In the Name of Love, a Small Corruption" 10-15; **1963** *G. E. True* "Defendant: Clarence Darrow" 1-13; *Perry Mason* "The Case of the Greek Goddess" 4-18; **1964** *Eleventh Hour* "Who Choppeth Down the Cherry Tree?" 1-29; *Kraft Suspense Theatre* "The Watchman" 5-14; **1965** *The Rogues* "Bless You G. Carter Huntington" 1-17; *Bonanza* "The Jonah" 5-9; **1966** *Bonanza* "Credit for a Kill" 10-23; *Iron Horse* "Explosion at Way Crossing" 11-21; **1967** *Dragnet* "The Big Badge Racket" 9-28; *Bonanza* "Justice Deferred" 12-17; **1968** *Lost in Space* "Fugitives in Space" 1-31; *The FBI* "The Flaw" 12-15; *Mannix* "Fear I to Fall" 12-21; **1969** *Wild Wild West* "The Night of the Tycoons" 3-28; *Land of the Giants* "Shell Game" 4-13; *The FBI* "Journey into Night" 12-14; **1970** *Mission: Impossible* "Flight" 10-17; **1971** *Mannix* "Round Trip to Nowhere" 1-2; *O'Hara, U. S. Treasury* "Operation: Bandera" 12-24; **1972** *Longstreet* "Field of Honor" 2-17; *Mission: Impossible* "Cocaine" 10-21; **1973** *Adam-12* "Night Watch" 2-14.

TELEFILMS

1973 *Set This Town on Fire* 1-8 NBC; *The Magician* 3-3 NBC; *The Marcus-Nelson Murders* 3-8 CBS.

Jerry Ayres

Baby-faced Jerry Ayres was visible on television from 1966 through 1979, primarily in sci-fi and detective series. His only big-screen film was made in 1971. He also did a stint on the soap *General Hospital*, appearing as David Hamilton, during 1977.

GUEST CREDITS

1966 *Blue Light* "Traitor's Blood" 2-9; *Combat* "One at a Time" 3-22; *Green Hornet* "Give 'Em Enough Rope" 9-16; **1967** *Star Trek* "Arena" 1-19; *Invaders* "Wall of Crystal" 5-2; *Star Trek* "Obsession" 12-15; **1968** *Mod Squad* "A Time to Love-A Time to Cry" 11-12; **1969** *The FBI* "The Maze" 2-9; *The FBI* "Gamble with Death" 10-19; *Adam-12* "Log 142-As High as You Are" 12-20; **1970** *Immortal* "The Rainbow Butcher" 10-22; **1971** *The FBI* "Eye of the Needle" 1-24; *Dan August* "Prognosis: Homicide" 4-1; **1972** *The FBI* "The Break-Up" 1-16; **1973** *Barnaby Jones* "Fatal Flight" 12-9; **1974** *Police Story* "Chain of Command" 1-8; **1977** *Barnaby Jones* "Circle of Treachery" 3-3; **1979** *Rockford Files* "The Return of the Black Shadow" 2-17.

TELEFILMS

1973 *Message to My Daughter* 12-12 ABC; **1975** *Attack on Terror: The FBI Versus the Ku Klux Klan* 2-20, 2-21 CBS; **1979** *Disaster on the Coastliner* 10-28 ABC.

Donna Baccala

(born 1945)

Donna made her screen debut in 1969 in *The Dunwich Horror*, following stage experience. She had come to television in 1967 in guest roles, followed by regular roles on two brief 1969-70 TV series, *The Survivors* and *The New People*. She also appeared for a time on the soap *General Hospital*, during 1978.

GUEST CREDITS

1967 *Jerico* episode 1-19; **1968** *Gunsmoke* "Blood Money" 1-22; *Cimarron Strip* "The Greeners" 3-7; *Judd, for the Defense* "My Client, the Fool" 11-22; **1969** *Mod Squad* "The Uptight Town" 2-18; *Big Valley* "A Passage of Saints" 3-10; *Daniel Boone* "A Pinch of Salt" 5-1; *High Chapparal* "A Time to Laugh, A Time to Cry" 9-26; *The FBI* "Blood Tie" 11-9; **1970** *Dan August* "The Soldier" 12-2; **1972** *Streets of San Francisco* "Bitter Wine" 12-23; **1973** *Mannix* "A Way to a Dusty

Death" 9-23; *New Perry Mason* "The Case of the Furious Father" 1-27; **1974** *Barnaby Jones* "Programmed for Killing" 1-27; **1977** *Rockford Files* "Trouble in Chapter Seventeen" 9-23; **1978** *Barnaby Jones* "Nest of Scorpions" 10-26.

Roy Barcroft

(born Howard H. Ravenscroft, September 7, 1902, Crab Orchard, Nebraska; died November 28, 1969)

Roy Barcroft was known as "King of the Heavies" a title earned in over 240 films, primarily westerns, in which he menaced virtually every western hero of the thirties-forties-fifties era. He also appeared in a staggering 34 episodic serials of that period. Joining the army at age 15, Roy served in the U. S. Army in France during World War I. He was wounded in action and discharged at age 16. Wandering around the country, he worked at a variety of jobs: dishwasher, cook, ranch hand, oil field worker, truck driver, railroad laborer and sailor on a tramp steamer. He did another Army hitch in Hawaii, where he learned to play saxophone. Leaving service, he joined dance bands in Chicago. The stock market crash in 1929 ended that employment and he headed for California.

His first acting job was as an extra in 1932. Some lean years of working at sales jobs followed before dramatic training and Little Theatre led to his first film acting at $66.00 per week. And as they say, "the rest is history".

Roy worked in most of the top-rated TV series and was a special favorite on *Gunsmoke* where he had a recurring role as Roy, a townsman (11 episodes). This wonderful western acting institution died of cancer on November 28, 1969.

GUEST CREDITS

1959 *Markham* "The Last Oasis" 4-21; *Have Gun-Will Travel* "Comanche" 5-16; *Have Gun-Will Travel* "Haunted Trees" 6-13; *Johnny Ringo* "The Arrival" 10-1; *M Squad* "The Human Bond" 10-23; *Deputy* "Proof of Guilt" 10-24; *Texan* "Stampede" 11-2; *Texan* "Showdown at Abilene" 11-9; **1960** *Riverboat* "The Wichita Arrows" 2-29; *Tales of Wells Fargo* "Forty Four-Four" 2-29; *Gunsmoke* "Ben Tolliver's Stud" 11-26; **1961** *Gunsmoke* "Bad Seed" 2-4; *Gunslinger* "Border Incident" 2-9; *Have Gun-Will Travel* "The Tax Gatherer" 2-11; *Wanted: Dead or Alive* "The Voice

Roy Barcroft (right) stands fast with Richard Boone in "The Long Weekend", an episode of *Have Gun-Will Travel*. Paige Adams in is the center.

of Silence" 2-l5; *Gunslinger* "The Buried People"
3-9; *Have Gun-Will Travel* "The Long Weekend" 4-
8; *Laramie* "The Debt" 4-l8; *Laramie* "Badge of the
Outsider" 5-23; *Rawhide* "Judgment at Hondo
Seco" l0-20; *Straightaway* "Heat Wave" l0-27; **1962**
Have Gun-Will Travel "Lazarus" 1-20; *Lawman*
"Change of Venue" 2-11; *National Velvet* "The
Rumor" 3-l9; *Rifleman* "Outlaw Shoes" 4-30;
Empire "The Fire Dancer" 11-l3; *Have Gun-Will
Travel* "Be Not Forgetful to Strangers" 12-22; **1963**
Gunsmoke "Cotter's Girl" l-l9; *Laramie* "The
Betrayers" 1-22; *Rawhide* "Incident of the Mountain
Men" l-25; *Virginian* "The Small Parade" 2-20;
Have Gun-Will Travel "Face of a Shadow" 4-20;
Rawhide "Incident at Alkali Sink" 5-24; *Rawhide*
"Incident at Confidence Creek" 11-28; **1964**
Gunsmoke "Once a Haggen" 2-l; **1965** *Gunsmoke*
"Thursday's Child" 3-6; *Gunsmoke* "Honey Pot" 5-
l5; *Rawhide* "Walk into Terror" l0-5; *Laredo* "The
Golden Trail" 11-4; *Laredo* "Jinx" 12-2; *Gunsmoke*
"Outlaw's Women" 12-11; *Wild Wild West* "The
Night of the Howling Light" 12-l7; **1967** *Gunsmoke*
"The Returning" 2-18; *Gunsmoke* "Cattle Barons" 9-
l8; *Iron Horse* "Leopards Try, But Leopards Can't"
l0-28; **1968** *Gunsmoke* "O'Quillan" l0-28; **1969**
Gunsmoke "The Mark of Cain" 2-3.

Rayford Barnes

(born l925)

One of the most familiar of television's western
series heavies, Rayford Barnes' smirk was his
trademark. Onstage from l950, he made a film debut
in l952 and began his TV career in l954. When not
appearing as a heavy, he was often cast as rural
sheriffs and deputies, and branched out to dramatic
series like *The Alfred Hitchcock Hour, The Twilight
Zone, The Fugitive* and *Cannon.*

Gunsmoke used his talents in 9 episodes and
Have Gun-Will Travel worked him in 6 episodes.
Rayford had a recurring role on *The Life and Times
of Wyatt Earp,* appearing as Billy Clanton.

GUEST CREDITS
1959 *Maverick* "Passage to Ft. Doom" 3-8; *Rin
Tin Tin* "Apache Stampede" 3-20; *Troubleshooters*

"Moment of Terror" l0-16; *Law of the Plainsman*
"Passenger to Mescalero" l0-29; *M Squad* "Death
by Adoption" 11-20; **1960** *Gunsmoke* "Till Death Do
Us" 1-l6; *Deputy* "Meet Sergeant Tasker" l0-l; *Have
Gun-Will Travel* "The Shooting of Jessie May" l0-
29; *Untouchables* "The Purple Gang" 12-l; *Wyatt
Earp* "Johnny Ringo's Girl" 12-13; **1961** *Have Gun-
Will Travel* "Long Way Home" 2-4; *Gunsmoke*
"Kitty Shot" 2-11; *Maverick* "Last Stop: Oblivion"
2-l2; *Wyatt Earp* "Apache Gold" 3-7; *Gunsmoke*
"Big Man" 3-25; *Lawman* "Fugitive" 4-2; *Maverick*
"The Devil's Necklace" 4-l6, 4-23; *Laramie*
"Widow in White" 6-l3; *Wyatt Earp* "Gunfight at O.
K. Corral" 6-20; *Wyatt Earp* "Outlaws Cry Murder"
6-27; *Have Gun-Will Travel* "The Revenger" 9-30;
Twilight Zone "A Quality of Mercy" 12-29; **1962**
Detectives "Point of No Return" 1-l2; *Rawhide*
"Incident of the Woman Trap' 1-26; *Laramie* "Fall
into Darkness" 4-l7; *Bonanza* "A Hot Day for a
Hanging" l0-l4; **1963** *Alfred Hitchcock Hour* "An
Out for Oscar" 4-5; *Have Gun-Will Travel* "Face of
a Shadow" 4-20; *Gunsmoke* "Carter Caper" 11-16;
1964 *Gunsmoke* "No Hands" 2-8; *Gunsmoke* "Old
Man" l0-l0; *Alfred Hitchcock Hour* "Water's Edge"
l0-l9; **1965** *Fugitive* "Masquerade" 3-23; **1966**
Laredo "Meanwhile Back at the Reservation" 2-l0;
Daniel Boone episode 11-3; **1967** *Big Valley* "Image
of Yesterday" l-9; *Invaders* "Panic" 4-11; *Cimarron
Strip* "The Roarer" 11-2; **1968** *High Chaparral* "The

Kinsman" 1-28; *Big Valley* "Shadow of a Giant" 1-29; *Cimarron Strip* "Sound of a Drum" 2-1; *Lancer* "Blood Rock" 10-1; **1969** *Guns of Will Sonnett* "Time Is the Rider" 1-10; *Gunsmoke* "Danny" 10-13; *High Chaparral* "Trail to Nevermore" 10-31; **1971** *Nichols* "The One Eyed Mule's Time Has Come" 11-23; **1972** *Gunsmoke* "Alias Festus Haggin" 3-6; *Nichols* episode 3-7; **1973** *Bonanza* "The Marriage of Theodora Duffy" 1-9; *Gunsmoke* "Kitty's Love Affair" 10-22; **1974** *Cannon* "The Conspirators" 1-1; *Kung Fu* "Night of the Owls" 2-14; *Bronk* "The Gauntlet" 10-5; **1976** *Little House on the Prairie* "The Bully Boys" 12-6.

TELEFILMS

1975 *The Daughters of Joshua Cabe* 2-20, 2-21 CBS; **1976** *James A. Michener's "Dynasty"* 3-13 NBC; **1982** *The Wild Women of Chastity Gulch* 10-13 ABC.

Ivor Barry

(born 1919)

Welsh-born actor Ivor Barry began his stage career in England in 1940, moving to Canada in 1953. His rather limited film career began in 1964 and he was first seen on U. S. television on a Canadian produced soap, *Moment of Truth.*

Ivor did the first of five *Mission: Impossible* episodes in 1967 and was seen intermittently in guest shots through much of the seventies. He was a regular on the brief *Mr. Deeds Goes to Town* (1969-70).

GUEST CREDITS

1966 *Bonanza* "Home from the Sea" 5-1; *Laredo* "The Price of a Ranger" 12-9; **1967** *Mission: Impossible* "The Diamond" 2-4; *Maya* "Twilight of the Empire" 10-21; **1968** *Mission: Impossible* "The Exilir" 11-24; **1969** *Daniel Boone* "Minnows for a Shark" 1-2; **1970** *Mission: Impossible* "Phantoms" 2-8; *Mission: Impossible* "Hunted" 11-21; **1971** *The FBI* "The Watch Dog" 10-31; **1972** *Mission: Impossible* "Two Thousand" 9-23; *McCloud* "The Bare-foot Stewardess Caper" 12-3; *Ironside* "Shadow Soldiers" 12-21; **1974** *Six Million Dollar Man* "Eye Witness to Murder" 3-3; *Streets of San Francisco* "Mask of Death" 10-3; *Hawaii Five-0* "A Gun for McGarrett" 11-26; **1976** *Rockford Files* "The Italian Bird Fiasco" 2-13; **1978** *Barnaby Jones* "Memory of a Nightmare" 12-14; **1982** *Father Murphy* episode 2-23; **1983** *A-Team* "The Taxicab Wars" 11-1.

TELEFILMS

1969 *Fear No Evil* 2-3 NBC; *Daughter of the Mind* 12-9 NBC; **1971** *Assault on the Wayne* 1-12 ABC; *Do You Take This Stranger?* 1-18 NBC; **1972** *Gidget Gets Married* 1-4 ABC; **1973** *Six Million Dollar Man* 3-7 ABC; *Death Race* 11-10 ABC.

Martine Bartlett

(born 1925)

Onstage from 1950, Martine didn't hit films and television until the early sixties. After a 1961 film debut in *Splendor in the Grass*, she guested on television series on a somewhat limited basis after a busy 1963-66 period. Her television debut was in a short-lived soap called *Ben Jerrod.*

GUEST CREDITS

1963 *Breaking Point* "And James Was a Very Small Snail" 11-ll; *Arrest and Trial* "Journey into Darkness" 12-8; **1964** *Twilight Zone* "Night Call" 2-7; *Lieutenant* "In the Highest Tradition" 2-29; *Fugitive* "The End Game" 4-21; *Eleventh Hour* "The Color of Sunset" 4-22; **1966** *Virginian* "One Spring, Like Long Ago" 3-2; *Mission: Impossible* "Zubrovnik's Ghost" 11-26; **1968** *Felony Squad* "The Love Victim" 2-5; **1969** *Then Came Bronson* "The Old Motorcycle Fiasco" 9-24; **1970** *Mod Squad* "Sweet Child of Terror" 1-6; *Immortal* "The Return" 12-17; **1972** *Sixth Sense* "Dear Joan, We're Going to Scare You to Death" 9-30; **1973** *Owen Marshall, Counselor at Law* "Sometimes Tough Is Good" 1-17; *Cannon* "He Who Digs a Grave" 9-12; **1974** *Toma* "The Friends of Danny Beecher" 3-29; *Manhunter* "The Lodester Ambush" 12-4; **1975** Kojak "Winner Takes Nothing" 12-14; **1976** *Cannon* "House of Cards" 1-14.

TELEFILMS

1975 *Attack on Terror: The FBI Versus the Ku Klux Klan* 2-20, 2-21 CBS; **1976** *Sybil* 11-14, 11-15 NBC; **1981** *Sizzle* 11-29 ABC.

Arthur (Art) Batanides

(born l925, Tacoma, Washington)

Art came from a family of eight children and was a natural mimic as he grew up. During World War II service with the U. S. Army he saw action in several major battles. His ability as a mimic got him into the Army Special Services branch as an entertainer during the post-war period.

Discharged from service, he did summer stock prior to a 1949 film debut. In l952 televison beckoned, and he worked regularly in 1953-54 on the children's show, *Rod Brown and the Rocket Rangers*. His only other series regular role was on a syndicated 1960 crime show called *Johnny Midnight*.

His swarthy complexion and stern look kept him in very strong demand in TV guest roles for two decades, often as a villain, and frequently in ethnic roles.

GUEST CREDITS

1959 *Richard Diamond* episode 6-7; *Twilight Zone* "Mr Denton on Doomsday" 10-l6; *Lawless Years* "The Joe Angelo Story" 11-l9; *Rawhide* "Incident of the Valley of the Shadow" 11-20; *Phillip Marlowe* "Hit and Run" 12-8; **1960** *Detectives* "Life in the Balance" l-l; *Detectives* "Anatomy of Fear" 2-26; *Deputy* "The Truly Yours" 4-9; *Wanted: Dead or Alive* "Vendetta" 4-9; *M Squad*

"Dead Parents Don't Talk" 5-3; *Chevy Mystery Show* "Dead Man's Walk" 7-10; **1961** *Detectives* "Power Failure" 1-13; *Bonanza* "The Spitfire" 1-14; *Islanders* "The World Is Her Oyster" 3-12; *Asphalt Jungle* "The Last Way Out" 5-7; *Rawhide* "Incident before Black Pass" 5-19; *Adventures in Paradise* "Show Me a Hero" 11-5; **1962** *87ᵗʰ Precinct* "The Pigeon" 1-29; *Rifleman* "The Wanted Man" 9-25; *Twilight Zone* "The Mirror" 10-20; **1963** *Perry Mason* "The Case of the Shoplifter's Shoe" 1-3; *Alcoa Premiere* "Million Dollar Hospital" 4-18; *Ben Casey* "My Enemy Is a Bright Green Sparrow" 4-29; *Combat* "The Long Way Home" 10-15; **1964** *Fugitive* "Search in a Windy City" 2-4; *Outer Limits* "Specimen Unknown" 2-23; *Great Adventure* "The Pathfinder" 3-6; *Rogues* "The Day They Gave the Diamonds Away" 9-20; **1965** *Amos Burke, Secret Agent* "Balance of Terror" 9-15; *Gunsmoke* "Taps for Old Jeb" 10-16; *Wild Wild West* "The Night of the Dancing Death" 11-5; *Honey West* "A Neat Little Package" 11-19; **1966** *Jerico* "Panic in the Piazza" 10-13; *Man from UNCLE* "The Thor Affair" 10-28; *I Spy* "To Florence with Love" 11-30; **1967** *Wild Wild West* "The Night of the Gypsy Peril" 1-20; *Mission: Impossible* "The Frame" 1-21; *Time Tunnel* "Attack of the Barbarians" 2-10; *I Spy* "The Mederra Block" 10-2; *Cimarron Strip* "The Hunted" 10-5; *I Spy* "Philotemo" 10-9; *Lost in Space* "The Space Primevals" 10-10; **1968** *Wild Wild West* "The Night of the Death Maker" 2-23; *Land of the Giants* "Terror-Go-Round" 11-3; *Wild Wild West* "The Night of Miguelito's Revenge" 12-13; **1969** *Star Trek* "That Which Survives" 1-24; *Mission: Impossible* "Doomsday" 2-16; *Mod Squad* "An Eye for an Eye" 10-7; *Mission: Impossible* "Commandante" 11-2; **1970** *Room 222* "Captain of the Team" 10-28; *Silent Force* "Take as Directed for Death" 11-30; **1971** *Hawaii Five-0* "The Gunrunner" 2-10; *Mission: Impossible* "The Party" 3-6; **1972** *Mission: Impossible* "Stone Pillow" 1-8; **1973** *Mannix* "The Man Who Wasn't There" 1-7; *McCloud* "Showdown at the End of the World" 1-7; **1974** *Columbo* "Mind over Mayhem" 2-10; **1975** *Police Story* "Face for a Shadow" 11-7; **1977** *Police Story* "Prime Rib" 4-5; **1978** *Wonder Woman* "Death in Disguise" 2-10; *Lou Grant* "Poison" 3-6; *Wonder Woman* "Pot O' Gold" 12-22; **1979** *Lou Grant* "Denial" 11-7.

TELEFILMS

1971 *The Feminist and the Fuzz* 1-26 ABC; *What's a Nice Girl Like You...?* 12-18 ABC; **1972** *Evil Roy Slade* 2-18 NBC; *The Heist* 11-29 ABC; **1976** *The Lindbergh Kidnapping Case* 2-26 NBC.

Hal Baylor (a.k.a. Hal Fieberling)
(born 1918)

Husky Hal Baylor was a boxer in his youth and his strong physique helped propel him into countless action oriented roles in television and films. He appeared in the first of eighty films in 1949, eventually having roles in *Sands of Iwo Jima, Jim Thorpe-All American, River of No Return, The Young Lions, Operation Petticoat, The Gnome Mobile, The Cheyenne Social Club, The Emperor of the North Pole, Herbie Rides Again* and *Hustle*.

Hal was well established in television by the mid-fifties; his only series regular role occured in 1955-56 in *The Life and Legend of Wyatt Earp*. He worked steadily thereafter in a variety of guest roles until the late seventies; he was particularly busy in western series, with 9 appearances on *Bonanza* and 6 guest shots on *Rawhide*.

GUEST CREDITS

1959 *Lawman* "The Gunman" 2-15; *Californians* "Act of Faith" 5-26; *Rawhide* "Incident of the Day of the Dead" 9-18; *Maverick* "The Sheriff of Duck 'N Shoot" 9-27; *Texan* "Blue Norther" 10-12; *Texan* "Cowards Don't Die" 11-30; **1960** *Bonanza* "The Stranger" 2-27; *Rawhide* "Incident of the Arana Scar" 4-22; *Bonanza* "Breed of Violence " 11-5; *Surfside 6* "The Frightened Canary" 12-12; **1961** *Deputy* "The Challenger" 2-25; *Rifleman* "Short Rope for a Tall Man" 3-28; *Rawhide* "The Black Sheep" 11-10; *Thriller* "The Remarkable Mrs. Hawk" 12-19; **1962** *Bonanza* "The Ride" 1-21; *Laramie* "The Runaway" 1-23; *Tales of Wells Fargo* "Incident at Crossbow" 2-3; *Lawman* "The Man Behind the News" 5-13; *77 Sunset Strip* "Pattern for a Bomb" 6-8; *Kraft Mystery Theatre* "Murder Is a Private Affair" 7-25; *Rawhide* "Incident of the Hunter" 9-28; *Wide Country* "What Are Friends For?" 10-18; *Rawhide* "Incident of the Querencias" 12-7; **1963** *Have Gun-Will Travel* "Bob Wire" 1-12; *Dakotas* "Mutiny at Ft. Mercy" 1-21; *Laramie* "The Fugitives" 2-12; *Virginian* "Ride a Dark Trail" 9-18; *Perry Mason* "The Case of the Devious Delinquent" 12-5; **1964** *Rawhide* "Incident of the Rusty Shotgun" 1-9; *Gunsmoke* "Now That April Is Here" 3-21; *Rawhide* "Incident at El Toro" 4-9; *Bonanza* "A Man to Admire" 12-6; **1965** *Perry Mason* "The Case of the Lover's Gamble" 2-18; *Virginian* "We've Lost a Train" 4-21; *Virginian* "The Brothers" 9-15; *Slattery's People* "A Sitting Duck Named Slattery" 9-17; *Perry Mason* "The Case of the Carefree Coronary" 10-17; *Man Called Shenandoah* "The Siege" 12-13; **1966** *Laredo* "Above the Law" 1-13; *Bonanza* "Shining in Spain" 3-20; *Bonanza* "Old Charlie" 11-6; **1967** *Big Valley* "Price of Victory" 2-13; *Invaders* "Vikor" 2-15; *Dragnet* "The Big Shooting" 3-30; *Star Trek* "The Edge of Terror" 4-6; *Guns of Will Sonnett* "The Natural Way" 9-29; *Judd, for the Defense* "The Confessional" 10-20; *Bonanza* "Six Black Horses" 11-26; *Gunsmoke* "Rope Fever" 12-4; *Tarzan* "Jai's Amnesia" 12-15; **1968** *The FBI* "Act of Violence" 1-21; *Bonanza* "Stronghold" 5-26; *Guns of Will Sonnett* "Home Free" 11-22; *Mod Squad* "A Quiet Weekend in the Country" 12-3; **1969** *Hawaii Five-0* "Along Came Joey" 2-12; *Mannix* "The Solid Gold Web" 3-22; **1969** *Mannix* "Who Killed Me?" 12-13; **1971** *Dan August* "The Assassin" 4-8; *Bonanza* "An Earthquake Called Callahan" 4-11; *Adam-12* "The Sniper" 10-6; *The D.A.* "The People vs. Ganda" 10-8; **1972** *Cannon* "Blood on the Vine" 1-18; *Gunsmoke* "Hostage!" 12-11; 1973 *Gunsmoke* "The Boy and the Sinner" 10-1; **1974** *Gunsmoke* "Thirty a Month and Found" 10-7; *Planet of the Apes* "The Deception" 11-1; **1975** *Emergency* episode 2-1; *Barbary Coast* "Arson and Old Lace" 11-14; **1978** *CHiPs* "Trick or Treat" 10-21.

TELEFILMS

1976 *The Macahans* 1-19 ABC; *The New Daughters of Joshua Cabe* 5-29 ABC.

Noah Beery, Jr.

(born August 10, 1913, New York City; died October 1, 1994)

The son of noted actor Noah Beery, Sr. (1884-1949) and nephew of film star Wallace Beery (1882-1949), Noah first appeared in one of his father's films at age 7 (1920). He made some episodic serials in 1937 and began hitting his stride in a career that totaled over 150 films.

He developed a low-keyed, laid-back and non-threatening style that served him well as a supporting player. Among his film roles were appearances in *Red River*, *The Spirit of St. Louis*, *Inherit the Wind*, *Little Fauss and Big Halsey* and *Walking Tall*.

In television from 1954, he had numerous series regular roles: *Circus Boy* (1956-58), *Riverboat* (1960-61), *Hondo* (1967) and *Doc Elliot* (1974). But the role that truly endeared him to a generation of television fans was his casting as Joseph "Rocky" Rockford, father of "Jim" in The *Rockford Files* (1974-80). His calm demeanor played off, and complimented James Garner's character in a truly excellent manner; Noah was twice nominated for an Emmy for his work on the series.

Following Rockford, Noah was a regular on *The Quest* (1982) and on *Yellow Rose* (1983-84). He

Virginian "You Can Lead a Horse to Water" 1-7; **1973** *Police Story* "The Big Walk" 12-4; **1974** *Waltons* "The Heritage" 1-17; *Streets of San Francisco* "The Hard Breed" 2-24; *Six Million Dollar Man* "Run, Steve, Run" 4-26; **1976** *Ellery Queen* "The Adventure of the Sinister Scenario" 2-8; *Six Million Dollar Man* "The Bionic Badge" 2-22; **1981** *Vegas* "Sourdough Suite" 1-14; *Magnum, P.I.* "J. Digger Doyle" 4-16.

Noah Berry, Jr. (right), in his featured role as Joseph "Rocky" Rockford, listens to series star James Garner, in an episode of *The Rockford Files* (NBC).

appeared on *Murder, She Wrote* in 1985 and on a *Love Boat* episode in 1986 as he wrapped up his career. Noah died on October 1, 1994 of complications from surgery to relieve bleeding of the brain. He was survived by his wife, two daughters, a son and three stepchildren.

GUEST CREDITS

1960 *Wagon Train* "The Jonas Murdock Story" 4-13; **1961** *Wagon Train* "Path of the Serpent" 2-8; *Adventures in Paradise* "Nightmare in the Sun" 6-19; **1962** *Route 66* "1800 Days to Justice" 1-26; *Wide Country* "A Guy for Clementine" 9-27; **1964** *Gunsmoke* "Prairie Wolfer" 1-18; *Wagon Train* "The Kate Crawley Story" 1-27; **1965** *Perry Mason* "The Case of the Golden Venom" 1-21; *Branded* "Now Join the Human Race" 9-19; **1966** *Gunsmoke* "Honor Before Justice" 3-5; *Monroes* "Lost in the Wilderness" 11-30; *Virginian* "The Long Journey Home" 12-14; **1967** *Combat* "A Little Jazz" 2-21; 1970

TELEFILMS

1973 *The Alpha Caper* 10-6 ABC; **1974** *Sidekicks* 3-21 CBS; *Savages* 9-11 ABC; **1976** *Francis Gary Powers: The True Story of the U-2 Incident* 9-29 NBC; **1980** *Gridlock* 10-2 NBC; **1982** *The Capture of Grizzly Adams* 2-21 NBC; *Mysterious Two* 5-31 NBC.

Fred Beir
(born 1927, died June 3, 1980)

Entering television in 1950 in a *Philco TV Playhouse* episode, Fred was a wonderful asset to the medium for 30 years as a leading man and supporting player. Perhaps his most memorable role was in the 1963 *Twilight Zone* episode "Death Ship" in which he played a young astronaut coming to grips with his own mortality.

Great versatitity marked his career, from western lawmen to outlaws to policemen and professionals to crime series criminals. He was good at light comedy in episodes of *Andy Griffith* and *The Dick Van Dyke Show*, and even found time to appear on

the soap *Days of Our Lives* (1977-78).

Married for a time to actress Sheilah Wells, Fred died of cancer in 1980, survived by his then wife Luci and two daughters.

GUEST CREDITS

1959 *Markham* "A Clear and Present Danger" 9-20; *Deputy* "Like Father" 10-17; *One Step Beyond* "Night of the Kill" 10-20; *Lineup* "Lonesome as Midnight" 11-18; *General Electric Theater* "Platinum on the Rocks" 11-29; *Wanted: Dead or Alive* "Man on Horseback" 12-5; **1960** *Men into Space* "The Space Satellite" 1-13; *Man and the Challenge* "Man in the Capsule" *Hawaiian Eye* "Shadow of the Blade" 5-4; *Rebel* "A Grave for Johnny Yuma" 5-1; *Detectives* "Song of Songs" 5-27; *Chevy Mystery Show* "Summer Hero" 6-12; *Bonanza* "Badge without Honor" 9-24; *Hawaiian Eye* "Sea Fire" 10-5; *Michael Shayne* "Murder and the Wanton Bride" 12-16; *Thriller* "Man in the Middle" 12-20; **1961** *Outlaws* "The Waiting Game" 1-19; *Perry Mason* "The Case of the Cowardly Lion" 4-8; *Bronco* "Guns of the Lawless" 5-8; **1962** *Cain's Hundred* "The Debasers" 1-16; *Maverick* "Epitaph for a Gambler" 2-11; *Wagon Train* "The Daniel Clay Story" 2-21; *Hawaiian Eye* "A Likely Story" 3-14; *87th Precinct* "New Man in the Precinct" 4-16; *Hawaiian Eye* "Pursuit of a Lady" 12-19; **1963** *Dick Powell Show* "The Rage of Silence" 1-29; *Wagon Train* "The Naomi Kaylor Story" 1-30; *Twilight Zone* "Death Ship" 2-7; *Ben Casey* "Rage Against the Dying Light" 4-15; *Ben Casey* "With the Rich and Mighty" 9-25; *Outer Limits* "The Man with the Power" 10-7; *Eleventh Hour* "You Shouldn't Have Done It, Steve Koslowski" 10-30; **1964** *Dr. Kildare* "Goodbye, Mr. Jersey" 2-20; **1965** *Fugitive* "A.P.B." 4-6; *Amos Burke, Secret Agent* "The Man with the Power" 10-13; **1966** *Honey West* "Like Visions and Omens" 2-4; *Virginian* "The Velvet Trap" 11-7; *T.H.E. Cat* "Crossing at Destiny Bay" 11-18; *Jerico* episode 12-15; **1967** *Time Tunnel* "Visitors from Beyond the Stars" 1-13; *Garrison's Gorillas* "The Death Sentence" 1-16; *Mod Squad* "The Teeth of the Barracuda" 9-24; **1969** *Mannix* "Death Run" 1-4; *Ironside* "A Drug on the Market" 3-6; *The FBI* "The Cober List" 3-23; *Virginian* "A Love to Remember" 10-29; **1970** *The FBI* "Pressure Point" 2-1; *Hawaii Five-0* "Nightmare Road" 2-18; *Mission: Impossible* "The Homecoming" 10-10; *Dan August* "The King Is Dead" 10-14; **1971** *Mannix* "What Happened to Sunday?" 1-9; *Interns* "The Secret" 1-22; *Longstreet* "A World of Perfect Complicity" 9-22; **1972** *Mannix* "To Draw the Lightning" 2-22; *Medical Center* episode 11-1; *Banyon* "Time to Kill" 11-10; *Medical Center* episode 2-28; *Owen Marshall, Counselor at Law* "Final Semester" 3-7; *Ironside* "All Honorable Men" 3-8; *Kung Fu* "The Third Man" 4-26; *Owen Marshall, Counselor at Law* "The Sin of Susan Gentry" 11-17; *Hawaii Five-0* "Try to Die on Time" 12-4; *Room 222* episode 12-7; *Mannix* "Cry Danger" 12-9; *Ironside* "The Last Payment" 12-20; *The FBI* "Ransom" 12-30; **1974** *Cannon* "Kelly's Song" 9-11; *Six Million Dollar Man* "Nuclear Alert" 9-13; *Rockford Files* "The Big Ripoff" 10-25; *Kolchak: The Night Stalker* "Firefall" 11-8; **1975** *Harry O* "For the Love of Money" 1-16; *Amy Prentiss* "Portrait in Evil" 2-2; *Barbary Coast* episode 10-6; *Petrocelli* "Face of Evil" 12-17; **1976** *Barnaby Jones* "Wipeout" 3-4; *Ellery Queen* "The Adventure of the Hard-Hearted Huckster" 3-21; **1977** *Man from Atlantis* "The Disappearances" 6-20; **1978** *CHiPs* "Rustling" 1-12; **1979** *Lou Grant* "Denial" 1-1; *CHiPs* "Counterfeit" 10-20; *Paris* "Friends and Enemies" 10-20; *Lou Grant* episode 11-5.

TELEFILMS

1969 *Trial Run* 1-8 NBC; 1971 *In Broad Daylight* 10-16 10-16 ABC; *Suddenly Single* 10-19 ABC; 1976 *Twin Detectives* 5-1 ABC; 1979 *Love's Dark Ride* 4-2 NBC.

Cal Bellini
(born 1936)

A swarthy complexion typecast Cal as American Indians, Latinos, Polynesians and men from India. He was a regular on the 1960 television series *Diagnosis: Unknown*, did a 1961 drama special "Cry Vengeance", then virtually disappeared from the medium until 1967. The following decade provided frequent guest roles, especially in crime dramas.

GUEST CREDITS

1967 *Coronet Blue* "The Assassins" 6-12; 1970 *Mod Squad* "Welcome to the Human Race, Levi Frazee" 11-10; *Dan August* "The Murder of a Small Town" 9-30; 1971 *Ironside* "Escape" 2-11; *Bold Ones: The Lawyers* "The Price of Justice" 2-21; 1972 *Mod Squad* "No More Leaves for Ernie Holland" 2-1; *Mod Squad* "Can You Hear Me Out

There?" 11-9; *Marcus Welby, M.D.* "Heartbeat for Yesterday" 12-12; 1973 *Streets of San Francisco* "Trail of the Serpent" 2-22; 1974 *Barnaby Jones* "Rendevous with Terror" 2-24; *King Fu* "The Predators" 10-5; 1975 *Cannon* "Tomorrow Ends at Noon" 3-19; 1976 *Streets of San Francisco* "Requiem for a Murder" 1-22; *Harry O* "Victim" 3-4; 1977 *Rockford Files* "Beamer's Last Case" 9-16; *Young Daniel Boone* "The Salt Licks" 9-26; *Big Hawaii* "Sun Children" 9-28; 1978 *Hawaii Five-0* "A Big Aloha" 1-12; *Hawaii Five-0* "A Distant Thunder" 11-9; *Project UFO* "Sighting 4022: The Island Incident" 11-30; 1979 *Hawaii Five-0* "Voice of Terror" 12-4; 1982 *Bring 'Em Back Alive* "The Warlord" 10-26.

TELEFILMS

1974 *Little House on the Prairie* 3-30 NBC; 1975 *Kate McShane* 4-11; 1976 *Law of the Land* 4-29 NBC; *Scott Free* 10-13 NBC; 1978 *Go West, Young Girl* 4-27 ABC; 1980 *Waikiki* 4-21 ABC.

Russ Bender
(born 1910; died August 16, 1969)

Following a film debut in 1956, Russ Bender found most of his screen roles in B pictures. He did have roles in *Lover, Come Back*, *That Touch of Mink* and *A Gathering of Eagles*. His television career

(from 1958) was more distinguished, with guest roles in a number of hit series. Russ died in 1969, survived by his wife and two sons.

GUEST CREDITS

1959 *Richard Diamond* episode 4-19; *Perry Mason* "The Case of the Petulant Parnter" 4-25; *Rawhide* "Incident of a Burst of Evil" 6-26; *Cheyenne* "The Prisoner of Moon Mesa" 11-16; **1960** *Twilight Zone* "The Hitchhiker" 1-22; *Black Saddle* "The Indian Tree" 2-19; *Hotel de Paree* "Sundance and the Good Luck Coat" 5-6; *Rawhide* "Incident of the Captive" 12-16; **1961** *Thriller* "Man in a Cage" 1-17; *Perry Mason* "The Case of the Barefaced Witness" 3-18; **1962** *Twilight Zone* "The Fugitive" 3-9; *Have Gun-Will Travel* "The Siege" 4-1; *Perry Mason* "The Case of the Skeleton's Closet" 5-5; *Virginian* "The Devil's Children" 12-5; *Ben Casey* "Pack Up All My Cares and Woes" 12-17; **1963** *Laramie* "The Wedding Party" 1-29; *Twilight Zone* "On Thursday We Leave for Home" 5-2; *Ben Casey* "The Last Splintered Spoke in the Old Burlesque Wheel" 12-25; **1965** *Gunsmoke* "Gold Mine" 12-25; **1967** *Mission: Impossible* "The Seal" 11-5; *Iron Horse* "Wild Track" 12-16.

Roxane Berard

With large and very striking eyes, French actress Roxane Berard was a busy young actress from 1959 until the mid sixties, frequently appearing as young French women who had ventured west in TV western dramas. She was a favorite guest on *Maverick* (4) and on *Have Gun-Will Travel* (3). Her last known TV appearance was on an October 1967 episode of *Get Smart*.

GUEST CREDITS

1959 *Maverick* "A Game of Chance 1-4; *General Electric Theater* "Man on a Bicycle" 1-11; *Colt .45* "The Man Who Loved Lincoln" 5-3; *77 Sunset Strip* "The Canine Caper" 5-15; *Markham* "The Human Factor" 5-30; *Maverick* "Royal Four Flush" 9-20; *Have Gun-Will Travel* "Les Girls" 9-26; *Untouch-*

ables "The Tri-State Gang" 12-10; **1960** *Deputy* "The Hidden Motive" 1-30; *Maverick* "The Resurrection of Joe November" 2-28; *Johnny Ringo* "The Rafferty" 3-3; *Markham* episode 3-10; *Bourbon Street Beat* "Wall of Silence" 3-28; *Rawhide* "Incident of the Last Chance" 6-10; *Have Gun-Will Travel* "The Fatalist" 9-10; **1961** *Maverick* "Diamond Flush" 2-5; *Have Gun-Will Travel* "A Drop of Blood" 12-2; **1962** *87th Precinct* "The Pigeon" 1-29; *Tales of Wells Fargo* "The Wayfarers 5-19; *Bronco* "Moment of Doubt" 4-2; **1964** *Perry Mason* "The Case of the Fifty Millionth Frenchman" 2-20.

Oscar Beregi, Jr.

(born 1918; died November 1, 1976)

The son of actor Oscar Beregi, Sr., Oscar was one of better character actors of his era. He made his film debut in 1953 in *Call Me Madam*. His large frame, strong features and stage presence made him a natural for authority figures, and he was very effective as brainy villains.

Frequently cast in European roles (Hungarian by birth), Oscar could handle strong dramatic roles but was also effective in sitcom roles of the period.

GUEST CREDITS

Girl from UNCLE "The Garden of Evil Affair" 10-1; *Mission: Impossible* "Odd Man Out" 10-8, 10-15; *Time Tunnel* "Devil's Island" 11-11; *I Spy* "Little Boy Lost" 12-14; *The FBI* "List for a Firing Squad" 12-18; **1967** *Man from UNCLE* "The Matterhorn Affair" 3-3; *Tarzan* "Tiger, Tiger" 9-15; *Wild Wild West* "The Night of the Running Death" 12-15; **1968** *Garrison's Gorillas* "War and Crime" *2-12;It Takes a Thief*

Oscar Beregi, Jr. (right), appearing as *The Cardinal*, offers a toast to Gregory Morton (left) and John Raynor. (Maurice Manson photo)

1959 *Have Gun-Will Travel* "An International Affair" 4-2; **1960** *Bat Masterson* "The Disappearance of Bat Masterson" 3-10; *Untouchables* "Clay Pigeon-The Jack 'Legs' Diamond Story" 10-20; *Have Gun-Will Travel* "Vernon Good" 12-31; **1961** *Untouchables* "The Organization" 1-26; *77 Sunset Strip* "Strange Bedfellows" 2-17; *Twilight Zone* "The Rip Van Winkle Story" 4-21; *Roaring 20's* "The Royal Tour" 6-3; *Twilight Zone* "Death's Head Revisited" 11-10; *Thriller* "The Return of Andrew Bentley" 12-15; **1962** *Bus Stop* "Turn Home Again" 1-28; *New Breed* "Policemen Die Alone" 2-6; *Dick Powell Show* "Safari" 4-3; *Untouchables* "The Contract" 5-31; *77 Sunset Strip* "The Reluctant Spy" 10-12; *Dick Powell Show* "The Great Anatole" 10-30; *77 Sunset Strip* "Shadow on Your Shoulder" 12-7; *77 Sunset Strip* "Adventure in San Dede" 12-14; **1963** *Twilight Zone* "The Mute" 1-31; *G.E. True* "Man with a Suitcase" 6-9; **1964** *Voyage to the Bottom of the Sea* "No Way Out" 11-30; **1965** *Man from UNCLE* "The Odd Man Affair" 4-19; *Wild Wild West* "The Night of the Glowing Corpses" 10-29; **1966**

"Totally by Design" *2-20; Mannix* "The Girl in the Frame" *3-16;* **1969** *Wild Wild West* "The Night of the Cassacks" *3-21;It Takes a Thief* "The Blue, Blue Danube" 10-30; *The FBI* "The Inside Man" 11-30; **1971** *McMillan and Wife* "Husbands, Wives and Killers" 11-10; **1972** *McCloud* "the Barefoot Stewardess Caper" 12-3; **1973** *Mannix* "Out of the Night" 1-21; *Cannon* "Press Pass to the Slammer" 3-14; *Mission: Impossible* "Imitation" 3-30; *Columbo* "The Most Dangerous Match" 4-4; *Cannon* "Murder by the Numbers" 11-28; **1974** *Police Story* "Glamour Boy" 10-29; **1975** *Caribe* "Counterfeit Killer" 4-28; **1976** *Kojak* "The Forgotten Room" 1-4.

TELEFILM

1967 *The Scorpio Letters* 2-19 NBC.

Lee Bergere

Onstage from 1950, Lee did a number of sixties TV guest appearances and was a regular on a short-lived 1975 sitcom called *Hot L Baltimore*. During 1981-83 he had the most visible role of his career, that of the Carrington's major domo on *Dynasty*.

GUEST CREDITS

1960 *Alaskans* "The Bride Wore Black" 4-10; *One Step Beyond* "The Storm" 6-21; *Law and Mr. Jones* "The Long Echo" 12-30; **1961** *New Breed* "Sweet Bloom of Death" 11-28; **1963** *Perry Mason* "The Case of the Deadly Verdict" 10-3; **1965** *Alfred Hitchcock Hour* " Wally the Beard" 3-1; *Perry Mason* "The Case of the Murderous Murderer" 11-18; *Man from UNCLE* "The Tigers Are Coming Affair" 11-5; **1966** *T.H.E. Cat* "Sandman" 9-23; *Jerico* "Have Traitor, Will Travel" 10-6; **1967** *Mission: Impossible* "The Legacy" 1-7; *Wild Wild West* "The Night of the Colonel's Ghost" 3-10; **1968** *Mannix* "The Falling Star" 1-6; *Run for Your Life* "The Exchange" 3-27; *Mannix* "Comes Up Roses" 10-5; **1969** *Star Trek* "The Savage Curtain" 3-7; *Mission: Impossible* "The Brothers" 12-14; **1970** *The FBI* "The Innocents" 11-1; *Young Lawyers* "The Russell Incident" 11-9; **1974** *Owen Marshall, Counselor at Law* "I've Promised You a Father" 3-5; **1978** *Wonder Woman* "Death in Disguise" 2-10.

Alan Bergmann

An effective character actor of the sixties and seventies, Alan Bergmann's permanent scowl and menacing persona resulted in his being cast in virtually all adversarial roles. He appeared in many of the era's top TV series and created some memorable villains, with a handful of sympathetic roles.

GUEST CREDITS

1966 *Bonanza* "Home from the Sea" 5-1; *Wild Wild West* "The Night of the Ready Made Corpse" 11-25; **1967** *Big Valley* "Court Martial" 3-6; *Run for Your Life* "East of the Equator" 3-20; **1968** *Star Trek* "The Empath" 12-6; *Bonanza* "Mark of Guilt" 12-15; **1969** *Land of the Giants* "Our Man O'Reilley" 12-28; **1970** *Mission: Impossible* "The Choice" 3-22; *Ironside* "Checkmate and Murder" 10-29, 11-5; *Mannix* "The Other Game in Town 10-31; **1972** *Mission: Impossible* "Committed" 1-22; *Search* "The Antidote" 11-1; *Mannix* "A Game of Shadows" 12-24; **1973** *Marcus Welby, M.D.* "Death Is a Side Effect" 11-18; **1974** *Mannix* "Race Against Time" 1-6, 1-13; **1975** *Rockford Files* "Just by Accident" 2-28; *Six Million Dollar Man* "The Bionic Badge" 2-22; *Cannon* "Mad Man" 3-3; *Spencer's Pilots* "The Explosives" 11-19; **1977** *Wonder Woman* "Wonder Woman in Hollywood" 2-16.

TELEFILM

1972 Welcome Home, Johnny Bristol l-30 CBS.

Bibi Besch

(born February l, 1942, Vienna, Austria)

Reared in Westchester County, New York, Austrian-born Bibi Besch began her television career during the early seventies in four soaps: *The Secret Storm, Love Is a Many Splendored Thing, Somerset* and *The Edge of Night*. She began doing guest work and telefilms in 1976 and continued into the nineties.

Bibi was a regular on *Secrets of Midland Heights* (1980-81) and *The Hamptons* (1983). Later eighties guest shots included *Cagney and Lacey* (2), *Trapper John, M.D., Dynasty* (2), *Dallas, Falcon Crest, Highway to Heaven, Murder, She Wrote, Family Ties*, and *J. J. Starbuck*.

She is the daughter of actress Gusti Huber; her daughter is actress Samantha Mathis.

GUEST CREDITS

1976 *Ellery Queen* "The Adventure of Caesar's Last Sleep" 3-14; *Police Story* "The Other Side of the Badge" 10-26; **1977** *Police Story* "The Blue Fog" 2-l; *Rockford Files* "Beamer's Last Case" 9-16; **1978** *Charlie's Angels* "Game, Set and Death" 1-4; *Police Woman* "Sunset" l-l8; *Six Million Dollar Man* "The Madonna Caper" 2-6; **1979** *Kate Loves a Mystery* "It Goes with the Territory" 10-25; *Eischied* "The Dancer" 11-23; **1981** *Hart to Hart* "Murder Takes a Bow" 5-19; **1982** *Trapper John, M.D.* "The Good Life" 11-28; **1983** *Scarecrow and Mrs. King* "There Goes the Neighborhood" 10-10; *Remington Steele* "Scene Stealers" 11-15.

TELEFILMS

1976 *Victory at Entebbe* 12-13 ABC; **1977** *Peter Lundy and the Medicine Hat Stallion* 11-6 NBC; **1978** *Betrayal* 11-13 NBC; **1980** *The Plutonium Incident* 3-11 CBS; **1981** *Death of a Centerfold: The Dorothy Stratten Story* 11-l NBC; **1983** *Secrets of a Mother and Daughter* 10-4 CBS; *The Day After* 11-20 ABC.

Zina Bethune

(born February 17, 1945, New York City)

While still a pre-teen, Zina became a regular on the soap The *Guiding Light* (1956-58), followed by a

stint on *Young Doctor Malone* (1959). During 1962-65 she co-starred on *The Nurses*. She subsequently returned to her soap roots on *The Love of Life* during the late sixties. Her television work was rather sporadic during the seventies and eighties.

A singer-dancer-actress, Zina worked on national tours of *Oklahoma!*, *Sweet Charity* and *Damn Yankees*. She has appeared with the New York City Ballet and in special performances at The White House and Kennedy Center.

GUEST CREDITS

1959 *U.S. Steel Hour* "Call It a Day" 5-20; **1960** *Route 66* "Swan Bed" 10-21; *Naked City* "The Human Trap" 11-30; **1961** *U.S. Steel Hour* "Famous" 5-31; **1962** *Cain's Hundred* "The Swinger" 4-3; *Route 66* "Kiss the Maiden, All Forlorn" 4-13; **1967** *Invaders* "The Prophet" 11-14; **1970** *Lancer* "Chad" 1-20; **1973** *Emergency* "The Old Engine" 9-29; **1974** *Gunsmoke* "Family of Killers" 1-14; *Planet of the Apes* "The Legacy" 10-11; **1976** *Emergency* "Grateful" 2-7; **1977** *CHiPs* "Aweigh We Go" 10-22; **1978** *Hardy Boys/Nancy Drew Mysteries* "Arson and Old Lace" 4-1.

Edward Binns

(born 1916, Pennsylvania; died 1990)

After training at Cleveland Playhouse, Ed hit Broadway in 1947 and entered films in 1951. Among his movies were roles in *North by Northwest*, *Fail Safe* and *Patton*. He was very active in television from 1952, appearing often in fifties productions like *Kraft Television Theatre* (6), *Robert Montgomery Presents*, *Danger*, *U.S. Steel Hour*, *Pond's Theater*, and *Inner Sanctum* (3).

Ed starred on a 1959 police series, *Brenner*, which was given new life in 1964 with new episodes filmed and inserted in a summer replacement slot. He became a semi-regular on *The Nurses* during 1962-63, appearing as Dr. Anson Kelly. *It Takes a Thief* provided Ed a recurring role during 1969-70.

His rich voice kept him in demand for narrations and voice-overs. He died of a heart attack in 1990.

GUEST CREDITS

1960 *Twilight Zone* "I Shot an Arrow into the Air" 1-15; *Alcoa Theater* "The Last Flight Out" 1-25; *One Step Beyond* "Vanishing Point" 2-2; *Route 66* "The Beryllium Eater" 12-9; *Detectives* "Big Poison" 12-16; **1961** *Wagon Train* "The Earl Packer Story" 1-4; *June Allyson Show* "Without Fear" 2-6; *Thriller* "The Merriweather File" 2-14; *Deputy* "The Lonely Road" 2-18; *Perry Mason* "The Case of the Angry Dead Man" 2-25; *General Electric Theater* "A Very Special Girl" 3-11; *Zane Grey Theater* "The Atoner" 4-6; *Stagecoach West* "A Place of Still Waters" 4-11; *Cain's Hundred* "Quick Brown Fox" 5-8; *Asphalt Jungle* "The McMasters Story" 5-14; *Perry Mason* "The Case of the Malicious Mariner" 10-7; *Investigators* "Style of Living" 11-8; *Dr. Kildare* "Holiday Weekend" 11-16; *Defenders* "The Treadmill" 11-25; **1962** *Wagon Train* "The Jud Steele Story" 5-2; *Checkmate* "The Bold and the Tough" 5-16; *Saints and Sinners* "Lucious Lois" 11-19; **1963** *Dakotas* "Return to Dry Dock" 1-7; *Dick Powell Show* "The Judge" 2-5; *Route 66* "The Cruelest Sea of All" 4-5; *Defenders* "A Taste of

Vengeance" 4-6; *Untouchables* "Junk Man" 6-11; *Defenders* "Weeping Baboon" 9-28; *Fugitive* "Glass Tightrope" 12-3; **1964** *Twilight Zone* "The Long Morrow" 1-10; *Defenders* "The Pill Man" 2-22; *Wagon Train* "The Santiago Quesada Story" 3-20; *Combat* "Rescue" 3-31; *Bob Hope Chrysler Theater* "The Command" 5-22; *Fugitive* "Cry Uncle" 12-1; *Slattery's People* "Question: Which One Has the Privilege?" *Virginian* "A Gallows for Sam Horn" 12-2; *Voyage to the Bottom of the Sea* "The Ghost of Moby Dick" 12-14; *12 O'Clock High* "The Suspected" 12-18; **1965** *Daniel Boone* "Doll of Sorrow" 4-22; *Man Called Shenandoah* "The Fort" 9-27; *Virginian* "Ring of Silence" 10-27; *Fugitive* "Set Fire to the Straw Man" 11-30; **1966** *Blue Light* "Target: David March" 1-19; *Loner* "Trouble in Paradise" 1-22; *Dr. Kildare* "A Few Hearts, a Few Flowers" 2-7; *Dr. Kildare* "Some Tales for Halloween" 2-8; *Dr. Kildare* "I Can Hear the Ice Melting" 2-14; *Dr. Kildare* "A Strange Sort of Accident" 3-29; *Hawk* "The Man Who Owned Everyone" 10-20; **1967** *Virginian* "Sue Ann" 1-11; *Laredo* "The Small Chance Ghost" 3-3; *Run for Your Life* "The Perils of Charity Jones" 3-10, 3-17; *Coronet Blue* "The Assassins" 6-12; **1968** *The FBI* "The Tunnel" 4-21; **1969** *Judd, for the Defense* "The Holy Ground" 2-14, 2-21; *It Takes a Thief* "Who'll Bid Two Million Dollars?" 10-2; *It Takes a Thief* "The King of Thieves" 11-30; **1970** *The FBI* "The Dollar" 2-22; *It Takes a Thief* "An Evening with Alexander Munday" 3-9; *Virginian* "The Price of Hanging" 11-11; *Bold Ones: The Senator* "The Continual Roar of Musketry" 11-29; *Name of the Game* "The Glory Shouter" 12-18; **1971** *Bold Ones: The Doctors* "An Absence of Lonliness" 1-24; *Ironside* "The Accident" 3-11; **1973** *Hawaii Five-0* "Jury of One" 3-13; **1974** *Chopper One* "The Copperhead" 3-7; *McCloud* "The Gang That Stole Manhattan" 10-13; *Cannon* "The Exchange" 10-23; **1975** *Police Story* "Year of the Dragon I, II" 1-21, 1-28; *Manhunter* "The Seventh Man" 1-29; *Caribe* "The Patriots" 4-21; **1976** *Police Woman* "Trial by Prejudice" 10-12; *Police Story* "Monster Manor" 11-30; *Lucan* "The Search" 12-26.

TELEFILMS

1971 *The Sheriff* 3-30 ABC; **1973** *Hunter* 1-9 CBS; **1979** *The Power Within* 5-11 ABC.

Sidney Blackmer

(born 1895; died October 5, 1973)

Following graduation from the University of North Carolina, and while trying to crack the New York stage, Sidney appeared in the famed episodic serial *The Perils of Pauline* (1914). He became a radio singer and acted in a DuMont experimental television programduring the late thirties.

After several years absence from the screen, from his 1914 debut, he began anew in 1929 and went on to appear in over 100 films. Included were roles in *Duel in the Sun, Saturday's Hero, The High and the Mighty, High Society* and *Rosemary's Baby*. He had an especially good part in the chilling latter film. Blackmer was noted for his portrayals of sly and dishonest characters.

Sidney was a staple of fifties television, with appearances on live dramas like *Armstrong Circle Theater, Goodyear Playhouse, U.S. Steel Hour, Philco Playhouse, The Web* and *Hallmark Hall of Fame*. He did guest work throughout the sixties before succumbing to cancer in October of 1973.

GUEST CREDITS

1961 *Thriller* "Premature Burial "10-2; **1962**
Alfred Hitchcock Presents "The Faith of Aaron
Menefee" 1-30; *Cain's Hundred* "The Manipulator"
1-30; *Target: The Corruptors* "The Malignant
Hearts" 3-23; *Dr. Kildare* "Operation Lazarus" 5-24;
1963 *DuPont Show of the Month*" Diamond Fever"
3-24; *Outer Limits* "The Hundred Days of the
Dragon" 9-23; *Defenders* "The Empty Heart" 10-5;
1964 *Reporter* "A Time to Be Silent" 12-4; **1966** *Ben
Casey* "For San Diego You Need a Different Bus" 1-
17; *Ben Casey* "Smile: It's Only Twenty Dols of
Pain" 1-24; *Ben Casey* "Fun and Games and Other
Tragic Things" 1-31; *Ben Casey* "Weave Nets to
Catch the Wind" 2-7; *Ben Casey* "Lullaby for a
Wind-Up Toy" 2-14; *Girl from UNCLE* "The
Atlantic Affair" 11-15; **1968** *Name of the Game*
"Pineapple Rose" 12-20; **1969** *Name of the Game*
"Chains of Command" 10-17.

TELEFILM

1971 *Do You Take This Stranger?* 1-18 NBC.

Whitney Blake

(born Los Angeles, Calif.)

Whitney made her television debut in 1956 and
had numerous late fifties guest credits on everything
from *Perry Mason* (2) to *Maverick* to *The Millionaire*. She was very busy during 1959-60 in guest
roles until she gained a long running regular role on
Hazel (1961-65).

Following *Hazel* she returned to occasional
guest work and was a regular on *The David Frost
Review* (1971). She and her husband, writer-producer
Alan Manings, created the long running hit sitcom
One Day at a Time.

Whitney's daughter, Meridith Baxter, has
become one of television's brightest stars and
appeared with her mother in a 1979 episode of
Family.

GUEST CREDITS

1959 *Gunsmoke* "Wind" 3-21; *Rawhide* "Incident
of the Curious Street" 4-10; *Loretta Young Show*
'Strictly Personal' 4-19; *Restless Gun* "One on the
House" 4-20; *Tales of Wells Fargo* "Doc Holliday"
5-14; *M Squad* "Model in the Lake" 5-15; *Markham*
"Round Trip to Mozambique" 11-14; *Richard
Diamond* "The Image" 11-30; **1960** *Riverboat*
"Blowup" 1-17; *77 Sunset Strip* " The One That Got
Away" 1-22; *M Squad* "The Velvet Stakeout" 3-8;
Michael Shayne "Dolls Are Deadly" 9-30; *Adven-
tures in Paradise* "The Krishmen" 10-31; *Thriller*
"The Fatal Impulse" 11-29; **1961** **Route 66** "Sheba"
1-6; *Aquanauts* "Niagra Drive" 1-11; *Bronco* "Yan-
kee Tornado" 3-13; *Route 66* "The Newborn" 5-5;
1962 *Kraft Mystery Theatre* "Two Counts of Mur-
der" 7-11; **1966** *Laredo* "One Too Many Voices" 11-
18; *Man from UNCLE* "The Take Me to Your Leader
Affair" 12-30; **1967** *Virginian* "Bitter Harvest" 3-15;
Mannix "Coffin for a Clown" 11-25; **1973**
Gunsmoke "A Game of Death…An Act of Love" 11-
5, 11-12; **1974** *Cannon* "The Deadly Trail" 10-16;
1977 *Hunter* "Mirror Image" 2-25; **1979** *Family* "The
Affair" 1-4.

TELEFILMS

1974 *The Stranger Who Looks Like Me* 3-6 ABC; *Strange Homecoming* 10-29 NBC; **1975** *Returning Home* 4-29 ABC; **1976** *Law and Order* 5-6 NBC.

Mari Blanchard
(born April 13, 1927; died May 10, 1970)

Mari Blanchard had severe polio at age 9 and took three years to recover the ability to walk. She later attended both U.C.L.A. and U.S.C. and, in 1949, signed a contract with Paramount. Universal had her under contract in later years.

Mari died of cancer in 1970 at age 43, survived by her husband, photographer Vincent Conti.

GUEST CREDITS

1959 *Incident of the Stalking Death* 11-13; *Sugarfoot* "Apollo with a Gun" 12-8; **1960** *Laramie* "Rope of Steel" 2-16; *Bronco* "Montana Passage" 4-5; **1961** *77 Sunset Strip* "The Positive Negative" 1-27; *Rawhide* "Incident of the Big Blowout" 2-10; *Roaring 20's* "The Vamp" 3-4; *Gunslinger* "Road of the Dead" 3-30; *Hawaiian Eye* "The Kapua of Coconut Bay" 10-4; *77 Sunset Strip* "The Cold Cash Caper" 11-10; **1962** *Detectives* "Night on the Town"

1-26; *Perry Mason* "The Case of theMelancholy Marksman" 3-24; **1964** *Breaking Point* "So Many Girls, So Little Time" 2-17; **1967** *Virginian* "Doctor Pat" 3-1.

Tiffany Bolling
(born 1946)

Tiffany debuted in films in 1967 in the Sinatra-starring *Tony Rome*. After her first TV guest role in 1969 it was apparent that the small screen would offer her more frequent work, and she stayed busy throughout the seventies. She was a regular on the short-lived *New People* (1969-70).

GUEST CREDITS

1969 *Bonanza* "Five Candles" 3-2; *Mod Squad* "A Seat by the Window" 4-15; **1970** *Ironside* "The Wrong Time, the Wrong Place" 2-5; *Marcus Welby, M.D.* "The Girl from Rainbow Beach" 11-17; **1971** *Mannix* "A Day Filled with Shadows" 2-13; **1972** *Bold Ones: The Lawyers* "Lisa, I Hardly Knew You" 2-13; *Sixth Sense* "Witch, Witch, Burning Bright" 3-11; **1973** *Toma* "The Oberon Contract" 10-4; *New Perry Mason* "The Case of the Deadly Deeds" 10-21; *Mannix* "A Matter of the Heart" 11-4; **1976** *Bronc* "The Vigilante" 3-28; **1977** *Switch*

"Portraits of Death" 1-4; *Man from Atlantis* "The Death Scouts" 5-7; *Barnaby Jones* "The Captives" 11-10; **1978** *Charlie's Angels* "Game, Set, Death" 1-4; *Vegas* "The Games Girls Play" 9-27; **1981** *Vegas* "Heist" 2-25.

TELEFILMS

1973 *Key West* 12-10 NBC; **1976** *Eleanor and Franklin* 1-11, 1-12.

Ivan Bonar

A character actor, in films from 1959, Ivan Bonar found most of his work in television. He was a regular during 1964-65 on The *Adventures of Ozzie and Harriet*, and subsequently worked mostly in guest roles. He also worked on the soap *General Hospital*, appearing as Chase Murdock.

GUEST CREDITS

1962 *Have Gun-Will Travel* "Penelope" 12-8; **1967** *Fugitive* "Goodbye My Love" 2-28; *Invaders* "The Betrayed" 3-26; **1969** *Medical Center* "The Adversaries" 12-31; **1971** *Men at Law* "The Truth, the Whole Truth and Anything Else That Works" 3-3; *Night Gallery* "A Question of Fear" 10-27; **1972** *Medical Center* episode 3-10; *Bonanza* "The Bucket Dog" 12-19; **1974** *Streets of San Francisco* "License to Kill" 12-5; **1975** *Harry O* "May Day" 10-23; *Medical Center* "Too Late for Tomorrow" 11-3; *Medical Center* "The Silent Witness" 12-29; **1976** *Medical Center* "The Stranger" 2-9; **1977** *Little House on the Prairie* "To Live with Fear" 2-14, 2-21; *Man from Atlantis* "The Killer Spores" 5-17; **1979** *Kaz* "Count Your Fingers" 2-29; *Lou Grant* "Hit" 3-5; **1980** *Lou Grant* episode 3-10; *Quincy, M.E.* "Last Rights" 9-16; *Little House on the Prairie* "The Silent Cry" 10-20; **1981** *Walking Tall* "The Protectors of the People" 1-24; *Walking Tall* "Deadly Impact" 2-21; *Quincy, M.E.* "D.U.I." 12-2; **1982** *Lou Grant* episode 3-1.

TELEFILMS

1973 *Hawkins on Murder* 3-13 CBS; *The President's Plane Is Missing* 10-23 ABC; **1977** *Spider Man* 9-14 CBS; *Mary Jane Harper Cried Last Night* 10-5 CBS; *The Storyteller* 12-5 NBC; **1978** *Cops and Robin* 3-28 NBC; **1982** *The Day the Bubble Burst* 2-7 NBC; **1983** *Packin' It In* 2-7 CBS; *Special Bulletin* 3-20 NBC; *Cave-In* 6-19 NBC; *The Haunting Passion* 10-24 NBC.

Ivan Bonar (left), in a scene with Joanne Linville from the 1976 Universal film, *Gable and Lombard*.

Carla Borelli

A lovely former model, Carla Borelli entered films in 1967's *The Gnome-Mobile*. She began her TV career in 1967, doing periodic guest roles until she became a regular on the soap *Days of Our Lives* during 1975-76. This was followed by additional work on soaps *Another World* and *Texas* (1980-82). She appeared in 6 episodes of *Falcon Crest* during 1985. She is a native of San Francisco.

GUEST CREDITS

1967 *Wild Wild West* "The Night of Montezuma's Hordes" 10-27; **1969** *It Takes a Thief* "The Family" 4-1; *Mannix* "Color Her Missing" 10-4; *Name of the Game* "Laurie Marie" 12-19; **1970** *Silent Force* "The Banker" 1-4, 1-11; *Adam-12* "Log Twenty Four-A Rare Occasion" 2-14; *Ironside* "Ransom" 2-19; *Name of the Game* "I Love You, Billy Baker" 11-20, 11-27; **1971** *Iron Side* "The Quincunx" 1-7; *Bold Ones: The Lawyers* "The Letter of the Law" 12-26; **1976** *Quincy, M.E.* "A Star Is Dead" 11-28; **1977** *Charlie's Angels* "The Vegas Connection" 2-9.

TELEFILMS

1970 *Ritual of Evil* 2-23 NBC; **1971** *Banyon* 3-15 NBC.

Phillip Bourneuf

(born 1907; died 1979)

Following a 1934 stage debut, Phillip made his first film, *Winged Victory*, in 1944. A stalwart of live television, Phillip made a memorable *Studio One* appearance in 1949, in *Julius Caesar*, playing Marc Antony. He later appeared in two more *Studio One* productions, and on *Philco Television Playhouse, Robert Montgomery Presents, Chevrolet Tele-Theater, Danger* (2) and *Kraft Mystery Theatre*. He worked often in TV guest roles during the fifties and through the mid-sixties, then tapered off to infrequent appearances.

GUEST CREDITS

1960 *Perry Mason* "The Case of the Prudent Prosecutor" 1-30; *One Step Beyond* "Who Are They?" 2-2; *Thriller* "The Return of Andrew Bentley" 12-11; **1962** *87th Precinct* "Step Forward" 3-26; *Wagon Train* "Swamp Devil" 4-4; *Dr. Kildare* "Horn of Plenty" 4-19; *Alcoa Premiere* "Cry Out in Silence" 5-15; *General Electric Theater* "The Roman Kid" 6-3; *U.S. Steel Hour* "Honor in Love" 7-25; *Defenders* "The Unwanted" 10-13; **1963** *Perry Mason* "The Case of the Lawful Lazarus" 3-14; *Ben Casey* "Father Was an Intern" 4-1; **1965** *Alfred Hitchcock Hour* "The Photographer and the Undertaker" 3-15; *Dr. Kildare* "Toast the Golden Couple"

11-1; *Dr. Kildare* "Wives and Losers" 11-2; *Dr. Kildare* "Welcome Home, Dear Anna" 11-8; *Dr. Kildare* "A Little Child Shall Lead Them" 11-9; *Dr. Kildare* "Hour of Decision" 11-15; *Dr. Kildare* "Aftermath" 11-16; *Perry Mason* "The Case of the Golden Girls" 12-19; **1966** *I Spy* "The Conquest of Maude Murdock" 3-2; *Big Valley* "The Martyr" 10-17; **1967** *Felony Squad* "Let Him Die" 9-11; **1970** *Immortal* "Reflections on a Lost Tomorrow" 10-8; **1975** *Medical Center* "Aftershock" 3-10; *Mobile One* "The Reporter" 10-10.

TELEFILMS

1968 *Istanbul Express* 10-22 NBC; **1971** *The Last Child* 10-5 ABC; **1973** *Frankenstein* 1-16, 1-17 ABC; **1975** *Babe* 10-23.

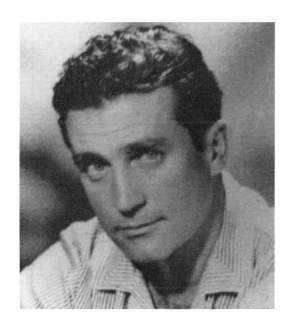

William Boyett

(born 1930)

For the two decades after a 1954 television debut William Boyett was very active in the medium. Typecast as policemen, he appeared in 7 *Perry Mason* episodes and 6 episodes of *Dragnet* as cops. His strong association with Jack Webb then led him into a long running semi-regular role on *Adam-12* as the commanding officer of the lead characters (1968-69. He is still a working actor in the nineties, appearing on the soap *General Hospital* in 1991.

GUEST CREDITS

1959 *Bat Masterson* "The Secret Is Death" 5-27; *Millionaire* "Millionaire Timothy MacKail" 12-30; **1960** *Perry Mason* "the Case of the Mythical Monkeys" 2-27; *Perry Mason* "The Case of the Larcenous Lady" 12-17; **1961** *Perry Mason* "The Case of the Renegade Refuge" 12-9; **1962** *Laramie* "Among the Missing" 9-25; *Perry Mason* "The Case of the Hateful Hero" 10-18; **1963** *Laramie* "The Wedding Party" 1-29; **1964** *Perry Mason* "The Case of the Ugly Duckling" 5-21; **1965** *Perry Mason* "The Case of the Mischievous Doll" 5-13; *Perry Mason* "The Case of the Candy Queen" 9-26; *Run for Your Life* "A Girl Named Sorrow" 11-22; **1967** *Dragnet*

"The Big Jade" 3-27; *Dragnet* "The Big Shooting Board" 9-21; *Dragnet* "The Big Listing" 11-16; **1967** "The Big Shipment" 12-28; **1970** *Dragnet* "Burglary: Baseball" 4-9; *Dragnet* "D.H.Q.-The Victims" 4-16; **1972** *Mission: Impossible* "Leona" 10-7; **1975** *Rockford Files* "Two into 5:56 Won't Go" 11-21; **1976** *Rookies* "Blue Movie, Blue Death" 2-24; **1978** *Rockford Files* "The Competitive Edge" 2-10; **1981** *Incredible Hulk* "Veteran" 10-16; **1982** *CHiPs* "Silent Partner" 2-28; **1983** *A-Team* "Steel" 11-28.

TELEFILMS

1971 *Vanished* 3-8, 3-9 NBC; **1975** *Mobile Two* 9-2 ABC; **1977** *Rosetti and Ryan: Men Who Love Women* 5-19 NBC; **1979** *The Golden Gate Murders* 10-3 CBS.

Lane Bradford

(born 1923; died 1973)

The son of well-known western film badman John Merton (1901-1959), Lane Bradford carved an outstanding film and television career of his own. Following a 1942 film debut, he appeared in 80 western movies and 5 episodic serials. Television viewers saw him often as heavies, especially on *Gunsmoke* (11), *Bonanza* (7) and *Laramie* (4).

GUEST CREDITS

1959 *Gunsmoke* "Jayhawkers" 1-31; *Maverick* "The Saga of Waco Williams" 2-15; *Restless Gun* "Code for a Killer" 4-27; *Colt .45* "The Devil's Godson" 10-18; **1960** *Law of the Plainsman* "The Imposter" 2-4; *Gunsmoke* "Moo Moo Raid" 2-13; *Maverick* "The Iron Hand" 2-21; *Texan* "Killer's Road" 4-25; *Texan* "Mission to Monterey" 6-13; *Tate* "Comanche Scalps" 8-10; *Bonanza* "The Mission" 9-17; *Gunsmoke* "The Peace Officer" 10-15; *Maverick* "Last Train from Stop Gap" 10-16; *Wagon Train* "The Candy O'Hara Story" 12-7; **1961** *Rawhide* "Incident on the Road Back" 2-24; *Bonanza* "The Rescue" 2-25; **1962** *Laramie* "The Hunt" 2-20; *Laramie* "The Day of the Savage" 3-13; *Perry Mason* "The Case of the Absent Artist" 3-17; *Rawhide* "The House of the Hunter" 4-20; *Gunsmoke* "Quint Asper Comes Home" 9-29; *Laramie* "Lost Allegiance" 10-30; *Gunsmoke* "Abe Blocker" 11-24; *Laramie* "Time of the Traitor" 12-11; **1963** *Bonanza* "Little Man-Ten Feet Tall" 5-26; *Fugitive* "See Hollywood and Die" 11-5; **1964** *Fugitive* "Angels Travel on Lonely Roads" 3-3; *Gunsmoke* "Caleb" 10-29; *Perry Mason* "The Case of the Nautical Knot" 10-29; *Bob Hope Chrysler Theater* "On the Outskirts of Town" 11-6; *Wagon Train* "The Last Circle Up" 12-27; **1965** *Bonanza* "Patchwork Man" 5-23; **1966** *Laredo* "The Treasure

of San Diablo "2-21; *Daniel Boone* "First in War, First in Peace" 10-13; *Lost in Space* "West of Mars" 11-30; **1967** *Iron Horse* "Volcano Wagon" 1-16; *Road West* "The Predators" 1-23; *Iron Horse* "Five Days to Washiba" 10-7; **1968** *Gunsmoke* "The Gunrunners" 2-5; *Bonanza* "In Defense of Honor" 4-28; *High Chaparral* "The Covey" 10-18; *Bonanza* "The Last Vote" 10-20; *Land of the Giants* "Double Cross" 12-8; **1969** *Gunsmoke* "Exodus 21:22" 3-24; **1971** *Bonanza* "Shadow of a Hero" 2-21; *Gunsmoke* "New Doctor in Town" 10-11; *Gunsmoke* "Lijah" 11-8; **1972** *Gunsmoke* "The Wedding" 3-13; **1973** *Hawaii Five-0* "Thanks for the Honeymoon" 1-9; *Search* "The Twenty-Four Carat Hit" 1-24; *Marcus Welby, M.D.* "Catch the Ring That Isn't There" 2-6.

Joycelyn Brando
(born San Francisco, Calif., 1919)

The older sister of Marlon Brando, Joycelyn was educated at Lake Forest College, and since she stayed out of the headlines, was not widely known

outside the acting profession.

   She debuted in television in 1948, appearing in several *Actor's Studio* productions of the early TV era.

   Joycelyn guested regularly on TV during the 1959-67 period, especially on western series. In 1968 she accepted a role on the soap *Love of Life* and disappeared from TV guest work until 1975. She appeared in two films with Marlon, *The Appaloosa* and *The Chase* (both 1966).

GUEST CREDITS

   1959 *M Squad* "The Terror of Dark Street" 4-24; *Alfred Hitchcock Presents* "True Account" 6-7; *Lux Playhouse* "The Miss and the Missiles" 6-12; *Alfred Hitchcock Presents* "Graduating Class" 12-27; **1960** *Riverboat* "The Night of the Faceless Men" 3-28; *Laramie* "Cemetery Road" 4-12; *Markham* "The Man from Saltzberg" 6-2; *Thriller* "Worse Than Murder" 9-27; *Riverboat* "The Water of Gorgeous Springs" 11-7; *General Electric Theater* "The Money Driver" 12-18; **1961** *Laramie* "Man from Kansas" 1-10; *Checkmate* "One for the Book" 3-18; *Tall Man* "The Legend and the Gun" 3-18; *Alfred Hitchcock Presents* "Make My Death Bed" 6-27; *Wagon Train* "The Kitty Albright Story" 10-4; *One Step Beyond* "People Need People" 10-10; *Tales of Wells Fargo* "Treasure Coach" 10-14; *Frontier Circus* "The Hunter and the Hunted" 11-2; *87th Precinct* "My Friend, My Enemy" 11-27; **1962** *Thriller* "Till Death Do Us Part" 3-12; **1963** *Wagon Train* "The Michael McGoo Story" 3-20; *Virginian* "Strangers at Sundown" 4-3; *Virginian* "To Make This Place Remembered" 9-25; *Wagon Train* "The Sam Pulaski Story" 11-4; *Dr. Kildare* "The Oracle" 12-19; **1964** *Alfred Hitchcock Hour* "The Jar" 2-14; **1967** *Virginian* "The Welcoming Town" 3-22; **1975** *Little House on the Prairie* "Money Crop" 2-19; **1979** *Dallas* episode 12-14; **1981** *Darkroom* "Catnip" 12-25.

TELEFILMS

   1978 *A Question of Love* 11-26 ABC; **1981** *Dark Night of the Scarecrow* 10-24 CBS; **1983** *Starflight: The Plane That Couldn't Land* 2-27 ABC.

Henry Brandon
(born Heinrich Von Kleinback, 1912, Germany; died February 15, 1990)

   Henry Brandon moved from his native Germany to California during childhood. He entered films in 1934, appearing in *Babes in Toyland*. He went on to appear in over 80 films, including *Trail of the Lonesome Pine, Beau Geste, The Paleface, Casanova's Big Night, The Searchers, Auntie Mame* and *Two Rode Together*. He appeared in his last film in 1983.

   Henry had varied roles, but his handsome yet cruel look often found him in adversarial roles. He retained a youthful look that belied his advancing years, and most of his later television guest appearances were on westerns or action-oriented series. He died in 1990 after a career that extended 50 years.

GUEST CREDITS

   1959 *Lawman* "To Capture the West" 2-7; *Wagon Train* "The Martha Barham Story" 11-4; **1960** *Rebel* "Gold Seeker" 1-17; *Gunsmoke* "The Deserter" 6-4; *Maverick* "A Bullet for the Teacher" 10-30; *77 Sunset Strip* "Trouble in the Middle East" 11-1; **1961** *Wagon Train* "The Patience Miller Story" 1-17; *Adventures in Paradise* "Angel of Death" 3-6; *Gunsmoke* "Stolen Horses" 4-8; *Whispering Smith*

"The Mortal Coil" 7-24; *Adventures in Paradise* "The Assassins" 11-26; **1962** *77 Sunset Strip* "The Diplomatic Caper" 1-26; **1964** *Temple Houston* "The Gun That Swept the West" 3-5; *Outer Limits* "The Chamelion" 4-27; *Combat* "Mountain Man" 9-15; **1965** *Branded* "Fill No Glass for Me" 11-7, 11-4; **1966** *Laredo* "Miracle at Massacre Mountain" 3-3; *Combat* "A Child's Game" 10-18; **1969** *Mission: Impossible* "The Brothers" 12-14; **1973** *Night Gallery* "Doll of Death" 5-20.

TELEFILMS

1978 *Bud and Lou* 11-15 NBC; **1981** *Evita Peron* 2-23, 2-24 NBC; **1983** *Little House: Back to Yesterday* 12-12 NBC.

Diane Brewster
(born 1931, Kansas City, Kansas)

Although she acted in only two episodes, Diane Brewster's inert from appeared in the opening scenes of each episode of *The Fugitive* for four seasons, playing the murdered wife of Dr. Richard Kimble. Diane's television career began in 1956 and she became a sermi-regular on *Leave It to Beaver* (1957-58), and had a regular role on *The Islanders* (1960-61). She retired from acting in 1968.

GUEST CREDITS

1959 *Cimarron City* "Runaway Train" 1-31; *Wanted: Dead or Alive* "Double Fee" 3-21; *General Electric Theater* "Nobody's Child" 5-10; *Lineup* "Thrills" 10-28; **1960** "The Lila Foldaire Story" 1-6; *Millionaire* "Millionaire Sylvia Merrick" 1-13; **1962** *Rifleman* "Jealous Man" 3-26; *Cheyenne* "Dark Decision" 11-5; *77 Sunset Strip* "The Dark Word" 11-30; **1963** *Dakotas* "Fargo" 2-25; *Perry Mason* "The Case of the Potted Planter" 5-9; *Fugitive* "The Girl from Little Egypt" 12-24; **1964** *Arrest and Trial* "Signs of an Ancient Flame" 1-12; *77 Sunset Strip* "Dead As in Dude" 1-31; **1967** *Fugitive* "The Judgment-Part II" 8-29; **1968** *Ironside* "Force of Arms" 1-4.

TELEFILM

1983 *Still the Beaver* 3-19 CBS.

Beth Brickell
(born 1941, Camden, Arkansas)

Basically a television actress, Beth Brickell became a regular on *Gentle Ben* (1967-69) early in

her acting career. Thereafter, she worked in guest roles until she left acting for directorial chores.

GUEST CREDITS

1967 *Man from UNCLE* "The Suburbia Affair" 1-6; **1969** *Bonanza* "Emily" 3-23; **1970** *Adam-12* "Log Seventy Four-Light Duty" 3-21; *Marcus Welby, M.D.* "The Worth of a Man" 9-29; *Dan August* "Passing Fair" 12-30; **1971** *Bonanza* "A Single Pilgrim" 1-3; *Alias Smith and Jones* "The Wrong Train to Brimstone" 2-4; *Hawaii Five-0* "No Bottles…No Cans…No People" 9-21; **1972** *Hawaii Five-0* "Good Night Baby-Time to Die" 2-15; **1973** *Gunsmoke* "The Widow and the Rogue" 10-29; *Chase* "A Bit of Class" 12-11; **1974** *Magician* "The Stainless Steel Lady" 1-28; *Nakia* "The Quarry" 9-28; *Kodiak* "The Last Enemy" 10-4; *Adam-12* "Earthquake" 11-19; *Ironside* "The Over-the-Hill Blues" 12-5; **1980** *Stone* "Just a Little Blow Among Friends" 3-3.

TELEFILMS

1970 *San Francisco International* 9-29 NBC; **1973** *The Great Man's Whiskers* 2-13 NBC; *Brock's Last Case* 3-5 NBC.

Burt Brinkerhoff

After a 1955 television debut, Burt was one of TV's busiest guest stars, frequently cast as angry or confused young men. He became a successful director, working on series like *Baretta* and *Hart to Hart*.

GUEST CREDITS

1960 *Hong Kong* "Clear for Action" 9-28; *Route 66* "Ten Drops of Water" 11-11; *Naked City* "Killer with a Kiss" 11-16; **1961** *Defenders* "Young Lovers" 10-14; *Naked City* "Show Me the Way to Go Home" 11-22; **1962** *New Breed* "The All-American Boy" 1-2; *Target: The Corruptors* "A Man Is Waiting to Be Murdered" 1-5; *Alcoa Premiere* "Of this Time, of That Place" 3-6; *Target: the Corruptors* "The Organizers" 5-18, 5-25; *DuPont Show* "The Betrayal" 10-21; **1963** *Fugitive* "Fatso" 11-19; **1964** *Slattery's People* "Question: Where Vanished the Tragic Piper?" 11-2; *Mr. Novak* "The People

Doll: You Wind It Up and It Makes Mistakes" 11-17; **1965** *Gunsmoke* "Run, Sheep, Run" 1-9; *Dr. Kildare* "Marriage of Convenience" 2-11; *12 O'Clock High* "The Mission" 4-2; *Dr. Kildare* "Behold the Great Man" 9-13; *Dr. Kildare* "A Life for a Life" 9-14; *Dr. Kildare* "Web of Hate" 9-20; *Dr. Kildare* "The Horizontal Hero" 9-21; *Combat* "Soldier of Fortune" 11-23; **1968** *The FBI* "The Harvest" 11-24.

Melindy Britt

A noted voice artist, Melendy made her film and television debuts in 1970, working in television until the eighties. Her voice was heard on *The New Adventures of Batman* (1977), *Flash Gordon* (1979-80) and *The Plasticman Comedy/Adventure Show* (1979-81).

GUEST CREDITS

1970 *Then Came Bronson* "The Mountain" 2-18; **1971** *Interns* episode 1-1; *Mannix* "With Intent to Kill" 1-23; *Psychiatrist* "In Death's Other Kingdom" 2-3; *Storefront Lawyers* "Yesterday Is But a Dream" 3-31; *Longstreet* "The Girl with a Broom" 11-4; **1972** *Mannix* "Portrait of a Hero" 10-15; **1973** *Ironside* "A Special Person" 1-11; **1974** *Kojak* "Slay Ride" 10-13; *Police Woman* "Requiem for Bored Wives" 11-29;

1975 *Rockford Files* "The Deep Blue Sleep" 10-10;
1976 *Rockford Files* "In Hazard" 2-6; *Bronk* "Target:
Unknown" 2-8; *Starsky and Hutch* "The Specialist"
11-13; **1977** *Rockford Files* "Just Another Polish
Wedding" 2-18; **1980** *Incredible Hulk* "Deathmask"
3-14; **1981** *Shannon* "Neither a Borrower" 11-18;
Shannon "Beating the Prime" 12-2; **1982** *Shannon*
"The Secret Rage" 3-31.

TELEFILMS

1975 *They Only Come Out at Night* 4-29 NBC;
1980 *Mother and Daughter: The Loving War* 1-25
ABC; *Reunion* 10-14 CBS.

Steve Brodie

(born John Stevens, November 25, 1919, El Dorado,
Kansas; died January 9, 1992)

A film career of over 80 movies began for Steve
in 1944, a career that included *Thirty Seconds Over
Tokyo, Winchester '73* and *The Caine Mutiny.* A
lenghty television career began in 1951, one that had
live television roles in productions like *Studio One,
Climax, Robert Montgomery Presents, Hallmark
Hall of Fame, Playhouse 90* and *Schlitz Playhouse
of Stars.*

He became a favorite of *Alfred Hitchcock*

Presents, with 4 appearances during 1956-58. In the
period 1959-61 he had a recurring role on *The Life
and Legend of Wyatt Earp*, appearing as Sheriff
Johnny Behan. He subsequently worked in guest
roles until 1978. Steve succumbed to cancer on
January 9, 1992, survived by his wife, 2 sons and 5
stepdaughters.

GUEST CREDITS

1959 *Rough Riders* " A Matter of Instinct" 2-19;
Richard Diamond episode 6-7; *Wanted: Dead or
Alive* "Montana Kid" 9-5; *Perry Mason* "The Case
of the Garrulous Gambler" 10-17; *June Allyson Show*
"Child Lost" 11-16; *Man with a Camera* "Missing"
11-23; *Millionaire* "Millionaire Mitchell Gunther"
12-2; **1960** *Rawhide* "Incident of the Wanted Painter"
1-29; *Alaskans* "Peril at Caribou Crossing" 2-28;
Perry Mason "The Case of the Slandered Submarine" 5-14; *Tightrope* "A Matter of Money" 5-24;
Stagecoach West "The Saga of Jeremy Boone" 11-
29; *Thriller* "The Fatal Impulse" 11-29; **1961** *Tales of
Wells Fargo* "Fraud" 3-13; *Americans* "The Invaders" 3-27; *Maverick* "The Devil's Necklace" 4-23;

Asphalt Jungle "The Nine-Twenty Hero" 5-21; *Stagecoach West* "The Guardian Angels"6-6; *Cheyenne* "Winchester Quarantine" 9-25; *Gunsmoke* "Old Yellow Boots" 10-7; *Surfside 6* "A Matter of Seconds" 11-27; *Cheyenne* "The Equalizer" 12-18; **1962** *Laramie* "The Confererate Express" 1-30; *Hawaiian Eye* "The Meeting on Molokai" 3-21; *Perry Mason* "The Case of the Angry Astronaut" 4-7; *Cheyenne* "Man Alone" 10-15; *Rawhide* "Incident of the Dogfaces" 11-9; *Wagon Train* "The Orly French Story" 12-12; **1963** *77 Sunset Strip* "Stranger from the Sea" 3-15; *Bonanza* "Any Friend of Walter's" 3-24; *Virginian* "Run Away Home" 4-24; *Perry Mason* "The Case of the Witless Witness" 5-16; *Rawhide* "The Case of the Two Graves" 11-7; **1964** *Bonanza* "Walter and the Outlaws" 5-24; **1965** *Burke's Law* "Who Killed Nobody Somehow?" 3-31; **1966** *Daktari* "Return of the Killer" 3-22, 3-29; *Man from Shenandoah* "Aces and Kings" 3-28; **1968** *Bonanza* "Trouble Town" 3-17; **1971** *Smith Family* "Winner Take All" 4-19; **1972**   Gunsmoke "No Tomorrow" 1-3; **1975** *Police Story* "Head Hunter" 1-14; **1978** *Police Story* "Sons" 2-15.

Hildy Brooks

Following significant stage training, Hildy made her film debut in 1968 and appeared in *Islands in the Stream* and *The Rose* before devoting most of her efforts to television. She began TV guest appearances in 1971, with most of her eighties work devoted to telefilms.

GUEST CREDITS

1971 *Mannix* "A Step in Time" 9-29; *Owen Marshall, Counselor at Law* "Voice from a Nightmare" 12-16; **1972** *Bold Ones: The Doctors* "A Very Strange Triangle" 10-31; **1973** *Ironside* "Armageddon Gang" 10-11; *Griff* "Her Name Was Nancy" 12-8; *Hawaii Five-0* "The One Hundred Thousand Dollar Nickel" 12-11; **1974** *Mannix* "Walk a Double Line" 2-10; *Toma* "A Pound of Flesh" 4-19; **1975** *Harry O* "Mayday" 10-23; **1978** *Starsky and Hutch* "The Avenger" 10-31; **1979** *Dear Detective* episode three 4-18.

TELEFILMS

1978 *The Critical List* 9-11, 9-12 NBC; **1979** *Silent Victory: The Kitty O'Neil Story* 2-24 CBS; *The Night Rider* 5-11 ABC; **1980** *To Race the Wind* 3-12 CBS; *A Perfect Match* 10-5 CBS; *The Baby Sitter* 11-28 ABC; **1982** *Forbidden Love* 10-18 CBS; **1983** *Rita Hayworth: The Love Goddess* 11-2 CBS.

Georg Stanford Brown

(born June 24, 1943, Havana, Cuba)

Reared in New York's Harlem District, Georg began his acting career in New York Shakespeare Festival productions and came to films in 1967. He made his TV debut the following year with the highlight coming during 1972-76 when he co-starred in *The Rookies.*

Married to Tyne Daly for many years, Georg began directing in television, winning an Emmy for his direction of a 1986 episode of *Cagney and Lacey.* He served as executive producer of HBO's *Vietnam War Story* and a stage work called *Kids Like These.* Much of his eighties acting work was in telefilms.

GUEST CREDITS

1968 *Dragnet* "The Big Problem" 3-28; *Judd, for the Defense* "The Ends of Justice" 10-11; *It Takes*

a Thief "Hans Across the Border" 11-12, 11-19; **1969** *Mannix* "Sometimes Don't Fly" 9-27; *Bold Ones: The Lawyers* "The Crowd Pleaser" 11-2; 1970 *Medical Center* "The Rebel in White" 4-8; *Bold Ones: The Doctors* "Killer on the Loose" 10-11; *Bold Ones: The Lawyers* "Cage for a Panther" 10-18; *Name of the Game* "The Time Is Now" 10-23; **1971** *Medical Center* "The Man in Hiding" 3-3; *Mannix* "A Choice of Evils" 11-10; **1972** *Room 222* "And in This Corner" 1-21; *Mission: Impossible* "Bag Woman" 1-29; **1979** *Paris* "Dead Men Don't Kill" 12-4.

TELEFILMS

1969 *The Young Lawyers* 10-28 ABC; **1970** *Ritual of Evil* 2-23 NBC; **1972** *Rookies* 3-7 ABC; **1976** *Dawn: Portrait of a Teenage Runaway* 9-27 NBC; **1980** *The Night the City Screamed* 12-14 ABC; **1982** *The Kid with the Broken Halo* 4-5 NBC; **1983** *In Defense of Kids* 4-6 CBS.

Lew Brown

(born 1925)

A bland appearance has enabled Lew to slip in and out of dozens of roles very readily. Yet each one was so well crafted. *Gunsmoke* used him in 18 episodes, but it is difficult to remember him for a particular one because of his smooth work.

He was also a member of Jack Webb's "stock company", doing several *Dragnet* and *Adam-12* guest roles. This versatile actor began his television career in 1956 after extensive stage work. He continued his career well into the eighties, including a 1984-85 regular slot on the soap *Days of Our Lives*.

GUEST CREDITS

1959 *Gunsmoke* "Print Asper" 5-23; **1960** *Maverick* "Maverick and Juliet" 1-17; *Gunsmoke* "The Ex-Urbanites" 4-12; *Twilight Zone* "A Thing About Machines" 10-28; 1961 *Gunsmoke* "Unloaded Gun" 1-14; *Twilight Zone* "Back There"1-21; *Gunsmoke* "Kitty Shot" 2-11; *Twilight Zone* "Long Distance Call" 3-31; *Rawhide* "Incident of the Running Man" 5-5; *Gunsmoke* "Hard Virtue" 5-6; **1962** *Ben Casey* "Imagine a Long Bright Corridor" 1-15; *Have Gun-Will Travel* "Invasion" 4-28; *Gunsmoke* "Chester's Indian" 5-12; *Virginian*

"Throw a Long Rope" 10-3; *Ben Casey* "The Night That Nothing Happened" 10-8; *Laramie* "Bad Blood" 12-4; **1963** *Virginian* "Duel at Shiloh" 1-2; *Virginian* "The Golden Door" 3-13; *Twilight Zone* "The 7ᵗʰ Is Made Up of Phantoms" 12-6; **1964** *Slattery's People* "Is Laura the Name of the Game?" 11-9; **1965** *Gunsmoke* "Double Entry" 1-2; *Voyage to the Bottom of the Sea* "Mutiny" 1-11; *Wild Wild West* "The Night of the Double-Edged Knife" 11-12; **1966** *Fugitive* "Ill Wind" 3-8; *Fugitive* "The Last Oasis" 9-13; **1967** *Gunsmoke* "Old Friend" 2-4; *Invaders* "Doomsday Minus One" 2-28; *Gunsmoke* "Ladies from St. Louis" 3-25; *Gunsmoke* "The Wreckers" 9-11; *Cimarron Strip* "The Legend of Jud Starr" 9-14; *Wild Wild West* "The Night Dr. Loveless Died" 9-29; **1968** *Cimarron Strip* "Fool's Gold" 1-11; *The FBI* "The Predators" 4-7; *Adam-12* "Log 141" 9-28; *Virginian* "The Orchard" 10-2; *Dragnet* "Management Services-DR-11" 10-10; *Gunsmoke* "Slocum" 10-21; *The FBI* "The Harvest" 11-24; **1969** *Dragnet* "Narcotics DR-21" 1-30; *Adam-12* "He Was Trying to Kill Me" 3-15; *Dragnet* "Burglary-Auto Showroom" 11-20; **1970** *Adam-12* "Log Forth-Three-Hostage" 1-3; *Adam-12* "Log Fourteen-S.W.A.T." 1-17; *Dragnet* "Narco-Pillmaker" 2-19; *Ironside* "No Game for Amateurs" 9-24; *Men from Shiloh* "Jenny" 9-30; *Gunsmoke* "McCabe" 11-30; *High Chaparral* "The Badge" 12-18; **1972** *Columbo* "Short Fuse" 1-19; *Gunsmoke* "The Predators" 1-31; *Gunsmoke* "Milligan" 11-6; *Ghost Story* "You Can Come Up Now, Mrs. Milligan" 11-12; **1973** *Emergency* episode 1-13; *Waltons* "The Deed" 2-8; *Mission: Impossible* "Imitation" 3-30; *Columbo* "Candidate for Crime" 11-4; **1974** *Mannix* "Walk a Double Line" 2-10; *Mannix* "The Man form Nowhere" 2-17; *Banacek* "Now You See Me…Now You Don't" 3-12; *Gunsmoke* "Cowtown Hustler" 3-11; *Cannon* "The Stalker" 3-20; **1975** *Baretta* "He'll Never See Daylight Again" 1-17; *McCloud* "Return to the Alamo" 3-30; *Mobile One* "The Bank Job" 10-3; *Ellery Queen* "The Adventure of the Mad Tea Party" 10-30; *Police Story* "the Test of Brotherhood" 11-14; **1977** *Waltons* "The Recluse" 9-29; **1978** *American Girls* "Haunting at Chickwood Bay" 10-7; **1979** *Man Called Sloane* "Architect of Evil" 12-15.

TELEFILMS

1970 *The Challenge* 2-10 ABC; **1971** *The D.A.: Conspiracy to Kill* 2-11 NBC; *O'Hara, U.S. Treasury* "Operation: Cobra" 4-2 CBS; **1972** *Emergency* 1-15 NBC; **1973** *Money to Burn* 10-27 ABC; **1974** *Planet Earth* 4-23 ABC; *Death Sentence* 10-2 ABC; **1976** *The Manhunter* 4-3 NBC; **1978** *The Clone Master* 9-13 NBC; *The Winds of Kitty Hawk* 12-17 NBC; **1980** *Kenny Rogers as the Gambler* 4-8 CBS; **1981** *A Matter of Life and Death* 1-13 CBS.

Kathie Browne

(born September 19, 1939, San Luis Obispo, Calif.)

Married to televison star Darren McGaven for many years, Kathie and Darren appeared together in several TV episodes. She debuted in films and TV in 1960 and had a busy two decades of guest work, plus series regular roles on *Slattery's People* (1965) and *Hondo* (1967). Her film career consisted of nine films, with roles in *Studs Lonigan* and *Come Blow Your Horn*.

GUEST CREDITS

1960 *Man From Blackhawk*"The Hundred Thousand Dollar Policy" 2-12; *Perry Mason* "The Case of the Provocative Protege" 11-12; **1961** *Bonanza* "Tax Collector" 2-18; *Rawhide* "Incident of the Phantom Bugler" 4-14; *Rawhide* "Judgment at Hondo Seco" 10-20; *Bronco* "The Harrigan" 12-25; **1962** *Bonanza* "The Tall Stranger" 1-7; *Perry Mason* "The Case of the Mystified Miner" 2-24; *Lawman* "Heritage of Hate" 3-18; *Ben Casey* "Monument to an Aged Hunter" 3-19; *Tales of Wells Fargo* "Who Lives by the Gun" 3-24; *77 Sunset Strip*"Green Bay Riddle" 4-23; *Surfside 6* "Pawn's Gambit" 6-4; *Have Gun-Will Travel* "Taylor's Women" 9-22; *77 Sunset Strip* "The Raiders" 11-2; *Have Gun-Will Travel* "Marshal of Sweetwater" 11-24; *Laramie* "Beyond Justice" 11-27; **1963** *Saints and Sinners* "Slug It, Miss Joyous" 1-14; *Wagon Train* "The Fort Pierce Story" 9-23; *Redigo* "Little MissAngel Blue Eyes" 10-29; *Perry Mason* "The Case of the Festive Falcon" 11-28; *Bonanza* "The Waiting Game" 12-8; **1964** *77 Sunset Strip* "Alimony League" 1-10; *Bonanza* "The Cheating Game" 2-9; *Bonanza* "The Pressure Game" 5-10; *Bonanza* "Triangle" 5-17; *Alfred Hitchcock Presents* "Bed of Roses" 5-22; **1965** *Perry Mason* "The Case of the Thermal Thief" 1-14; **1966** *Branded* "Call to Glory" 2-27, 3-6, 3-13; *Laredo* "The Sweet Gang" 11-4; **1967** *Felony Squad* "The Strangler" 1-30; *Wild Wild West* "The Night of the Colonel's Ghost" 3-10; **1968** *Ironside* "The Lonely Hostage" 2-1; *Big Valley* "Deathtown" 10-28; *Name of the Game* "Shine On, Jesse Gill" 11-1; *Star Trek* "Wink of an Eye" 11-22; *Ironside* "The Macabre Mr. Micawber" 11-28; **1971** *Bold Ones: The Lawyers* "The Invasion of Kevin Ireland" 9-26; *Mannix* "The Man Outside" 11-24; **1972** *Longstreet* "Anatomy of a Mayday" 2-3; *Cade's County* "Inferno" 2-27; **1974** *Police Story* "Ripper" 2-12; *Evil Touch* "Gornak's Prison" 3-3; *Banacek* "Now You See Me...Now You Don't" 3-12; *Ironside* "Act of Vengeance" 11-14; **1975** *Kolchak: The Night Stalker* "Sentry" 3-28; *Rockford Files* "Pastoria Prime Pick" 11-28; **1978** *Eddie Capra Mysteries* "And the Sea Shall Give Up Her Dead" 10-28.

TELEFILM

1970 *Berlin Affair* 11-2 ABC.

William Bryant

(born 1924, Detroit, Michigan)
   Following a distinguished World War II record, William Bryant made a film debut in *Twelve O'Clock High* (1950). Subsequent films included *The Pink Panther, Good Neighbor Sam, The Great Race, Chism* and *Walking Tall-Part 2*.
   He narrated the 1957 dramatic TV series *The*

Web and was a regular on *Hondo* (1967) and *Switch* (1976-77). He also acted in numerous telefilms.

GUEST CREDITS

1959 *Rifleman* "The Shivaree" 2-3; *Gunsmoke* "The Constable" 5-30; *Have Gun-Will Travel* "Charlie Red Dog" 1-12; **1960** *Rebel* "You Steal My Eyes" 3-20; **1961** *Michael Shayne* " Final Settlement" 2-10; *Outlaws* "Rape of Red Sky" 2-23; *Peter Gunn* "The Deep End" 3-6; *Laramie* "Ladie's Day" 10-3; **1962** *Rifleman* "Gunfire" 1-15; *Rifleman* "The Assailants" 11-12; *Laramie* "Double Eagles" 11-20; *Gunsmoke* "False Front" 12-22; **1966** *Combat* "The

Leader" 4-12; *Monroes* "Court Martial" 11-16; *Gunsmoke* "Quaker Girl" 12-10; **1967** *Man from UNCLE* "the Five Daughters Affair" 3-31, 4-7; **1968** *Garrison's Gorillas* "War and Crime" 2-13, 2-20; *Mannix* "Eight to Five, It's a Miracle" 2-17; *Bonanza* "The Stronghold" 5-26; *Lancer* "The Last Train for Charlie Poe" 11-26; **1969** *Bonanza* "Company of Forgotten Men" 2-2; *Lancer* "Zec" 9-30; *Mission: Impossible* "Mastermind" 11-23; **1970** *Gunsmoke* "Chato" 9-14; **1971** *Alias Smith and Jones* "Jailbreak at Junction City" 9-30; **1972** *Sixth Sense* "The House That Cried Murder" 2-5; *Gunsmoke* "Alias Festus Haggin" 3-6; *O'Hara, U.S. Treasury* "Operation: Smoke Screen" 3-10; *Mannix* "Portrait of a Hero" 10-15; *Banacek* "A Million the Hard Way" 11-1; *Ironside* "Riddle Me to Death" 11-2; **1973** *The FBI* "Desperate Journey" 1-28; *Rookies* "Three Hours to Kill" 2-12; *Chase* "Foul-Up" 9-25; *Barnaby Jones* "Fatal Flight" 12-9; **1974** *McMillan and Wife* "Man without a Face" 1-6; *Columbo* "Mind over Mayhem" 2-10; *Ironside* "Class of '40" 2-14; *Gunsmoke* "The Iron Man" 10-21; **1975** *Rockford Files* "The Girl in the Bay City Boys Club" 12-19; **1976** *Waltons* "The Cloudburst" 11-11; *Bionic Woman* "Jaimie's Shield" 12-15, 12-22; **1978** *Lou Grant* "Hero" 1-17; *Buck Rogers* "The Hand of Goral" 3-26; *Hawaii Five-0* "Small Potatoes" 10-26; **1982** *Bret Maverick* "Dateline: Sweetwater" 1-12; *Fall Guy* "Goin' for It" 1-27; *Fall Guy* "Colt's Outlaws" 11-10; *Fall Guy* "Hell on Wheels" 12-8; **1983** *Fall Guy* "Spaced Out" 2-16; *Fall Guy* "P.S., I Love You" 3-16; *Fall Guy* "Trauma Center" 9-28.

TELEFILMS

1971 *City Beneath the Sea* 1-25 NBC; *Powderkeg* 4-16 CBS *Sweet, Sweet Rachel* 10-2 ABC; *Black Noon* 11-5 CBS; **1972** *Killer by Night* 1-7 CBS; *Women in Chains* 1-25 ABC; **1973** *The Stranger* 2-26 NBC; **1974** *The Hanged Man* 3-13 ABC; **1975** *The Last Survivors* 3-4 NBC; *Death Scream* 9-26 ABC; **1976** *The Macahans* 1-19 ABC; *Mayday at 40,000 Feet* 11-12 CBS; **1977** *Nowhere to Hide* 6-5 CBS; **1978** *Steel Cowboy* 12-6 NBC; **1979** *The Child Stealer* 3-9 ABC; *The Legend of the Golden Gun* 4-10 NBC; *The Billion Dollar Threat*

4-15 ABC; **1980** *Gridlock* 10-2 NBC; **1982** *Rooster* 8-19 ABC; **1983** *Cave-In!* 6-19 NBC.

Claudia Bryar

(born 1918)

Married to actor Paul Bryar since 1941, Claudia appeared in some excellent films following a 1956 screen debut. Among her credits were roles in *Elmer Gantry* and *The Days of Wine and Roses*. She turned mainly to television work during the seventies and had a regular role on *The Manhunter* (1974-75).

GUEST CREDITS

1960 *Wanted: Dead or Alive* "The Cure" 9-28; *Wagon Train* "The River Crossing" 12-14; **1961** *Bus Stop* "The Glass Jungle" 11-5; **1963** *Fugitive* "The Witch" 9-24; *Mr. Novak* "Hello, Miss Phipps" 11-5; **1965** *Fugitive* "A.P.B." 4-6; **1966** *The FBI* "The Other Side of the Coin" 1-10; *Laredo* "A Very Small Assignment" 3-17; **1967** *Guns of Will Sonnett* "Meeting at Devil's Fork" 10-27; *Bonanza* "Justice Deferred" 12-17; **1969** *Mod Squad* "Child of Sorrow, Child of Light" 3-18; **1970** *Mod Squad* "The Deadly Sin" 2-24; **1971** *Alias Smith and Jones* "The Girl in Boxcar No. 3" 2-17; **1973** *Mannix* "Climb a Deadly Mountain" 9-30; *Barnaby Jones* "Catch Me If You

Can" 10-21; **1974** *Marcus Welby, M.D.*
"The Faith of Childish Things" 9-17;
Marcus Welby, M.D. "Child of Silence"
9-17; **1975** *Waltons* "The Venture" 3-6;
Barnaby Jones "Blood Relations" 11-
28; *Blue Knight* "Two to Make Deadly"
12-17; **1976** *Streets of San Francisco*
"Alien Country" 3-11; **1977** *Barnaby*
Jones "Sister of Death" 1-6; *Barnaby*
Jones "The Devil's Handmaiden" 12-1;
Quincy, M.E. "Aftermath" 2-7.

TELEFILMS

1969 *The Immortal* 9-30 ABC; *The*
Ballad of Andy Crocker 11-18 ABC;
1972 *Jigsaw* 3-26 ABC; *The Daughters*
of Joshua Cabe 9-13 ABC; *Welcome*
Home, Johnny Bristol 1-30 CBS; **1973**
Letters from Three Lovers 10-3 ABC;
A Summer without Boys 12-4 ABC; **1974**
Manhunter 2-26 CBS; *The FBI Story:*
The FBI versus Alvin Karpis, Public
Enemy Number One 11-8 CBS; **1975**
The Family Nobody Wanted 2-19 ABC;
1977 *Green Eyes* 1-3 ABC; *Alexander:*
The Other Side of Dawn 5-16 NBC;
1978 *Suddenly, Love* 12-4 NBC.

Walter Burke (left) and Steve Raines are scrutinizing the situation in a 1966 episode of *Bonanza*, "Destiny's Child" (NBC).

Walter Burke

(born 1909; died 1984)

A wiry little leprechaun-like charac-
ter actor, Walter was a veteran of radio, stage, screen
and television. He made his screen debut in 1945 in
The Naked City. Especially visible in television
roles during the sixties, he worked in the medium
until 1981.

GUEST CREDITS

1959 *Gunsmoke* "Wind" 3-21; *One Step Beyond*
"Front Runner" 6-9; *Man from Blackhawk* "Death Is
the Best Policy" 11-18; *Law of the Plainsman* "The
Gibbet" 11-26; *One Step Beyond* "The Stonecutter"
12-8; **1960** *Gunsmoke* "Hinka Do" 1-30; *Twilight*
Zone "The Big Tall Wish" 4-8; *Alaskans* "The Devil
Made Five" 6-19; *Islanders* "The Phantom Captain"
11-13; *77 Sunset Strip* "The Double Death of
Benjamin Martin" 11-25; *Klondike* "Bathhouse
Justice" 12-26; **1961** *Perry Mason* "The Case of the
Missing Melody" 9-30; **1962** *Thriller* "The Hollow
Watcher" 2-12; *Ben Casey* "The Fireman Who
Raised Rabbits" 11-26; *Wide Country* "Good Old
Uncle Walt" 12-13; **1963** *Gunsmoke* "Extradition" 12-
7, 12-14; **1964** *Outer Limits* "The Invisibles" 2-3;
Outer Limits "The Mutants" 6-16; *Dr. Kildare* "A
Candle in the Window" 11-5; *Perry Mason* "The

Case of the Wooden Nickels" 12-10; **1965** *Gunsmoke* "Circus Trick" 2-6; *I Spy* "Dragon's Teeth" 10-13; **1966** *Bonanza* "Destiny's Child" 1-30; **1967** *Lost in Space* "The Toymaker" 1-25; *Wild Wild West* "The Night of the Cut Throats" 11-17; *Wild Wild West* "The Night of the Legion of Death" 11-24; 1968 *Voyage to the Bottom of the Sea* "The Terrible Leprechaun" 1-7; *Big Valley* "Fall of a Hero" 2-5; *Guns of Will Sonnett* "The Trap" 10-4; *Guns of Will Sonnett* "The Straw Man" 11-8; **1969** *Gunsmoke* "Roots of Fear" 12-15; **1972** *Night Gallery* "Deliveries in the Rear" 1-29; *Adam-12* "Back-Up One L-20" 2-23; *Ghost Story* "The Concrete Captain" 9-22; **1975** *Streets of San Francisco* "Runaway" 12-18.

TELEFILMS

1967 *Stranger on the Run* 10-31 NBC; **1970** *The Over-the-Hill Gang Rides Again* 11-17 ABC; **1972** *Goodnight My Love* 10-17 ABC; **1973** *Murdock's Gang* 3-20 CBS; **1976** *Time Travelers* 3-19 ABC.

Normann Burton

(born 1923)

Normann Burton got his acting start in 1950 U. S. Signal Corps films, with his first Hollywood film in 1957. He subsequently appeared in *Planet of the Apes, Diamonds Are Forever, Save the Tiger* and *Inferno*. His television guest appearances were rather scattered from 1961 on through the seventies. He was a regular on the abbreviated *Ted Knight Show* (1978) and had a more visible role on *The New Adventures of Wonder Woman* (1978-79).

GUEST CREDITS

1961 *New Breed* "Death of a Ghost" 10-17; *Checkmate* "Kill the Sound" 11-13; **1962** *Untouchables* "The Floyd Gibbons Story" 12-11; **1963** *Fugitive* "See Hollywood and Die" 11-5; **1965** *Gunsmoke* "The Reward" 11-6; **1968** *I Spy* "Tag, You're It" 1-22; **1969** *Land of the Giants* "The Chase" 4-20; **1974** *Magician* "The Illusion of Black Gold" 2-11; *Rockford Files* "The Big Ripoff" 10-25; *Planet of the Apes* "The Interrogation" 11-15; *Kojak*

"The Best War in Town" 11-24; **1975** *Baretta* "The Good-Bye Orphan Blues" 9-10; **1976** *Harry 0* "Death Certificate" 4-29; *Rockford Files* "Return to the Thirty-Eighth Parallel" 12-10; **1977** *Dog and Cat* "Dead Skunk" 4-23; **1978** *Eddie Capra Mysteries* "Who Killed Lloyd Wesley Jordan?" 9-29; **1978** *Lou Grant* "Conflict" 12-18; **1982** *Simon and Simon* "Foul Play" 12-16; **1983** *Knight Rider* "A Nice Indecent Little Town" 2-18.

TELEFILMS

1971 *They Call It Murder* 12-17 NBC; **1972** *A Great American Tragedy* 10-18 ABC; **1975** *Force Five* 3-28 CBS; *Conspiracy of Terror* 12-29 NBC; **1977** *Murder in Peyton Place* 10-3 NBC; **1979** *The Ultimate Imposter* 5-12 CBS; **1980** *Bogie* 3-2 ABC; *To Race the Wind* 3-12 CBS.

Billy Green Bush

(born 1935)

Following a stage career that began in 1955, Billy began a film career in 1968, with eventual roles in *Five Easy Pieces, Monte Walsh, The Culpepper Cattle Company, Forty Carats, Electra Glide in Blue, Alice Doesn't Live Here Anymore* and *Tom Horn*. He continued to appear in films well into the nineties.

His mainly seventies television career began in 1970, with most roles utilizing his southwestern

drawl as cowboys or sly southerners. His only series regular role came in 1980, playing Elvis Presley's father on *Elvis*.

Billy is the father of twins Lindsay and Sidney Green Bush who alternated in the role of Carrie on *Little House on the Prairie*.

GUEST CREDITS

1970 *Bonanza* "Long Way to Ogden" 2-22; **1971** *Alias Smith and Jones* "The Legacy of Charlie O'Rourke" 4-22; **1972** *Sarge* "An Accident Waiting to Happen" 1-4; *Banyon* "Dead End" 11-3; *The FBI* "The Loner" 11-19; *Cannon* "The Endangered Species" 12-13; 1973 *Gunsmoke* "The Hanging of Newly O'Brien" 11-26; **1974** *Manhunter* "Terror from the Skies" 10-16; **1975** *Streets of San Francisco* "Runaway" 12-18; **1976** *Baretta* "The Left Hand of the Devil" 1-7; *Barbary Coast* "The Dawson Marker" 1-9; *City of Angels* "The House on Orange Grove Avenue" 3-16; *Serpico* "Country Boy" 9-24; **1977** *Westside Medical* "The Devil and the Deep Blue Sea" 7-14; *Oregon Trail* "Hannah's Girls" 10-26; **1978** *Starsky and Hutch* "Moonshine" 10-17; **1979** *Incredible Hulk* "Wildfire" 1-17; **1981** *Incredible Hulk* "The First" 3-6, 3-13; **1982** *Strike Force* "Ice" 1-15; **1983** *A-Team* "Till Death Do Us Part" 4-19.

TELEFILMS

1974 *Skyway to Death* 1-19 ABC; **1975** *Attack on Terror: The FBI vs. the Ku Klux Klan* 2-20, 2-21 CBS; **1976** *The Call of the Wild* 5-22 NBC; *The Invasion of Johnson County* 7-31 NBC; **1978** *The Beasts Are on the Street* 5-18 NBC; **1979** *The Jerico Mile* 3-18 ABC.

Alan Caillou
(born 1914, England)

Alan Caillou began his stage career in England at age 9. Living in the U. S. for years, he has been prominent in radio, films, stage and television. His film debut came in 1959 in the epic *Journey to the Center of the Earth*.

The sixties were a busy decade of TV guest roles for Alan. He is also a prolific writer, with over 40 novels and numerous screenplays to his credit. Alan was a series regular on *Tarzan* (1966-68) and on *Quark* (1978).

GUEST CREDITS

1959 *Maverick* "Passge to Fort Doom" 10-31; *Californians* "A Hundred Barrels" 4-21; *Have Gun-Will Travel* "Fragile" 10-31; **1960** *Thriller* "The

Prediction" 11-22; **1961** *Cheyenne* "Duel at Judas Basin" 1-30; *Hong Kong* "Double Jeopardy" 2-1; *Thriller* "Hay-Fork and Bill-Hook" 2-7; *Adventures in Paradise* "Errand of Mercy" 5-29; **1962** *Dick Powell Show* "The Prison" 2-6; *Checkmate* "A Chant of Silence" 3-21; **1965** *Burke's Law* "Who Killed Wimbledon Hastings?" 2-3; *Kraft Suspense Theatre* "The Last Clear Chance" 3-11; *Man from UNCLE* "The Tigers Are Coming Affair" 11-5; *Amos Burke, Secret Agent* "Deadlier Than the Male" 11-12; **1966** *Girl from UNCLE* "The Jewels of Ubango Affair" 12-20; *Jerico* episode 12-29; **1967** *Girl from UNCLE* "The Phi Beta Killer Affair" 3-14; *Daniel Boone* "Fort West Point" 3-23; *Daniel Boone* "Beaumarchais" 10-12; **1968** *Daniel Boone* "The Who Will They Hang from the Yardarm if Willy Gets Away?" 2-8; **1969** *It Takes a Thief* "A Matter of Gray Matter" 2-4, 2-11; *Mod Squad* "Captain Greer, Call Surgery" 3-7; *Daniel Boone* "The Printing Press" 10-23; **1970** *Bonanza* "The Big Jackpot" 1-18; *High Chaparral* "The Forge of Hate" 11-13; **1972** *Mannix* "One Step to Midnight" 11-12; **1975** *Six Million Dollar Man* "Outrage in Balinderry" 4-19; *Caribe* "The Patriots" 4-21.

TELEFILMS

1970 *Sole Survivor* 1-9 CBS; *The Challengers* 2-20 CBS; **1972** *Hound of the Baskervilles* 2-12 ABC; **1974** *The Questor Tapes* 1-23 NBC; **1980** *Gauguin The Savage* 4-29 CBS.

Pepe Callahan

Pepe made a 1965 film debut in *Ship of Fools*, but had first appeared on television five years previously. His other films of note were *McKenna's Gold, Joe Kidd* and *The Apple Dumpling Gang*. Castings were as Native-Americans and Hispanics. He continued to do occasional acting jobs into the mid-eighties.

GUEST CREDITS

1960 *Westerner* "Ghost of a Chance" 12-2; **1965** *Virginian* "Ring of Silence" 10-27; **1966** *Big Valley* "Teacher of Outlaws" 1-26; *I Spy* "the Conquest of Maude Murdock" 3-2; **1967** *Fugitive* " The One That

Got Away" 1-17; *The FBI* "Line of Fire" 11-26; **1968** *Bonanza* "Salute to Yesterday" 9-29; **1969** *Wild Wild West* "The Night of the Spanish Curse" 1-3; *Mission: Impossible* "Commandante" 11-2; **1970** *Gunsmoke* "The Noon Day Devil" 12-7; *Mission: Impossible* "The Hostage" 12-19; **1971** *Mission: Impossible* "The Fountain" 1-26; *Gunsmoke* "Gold Train: The Bullet" 11-29; 12-6; 12-13; **1975** *Invisible Man* "The Fine Art of Diplomacy" 9-15.

TELEFILMS

1970 *Wild Women* 10-20 ABC; **1978** *Go West, Young Girl* 4-27 ABC.

John Calvin

(born November 29, Staten Island, New York)

A seventies/eighties television actor, John broke into the medium in 1971. He gained a prominent role as an obnoxious son-in-law on *The Paul Lynde Show* (1972-73). For the balance of the seventies he worked primarily in crime series guest roles.

Highly visible during the eighties, John had one series regular role, on *Tales of the Gold Monkey (1982-83)*. His prolific post-1983 guest shots included *Night Rider, A-Team, Hardcastle and McCormick, Scarecrow and Mrs. King, T. J.*

Hooker, Moonlighting, Cheers, Night Court, Simon and Simon (2), *Murder, She Wrote, Dallas* (2), *Highway to Heaven, Magnum, P.I.* and *Our House.*

GUEST CREDITS

1971 *Cade's County* "Violent Echo" 10-24; *Cannon* "A Lonely Place to Die" 11-16; **1972** *Mod Squad* "Outside Position" 2-29; **1975** *Kate McShane* "Murder Comes in Little Pills" 10-1; *Harry O* "The Acolyte" 10-16; *Bronk* "The Fifth Victim" 10-19; **1976** *Jigsaw John* "Death of the Partly" 3-22; **1977** *Charlie's Angels* "Dirty Business" 2-2; *Most Wanted* "The Spellbinder" 3-7; *Rockford Files* "Crack Back" 3-25; **1978** *Amazing Spider Man* "The Curse of Rava" 4-19; *Incredible Hulk* "Never Give a Trucker an Even Break" 4-28; *Kaz* "Which Side You On?" 11-5; *Barnaby Jones* "Deadly Sanctuary" 12-10; **1979** *Quincy, M.E.* "The Eye of the Needle" 4-12; **1981** *Hart to Hart* "Slow Boat to Murder" 2-17; *Magnum, P.I.* "Wave Goodbye" 11-19; *Strike Force* "The Predator" 12-4; **1982** *Matt Houston* "Who Killed Ramona?" 10-10; *Devlin Connection* "Arsenic and Old Caviar" 12-4; **1983** *Magnum, P.I.* "Birds of a Feather" 3-17.

TELEFILMS

1974 *Winter Kill* 4-15 ABC; **1975** *The Hatfields and the McCoys* 1-15 ABC; **1978** *The Dark Secret of Harvest Home* 1-23, 1-24 NBC; **1979** *The Last Ride of the Dalton Gang* 11-20 NBC; *Beggarman, Thief* 11-26, 11-27 NBC; **1982** *The Ambush Murders* 1-5 CBS.

Rafael Campos

(born 1936, Dominican Republic; died July 7, 1985.

Rafael came to the U. S. in 1949 from his native Dominican Republic and enrolled in the New York School for the Performing Arts. He made his film debut in *The Blackboard Jungle*, appearing as one of the delinquents. Other films included *Mr. Buddwing, The Appaloosa* and *Oklahoma Crude.*

Campos began appearing in live television dramas like *Studio One* and *Playhouse 90* during the fifties; his career extended until 1984 when he last appeared on an episode of *The A-Team*. Rafael died of cancer at age 49.

GUEST CREDITS

1959 *Goodyear Theater* "Afternoon of the Beast" 1-19; *Restless Gun* "Ride with the Devil" 5-18; *Have Gun-Will Travel* "Pancho" 10-24; *Wanted: Dead or Alive* "Desert Seed" 11-14; **1960** *Wagon Train* "Dr. Swift Cloud" 5-25; **1962** *Alfred*

Hitchcock Presents "The Big Score" 3-6; *Have Gun-Will Travel* "A Miracle for St. Francis" 11-17; **1965** *Gunsmoke* "Ten Little Indians" 10-9; **1966** *Branded* "The Ghost of Murrieta" 3-20; *Combat* "The Losers" 9-20; *Girl from UNCLE* "The Prisoner of Zalomar" 9-20; *Gunsmoke* "The Mission" 10-8; *T.H.E. Cat* "King of Limpets" 12-9; **1967** *Big Valley* "Four Days to Furnace Hill" 12-4; *Hondo* "The Rebel Hat" 12-29; **1968** *Ironside* "The Sacrifice" 10-3; **1970** *Adam-12* "Log Sixty-Four-Bottom of the Bottle" 1-31; *Marcus Welby, M.D.* "Nobody Wants a Fat Jockey" 2-17; **1971** *Adam-12* "Log 115-Gang War" 1-9; **1973** *Rookies* "Point of Impact" 2-5; *Ironside* "The Best Laid Plans" 3-15; **1974** *Streets of San Francisco* "Rampage" 2-28; *McCloud* "The 42nd Street Calvary" 11-17; **1975** *Streets of San Francisco* "False Witness" 1-9; **1976** *Jigsaw John* "The Mourning Line" 3-15; **1977** *Streets of San Francisco* "Hang Tough" 2-17; **1979** *Lou Grant* "Sweep" 2-5.

TELEFILMS

1974 *The Hanged Man* 3-13 ABC; **1977** *Killer on Board* 10-10 NBC; **1979** *The Return of the Mod Squad* 5-18 ABC; **1980** *The Return of Frank Cannon* 11-1 CBS; **1983** *V* 5-1, 5-2 NBC.

Anthony Carbone

(born 1927)

From his 1959 film debut Anthony Carbone was frequently cast as violent mobsters and syndicate bosses. He was absent from television for several years, resurfacing during the mid-seventies in typical roles as hoods.

GUEST CREDITS

1960 *Untouchables* "Clay Pigeon: the Jack 'Legs' Diamond Story" 10-20; *Thriller* "The Fatal Impulse" 11-29; **1961** *Dante's Inferno* "Dante Rises Again" 1-30; *Twilight Zone* "The Mirror" 10-20; *Untouchables* "The Genna Brothers" 11-2; *Detectives* "Hit or Miss" 12-1; *Target: The Corruptors* "Silent Partner" 12-8; **1962** *87th Precinct* "King's Ransom" 2-19; **1964** *Bonanza* "The Campaigners" 4-

29; **1966** *High Chaparral* "A Way of Justice" 12-3; **1971** *McCloud* "Top of the World, Ma?" 11-3; **1974** *Police Story* "Chain of Command" 1-8; *Chopper One* "Bust Out" 1-31; *Rookies* "Johnny Lost His Gun" 11-4; **1975** *Police Story* "The Witness" 3-11; *Streets of San Francisco* "Solitaire" 3-13; *Rookies* "Lamb to the Slaughter" 9-9; **1976** *Police Woman* "Generation of Evil" 2-10; *Police Story* "Eamon Kinsella Royce" 2-20; *Police Story* "Payment Deferred" 9-21; *Rockford Files* "Drought in Indianhead River" 11-5; **1977** *McMillan* "Dark Surface" 1-2; *Switch* "For Broke" 12-12; **1980** *Stone* "Race Against Time" 3-17.

TELEFILM

1974 *A Case of Rape* 2-20 NBC.

Harry Carey, Jr.

(born May 16, 1921, Newhall, California)

Educated at Black Fox Academy in Hollywood, Harry served in the U. S. Navy from 1941 until 1946.

The son of actors Harry Carey, Sr. and Olive Deering, Harry began appearing in summer stock after leaving military service. He began working in John Ford films like *Red River, She Wore a Yellow Ribbon, Rio Grande* and *The Searchers*, but evolved into some non-western films like *Mr. Roberts* and *Niagara.*

    The vast majority of his films were westerns and it was only natural that most of his television work was also in the western genre. *Gunsmoke* used him in 10 episodes and he worked in 5 episodes of *Have Gun-Will Travel.* Harry was active during 5 decades as he continued to act into the eighties.

GUEST CREDITS

1959 *Gunsmoke* "Horse Deal" 9-26; *Rawhide* "Incident of the Shambling Man" 10-9; **1960** *Men into Space* episode 3-30; *Hotel de Paree* "Sundance and the Long Trek" 4-22; *Have Gun-Will Travel* "The Legacy" 12-10; **1961** *Gunsmoke* "Bad Sheriff" 1-7; *Tales of Wells Fargo* "Gunmen's Revenge" 5-22; *Have Gun-Will Travel* "The Revenger" 9-30; **1962** *Laramie* "The Barefoot Kid" 1-9; *Have Gun-Will Travel* "The Jonah" 5-26; *Gunsmoke* "Quint Asper Comes Home" 9-29; *Gunsmoke* "Abe Blocker" 11-24; *Laramie* "The Time of the Traitor" 12-11; **1963** *Have Gun-Will Travel* "Face of a Shadow" 4-20; *Have Gun-Will Travel* "The Sanctuary" 6-22; *Wagon Train* "The Molly Kincaid Story" 9-16; **1965** *Bonanza* "The Flannel-Mouth Gun" 1-31; *Branded* "The Vindicated" 1-31; *Gunsmoke* "Bank Baby" 5-20; **1967** *Gunsmoke* "Baker's Dozen" 12-25; **1968** *Cimarron Strip* "Sound of a Drum" 2-1; *Gunsmoke* "Waco" 12-9; **1969** *Mannix* "Missing: Sun and Sky" 12-20; **1971** *Gunsmoke* "The Lost" 9-13; *Gunsmoke* "Gold Train: The Bullet" 11-29, 12-6; 12-13; **1974** *Streets of San Francisco* "The Hard Breed" 2-21; *Gunsmoke* "Trail of Bloodshed" 3-4; *Banacek* "Horse of a Slightly Different Color" 1-22; **1982** *CHiPs* "Flare-Up" 3-7.

TELEFILMS

1978 *Kate Bliss and the Ticker Tape Kid* 5-26 ABC; **1982** *Louis L'Amour's "The Shadow Riders"* 9-28 CBS.

Michelle Carey
(born 1943)

A striking former Powers model, and child prodigy at piano, Michelle broke into films and television in 1964. In her early television years she guested on many of the era's most popular dramatic series, and appeared in some sitcom roles as well. Her distinctive voice earned her a series role as the computer voice, Effie, in *A Man Called Sloane* (1979).

GUEST CREDITS

1964 *Man from UNCLE* "The Double Affair" 11-17; **1965** *Amos Burke, Secret Agent* "Balance of Terror" 9-15; *T.H.E. Cat* "Ring of Anasis" 12-30; **1967** *Wild Wild West* "Night of the Feathered Fury" 1-13; *Run for Your Life* "Tell It to the Dead" 4-30; **1969** *Wild Wild West* "Night of the Winger Terror" 1-17, 1-24; *Name of the Game* "Blind Man's Bluff" 10-3; *Mission: Impossible* "The Brothers" 12-7; *The FBI* "Tug of War" 12-28; **1970** *It Takes a Thief* "Nice Girls Marry Stockbrokers" 1-15; **1972** *Gunsmoke* "Tara" 1-17; **1973** *Six Million Dollar Man* "Wine, Women and War" 10-20; **1977** *Starsky and Hutch* "Starsky and Hutch Are Guilty" 4-16; *Man from Atlantis* "C.W. Hyde" 1-13; *Starsky and Hutch* "Class in Crime" 2-15; **1982** *Fall Guy* "No Way Out" 1-6.

TELEFILMS

1973 *The Norliss Tapes* 2-21 NBC; *Savage* 3-31 NBC; **1977** *Delta County, U.S.A.* 5-20 ABC; **1979** *Legend of the Golden Gun* 4-10 NBC; *Undercover with the KKK* 10-23 ABC; **1982** *Rooster* 8-19 ABC.

Tim Carey

(born 1929; died May 11, 1994)

In films from 1952, Timothy Carey has often been cast as vicious killers or underworld figures. His infrequent television guest work was scattered over several decades.

Timothy was a writer, directed B films and was a well-known acting teacher. He died from a stroke in 1994, survived by his wife and 6 children.

GUEST CREDITS

1965 *Rawhide* "Encounter at Boot Hill" 9-14; **1966** *Big Valley* "Teacher of Outlaws" 1-26; *Gunsmoke* "Quaker Girl" 12-10; **1967** *Man from UNCLE* "The Deadly Quest Affair" 10-30; **1968** *Cowboy in Africa* "The Red Hand of Michael O'Neill" 2-5; *Cimarron Strip* "Big Jesse" 2-8; *Daniel Boone* "The Blackbirder" 10-3; **1971** *Columbo* "Dead Weight" 10-27; **1974** *Toma* "A Funeral for Max Fabian" 2-22; **1975** *Baretta* "He'll Never See Daylight Again" 1-17; *Kung Fu* "The Last Raid" 4-5; *Baretta* "Set-Up City" 10-29; **1976** *Columbo* "Fade In to Murder" 10-10; **1977** *Baretta* "This Sister Ain't No Cousin" 1-19; *Charlie's Angels* "Angels on Ice" 9-21; **1978** *Baretta* "The Marker" 2-16; **1980** *CHiPs* "Kidnap" 1-26.

TELEFILMS

1971 *Ransom for a Dead Man* 3-1 NBC; **1973** *The Bait* 3-13 ABC; **1980** *Nightside* 6-8 ABC.

Carmini Caridi

(born 1933)

A seventies film and television actor, gruff-acting Carmine Caridi frequently played Italian roles, often as criminal types. But he could be effective in comedy roles as evidenced by his regular slot on *Phyllis* (1976-77). He also had a series regular role on *Fame* (1982-83).

GUEST CREDITS

1975 *Kojak* "Unwanted Partners" 2-16; **1976** *Police Woman* "The Melting Point of Ice" 1-6; **1977** *Kojak* "Cry for the Kids" 10-23; *Quincy, M.E.* "The Hero Syndrome" 11-18; **1978** *Starsky and Hutch* "The Action" 1-7; *Sword of Justice* "The Gemini Connection" 10-21; *Eddie Capra Mysteries* "The Intimate Friends of Jenny Wilde" 11-10; **1979** *Dear Detective* "episode 1" 4-4; **1979** *Rockford Files* "Lions, Tigers, Monkeys and Dogs" 10-12; **1980** *Barnaby Jones* "Deadline for Murder" 3-27; **1981** *Today's FBI* "El Paso Murders" 12-13; **1982** *Cassie and Company* "A Ring Ain't Always a Circle" 8-20.

TELEFILMS

1973 *Honor Thy Father* 3-1 CBS; **1975** *Kate McShane* 4-11 CBS; **1978** *KISS Meets the Phantom*

of the Park 10-28 CBS; **1980** *Children of Divorce* 11-24 NBC.

Robert Carricart

(born 1917, Bordeaux, France)

Robert debuted in films in 1958 and began receiving significant numbers of television guest roles during that same time frame. After numerous guest appearances he gained his only series regular role during 1966-67, on *T.H.E. Cat.* He frequently played Europeans or Hispanics.

GUEST CREDITS

1959 *Yancy Derringer* "Five on the Frontier" 4-2; *One Step Beyond* "The Aerialist" 4-28; *Lawless Years* "The Ray Baker Story" 8-6; *Lawless Years* "The Morrison Story" 8-20; *Detectives* "Shot in the Dark" 10-23; *Peter Gunn* "The Price Is Murder" 12-14; **1960** *M Squad* "Diary of a Bomber" 3-29; *Hallmark Hall of Fame* "Captain Brassbound's Conversion" 5-2; *Johnny Ringo* "Cobo Lawman" 6-23; *Wrangler* "Encounter at Elephant Butte" 9-15;

Islanders "Five O'Clock Friday" 10-2; *Checkmate* "Lady on the Brink" 10-15; *Untouchables* "The Jack 'Legs' Diamond Story" 10-20; *Tales of Wells Fargo* "Leading Citizen" 11-24; *Zane Grey Theater* "The Last Bugle" 11-24; *Thriller* "The Big Blackout" 12-6; **1961** *Have Gun-Will Travel* "A Quiet Night in Town" 1-7, 1-14; *Hong Kong* "Lesson in Fear" 1-11; *Roaring 20's* "Big Town Blues" 1-21; *Perry Mason* "The Case of the Waylaid Wolf" 2-4; *Shirley Temple Theatre* "The Return of Long John Silver" 2-19; *Roaring 20's* "The Salvation of Killer McFadden" 4-1; *Have Gun-Will Travel* "The Duke of Texas" 4-22; *National Velvet* "The Desparado" 11-27; *Have Gun-Will Travel* "A Knight to Remember" 12-9; *Roaring 20's* "Blondes Prefer Gentlemen" 12-16; *Untouchables* "Hammerlock" 12-21; **1962** *87ᵗʰ Precinct* "Main Event" 1-1; **1963** *Lloyd Bridges Show* "A Personal Matter" 2-5; *Bonanza* "A Stranger Passed This Way" 3-3; *Lloyd Bridges Show* "Without Wheat There Is No Bread" 5-14; *Combat* "Thunder from the Hill" 12-17; **1965** *Combat* "The Convict" 2-16; *Honey West* "In the Bag" 11-5; **1966** *I Spy* "A Day Called 4 Jaguar" 3-9; *Girl from UNCLE* "The Little John Doe Affair" 12-13; *Time Tunnel* "Invasion" 12-23; **1967** *Big Valley* "Joaquin" 9-11; *High Chaparral* "the Firing Wall" 12-31; **1969** *Hawaii Five-0* "Episode 21" 3-12; **1970** *Mission: Impossible* "Gitano" 2-1; **1975** *Kojak* "Life, Liberty and the Pursuit of Death" 10-26; **1976** *Columbo* "A Matter of Honor" 2-1; *Streets of San Francisco* "Alien Country" 3-11.

TELEFILMS

1964 *See How They Run* 10-7 NBC; **1974** *The Mark of Zorro* 10-29 ABC; **1978** *Donner Pass: The Road to Survival* 11-24 NBC.

John Carter

(born November 26, 1927, Center Ridge, Arkansas)

Best known for his long running role (1974-80) as Lt. Biddle on *Barnaby Jones*, John's television career began in 1967. He had a regular slot on *The Smith Family* (1971-72), also as a cop. His acting career extended well into the eighties, including a film role on *Scarface*. John also made several

appearances on *Falcon Crest* during 1984-85.

GUEST CREDITS

1967 *Combat* "Nightmare on the Red Ball Run" 2-28; *Gunsmoke* "Ladies from St. Louis" 3-25; *Invaders* "Moonshot" 4-18; *Garrisons's Gorillas* "Black Market" 11-28; **1968** *Cimarron Strip* "The Assassin" 1-11; *Bonanza* "The Survivors" 11-10; **1969** *Mod Squad* "Shell Game" 1-28; *Hawaii Five-0* episode 18 2-19, 2-26; **1971** *Mod Squad* "Welcome to Our City" 3-2; *Bold Ones: The Doctors* "The Glass Cage" 12-5; **1973** *Gunsmoke* "Shadler" 1-15; *Cannon* "Memo from a Dead Man" 9-19; **1974** *The FBI* "The Lost Man" 3-24; *Kodiak* "Red Snow, White Death" 9-13; *Rockford Files* "Profit and Loss" 12-20, 12-27; **1976** *Waltons* "The Cloudburst" 11-11; **1977** *Little House on the Prairie* "Blizzard" 1-3; *Hardy Boys/Nancy Drew Mysteries* "The Secret of the Whispering Walls" 3-13; **1981** *Freebie and the Bean* "Highway Robbery" 1-17; *Waltons* "The Hot Rod" 2-19; *Waltons* "The Victims" 3-19; *Flamingo Road* "Bad Chemistry" 12-13; **1982** *Fall Guy* "Bail and Bond" 10-27; **1983** *A-Team* "Children of Jamestown" 1-30.

TELEFILMS

1970 *Night Chase* 11-20 CBS; **1971** *Earth II* 11-28 ABC; **1975** *Winner Take All* 3-3 NBC; *Guilty or Innocent: The Sam Sheppard Murder Case* 11-17 NBC; **1976** *James A. Michener's "Dynasty"* 3-13; **1979** *The House on Garibaldi Street* 5-28 ABC; **1980** *Little Lord Fauntleroy* 11-25 CBS; **1983** *The Other Woman* 3-22 CBS.

John Chandler (a.k.a. John Davis Chandler)
(born 1937)

The heavy lidded eyes of John Chandler helped to generate frequent castings as furtive criminal types throughout much of his film and television career (from 1961).

GUEST CREDITS

1961 *Straightaway* "The Stranger" 11-17; **1962** *Detectives* "Never the Twain" 3-23; *Rifleman* "The Executioner" 5-7; *Virginian* "The Brazen Bell"10-17; **1963** *Fugitive* "The Other Side of the Mountain" 10-1; **1965** *Man Called Shenandoah* "Survival" 9-20; **1967** *Fugitive* "Run the Man Down" 1-3; **1971** *Adam-12* "Log Sixteen-Child in Danger" 3-4; *Adam-12*

"The Sniper" 10-6; *The D.A.* "The People vs. Gayda" 10-8; **1973** *Gunsmoke* "Shadler"1-15; *Adam-12* "Killing Ground" 2-7; *Toma* "Frame-Up" 11-15; **1974** *Adam-12* "The Sweet Smell..." 1-9; *Columbo* "Publish or Perish" 1-13; *Gunsmoke* "Cowtown Hustler" 3-11; **1975** *Police Story* "War Games" 3-4; **1977** *Quincy, M.E.* "The Thigh Bones Connected to the Hip Bone" 2-11; *Police Story* "The Six Foot Stretch" 3-22; *Police Woman* "Guns" 11-1.

TELEFILMS

1972 *Moon of the Wolf* 9-26 ABC; **1973** *Chase* 3-24 NBC; **1975** *The Desperate Miles* 3-5 ABC.

Judith Chapman
Judith's television career began during 1975-78 with a strong role on the soap *As the World Turns.* Beginning in 1977, she worked steadily in television guest roles until 1984, when she did a turn on the soap *Ryan's Hope.* Thereafter, she worked often in soap roles, on *General Hospital (1984), One Life to Live,* and *Days of Our Lives* (1988-89). During 1987-89 she took time off from soaps to guest on *Highway to Heaven, Murder, She Wrote, McGyver, Law and Harry McGraw* and *In the Heat of the Night.*

GUEST CREDITS

1977 *Kojak* "The Condemned" 1-11; **1978** *Barnaby Jones* "The Picture Pirates" 12-21; **1979** *Paper Chase* "Once More with Feeling" 2-27; **1980** *Incredible Hulk* "Sideshow" 1-25; *B. J. and the Bear* "Through the Past Darkly" 1-26; *Buck Rogers* "Olympiad" 2-7; *Beyond Westworld* "Destroyed" 3-5; *Galactica 1980* "Starbuck's Great Journey" 5-4; **1981** *Flamingo Road* "The Hostages" 1-6; *Magnum, P.I.* "The Black Orchid" 4-2; *Magnum, P.I.* "Woman on the Bench" 10-22; *Fitz and Bones* episode 10-24; *Fall Guy* "The Rich Get Richer" 11-11; **1982** *Darkroom* "The Rarest of Wines" 1-15; *McClain's Law* "A Matter of Honor" 1-15; *Fall Guy* "Goin' For It" 1-27; *Fall Guy* "Three for the Road" 4-14; *Knight Rider* "Inside Out" 11-26; **1983** *Fall Guy* "Death Boat" 2-2; *Simon and Simon* "What's in a Gnome?" 2-24; *Trapper John, M.D.* "The Final List" 11-6; *Remington Steele* "My Fair Steele" 12-6.

TELEFILMS

1980 *Flamingo Road* 5-12 NBC; **1981** *Thin Ice* 2-17 CBS; *The Five of Me* 5-12 CBS; **1982** *Farrell for the People* 10-18 NBC; **1983** *The Return of the Man from UNCLE: The 15 Years Later Affair* 4-5 CBS.

Lewis Charles

(born September 2, 1920, New York City; died November 9, 1979)

After stage and vaudeville experience, Lewis Charles came to films in 1950. He eventually appeared in screen gems like *The Rose Tattoo, The Birdman of Alcatraz* and *Topaz*. He worked in television through three decades in guest roles, with but one regular role, that in *The Feather and Father Gang* (1977). He was effectively cast as mobsters in many of his TV roles.

Lewis was also a very skilled ballroom dancer.

GUEST CREDITS

1959 *Peter Gunn* "The Ugly Frame" 3-9; *Rifleman* "One Went to Dinner" 3-17; *Richard Diamond* episode 4-5; *Richard Diamond* episode 12-21; **1960** *Johnny Staccato* "The List of Death" 5-1; *Peter Gunn* "Letter of the Law" 5-30; *Wanted: Dead or Alive* "One Mother Too Many" 12-7; *Hong Kong* "The Dragon Cup" 12-14; **1961** *Wanted: Dead or Alive* "Epitaph" 2-8; *Roaring 20's* "The Vamp" 3-4; *Hawaiian Eye* "Pill in a Box" 11-1; **1962** *Rifleman* "Skull" 1-1; *77 Sunset Strip* "Penthouse on Skid Row" 1-19; **1963** *Perry Mason* "The Case of the Lover's Leap" 4-4; **1964** *Fugitive* "Search in a Windy City" 2-4; *Alfred Hitchcock Hour* "A Matter of Murder" 4-3; **1965** *Fugitive* "Set Fire to a Strawman" 11-30; **1966** *Loner* "Pick Me Another Time to Die" 2-26; *Big Valley* "Into the Widow's Web" 3-23; **1969** *Mod Squad* "The Sunday Drivers" 1-7; *Adam-12* "Log Ninety Three-Once a Junkie" 11-22; **1970** *Adam-12* "Log 104-The Bomb" 3-14; **1971** *Mission: Impossible* "The Puppet" 12-22; **1972** *Sixth Sense* "Whisper of Evil" 4-8; **1974** *Kolchak: The Night Stalker* "The Werewolf" 11-1; **1975** *Streets of San Francisco* "The Cat's Paw" 12-4; **1976** *Ellery Queen* "The Adventure of the Black Falcon" 1-4; **1978** *Hawaii Five-0* "Small Potatoes" 10-26.

TELEFILMS

1972 *Man on a String* 2-18 CBS; *I Love a Mystery* 2-27 NBC; **1975** *Queen of the Stardust*

Ballroom 2-13 CBS; *Cage without a Key* 3-14 CBS; **1979** *The Gift* 12-15 CBS.

Suzanne Charney

(born 1940)

A seventies television actress and dancer, Suzanne had but one sixties TV appearance, on *That Girl* (1967). She worked primarily in seventies crime series guest roles. After 1981 guest roles she disappeared from the medium.

GUEST CREDITS

1970 *Bracken's World* "A Preview in Samarkind" 10-16; **1973** *Ironside* "A Game of Showdown" 3-22; *Marcus Welby, M.D.* "Blood Kin" 10-2; **1974** *Toma* "The Madame" 4-12; *Kolchak: The Night Stalker* "Vampire" 10-4; *Manhunter* "The Lodester Ambush" 12-4; **1975** *Rookies* "Angel" 2-3; *Starsky and Hutch* "Death Notice" 10-15; *Blue Knight* "The Creeper" 12-17; **1976** *Kojak* "A Wind from Corsica" 1-18; *Streets of San Francisco* "Underground" 1-29; *Rockford Files* "Johnny Blue Eyes" 1-30; **1977** *Six Million Dollar Man* "Privacy of the Mind" 2-27; **1978** *Bionic Woman* "The Antidote" 1-21; *Starsky and Hutch* "The Game" 9-19; **1981** *Quincy, M.E.* "Headhunter" 2-4; *Incredible Hulk* "Two Godmothers" 10-9.

TELEFILM

1972 *Short Walk to Daylight* 10-24.

Don Chastain

(born September 2, 1935, Oklahoma City, Oklahoma)

Don Chastain was a multi-faceted performer of stage, screen and television. During his debut year in films (1958), he appeared in *South Pacific* and *The Young Lions*. A fine singer, he became a regular on *The Edie Adams Show* (1963-64) and *The Debbie Reynolds Show* (1969-70).

Don spent a considerable amount of time on soaps *As the World Turns* (early sixties and 1987), *General Hospital* (1976) and *Search for Tomorrow*. He became a dubbing artist and was also a prolific screenwriter.

GUEST CREDITS

1960 *Colt .45* "Trial by Rope" 5-3; **1967** *Big Valley* "Image of Yesterday" 1-9; *Big Valley* "Turn of a Card" 3-20; *Big Valley* "Four Days to Furnace Hill" 12-4; **1968** *Gunsmoke* "The Miracle Man" 12-2; **1969** *Mannix* "Killjoy" 1-25; *The FBI* "Conspiracy of

Silence" 3-2; **1971** *Hawaii Five-0* "The Grandstand Play" 3-3, 3-10; *Marcus Welby, M.D.* "The House of Alquist" 3-30; *Hawaii Five-0* "Air Cargo-Dial for Murder" 10-26; *Cannon* "Stone, Cold Dead" 11-30; **1973** *Cannon* "Murder for Murder" 2-7; **1976** *S.W.A.T.* "Lessons in Fear" 1-31; **1978** *Rockford Files* "South by Southwest" 2-3; **1983** *Hart to Hart* "Hartstruck" 4-12.

TELEFILM

1979 *Son Rise: A Miracle of Love* 5-14 NBC.

Al Checco

(born July 21, 1925, Pittsburgh, Pa.)

Educated at Carnegie-Mellon, Al Checco earned a B.A. at that institution. He began working in films in 1964 in *The Incredible Mr. Limpet*. Al appeared in comedy and light films like *The Ghost and Mr. Chicken* and *Angel in My Pocket*, and appeared in more serious films like *Bullitt*.

He was effective in over-the-top portrayals and worked onstage as well as films and television. Checco was featured in a 1975-76 Saturday morning live-action sitcom, *Far Out Space Nuts*.

GUEST CREDITS

1965 *Perry Mason* "The Case of the Hasty Honeymooner" 10-24; *Run for Your Life* "The Voice of Gina Milan" 11-29; **1969** *Adam-12* "Log Fifteen-Exactly One Hundred Miles" 9-20; *The FBI* "Blood Tie" 11-9; **1970** *Bonanza* "The Big Jackpot" 1-18; **1971** *Bonanza* "Rockaby Hoss" 10-10; **1973** *Adam-12* "Harbor Division" 9-12; *1975 Kolchak: The Night Stalker* "The Primal Scream" 1-17; *Kung Fu* "Barbary House" 2-15; *Six Million Dollar Man* "One of Our Running Backs Is Missing" 11-2; **1976** *Rockford Files* "Foul on the First Play" 3-12; **1977** *Rockford Files* "Trouble in Chapter Seventeen" 9-23; **1978** *Quincy, M.E.* "No Way to Treat A Body" 12-7.

TELEFILMS

1973 *Go Ask Alice* 1-24 ABC; **1976** *Helter Skelter* 4-1, 4-2 CBS; *The Million Dollar Rip-Off* 9-22 NBC; **1978** *The Other Side of Hell* 1-17 NBC; *Happily Ever After* 9-5 CBS; **1979** *Some Kind of Miracle* 1-3 CBS.

Virginia Christine

(born March 5, 1920, Stanton, Iowa; died July 24, 1996)

To most television viewers, Virginia Christine will forever be Mrs. Olson of Folger's Coffee commercials, "It's the richest kind". An accomplished pianist, Virginia migrated to Hollywood and married prominent character actor Fritz Feld. She made her film debut in 1942, ultimately appearing in *Cyrano de Bergerac, The Killers, High Noon, Not As a Stranger, Judgment at* Nurenberg, *A Rage to Live* and *Guess Who's Coming to Dinner?*.

She worked in fifties television productions, but became more prominent in dozens of sixties guest roles, with numerous roles in westerns series like *Wagon Train* (4). Virginia was a regular on *Tales of Wells Fargo* during 1961-62. Her fame as Mrs. Olson nearly crowded out her decades of strong film and television work.

GUEST CREDITS

1959 *Wanted: Dead or Alive* "Rope Law" 1-3; *Loretta Young Show* "Seed from the East" 2-1; *Lawless Years* "The Immigrant" 4-23; *Twilight Zone* "Escape Clause" 11-6; *Man from Blackhawk* "Death Is the Best Policy" 11-18; *Rifleman* "The Spiked Rifle" 11-24; **1960** *Loretta Young Show* "Faith, Hope and Mr. Flaherty" 5-8; *Thriller* "Twisted Image" **1961** *Perry Mason* "The Case of the Fickle Fortune" 1-21; *Wagon Train* "The Prairie Story" 2-1; *Deputy* "Tension Point" 4-8; *Rawhide* "Incident of the Black Storms" 5-26; **1962** *Target: The Corruptors* "A Book of Faces" 4-27; *Wagon Train* "The Martin Gatsby Story" 10-10; *Perry Mason* "The Case of the Double Entry Mind" 11-1; *Stoney Burke* "A Matter of Pride" 11-5; **1963** *Bonanza* "Song in the Dark" 1-6; *Eleventh Hour* "My Name Is Judith, I'm Lost, You See" 1-16; *Ben Casey* "Rigadoon for Three Pianos" 3-4; *Wagon Train* "The Blane Wessels Story" 4-17; **1964** *Ben Casey* "Say Goodbye to Blue Elephants and Such" 2-5; *Bonanza* "The Saga of Outlaw Charlie" 12-27; **1965** *Fugitive* "Moon Child" 2-16; *Gunsmoke* "Bank Baby" 3-20; *Wagon Train* "The Katy Piper Story" 4-11; *Big Valley* "Young Marauders" 10-6; **1966** *The FBI* "Quantico" 1-30; *Jerico* "Long Journey Across a Short Street" 12-8; **1967** *The FBI* "Passage into Fear" 1-8; *Judd, for the Defense* "A Civil Case of Murder" 9-29; *Invaders* "Labyrinth" 11-21; *Virginian* "A Small Taste of

Justice" 12-20; **1968** *Daniel Boone* "Thirty Pieces of Silver" 3-28; *The FBI* "The Hero" 12-22; **1976** *Kojak* "By Silence Betrayed" 11-14.

TELEFILMS

1969 *Daughter of the Mind* 12-9 ABC; **1970** *The Old Man Who Cried Wolf* 10-1 ABC; **1976** *Woman of the Year* 7-28 CBS.

Dort Clark

(born 1917)

Dort Clark worked extensively in television's live dramas during the fifties following a stage background, and TV debut in 1949. His film roles, from 1951, were rather limited, but he worked in *Bells Are Ringing, Fate Is the Hunter, The Loved One* and *In Harm's Way*. He wound down his television career with small guest roles.

GUEST CREDITS

1961 *Armstrong Circle Theater* "The Crime

without a Country" 3-29; **1962** *Hallmark Hall of Fame* "Arsenic and Old Lace" 2-5; **1963** *Empire* "Between Friday and Monday" 5-7; *Fugitive* "Glass Tightrope" 12-3; **1964** *Fugitive* "Man in a Chariot" 9-15; **1965** *Perry Mason* "The Case of the Sad Sicilian" 3-11; **1967** *Fugitive* "The Judgment" 8-22; *Wild Wild West* "The Night of the Circus of Death" 11-3; *Daniel Boone* "The Value of a King" 11-9; **1968** *Wild Wild West* "The Night of Miguelito's Revenge" 12-13; **1972** *Nichols* "About Jesse James" 2-15; *Night Gallery* "Finnegan's Flight" 12-17; **1974** *Kolchak: The Night Stalker* "The Werewolf" 11-1.

TELEFILMS

1976 *Time Travelers* 3-19 ABC; *Brink's: The Great Robbery* 3-26 CBS.

Sidney Clute

(born April 21, 1916, Brooklyn, New York; died October 2, 1985)

Sid Clute received early dramatic training in summer stock and moved to Hollywood for film and television work during the early fifties. He made his screen debut in 1952 in *Red Ball Express* and later had prominent roles in *The Russians Are Coming, The Russians Are Coming* and *Walking Tall*. His first TV work was in the *Superman* series.

He became one of television's more familiar faces, from 1956, with 9 guest credits on *McCloud* (recurring role) and 5 on *Dragnet*. Sid did a good deal of sitcom work on shows like *Bewitched* (4), *Hogan's Heroes, Get Smart, Beverly Hillbillies, Petticoat Junction, Here's Lucy* and *The Mary Tyler Moore Show*. He become a regular on *Lou Grant* in 1977 and played Detective Paul La Guardia on *Cagney and Lacey* (1982-85).

Sid succumbed to cancer in 1985 at age 69, survived by 2 sisters and a brother.

GUEST CREDITS

1959 *M Squad* "The Star Witness" 2-20; *Millionaire* "Millionaire Gilbert Burton" 4-29; **1961** *Perry Mason* "The Case of the Blind Man's Bluff"

3-11; *Dick Powell Show* "Open Season" 12-26; **1962** *Ben Casey* "The Fireman Who Raised Rabbits" 11-26; **1963** *Wagon Train* "the Nancy Palmer Story" 10-21; *Ben Casey* "Little Drops of Water, Little Grains of Sand" 10-30; **1964** *Ben Casey* "The Lonely Ones" 3-4; *Wagon Train* "The Zebedee Titus Story" 4-20; **1965** *Perry Mason* "The Case of the Frustrated Folk Singer" 1-7; *Slattery's People* "How Do You Catch a Cool Bird of Paradise?" 2-12; *Ben Casey* "A Dipperful of Water from a Poisoned Well" 3-1; *Slattery's People* "What's a Swan Song for a Sparrow?" 4-16; *Ben Casey* "A Nightingale Named Nathan" 9-27; *Laredo* "Three's Company" 10-4; **1966** *Fugitive* "Second Sight" 10-25; **1967** *The FBI* "Passage into Fear" 1-8; *Fugitive* "There Goes the Ball Game" 2-7; *Iron Horse* "Wild Track" 12-16; **1968** *Dragnet* "The Big Search" 1-11; *Mannix* "Deadfall" 1-20; *Big Valley* "Run of the Savage" 3-11; *Big Valley* "In Silent Battle" 9-23; **1969** *Dragnet* "Frauds-DR-28" 2-20; *It Takes a Thief* "Totally by Design" 4-1; *Room 222* "Richie's Story" 9-17; *Dragnet* "Bunco-$9,000" 12-11; *Medical Center* "The Adversaries" 12-31; **1970** *Dragnet* "D.H.Q.-Night School" 3-19; *Dragnet* "The Harassing Wife" 4-2; **1971** *Night Gallery* "Make Me Laugh" 1-16; *Mission: Impossible* "The Tram" 10-2; *Alias Smith and Jones* "The Posse That Wouldn't Quit" 10-14; **1972** *McMillan and Wife* "The Face of Murder" 1-5; *Marcus Welby, M.D.* "All the Pretty People" 1-25;

McCloud "The New Mexican Connection" 10-1; *McCloud* "The Barefoot Stewardess Caper" 12-3; **1973** *Cannon* "Hard Rock Roller Coaster" 1-3; *Bold Ones: The Doctors* "A Tightrope to Tomorrow" 1-9; *Kojak* "The Girl in the River" 11-21; **1974** *Chase* "Vacation for a President" 2-6; *McCloud* "This Must Be the Alamo" 3-24; *McCloud* "The Gang That Stole Manhattan" 10-13; *Streets of San Francisco* "Jacob's Boy" 10-24; *McCloud* "The Concrete Jungle Caper" 11-24; **1975** *McCloud* "Killer on the Hill" 1-29; *McCloud* "The Park Avenue Pirates" 9-21; *McCloud* "Three Guns for New York" 11-23; *Kojak* "Money Back Guarantee" 12-7; **1976** *Doctor's Hospital* "Lullaby" 1-13; *McCloud* "The Day New York Turned Blue" 2-22; *Jigsaw John* "Dry Ice" 3-1; **1977** *McCloud* "The Great Taxicab Stampede" 1-16; *Charlie's Angels* "Dirty Business" 2-2; *Rockford Files* "Just Another Polish Wedding" 2-18; *Hawaii Five-0* "Tounai" 12-22; **1978** *Quincy, M.E.* "Gone, But Not Forgotten" 2-17; **1979** *CHiPs* "High Octane" 10-6.

GUEST CREDITS

TELEFILMS

1971 *Terror in the Sky* 9-17 CBS; **1974** *The Death Squad* 1-8 ABC; *Thursday's Game* 1-8 ABC; **1976** *Helter Skelter* 4-1, 4-2 CBS; **1980** *Fugitive Family* 10-1 CBS; *Alcatraz: The Whole Shocking Story* 11-5, 11-6 NBC; **1981** *Terror Among Us* 1-12 CBS.

Julie Cobb

(born Los Angeles, Calif.)

The daughter of the late actor Lee J. Cobb (1911-76), Julie first appeared on television in 1968. She became a regular on *The D. A..* in 1971-72, did some guesting, then was a regular on the abbreviated sitcom, *A Year at the Top* (1977).

The eighties were a very busy period for Julie, peaked by a series regular role on *Charles in Charge* (1984-85). Thereafter, she guested on *MacGruder and Loud, T. J. Hooker, Magnum, P.I.* (2), *McGyver, St. Elsewhere, Growing Pains* (2), *Jake and the Fatman, Our House* and *Heart Beat*.

1968 *Star Trek* "By Any Other Name" 2-23; **1973** *Cannon* "The Prisoners" 2-21; *Gunsmoke* "Lynch Town" 11-19; *Waltons* "The Air Mail Man" 12-13; **1974** *Gunsmoke* "The Colonel" 12-16; *Petrocelli* "Covenant with Evil" 12-18; **1975** *Little House on the Prairie* "Money Crop" 2-19; *Marcus Welby, M.D.* "Tomorrow May Never Come" 9-9; *Medical Story* "Million Dollar Baby" 10-23; *Marcus Welby, M.D.* "The Fruitfulness of Mrs. Steffie Rhodes" 12-23; **1977** *Fantastic Journey* "Turnabout" 4-7; *Rosetti and Ryan* "Rosetti and Ryan" 9-22; **1978** *CHiPs* "Rainy Day" 3-2; *Incredible Hulk* "Stop the Presses" 11-24; **1979** *Kaz* "Conspiracy in Blue" 1-24; *Lou Grant* "Expose" 9-24; **1980** *Hart to Hart* "Color Jennifer Dead" 1-8; *Concrete Cowboys* episode 3-21; *Riker* "Sisters" 3-21; *Knot's Landing* episode 4-1; **1982** *Today's FBI* "Energy Fraud" 4-26; **1983** *Mississippi* episode 3-25; *Tucker's Witch* "Living and Presumed Dead" 5-5; *Mississippi* episode 12-6.

TELEFILMS

1979 *Salem's Lot* 11-17, 11-24 CBS; **1982** *Uncommon Valor* 1-22 CBS.

Peter Coe

(born 1918, Yugoslavia)

Yugoslavian-born Peter Coe made a film debut in 1943, doing war films like *Gung Ho*, and later, *Sands of Iwo Jima* (1949). He also did some horror flicks like *The Mummy's Curse* and *The House of Frankenstein* (1944). After a 1956 TV debut, he worked in guest roles exclusively, including 3 episodes of *Mission: Impossible*.

GUEST CREDITS

1959 *Have Gun-Will Travel* "Heritage of Anger" 6-6; **1960** *Twilight Zone* "Man in the Bottle" 10-7; **1961** *Wyatt Earp* "Wyatt Takes the Primrose Path" 3-28; *Hong Kong* "The Runaway" 3-29; *Follow the Sun* "Busman's Holiday" 10-22; *Untouchables* "The Genna Brothers" 11-2; *Adventures in Paradise* "The Assassins" 11-26; **1964** *Fugitive* "Somebody to Remember" 3-24; *Daniel Boone* "My Brother's Keeper" 10-8; **1965** *Combat* "Odyssey" 4-20; *Bob*

Hope Chrysler Theater "Escape into Jeopardy" 5-28; *Daniel Boone* "A Rope for Mingo" 12-2; **1966** *Combat* "The Flying Machine" 2-22; **1967** *Mission: Impossible* "Operation...Heart" 10-27; *Invaders* "The Captive" 11-28; **1968** *Mission: Impossible* "Recovery" 3-17; **1969** *Mission: Impossible* "Nitro" 3-23; *It Takes a Thief* "The Great Chess Gambit" 4-15; **1974** *Police Story* "Fathers and Sons" 10-1.

Russell Collins

(born 1897; died 1965)

Russell studied drama at Carnegie Tech and subsequently joined the Cleveland Playhouse in 1922. Ten years later he made his Broadway debut and eventually made his way to Hollywood. He became a character actor and had roles in significant films like *Bad Day at Black Rock*, *Raintree County* and *Fail-Safe*. He debuted on television in 1948 and worked often in the medium; during 1961-65 he appeared in over three dozen guest roles.

GUEST CREDITS

1961 *Checkmate* "Don't Believe a Word She Says" 1-28; *Islanders* "A Rope for Charlie Munday" 3-5; *Untouchables* "Ring of Terror" 4-13; *Alfred Hitchcock Presents* "Death Mate" 4-18; *Peter Gunn*

"The Murder Bond" 4-24; *Naked City* "A Kettle of Precous Fish" 5-31; *DuPont Show of the Week* "The Battle of the Paper Bullets" 10-15; *Detectives* "Escort" 12-15; *DuPont Show of the Week* "Trick or Treason" 12-17; *Alfred Hitchcock Presents* "The Right Kind of Medicine" 12-19; **1962** *Twilight Zone* "Kick the Can" 2-9; *87ᵗʰ Precinct* "The Lover" 4-30; *Target: The Corruptors* "Nobody Gets Hurt" 6-1; **1963** *Sam Benedict* "Image of a Toad" 2-23; *Nurses* "They Are As Lions" 6-6; *Alfred Hitchcock Hour* "Starring the Defense" 11-15; *Great Adventure* "The Man Who Stole New York City" 12-3; **1964** *Outer Limits* "Don't Open Till Doomsday" 1-20; *Breaking Point* "Shadow of a Starless Night" 3-9; *Great Adventure* "The President Vanishes" 3-13; *Bob Hope Chrysler Theater* "A Case of Armed Robbery" 4-3; *Nurses* "The Bystanders" 5-28; *Fugitive* "Man on a String" 9-29; **1965** *Slattery's People* "Question: What's a Swan Song for a Sparrow?" 4-16; *Dr. Kildare* "Duet for One Hand" 12-28.

Booth Colman

(born March 8, 1923, Portland, Oregon)

Following a 1952 film debut Booth divided his time between stage, film and television work, coming to television in 1953. His films included roles in *The Big Sky, Auntie Mame, The Commancheros* and *Fate Is the Hunter*.

Booth's rather sober demeanor often found him cast as authority figures or professionals. His only TV series regular role was in *Planet of the Apes* (1974); he also did a stint on the soap *General Hospital*.

GUEST CREDITS

1959 *Californians* "The Fugitive" 4-28; **1961** *Thriller* "Man in a Cage" 1-17; *Rifleman* "The High Country" 12-18; **1962** *Thriller* "Waxworks" 1-8; *Route 66* "Even Stones Have Eyes" 3-30; **1963** *Gunsmoke* "The Bad One" 1-26; *Dick Powell Show* "Tissue of Hate" 2-26; **1964** *Outer Limits* ""Zzzz" 1-27; *Perry Mason* "The Case of the Nervous Neighbor" 2-13; *Perry Mason* "The Case of the Paper Bullets" 10-1; *Voyage to the Bottom of the Sea* "The

Mist of Silence" 10-5; *Bonanza* "A Man to Admire" 12-6; *Ben Casey* "Courage at 3:00 a.m." 12-7; **1965** *Fugitive* "Trial by Fire" 10-5; *Run for Your Life* "Where Mystery Begins" 11-1; **1966** *The FBI* "The Scourge" 10-23; **1967** *Daniel Boone* "The Williamsburg Cannon" 1-12, 1-19; *Mission: Impossible* "The Train" 3-18; *The FBI* "Counterstroke" 10-1; **1968** *Invaders* "The Possessed" 1-2; **1969** *Mannix* "Return to Summer Grove" 10-11; **1970** *Mission: Impossible* "Orpheus" 3-1; *Mod Squad* "Who Are the Keepers-Who Are the Inmates?"10-6; **1971** *Smith Family* "Winner Take All" 4-19; *The D. A.* "The People vs. Drake" 9-17; *McCloud* "Encounter with Aries" 9-22; **1972** *Gunsmoke* "Alias Festus Haggin" 3-6; *Cannon* "That Was No Lady" 10-4; *Streets of San Francisco* "Timelock" 11-11; **1973** *Barnaby Jones* "The Murdering Class" 3-4; *Police Story* "The Ripper" 2-12; *Police Story* "Requiem for C. Z. Smith" 9-17; **1973** *Kung Fu* "The Tong" 11-1; **1975** *Switch* "Death Heist" 10-21; *Barbary Coast* "The Day Cable Was Hanged" 12-26; **1976** *Delvecchio* "A Madness Within" 2-20, 2-27; *City of Angels* "The Bloodshot Eye" 5-11; *Lou Grant* "Hoax" 10-4; *Quincy, M.E.* "Touch of Death" 11-25; **1979** *Quincy, M.E.* "An Ounce of Prevention" 3-22.

TELEFILMS

1972 *The Adventures of Nick Carter* 2-20 NBC;

1974 *I Love You...Goodbye* 2-12 CBS; *A Tree Grows in Brooklyn* 3-27 NBC; **1975** *Returning Home* 4-29 ABC; **1976** *Time Travelers* 3-19 ABC; *The Return of the World's Greatest Detective* 6-16 NBC; *Frances Gary Powers: The True Story of the U-2 Incident* 9-29 NBC; **1977** *Yesterday's Child* 2-3 NBC; *In the Glitter Palace* 2-27 NBC; **1979** *The Best Place to Be* 5-27 NBC; *Marciano* 11-21 ABC.

Jack Colvin

Jack is perhaps best known for his TV role on *The Incredible Hulk* (1978-82), playing a reporter trying for years to expose the Hulk. In television from the mid-sixties, he found most of his television and film work during the seventies. He also directed in the theater.

GUEST CREDITS

1966 *Blue Light* "The Other Fuehrer" 4-27; **1967** *Rat Patrol* "The This One That Got Away Raid" 1-9; **1974** *Kojak* ""Eighteen Hours of Fear" 2-20; *Invisible Man* "Man of Influence" 9-22; *Baretta* "Double Image" 10-15; *Rookies* "episode 79" 11-15; **1976** *McCoy* "In Again, Out Again" 1-4; *Six Million Dollar Man* "Hocus Pocus" 1-18; *Switch* "The Girl on the Golden Strip" 3-16; *Rockford Files* "Bad Deal

in the Valley" 3-19; *City of Angels* "Say Goodbye to Yesterday" 5-4; *Bionic Woman* "Kill Oscar" 10-27; **1977** *Quincy, M.E.* "Hit and Run at Danny's" 3-11; *Westside Medical* "The Mermaid" 7-7; *Switch* "The Legend of Macanuse" 10-21; *Six Million Dollar Man* "The Dark Side of the Moon" 11-6, 11-13.

TELEFILMS

1972 *Footsteps* 10-3 CBS; **1974** *Hurricane* 9-10 ABC; **1976** *Amelia Earhart* 10-25 NBC; **1977** *Benny and Barney: Las Vegas Undercover* 1-9 NBC; *The Spell* 2-20 NBC; *Exo-Man* 6-18 NBC; *The Incredible Hulk* 11-4 CBS.

Forrest Compton
(born September 15, 1925, Reading, Pa.)

Following early sixties TV guest roles, Forrest became a regular on *Gomer Pyle, U.S.M.C.* from 1964 until 1969, playing the commanding officer. In 1971 he took over the Mike Karr role on *The Edge of Night*, a part he played until 1984.

GUEST CREDITS
1959 *Troubleshooters* "The Big Squeeze" 11-20; **1961** *Roaring 20's* "Dance Marathon" 1-14; *Route*

66 "An Absence of Tears" 3-3; *Checkmate* "A Slight Touch of Venom" 6-l7; *General Electric Theater* "Call to Danger" 12-l0; **1962** *Hawaiian Eye* "My Love, But Lightly" 1-3l; *77 Sunset Strip* "The Bridal Trail Caper" 2-2; **1963** *Twilight Zone* "The Thirty Fathom Grave" 10-l0' **1965** *12 O'Clock High* "The Mission" 4-2; *The FBI* "Pound of Flesh" 12-19; **1967** *The FBI* "Passage into Fear" 1-8; *Invaders* "Condition: Red" 9-5; *The FBI* "False Witness" 12-l0; **1968** *The FBI* "Wind It Up and It Betrays You" 9-22; **1969** *The FBI* "The Challenger" 11-2; **1970** *Mannix* "One for the Lady" 9-26; *The FBI* "The Traitor" 9-27; **1971** *The FBI* "The Hitchhiker" 2-28; **1973** *The FBI* "Desperate Journey" 1-28.

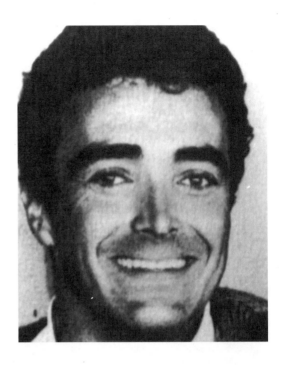

John Considine

(born 1937)

The son of the late producer John W. Considine, Jr., John made his film debut at age 5, but didn't appear in another movie until l965. He was primarily a television actor, from l960 until well into the eighties decade. Graying and mustachioed, his eighties appearance was quite unlike his darkly handsome early sixties look.

GUEST CREDITS

1960 *Michael Shayne* "Murder Plays Charades" 12-9; **1961** *Adventures in Paradise* "The Feather Cloak" 2-27; *Straightaway* "The Bribe" 12-29; **1962** *Combat* "Rear Echelon Commands" 10-9; *Combat* "I Swear by Apollo" 12-11; **1963** *Twilight Zone* "The Thirty Fathom Grave" 1-l; *Outer Limits* "The Man Who Was Never Born" 10-28; *Lieutenant* "The Art of Discipline" 12-21; **1964** *Fugitive* "Bloodline" 2-11; **1966** *Combat* "The Losers" 9-20; **1967** *The FBI* "Overload" 11-12; **1968** *Mannix* "Fear I to Fall" 12-21; **1970** *Marcus Welby, M.D.* "Aura of a New Tomorrow" 11-24; *Mannix* "Duet for Three" 12-19; **1971** *Mannix* "Woman in the Shadows" 10-13; **1973** *Mannix* "The Faces of Murder" 2-4; *Cannon* "Dead Ladie's Tears" 11-7; **1979** *Rockford Files* "A Different Drummer" 4-13; **1981** *Hart to Hart* "Harts and Flowers" 10-6; **1983** *Hart to Hart* "Pandora Has Wings" 10-25.

TELEFILMS

1971 *Incident in San Francisco* 2-28 ABC; **1978** *See How She Runs* 2-l CBS; **1980** *The Shadow Box* 12-28 CBS; **1981** *Mickey Spillane's "Margin for Murder"* 10-15; **1982** *Marian Rose White* 1-l9 CBS; *Mother's Day on Walton's Mountain* 5-9 NBC; *Forbidden Love* 10-19 CBS; **1983** *Dixie: Changing Habits* 2-16 CBS; *Rita Hayworth: The Love Goddess* 11-2 CBS.

Richard Conte

(born Nicholas Peter Conte, March 24, 1910, Jersey City, N. J.; died April 15, 1975)

Drifting and working in menial jobs, Richard became interested in acting and obtained a scholarship to The Group Theatre and Playhouse in Connecticut. He made his stage debut in 1935, moving to Broadway in 1940. After a medical discharge from the Army he signed a contract with Twentieth Century Fox and moved to Hollywood, in 1943. He scored well in forties films like *Guadalcanal Diary, The Purple Heart, A Bell for Adano, Captain Eddie* and *A Walk in the Sun.*

Richard eventually starred in 65 films, with later appearances in *They Came to Cordura, The Greatest Story Ever Told* and *The Godfather*. His role in the latter film, as the sinister mafia chieftain Barzini, was critically acclaimed. Throughout much of his film and television career Richard was cast in villainous underworld and mobster roles.

He came to television in 1953 in a *General Electric Theater* production and worked in other fifties shows like *Ford Theater* (2), *20th Century Fox Hour* (2) and *The Twilight Zone*. He worked regularly in guest roles during the sixties and had a series regular role on *The Jean Arthur Show* (1966).

From 1972 to 1975 he starred in a dozen Italian and Spanish films, playing typical gangster types. He died in 1975, from a heart attack and stroke, survived by his second wife and an adopted son.

GUEST CREDITS

1960 *Checkmate* "Moment of Truth" 11-26; **1961** *Untouchables* "The Organization" 1-26; *Alfred Hitchcock Presents* "The Old Pro" 11-28; **1962** *Bus Stop* "Cry to Heaven" 1-14; *Naked City* "One of the

Most Important Men in the Whole World" 1-31; *Checkmate* "An Assassin Arrives, Andante" 2-21; *DuPont Show of the Month* "The Outpost" 9-16; *Untouchables* "The Chess Game" 10-9; *Alcoa Theater* "Ordeal in Darkness" 11-15; *Going My Way* "A Saint for Mama" 12-26; **1963** *77 Sunset Strip* "5" 9-20, 9-27, 10-4; 10-11, 10-18; **1964** *Arrest and Trial* "Tigers Are for Jungles" 3-22; *Reporter* "Hideout" 10-2; **1965** *Kraft Suspense Theatre* "The Green Felt Jungle" 4-1; **1967** *Danny Thomas Hour* "Fame Is a Four-Letter Word" 10-30; **1970** *Bold Ones: The Lawyers* "Trial of a Mafiosa" 1-4; *Name of the Game* "The Enemy Before Us" 10-16.

TELEFILM

1969 *The Challengers* 3-28 CBS.

Carole Cook

A seventies/eighties television actress, Carole often played boisterous and coarse middle-aged ladies. She was a regular on the soap *Capitol* during 1987. Carole was married to actor Tom Troupe.

GUEST CREDITS
1966 *Daniel Boone* "The Symbol" 12-29; **1972** *McMillan and Wife* "The Night of the Wizard" 9-24;

1973 *McMillan and Wife* "Free Fall to Terror" 11-11; **1974** *McMillan and Wife* "Reunion in Terror" 1-27; **1975** *Baretta* "Woman in the Harbor" 1-31; **1976** *Charlie's Angels* "The Seance" 12-15; **1977** *Kojak* "The Queen of Hearts Is Wild" 10-2; *Kojak* "Laid Out" 10-16; **1977** *Charlie's Angels* "Angel in Love" 10-26; **1982** *Strike Force* "Lonely Ladies" 3-15; *Knight Rider* "Deadly Maneuvers" 10-1; *Knight Rider* "Just My Bil" 10-24; *Trapper John, M.D.* "The Object of My Affliction" 10-24; *Hart to Hart* "One Hart Too Many" 12-7; **1983** *Quincy, M.E.* "Quincy's Wedding" 2-16, 2-23.

TELEFILMS

1977 *In the Glitter Palace* 2-27 NBC; **1980** *Make Me an Offer* 1-11 ABC; **1982** *Something So Right* 11-30 CBS; *Remembrance* of Love 12-6 NBC.

Ben Cooper

(born September 30, 1933, Hartford, Conn.)

Ben first appeared onstage at the age of 9 (1942), in *Life with Father*. Later educated at Columbia University, he went on to appear in a number of fifties and sixties mostly western films (beginning in 1950). He left acting in 1972 in favor of a business career after 30 years of acting, returning in 1981-82 for two guest shots on *The Fall Guy*.

GUEST CREDITS

1959 *Millionaire* "Millionaire Alicia Osante" 3-18; *One Step Beyond* "Front Runner" 6-9; **1960** *Zane Grey Theatre* "Desert Flight" 10-13; **1961** *Americans* "The Sentry" 4-10; *Perry Mason* "The Case of the Impatient Partner" 9-16; *Twilight Zone* "Still Valley" 11-24; *Gunsmoke* "Apprentice Doc" 12-9; *Adventures in Paradise* "The Trial of Adam Troy" 12-17; **1962** *Perry Mason* "The Case of the Promoter's Pillbox" 5-19; *Perry Mason* "The Case of the Polka Dot Pony" 12-20; *Laramie* "Gun Duel" 12-25; **1963** *Combat* "Next in Command" 2-5; **1964** *Rawhide* "The Photographer" 12-11; **1965** *Gunsmoke* "Breckenridge" 3-13; *Kraft Suspense Theatre* "Won't It Ever Be Morning?" 3-18; *Gunsmoke* "Two

Tall Men" 5-8; *Perry Mason* "The Case of the Mischievous Doll" 5-13; *Combat* "Main Event" 9-14; *Perry Mason* "The Case of the Baffling Bug" 12-12; **1966** *Time Tunnel* "One Way to the Moon" 9-16; **1969** *It Takes a Thief* "The Great Chess Gambit" 4-15; *Mannix* "Playground" 10-18; **1970** *Marcus Welby, M.D.* "Sea of Security" 3-10; *Adam-12* "Log Ninety-Five-Purse Snatcher" 3-10; *Mannix* "To Cage a Seagull" 11-21; **1981** *Fall Guy* "The Human Torch" 12-9; **1982** *Fall Guy* "No Way Out" 1-6.

Jeanne Cooper

(born 1928, Taft, California)

Jeanne made her film debut in 1953; the following year she gave birth to a son who would grow up to become a noted film and TV actor, Corbin Bernsen. She worked often in television during the late fifties and became one of the sixties most prolific female guest stars on TV dramas.

Following a series regular role on *Bracken's World*, in 1970, she began a long running part on the soap *The Young and the Restless*, beginning in 1973 and running currently. In 1986 she appeared on an episode of *L. A. Law* with her son Corbin.

GUEST CREDITS

1961 *Lawman* "The Reversed Blade" 2-4;
Maverick "Flood's Folly" 2-19; *Ben Casey* "But
Linda Only Smiled" 10-9; *87ᵗʰ Precinct* "Killer's
Payoff" 11-6; *New Breed* "The Butcher" 11-14;
Roaring 20's "Asparagus Tips" 12-9; **1962** *Surfside 6*
"Anniversary Special" 1-29; *Hawaiian Eye* "My
Love, But Lightly" 1-31; *Perry Mason* "The Case of
the Glamorous Ghost" 2-3; **1963** *Eleventh Hour* "My
Name Is Judith, I'm Lost, You See" 1-16; *Stoney
Burke* "Web of Fear" 2-18; *Hawaiian Eye* "The Long
Way Home" 2-19; *Channing* "The Potato Bash
World" 10-30; *Gunsmoke* "The Ex-Con" 11-30; *Mr.
Novak* "The Boy without a Country" 12-10; **1964**
Virginian "The Fortunes of J. Jimmerson Jones" 1-
15; *77 Sunset Strip* "The Target" 1-24; *Perry Mason*
"The Case of the Nervous Neighbor" 2-13; *Dr.
Kildare* "The Child Between" 3-5; **1965** *Man from
UNCLE* "The Children's Day Affair" 12-10; **1966**
Perry Mason "The Case of the Vanishing Victim" 1-
23; *Daniel Boone* "Crisis by Fire" 1-27; *Ben Casey*
"Weave Nets to Catch the Wind" 2-7; *Big Valley*
"Tunnel of Gold" 4-20; **1968** *Ironside* "Officer
Bobby" 3-14; **1970** *Silent Force* "A Cry in Concrete"
11-16; **1971** *Mannix* "A Walk in the Shadows" 2-9;
Storefront Lawyers "The Dark World of Harry
Anders" 2-17; *Hawaii Five-0* "…And I Want Some
Candy and a Gun That Shoots" 10-19; **1972**
Longstreet "Sad Songs and Other Conversations" 2-
10; *Hawkins* "A Life for a Life" 9-13; **1973** *Ironside*

"Confessions from a Lady of the Night" 9-13; **1974**
Doc Elliot "The Carrier" 2-20; *Kolchak: The Night
Stalker* "The Devil's Platform" 11-15; **1975** *Emergency* episode 10-11.

TELEFILMS

1975 *Sweet Hostage* 10-10 ABC; **1977** *The San
Pedro Beach Bums* 5-13 ABC.

Regis J. Cordic

Primarily a seventies television actor, Rege did
20 telefilms and over 3 dozen guest roles during the
decade; he also found time to appear in 3 miniseries.
His strong and distinguished presence frequently
found him cast as judges and other authority figures.

GUEST CREDITS

1969 *Mannix* "Penny for the Peepshow" 11-1;
Ironside "Five Miles High" 11-27; **1971** *Name of the
Game* "L. A.: 2017: 1-15; *Sarge* "A Company of
Victims" 12-7; *Sixth Sense* "The Eyes That Would
Not Die" 12-23; **1972** *Owen Marshall, Counselor at
Law* "Warlock at Mach 3" 1-6; *Gunsmoke*
"Bohannon" 9-25; *Bold Ones: The Doctors* "Is
This Operation Necessary?" 9-26; *Gunsmoke* "The

Brothers" 11-27; *Waltons* "The Minstrel" 12-21; **1973** *The FBI* "The Disinherited" 1-21; *Gunsmoke* "Jesse" 2-19; *Ironside* "All Honorable Men" 3-8; *Emergency* episode 3-10; *Cannon* "Memo from a Dead Man" 9-19; *Columbo* "Any Old Port in a Storm" 10-7; *Columbo* "Candidate for Crime" 11-4; *New Perry Mason* "The Case of the Furious Father" 11-11; **1974** *Toma* "The Big Dealers" 3-1; *Six Million Dollar Man* "Eyewitness to Murder" 3-8; *Mannix* "The Ragged Edge" 3-31; *Barnaby Jones* "A Gathering of Thieves" 9-10; *Manhunter* "Terror from the Skies" 10-16; *Gunsmoke* "Island in the Desert" 12-2, 12-9; **1975** *Kolchak: The Night Stalker* "The Primal Scream" 1-17; *Rockford Files* "Say Goodbye to Jennifer" 2-7; *McCloud* "Return to the Alamo" 3-30; *Streets of San Francisco* "Deadly Silence" 10-16; *Marcus Welby, M.D.* "Calculated Risk" 11-11; *Medical Center* "One Last Rebellion" 11-24; **1977** *Quincy, M.E.* "Let Me Light the Way" 5-27; *Six Million Dollar Man* "Bigfoot V" 10-9; **1978** *Logan's Run* "Carousel" 1-16; *Bionic Woman* "Which One Is Jaimie?" 2-25; *Richie Brockelman* "The Framing of Perfect Sidney" 3-17; **1979** *Barnaby Jones* "Design for Madness" 10-18; *Quincy, M.E.* "Mode of Death" 11-1; *Waltons* "The Waiting" 11-22; *Incredible Hulk* "Homecoming" 11-30.

TELEFILMS

1970 *Ritual of Evil* 2-23 NBC; **1971** *Travis Logan, D. A.* 3-11 CBS; *The Priest Killer* 9-14 NBC; *The Face of Fear* 10-8 CBS; *Death Takes a Holiday* 10-23 ABC; *A Death of Innocence* 11-26 CBS; **1974** *The Death Squad* 1-8 ABC; *Murder or Mercy* 4-10 ABC; *The Law* 10-22 NBC; **1975** *Target Risk* 1-6 NBC; *The Dream Makers* 1-7 NBC; *Crime Club* 4-3 CBS; **1976** *Law of the Land* 4-29 NBC; *Woman of the Year* 7-28 CBS; **1977** *The Man with the Power* 5-24 NBC; *Panic in Echo Park* 6-23 NBC; *Intimate Strangers* 11-11 ABC; **1978** *Standing Tall* 1-21 NBC; *The Critical List* 9-11, 9-12 NBC; **1979** *The Golden Gate Murders* 10-3 CBS.

Jeff Corey
(born August 10, 1914, New York City)

Jeff Corey's stage career began in 1938, with a film debut in 1941. His screen career would total 80

movies, including roles in *Miracle on 34th Street*, *True Grit*, *Butch Cassidy and the Sundance Kid* and *Oh, God!* A U. S. Navy combat photographer from 1943-45, Jeff was given a citation from the Navy.

From 1952 until 1963, Jeff was blacklisted and unable to find roles during the House Un-American Activities Committee era. He founded an acting school and became a notable dramatic coach and teacher. Upon his return to acting Jeff worked steadily throughout the balance of the sixties/ seventies era.

The eighties were one of his most productive television acting periods, with series regular roles in *Hell Town* (1985) and *Morningstar/Evening Star* (1986). He had eighties guest roles on *Newhart*, *Night Court* and *Perfect Strangers*. Corey also directed many TV episodes, including *Police Story* and *The Bob Newhart Show*.

GUEST CREDITS

1963 *Outer Limits* "O.B.I.T." 11-4; **1964** *Doctors and Nurses* "No Shadow Where There Is No Sun" 10-20; *Perry Mason* "The Case of the Reckless Rock Hound" 11-25; **1965** *Wild Wild West* "The Night of a Thousand Eyes" 10-22; **1966** *Run for Your*

Life "Who's Watching the Fleshpot?"3-7; **1967**
Garrison's Gorillas "The Grab" 9-19; *Judd for the
Defense* "The Other Face of the Law" 9-22; *Iron
Horse* "Gallows for Bill Pardew" 9-30; *Run for Your
Life* "At the End of the Rainbow, There's Another
Rainbow" 10-10; **1968** *Wild Wild West* "The Night of
the Underground Terror" 1-19; **1969** *Hawaii Five-0*
"King of the Hill" 1-8; *Gunsmoke* "The Night
Riders" 2-24; *Star Trek* "The Cloud Minders" 2-28;
1970 *Night Gallery* "The Dead Man" 12-16; **1971**
Psychiatrist "Such Civil War in My Love and Hate"
2-17; *Mannix* "Overkill" 3-13; *Hawaii Five-0* "High-
est Castle, Deepest Grave" 9-14; **1972** *Search* "Short
Circuit" 9-27; **1973** *Streets of San Francisco* "Shat-
tered Image" 3-22; *Police Story* "The Big Walk" 12-
4; **1974** *Hawkins* "Murder on the Thirteenth Floor"
2-5; **1975** *Six Million Dollar Man* "Lost Love" 1-17;
Doctor's Hospital "Point of Maximum Pressure" 9-
10; *Starsky and Hutch* "Death Ride" 9-24; **1976**
McCloud "The Shiek of Arami" 1-11; *Switch* "The
Lady from Liechtenstein" 11-23, 11-30; **1977** *Bionic
Woman* "The Daemon Creature" 3-23; **1979** *Little
House on the Prairie* "Barn Burner" 2-19; *Quincy,
M.E.* "Promises to Keep" 3-1; **1982** *Lou Grant*
"Blacklist" 4-5; **1983** *Manimal* "Night of the Beast"
12-10.

TELEFILMS

1970 *The Movie Murderer* 2-2 NBC; *A Clear
and Present Danger* 3-21 NBC; **1972** *Something Evil*
1-21 CBS; **1973** *Set This Town on Fire* 1-8 NBC; **1974**
The Gun and the Pulpit 4-3 ABC; **1976** *Banjo
Hackett: Roamin' Free* 5-3 NBC; *Curse of the
Black Widow* 9-16 ABC; *Captains Courageous* 12-4
ABC; *Harold Robbins' "The Pirate"* 11-21, 11-22;
1980 *Homeward Bound* 11-19 CBS; **1982** *Cry for the
Strangers* 12-11 CBS.

Robert Cornthwaite

(born April 28, 1917, St. Helens, Oregon)
    Robert made his film debut during 1951 in *The
Thing*. His prolific television career began in 1954
and has extended into the nineties. A dead-pan
manner has made him quite valuable to stage, screen

and television in a wide variety of roles.
    Eighties guest credits included guest shots on
Cagney and Lacey and on *Perfect Strangers*.

GUEST CREDITS

1959 *Rawhide* "Incident of the Thirteenth Man"
10-23; *Perry Mason* "The Case of Paul Drake's
Dilemma" 11-4; **1960** *Rifleman* "The Deserter" 3-15;
Maverick "Last Wire from Stop Gap" 10-16; *Perry
Mason* "The Case of the Wandering Widow" 10-22;
Law and Mr. Jones "The Storyville Gang" 11-25;
1961 *Maverick* "Family Pride" 1-8; *Hong Kong* "The
Hunted" 2-15; *Adventures in Paradise* "The Secret
Place" 2-25; *Acapulco* "The Gentlemen from Brazil"
3-13; *Tales of Wells Fargo* "Remember the Yazoo" 4-
14; *Roaring 20's* "The Red Carpet" 4-15; *Wagon
Train* "The Mark Minor Story" 11-15; **1962** *Rawhide*
"The Long Count" 1-5; *Twilight Zone* "Showdown
with Rance McGrew" 2-2; *Perry Mason* "The Case
of the Ancient Romeo" 5-12; *Wagon Train* "The Orly
French Story" 12-12; **1963** *Laramie* "Naked Steel"1-
1; *Twilight Zone* "No Time Like the Past" 3-7;
Wagon Train "The Fenton Canaby Story" 12-30;
1964 *Alfred Hitchcock Hour* "Three Wives Too
Many" 1-3; *Destry* "Stormy Is a Lady" 3-6; *Voyage
to the Bottom of the Sea* "Turn Back the Clock 10-
31; *Perry Mason* "The Case of a Place Called
Midnight" 11-12; *Mr. Novak* "A as in Anxiety" 12-8;

1965 *Combat* "The Steeple" 2-9; *Dr. Kildare* "Behold the Great Man" 9-13; *Dr. Kildare* "A Life for a Life" 9-14; *Dr. Kildare* "A Web of Hate" 9-20; *Fugitive* "Conspiracy of Silence" 10-12; *Amos Burke, Secret Agent* "The Prisoners of Mr. Sin" 10-27; *Voyage to the Bottom of the Sea* "The Deadliest Game" 10-31; *Laredo* "Pride of the Rangers" 12-16; 1966 *Big Valley* "A Time to Kill" 1-19; *The FBI* "The Defector" 3-27, 4-3; 1967 *Jerico* episode 1-5; *Dragnet* "The Big Pyramid" 11-30; 1968 *Garrison's Gorillas* "The Big Lie" 1-23; *Ironside* "Little Bear Died Running" 11-6; *Lancer* "The Last Train for Charlie Roe" 11-26; *The FBI* "The Flaw" 12-15; 1970 *Bonanza* "What Are Partners For?" 4-2; 1971 *The FBI* "Center of Evil" 1-13; *Gunsmoke* "Cleavus" 2-15; 1973 *The FBI* "Break-In" 10-7; 1974 *Kolchak: The Night Stalker* "The Energy Eater" 12-13; 1975 *Manhunter* "To Kill a Tiger" 2-26; 1979 *Quincy, M.E.* "Hot Ice" 10-18; *Buck Rogers* "Unchained Woman" 11-1.

TELEFILMS

1971 *Two on a Bench* 11-2 ABC; 1972 *Killer by Night* 1-7 CBS; *The Longest Night* 9-12 ABC; 1973 *The Devil's Daughter* 1-9 ABC; *The Six Million Dollar Man* 3-7 ABC; 1979 *Love's Savage Fury* 5-20 ABC; *Beggarman, Thief* 5-26, 5-27 NBC; 1982 *The Day the Bubble Burst* 2-7 NBC.

Nicholas Coster

(born December 30, 1934, London, England)

Nicholas Coster has gained great fame as a soap actor, on: *Young Doctor Malone* (1958-63), *The Secret Storm* (1964, 1968-69), *Our Private World* (1965), *As the World Turns* (1966), *Somerset* (1970-73), *Another World* (1973-76) *One Life to Live* (1983-84) and *Santa Barbara* (1984-88, 1990-).

A very hardworking actor, Nicholas found time for a great deal of prime time television between his lengthy soap stints. From 1959 on through the eighties he made numerous guest appearances and was a regular on *Lobo* (1980-81) and *Ryan's Four* (1983).

During the late eighties he guested on *L. A. Law, Hooperman, Murder, She Wrote, thirtysomething* and *Who's the Boss?*

Trained at The Royal Academy of Dramatic Arts, his film career began in 1952 in *Stars and Stripes Forever*. He also appeared in *The Robe, Desiree, The Electric Horseman, The Concorde--Airport 79*, and *The Pursuit of D. B. Cooper*.

GUEST CREDITS

1959 *U.S. Steel Hour* "No Leave for the Captain" 6-17; 1961 *Defenders* "The Accident" 11-4; 1967 *Green Hornet* "Ace in the Hole" 2-10; 1977 *Charlie's Angels* "Angels on the Air" 11-9; 1978 *Baretta* "The Dream" 5-4; *Rockford Files* "A Good Clean Bust with Serial Rights" 5-30; *Spider Man* "A Matter of State" 9-12; *Wonder Woman* "The Deadly Dolphin" 12-1; 1979 *Incredible Hulk* "Blind Rage" 9-28; *Kate Loves a Mystery* "A Chilling Surprise" 11-22; 1980 *Paris* "The Ghost Maker" 1-8; *Buck Rogers* "Olympiad" 2-7; *Tenspeed and Brownshoe* "Loose Larry's Nest of Lovers" 5-30; 1981 *Simon and Simon* "The Least Dangerous Game" 12-29; 1982 *Today's FBI* "Blue Collar" 2-21; *Hart to Hart* "Blue and Broken Hearted" 2-23; *Shannon* "The Untouchable" 3-24; *Quincy, M.E.* "A Ghost of a Chance" 10-6; 1983 *Magnum, P.I.* "I Do?" 2-17; *Hardcastle and McCormick* "The Crystal Duck" 10-

2; *T. J. Hooker* episode l0-22; *Knight Rider* "Return to Cadiz" l0-30.

TELEFILMS

1978 *A Fire in the Sky* 11-26 NBC; *Long Journey Back* 12-l5 ABC; **1979** *Friendly Fire* 4-22 ABC; *Ebony, Ivory and Jade* 8-3 CBS; *The Solitary Man* l0-9 CBS; **1982** *The Day the Bubble Burst* 2-7 NBC; **1983** *M.A.D.D.: Mothers Against Drunk Driving* 3-l4 NBC; *Princess Daisy* 11-6, 11-7 NBC.

Kevin Coughlin
(born 1945; died 1976)

First a Conover model (at age 3), then a juvenile actor, Kevin appeared in l954 productions of *Armstrong Circle Theater* and *Goodyear Playhouse* prior to being cast in the early sitcom, *Mama*, from 1954-57. He continued to appear in live fifties dramas like *U.S. Steel Hour* (2), *Philco Television Playhouse* and *Studio One*. As the sixties progressed, Kevin began taking teenager roles that continued until his accidental death in l976. He also produced and hosted an L. A. talk show called *The Age of Acquarius*.

Kevin was killed in a hit-and-run accident while cleaning the windshield on his car. He was survived by his wife, mother and sister.

GUEST CREDITS

1962 *Armstrong Circle Theater* "Runaway Reed: Story of Missing Persons" l-3; **1965** *Combat* "The First Day" 9-2l; **1967** *Fugitive* "The Savage Street" 3-l4; *Invaders* "The Spores" l0-17; **1968** *Dragnet* "The Big Departure" 3-7; *Name of the Game* "High on a Rainbow" 12-6; **1969** *Gunsmoke* "The Mark of Cain" 2-3; *Judd, for the Defense* "Between the Dark and the Daylight" 2-7; *Dragnet* "Homicide-The Student" 9-25; *Gunsmoke* "Coreyville" l0-6; **1970** *Gunsmoke* "The Gun" 1 1-9; **1971** *O'Hara, U. S. Treasury* "Operation: Time Fuse" l0-15; **1973** *Gunsmoke* "This Golden Land" 3-5; *The FBI* "Break-In" l0-7; **1975** *Gunsmoke* "Hard Labor" 2-24.

Dennis Cross
(born 1924)

In television from l949, Dennis had a starring role in the syndicated adventure series *The Blue Angels* (1960). He appeared in numerous TV guest roles, especially in the western genre. Following retirement from acting Dennis became a dialogue director for Spelling Productions.

Dennis is the father of professional football player Randy Cross, recently retired from a fine career with the San Francisco 49ers, and now a broadcaster.

GUEST CREDITS

1959 *Rawhide* "Incident of the Curious Street" 4-10; *Gunsmoke* "Cheyennes" 6-13; *Rifleman* "The Patsy" 9-29; **1960** *Rifleman* "Hero" 2-2; *Gunsmoke* "Doc Judge" 2-6; *Black Saddle* "The Indian Tree" 2-19; *Rifleman* "The Vision" 3-22; *Hotel de Paree* "Sundance and the Black Widow" 4-1; **1961** *Rawhide* "Incident before Black Pass" 5-19; **1963** *Rawhide* "The Captain's Wife" 1-12; *Rifleman* "The Quiet Fear" 1-22; *Rawhide* "Incident at Two Graves" 11-7; *Gunsmoke* "Carter Caper" 11-16; **1964** *Fugitive* "Search in a Windy City" 2-4; *Fugitive* "Iron Maiden" 12-15; **1965** *Big Valley* "Palms of Glory" 9-15; *Legend of Jesse James* "The Pursuers" 10-11; **1966** *Big Valley* "Teacher of Outlaws" 1-26; *Big Valley* "The Fallen Hawk" 3-2; *Tarzan* "The Ultimate Weapon" 9-16; *Big Valley* "Last Train to Salt Flats" 12-5 *Iron Horse* "Town Full of Fear" 12-5; **1968** *Land of the Giants* "Framed" 10-6; **1969** *Gunsmoke* "The Reprisal" 2-10; *Outcasts* "The Town That Wouldn't Die" 3-31; **1970** *Mod Squad* "The Deadly Sin" 2-24; **1971** *Mission: Impossible* "Mindbend" 10-9; **1972** *Mission: Impossible* "Underground" 10-28; **1976** *Waltons* "The Cloudburst" 11-11; *Magician* "Man on Fire" 11-20.

TELEFILMS

1969 *The Over-the-Hill Gang* 10-7 ABC; **1970** *Crowhaven Farm* 11-24 ABC; **1972** *The Bounty Man* 10-31 ABC; **1974** *Betrayal* 12-3 ABC.

Kathleen Crowley

(born December 26, 1931, Green Bank, N. J.)
A striking beauty contest winner, Kathleen attended American Academy of Dramatic Arts (AADA) in 1949, and studied with Lee Strasberg at Actor's Studio. She made her TV debut in 1951, a starring role in a Robert Montgomery presentation

of *Jane Eyre*. 20th Century Fox signed her to a contract and her career was off and running. In 1953 she garnered a series regular role on *Waterfront* (1953-56).

During the late fifties and early sixties she was one of television's busiest actresses, frequently appearing in western series like *Maverick* (7) and *Bonanza* (4). In 1970 she married a wealthy textile executive and left acting.

GUEST CREDITS

1959 *Bat Masterson* "Incident in Leadville" 3-18; *Rawhide* "Incident below the Brazos" 5-15; *Markham* "Forty-Two on a Rope" 7-11; *Bourbon Street Beat* "Invitation to Murder" 11-23; *77 Sunset Strip* "Secret Island" 12-4; *Maverick* "Maverick Springs" 12-6; **1960** *Hawaiian Eye* "Kamehameha Cloak" 1-13; *Maverick* "The Misfortune Teller" 3-6; *Bonanza* "San Francisco Holiday" 4-2; *77 Sunset Strip* "The Attic" 9-16; *Deputy* "The Fatal Urge" 10-15; *Maverick* "A Bullet for the Teacher" 10-30; *Bat Masterson* "Murder Can Be Dangerous" 11-3; *Maverick* "Kiz" 12-4; *77 Sunset Strip* "The Valley

Kathleen Crowley uses her wiles on a receptive Clint Eastwood, while trail boss Eric Fleming registers disapproval in a 1959 episode of *Rawhide*, **"Incident Below the Brazos" (CBS).**

Howard Culver
(born 1918, Colorado; died August 5, 1984)

Most visible on *Gunsmoke* in a long running recurring role (1957-1974) as Howie the desk clerk, Howard was also a member of Jack Webb's stock company, appearing in several episodes of *Dragnet* and *Adam-12*. He was also active in radio, in the featured role of *Ellery Queen*, and in radio versions of *Gunsmoke*.

GUEST CREDITS

1960

Caper" 12-16; **1961** *77 Sunset Strip* "Strange Bedfellows" 2-17; *Surfside 6* "Black Orange Blossoms" 2-20; *Thriller* "The Ordeal of Dr. Cordell" 3-7; *Maverick* "Dade City Dodge" 9-17; *77 Sunset Strip* "The Desert Spa Caper" 9-22; *Surfside 6* "Prescription for Panic" 12-4; *Hawaiian Eye* "The Classic Cab" 12-22; **1963** *Bronco* "Destinies West" 2-26; *Maverick* "The Troubled Heir" 4-1; *Maverick* "One of Our Trains Is Missing" 4-22; *Tales of Wells Fargo* "Royal Maroon" 4-28; *Checkmate* "Rendevous in Washington" 5-9; *Perry Mason* "The Case of the Lonely Eloper" 5-26; **1963** *Route 66* "Shall Forfeit His Dog and Ten Shillings to the King" 2-22; *Bonanza* "The Actress" 2-24; *Bonanza* "Five into the Wind" 4-21; *Perry Mason* "The Case of the Drowsy Mosquito" 10-17; *Redigo* "Shadow of the Cougar" 11-26; **1965** *Virginian* "Farewell to Honesty" 3-24; **1966** *Perry Mason* "The Case of the Bogus Buccaneers" 1-9; **1968** *Bonanza* "Stage Door Johnnies" 7-28; **1969** *High Chaparral* "Once, on a Day in the Spring" 2-14.

Gunsmoke "The Worm" 10-29; **1961** *Gunsmoke* "Harriet" 3-4; *Twilight Zone* "Shadow Play" 5-5; **1962** *Gunsmoke* "Durham Bull" 3-31; **1963** *Gunsmoke* "Old York" 5-4; **1964** *Gunsmoke*

"Doctor's Wife" 10-24; **1965** *Gunsmoke* "Dry Road to Nowhere" 4-3; *Gunsmoke* "The Avengers" 12-18; **1967** *Gunsmoke* "Muley" 1-21; *Dragnet* "The Big Bank Examiners" 2-23; *Gunsmoke* "Nitro I, II" 4-8, 4-15; **1968** *Dragnet* "The Big Departure" 3-7; *Adam-12* "Log One-The Impossible Mission" 9-21; *Dragnet* "Narcotics-DR-16" 12-5; *Land of the Giants* "Double Cross" 12-8; **1969** *Gunsmoke* "Mannon" 1-20; *Dragnet* "Frauds-Dr-28" 2-20; *Dragnet* "Juvenile-DR-35" 4-3; **1970** *Gunsmoke* "Doctor Herman Schultz, M.D" 1-26; *Dragnet* "Missing Persons-The Body"3-5; *Dragnet*-D.H.Q.-The Victims" 4-16; *Gunsmoke* "Luke" 11-2; *Adam-12* "Log Eighty Five-Sign of the Twins" 12-26; **1971** *Gunsmoke* "Lijah" 11-8; **1972** *Gunsmoke* "The School Marm" 2-25; **1978** *Project UFO* "Sighting 4010: The Academy Incident" 5-7; **1983** *Hart to Hart* "Harts at High Noon" 11-9.

Ken Curtis, in his wonderful role as "Festus", appears dubious of the effectiveness of new deputy Harry Townes. The 1965 episode of *Gunsmoke* **(CBS) was called "Malachi".**

TELEFILMS

1981 *Code Red* 9-20 ABC; *Return of the Beverly Hillbillies* 10-6 CBS.

Ken Curtis

(born Curtis Gates, July 2, 1916, Lamar, Colorado; died April 28, 1991)

Ken Curtis, alias deputy Festus Haggen on *Gunsmoke* 1964-75, had a most remarkable career in the world of entertainment. A pre-med student at Colorado College, he subsequently worked for NBC prior to joining the Tommy Dorsey orchestra as band vocalist, later moving over to Shep Fields as his vocalist.

He then joined The Sons of the Pioneers western singing group for a time before World War II service. After service he became a singing cowboy lead for Columbia Pictures westerns (1945-47). Leaving the low-budget western scene, Ken had a major role in *Mr. Roberts* in 1955; eventually he appeared in *The Searchers, The Alamo, How the West Was Won* and *Cheyenne Autumn.*

Following a number of TV western series guest roles, including 5 on *Have Gun-Will Travel*, he co-starred on a syndicated adventure series, *Ripcord* (1961-63). He appeared in 5 guest roles on

Gunsmoke, including his first appearance as Festus, in 1962. When Dennis Weaver left the *Gunsmoke* cast, Curtis established his Festus character as a TV institution. His scruffy appearance, twangy drawl and loyalty to the other characters earned him millions of fans during the 1964-75 period that he played the role.

When *Gunsmoke* left the air, Curtis did a couple of guest shots before taking a series regular role on The *Yellow Rose* (1983-84). He died in his sleep of natural causes on April 28, 1991 in Fresno, California. Ken was survived by his widow, Torie, 2 children and 8 grandchildren.

GUEST CREDITS

1959 *Gunsmoke* "Jawhawkers" 1-31; *Gunsmoke* "Change of Heart" 4-25; *Have Gun-Will Travel* "The Posse" 10-3; *Have Gun-Will Travel* "Naked Gun" 12-19; **1960** *Gunsmoke* "The Ex-Urbanites" 4-9; *Gunsmoke* "Speak Me Fair" 5-7; *Have Gun-Will Travel* "Love's Young Dream" 9-17; *Wagon Train* "The Horace Best Story" 10-5; *Perry Mason* "The Case of the Clumsy Clown" 11-5; **1961** *Have Gun-Will Travel* "Soledad Crossing" 6-10; **1962** *Have Gun-Will Travel* "Pandora's Box" 5-19; *Gunsmoke* "Us Haggens" 12-8; **1963** *Gunsmoke* "Lover Boy" 10-5; **1976** *Petrocelli* "Falling Star" 1-21; **1979** *Vegas* "Death Mountain" 1-31.

Jon Cypher

(born 1932)

Primarily a television actor, with much stage experience, Jon starred in a 1957 production of *Cinderella* with Julie Andrews, then was largely absent the medium until the early seventies when he began guesting on dramatic series. He appeared on *Hill Street Blues* as the Chief of Police from 1981 to 1987 in a semi-regular role. From 1990 to 1994 he attained his greatest TV exposure as a regular on *Major Dad*, playing the blustery General. He also worked on soaps *As the World Turns* (1977-79), *General Hospital* (1981) and *Santa Barbara*.

GUEST CREDITS

1972 *McMillan and Wife* "The Face of Murder" 1-5; *Mannix* "The Sound of Murder" 1-12; *Mission: Impossible* "Trapped" 2-26; *Bonanza* "A Place to Hide" 3-19; *Mannix* "Broken Mirror" 10-8; **1973** *Circle of Fear* "Night of Daemons" 2-2; **1974** *Cannon* "Bobby Loved Me" 2-27; *The FBI* "Survival" 4-28; *Rookies* "Key Witness" 9-23; **1975** *Marcus Welby, M.D.* "The Lie" 9-23; *Marcus Welby, M.D.* "The Covenant" 9-30; **1976** *Barnaby Jones* "Dangerous Gambit" 2-26; **1977** *Police Woman* "Disco Killer" 1-25; *Rockford Files* "To Serve and Protect" 3-11, 3-18; *Feather and Father Gang* "Sun, Sand and Death" 3-14; **1981** *Trapper John, M.D.* "The Albatross" 5-10; **1982** *Today's FBI* "Spy" 1-10; *Greatest American Hero* "Now You See It" 1-20; **1983** *Knight Rider* "Soul Survivor" 11-27.

TELEFILMS

1974 *Night Games* 3-16 NBC; **1981** *Evita Peron* 2-23, 2-24 NBC.

Charles Cyphers

(born 1939)

A stage, screen and television actor of the seventies, Charles Cyphers had one TV series

regular role, on *The Betty White Show* (1977-78). Among his film credits were appearances in *Gray Lady Down, The Onion Field, Escape from New York* and *Halloween II*.

GUEST CREDITS

1967 *Coronet Blue* "A Time to Be Born" 5-29; **1973** *Barnaby Jones* "Requiem for a Son" 1-28; *The FBI* "Break-In" 10-7; **1976** *Six Million Dollar Man* "Secret of Bigfoot" 2-1, 2-4; *Six Million Dollar Man* "The Return of Big Foot" 9-19; *Bionic Woman* "The Return of Big Foot" 9-22; *Starsky and Hutch* "The Specialist" 11-13; *Gibbsville* "Trapped" 12-9; **1977** *Charlie's Angels* "Angels on a String" 1-19; *Wonder Woman* "Wonder Woman in Hollywood" 2-16; *Dog and Cat* "Dead Skunk" 4-23; **1978** *Starsky and Hutch* "The Avenger" 10-31; **1979** *Starsky and Hutch* "Birds of a Feather" 1-30; **1981** *Hart to Hart* "Hart-Shaped Murder" 2-10.

TELEFILMS

1974 *The FBI Story: The FBI Versus Alvin Karpis, Public Enemy Number One* 11-8 CBS; **1977** *The Trial of Lee Harvey Oswald* 9-30; 10-2 ABC; **1978** *Someone's Watching Me* 11-29 NBC; **1979** *Elvis* 2-11 ABC; *Friendly Fire* 4-22 ABC; **1982** *The Executioner's Song* 11-28, 11-29 NBC; **1983** *Little*

House: Look Back to Yesterday 2-12 NBC; *Memorial Day* 11-27 CBS.

Royal Dano

(born November 16, 1922, New York City; died May 15, 1994)

Royal began acting in the U. S. Army Special Services during World War II. He debuted in films in 1950, eventually appearing in over 60 movies, with numerous credits in western flicks. He did a great deal of early fifties television and went on to become one of TV's most familiar and enduring character actors. Perhaps best known for his work in television westerns, Royal appeared in over 30 western series episodes, including 13 guest shots on *Gunsmoke*, and multiple appearances on *Rawhide, The Virginian, Big Valley* and *Bonanza*.

His somber look found him frequently cast as harassed victims, preachers, fugitives, and sometimes, cunning criminals. He forged some truly unforgettable performances.

Royal died May 15, 1994, of heart failure, in

Santa Monica, California, survived by his wife and a son.

GUEST CREDITS

1959 *Rifleman* "The Sheridan Story" 1-13; *Loretta Young Show* "810 Franklin Street" 4-7; *Wanted: Dead or Alive* "The Matchmaker" 9-19; *Rebel* "The Scavengers" 10-18; **1960** *Tales of Wells Fargo* "Cole Younger" 1-4; *Johnny Ringo* "Black Harvest" 4-7; *Zane Grey Theater* "Image of a Drawn Sword" 5-11; *Alfred Hitchcock Presents* "Party Line" 5-29; *Tate* "Home Town"6-8; **1961** *Gunslinger* "Border Incident" 2-9; *Have Gun-Will Travel* "The Fatal Flaw" 2-25; *Gunslinger* "The Buried People" 3-9; *Rebel* "The Proxy" 4-16; *Frontier Circus* "The Patriarch of Purgatory" 11-30; *Target: The Corruptors* "To Wear a Badge" 12-1; **1962** *New Breed* "Care Is No Cure" 1-23; *Bonanza* "Gift of Water" 2-11; *Rifleman* "Day of Reckoning" 4-9; *Target: The Corruptors* "Journey into Mourning" 4-13; *Tales of Wells Fargo* "Don't Wake a Tiger" 5-12; *Virginian* "The Brazen Bell" 10-17; *Rawhide* "Incident at Quivara" 12-14; **1963** *Virginian* "Say Goodbye to All That" 1-23; *Dakotas* "Terror at Heart River" 4-15; *Temple Houston* ""Toll the Bell Slowly" 10-7; *Wagon Train* "The Robert Harrison Clark Story" 10-14; **1964** *Rawhide* "Incident at Ten Trees" 1-2; *Ben Casey* "There Was Once a Man in the Land of Oz"1-12; *Gunsmoke* "Now That April's Here" 3-21; *Gunsmoke* "Crooked Mile" 10-3; *Alfred Hitchcock Hour* "Change of Address" 10-12; *Fugitive* "When the Bough Breaks" 10-13; *Rawhide* "Incident of the Lost Herd" 10-16; **1965** *Gunsmoke* "Deputy Festus" 1-16; *Virginian* "We've Lost a Train" 4-21; *Legend of Jesse James* "Jail Break" 11-15; *Bonanza* "The Reluctant Rebel" 11-21; *Long Hot Summer* "Track the Man Down" 12-30; **1966** *Gunsmoke* "Sweet Billy, Singer of Songs" 1-15; *Big Valley* "The Death Merchant" 2-23; *Daniel Boone* "Cibola" 3-31; *Lost in Space* "Lost Civilization" 4-13; *Virginian* "A Bald-Faced Boy" 4-13; *Big Valley* "Hide the Children" 12-19; **1967** *Iron Horse* "Welcome to the General" 1-2; *Bonanza* "A Man without Land" 4-9; *Cimarron Strip* "Broken Wing" 9-21; *Gunsmoke* "Vengeance I, II" 10-2, 10-9; *Big Valley* "Lady Killer" 10-16; *Gunsmoke* "Hard Luck Henry" 10-23; *Cimarron Strip* episode 11-30; *The FBI* "The Legend of John Rim" 12-31; **1968** *Guns of Will Sonnett* "The Trap" 10-4; **1969** *Big Valley* "Joshua Watson" 1-20; *Gunsmoke* "Stryker" 9-29; **1970** *Gunsmoke* "The Thieves" 3-9; *The FBI* "The Condemned" 9-20; *Hawaii Five-0* "Paniolo" 12-30; **1971** *Gunsmoke* "Captain Sligo" 1-4; *Alias Smith and Jones* "The Girl in Boxcar 3" 2-17; *Gunsmoke* "The Lost" 9-13; *Man and the City* "The Cross Country Man" 12-1; **1972** *Night Gallery* "I'll Never Leave You, Ever" 2-16; **1973** *Cannon* "He Who Digs a Grave" 9-12; **1974** *Doc Elliot* "The Touch of God" 1-23; *Chase* episode 10 4-10; *Planet of the Apes* "Escape from Tomorrow" 9-13; **1975** *Adam-12* "Follow-Up" 3-11; *Police Story* "The Test of Brotherhood" 11-14; **1977** *Quincy, M.E.* "Tissue of Truth" 10-28; **1979** *Quincy, M.E.* "A Question of Death" 1-4; **1981** *Little House on the Prairie* episode 2-9.

TELEFILMS

1966 *The Dangerous Days of Kiowa Jones* 12-25 ABC; **1970** *Run, Simon, Run* 12-1 ABC; **1972** *Moon of the Wolf* 9-26 ABC; *Huckleberry Finn* 3-25 ABC; **1976** *The Manhunter* 4-3 NBC; **1977** *Murder in Peyton Place* 10-3 NBC; **1978** *A Love Affair: The Eleanor and Lou Gehrig Story* 1-15 NBC; *Donner Pass: The Road to Survival* 10-24 NBC; *Crash* 10-29 ABC; **1979** *Strangers: The Story of a Mother and Daughter* 5-13 CBS; *The Last Ride of the Dalton Gang* 11-20 ABC; **1983** *Will There Really Be a Morning?* 2-22 CBS; *Murder 1, Dancer 0* 6-5 NBC.

Michael Dante

(born Ralph Vitte, 1935, Stamford, Conn.)

An excellent baseball player, Ralph Vitte was signed to a contract by the Boston Braves, and was with the Washington Senators briefly. He left baseball and attended the University of Miami, majoring in drama. He signed with MGM and debuted in the 1956 film *Somebody Up There Likes Me*. He later appeared in *Raintree County, Kid Galahad, Harlow* and *Willard*.

Vitti, now Michael Dante, began working in television during the late fifties. His swarthy complexion frequently created castings as Hispanics and Native Americans. In fact, he played Sioux chief Crazy Horse in *Custer* (1967), his only TV series regular role. Dante continued to act on television during the eighties with a 1984 stint on the soap *Days of Our Lives*, and guesting on shows like *Cagney and Lacey*.

GUEST CREDITS

1959 *Maverick* "Betrayal" 3-22; *Perry Mason* "The Case of the Dangerous Dowager" 5-9; *Texan* "Stampede" 11-2; *Texan* "Showdown at Abilene" 11-9; *Texan* "The Reluctant Bridegroom" 11-16; *Texan* "Trouble on the Trail" 11-23; **1961** *Detectives* "The Champ" 5-19; *Cain's Hundred* "Cain's Final Judgment" 12-9; **1962** *87th Precinct* "Idol in the Dust" 4-2; **1963** *Hawaiian Eye* "Go Steady with Danger" 1-1; **1965** *Perry Mason* "The Case of the Feather Cloak" 2-11; *Bonanza* "The Brass Box" 9-26; *Branded* "Mightier Than the Sword" 9-26; **1967** *Star Trek* "Friday's Child" 12-1; **1968** *Big Valley* "Deathtown"10-28; **1969** *Daniel Boone* "For a Few Rifles" 4-10; **1974** *Six Million Dollar Man* "Dr. Wells Is Missing" 3-29; **1983** *Fall Guy* "Hollywood Shorties" 11-30.

Severn Darden

(born November 9, 1929; died May 26, 1995)

Few actors of the modern era have done as many offbeat roles as Severn Darden. He began working in TV guest roles in 1961, before his 1965 film debut. He worked throughout the eighties, guesting on shows like *Cheers* and *Beauty and the Beast*. He had his only series regular roles during the decade on abbreviated series *Beyond Westworld* (1980) and *Take Five* (1987).

He died in Santa Fe, New Mexico on May 26, 1995.

GUEST CREDITS

1961 *Alfred Hitchcock Presents* "Beta Delta Gamma" 11-14; **1964** *East Side/West Side* "The Beatnik and the Politician" 1-20; **1966** *Honey West* "Little Green Robin Hood" 3-18; **1968** *Daniel Boone* "The Valley of the Sun" 11-28; **1971** *Name of the Game* "L. A. 2017" 1-15; *Man and the City* "I Should Have Let Him Die" 9-29; **1972** *Cannon* "Bad Cats and Sudden Death" 9-13; *Banyon* "Completely Out of Print" 10-6; **1974** *Kolchak: The Night Stalker* "The Spanish Moss Murders" 12-6; **1975** *Baretta* "Woman in the Harbor" 1-31; *Harry O* "The Acolyte" 10-16; **1976** *Six Million Dollar Man* "Bigfoot" 1-28, 2-4; *Jigsaw John* "Follow the Yellow Brick Road" 3-8; *City of Angels* "The House on Orange Grove

Avenue" 3-16; *Six Million Dollar Man* "The Return of Bigfoot" 9-19, 9-26; **1978** *Starsky and Hutch* "Hutchinson for Murder One" 2-22; **1979** *Salvage I* "The Bugatti Map" 3-5; **1981** *Fall Guy* "The Human Torch" 12-9.

TELEFILMS

1970 *The Movie Murderer* 2-2 NBC; **1972** *Playmates* 10-3 ABC; **1973** *The Man Who Died Twice* 4-13 ABC; **1974** *Skyway to Death* 1-19 ABC; **1975** *New, Original Wonder Woman* 11-7 ABC; **1976** *The Disappearance of Aimee* 11-17 NBC; *Victory at Entebbe* 12-13 ABC; **1979** *Rendevous Hotel* 7-11 CBS; *Orphan Train* 12-22 CBS; **1981** *Evita Peron* 2-23, 2-24 NBC; **1982** *Rooster* 8-19 ABC; **1983** *Quarterback Princess* 12-3 CBS.

Richard Davalos
(born November 5, 1935, New York City)

A fine role in *East of Eden* marked Richard Davalos' film debut in 1955, and he entered TV the same year. Tough appearing, he was often cast as heavies in crime stories. He co-starred in the 1961 TV Civil War series, *The Americans*.

Richard is the father of actress Elyssa Davalos.

GUEST CREDITS

1960 *One Step Beyond* "The Return" 10-11; *Bonanza* "The Trail Gang" 11-26; **1961** *Hawaiian Eye* "A Touch of Velvet" 1-11; *Laramie* "The Last Journey" 10-31; **1962** *Alcoa Premiere* "All My Clients Are Innocent" 4-17; *Perry Mason* "The Case of the Hateful Hero" 10-18; *Hawaiian Eye* "Lament for a Saturday Warrior" 10-30; *Dr. Kildare* "An Ancient Office" 12-6; **1964** *Perry Mason* "The Case of the Ice Cold Hands" 1-23; **1966** *Blue Light* "Agent of the East" 2-16; **1968** *Rat Patrol* "The Decoy Raid" 1-22; **1969** Mannix "Missing: Sun and Sky" 12-20; **1971** *The FBI* "The Replacement" 2-7; **1973** *Toma* "Frame-Up" 11-15; **1975** *Petrocelli* "The Kidnapping" 2-5; *S.W.A.T.* "Ordeal" 11-8; *Bronk* "The Pickoff" 11-23; *Blue Knight* "Odds Against Tomorrow" 1-31; **1976** *Rockford Files* "Foul on the First Play" 3-12; **1977** *Hawaii Five-0* "A Capital Crime" 2-17; *Starsky and Hutch* "Death in a Different Place" 10-15; **1981** *Hart to Hart* "Hart-Shaped Murder" 2-10.

TELEFILM

1973 *Snatched* 1-31 ABC.

Thayer David
(born 1926; died 1978)

Perhaps best known for his spooky roles in *Dark Shadows* (1967-71), the booming voice and portly appearance of Thayer David came to films in 1957. His movies included *Journey to the Center of the Earth, The Eiger Sanction, The Duchess and the Dirtwater Fox* and *Fun with Dick and Jane.*

Initially on television in 1959, Thayer was more active in TV guest roles following his stint on *Dark Shadows.*

GUEST CREDITS

1959 *Goodyear Theater* "Any Friend of Julie's" 10-19; **1965** *Trials of O'Brien* "Leave It to Me" 12-17; **1966** *Hallmark Hall of Fame* "Lamp at Midnight" 4-

27; **1967** *Wild Wild West* "Night of the Samurai" 10-13; **1969** *Wild Wild West* "Night of the Spanish Curse" 1-3; **1975** *Kojak* "Close Cover Before Killing" 1-5; *Rockford Files* "Say Goodbye to Jennifer" 2-7; *Ellery Queen* "The Adventure of Auld Lang Syne" 9-11; *Invisible Man* "Eyes Only" 9-29; *Harry O* "Shades" 10-2; **1976** *Petrocelli* "The Night Visitor" 2-4; *Columbo* "Now You See Him" 2-29; *Switch* "The 12th Commandment" 9-28; *Charlie's Angels* "Target Angels" 10-27; *Hawaii Five-0* "Double Exposure" 12-2; **1977** *Hardy Boys Mysteries* "The Strange Fate of Flight 608" 11-6.

TELEFILMS

1975 *The Secret Night Caller* 2-18 NBC; **1976** *Frances Gary Powers: The True Story of the U-2 Incident* 9-29 NBC; **1977** *The Amazing Howard Hughes* 4-13, 4-14 CBS; *Spider-Man* 9-14 CBS; **1979** *Nero Wolfe* 12-18 ABC.

Roger Davis

(born April 5, 1939, Louisville, Kentucky)

Roger got his television career kick-started in 1962-63 with a featured role in *The Gallant Men*. He followed up with a regular role on the modern western series *Redigo* (1963).

A lengthy run as a regular on the cult soap *Dark Shadows* kept Roger well employed from 1966 to 1971. The tragic death of Peter Deuel in December of 1971 resulted in Davis being moved from narrator of *Alias Smith and Jones* to a co-starring role with Ben Murphy, from January 1972 until 1973.

GUEST CREDITS

1964 *Twilight Zone* "Spur of the Moment" 2-21; **1965** *Dr. Kildare* "Marriage of Convenience" 2-11; **1970** *Bold Ones: The Lawyers* "Point of Honor" 1-25; *Most Deadly Game* "Little David" 10-10; **1971** *Medical Center* "The Idol Maker" 10-13; **1972** *Bold Ones: The Lawyers* "The Long Morning After" 1-9, 1-16; *Night Gallery* "You Can Come Up Now, Mrs. Milliken" 11-12; **1973** *Owen Marshall, Counselor at Law* "Some People in a Park" 2-21; *McCloud* "Butch Cassidy Rides Again" 10-14; *New Perry Mason* "The Case of the Murdered Murderer" 10-28; *Faraday and Company* "Fire and Ice" 12-12; **1974** *Ironside* "One More for Joey" 1-17; *Rockford Files* "The Kirkhoff Case" 9-13; **1976** *Six Million Dollar Man* "Welcome Home, Jaimie" 1-11; **1977** *Hardy Boys/Nancy Drew Mysteries* "The Mystery of the Haunted House" 1-30; *Quincy, M.E.* "Visitors in Paradise" 2-18; *Wonder Woman* "The Man Who Made Volcanoes" 11-18.

TELEFILMS

1971 *The Young Country* 3-17 ABC; *River of Gold* 3-9 ABC; **1974** *Killer Bees* 2-26 ABC.

Rosemary DeCamp
(born November 14, 1914, Prescott, Arizona)

Early television fans will remember Rosemary as Peg Riley in the 1949-50 sitcom *The Life of Riley*. She became a commercial spokeswoman for *Death Valley Days* in 1952, a function that lasted well into the sixties. A regular on *The Bob Cummings Show* (1955-59), she found time during the fifties to appear on *Ford Theater* (4), *Studio One* (2) and *Climax*.

In addition to sixties dramatic TV series guest roles, Rosemary made guest appearances on *Petticoat Junction* (5), *Beverly Hillbillies* (2), *Ensign O'Toole, Hazel* and *The Baileys of Balboa*. In 1966 she joined the cast of *That Girl*, playing the lead character's mother.

She worked well into the eighties, with guest appearances on *Fantasy Island* and *Hotel*.

GUEST CREDITS

1959 *General Electric Theater* "Night Club" 10-11; **1961** *Rawhide* "Incident Near Gloomy River" 3-17; **1962** *87th Precinct* "Killer's Choice" 3-5; *Follow the Sun* "Chalk One Up for Johnny" 4-8; **1964** *Breaking Point* "A Little Anger Is a Good Thing" 1-6; **1965** *Dr. Kildare* "Music Hath Charms" 4-15; *Amos Burke, Secret Agent* "Operation Long Shadow" 9-22; **1971** *Mannix* "The Crime That Wasn't" 1-30; *Night Gallery* "The Painted Mirror" 12-15; *Longstreet* "Long Way Home" 12-30; **1973** *Mannix* "Little Girl Lost" 10-7; *Police Story* "Collision Course" 11-20; **1975** *Marcus Welby, M.D.* "Dark Corridors" 3-4; *Rockford Files* "Gear Jammers" 9-26, 10-3; *Petrocelli* "Chain of Command" 10-8; *Police Story* "Breaking Point" 12-12; **1976** *Medical Story* "The Moonlight Healer" 10-30; **1981** *Buck Rogers* "The Guardians" 1-29; *B. J. and the Bear* "Adults Only" 3-10; **1982** *Simon and Simon* "The Dead Letter Files" **1983** *Quincy, M.E.* "Whatever Happened to Morris Perlmutter?" 5-4.

TELEFILM

1978 *The Time Machine* 11-5 NBC.

Ted DeCorsia
(born September 29, 1904, Brooklyn, New York; died April 11, 1973)

Hefty Ted DeCorsia made his film debut in 1948 in *The Naked City*. In keeping with his physical appearance, he usually played tough characters in film and television roles; he also worked in radio and on the stage. He appeared in films like *Twenty Thousand Leagues Under the Sea, Gunfight at the O.K. Corral, From the Terrace* and *Spartacus*.

His only TV series regular role was in *Steve Canyon* (1959). His sixties guest roles were mostly in the sci-fi and crime genres.

GUEST CREDITS

1959 *Rough Riders* "Forty-Five Calibre Vow" 5-14; *Markham* "Thirteen Avenida Muerte" 7-7;

Lawless Years "The Poison Ivy Story" 8-27; *Tightrope* "The Patsy" 11-10; *Untouchables* "Ain't We Got Fun?" 11-12; **1960** *Tightrope* "The Chinese Pendant" 3-29; *Peter Gunn* "The Passenger" 10-3; *Surfside 6* "The Clown" 10-17; *Wanted: Dead or Alive* "The Medicine Man" 11-23; **1961** *Loretta Young Show* "Emergency in 114" 4-23; *Alfred Hitchcock Presents* "You Can't Be a Little Girl All Your Life" 11-21; **1962** *Gunsmoke* "He Learned About Women" 2-24; *87ᵗʰ Precinct* "Feel of the Trigger" 2-26; *Dick Powell Show* "The Hook" 3-6; *Cain's Hundred* "A Creature Lurks in Ambush" 4-17; *Untouchables* "Come and Kill Me" 11-27; **1963** *Stoney Burke* "King of the Hill" 1-21; *Outer Limits* "It Crawled Out of the Woodwork" 12-9; **1964** *Outer Limits* "The Inheritors" 1-21, 1-28; *Twilight Zone* "The Brain Center at Whipples" 5-15; *Perry Mason* "The Case of the Reckless Rockhound" 11-26; **1965** *Voyage to the Bottom of the Sea* "The Human Computer" 2-15; *Daniel Boone* "Cain's Birthday" 4-1; 4-8; **1966** *Man from UNCLE* "The Indian Affairs Affair" 4-15; *Perry Mason* "The Case of the Positive Negative" 5-1; *Jerico* "Long Journey Across a Short Street" 12-8; *1969* Wild Wild West "The Night of the Spanish Curse" 1-3; *Wild Wild West* "The Night of the Sabatini Death" 2-2; *Daniel Boone* "For a Few Rifles" 4-10.

John Dehner

(born John Forkum, November 23, 1915, Staten Island, New York; died February 4, 1992)

Following a stage acting debut in the early thirties, John turned animator and worked on Disney classics like *Bambi* and *Fantasia*. He returned to radio acting and worked extensively on *The Lone Ranger, Gunsmoke* and *Have Gun-Will Travel* (as Palladin) radio shows.

A lengthy screen career, from 1937, included over 100 movies. He was especially busy on TV during the sixties, with over 75 guest appearances. During that decade he was a series regular on *The Roaring 20's, The Baileys of Balboa,* and *The Virginian* (1966 only).

During the seventies he became a regular on *The Doris Day Show* (1971-73), *The New Temperatures Rising* (1973-74), *Big Hawaii* (1977) and *Young Maverick* (1979-80). In the eighties he was a regular on *Enos* (1980-81) and *Bare Essence* (1983). His last guest appearances were on *The Colbys* in 1986 and 1987.

John died of emphysema on February 4, 1992 in Santa Barbara, California, survived by his wife, 2 daughters, a step daughter and 2 stepsons. Of special note is the fact that John guested on 70 TV western episodes.

GUEST CREDITS

1959 *Black Saddle* "Client: Robinson" 2-21; *Wanted: Dead or Alive* "Angels of Vengeance" 4-18; *Restless Gun* "The Hill of Death" 6-22; *Tales of Wells Fargo* "Young Jim Hardie" 9-7; *Goodyear Theater* "Hello, Charlie" 9-28; *Riflelman* "The Blowout" 10-13; *Bat Masterson* "Wanted—Dead" 10-15; *Alaskans* episode 10-18; *Alaskans* "Big Deal" 11-8; *Twilight Zone* "The Lonely" 11-13; *Wanted: Dead or Alive* "Twelve Hours to Crazy Horse" 11-21; *Phillip Marlowe* "The Temple of Love" 11-24; *Rifleman* "The Baby Sitter" 12-15; *Wichita Town* "Death Watch" 12-16; *Law of the Plainsman* "Clear Title" 12-17; *Alaskans* "Remember the Maine" 12-20; **1960** *Texan* "Friend of the Family" 1-4; *Laramie* "Company Man" 2-9; *Rawhide* "Incident at Sulphur Creek" 3-11; *Black Saddle* "A Case of the Slow" 4-

15; *Westerner* "Brown" 10-21; *Gunsmoke* "The Badge" 11-12; *Zane Grey Theater* "So Young This Savage Land" 11-21; *Tales of Wells Fargo* "Jeff Davis' Treasure" 12-5; *Rebel* "The Scalp Hunter" 12-11; *Westerner* "The Painting" 12-30; **1961** *Stagecoach West* "Image of a Man" 1-13; *Rebel* "Jerkwater" 1-22; *Bat Masterson* "The Prescott Campaign" 2-2; *Stagecoach West* "The Root of Evil" 2-28; *Rawhide* "Incident of the New Start" 3-3; *Rifleman* "The Prisoner" 3-14; *Stagecoach West* "The Butcher" 3-28; *Maverick* " Devil's Necklace" 4-23; *Untouchables* "The Nero Rankin Story" 5-11; *Malibu Run* "The Stakeout Adventure" 5-24; *Tales of Wells Fargo* "A Quiet Little Town" 6-5; *Checkmate* "The Heat of Passion" 10-18; *77 Sunset Strip* "The Unremembered" 10-27; *Gunsmoke* "The Squaw" 11-11; *Twilight Zone* "The Jungle" 12-1; *Surfside 6* " A Slight Case of Chivalry" 12-18; **1962** *Lawman* "The Long Gun" 3-4; *Hawaiian Eye* "A Scent of Whales" 3-7; *Maverick* "Marshall Maverick" 3-11; *77 Sunset Strip* "The Disappearance" 4-7; *Gunsmoke* "Root Down" 10-6; *Empire* "Ride to a Fall" 10-16; *Gallant Men* "One Moderately, Peaceful Sunday" 11-2; **1963** *Stoney Burke* "King of the Hill" 1-21; *Rawhide* "Incident at Judgment Day" 2-8; *Gunsmoke* "Ash" 2-16; *Virginian* "Echo of Another Day" 3-27; *77 Sunset Strip* "Reunion at Balboa" 4-12; *Virginian* "Make This Place Remember" 9-25; *Temple Houston* "Enough Rope" 12-19 **1964** *Greatest Show on Earth* "Where the Wire Ends" 1-7; *Combat* "The General and the Sergeant" 1-14; *Bonanza* "The Gentleman from New Orleans" 2-2; *Rawhide* "Incident of the Swindler" 2-20; *Great Adventure* "Plague" 2-28; *Temple Houston* "The Gun That Swept the West" 3-5; *Gunsmoke* "The Homecoming" 3-28; *East Side/West Side* "The Givers" 4-13; *Twilight Zone* "Mr. Garrity and the Graves" 5-8; *Rogues* "The Personal Touch" 9-13; **1965** *Gunsmoke* "The Pariah" 4-17; *Branded* "One Way Out" 4-18; *Wild Wild West* "The Night of the Casual Killer" 10-15; *Man Called Shenandoah* "The Young Outlaw" 12-27; *Big Valley* "Invaders" 12-29; **1966** *Wild Wild West* "The Night of the Steel Assassin" 1-7; *Voyage to the Bottom of the Sea* "The Manfish" 3-6; *Jerico* "Wall to Wall Kaput" 10-27; *Run for Your Life* "Edge of the Volcano" 10-31; *T.H.E. Cat* "King of Limpets" 12-9; *Road West* "Power of Fear" 12-26;

1967 *Monroes* "Gun Bound" 1-25; *Judd, for the Defense* "A Civil Case of Murder" 9-29; *Man from UNCLE* "The Prince of Darkness Affair" 10-2, 10-9; *Tarzan* "Jai's Amnesia" 12-15; **1968** *Gunsmoke* "Nowhere to Run" 1-8; *Outcasts* "Take Your Lover in the Ring" 10-28; *Ironside* "Officer Mike" 12-12; **1969** *Mannix* "Only Giants Can Play" 1-18; *Judd, for the Defense* "The Holy Ground" 2-14, 2-21; *High Chaparral* "Surtee" 2-28; *High Chaparral* "The Legacy" 11-28; **1970** *Then Came Bronson* "The Gleam of the Eagle Mind" 1-21; *Land of the Giants* "The Deadly Dart" 2-1; *Silent Force* "The Judge" 10-19; **1974** *Columbo* "Swan Song" 3-3; *Magician* "Illusion of the Cat's Eye" 3-25; **1975** *Petrocelli* "Once Upon a Victim" 1-29; *Kolchak: The Night Stalker* "The Knightly Murders" 3-7; *Switch* "Story from Behind" 9-30; *S.W.A.T.* "Pressure Cooker" 11-15; *Movin' On* "Please Don't Talk to the Driver" 11-25; *Ellery Queen* "The Adventure of the Blunt Instrument" 12-18; *Barbary Coast* "The Day Cable Was Hanged" 12-26; **1976** *Columbo* "Last Salute to the Commodore" 5-2; **1977** *Rockford Files* "There's One in Every Port" 1-7; **1979** *Quincy, M.E.* "Physician, Heal Thyself" 2-22; **1980** *Hawaii Five-0* "A Bird in Hand" 3-22; **1981** *Hart to Hart* "Harts Under Glass" 11-11.

TELEFILMS

1967 *Winchester '73* 3-14 NBC; **1968** *Something*

for a Lonely Man 11-26 NBC; **1970** *Quarantined* 2-24 NBC; **1974** *Honky Tonk* 4-1 NBC; **1975** *The Big Ripoff* 3-11; **1976** *The New Adventures of Joshua Cabe* 5-29 ABC; **1977** *Danger in Paradise* 5-12 NBC; **1981** *California Gold Rush* 7-30 NBC; **1982** *Bare Essence* 10-4, 10-5 CBS.

Frank De Kova

(born 1910; died October 15, 1981)

A language teacher in New York City before becoming an actor, Frank did numerous Shakespearian plays in repertory theater. While

Frank De Kova (left), is finding the situation amusing in a 1973 episode of *The FBI*, "Night of the Long Knives" (ABC). Series star Efrem Zimbalist, Jr. (center) and guest star Alex Cord look on.

appearing on Broadway, he was brought to Holly-wood by Elia Kazan to assume a major role in *Viva Zapata* (1952). His film career would total over 50 movies, including roles in *The Robe, The Ten Commandments* and *The Greatest Story Ever Told.*

He began working on television during the early fifties and frequently played mobsters in sixties series like *The Untouchables and The Roaring 20's.* He continued this type of role in seventies detective series guest shots.

His swarthy complexion also found him cast as American Indians and Arabs in both television and film roles. This sort of casting brought him his greatest TV exposure and fame as the hilarious Chief Wild Eagle on the 1965-67 sitcom, *F Troop.*

After *F Troop*, Frank resumed a strong schedule of TV guest work that continued until shortly before his death in 1981. While his family was in England he was found dead of natural causes on October 15, 1981. He was survived by a wife and daugher.

GUEST CREDITS

1959
Rifleman "The Indian" 2-17; *Peter Gunn* "Breakout" 3-30; *Lawless Years* "the Posion Ivy Story" 8-27; *Gunsmoke* "Target" 9-5; *Deputy* "Back to Glory" 9-26; *Cheyenne* "Rebellion" 10-12; *Alaskans* "Contest at Gold Bottom" 11-15; *Rawhide* "Incident at Spanish Rock" 12-18; **1960** *Johnny Staccato* "Night of Jeopardy" 1-21; *Hotel de Paree* "Sundance and the Hero of Bloody Blue Creek" 3-11; *Untouchables* "The Frank Nitti Story" 4-28; *Rifleman*

"Meeting at Midnight" 5-17; *Surfside 6* " Country Gentleman" 10-3; *Untouchables* "The Waxey Gordon Story" 11-10; *Hawaiian Eye* "The Contenders" 11-30; *Roaring 20's* "The White Carnation" 12-3; *Lawman* "Cornered" 12-11; *Islanders* "The Widow from Richmond" 12-18; **1961** *Hong Kong* "Double Jeopardy" 2-1; *Untouchables* "The Underground Court" 2-16; *Hawaiian Eye* "The Stanhope Brand" 2-22; *Rawhide* "Incident of the Boomerang"3-24; *Route 66* "Almost Vanquished, Most Victorious" 4-14; *Tall Man* "The Cloudbuster" 4-29; *Gunslinger* "The New Savannah Story" 5-18; *Roaring 20's* "Million Dollar Suit" 5-27; *Bronco* "Trouble Street" 10-2; *Cheyenne* "Cross Purpose" 10-9; *Laramie* "Wolf Cub" 11-21; *Maverick* "A Technical Error" 11-26; **1962** *Thriller* "La Strega" 1-15; *Alfred Hitchcock Presents* "Strange Miracle" 2-13; *Outlaws* "Charge!" 3-22; *Wagon Train* "The George B. Hanrahan Story" 3-28; *Untouchables* "The Maggie Storm Story" 3-29; *77 Sunset Strip* "Pattern for a Bomb" 6-8; *Gallant Men* "The Ninety-Eight Cent Man" 10-26; *Cheyenne* "Pocketful of Stars" 11-12; *Untouchables* "A Fist of Five" 12-4; **1963** *Laramie* "The Unvanquished" 3-12; *Dakotas* "A Nice Girl from Goliath" 5-13; *77 Sunset Strip* "Bonus Baby" 12-20; **1964** *Greatest Show on Earth* "Corsicans Don't Cry" 1-14; *Daniel Boone* "The Sound of Wings" 3-25; **1965** *Ben Casey* "Make the First American" 1-21; *Wagon Train* "The Isiah Quickfox Story" 1-31; *Daniel Boone* "Four Leaf Clover" 3-25; **1968** *It Takes a Thief* "Hands Across the Border" 11-12, 11-19; **1969** *Hawaii Five-0* "Along Came Joey" 2-12; **1973** *The FBI* "The Night of the Long Knives" 3-25; *The FBI* "The Bought Jury" 12-16; **1974** *Toma* "The Contract on Alex Cordeen" 3-8; *Police Story* "Across the Line" 11-12; **1975** *Police Woman* "The Company" 2-21; **1976** *Cannon* "Revenge" 1-21; **1977** *Rockford Files* "Hotel of Fear" 12-2; **1979** *Little House on the Prairie* "The Craftsman" 1-8; *Little House on the Prairie* "The Halloween Dream" 10-29.

TELEFILM

1975 *Crossfire* 3-24 NBC.

Lee Delano

(born January 18)

A television and film actor since 1966, Lee has also done some stage work and performed as a night club comic. Sci-fi and detective series guest shots were the staple of his television experience.

GUEST CREDITS

1966 *Man from UNCLE* "The Waverly Ring Affair" 1-28; *Felony Squad* "A Date with Terror" 10-10; *Mission: Impossible* "Fakeout" 12-3; *Voyage to the Bottom of the Sea* "Monster from Outer Space" 12-19; **1968** *Star Trek* "A Piece of the Action" 1-12; **1971** *Bold Ones: The Lawyers* "The Price of Justice" 2-21; *Mission: Impossible* "The Miracle" 10-23; **1973** *Police Story* "Man on the Rack" 12-11; **1974** *Get Christie Love!* "For the Family Honor" 10-23; *Ironside* "Speak No Evil" 12-12; **1975** Police Woman "Cold Wind" 10-17; *Police Story* "Company Man" 12-19; **1976** *Joe Forrester* "Squeeze Play" 2-9; *Jigsaw John* "Sand Trap" 2-9; *Jigsaw John* "The Mourning Line" 3-15; *Jigsaw John* "The Executioner" 4-5; *Police Story* "The Jar" 12-14, 12-21; **1977** *Charlie's Angels* "Angels on Ice" 9-21; **1978** *Baretta* "The Bundle" 5-18; *Rockford Files* "The Empty

Frame" 11-3; **1979** *Charlie's Angels* "Angels on Vacation" 1-10; *Sword of Justice* "Blackjack" 7-11; **1980** *Charlie's Angels* "Dancin' Angels" 2-6.

TELEFILMS

1974 *Bloodsport* 12-5 ABC; **1977** *In the Glitter Palace* 2-27 NBC; *Don't Push, I'll Charge When I'm Ready* 12-18 NBC; **1978** *Doctors' Private Lives* 3-20 ABC; **1980** *Power* 1-14, 1-15 NBC; **1981** *Sizzle* 11-29 ABC.

Cyril Delevanti
(born 1887, England; died December 13, 1975)

A rail-thin character actor, Cyril began a film career in 1930. Many of his forties films were of the horror genre: *Frankenstein and the Wolf Man, Son of Dracula, The House of Fear* and *The Phantom of 42ⁿᵈ Street*. However in later years he acted in much lighter film fare, in *Bye Bye Birdie, Mary Poppins* and *Bedknobs and Broomsticks*. He also appeared in *Night of the Iguana* and *Soylent Green*.

Much of his television work was compressed into the sixties following his only TV series regular role, in *Jefferson Drum* (1958-59).

1959 *Peter Gunn* "Protection" 9-21; **1960** *Alfred Hitchcock Presents* "A Letter of Credit" 6-19; *Adventures in Paradise* "Hangman's Island" 11-23; **1961** *Gunsmoke* "Love Thy Neighbor" 1-28; *Twilight Zone* "A Penny for Your Thoughts" 2-3; *Twilight Zone* "The Silence" 4-28; **1962** *Twilight Zone* "A Piano in the House" 2-16; *Thriller* "Cousin Tundifer" 2-19; **1963** *Twilight Zone* "Passage on the Lady Anne" 5-9; **1964** *Fugitive* "Man on a String" 9-29; **1965** *Gunsmoke* "Double Entry" 1-2; *Bob Hope Chrysler Theater* "The Game" 9-15; *Voyage to the Bottom of the Sea* "The Left-Handed Man" 10-24; *Run for Your Life* "Where Mystery Begins" 11-1; *Perry Mason* "The Case of The Silent Six" 11-26; **1966** *Gunsmoke* "Killer at Large" 2-5; *Mission: Impossible* "Odd Man Out" 10-8, 10-15; **1967** *I Spy* "A Rome with a Rack" 2-8; **1969** *It Takes a Thief* "The Family" 4-1; *Dragnet* "D.H.Q. Medical" 10-9; **1970** *Dragnet* "Burglary-Helpful Woman" 1-22.

TELEFILMS

1970 *Crowhaven Farm* 11-24 ABC; **1973** *The Girl Most Likely To...* 11-6 ABC.

Danielle de Metz
In films from 1959, beautiful auburn-haired French actress Danielle de Metz guested sporadically on American television for a dozen years before leaving acting.

1959 *Have Gun-Will Travel* "Les Girls" 9-26; **1960** *Alfred Hitchcock Presents* "The Icon of Elijah" 1-10; *Adventures in Paradise* "Sink or Swim" 12-19; **1961** *Thriller* "Guillotine" 9-25; *Combat* "The Party" 12-24; **1964** *Voyage to the Bottom of the Sea* "No Way Out" 11-30; **1966** *I Spy* "Bet Me a Dollar" 2-16; *Man from UNCLE* "The Foreign Legion Affair" 2-18; *Man from UNCLE* "The Come with Me to the Casbah Affair" 11-11; **1967** *Girl from UNCLE* "The Catacombs and Dogma Affair" 1-24; *Man from*

UNCLE "The Five Daughters Affair" 3-31, 4-7; **1971** *Longstreet* "There Was a Crooked Man" 12-9; **1972** *Cool Million* "The Abduction of Bayard Barnes" 12-6.

John Dennis

(born 1925)

After a stage career that began in 1945, John made his film debut during 1953 in *From Here to Eternity*. His stocky build and stern appearance usually found him playing rugged roles in nearly 70 movies, including *Earthquake, Airport* and *Soylent Green*. His television roles (from 1954) found him in similar castings.

GUEST CREDITS

1959 *Maverick* "Betrayal" 3-22; *Lawless Years* "The Dutch Schultz Story" 5-14; **1960** *Perry Mason* "The Case of the Violent Village" 1-2; *M Squad* "Pitched Battle at Blue Bell Acres" 1-22; *Man with a Camera* "Kangaroo Court" 2-8; *77 Sunset Strip* "Double Trouble" 11-4; **1961** *Roaring 20's* "Big Town Blues" 1-20; *Deputy* "The Hard Decision" 1-28; *Lawless Years* "Louey K" 5-26, 6-2, 6-9, 6-16, 6-23; *Lawless Years* "Mad Dog Coll" 7-28; *Lawless Years* "Ike, the Novelty King" 9-22; *87th Precinct* "Occupation:

Citizen" 10-23; **1962** *Perry Mason* "The Case of the Shapely Shadow" 1-6; **1963** *Wagon Train* "The Kitty Pryor Story" 11-18; **1965** *Fugitive* "Masquerade" 3-23; **1968** *Dragnet* "Police Commission-DR-13" 10-17; **1969** *Dragnet* "Administrative Vice-DR-29" 2-6; *Cimarron Strip* "The Town That Wouldn't" 3-31; *Dragnet* "Internal Affairs-Parolee" 11-27; *Mod Squad* "The Healer" 12-9; **1970** *Adam-12* "Log Sixty Four-Bottom of the Bottle" 1-31; *Mannix* "Who Is Sylvia?" 2-7; **1971** *Mission: Impossible* "The Missile" 1-16; *O'Hara, U.S. Treasury* "Operation: Bandera" 9-24; **1972** *Mod Squad* "Corbey" 11-2; **1973** *Emergency* episode 9-22; *Rookies* "Code 261" 11-5; *Police Story* "Collision Course" 11-20; *Emergency* episode 12-15; **1974** *Chase* "Joe Don Ducks" 1-16; **1975** *Adam-12* "Follow Up" 3-11; *S.W.A.T.* "Time Bomb" 4-21; *Mobile One* "Not by Accident" 10-17; *Harry O* "APB Harry Orwell" 11-6; *Police Story* "Face for a Shadow" 11-7; **1976** *Ellery Queen* "The Adventure of Veronica's Veils" 3-13; **1977** *Quincy, M.E.* "Let Me Light the Way" 5-27; *Man from Atlantis* "Giant" 10-25; *Quincy, M.E.* "The Last of the Dinosaurs" 12-6; **1978** *Quincy, M.E.* "Speed Trap" 10-12; *CHiPs* "Trick or Treat" 10-21;

1979 *Eischied* "Who Is the Missing Woman?" 11-30; **1981** *Quincy, M.E.* "Dead Stop" 12-31; **1982** *Magnum, P.I.* "The Elmo Ziller Story" 3-18.

TELEFILMS

1971 *Dead Men Tell No Tales* 12-17 CBS; **1973** *The Bait* 3-13 ABC; **1975** *The Blue Knight* 5-9 CBS; **1977** *The Amazing Howard Hughes* 4-13, 4-14 CBS; **1978** *Doctor's Private Lives* 3-20 ABC; **1979** *The Seeding of Sarah Burns* 4-7 CBS; *The Power Within* 5-11 ABC; **1980** *Moviola: This Year's Blonde* 5-18 NBC.

Bruce Dern

(born June 3, 1936, Winnetka, Illinois)

One of films' and television's best remembered psychotic and murderous heavies of the sixties, Bruce graduated from Actor's Studio in 1960 and plunged into an extemely busy schedule of television guest roles. He was a regular on *Stoney Burke* in 1962-63 before resuming his bad-guy roles.

By 1970 he had enough major film offers to leave television, and received an Oscar Nomination in 1978 for his work in *Coming Home*. Bruce is the father of the talented young actress Laura Dern, who earned an Oscar Nomination of her own in 1992.

GUEST CREDITS

1960 *Route 66* "The Man on the Monkey Board" 10-28; **1961** *Naked City* "Bullets Cost Too Much" 1-4; *Naked City* "The Fault in Our Stars" 3-22; *Surfside 6* "Daphne, Girl Detective" 10-9; *Ben Casey* "Dark Night for Bill Harris" 12-18; *Thriller* "The Remarkable Mrs. Hawk" 12-18; *Detectives* "An Act of God" 12-29; **1962** *Law and Mr. Jones* "Poor Eddie's Dad" 7-12; **1963** *Dick Powell Show* "Old Man and the City" 4-23; *Fugitive* "The Other Side of the Mountain" 10-1; *Wagon Train* "The Eli Bancroft Story" 11-11; *Kraft Suspense Theatre* "The Hunt" 12-19; *Outer Limits* "The Zanti Misfits" 12-30; **1964** *77 Sunset Strip* "Lover's Lane" 1-3; *Fugitive* "Come Watch Me Die" 1-21; *Alfred Hitchcock Hour* "Night Caller" 1-31; *Virginian* "First to Thy Own Self" 2-12; *Greatest Show on Earth* "The Last of the Strongmen" 3-3; *Wagon Train* "Those Who Stay Behind" 11-8; *Alfred Hitchcock Hour* "Lonely Place" 11-16; *Virginian* "The Payment" 12-16; **1965** *12 O'Clock High* "The Lorelei" 1-22; *Fugitive* "Corner of Hell" 2-9; *Wagon Train* "The Indian Girl Story" 4-18; *Rawhide* "Walk into Terror" 10-5; *Laredo* "Rendezvous at Arillo" 10-7; *Gunsmoke* "Ten Little Indians" 10-9; *Man Called Shenandoah* "The Verdict" 11-1; *Gunsmoke* "South Wind" 11-27; *12 O'Clock High* "The Jones Boys" 12-6; *Fugitive* "The Good Guys and the Bad Guys" 12-14; *The FBI* "Pound of Flesh" 12-19; **1966** *Branded* "The Wolfers" 1-9; *Big Valley* "Under a Dark Star" 2-9; *Loner* "To Hang a Dead Man" 3-12; *Big Valley* "By Force of Violence" 3-30; *Big Valley* "The Lost Treasure" 9-12; *Gunsmoke* "The Jailer" 10-1; *Run for Your Life* "The Treasure Seekers" 11-14; *Fugitive* "The Devil's Disciples" 12-6; **1967** *Run for Your Life* "Trip to the Far Side" 10-11; *Run For Your Life* "At the End of the Rainbow There's Another Rainbow" 10-25; *Big Valley* "Four Days to Furnace Hill" 12-4; **1968** *Bonanza* "The Trackers" 1-7; *Lancer* "Julie" 10-29; *The FBI* "Nightmare" 11-10; *Big Valley* "The

Prize" 12-16; **1969** *Gunsmoke* "The Long Night" 2-17; *Then Came Bronson* "Amid Splinters of the Thunderbolt" 10-22; *Lancer* "A Person Unknown" 11-25; **1970** *Land of the Giants* "Wild Journey" 3-6; *Bonanza* "The Gold Mine" 3-8; *High Chaparral* "Only the Bad Come to Sonora" 10-2; *Immortal* "To the Gods Alone" 10-2.

TELEFILM

1971 *Sam Hill: Who Killed the Mysterious Mr. Foster?* 2-1 NBC.

Joe DeSantis

(born 1909, New York City; died August 30, 1989)

Born of Italian immigrant parents in New York City, Joe began his acting career in 1931 with Italian companies in New York. After touring with repertory companies for three years, he began a lengthy radio career in 1936. His work with language and dialects made him one of radio's most sought after performers; he was active on Broadway as well.

Joe debuted in films and television in 1949, and he became a regular on a 1949 TV series called *Photocrime*. He worked regularly on TV during the fifties and was a regular on a 1954-55 soap, *Golden Windows*.

During the decade from 1960 to 1970 he was one of television's busiest guest stars, appearing in over 40 episodes. He was frequently cast as underworld bosses and also had a number of parts as various ethnics: Spaniards, Italians and Mexicans.

DeSantis' marvelous experience and talent helped him create many memorable roles and his rich voice gained him work as a narrator.

GUEST CREDITS

1959 *Perry Mason* "The Case of the Borrowed Brunette" 1-10; *Rawhide* "Incident at Alabaster Plain" 1-16; *77 Sunset Strip* "In Memoriam" 2-27; *Cheyenne* "The Rebellion" 10-12; *Phillip Marlowe* "Child of Virtue" 11-10; *Rawhide* "Incident of the Blue Fire" 12-11; **1960** *Tightrope* "Gangster's Daughter" 4-12; *Bourbon Street Beat* "Green Hell"

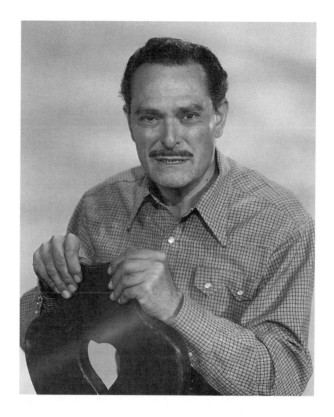

5-30; *Chevy Mystery Show* "Femme Fatale" 8-28; *77 Sunset Strip* "The Fanatics" 9-23; *Untouchables* "Nicky" 11-3; *Riverboat* "Chicota Landing" 12-5; *Rawhide* "Incident of the Captive" 12-16; **1961** *Maverick* "A State of Siege" 1-1; *Untouchables* "The Nick Moses Story" 2-23; *Bonanza* "The Rival" 4-15; *Tall Man* "Death or Taxes" 5-27; *Naked City* "A Corpse Ran Down Mulberry Street" 10-10; **1962** *Bonanza* "Look to the Stars" 3-18; *77 Sunset Strip* "Flight from Escondido" 5-18; *Sam Benedict* "A Split Week in San Quentin" 9-22; *Sam Benedict* "Nothing Equals Nothing" 10-6; *77 Sunset Strip* "Adventure in San Dede" 12-14; **1963** *Untouchables* "Junk Man" 2-26; *Virginian* "The Mountain of the Sun" 4-17; *Untouchables* "Line of Fire" 5-14; *Nurses* "Helping Hand" 11-7; *77 Sunset Strip* "Don't Wait for Me" 11-8; *Outer Limits* "The Human Factor" 11-11; **1964** *Dr. Kildare* "Onions, Garlic and Flowers That Bloom in the Spring" 2-6; *Bob Hope Chrysler Theater* "A Wind of Hurricane Force" 2-7; *East Side/West Side* "Don't Grow Old" 2-17; *Great Adventure* "The Pathfinder" 3-6; *Wagon Train* "The Last Circle-Up" 4-27; *Fugitive* "The Cage" 11-24; **1965** *Voyage to the Bottom of the Sea* "The Last

Battle" 1-4; *Branded* "The Test" 2-7; *Ben Casey* "Minus That Old Rusty Hacksaw" 3-15; *Doctors and Nurses* "The Politician" 3-16; *Perry Mason* "The Case of the Deadly Debt" 4-1; *Alfred Hitchcock Hour* "Night Fever" 5-5; **1966** *Dr. Kildare* "The Art of Taking a Powder" 3-14; *Dr. Kildare* "Read the Book, Then See the Picture" 3-15; **1967** *Mission: Impossible* "The Frame" 1-21; *Road West* "A War for Gravediggers" 4-10; *Bonanza* "Second Chance" 9-17; *Run for Your Life* "The Naked Half Truth" 11-8; **1968** *Gunsmoke* "The Jackals" 2-12; *Gunsmoke* "Lyle's Kid" 9-23; *Name of the Game* "Witness" 9-27; *Lancer* "The Escape" 12-31; **1969** *Hawaii Five-0* "Leopard on the Rock" 12-3; **1970** *Bold Ones: The Lawyers* "Trial of a Mafioso" 1-4; *Mission: Impossible* "Terror" 2-15; *Bonanza* "Decision at Los Robles" 3-22; *High Chaparral* "A Good Sound Profit" 10-30; *Dan August* "The Union Forever" 11-19; **1971** *Name of the Game* "Appointment in Palermo" 2-26; *Sarge* "Ring Out, Ring In" 9-28; **1972** *Mannix* "Harvest of Death" 11-19; **1973** *Toma* "Frame-Up" 11-15; **1975** *Cannon* "Nightmare" 9-10.

TELEFILMS

1970 *Night Chase* 11-20 CBS; **1971** *Powderkeg* 4-16 CBS; **1973** *Honor Thy Father* 3-1 CBS; **1974** *It's Good to Be Alive* 2-22 CBS; **1975** *Katherine* 10-5 NBC; **1977** *Contract on Cherry Street* 11-19 NBC.

Geoffrey Deuel

The younger brother of the late Peter Deuel (1940-1971), Geoffrey did a number of late sixties/early seventies TV crime series guest roles before disappearing from acting. In many of his roles he played troubled teenagers or college students.

GUEST CREDITS

1967 *Invaders* "The Condemned" 5-9; **1968** *High Chaparral* "The Assassins" 1-7; **1969** *Adam-12* "I'm Still a Cop" 2-22; *Mannix* "Sometimes Eagles Don't Fly" 9-27; *Mod Squad* "A Place to Run, a Heart to Hide In" 12-2; **1970** *The FBI* "Time Bomb"

10-25; *Medical Center* "The Savage Image" 12-30; **1973** *Mission: Impossible* "The Fighter" 2-9; *Streets of San Francisco* "Deadline" 2-15; *The FBI* "Memory of a Legend" 3-11; *Cannon* "Hounds of Hell" 9-26; *Toma* "Ambush of Seventh Avenue" 10-11; *Magician* "Lightning on a Dry Day" 10-30; **1974** *Streets of San Francisco* "Commitment" 1-3; *Ironside* "Once More for Joey" 1-17; *Petrocelli* "A Life for a Life" 10-9; *Nakia* "The Driver" 11-2; *Manhunter* "A.W.O.L. to Kill" 12-11; **1975** *Mannix* "Chance Meeting" 1-19; *Joe Forrester* "Stake Out" 9-9.

TELEFILM

1970 *House on Greenapple Road* 1-11 ABC.

Val De Vargas

Valentin De Vargas always played either Hispanics or Native Americans in his screen and television career which began in 1958. He wound down his acting career in the late seventies.

GUEST CREDITS

1962 *Ben Casey* "Image of a Long Bright Corridor" 1-15; *Tall Man* "The Woman in Black" 5-12; *Ben Casey* "The Night That Nothing Happened"

his villainy in adventure and crime series like *Mission: Impossible, The FBI* and *Perry Mason*.

His film career, from 1954, consisted mainly of sci-fi and B films, but his principal fame came from his numerous and memorable TV roles.

GUEST CREDITS

1959 *Loretta Young Show* "Incident in India" 1-25; *Wanted: Dead or Alive* " Eager Man" 2-28; *Yancy Derringer* "Duel at the Oaks" 4-9; *Roughriders* "Paradise Gap" 4-16; *Yancy Derringer* "The Quiet Firecracker" 5-21; *Wanted: Dead or Alive* "The Montana Kid" 9-5; *Law of the Plainsman* "Prairie Incident" 10-1; *Johnny Ringo* "The Hunters" 10-29; *Colt .45* "Yellow Terror" 11-15; *Richard Diamond* "The Messenger" 11-16; *Rifleman* "Spiked Rifle" 11-24; *Richard Diamond* "The Image" 11-30; *Detectives* "Backseat Driver" 12-4; **1960** *Texan* "The Taming of Rio Nada" 1-11; *Texan* "Six Gun Street" 1-18; *Texan* "The Terrified Town" 1-25; *Hotel de Paree* "Sundance and the Greenhorn Trader" 2-26; *Rifleman* "The Grasshopper" 3-1; *Bonanza* "The Avenger" 3-19; *Phillip Marlowe* "You Kill Me" 3-29; *Sugarfoot* "Vigaroon" 3-29; *Law of the Plainsman* "Stella" 3-31; *Islanders* "Operation Dollar Sign" 10-30; *Rifleman* "Miss Milly" 11-15; *Rifleman* "The Silent Knife" 12-20; **1961** *One Step Beyond* "Where Are They?" 2-7; *Untouchables* "The Underground Court" 2-16; *Stagecoach West* "Songs

10-8; **1965** *Bonanza* "Woman of Fire" 1-17; **1966** *Mission: Impossible* "Elena" 12-10; **1967** *Gunsmoke* "Old Friend" 2-4; *Fugitive* "Death of a Very Small Killer" 3-21; **1969** *Gunsmoke* "The Devil's Outpost" 9-22; **1970** *Mission: Impossible* "Death Squad" 3-15; **1971** *Storefront Lawyers* "We Get Rid of the Principal" 1-13; *O'Hara, U.S. Treasury* "Operation: Heroin" 10-29; *Mission: Impossible* "Run for the Money" 12-11; **1972** *Streets of San Francisco* "Hall of Mirrors" 11-4; **1973** *The FBI* "Desperate Journey" 1-28; *Streets of San Francisco* "The Victims" 11-29; **1974** *Police Story* "Across the Line" 11-12; **1978** *Project UFO* "Sighting 4013" 6-4; *Switch* "Mexican Standoff" 7-30; *Police Story* "Broken Badge" 8-27.

TELEFILMS

1971 *They Call It Murder* 12-17 NBC; **1972** *Visions...*10-10 CBS; **1973** *Incident on a Dark Street* 1-13 NBC; *Chase* 3-24 NBC; **1974** *The Gun* 11-13 ABC; **1976** *Perilous Voyage* 7-29 NBC.

Richard Devon

(born December 11, 1931, Glendale, California)

A tough and sober looking heavy, Richard Devon guested in virtually every major western TV series from 1958 through 1969, and often practiced

My Mother Taught Me" 2-21; *Stagecoach West* "The Remounts" 3-14; *Stagecoach West* "The Renegades" 6-20; *Rifleman* "The Stand-In" 10-23; **1962** *Twilight Zone* "Dead Man's Shoes" 1-19; *Detectives* "Finders Keepers" 4-13; *77 Sunset Strip* "Framework for a Badge" 6-1; *Rifleman* "The Most Amazing Man" 11-26; *Laramie* "Gun Duel" 12-25; **1963** *Rawhide* "Incident of the Buryin' Man" 1-4; *Wagon Train* "The Emmitt Lawton Story" 3-6; *Gunsmoke* "The

Khigh Dhiegh (left), appearing as Wo-Fat in 11 episodes of the CBS hit series *Hawaii Five-0*, is arrested by McGarrett (Jack Lord).

Quest for Asa Janin" 6-1; *Virginian* "Brother Thaddeus" 10-30; *Gunsmoke* "Ex-Con" 11-30; **1964** *Perry Mason* "The Case of the Frightened Fisherman" 2-27; *Destry* "Big Deal at Little River" 3-20; *Breaking Point* "Confounding Her Astronomers" 4-6; *Ben Casey* "A Bird in Solitude Singing" 9-21; *Burke's Law* "Who Killed the Horn of Plenty?" 10-7; *Bonanza* "The Scapegoat" 10-25; *Daniel Boone* "The Choosing" 10-29; **1965** *Fugitive* "The Survivors" 3-2; *Perry Mason* "The Case of the Fatal Fetish" 3-4; *Ben Casey* "A War of Nerves" 9-13; *Man Called Shenandoah* "The Onslaught" 9-13; *Big Valley* "Boots with My Father's Name" 9-29; *Laredo* "Jinx" 12-2; **1966** *Daniel Boone* "Seminole Territory" 1-13; *Perry Mason* "The Case of the Scarlet Scandal" 2-20; *Laredo* "No Bugles, One Drum" 2-24; *Daniel Boone* "The Loser's Race" 11-10; *Mission: Impossible* "A Spool There Was" 11-12; **1967** *Iron Horse* "Shadow Run" 1-30; *High Chaparral* "A Quiet Day in Tuscon" 10-1; **1968** *Guns of Will Sonnett* "End of a Rope" 1-12; *The FBI* "The

Quarry" 10-6; *Daniel Boone* "The Plague That Came to Ford's Run" 10-31; *Big Valley* "A Stranger Everywhere" 12-9; **1969** *Lancer* "Warburton's Edge" 2-4; *Daniel Boone* "The Traitor" 10-30; **1970** *The FBI* "Return to Power" 2-15; **1971** *Man and the City* "The Cross-Country Man" 12-1; **1972** *Mannix* "Cry Pigeon" 1-26; *Mission: Impossible* "Casino" 2-19; *Mission: Impossible* "The Puppet" 12-22; **1974** *Planet of the Apes* "The Horse Race" 11-8; **1978** *Richie Brockelman, Private Eye* "Escape from Caine Abel" 4-14.

Khigh Dhiegh

(born 1910, New Jersey)

Of Egyptian-Sudanese extraction, Khigh Dhiegh (pronounced Ki-Dee) was known primarily for Oriental roles in films and television. He made a 1962 film debut in *The Manchurian Candidate* and came to television in 1966. Khigh was best known to television audiences in a recurring role as "Wo-Fat", arch-enemy of Jack Lord on *Hawaii Five-0*.

He also made multiple appearances on *Kung Fu*. His menacing appearance made him a superb villain, although he played a detective on the thankfully brief 1975 series *Khan*. Dhiegh despised the show so much that he didn't want his name to appear in the credits.

He appeared in the final episode of *Hawaii Five-0* in 1980, guested on *Matt Houston* in 1984 and made his last TV appearance during 1988 in a miniseries.

GUEST CREDITS

1966 *Girl from Uncle* "The Atlantis Affair" 11-15; **1967** *Wild Wild West* "Night of the Samurai" 10-13; **1968** *Wild Wild West* "Night of the Pelican" 12-27; **1969** *Mission: Impossible* "Doomsday" 2-16; *Hawaii Five-0* "Forty Feet High and It Kills" 10-8; *Hawaii Five-0* "A Bullet for McGarrett" 10-29; **1970** *Hawaii Five-0* "And a Time to Die" 9-16; *Mission: Impossible* "Butterfly" 10-31; **1971** *Hawaii Five-0* "F.O.B. Honolulu" 1-27, 2-3; **1972** *Hawaii Five-0* "The Ninety Second War" 1-11; *Hawaii Five-0* "Skinhead" 1-25; *Hawaii Five-0* "The Jinn Who Clears the Way" 12-5; **1973** *Kung Fu* "The Spirit Helper" 11-8; **1974** *The FBI* "The $2,000,000 Hit" 2-24; *Kung Fu* "Besieged: Death on a Cold Mountain" 11-15; *Kung Fu* "Besieged: Cannon at the Gate" 11-22; *Hawaii Five-0* "Presenting...In the Center Ring—Murder" 12-10; **1975** *Hawaii Five-0* "Murder—Eyes Only" 9-12; **1976** *Hawaii Five-0* "Nine Dragons" 9-30; **1980** *Hawaii Five-0* "Woe to Wo Fat" 4-5.

TELEFILMS

1968 *Hawaii Five-0* 9-20 CBS; **1974** *Judge Dee in the Monastery Murders* 12-19 ABC.

Charles Dierkop

(born September 11, 1936, La Crosse, Wisconsin) In films from 1961, Charles usually played

pugnacious little tough guys. He first appeared on television in 1965, with the high point of his career being his featured role as the undercover detective Pete Royster on *Police Woman* (1974-78).

GUEST CREDITS

1965 *Trials of O'Brien* "Bargain Day on the Street of Regret" 9-25; *Voyage to the Bottom of the Sea* "The Left-Handed Man" 10-24; **1966** *Gunsmoke* "My Father's Guitar" 2-12; *Girl from UNCLE* "The Mother Muffin Affair" 9-27; *Man from UNCLE* "The Off-Broadway Affair" 9-27; *Gunsmoke* "The Newcomers" 12-3; **1967** *Custer* episode 11-8; **1968** *Cimarron Strip* "The Judgment" 1-4; *Lancer* "Blood Rock" 10-1; *Adam-12* "I Feel Like a Fool, Malloy" 11-2; *Outcasts* "My Name Is Jamal" 11-18; **1969** *Ironside* "A World of Jackals" 2-13; *Lancer* "Devil's Blessing" 4-22; *Bonanza* "The Fence" 4-27; **1970** *High Chaparral* "Friends and Partners" 1-16; *Land of the Giants* "Doomsday" 2-15; **1971** *Bonanza* "A Deck of Aces" 1-31; *Cannon* "Scream of Silence" 10-12; *Nichols* "The Dirty Half Dozen Run Amok" 10-28; *Cade's County* "The Mustangers" 11-14; *Bearcats!* "Bitter Flats" 11-18; **1972** *Mission: Impossible* "The Bride" 1-1; *Bonanza* "New Man" 10-10; *Alias Smith and Jones* episode 11-25; **1973** *Chase* "The Winning Ticket Is a Loser" 10-2; *Police Story* "Dangerous Games" 10-2; *Gunsmoke* "The

Deadly Innocent" 12-17; **1974** *Cannon* "The Sounds of Silence" 12-4; **1978** *Vegas* "Lost Women" 11-22; **1980** *CHiPs* "Satan's Angels" 12-14.

TELEFILMS

1971 *Alias Smith and Jones* 1-5 ABC; *City Beneath the Sea* 1-25 NBC; *Lock, Stock and Barrel* 9-24 NBC; *The Face of Fear* 10-8 CBS; **1973** *Female Artillery* 1-17 ABC; *Murdock's Gang* 3-20 CBS; **1977** *Captains Courageous* 12-4 ABC; **1978** *The Deerslayer* 12-18 NBC.

Peter Donat

(born January 20, 1928, Kentville, Novia Scotia, Canada)

Educated at Acadia University, Peter did graduate work at Yale. Early in his acting career he received the Theatre World Award as Best Featured Actor (1957). Shortly after making a 1955 television debut Peter gained a role on soap *The Brighter Day*. During the late sixties he began guesting on TV and is still active during the nineties with recent guest shots on *Murder, She Wrote*. He was a regular on the *Rich Man-Poor Man, Book II* series (1976-77) and on *Flamingo Road* (1981-82).

Peter was married to popular television actress Michael Lerned from 1956 until a 1974 divorce.

GUEST CREDITS

1968 *Mission: Impossible* "The Condemned" 1-28; *I Spy* "Turnabout for Traitors" 2-9; *Run for Your Life* "Life Among the Man-Eaters" 3-13; **1969** *Judd, for the Defense* "Epitaph on a Computer Card" 1-17; *Mannix* "Only Giants Can Play" 1-18; *The FBI* "The Swindler" 9-28; *Medical Center* "Thousands and Thousands of Miles" 11-11; *Bracken's World* "Move in for a Close Up" 12-12; **1970** *Young Lawyers* "The Legacy of Miles Turner" 12-7; **1972** *Banacek* "No Sign of the Cross" 10-11; **1973** *Waltons* "The Prize" 10-25; **1974** *Hawaii Five-0* "Murder with a Golden Touch" 1-29; **1975** *Kate McShane* "Conspiracy of Silence" 10-29; *Invisible Man* "The Klae Dynasty" 12-8; **1977** *Future Cop* "The Carlisle Girl" 4-22; *McMillan and Wife* "Have You Heard About Vanessa?" 4-24; **1978** *Charlie's Angels* "Haunted Angels" 10-25; *Lou Grant* "Singles" 12-4; *Eddie Capra Mysteries* "Breakout to Murder" 12-1; **1979** *Salvage 1* "Energy Solution" 5-21; *Kate Loves a Mystery* "It Goes with the Territory" 10-25.

TELEFILMS

1975 *Last Hours Before Morning* 4-19 NBC; *The First 36 Hours of Dr. Durant* 5-13 NBC; **1976** *The Lindbergh Kidnapping Case* 2-26 NBC; **1977** *Delta County U.S.A.* 5-20 ABC; **1979** *Hanging by a Thread* 5-8, 5-9 NBC; *The Suicide's Wife* 11-7 CBS; **1980** *Fun and Games* 5-26 ABC; **1981** *A Matter of Life and Death* 1-13 CBS; *Golden Gate* 9-25 ABC; *The Princess and the Cabbie* 11-3 CBS; **1982** *Rona Jaffe's "Mazes and Monsters"* 12-28 CBS.

Patricia Donohue

(born 1930)

In films from 1957, Patricia was a regular during 1958-59 on a TV detective series, *The Thin Man*.

She also had a regular slot on *Michael Shayne* in 1960-61. Patricia spent much of the mid and late sixties in England, returning to America for scattered seventies guest roles and telefilms.

GUEST CREDITS

1959 *Markham* episode 2-25; *Trackdown* "False Witness" 4-8; *Millionaire* "Millionaire Martha Halloran" 5-27; *Richard Diamond* "Act of Grace" 10-12; *Man with a Camera* "The Man Below" 11-2; *Perry Mason* "The Case of the Artful Dodger" 12-12; *77 Sunset Strip* "The Juke Box Caper" 12-25; **1960** *Bat Masterson* "A Picture of Death" 1-14; *Black Saddle* "Means to an End" 1-29; *Twilight Zone* "A Stop at Willoughby" 1-29; *Man from Blackhawk* "The Man Who Wanted Everything" 6-3; *Loretta Young Show* "The Misfit" 6-5; *Loretta Young Show* "At the Edge of the Desert" 9-25; *Bonanza* "The Hopefuls" 10-8; **1961** *Checkmate* "Jungle Castle" 4-1; *Alfred Hitchcock Presents* "A Secret Life" 5-30; *Tall Man* "The Liberty Belle" 9-16; *87th Precinct* "Lady Killer" 10-9; *Bus Stop* "The Glass Jungle" 11-5; **1962**

Perry Mason "The Case of the Angry Astronaut" 4-7; **1963** *Alfred Hitchcock Hour* "Dear Uncle George" 5-10; **1966** *Virginian* "Dead-Eye Dick" 11-9; *The FBI* "Anatomy of a Prison Break" 11-27; **1970** *Bold Ones: The Lawyers* "The Lonliness Racket" 12-20; **1971** *Night Gallery* "The Hand of Borgus Weems" 9-15; *Night Gallery* "The Dear Departed" 12-1; *The FBI* "The Recruiter" 12-19; **1973** *Barnaby Jones* "See Some Evil…Do Some Evil" 4-8; **1978** *Rockford Files* "The Paper Palace" 1-20; *Barnaby Jones* "Stages of Fear" 11-23.

TELEFILM

1978 *Harold Robbins' "The Pirate"* 11-21, 11-22 CBS.

Robert DoQui

(born 1934, Stillwater, Oklahoma)

Robert earned a music scholarship to Langston University (Oklahoma) and sang with The Langstonaires. Following a four year U. S. Army stint Robert pursued an acting career in New York City. He came to television in 1964 and made his film debut in 1965. He later appeared in films like *The Fortune Cookie, Nashville, Walking Tall, Part 2, Robocop, Robocop 2* and *Robocop 3*.

DoQui also worked on the stage, in radio and was visible in numerous commercials. He served on The Screen Actors' Guild Board of Directors for ten years. During 1968-69 he was a regular on *Felony Squad*. In the later eighties he guested on *The Fall Guy, Webster, Cagney and Lacey* and *Frank's Place*.

GUEST CREDITS

1964 *Outer Limits* "The Invisible Enemy" 10-31; **1966** *Daktari* "Trail of the Cheetah" 2-8; *Fugitive* "The White Knight" 3-22; *Tarzan* "The Deadly Silence" 10-28, 11-4; **1968** *Daktari* "The Monster of Wameru" 2-6; *Ironside* "Shell Game" 9-19; *Guns of Will Sonnett* "The Trap" 10-4; **1969** *Gunsmoke* "The Mark of Cain" 2-3; *Gunsmoke* "The Good Samaritans" 3-10; *Ironside* "Five Miles High" 11-27; **1971** *Mission: Impossible* "Kitara" 2-20; *Longstreet* "Elegy in Brass" 10-14; **1972** *O'Hara, U. S. Treasury* "Operation: White Fire" 1-28; **1974** *Adam-12* "Routine Patrol" 2-12; **1975** *Adam-12* "Pressure Point" 2-4; *Six Million Dollar Man* "Look Alike" 2-23; *Blue Knight* "Two to Make Deadly" 12-17; **1977** *Rockford Files* "The Trees, the Bees and T. T. Flowers" 1-21, 1-28; **1978** *Quincy, M.E.* "Death by Good Intention" 10-26; **1981** *Concrete Cowboys* episode 3-21.

TELEFILMS

1972 *Visions* 10-10 CBS; *Lieutenant Schuster's Wife* 10-11 ABC; **1973** *A Dream for Christmas* 12-24 ABC; **1974** *Heat Wave!* 1-26 ABC; **1977** *Green Eyes* 1-3 ABC; **1979** *The Child Stealer* 3-9 ABC; **1983** *Making of a Male Model* 10-9 ABC.

John Doucette

(born January 21, 1921, Brockton, Mass.; died May 11, 1994)

A screen career of over 90 films for John Doucette began in 1943. Over the years he appeared in such well known movies as *High Noon, Winchester '73, Cleopatra, True Grit* and *Patton*. Many of his film roles were in westerns, playing characters

on both sides of the law.

Following a 1952 TV debut John was a regular on the drama series *Big Town* and on the 1959 crime show *Lock Up*. His last series regular role came in 1971-72 in a sitcom called *The Partners*. Many of his TV guest roles were in western series, with *Wagon Train* (7) being a particular favorite.

John died of cancer in 1994 in Cabazon, California, surivived by 8 children.

GUEST CREDITS

1959 *Lawman* "The Chef" 3-1; *Tombstone Territory* "Surrender at Sunset" 5-15; *Tales of Wells Fargo* "The Train Robbery" 10-12; **1960** *Bat Masterson* "A Grave Situation" 5-12; **1961** *Americans* "The Regular" 2-6; *Americans* "On to Richmond" 2-20; **1962** *Tales of Wells Fargo* "Reward for Gaine" 1-20; *Rawhide* "Incident of the Dogfaces" 11-9; *Bonanza* "Knight Errant" 11-18; *Wagon Train* "The Orly French Story" 12-12; **1963** *Laramie* "Naked Steel" 1-1; *Wide Country* "The Man Who Ran Away" 2-7; *Wagon Train* "The Michael McGoo Story" 3-20; *Lieutenant* "A Million Miles from Clary" 9-14; *Wagon Train* "The Fort Pierce Story" 9-23; **1964** *Wagon Train* "The Ben Engel Story" 3-16; *Fugitive* "Nemesis" 10-13; *Wagon Train* "Little Girl Lost" 12-6; **1965** *Wagon Train* "The Chottsie Gubenheimer Story" 1-10; *Rawhide* "Josh" 1-15;

Virginian "Six Graves at Cripple Creek" 1-27; *Wagon Train* "The Isaiah Quickfox Story" 1-31; *Bonanza* "Devil on Her Shoulder" 10-17; **1966** *Rat Patrol* "The Deadly Double Raid" 11-21; **1967** *Wild Wild West* " The Night of the Surreal McCoy" 3-3; *Judd, for the Defense* "The Other Face of the Law" 9-22; *Tarzan* "Voice of the Elephant" 9-22; **1968** *Bonanza* "The Price of Salt" 2-4; *Big Valley* "The Devil's Masquerade" 3-4; **1969** *Outsider* "Service for One" 4-9; *Virginian* "The Stranger" 4-9; **1973** *Kung Fu* "The Soul Is the Warrior" 2-8; *Mannix* "Desert Run" 10-21; *Ironside* "Mind for Murder" 11-15; **1974** *Tenafly* "Man Running" 1-2; *Harry O* "Mortal Sin" 10-3; *Kolchak: The Night Stalker* "The Vampire" 10-4; *Lucas Tanner* "Echoes" 11-13.

TELEFILMS

1967 *Winchester '73* 3-14 NBC; **1976** *Panache* 5-15 ABC; **1978** *Donner Pass: The Road to Survival* 10-24 NBC; *The Time Machine* 11-5 NBC; **1983** *Heart of Steel* 12-4 ABC.

David Doyle

(born December 1, 1925, Omaha, Nebraska)

Trained to be a lawyer, David opted for an acting career and began working on Broadway during the

fifties, making a film debut in 1963. He first worked in television guest roles in 1961, appearing only sporadicallly in the medium until he gained simultaneous series regular roles during 19772-72 in *Bridget Loves Bernie* and *The New Dick Van Dyke Show*.

In 1976 he was cast as John Bosley in the pilot for a new Aaron Spelling TV series, *Charlie's Angels*. The series began airing in September of 1976 and lasted five seasons, reaching No. 4 in the Neilson ratings in 1977-78. He was an ideal casting as the light-hearted supervisor and protector of the angels. He later became a regular on an abbreviated 1987 series, *Sweet Surrender*.

David was a frequent visitor to *Fantasy Island* (4), and took six cruises on *The Love Boat* (1978-87). During the later eighties he also guested on *Starman* and *Murder, She Wrote*.

GUEST CREDITS

1961 *Naked City* "Murder Is a Face I Know" 1-11; **1962** *General Electric Theater* "Acres and Pains" 5-12; **1964** *Defenders* "The 700-Year Old Gang" 9-24, 10-1; **1965** *For the People* "Dangerous to the Public Peace and Safety" 3-28; *Trials of O'Brien* "A Gaggle of Girls" 10-30; **1970** *Storefront Lawyers* "Episode 10" 11-18; **1971** *Cade's County* "A Gun for Billy" 11-28; **1972** *Hawaii Five-0* "Follow the White Brick Road" 2-1; **1973** *Banacek* "$10,000 a Page" 1-10; **1974** *Petrocelli* "Music to Die By" 9-18; *Police Story* "A World Full of Hurt" 10-8; *Police Story* "Glamour Boy" 10-29; *Kolchak: The Night Stalker* "The Doppleganger" 11-8; *Kojak* "The Best War in Town" 11-24; **1975** *Ellery Queen* "The Adventure of Auld Lang Syne" 9-11; *McCoy* "Bless the Big Fish" 10-5; *Police Story* "Vice: Twenty-Four Hours" 12-5; **1981** *Hart to Hart* "Hartland Express" 11-3; **1983** *Fall Guy* "Wheels" 12-21.

TELEFILMS

1973 *The Police Story* 3-20 NBC; *Money to Burn* 10-27 ABC; *Blood Sport* 12-5 ABC; *Miracle on 34th Street* 12-14 CBS; **1974** *The Stranger Within* 10-1 ABC; **1975** *The First 36 Hours of Dr. Durant* 5-13 ABC; **1976** *Charlie's Angels* 3-21 ABC; **1977**

Black Market Baby 10-7 ABC; **1983** *Wait Till Your Mother Gets Home* 1-17 NBC.

Keir Dullea
(born May 30, 1936, Cleveland, Ohio)

From 1960 until 1965, Keir appeared frequently in TV guest roles. He re-appeared briefly during the mid-seventies, and was a regular on the syndicated Canadian series, *The Starlost* (1973-74). This role may have been set in motion by his role in the 1968 sci-fi film *2001: A Space Odyssey*. His later television work consisted of telefilms only.

GUEST CREDITS

1960 *Route 66* "Black November" 10-7; **1961** *Naked City* "Murder Is a Face I Know" 1-11; *U.S. Steel Hour* "The Big Splash" 2-8; *Hallmark Hall of Fame* "Give Us Barabbas" 3-26; *U.S. Steel Hour* "The Golden Thirty" 8-9; *Alcoa Premiere* "People Need People" 10-10; *New Breed* "Prime Target" 10-10; **1962** *U.S. Steel Hour* "Far from the Shade Tree" 1-10; *Checkmate* "A Very Rough Sketch" 1-24; *Alcoa*

Premiere "Tiger" 3-20; *Cain's Hundred* "A Creature Lurks in Ambush" 4-17; *Kraft Mystery Theatre* "Cry Ruin" 8-15; *DuPont Show of the Month* "The Outpost"9-16; *Alcoa Premiere* "Ordeal in Darkness" 11-15; *Eleventh Hour* "Cry a Little for Mary Too" 11-28; **1963** *Empire* "Stopover on the Moon" 1-1; *U.S. Steel Hour* "The Young Avengers" 1-9; *Naked City* "The Apple Falls Not Far from the Tree" 1-23; *Going My Way* "One Small, Unhappy Family" 2-13; *Alcoa Premiere* "The Broken Year" 4-4; **1964** *Channing* "The Trouble with Girls" 3-11; **1965** *12 O'Clock High* "To Heinie with Love" 2-5; **1973** *McMillan and Wife* "Blues for Sally M" 5-13; **1975** *Switch* "The James Caan Con" 9-9.

TELEFILMS

1970 *Black Water Gold* 1-6 ABC; **1976** *Law and Order* 5-6 NBC; **1979** *Legend of the Golden Gun* 4-10 NBC; **1980** *Brave New World* 3-7 NBC; *The Hostage Tower* 5-13 CBS; **1981** *No Place to Hide* 3-4 CBS.

James Dunn
(born November 2, 1905, New York City; died September 1, 1967)

After a busy film career during the thirties, James Dunn came to television in 1948. He was very

prominent in the medium during the fifties, appearing on *Studio One* (4), *Schlitz Playhouse of Stars* (3), *Goodyear Playhouse* (2), *Robert Montgomery Presents* (3), *Climax* (2), *Wagon Train* and *Armstrong Circle Theater*. James was also a series regular on the sitcom, *Its a Great Life*, in 1954-55.

He worked in guest roles until shortly before his death in 1967. His only telefilm aired after his death.

GUEST CREDITS

1959 *Wanted: Dead or Alive* "Call Your Shot" 2-7; **1960** *Rawhide* "Incident at Red River Station" 1-15; *Playhouse 90* "Journey to the Day" 4-22; **1961** *Stagecoach West* "The Arsonist" 2-14; *Acapulco* "Death Is a Smiling Man" 3-27; *Naked City* "Sweet Prince of Delancey Street" 6-7; *Route 66* "Bridge Across Five Days" 11-17; *Investigators* "The Mind's Own Fire" 12-14; **1962** *Bonanza* "The Auld Sod" 2-4; *Follow the Sun* "Run, Clown, Run" 4-1; *Route 66* "Across Walnuts and Wine" 11-2; *Ben Casey* "Between Summer and Winter, The Glorious Season" 12-3; *Going My Way* "Keep an Eye on Santa Claus" 12-12; *Ben Casey* "Saturday, Surgery and Stanley Schultz" 12-31; **1963** *Great Adventure* "The Death of Sitting Bull" 10-4; *Great Adventure* "Massacre at Wounded Knee" 10-11; *Fugitive* "Decision in the Ring" 10-22; *Ben Casey* "Dispel the Black Cyclone That Shakes the Throne" 11-27; **1964** *Bob Hope Chrysler Theater* "A Slow Fade to Black" 3-27; *Virginian* "Man of the People" 12-23; **1965** *Slattery's People* "Question: How Do You Fall in Love with a Town?" 1-22; *Branded* "The First Kill" 4-4; **1966** *T.H.E. Cat* "The Canary Who Lost His Voice" 11-23; **1967** *Dundee and the Culhane* "Death of a Warrior Brief" 11-15.

TELEFILM

1968 *Shadow over Elveron* 3-5 NBC.

Michael Dunn

(Gary Neil Miller, October 20, 1934, Shattuck, Oklahoma; died 1973.)

A marvelous dwarf-actor, Michael entered films in 1960 and received an Academy Award Nomination

in 1965 for his work in *Ship of Fools*. Television fans will forever remember his wonderful recurring role in *Wild Wild West* as the evil Miguelito Loveless. Michael died in 1973, an apparent suicide.

GUEST CREDITS

1964 *Arrest and Trial* "Revenge of the Worm" 3-29; *East Side/West Side* "Here Today" 4-27; **1965** *Wild Wild West* "The Night the Wizard Shook the Earth" 10-1; *Amos Burke, Secret Agent* "The Prisoners of Mr. Sin" 10-27; *Wild Wild West* "The Night the Terror Stalked the Town" 11-19; **1966** *Wild Wild West* "The Night of the Whirring Death" 2-18; *Wild Wild West* "The Night of the Murderous Spring" 4-15; *Wild Wild West* "The Night of the Raven" 9-30; *Run for Your Life* "The Dark Beyond the Door" 10-10; *Wild Wild West* "The Night of the Green Terror" 11-18; **1967** *Wild Wild West* "The Night of the Surreal McCoy" 3-3; *Voyage to the Bottom of the Sea* "The Waxman" 3-5; *Wild Wild West* "The Night of the Bogus Bandits" 4-7; *Wild Wild West* "The Night Dr. Loveless Died" 9-29; **1968** *Tarzan* "Alex the Great" 3-22; *Star Trek* "Plato's Stepchildren" 11-22; *Wild Wild West* "The Night of Miguelito's Revenge" 12-13; **1972** *Night Gallery* "The Sins of the Fathers" 2-22.

TELEFILM

1972 *Goodnight My Love* 10-17 ABC.

John Durren

In television guest roles sporadically from 1959 through 1980, John is one of those faces remembered for a number of roles but none so memorable that his name ever caught on—a working actor doing his best, but never quite getting to the top of the cast list. He disappeared from televison from 1965 until 1975, then worked most years thereafter until the end of the decade. He had a significant role in *Arthur Hailey's "Wheels"*, a 1978 miniseries.

GUEST CREDITS

1959 *Rifleman* "The Challenge" 4-7; *Rifleman* "Bloodlines" 10-6; **1960** *Rawhide* "Incident of the Music Maker" 5-20; **1962** *Surfside 6* "The Affairs of Hotel Delight" 11-6; *Perry Mason* "The Case of the Lurid Letter" 12-6; **1964** *Fugitive* "Angels Travel on Lonely Roads" 2-25; **1965** *Fugitive* "Trial by Fire" 10-5; **1975** *Manhunter* "Man in a Cage" 1-22; *Matt Helm* "Panic" 12-27; **1976** *City of Angels* "Say Goodbye to Yesterday" 3-4; *Delvecchio* "The Avenger" 9-26; *Rockford Files* "Rattlers Class of '63" 11-26; *Kojak* "Dead Again" 12-19; **1977** *Feather and Father Gang* "Sun, Sand and Death" 3-14; **1978** *David Cassidy, Man Undercover* "Flashpoint" 12-7; *Eddie Capra Mysteries* "Dying Declaration" 12-15.

TELEFILMS

1975 *Crime Club* 4-3 CBS; *The Turning Point of Jim Malloy* 4-12 NBC; **1976** *The Lindbergh Kidnapping Case* 2-26 NBC; **1977** *Killer on Board* 10-10 NBC; *The Girl Called Hatter Fox* 10-12 CBS; **1979** *Mr. Horn* 2-1, 2-3 CBS; *High Midnight* 11-27 CBS; **1980** *Power* 1-14, 1-15 NBC; *Rage* 9-25 NBC.

Gene Dynarski

(born 1933)

Gene Dynarski made his film and television debuts in 1965. He made guest appearances on many hit TV series, especially crime dramas. Among Gene's film credits were roles in *Airport*, *Earthquake* and *Close Encounters of the Third Kind*.

In 1979 he founded and became director of The Gene Dynarski Theater in Los Angeles. During 1983 he tried his hand at soaps, appearing on *General Hospital*.

GUEST CREDITS

1965 *Ben Casey* "A Slave Is on the Throne" 4-12; *Big Valley* "The Guilt of Matt Bentell" 12-8; **1966** *Mission: Impossible* "Memory" 9-24; *Star Trek* "Mudd's Women" 10-13; **1967** *Felony Squad* "Deadly Partner" 1-9; *Mission: Impossible* "The Bank" 10-1;

Adam-12 "Log 131-Reed, The Dicks Have Their Jobs, and We Have Ours" 10-12; **1969** *Star Trek* "The Mark of Gideon" 1-17; *Land of the Giants* "Deadly Lodestone" 2-2; *Bonanza* "Silence at Stillwater" 9-28; **1970** *Mannix* "Fly, My Little One" 2-21; **1973** *Banacek* "The Greatest Collection of Them All" 1-24; *The FBI* "The Payoff" 10-14; *Cannon* "Come Watch Me Die" 10-24; **1974** *Banacek* "Now You See Me…Now You Don't" 3-12; *Kung Fu* "The Last Raid" 4-5; **1976** *Bronk* "Jailbreak" 2-15; *Starsky and Hutch* "Coffin for Starsky" 3-5; *City of Angels* "The Bloodshot Eye" 3-11; **1978** *Vegas* "The Games Girls Play" 9-27.

TELEFILMS

1968 *The Sound of Anger* 12-10 NBC; **1969** *Then Came Bronson* 3-24 CBS; **1971** *Duel* 11-13 ABC; **1973** *Banacek: Detour to Nowhere* 3-20 NBC; *Partners in Crime* 3-24 NBC; *Double Indemnity* 10-13 ABC; **1975** *Guilty or Innocent: The Sam Sheppard Murder Case* 11-17 NBC.

Richard Eastham

(born June 22, 1918, Opelousas, Louisiana)

In films from 1954, Richard got his first TV series regular role during 1957-60 in *Tombstone Territory*. After scattered guest work and a soap role (in *Bright Promise* 1969-70), he hit his stride in television during the seventies with frequent guest shots and a regular slot on *Wonder Woman* (1976-77). He later became a regular on *Falcon Crest* (1982-83).

GUEST CREDITS

1960 *Aquanauts* episode 10-26; **1961** *Perry Mason* "The Case of the Pathetic Patient" 10-28; **1962** *DuPont Show of the Month* " The Richest Man in Bogota" 8-5; **1965** *Perry Mason* "The Case of the Runaway Racer" 11-14; **1967** *Invaders* "The Summit Meeting" 10-31, 11-7; *Cowboy in Africa* "The Hesitant Hero" 12-18; **1970** *Mod Squad* "A Time for Remembering" 3-3; *Adam-12* "Log 173-Shoplift" 5-9; *Young Lawyers* "Where's Aaron?" **1971** *Owen Marshall, Counselor at Law* "Legacy of Fear" 9-16; **1972** *Cade's County* "Shakedown" 1-9; *Cannon* "The Shadow Man" 11-22; *Streets of San Francisco* "In the Midst of Strangers" 11-25; **1974** *Toma* "50 Per Cent Normal" 1-18; *Owen Marshall, Counselor at Law* "A Foreigner Among Us" 2-2; *Streets of San Francisco* "Flags of Terror" 10-31; **1975** *Barnaby Jones* "Murder Once Removed" 1-21; **1977** *Waltons* "The Warrior" 10-13; **1979** *Quincy, M.E.* "Aftermath" 2-7; *Salvage 1* "Energy Solution" 5-21; *Salvage 1* "Hard Water" 11-4, 11-11; **1981** *Quincy, M.E.* "By the Death of a Child" 4-8; *Waltons* "The Lumberjack" 5-21; **1982** *Tales of the Gold Monkey* "Trunk from the Past" 11-3.

TELEFILMS

1969 *Silent Night, Lonely Night* 12-16 NBC; **1973** *The President's Plane Is Missing* 10-23 ABC; **1975** *Attack on Terror: The FBI Versus the Ku Klux Klan* 2-20, 2-21; **1976** *Mallory: Circumstantial Evidence* 2-8 NBC; **1982** *A Wedding on Walton's Mountain* 2-22 NBC.

Walker Edmiston

A renowed voice artist, Walker Edmiston appeared in television guest roles from 1958 well into the eighties. He was a favorite guest on *Wild Wild West, Gunsmoke* and *Mission: Impossible,* appearing in multiple episodes of those series.

GUEST CREDITS

1962 *Thriller* "Till Death Do Us Part" 3-12; **1965** *Big Valley* "Forty Rifles" 9-22; *Wild Wild West* "The Night of the Fatal Trap" 12-24; **1967** *Big Valley* "Price of Victory" 2-13; *Wild Wild West* "The Night of the Colonel's Ghost" 3-10; *Wild Wild West* "The Night of the Turncoat" 12-1; **1968** *Wild Wild West* "The Night of the Camera" 11-29; **1970** *Gunsmoke* "Celia" 2-23; **1971** *Gunsmoke* "The Tycoon" 1-25; **1972** *Mission: Impossible* "Casino" 2-19; *Mission: Impossible* "Movie" 11-4; **1973** *Gunsmoke* "A Quiet Day in Dodge" 1-29; *Mission: Impossible* "The Fighter" 2-9; *Columbo* "Any Old Port in a Storm" 10-7; *Griff* "Don't Call Us, We'll Call You" 10-20; *Gunsmoke* "The Widow and the Rogue" 10-29; **1974** *Six Million Dollar Man* "Doomsday and Counting" 3-1; **1976** *Six Million Dollar Man* "Love Song for Tanya" 2-15; **1977** *Waltons* "The Hiding Place" 3-3; *Waltons* "The Recluse" 9-22; **1978** *Waltons* "The

Beau" 11-23; **1981** *Little House on the Prairie* "Goodbye Mrs Wilder" 2-2; *Buck Rogers* "The Dorian Secret" 4-16.

TELEFILMS

1969 *The Silent Gun* 12-16 ABC; **1972** *Short Walk to Daylight* 10-24 ABC; **1973** *Partners in Crime* 3-24 NBC; **1974** *Live Again, Die Again* 2-16 ABC; **1975** *The Night That Panicked America* 10-31 ABC; **1976** *Oregon Trail* 1-10 NBC; *The Lonliest Runner* 12-20 NBC; **1977** *Mad Bull* 12-21 CBS; **1979** *Some Kind of Miracle* 1-3 CBS; *Breaking Up Is Hard to Do* 9-5, 9-7 ABC; **1981** *Sizzle* 11-29 ABC; **1983** *Confessions of a Married Man* 1-31 ABC; *Grace Kelly* 2-21 ABC; *Dempsey* 9-28 CBS.

Sam Edwards

(born 1918)

The son of vaudevillians, Sam Edwards worked extensively in radio and onstage prior to his 1940 film debut. His parents produced a radio show in San Antonio, with Sam and his brother playing primary roles. A family move to California brought him into radio there, and into the family of CBS radio programs. He began playing on the *Gunsmoke* radio program in 1952 and continued throughout it's run (until 1961).

Edwards moved over into *Gunsmoke's* television show in 1958, with 4 subsequent guest roles on the series. He worked often on Jack Webb's television productions, on *Dragnet* and *Adam-12*. Sam's lengthy film and television career extended into the eighties.

GUEST CREDITS

1960 *Texan* "The Mountain Man" 5-23; **1961** *Zane Grey Theater* "Little Lou" 10-25; **1963** *Wagon Train* "The Cassie Vance Story" 12-23; **1965** *Laredo* "Yahoo" 9-30; *Gunsmoke* "The Pretender" 11-20; **1967** *Dragnet* "The Big Pyramid" 11-30; **1968** *Dragnet* "Homicide-DR-06" 10-24; **1969** *Mod Squad* "A Run for the Money" 3-11; *Dragnet* "Frauds-DR-36" 4-10; *Gunsmoke* "The Devil's Outpost" 9-22; *Gunsmoke* "McGraw" 12-8; *Adam-12* "Log 143-Cave" 12-13; **1970** *Dragnet* "Narco-Pillmaker" 2-19; **1971** *Mission: Impossible* "Encore" 9-25; *Mod Squad* "Whatever Happened to Linc Hayes?" 11-16; **1972** *Hawaii Five-0* "Fools Die Twice" 10-17; **1973** *Adam-12* "Training Division" 11-7; *Griff* "The Last Ballad" 11-10; **1976** *Barnaby Jones* "Dangerous Gambit" 2-26; *Streets of San Francisco* "Hot Dog" 12-9; **1979** *Project UFO* "Sighting 4026" 7-12; *Little House on the Prairie* "Crossed Connections" 12-10; **1981** *Little House on the Prairie* "The Legend of Black Jake" 11-16; **1982** *Little House on the Prairie* "Little Lou" 10-25.

TELEFILMS

1971 *In Broad Daylight* 10-16 ABC; *The Death of Me Yet* 10-27 ABC; **1973** *Set This Town on Fire* 1-8 NBC; *Chase* 2-24 NBC; **1974** *Hurricane* 9-10 ABC; *Hit Lady* 10-8 ABC; **1976** *The New Daughters of Joshua Cabe* 5-29 ABC; **1977** *The Incredible Rocky Mountain Race* 12-17 NBC; **1978** *Just You and Me* 5-22 NBC; **1980** *The Great Cash Giveaway Getaway* 4-21 NBC.

Lisa Eilbacher

(born May 5, 1959, Saudi Arabia)
The daughter of an oil executive, Lisa spent her

early years in Europe and the middle east before the family returned to Los Angeles. The older sister of actress Cindy Eilbacher, Lisa began her television career in 1965 doing TV commercials, then playing juvenile roles in various TV series. She became a series regular on *The Texas Wheelers* (1974-75) and *The Hardy Boys Mysteries* (1977-78). She followed those roles with a strong part in the miniseries *Wheels* (1978), then had the lead role in a 1979 telefilm, *The Ordeal of Patty Hearst*.

Lisa graduated to some good film roles in *An Officer and a Gentleman*, and in *Beverly Hills Cop*. She continued to work steadily in television throughout the eighties, in guest roles, in the miniseries *The Winds of War*, and in two abortive series, *Ryan's Four* and *Me and Mom*. In 1990 she joined the cast of *The Midnight Caller*.

GUEST CREDITS

1965 *Laredo* "Rendevous at Arrilo" 10-7; **1968** *Guns of Will Sonnett* "Where There's Hope" 12-20; **1971** *Alias Smith and Jones* "The Posse That Wouldn't Quit" 10-14; **1972** *Bonanza* "First Love" 12-26; **1973** *Waltons* "The Fire" 1-11; *Gunsmoke* "Kimbrough" 2-12; *Owen Marshall, Counselor at Law* "The Pool House" 9-26; **1974** *Doc Elliot* "Time to Grow" 3-6; **1975** *Movin' On* "Landslide" 1-16; *Gunsmoke* "The Sharecroppers" 3-31; *Caribe* "The

Patriots" 4-21; **1976** *Streets of San Francisco* "Dead or Alive" 10-21; **1977** *Man from Atlantis* "The Naked Montague" 12-6; *Hawaii Five-0* "Tall on the Wave" 3-2; *Richie Brockelman* "Junk It to Me Baby" 3-24; **1982** *Simon and Simon* "Earth to Stacey" 2-9; *Simon and Simon* "Sometimes Dreams Do Come True" 12-2.

TELEFILMS

1969 *In Name Only* 11-25 ABC; **1974** *Bad Ronald* 10-23 ABC; *Spider Man* 9-14 CBS; **1979** *The Ordeal of Patty Hearst* 3-4 ABC; *Love for Rent* 11-11 ABC; **1980** *To Race the Wind* 3-12 CBS; **1982** *This House Possessed* 2-6 ABC.

Jack Elam

(born November 16, 1916, Miami, Arizona)

Considered by most television and western film fans to be one of the meanest looking villains of the genre, Jack Elam was initially a C.P.A. in Los Angeles. His business contacts helped to finance a movie; the favor was returned with an opportunity for Jack to move into acting (1949). He ultimately made over 90 films, with roles in *The Sundowners, High Noon, Shane, Vera Cruz, Kismet, Jubal, Gunfight at O. K. Corral, The Comancheros, The Last Sunset, Firecreek* and *Support Your Local Sheriff*.

Jack's TV career kicked into gear in 1952. With the advent of television western series, Jack worked constantly, with over 70 western guest roles, beginning with a 1954 episode of *The Lone Ranger*. He found time to appear as a series regular on *The Dakotas* (1963) and *Temple Houston* (1963-64).

In later years, with added bulk, Jack did more comic roles and was a regular on brief series like *The Texas Wheelers* (1974-75), *Struck by Lightning* (1979), *Detective in the House* (1985) and *Easy Street* (1986-87). Jack appeared in guest roles as late as 1988, last working on an episode of *J. J. Starbuck*.

GUEST CREDITS

1959 *Gunsmoke* "The Jayhawkers" 1-31; *Have*

Gun-Will Travel "The Man Who Lost" 2-7; *Tombstone Territory* "Day of the Amnesty" 4-3; *Have Gun-Will Travel* "Hunt the Man Down" 4-25; *Lawman* "The Senator" 5-17; *Texan* "South of the Border" 5-19; *Desilu Playhouse* "Six Guns for Donegan" 10-16; *Richard Diamond* "One Dead Cast" 12-28; **1960** *Untouchables* "Syndicate Sanctuary " 1-7; *Rebel* "Angry Town" 1-10; *Tightrope* "Broken Rope" 1-12; *Gunsmoke* "Where'd They Go?" 3-12; *Mr. Lucky* "The Big Squeeze" 3-12; *Rifleman* "Shotgun Man" 4-12; *Texan* "Lady Tenderfoot" 5-9; **1961** *Zane Grey Theater* "Ambush" 1-5; *Bonanza* "Spitfire" 1-14; *Sugarfoot* "Toothy Thompson" 1-16; *Klondike* "Queen of the Klondike" 1-23; *Gunsmoke* "Love Thy Neighbor" 1-28; *Gunslinger* "The Hostage Fort" 2-16; *Sugarfoot* "Angel" 3-6; *Untouchables* "Testimony of Evil" 3-30; *Americans* "The Gun" 4-3; *Rebel* "Helping Hand" 4-30; *Cheyenne* "Massacre at Gunsight Pass" 5-1; *Laramie* "The Tumbleweed Wagon" 5-9; *Twilight Zone* "Will the Real Martian Please Stand Up" 5-26; *Lawman* "The Four" 10-1; *Rifleman* "Knight Errant" 11-30; *National Velvet* "The Desperado" 11-27; *Rifleman*

"The Shattered Idol" 12-4; *Outlaws* "The Outlaw Marshals" 12-14; *Bronco* "The Equalizer" 12-18; **1962** *Have Gun-Will Travel* "One, Two, Three" 2-17; *Rawhide* "The Pitchwagon" 3-2; *Target: The Corruptors* "A Man's Castle" 3-30; *Cheyenne* "A Man Called Ragan" 4-23; *Untouchables* "Pressure" 6-14; *Cheyenne* "The Durango Brothers" 9-24; *Ben Casey* "The Night That Nothing Happened" 10-8; *Laramie* "Gun Duel" 12-25; **1964** *Gunsmoke* "Orvall Bass" 5-23; *Gunsmoke* "Help Me, Kitty" 11-2; **1965** *Daniel Boone* "The Sound of Fear" 2-11; *Legend of Jesse James* "Three Men from Now" 9-13; *Gunsmoke* "Clayton Thaddeus Greenwood" 10-2; *Gunsmoke* "Malachi" 11-13; **1966** *Gunsmoke* "My Father, My Son" 4-23; **1967** *Bonanza* "A Bride for Buford" 1-15; *Tarzan* "The Circus" 3-24; *Guns of Will Sonnett* "A Son for a Son" 10-20; *Wild Wild West* "The Night of Montezuma's Hordes" 10-27; *Hondo* "Hondo and the Rebel Hat" 12-29; **1968** *Cimarron Strip* "Big Jesse" 2-8; *Gunsmoke* "The First People" 2-19; *High Chaparral* "North to Tucson" 11-8; **1969** *Outcasts* "The Glory Wagon" 2-3; *Lancer* "Zee" 9-30; *Gunsmoke* "The Sisters" 12-29; **1970** *Virginian* "Rich Man, Poor Man" 3-11; *Bonanza* "Honest John" 12-20; **1971** *Gunsmoke* "Murdock" 2-8; *Gunsmoke* "P.S. Murry Christmas" 12-27; **1972** *Nichols* "About Jesse James" 2-15; *Alias Smith and Jones* "Bad Night in Big Butte" 3-2; *Gunsmoke* "The River" 9-11, 9-18; **1973** *Kung Fu* "The Squaw Man" 11-1; **1978** *Life and Times of Grizzly Adams* episode 3-1; **1981** *Father Murphy* "By the Bear That Bit Me" 12-1, 12-8.

TELEFILMS

1969 *The Over-the-Hill Gang* 10-7 ABC; **1972** *The Daughters of Joshua Cabe* 9-13 ABC; **1973** *The Red Pony* 3-18 NBC; **1974** *Shoot-Out in a One-Dog Town* 1-9 CBS; *Sidekicks* 3-21 CBS; **1975** *Huckleberry Finn* 3-25 ABC; **1976** *The New Daughters of Joshua Cabe* 5-29 ABC; **1978** *Lacy and the Mississippi Queen* 5-1 NBC; **1979** *The Sacketts* 5-16 CBS.

In his very first film, in 1953, Biff Elliott starred as Mike Hammer in *I, The Jury*. His roles as a leading man were limited, but he did become an effective character and supporting player, through the sixties and seventies. His television guest roles were mainly action-oriented.

GUEST CREDITS

1960 *Alfred Hitchcock Presents* "The Day of the Bullet" 2-14; **1961** *Alfred Hitchcock Presents* " A Crime for Mothers" 1-24; *Roaring 20's* "The Salvation of Killer McFadden" 4-1; *Surfside 6* "Little Mister Kelly" 5-1; *Alfred Hitchcock Presents* "Bang, You're Dead" 10-17; *77 Sunset Strip* "Big Boy Blue" 11-3; **1962** *Route 66* "From an Enchantress Fleeing" 6-1; **1963** *Combat* "The Party" 12-24; **1967** *Mission: Impossible* "The Confession" 2-25; *Star Trek* "Devil in the Dark" 3-9; *Mission: Impossible* "The Contender" 10-6, 10-13; *Mission: Impossible* "Casino" 2-19; *Cannon* "That Was No Lady" 10-4; **1973** *The FBI* "The Double Play" 2-4; **1974** *Magician* "The Stainless Steel Lady" 1-28; *Planet of the Apes* "Escape from Tomorrow" 9-13.

Biff Elliott

(born 1923)

Stephen Elliott

(born November 27, 1918)

A graduate of New York's Neighborhood Playhouse, Stephen developed a no-nonsense personna, often backed by bombast and bluster. It's kept him working on stage, screen and television since his 1954 film debut. His first television exposure was on the soap *Young Doctor Malone* from 1958 to 1963; he was also on *A World Apart* in 1970-71. TV guest roles were very infrequent until 1974. He was a regular on a brief series called *Beacon Hill* in 1975, then moved over into *Executive Suite* in a nice 1976-77 role.

He had a recurring role on *Falcon Crest* in 1982, was a regular for a time during 1985 on *Dallas* and was in a brief 1988 series, *Trial and Error*. Stephen had featured roles in the popular *Beverly Hills Cop* films, appearing as the police commissioner.

GUEST CREDITS

1960 *Armstrong Circle Theater* "Raid in Beatnik Village" 3-2; **1963** *Nurses* "Night Sounds" 1-24; **1966** *Hawk* "H is for a Dirty Letter" 12-1; **1974** *Barnaby Jones* "Web of Deceit" 12-10; *Manhunter* "A.W.O.L. to Kill" 12-11; **1975** *Kojak* "Elegy in an Asphalt Graveyard" 2-2; *Petrocelli* "Death in Small Doses" 3-27; *Columbo* "A Deadly State of Mind" 4-27; *Bronk* "There's Gonna Be a War" 12-21; **1976** *City of Angels* "The November Plan" 2-3, 2-10, 2-17; **1978** *Rockford Files* "The Competitive Edge" 2-10;

Hawaii Five-0 "The Deadly Courier" 10-12; **1979** *Vegas* "Touch of Death" 3-14; *Quincy, M.E.* "Mode of Death" 11-1; **1982** *Falcon Crest* "Kindred Spirits" 1-1; *Falcon Crest* "House of Cards" 3-2; *Falcon Crest* "The Good, the Bad and the Profane" 4-2; *Falcon Crest* "Pentultimate Questions" 4-9; *Magnum, P.I.* "Almost Home" 12-9; **1983** *Mississippi* episode 11-15; *Remington Steele* "My Fair Steele" 12-13.

TELEFILMS

1974 *The Gun* 11-13 ABC; **1976** *The Invasion of Johnson County* 7-31 NBC; **1977** *Young Joe, the Forgotten Kennedy* 9-18 ABC; **1978** *Sergeant Matlovich vs. the U. S. Air Force* 8-21 NBC; *Overboard* 9-25 NBC; *Betrayal* 11-13 NBC; **1979** *Some Kind of Miracle* 1-3 CBS; *Son Rise: A Miracle of Love* 5-14 NBC; *Can You Hear the Laughter?: The Story of Freddie Prinze* 9-11 CBS; *Mrs. R's Daughter* 9-19; **1981** *Jacqueline Bouvier Kennedy* 10-14 ABC; **1982** *My* Body, *My Child* 4-12; **1983** *Prototype* 12-7 CBS.

Cliff Emmich

(born 1936)

A chubby character actor, Cliff got his acting start in 1960, touring extensively. After a film debut during 1969 in *Gaily, Gaily*, he began doing television guest work in the early seventies, often as villains or snitches. He has been active in telefilms, from 1971.

GUEST CREDITS

1972 *Cool Million* "The Million Dollar Misundestanding" 12-20; **1974** *Police Woman* "The Child Buyers" 12-13; **1975** *Police Woman* "The Hit" 12-9; **1977** *Police Story* "Spitfire" 1-11; *Starsky and Hutch* "Psychic" 1-15; *Police Woman* "Shark" 2-15; *Charlie's Angels* "Angels in Paradise" 9-14; **1978** *CHiPs* "Rainy Day" 3-2; *Little House on the Prairie* "The Man Inside" 10-2; **1979** *Salvage 1* "Mermadon" 4-16; *Vegas* "The Macho Murders" 11-21; **1981** *CHiPs* "The Poachers" 6-21; **1982** *Bret Maverick* "The Ballad of Bret Maverick" 2-16; *Trapper John, M.D.* "The Good Life" 11-28; **1983** *CHiPs* "Country Action" 1-23; *Matt Houston* episode 9-16.

TELEFILMS

1971 *The Feminist and the Fuzz* 1-26 ABC; **1975** *Shell Game* 5-9 CBS; **1976** *Mallory: Circumstantial Evidence* 2-8 NBC; *McNaughton's Daughter* 3-4 NBC; **1979** *Undercover with the KKK* 10-23 CBS; *The Streets of L.A.* 11-13; **1980** *The $5.20 an Hour Dream* 1-26 CBS; **1983** *I Want to Live* 5-9 ABC; *Dempsey* 9-28 CBS.

Roy Engel

(born September 13, 1913, Missouri; died February 19, 1981)

Roy Engel started his career in radio, and was the voice of the orignial *Sky King*; he was also on *The Whistler*. He made his film debut in 1949 and later appeared in *Spartacus, Silent Running* and *Skyjacked*. After making a television debut in 1955, Roy gained a series regular role during 1957-58 in *A Date with the Angels*.

Following early sixties guest work he became a regular on *My Favorite Martian*, playing the police

chief. During 1966-68 he had a recurring role on The *Wild Wild West*, appearing as President Grant. He died in 1981, survived by his wife and a daughter.

GUEST CREDITS

1959 *Gunsmoke* "Wind" 3-21; *Restless Gun* "One on the House" 4-20; *Black Saddle* "Client: Reynolds" 5-29; **1960** *Maverick* "Greenbacks Unlimited" 3-13; *Millionaire* "Millionaire Tony Rogers" 3-30; *Wagon Train* "The Countess Baranoff Story" 5-11; *Bonanza* "Day of Reckoning" 10-22; *Gunsmoke* "Don Matteo" 10-22; *Barbara Stanwyck Show* "Ironback's Bride" 11-28; **1961** *Bonanza* "Vengeance" 2-11; *Bonanza* "The Dark Gate" 3-4; *Wyatt Earp* "Hiding Behind a Star" 3-21; *Wanted: Dead or Alive* "Dead Reckoning" 3-22; *Have Gun-Will Travel* "Everyman" 3-25; *Bonanza* "The Secret" 5-6; *Have Gun-Will Travel* "The Gospel Singers" 10-21; *Detectives* "Beyond a Reasonable Doubt" 11-17; *Bus Stop* "A Lion Walks Among Us" 12-3; *Have Gun-Will Travel* "Squatter's Rights" 12-23; **1962** *Gunsmoke* "The Do-Badder" 1-6; *Virginian* "Say Goodbye to All That" 1-23; *Alcoa Premiere* "The

Long Walk Home" 10-18; *Stoney Burke* "The Wanderer" 12-3; **1963** *Virginian* "Duel at Shiloh" 1-2; *Virginian* "A Distant Fury" 3-20; *Virginian* "The Invaders" 1-1; *Bonanza* "The Campaneros" 4-19; *Virginian* "Man of the People" 12-22; **1965** *Virginian* "You Take the High Road" 2-17; **1966** *Wild Wild West* "The Night of the Steel Assassin" 1-7; *Perry Mason* "The Case of the Fanciful Frail" 3-27; *The FBI* "The Bomb That Walked Like a Man" 5-1; **1967** *Fugitive* "Run the Man Down" 1-3; *Wild Wild West* "The Night of the Colonel's Ghost" 3-10; *Invaders* "Condition: Red" 9-5; *Virginian* "Ah Sing vs. Wyoming" 10-25; *Judd, for the Defense* "To Love and Stand Mute" 12-8; *Wild Wild West* "The Night of the Arrow" 12-29; **1968** *The FBI* "Act of Violence" 1-21; *Mission: Impossible* "The Counterfeiter" 2-4; *Wild Wild West* "The Night of the Death Maker" 2-23; *Judd, for the Defense* "You Remember Joe Maddox" 3-22; *Wild Wild West* "The Night of the Big Blackmail" 9-27; *Lancer* "The Prodigal" 11-12; **1969** *Wild Wild West* "The Night of the Winged Terror" 1-17; *The FBI* "Nightmare Road" 9-21; **1971** *Owen Marshall, Counselor at Law* "Eighteen Years Next April" 11-24; **1972** *The FBI* "The Engineer" 10-29; **1974** *Waltons* "The Ring" 10-17.

TELEFILMS

1971 *The Last Child* 10-5 ABC; **1977** *The Amazing Howard Hughes* 4-13, 4-14 CBS.

Jena Engstrom

(born 1941)

The daughter of actress Jean Engstrom, Jena frequently donned calico to portray young frontier ladies in television series like *Have Gun-Will Travel* (5), *Gunsmoke* (2) and *Rawhide* (2). She appeared in several episodes with her mother prior to leaving the medium after 1964 guest work.

GUEST CREDITS

1961 *Gunslinger* "The Hostage Fort" 2-16; *Have Gun-Will Travel* "The Fatal Flaw" 2-25; *Have Gun-*

Will Travel "The Gold Bar" 3-18; *Rawhide* "The Incident of the Lost Idol" 4-28; *Have Gun-Will Travel* "The Education of Sara Jane" 9-23; *Bonanza* "Springtime" 10-1; *Tall Man* "An Item for Sale" 10-14; *87th Precinct* "The Modus Man" 10-16; *Outlaws* "The Braithwaite Brothers" 11-9; *Gunsmoke* "Milly" 11-25; **1962** *New Breed* "To Sell a Human Being" 1-16; *Have Gun-Will Travel* "Alive" 3-17; *Rawhide* "The Child Woman" 3-23; *Gunsmoke* "Chester's Indian" 5-12; *Have Gun-Will Travel* "A Place for Abel Hix" 10-6; *Stoney Burke* "A Matter of Pride" 11-5; *Laramie* "The Sunday Shoot" 11-13; **1963** *Route 66* "You Can't Pick Cotton in Tahiti" 1-11; *Eleventh Hour* "Try to Keep Alive Until Next Tuesday" 4-17; *Nurses* "Bitter Pill" 5-23; **1964** *77 Sunset Strip* "Queen of Cats" 2-7; *Wagon Train* "The Santiago Quesada Story" 3-23; *Virginian* "The Black Stallion" 9-30.

Richard Erdman

(born June 1, 1925, Enid, Oklahoma)

A very busy film actor, from 1944, Richard Erdman estimates that he has appeared in over 500 films, including a memorable role in *Stalag 17*. He also appeared in *The Blue Gardenia* and *Tora! Tora! Tora!* His first visible television role was as a regular on *The Ray Bolger Show* (1953-55), followed

by a stint on a sitcom, *The Tab Hunter Show* (1960-61). During 1962-63 he was a regular on *Saints and Sinners*.

He began directing in 1966 with a couple of *Dick Van Dyke Show* episodes. His guest roles thereafter were somewhat limited, but he did a number of sitcom guest shots on *Mr. Ed, Gomer Pyle, U.S.M.C; Green Acres, The Beverly Hillbillies* and *Here's Lucy*. He had a recurring role on *Dallas* (1988-89) and guested during the eighties on *Murder, She Wrote*.

GUEST CREDITS

1959 *Perry Mason* "The Case of the Lost Last Act" 3-21; **1962** *Perry Mason* "The Case of the Absent Artist" 3-17; **1963** *Twilight Zone* "A Kind of Stopwatch" 10-10; **1967** *Man from UNCLE* "The Suburbia Affair" 1-6; **1969** *Wild Wild West* "The Night of the Bleak Island" 3-14; **1975** *Six Million Dollar Man* "Outrage in Balinderry" 4-19; **1976** *Six Million Dollar Man* "The Bionic Boy" 11-7; **1977** *Bionic Woman* "Over the Hill" 12-17; **1978** *Lou Grant* "Sect" 2-6; **1979** *Spiderman* "The Chinese Web" 7-6; **1980** *Lou Grant* "Nightside" 9-22; **1981** *Lou Grant* "Jazz" 1-4; *Lou Grant* "Business" 3-23.

TELEFILMS

1972 *Visions*...10-10 CBS; **1973** *The Great Man's Whiskers* 2-13 NBC.

Devon Erickson

(born December 21, Salt Lake City, Utah)

Following her 1974 debut, Devon became a busy television actress, guesting in numerous episodes, and appearing in a featured role in the abbreviated 1977 series *Young Dan'l Boone*. She also appeared in 3 miniseries: *The Awakening Land* (1978), *Testimony of Two Men* (1978) and *Studs Lonigan* (1979).

During the mid and late eighties Devon guested on *Hotel, The Love Boat, Airwolf* (2), *Hunter, Trapper John, M.D., It's a Living* and *St. Elsewhere* (2).

GUEST CREDITS

1974 *Waltons* "First Day" 9-19; *Manhunter* "A.W.O.L. to Kill" 12-11; **1975** *Barnaby Jones* "Bond of Fear" 4-15; *Streets of San Francisco* "Most Likely to Succeed" 12-13; **1976** *Movin' On* "The Old South Will Rise Again" 1-6; *Barnaby Jones* "Band of Evil" 11-18; **1977** *Police Story* "The Malflores" 1-25; *Most Wanted* "The Ritual Killer" 2-12; *Streets of San Francisco* "Once a Con" 3-3; *Westside Medical* "Red Blanket for a City" 3-31; **1979** *Barnaby Jones* "Nightmare in Hawaii" 9-27; **1980** *CHiPs* "Wheels of Justice" 12-21; **1981** *Quincy, M.E.* "To Kill in Plain Sight" 3-4; *Buck Rogers* "The Dorian Secret" 4-16; *Magnum, P.I.* "Tropical Mad-

ness" 11-12; **1982** *Knight Rider* "Deadly Maneuvers" 10-1; **1983** *A-Team* "West Coast Turnaround" 4-5.

TELEFILMS

1975 *The Dream Makers* 1-7 NBC; *The Runaway Barge* 3-24 NBC; **1976** *Eleanor and Franklin* 1-11, 1-12 ABC; **1978** *Ishi: The Last of His Tribe* 12-20 NBC; **1979** *Can You Hear the Laughter?: The Story of Freddie Prinze* 9-11 CBS; **1980** *Baby Comes Home* 10-16 CBS.

Maurice Evans
(born June 3, 1901, Dorchester, England; died 1989)

A noted Welsh stage actor (from 1926), Maurice made his first film in 1929. He came to the U. S. in 1941 and established himself on the American stage. He became noted on television during the fifties in *Hallmark Hall of Fame* Shakespearean classics: Hamlet (1953), King Richard II (1954), Macbeth (1954), The Taming of the Shrew (1956) and The Twelfth Night (1957). He also had fifties credits on *General Electric Theater* and *The U.S. Steel Hour*.

He received a Best Actor Emmy in 1960 for a restaged *Hallmark Hall of Fame* version of

Macbeth. In 1964 he changed pace to display his comedic talents in a long running role on *Bewitched* (1964-72), as the warlock father of the lead character, Samantha.

After *Bewitched*, Maurice did some guesting on crime series episodes and on *Fantasy Island* and *The Love Boat*.

GUEST CREDITS

1960 *Hallmark Hall of Fame* "The Tempest" 2-3; *Hallmark Hall of Fame* "Macbeth" 11-20; **1961** *Westinghouse Playhouse* "Come Again to Carthage" 12-8; **1962** *U.S. Steel Hour* "The Loves of Claire Ambler" 4-4; **1965** *Bob Hope Chrysler Theater* "The Game" 9-15; **1966** *Man from UNCLE* "The Bridge of Lions Affair" 2-4, 2-11; **1967** *Tarzan* "Basil of the Bulge" 2-10; *Tarzan* "Algie B for Brave" 4-7; *Daniel Boone* "Beaumarchais" 10-12; *I Spy* "Oedipus at Colonus" 11-27; *Hallmark Hall of Fame* "St. Joan" 12-4; **1968** *Tarzan* "Four O'Clock Army" 3-1, 3-8; *The FBI* "The Intermediary" 12-1; **1969** *Name of the Game* "Agent of the Plaintiff" 3-21; *Mod Squad* "Never Give the Fuzz an Even Break" 12-23; **1972** *Search* "The Murrow Disappearance" 9-13; **1973** *Six Million Dollar Man* "The Solid Gold Kidnapping" 11-17; **1974** *Snoop Sisters* "Fear Is a Free Throw" 1-29; **1975** *Caribe* "The Patriots" 4-21; *Columbo* "Forgotten Lady" 9-14; *Streets of San Francisco* "School of Fear" 10-9; **1980** *Hagen* "Jeopardy" 4-10.

TELEFILMS

1969 *U.M.C.* 4-17 CBS; **1970** *The Brotherhood of the Bell* 9-17 CBS; **1983** *Agatha Christie's "A Caribbean Mystery"* 10-22 CBS.

Richard Evans
(born 1935)

Richard Evans began a stage career in 1957, debuted in films in 1959 and came to television in 1960. He was a regular on *Peyton Place* in 1965, then spent the balance of the sixties/seventies era in action-related guest roles and telefilms.

Thin and intense looking, Richard often played

troubled young men struggling with inner devils.

GUEST CREDITS

1960 *Gunsmoke* "Moo Raid" 2-13; *Rifleman* "Sins of the Father" 4-19; *Zane Grey Theater* "Image of a Manhunt" 5-11; *Lawman* "The Town Boys" 9-18; *Detectives* "Razor's Edge" 12-30; **1961** *Checkmate* "Through a Dark Glass" 11-1; **1962** *Eleventh Hour* "Hooray, Hooray, The Circus Is Coming to Town" 11-21; **1963** *Empire* "The Tiger Inside" 2-12; *Redigo* "The Blooded Bull" 10-1; **1964** *Ben Casey* "The Sound of One Hand Clapping" 2-19; *Dr. Kildare* "Man Is a Rock" 9-24; *Fugitive* "The Cage" 11-24; **1965** *Gunsmoke* "The Storm" 9-25; *Perry Mason* "The Case of the Hasty Honeymooner" 10-24; **1966** *Gunsmoke* "Death Watch" 1-8; **1967** *Bonanza* "Dark Enough to See the Stars" 3-12; *Gunsmoke* "The Prodigal" 9-25; **1968** *High Chaparral* "The Hair Hunter" 3-10; *Guns of Will Sonnett* "Home Free" 11-22; *Mod Squad* "Twinkle, Twinkle, Little Starlet" 12-17; **1970** *Bonanza* "What Are Partners For?" 4-12; *The FBI* "Incident in the Desert" 12-20; **1972** *The FBI* "The Outcast" 12-17; **1974** *Barnaby Jones* "The Deadly Jinx" 1-13; *Magician* "The Illusion of Evil Spikes" 4-15; *Barnaby Jones* "A Gathering of Thieves" 9-10; **1975** *Cannon* "Coffin Corner" 1-15; **1977** *Barnaby Jones* "The

Killer on Campus" 5-19; **1978** *Barnaby Jones* "Blind Jeopardy" 9-21; **1981** *Hart to Hart* "A Couple of Harts" 10-13.

TELEFILMS

1972 *Welcome Home, Johnny Bristol* 1-30 CBS; **1973** *Cry Rape!* 11-27 CBS; **1974** *Honky Tonk* 4-1 NBC; **1979** *When Hell Was in Session* 10-8 NBC.

Jason Evers
(born January 2, 1927, New York City)

The son of William Everin, a New York theatrical ticket broker, the younger Everin often attended 15 or 20 plays a season as a youngster. That probably caused the acting "bug" to bite early, for he dropped out of high school after two years to study acting with Maria Ouspenskaya. After a year's training he toured with Ethel Barrymore's repertory company and eventually came to Broadway, in 1944. He entered the U. S. Army that same year and served until the end of World War II.

Returning to acting, he had a two year run of *Dear Ruth* in Chicago, then did more touring. He met and fell in love with actress Shirley Ballard; the couple were married on December 24, 1953. They

struggled through some lean years in New York, then moved to Hollywood and he changed his stage name from Herb, to Jason, Evers. He was cast almost immediately for the leading role in *The Wrangler* (1959).

Numerous guest roles followed *The Wrangler*, and in 1963, Jason was cast in the starring role in *Channing* (1963-64), his best known role. Thereafter, he did a number of guest shots before beginnng a recurring role (1967-69) on *The Guns of Will Sonnett*, 12 episodes in all.

During the period from 1969 to 1985 Jason appeared on virtually every major detective and crime series, often playing crooked businessmen or various criminal types. One of Hollywood's consumate professionals, Jason's early training and dedication paid huge dividends to him, and to his craft.

GUEST CREDITS

1961 *Hong Kong* "Suitable for Framing" 1-4; *Bonanza* "The Duke" 3-11; *Perry Mason* "The Case of the Difficult Detour" 3-25; *Rebel* "Miz Purdy" 4-2; *Laramie* "The Debt" 4-18; *Lawman* "Blind Hate" 5-14; *Surfside 6* "Count Seven" 9-18; *Lawman* "The Mountain Men" 10-17; *Perry Mason* "The Case of the Posthumous Painter" 11-11; *Cheyenne* "Retaliation" 11-13; **1962** *Adventures in Paradise* "Please Believe Me" 2-4; *Alcoa Premiere* "Of This Time, Of That Place" 3-6; *Gunsmoke* "Reprisal" 3-10; *Laramie* "Trial by Fire" 4-10; *Tales of Wells Fargo* "Remember the Yazoo" 4-14; *Gunsmoke* "Collie's Free" 10-20; *Defenders* "The Bigamist" 11-3; **1964** *Gunsmoke* "Cornelia Conrad" 6-13; *Perry Mason* "The Case of the Latent Lover" 12-3; *Gunsmoke* "Innocence" 12-12 **1965** *Branded* "The Test" 2-7; *Big Valley* "The Odyssey of Jubal Tanner"10-13; *The FBI* "The Problem of the Honorable Wife" 10-31; **1966** *The FBI* "Flight to Harbin" 2-27; *T.H.E. Cat* "To Kill a Priest" 9-16; *Virginian* "An Echo of Thunder" 10-5; *Green Hornet* "Eat, Drink and Be Dead" 10-14; *Combat* "The Outsider" 11-22; **1967** *Felony Squad* "The Strangler" 1-30; *Bonanza* "Journey to Terror" 2-5; *Road West* "The Insider" 2-13; *Invaders* "Condition: Red" 9-5; *Tarzan* "The Blue Storm of Heaven" 10-6, 10-13; *Guns of Will Sonnett* "Message

at Noon" 10-13; *Guns of Will Sonnett* "Meeting at Devil's Fork" 10-27; **1968** *Guns of Will Sonnett* "End of a Rope" 1-12; *Judd, for the Defense* "No Law Against Murder" 1-19; *Guns of Will Sonnett* "Alone" 2-9; *Guns of Will Sonnett* "Reunion" 9-27; *Mannix* "The Silent Cry" 9-28; *Felony Squad* "Dark Memory" 10-25; *Big Valley* "Death Town" 10-28; *Guns of Will Sonnett* "Joby" 11-1; *Wild Wild West* "the Night of the Kraken" 11-1; *Star Trek* "Wink of an Eye" 11-29; *Guns of Will Sonnett* "Meeting in a Small Town" 12-6; *It Takes a Thief* "Glass Riddle" 12-17; **1969** *Guns of Will Sonnett* "Time Is the Rider" 1-10; *Mission: Impossible* "The Mind of Stefan Miklos" 1-12; *Guns of Will Sonnett* "A Town in Terror" 2-7, 2-14; *Mod Squad* "The Up-Tight Town" 2-18; *Guns of Will Sonnett* "Jim Sonnett's Lady" 2-21; *Guns of Will Sonnett* "The Trial" 2-28; *Guns of Will Sonnett* "Three Stand Together" 9-15; *Mannix* "Color Her Kissing" 10-4; *Bold Ones: The Doctors* "What's the Price of a Pair of Eyes?" 10-5; *Mission: Impossible* "Double Circle" 11-9; *Hawaii Five-0* "All the King's Horses" 11-26; **1970** *Marcus Welby, M.D.* "The Merely Syndrome" 3-3; *Medical Center* "Scream of Silence" 10-28; **1971** *Mannix* "A Gathering of Ghosts" 2-6; *Mission: Impossible* "Blind" 9-18; *Cannon* "Scream of Silence" 10-12; **1972** *Hawaii Five-0* "Cloth of Gold" 2-8; *Mannix* "Death in the Fifth Gear" 3-8; **1973** *Mission: Impossible* "The Question" 1-19; *Streets of San Francisco* "An Eye for an Eye" 1-25; *Mannix* "Carol Lockwood, Past Tense" 1-28; *Banacek* "The Two Million Clams of Cap'n Jack" 2-7; *Cannon* "Murder for Murder" 2-7; *Owen Marshall, Counselor at Law* "Once a Lion" 9-19; *Cannon* "The Limping Man" 11-14; *Rookies* "The Sound of Silence" 12-17; **1974** *Ironside* "Class of '40" 2-7; *Barnaby Jones* "Gold Record for Murder" 2-10; *Hec Ramsey* "Scar Tissue" 3-16; *Cannon* "Voice from the Grave" 9-25; *Manhunter* "The Doomsday Gang" 10-23; **1975** *Caribe* "Vanished" 2-24; *Matt Helm* "Scavenger's Paradise" 10-11; *Marcus Welby, M.D.* "An End and a Beginning" 10-21; *Mobile One* episode 12-15; **1976** *Switch* "Come Die with Me" 1-27; *Streets of San Francisco* "Underground" 1-29; *McMillan and Wife* "All Bets Are Off" 12-5; *Barnaby Jones* "The Bounty Hunter" 12-16; **1977** *Fantastic Journey* "Vortex" 2-3; *Most Wanted* "The Spellbinder" 3-7; *Bionic Woman*

"Rodeo" 10-15; *Rockford Files* "Requiem for a Funny Box" 11-4; **1978** *Rockford Files* "White on White and Nearly Perfect" 10-20; *CHiPs* "Supercycle" 12-2; **1979** *Hawaii Five-0* "Good Help Is Hard to Find" 11-1; **1980** *Vegas* "A Deadly Victim" 12-3; **1981** *Hart to Hart* "Ex-Wives Are Murder" 1-20; **1982** *Fall Guy* "Guess Who's Coming to Town?"3-17; *Knight Rider* "Not a Drop to Drink" 11-5; **1983** *Fall Guy* "Spaced Out" 2-16.

TELEFILMS

1969 *The Young Lawyers* 10-24 ABC; **1974** *Fer-De-Lance* 10-18 CBS; **1981** *Golden Gate* 9-25 ABC.

Myrna Fahey
(born 1936, Maine; died May 6, 1973)

Beautiful Myrna Fahey starred in a 1961-62 sitcom, *Father of the Bride.* This was the highlight of her all too brief television career. She died on May 6, 1973 in Santa Monica, California, of un-stated causes, at age 34. She was survived bly her parents and a brother. During the early sixties she was seen frequently in guest roles, and seemed to be headed to a fine career.

GUEST CREDITS

1959 *Maverick* "Duel at Sundown" 2-1; *Line Up* "Dangerous Eden" 11-4; **1960** *Maverick* "A Flock of Trouble" 2-14; *Perry Mason* "The Case of the Nimble Nephew" 4-23; *Alaskans* "Calico"5-22; *Maverick* "Mano Nera" 10-23; *Thriller* "Girl with a Secret" 11-15; *Hawaiian Eye* "The Contenders" 11-30; *77 Sunset Strip* "The Dresden Doll" 12-23; **1961** *Acapulco* episode 3-27; *Checkmate* "Jungle Castle" 4-1; *Perry Mason* "The Case of the Violent Vest" 4-29; *Straightaway* "Troubleshooter" 12-22; *Surfside 6* "Pattern for a Frame" 12-25; **1962** *Laramie* "the Last Allegiance" 10-30; **1963** *77 Sunset Strip* "The Night Was Six Years Long" 2-8; *Hawaiian Eye* "The Sisters" 3-19; **1964** *Reporter* "Vote for Murder" 12-18; **1965** *Daniel Boone* "The Price of Friendship" 2-18; *Kraft Suspense Theatre* "Nobody Will Ever Know" 3-25; **1965** *Perry Mason* "The Case of the Gambling Lady" 4-8; 1966 *Perry Mason* "The Case of the Midnight Howler" 1-16; **1967** *Time Tunnel* "The Walls of Jerico" 1-27.

TELEFILM

1973 *The Great American Beauty Contest* 2-13 ABC.

Ron Feinberg

Primarily a seventies television actor, Ron's huge body and fierce countenance usuallly resulted in castings as thugs and merciless killers. *Mission: Impossible* used him in four episodes.

GUEST CREDITS

Alan Feinstein (a.k.a Alan Yorke)

(born September 8, 1941, New York City)

Primarily a television actor, Alan brought stage experience to two consecutive soap roles, in *Love of Life* (1965-68) and *The Edge of Night* (1969-74). He mixed seventies guest work with two series regular roles, on *Jigsaw John* (1976) and *The Runaways* (1979)

The eighties brought two additional regular roles in two abbreviated series, *The Family Tree* (1983) and *Berringers* (1985). He also had guest shots on *St. Elsewhere, Hardcastle and McCormick* and *Remington Steele* during the eighties. In 1988 he became a cast member of the soap *General Hospital*.

GUEST CREDITS

1974 *Kojak* "Wall Street Gunslinger" 10-6; **1975** *Rookies* "Death Lady" 10-21; *Cannon* "Fall Guy" 11-5; *Baretta* "When Dues Come Down" 11-12; *Harry O* "Portrait of a Murder" 11-20; *Bronk* "Deception" 12-7; *Medical Story* "Woman in White" 12-11; *Barnaby Jones* "Portrait of Evil" 12-18; **1977** *Charlie's Angels* "Dirty Business" 2-2; *Dog and Cat* "Live Bait" 3-19; *Streets of San Francisco* "Interlude" 4-28; **1978** *Charlie's Angels* "The Sand Castle Murders" 2-1; **1979** *Trapper John, M.D.*

1967 *I Spy* "Tonia" 1-4; **1968** *Cowboy in Africa* "African Rodeo" 1-15, 1-22; *Run for Your Life* "The Dead on Furlough" 2-21; **1969** *Hawaii Five-0* "Pray Love Remember, Pray Love Remember" 1-1; *High Chaparral* "Apache Trust" 11-7; **1970** *Mission: Impossible* "Terror" 2-15; *Mission: Impossible* "The Amateur" 11-14; **1971** *Hawaii Five-0* "No Bottles...No Cans...No People" 9-21; *Mission: Impossible* "The Miracle" 10-23; **1972** *The FBI* "Escape to Nowhere" 3-19; *Mission: Impossible* "Boomerang" 1-12; *Hawaii Five-0* "Little Girl Blue" 2-13; **1974** *Chase* "Hot Beef" 2-12; **1977** *Delvecchio* "A Madness Within" 2-27; *Switch* "The Legend of Macanuse" 10-21; **1978** *American Girls* "A Crash Course in Survival" 10-21.

TELEFILMS

1971 *Brian's Song* 11-30 ABC; **1973** *Dying Room Only* 9-18 ABC; *Hi Jack!* 9-26 ABC; *Money to Burn* 10-27 ABC; **1979** *The Man in the Santa Claus Suit* 12-22 NBC.

"Whose Little Hero Are You?" l2-30; **1980** *Vegas* "Judgment Pronounced" 5-27; **1982** *Cassie and Company* "Man Overboard" 6-29; **1983** *Fall Guy* "Death Boat" 2-2.

TELEFILMS

1977 *Alexander: The Other Side of Dawn* 5-16 NBC; *The Hunted Lady* ll-22; **1978** *The Users* l0-1 ABC; **1979** *The Two Worlds of Jennie Logan* l0-31 CBS.

Frank Ferguson
(born December 25, 1899; died September l2, 1978)

A staple of TV western series guest work, Frank Ferguson was a regular on *My Friend Flicka* (1956-57). But it was his 1964-69 role as the family patriarch on *Peyton Place* that established him so solidly in the national TV consciousness. His last television work was in a 1976 telefilm.

Frank's film career, dating from 1940, included roles in *They Died with Their Boots On, Rhapsody in Blue, Bend of the River, Battle Cry, Sunrise at Campobello, Pocketful of Miracles* and *Hush...Hush...Sweet Charlotte.*

GUEST CREDITS

1959 *Trackdown* "Terror" 2-4; *Texan* "Race for Life" 3-l6; *Tales of Wells Fargo* "Toll Road" 3-23; *Colt .45* "Law West of the Pecos" 6-7; *Alaskans* "Cheating Cheaters" l0-11; *Maverick* "Easy Mark" 11-l5; **1960** *Bonanza* "The Fear Merchants" 1-30; *Rifleman* "Hero" 2-2; *Wichita Town* "The Frontiersman" 3-2; *Perry Mason* "The Case of the Perjured Parrot" 3-19; *Sugarfoot* "Vinegaroon" 3-29; *Texan* "Quarantine" 7-4; *Lawman* "The Mad Bunch" l0-2; *Maverick* "Destination: Devil's Flat" l2-25; **1961** *Broncho* "Ordeal at Dead Tree" l-2; *Hawaiian Eye* "Made in Japan" l-4; *Perry Mason* "The Case of the Angry Dead Man" 2-25; *Destry* "Ride to Rio Verde" 4-l0; *Lawman* "Grub Stake" 4-16; *Wyatt Earp* "Wyatt Earp's Baby" 4-25; *Have Gun-Will Travel* "Bear Bait" 5-l3; *Tall Man* "The Great Western" 6-3; *Wagon Train* "The Ah Chung Story" 6-14; *Maverick* "Three Queens Full" 11-l2; *Target: The Corruptors* "Prison Empire" l2-15; **1962** *Lawman* "A Friend of the Family" 1-l4; *Maverick* "The Troubled Heir" 4-l; *National Velvet* "The Clown" 4-2l; *Alcoa Premiere* "A Place to Hide" 5-22; *Alfred Hitchcock Hour* "Night of the Owl" l0-4; **1963** *Perry Mason* "The Case of the Bluffing Blast" 1-l0; *Virginian* "If You Have Tears" 2-l3; **1964** *Temple Houston* "Sam's Boy" 1-23; *Twilight Zone* "Queen of the Nile" 3-6; *Wagon Train* "The Ben Engel Story" 3-16; *Voyage to the Bottom of the Sea* "The Sky Is Falling" l0-19; **1965** *Perry Mason* "The Case of the Golden Venom" 1-2l; **1970** *Land of the Giants* "The Marionettes" 3-l; **1971** *Adam-12* "The Sniper" l0-6; *The D. A.* "The People vs. Gayda" l0-8.

TELEFILMS

1969 *The Silent Gun* l2-16 ABC; **1976** *The Macahans* 1-19 ABC.

George "Shug" Fisher
(born 1907)

A most familiar character actor, George "Shug" Fisher entered films in 1943, ultimately appearing in

1-29; **1974** *Gunsmoke* "The Guns of Cibola Blanca"9-23, 9-30; **1975** *Kolchak: The Night Stalker* "The Knightly Murders" 3-7; *Petrocelli* "episode 20" 3-12; **1976** *City of Angels* "The House on Orange Grove Avenue" 3-16; **1978** *Starsky and Hutch* "Moonshine" 10-17.

TELEFILMS

1970 *Cutter's Trail* 2-10 CBS; **1973** *Key West* 12-10 NBC; **1975** *The Last Day* 2-15 NBC; *Huckleberry Finn* 3-25; **1976** *Richie Brockelman: Missing 24 Hours* 11-27 NBC; **1977** *The 3,000 Mile Chase* 6-16 NBC; **1979** *Louis L'Amour's "The Sacketts"* 5-15, 5-16 NBC.

films like *Mr. Roberts* and *The Man Who Shot Liberty Valance*. He became a regular on the country music show *Ozark Jubilee* in 1960, and followed with a regular slot on the syndicated 1961 adventure series *Ripcord*. Thereafter, he became a frequent guest on *Gunsmoke*, appearing in 18 episodes between 1962 and 1974.

In 1969 he began the recurring role of the rollicking character Shorty Kellems on *The Beverly Hillbillies*.

GUEST CREDITS

1961 *Have Gun-Will Travel* "The Revenger" 9-30; **1962** *Gunsmoke* "Chester's Indian" 5-12; **1963** *Have Gun-Will Travel* "Brotherhood" 1-5; **1964** *Gunsmoke* "No Hands" 2-8; *Gunsmoke* "Kitty Cornered" 4-18; **1965** *Gunsmoke* "Deputy Festus" 1-16; *Gunsmoke* "The Storm" 9-25; **1966** *Gunsmoke* "The Good People" 10-15; *Wild Wild West* "The Night of the Poisonous Posey" 10-28; **1967** *Gunsmoke* "Fandango" 2-11; *Wild Wild West* "The Night of the Cut Throats" 11-17; **1968** *Gunsmoke* "A Noose for Dobie Price" 3-4; *Gunsmoke* "Railroad" 11-25; *Gunsmoke* "Johnny Cross" 12-23; **1969** *Gunsmoke* "The Still" 11-10; **1970** *Gunsmoke* "Gentry's Law" 10-12; *Bonanza* "El Jefe" 11-15; **1971** *Gunsmoke* "The Tycoon" 1-25; *Gunsmoke* "Waste"

Ed Flanders

(born December 29, 1934, Minneapolis, Minnesota; died Feburary 22, 1995)

The receipient of three Emmy Awards, Ed

Flanders got his acting start in his hometown of Minneapolis during the fifties, eventually working his way to Broadway. He received a Tony in 1974 for his work in *A Moon for the Misbegotten*; a repeat of this on *ABC Theatre* earned him his first Emmy in 1976 (Best Supporting Actor in a Special).

Ed began his television career in a 1969 episode of *Hawaii Five-0*; he ultimately did four additional guest shots on that series. Much of his seventies work was in telefilms, miniseries and specials; he won a second Emmy for his impersonation of Harry S. Truman on the PBS production of *Harry S. Truman: Plain Speaking* (1977).

A third Emmy was earned for his excellent portrayal of the wise senior physician on *St. Elsewhere* (Best Actor in a Drama Series, 1983).

He died February 22, 1995; his family requested that details of his death not be released.

GUEST CREDITS

1969 *Hawaii Five-0* "Up Tight" 1-15; *Daniel Boone* "The Traitor" 10-30; **1970** *Hawaii Five-0* "Three Dead Cows at Makapu" 2-25, 3-4; **1971** *Name of the Game* "Beware of the Watch Dog" 3-5; *Bearcats!* "Hostage" 10-14; *McMillan and Wife* "Husbands, Wives and Killers" 11-10; 1*Mission: Impossible* "Blues" 11-20; **1972** *Hawaii Five-0* "While You're At It, Bring in the Moon" 2-1; *Mannix* "A Walk in the Shadows" 2-9; *Cade's County* "Blackout" 3-26; *Banyon* "Just Once" 12-22; **1974** *Marcus Welby, M.D.* "The Comeback" 1-1; *Hawaii Five-0* "One Born Every Minute" 1-8; *Barnaby Jones* "Death on Deposit" 12-3; **1975** *Hawaii Five-0* "And the Horse Jumped Over the Moon" 2-18.

TELEFILMS

1971 *Travis Logan, D.A.* 3-11 CBS; *Goodbye Raggedy Ann* 10-22 CBS; **1972** *The Snoop Sisters* 12-18 NBC; **1973** *Hunter* 1-9 CBS; **1974** *Indict and Convict* 1-6 ABC; *Things in Their Season* 11-27 CBS; **1975** *The Legend of Lizzie Borden* 2-10 ABC; *Attack on Terror: The FBI Versus The Ku Klan* 2-20, 2-21 CBS; *Eleanor and Franklin* 1-11, 1-12 ABC; **1977** *The Amazing Howard Hughes* 4-13, 4-14

CBS; *Mary White* 11-18 ABC; **1979** *Salem's Lot* 11-17, 11-24 CBS; **1981** *Skokie* 11-17 CBS; **1982** *Tomorrow's Child* 3-22 ABC; **1983** *Special Bulletin* 3-20 NBC.

Bill Fletcher

(born 1922)

Angular and thin-faced, Bill Fletcher often played conniving characters during a television career that dated from 1949. Absent from television during the early sixties, he was seen often in guest roles, beginning in 1967.

GUEST CREDITS

1967 *Mission: Impossible* "The Legacy" 1-7; *Invaders* "The Betrayed" 3-28; *Ironside* "Light at the End of the Journey" 11-9; *Wild Wild West* "The Night of the Iron Fist" 12-8; **1969** *Land of the Giants* "Deadly Lodestone" 2-2; *The FBI* "Moment of Truth" 3-30; **1970** *McCloud* "Our Man in Paris" 10-21; **1971** *Alias Smith and Jones* "Never Trust an Honest Man" 4-15; *Mission: Impossible* "Mindbend" 10-9; *Sarge* "Identity Crisis" 10-12; **1972** *Mod Squad* "Deal with the Devil" 1-11; *Ghost Story* "Bad Connection" 10-6; *Alias Smith and Jones* "The Ten Days That Shocked Kid Curry" 11-4; *Search* "The Bullet" 12-20; **1973** *Kung Fu* "A Praying

Mantis Kills" 3-22; *Griff* "Her Name Was Nancy" 12-8; *McCloud* "The Barefoot Girls on Bleeker Street" 9-22; *Rockford Files* "In Pursuit of Carol Thorne" 11-8; **1974** *Mannix* "The Ragged Edge" 3-31; **1975** *Manhunter* "Web of Fear" 1-1; *Cannon* "Killer on the Hill" 1-29; *Six Million Dollar Man* "Taneha" 2-2; *S.W.A.T.* "Courthouse" 11-1; *Switch* "The Cold War Con" 12-9; *Blue Knight* "Two to Make Deadly" 12-17; **1976** *Police Story* "Eamon Kinsella Royce" 2-20; **1977** *Six Million Dollar Man* "Death Probe" 1-9, 1-16; *Switch* "Camera Angles" 1-30; *Bionic Woman* "Max" 12-3; **1978** *Lucan* "How Do You Run Forever?" 1-9; **1979** *Charlie's Angels* "Angels in a Box" 2-14; **1980** *Vegas* "The Man Who Was Twice".

TELEFILMS

1971 *Alias Smith and Jones* 1-5 ABC; **1973** *Murdock's Gang* 3-20 CBS; **1977** *The Man with the Power* 5-24 NBC; **1978** *Keefer* 3-16 ABC.

Jay C. Flippen

(born March 6, 1898, Little Rock, Arkansas; died February 3, 1971)

Beginning in 1915, Jay C. began traveling in minstrel shows, doing vaudeville and performing as a comic. In 1928 and 1929 he made a couple of two-reeler comedy films and later appeared in a couple of 1934 movies. During his early years he understudied Al Jolson for a time.

He turned to films strongly in 1947 in Brute Force; his later films included *Winchester '73, The Lemon Drop Kid, Bend of the River, Six Bridges to Cross, Strategic Air Command, Oklahoma!, Kismet, Run of the Arrow, Cat Ballou, Firecreek* and *Hello Dolly*.

Jay C. began working in television in 1954 and was a favorite on *Climax*, doing 4 episodes. He also had credits on *Playhouse 90* and *Goodyear Playhouse* in the pre-1959 period. He became a regular on *Ensign O'Toole* during 1962-63.

The loss of a leg from gangrene in 1965 did not sideline Jay C. for long and he continued his fine work. He died of an aneurysm in 1971, survived by his wife.

GUEST CREDITS

1959 *Rawhide* "Incident of the Widowed Dove" 1-30; *Alcoa Theater* "The Best Way to Go" 6-15; *Untouchables* "You Can't Pick the Numbers" 12-24; **1960** *Thriller* "The Guilty Men" 10-18; *Route 66* "Legacy for Lucia" 11-25; **1962** *Untouchables* "Fall Guy" 1-11; *Follow the Sun* "The Last of the Big Spenders" 1-14; *Bus Stop* "Verdict of Twelve" 3-1; **1963** *Dick Powell Show* "Last of the Private Eyes" 4-30; *Burke's Law* "Who Killed Wade Walker?" 11-15; *Bonanza* "The Prime of Life" 12-29; **1964** *Rawhide* "Incident at Hourglass" 3-12; *Burke's Law* "Who Killed Molly?" 3-27; *Gunsmoke* "Owney Tupper Had a Daughter" 4-4; **1965** *Rawhide* "Josh" 1-15; **1966** *Virginian* "The Wolves Up Front, the Jackals Behind" 3-23; *Man Called Shenandoah* "The Imposter" 4-4; **1967** *Road West* "Charade of Justice" 3-27; *Virginian* "The Barren Ground" 12-6; **1968** *Virginian* "Stopover" 1-8; **1969** *Judd, for the Defense* "Borderline Girl" 1-10; *Name of the Game* "The Incomparable Connie Walker" 1-24; *Bracken's World* "King David" 10-3; *Name of the Game* "Chains of Command" 10-17.

TELEFILMS

1970 *The Old Man Who Cried Wolf* 10-13 ABC; **1971** *Sam Hill: Who Killed the Mysterious Mr. Foster* 2-1 NBC.

Med Flory

Med's first significant television exposure came in 1956-57 as a vocalist on *The Ray Anthony Show*. That was his last series regular stint until 1988 when he played a sheriff on *High Mountain Rangers*. In between, he guested on numerous action oriented series, including 4 episodes of *Daniel Boone*. Tall and raw-boned, Med was well suited to action roles. He is also a composer.

GUEST CREDITS

1960 *Maverick* "Dodge City or Bust" 12-11; **1961** *Bonanza* "The Dark Gate" 3-4; *Lawman* "Whiphand" 4-23; *Perry Mason* "The Case of the Misguided Missile" 5-6; *Perry Mason* "The Case of the Crying Comedian" 10-14; *Surfside 6* "Affairs at Hotel Delight" 11-6; **1962** *77 Sunset Strip* "Mr. Bailey's Honeymoon" 1-12; *Maverick* "Marshall Maverick" 3-11; **1963** *Law Man* "Mountain Man" 3-25; *Bonanza* "The Saga of Whizzer White" 4-23; **1965** *Daniel Boone* "A Rope for Mingo" 12-2; **1966** *The FBI* "The Forests of the Night" 1-2; *12 O'Clock High* "Which Way the Wind Blows" 1-24; **1967** *Monroes* "Wild Bull" 2-15; *Cimarron Strip* "The Roarer" 11-2; **1968** *Daniel Boone* "Orlando, the Prophet" 2-29; *Daniel Boone* "The Far Side of Fury" 3-7; **1969** *Daniel Boone* "Love and Equity" 3-

3; **1970** *Mannix* "War of Nerves" 3-14; *Gunsmoke* "Sergeant Holly" 12-14; **1971** *Alias Smith and Jones* "Journey from San Juan" 4-8; *Bonanza* "The Grand Swing" 9-19; *Nichols* "Peanuts and Crackerjacks" 11-4; **1972** *Mission: Impossible* "Break!" 9-16; **1974** *Gunsmoke* "A Town in Chains" 9-16; *Police Woman* "The Stalking of Joey Marr" 11-22; **1975** *Starsky and Hutch* "The Texas Longhorn" 9-17; *Switch* "Mistresses, Murder and Millions" 12-23; **1979** *Salvage-1* "Confederate Gold" 5-28; **1980** *Lou Grant* "Goop" 11-24; **1982** *Lou Grant* "Jazz" 1-4; *Magnum, P.I.* "The Elmo Zeller Story" 3-18.

TELEFILMS

1972 *Home for the Holidays* 11-28 ABC; **1974** *Things in Their Season* 11-27 CBS; **1977** *Deadly Game* 12-3; *It Happened One Christmas* 12-11 ABC; **1978** *Wild and Wooly* 2-20 ABC; **1981** *The Killing of Randy Webster* 3-11 CBS.

Dick Foran

(born John Nicholas Foran, June 18, 1910, Flemington, N. J.; died August 10, 1979)

The son of a U. S. Senator, Dick was educated at Princeton University. With some experience as a band vocalist, Dick made his film debut in 1934.

The following year Warner Bros. made him their only singing cowboy in a series of a dozen westerns, running through 1937. He then turned to non-western films, although he starred in a 1942 episodic serial, *Riders of Death Valley*, that featured a very expensive cast including Buck Jones, Charles Bickford, Leo Carillo, Noah Beery, Jr. and Guinn "Big Boy" Williams.

Dick was in television early on, appearing in 5 *Studio One* productions in the 1950-54 period, with multiple appearances on *Kraft Television Theatre, Science Fiction Theatre, Climax* and *Crossroads*. He had a recurring role on Walt Disney's *The Swamp Fox* and was in strong demand for guest roles on western TV series from 1958 through the sixties. He also appeared in 5 episodes of the syndicated *Death Valley Days*.

His only series regular slot was on the sitcom *O. K. Crackerby* (1965-66).

Dianne Foster watches as Richard Boone, as Palladin, registers concern over the handkerchief in his hand. Kent Smith, at right, observes. This scene is from a 1961 episode of *Have Gun--Will Travel* called "Shadow of a Man" (CBS).

GUEST CREDITS

1959 *Yancy Derringer* "Two of a Kind" 1-1; *Perry Mason* "The Case of the Bedeviled Doctor" 4-4; *Playhouse 90* The Sound of Eden" 10-15; *Perry Mason* "The Case of the Garrulous Gambler" 10-17; **1960** *Untouchables* "The Frank Nitti Story" 4-28; *Wanted: Dead or Alive* "The Choice" 12-14; *Laramie* "A Sound of Bells" 12-27; **1961** *Deputy* "The Dream" 2-4; *Dante's Inferno* "Aces and Eights" 2-13; *Laramie* "Bitter Glory" 5-2; *Perry Mason* "The Case of the Renegade Refugee" 12-8; *Laramie* "Bitter Glory" 5-2; *Perry Mason* "The Case of the Renegade Referee" 12-8; *Laramie* "The Killer Legend" 12-12; *Dr. Kildare* "Hit and Run" 12-14; **1962** *77 Sunset Strip* "The Gang's All Here" 6-29; *Lawman* "The Wanted Man" 9-25; *Laramie* "Double Eagles" 11-20; *Cheyenne* "Wanted for the Murder of Cheyenne Bodie" 12-10; **1963** *Dakotas* "Requiem at Dancer's Hill" 2-18; *Gunsmoke* "With a Smile" 3-30; *Great Adventure* "The Great Diamond Mountain" 11-8; **1964** *Virginian* "A Man Called Kane" 5-6; **1965** *Rawhide* "The Testing Post" 11-30; *Daniel Boone* "Dan'l Boone Shot a B'ar" 9-15; **1967** *Virginian* "Requiem for a Country Doctor" 1-25; *Virginian* "Reckoning" 9-13; **1968** *Bonanza* "Mark of Guilt" 12-15; *Virginian* "Big Tiny" 12-8; *Adam-12* "Log 122" 12-22.

Dianne Foster

(born October 31, 1928, Edmonton, Alberta, Canada)

Dianne began her film career in 1952 and began receiving television guest roles in the late fifties. During the 1960-61 period she was one of TV's most-seen actresses, especially in westerns and detective series.

GUEST CREDITS

1960 *Riverboat* "Path of an Eagle" 2-1; *Overland Trail* "Lawyer in Petticoats" 3-27; *General Electric Theater* "Mystery of Malibu" 4-10; *Hawaiian Eye* "Dead Ringer" 5-11; *Bourbon Street Beat* "Reunion" 5-27; *Peter Gunn* "Mask of Murder" 10-10; *Outlaws* "The Fortune Stone" 12-15; **1961** *Have Gun-Will Travel* "Shadow of a Man" 1-28; *Laramie* "Bitter Glory" 5-2; *Checkmate* "Kill the Sound" 11-15; *Outlaws* "Roly" 11-23; *Detectives* "Crossed Wires" 1-19; *Ben Casey* "He Thought He Saw an Albatross" 2-4; *77 Sunset Strip* "To Catch a Mink" 5-10; **1964** *Perry Mason* "The Case of the Betrayed Bride" 10-22; **1965** *Rogues* "The Diamond-Studded Pie" 1-31; *Fugitive* "Scapegoat" 2-2; *Ben Casey* "A Little Fun to Match the Sorrow" 3-8; *Slattery's People* "Question: What Time Is the Next Bandwagon?" 4-9; *Honey West* "A Matter of Wife and Death" 10-8; *Perry Mason* "The Case of the Silent Six" 11-21; **1966** *Big Valley* "Caesar's Wife" 10-3.

Ron Foster

Primarily a television actor, Ron appeared in guest roles sporadically from 1958. His best known role was a starring vehicle in a *Twilight Zone* episode called "The Seventh Is Made Up of Phantoms". During 1982 he appeared on the soap *As the World Turns*.

GUEST CREDITS

1959 *Rawhide* "Incident in No Man's Land" 6-12; *Men into Space* "Space Trap" 11-18; **1961** *Gunsmoke* "Bless Me Till I Die" 4-22; *Bat Masterson* "The Fatal Garment" 5-25; *Gunsmoke* "Nina's Revenge" 12-16; **1963** *Twilight Zone* "The

Seventh Is Made Up of Phantoms" 12-6; **1964** *Outer Limits* "The Mice" 1-6; *Bonanza* "Invention of a Gunfighter" 9-20; **1965** *Combat* "Crossfire" 11-2; **1966** *Bonanza* "Peace Officer" 2-6; *12 O'Clock High* "Gauntlet of Fire" 9-9; **1967** *Run for Your Life* "Rendevous in Tokyo" 2-13; *Bonanza* "Sense of Duty" 9-24; **1971** *O'Hara, U. S. Treasury* "Operation: Crystal Strings" 12-3; **1974** *Petrocelli* " Double Negative" 10-30; **1976** *Petrocelli* "Deadly Journey" 3-3.

TELEFILMS

1977 *Relentless* 9-14 CBS; **1980** *Attica* 3-2 ABC.

Byron Foulger

(born 1900; died 1970)

A mild looking little man with wire rimmed glasses, Byron's lengthy film and television career found him much in demand for milquetoast charaters, some with remarkable inner strength.

He attended The University of Utah and, following little theatre experience, landed on Broadway during the early twenties. Byron toured the Northwest and came to the Pasadena Playhouse around 1930. He made a film debut in 1937 in *The Prisoner*

of Zenda, and went on to act in nearly 300 films and several episodic serials.

His television credits (from 1950) were more modest but he worked sparingly in the medium until shortly before his death, of a heart condition, in 1970. Byron was a semi-regular on *Petticoat Junction* during 1968-70, playing a train engineer. He was the father of actress Rachael Ames.

GUEST CREDITS

1959 *Rin Tin Tin* "The Failure" 5-8; *Markham* "The Bay of the Dead" 8-8; *Twilight Zone* "Walking Distance" 10-30; **1960** *Rawhide* "Incident of the Druid's Curse" 1-8; **1962** *Gunsmoke* "The Hunger" 11-17; **1963** *Rawhide* "Incident at Confidence Creek" 11-28; **1964** *Wagon Train* "The Geneva Balfour Story" 1-20; *Bonanza* "King of the Mountain" 2-23; **1966** *Laredo* "A Taste of Money" 4-28; *Gunsmoke* "The Hanging" 12-31; **1967** *Time Tunnel* "Visitors from Beyond the Stars" 1-13; **1968** *Wild Wild West* "The Night of the Juggernaut" 10-11; *Adam-12* "Log 161-And You Want Me to Get Married?" 10-26; *Mod Squad* "You Can't Tell the Players without a Programmer" 10-29; **1969** *Mod Squad* "Lisa" 11-4.

TELEFILM

1970 *The Love War* 3-10 ABC.

Michael Fox

(born 1921; died June 1, 1996)

Following a 1946 stage debut, Michael Fox began a film career of over 100 movies in 1952. A character actor, he has frequently been cast as a heavy. His only television series regular role came in 1955-56, in *Casablanca*. He did have a recurring role on *Perry Mason*, appearing in 13 episodes (1959-1963).

He was still going strong in the late eighties with a stint on the soap *The Bold and the Beautiful*.

GUEST CREDITS

1959 *Perry Mason* "The Case of the Caretaker's Cat" 3-7; *Richard Diamond* episode 4-5; *Perry Mason* "The Case of the Lame Canary" 6-27; *Perry Mason* "The Case of the Spurious Sister" 10-3; **1960** *Perry Mason* "The Case of the Prudent Prosecutor" 1-30; *Twilight Zone* "Nightmare As a Child" 4-29; *Perry Mason* "The Case of The Singular Double" 10-8; **1961** *Perry Mason* "The Case of the Wintry Wife" 2-18; *Twilight Zone* "Mr. Dingle, the Strong" 3-3; *Perry Mason* "The Case of the Duplicate Daughter" 5-20; **1962** *Perry Mason* "The Case of the Promoter's Pillbox" 5-19; *Perry Mason* "The Case of the Bogus Books" 9-27; *Virginian* "The Brazen Bell" 10-10; *Perry Mason* "The Case of the Stand-In

Sister" 11-29; **1963** *Perry Mason* "The Case of the Golden Oranges" 3-7; *Perry Mason* "The Case of the Witless Witness" 5-16; *Burkes Law* "Who Killed Wade Walker?" 11-15; *Gunsmoke* "Carter Caper" 11-16; *Perry Mason* "The Case of the Festive Falcon" 11-28; **1964** *Twilight Zone* "Sounds of Silence" 5-4; **1965** *Burke's Law* "Who Killed Rosie Sunset?" 1-27; *Big Valley* "Forty Rifles" 9-22; **1966** *Gunsmoke* "Wishbone" 2-19; *Lost in Space* "The Ghost Planet" 9-28; *Voyage to the Bottom of the Sea* "Deadly Invasion" 11-20; **1967** *Lost in Space* "Cave of the Wizards" 2-22; *Gunsmoke* "Hard Luck Henry" 10-23; **1968** *Wild Wild West* "The Night of the Death Maker" 2-23; **1971** *Mod Squad* "And a Little Child Shall Bleed Them" 11-23; **1972** *O'Hara, U. S. Treasury* "Operation: Dorais" 2-4; *Rookies* "The Good Die Young" 11-13; **1973** *Columbo* "The Most Dangerous Match" 3-4; **1974** *Lucas Tanner* "Cheers" 12-4; *Kolchak: The Night Stalker* "The Energy Eater" 12-13; **1971** *Rockford Files* "Just by Accident" 2-28; **1981** *Buck Rogers* "Time of the Hawk" 1-15; *Quincy,M.E.* "Jury Duty" 2-18.

TELEFILMS

1968 *Now You See It, Now You Don't* 11-11 NBC; **1969** *Seven in Darkness* 9-23 ABC; **1971** *If Tomorrow Comes* 12-7 ABC; **1972** *Two for the Money* 2-26; *The Judge and Jake Wyler* 12-2 NBC; **1980** *Trouble in High Timber Country* 6-27 ABC; **1983** *Dempsey* 9-28 CBS.

Ivor Francis

(born 1918, Toronto, Canada; died October 22, 1986)

Charactor actor Ivor Frances frequently appear as befuddled professional men in stage, film and television roles. He was especially busy during the seventies in television guest roles and was a regular on the abbreviated sitcom *Dusty's Trail*. He guested on numerous sitcoms: *Get Smart, Flying Nun, The Mary Tyler Moore Show, The Odd Couple, Love, American Style, The Partridge Family, The Jeffersons* and *Barney Miller*.

Ivor was the father of Genie Francis, noted star of several soap operas.

GUEST CREDITS

1962 *Defenders* "The Locked Room" 2-18; **1969** *Judd, for the Defense* "The View from the Ivy Tower" 3-7; **1971** *Men at Law* "Yesterday is But a Dream" 3-31; *Bold Ones: The Doctors* "Broken Melody" 9-19; *Bonanza* "Rock-a-Bye Hoss" 10-10; *Night Gallery* "The Phantom Farmhouse" 10-20; **1972** *Cannon* "Blood on the Vine" 1-18; *Bold Ones: The Lawyers* "Lisa, I Hardly Knew You" 2-13; *Night Gallery* "Little Girl Lost" 3-1; **1973** *Search* "The Mattson Papers" 2-28; **1974** *Kojak* "Deliver Us Some Evil" 2-13; *Kung Fu* "The Passion of Cher Yi" 2-28; *Magician* "The Illusion of Lethal Playthings" 3-18; *Hawaii Five-0* "I'll Kill 'Em Again" 9-24; **1975** *Kojak* "Night of the Piraeus" 1-26; *Starsky and Hutch* "Death Notice" 10-15; *Waltons* "The Breakdown" 10-16; *Six Million Dollar Man* "Target in the Sky" 10-26; **1976** *McCoy* "New Dollar Day" 1-25; *Bronk* "Ordeal" 3-7; *Quest* "Portrait of a Gunfighter" 12-22; **1977** *Barnaby Jones* "Duet for Dying" 2-24; *Little House on the Prairie* "Here Come the Brides" 12-5; **1978** *Eddie Capra Mysteries* "Who Killed Charles Pendragon?" 9-8; **1979** *Lou Grant* "Hit" 3-5; *Waltons* "The Burden" 1-25; **1980** *Waltons* "The Remembrance" 1-24; *Lou Grant* "Pack" 10-27; **1981** *240-Robert* "Hostages" 3-21; *Waltons* "The Threshold" 4-2; *Quincy, M.E.* "Memories of Allison" 10-2.

TELEFILMS

1970 *Hunters Are for Killing* 3-12 CBS; **1973** *The Suicide Club* 2-13 ABC; **1973** *Outrage* 11-28 ABC; **1977** *Spider-Man* 1-14 CBS.

Eduard Franz

(born October 31,, 1902, Milwaukee, Wisconsin; died February 10, 1983)

Onstage from the late twenties, Eduard made his screen debut in 1947. His dignified manner and deep voice frequently brought castings as professionals and kindly parents and advisors. During 1958-59 he became a regular on the television version of *Zorro*, but his most famous role was as the wise clinic director on *Breaking Point* (1963-64).

GUEST CREDITS

1960 *June Allyson Show* "The Test" 10-20; **1961** *Barbara Stanwyck Theatre* "Shock" 3-6; **1963** *Wide Country* "Whose Hand at My Throat?" 2-14; **1964** *Bob Hope Chrysler* Theater "Murder in the First "10-9; **1966** *Fugitive* "The Sharp Edge of Chivalry" 10-4; *The FBI* "The Plague Merchant" 10-30; **1967** *Invaders* "Summit Meeting" 10-31, 11-7; **1968** *The*

FBI "Region of Peril" 2-25; **1969** *Mannix* "Death Run" 1-4; *The FBI* "Target of Interest" 9-14; **1970** *Interns* "The Fever" 12-4; *Medical Center* "The Savage Image" 12-30; **1974** *Rookies* "Judgment" 10-28; *Gunsmoke* "In the Performance of Duty" 11-18; **1975** *Streets of San Francisco* "Murder by Proxy" 10-23; **1978** *Bionic Woman* "The Pyramid" 1-14; *Hawaii Five-0* "A Stranger in His Grave" 3-23; **1979** *Hawaii Five-0* "The Spirit Is Willie" 1-25; *Vegas* "An Eastern Princess" 5-9.

TELEFILMS

1970 *Brotherhood of the Bell* 9-17 CBS; **1974** *Panic on the 5:22* 11-20 ABC.

Charles Fredericks

(born 1919; died 1970)

A hefty villain in numerous television westerns, Charles' talents were especially used on *Gunsmoke* (4) and *Maverick* (4). He made a television debut in 1952, and worked in films like *Tender Is the Night* and *To Kill a Mockingbird*.

GUEST CREDITS

1959 *Rifleman* "The Boarding House" 2-24; *Rough Riders* "The Promise" 4-2; *Gunsmoke* "Fawn"4-4; *Colt .45* "Don't Tell Joe" 6-14; *77 Sunset Strip* "Clay Pigeon" 10-23; *Wyatt Earp* "Behan Shows His Hand" 10-27; *Wyatt Earp* "The Ring of Death" 11-3; **1960** *Maverick* "The Cruise of the Cynthia B" 1-10; *Goodyear Theater* "Capital Gains" 2-1; *Rawhide* "Incident of the Arana Scar" 4-22; *Colt .45* "The Gandy Dancers" 5-10; *Gunsmoke* "The Deserter" 6-4; *Klondike* " 88 Keys to Trouble" 11-4; *Maverick* "The Maverick Line" 11-20; *Maverick* "Bolt From the Blue" 11-27; *Bat Masterson* "Last Stop to Austin" 12-1; **1961** *Rawhide* "Incident in the Middle of Nowhere" 4-7; *Tall Man* "An Item for Sale" 10-14; **1962** *Bonanza* "Inga, My Love" 4-15; *Maverick* "The Money Machine" 4-8; *Gunsmoke* "False Front" 12-22; **1963** *Laramie* "The Fugitive" 2-12; *Rifleman* "Requiem at Mission Springs" 3-4; *Virginian* "Ride a Dark Trail" 9-18; *Dr. Kildare* "The Ratpack and the Prima Donna" 11-28; **1969** *Gunsmoke* "Coreyville" 10-6.

Joan Freeman

(born 1942, Council Bluffs, Iowa)

Raised in Burbank, California, beautiful Joan Freeman naturally gravitated to acting. She made her film debut in 1956, but is best remembered for her starring role in Don Knotts' *The Reluctant Astronaut* (1967). During 1961-62 Joan co-starred in *Bus Stop*, her only television series regular role. Thereafter, she worked in guest roles for over two decades. She still works occasionally on television, doing guest appearances.

GUEST CREDITS

1961 *National Velvet* "The Beauty Contest" 3-12; *Wagon Train* "Alias Bill Hawks" 5-15; **1962** *Gunsmoke* "Phoebe Strunk" 11-10; *Virginian* "The Devil's Children" 12-5; *Perry Mason* "The Case of the Fickle Filly" 12-13; **1963** *Dakotas* "Trouble at French Creek" 1-28; *Hawaiian Eye* "Blow Low, Blow Blue" 3-5; *Greatest Show on Earth* "Lion on Fire" 9-17; *Arrest and Trial* "Whose Little Girl Are You?" 10-27; *Virginian* "Stopover in a Western Town" 11-27; **1964** *Travels of Jaimie McPheeters* "The Day of the 12 Candles" 2-23; *Outer Limits* "Behold, Eck!" 10-3; **1965** *Bonanza* "The Trap" 2-28; *Virginian* "Timberland" 3-10; *Loner* "The Vespers" 9-25; *Virginian* "Blaze of Glory" 12-29; **1966** *Man from UNCLE* "The Bat Cave Affair" 4-1; **1969** *Land of the Giants* "Chamber of Fear" 11-16; *Lancer* "Legacy" 12-9; **1974** *Adam-12* "X-Force" 12-3; **1978** *Project UFO* "Sighting 4005: The Medicine Bow Incident" 3-26; **1979** *Quincy, M.E.* "No Way to Treat a Flower" 9-20; **1980** *CHiPs* "Dynamite Alley" 3-29; **1982** *Chicago Story* "Bad Blood" 4-30.

TELEFILM

1978 *Death Moon* 5-31 CBS.

Kathleen Freeman

(born February 17, 1919, Chicago, Illinois)

The daughter of vaudevillians, Kathleen was a part of the act at age 2. A veteran television performer in 5 sitcom series regular roles, dating from

1953, Kathleen has helped keep TV audiences giggling for forty years. She has also done a number of dramatic series guest appearances to compliment her comedic emphasis.

Her film career, encompassing 80 movies, began in 1948, with *Naked City*. She has had roles in *Singin' In the Rain, The Greatest Show on Earth, North to Alaska, The Nutty Professor, Myra Breckenridge* and *The Blues Brothers*. Freeman appeared in four films with Jerry Lewis, serving as a foil for his goofy personna.

Kathleen has had a remarkable number of guest shots on sitcoms over the years: *The Donna Reed Show* (2), *Margie* (2), *Beverly Hillbillies* (6), *The Lucy Show* (2), *The Dick Van Dyke Show* (2), *Hogan's Heroes* (3), *Gomer Pyle, U.S.M.C.* (2), *Growing Pains, ALF, Mr. Belvedere* and *Head of the Class.* Two of her *Beverly Hillbillies* episodes were classics: she teamed with Phil Silvers to sell the Clampetts The Washington Monument, The Pentagon and The Lincoln Memorial during their visit to Washington.

GUEST CREDITS

1960 *Hawaiian Eye* "And Then There Were Three" 1-27; **1961** *Bus Stop* "The Man from Bootstrap" 11-26; **1962** *Detectives* "Pandora's Box" 2-2; *Rawhide* "The Greedy Town" 2-16; **1963** *Alfred Hitchcock Hour* "You'll Be the Death of Me" 10-18;

1965 *Slattery's People* "Question: Bill Bailey, Why Did You Come Home?" 4-2; *Alfred Hitchcock Hour* "The World's Oldest Motive" 4-12; **1967** *Laredo* "Scourge of San Rosa" 1-20; *Man from UNCLE* "The When in Roma Affair" 3-17; *Dragnet* "The Big Gun" 4-27; *Bonanza* "Maestro Hoss" 5-7; *Ironside* "Message from Beyond" 9-14; *Man from UNCLE* "The Prince of Darkness Affair" 10-2, 10-9; **1968** *Daniel Boone* "The Fleeing Nuns" 10-24; *High Chaparral* "A Way of Justice" 12-13; **1970** *Bonanza* "Long Way to Ogden" 2-22; **1972** *Cannon* "The Big Rip-Off" 11-1; **1975** *Kolchak: The Night Stalker* "The Youth Killer" 3-14; **1977** *Kojak* "Case without a File" 12-17.

TELEFILMS

1970 *But I Don't Want to Get Married* 10-6 ABC; **1972** *Call Her Mom* 2-15 ABC; **1973** *Hitched* 3-31 NBC; **1975** *The Daughters of Joshua Cabe* 1-28 NBC; **1979** *The Last Ride of the Dalton Gang* 11-20 NBC.

Mona Freeman

(born June 9, 1926, Baltimore, Maryland)

Mona became a Powers Model and, after seeing her picure on a magazine cover, Howard Hughes signed her to a film contract. Paramount bought the contract and she made the first of 36 films in 1944. Her baby face resulted in teen-age castings for years, usually playing daughters or sisters to the lead actresses.

She made her television debut in 1955 and worked often in the medium in the following ten years. Freeman stated that she much preferred television acting to films. Her fifties credits included appearances on *Climax* (5), *Studio '57, Playhouse 90* (2), *Ford Theater* (2), *Lux Video Theater, Matinee Theater, Wagon Train* and *Pursuit*.

Her sixties work included 7 appearances on the acclaimed *U.S. Steel Hour*.

GUEST CREDITS

1959 *Wanted: Dead or Alive* "Breakout" 9-26;

Penny Fuller

(born 1940, Durham, North Carolina)

Penny made her television debut in 1962, becoming a regular on the soap *The Edge of Night* in 1964. She was seen in a variety of seventies TV series guest roles, often in very assertive roles.

In 1982 Penny received an Emmy as Outstanding Supporting Actress for her role in a telefilm, *The Elephant Man*. She later became a regular on two brief eighties series, *Bare Essence* (1983) and *Fortune Dane* (1986). Later eighties guest shots included *Simon and Simon*, *Love Boat* (2), *McGruder and Loud*, *Matlock*, *Murder, She Wrote* and *China Beach*.

GUEST CREDITS

1963 *East Side/West Side* "Age of Consent" 9-30; **1969** *Judd, for the Defense* "The Crystal Maze" 1-3; *The FBI* "The Doll Courier" 12-21; **1972** *The FBI* "Deadly Species" 3-5; **1973** *Banacek* "The Greatest Collection of Them All" 1-24; *The FBI* "The Wedding Gift" 2-11; **1974** *Six Million Dollar*

Maverick "Cat of Paradise" 10-11; *June Allyson Show* "The Pledge" 10-26; **1960** *Maverick* "Curse of the Cynthia B" 1-10; *Millionaire* "Millionaire Margaret Stoneham" 2-3; *Johnny Ringo* "Mrs. Ringo" 2-11; *U.S. Steel Hour* "The Women of Hadley" 2-24; *U.S. Steel Hour* "Revolt in Hadley" 3-9; *U.S. Steel Hour* "The Girl Who Knew Too Much" 4-20; *Chevy Mystery Show* "Fear Is the Parent" 6-26; *Thriller* "The Mark of Hand" 10-4; *Michael Shayne* "Blood on Biscayne Bay" 12-2; *U.S. Steel Hour* "Operation Northstar" 12-28; **1961** *Checkmate* "Don't Believe a Word She Says" 1-28; *U.S. Steel Hour* "The Two Worlds of Charlie Gordon" 2-22; *Tall Man* "Petticoat Crusade" 11-18; *U.S. Steel Hour* "The Bitter Sex" 12-27; **1962** *U.S. Steel Hour* "Murder on the Agenda" 8-22; *Perry Mason* "The Case of the Lurid Letter" 12-6; **1964** *Perry Mason* "The Case of the Illicit Illusion" 4-9; *Perry Mason* "The Case of the 12th Wildcat" 10-30; **1966** *Branded* "McCord's Way" 1-30.

TELEFILM

1972 *Welcome Johnny Bristol* 1-30 CBS.

Man "Population Zero" 1-18; *Barnaby Jones* "The Platinum Connection" 1-20; *Chopper One* "Deadly Carrier" 3-21; **1975** *Medical Center* "The Invisible Wife" 2-10; *Barnaby Jones* "Poisoned Pigeon" 3-25; **1976** *McNaughton's Daughter* "The Smashed Lady" 3-31; *Family* episode 12-7; *Movin' On* "Woman of Steel" 3-31; **1979** *Trapper John, M.D.* "One for My Baby" 11-18; **1981** *Trapper John, M.D.* "Have I Got a Girl for You" 2-1; **1983** *Simon and Simon* "Design for Killing" 2-10.

TELEFILMS

1972 *Women in Chains* 1-25 ABC; **1979** *Ebony, Ivory and Jade* 8-3 CBS; **1980** *Amber Waves* 3-9 ABC; **1981** *The Elephant Man* 1-4 ABC; **1982** *A Piano for Mrs. Cimono* 2-3 CBS; *Lois Gibbs and The Love Canal* 2-17 CBS; **1983** *Your Place or Mine* 3-2 CBS; *Intimate Agony* 3-21 ABC.

James Gammon

(born 1940)

James became involved in television during the early sixties as a cameraman and director at TV stations in Orlando, Florida. He made a film debut in 1967 in *Cool Hand Luke* and began appearing on television in the same time frame. He worked in television throughout the seventies and well into the eighties, specializing in roles as rurals and rednecks. James was a favorite guest star on *The Waltons*, with 8 guest appearances.

After his move to California he purchased a theater and became co-founder of MET Theatre (1972-83). He was honored as Best Actor in 1974, by the L. A. Drama Critics Award, for his work in *Dark at the Top of the Stairs*.

His film work picked up during the eighties, with roles in *Urban Cowboy, The Milagro Beanfield War* and *Major League*.

GUEST CREDITS

1966 *Wild Wild West* "The Night of the Freebooters" 4-1; *Monroes* "Night of the Wolf" 9-14; **1967** *Invaders* "The Spores" 10-17; *Virginian* "A Small Taste of Justice" 12-20; **1969** *Lancer* "Blind Man's Bluff" 9-23; **1970** *High Chaparral* "Only the Bad Come to Sonora" 10-2; **1973** *Waltons* "The Fawn" 11-8; *Gunsmoke* "Susan Was Evil" 12-3; **1974** *Barnaby Jones* "The Deadly Jinx" 1-13; *Waltons* "The Ghost Story" 2-14; *The FBI* "Diamond Run" 3-10; *Waltons* "The Thoroughbred" 9-26; **1975** *Waltons* "The Shivaree" 1-30; *Streets of San Francisco* "River of Fear" 2-13; *Waltons* "The Song" 2-20; *Waltons* "The Venture" 3-6; *Waltons* "The Fighter" 9-25; *Barnaby Jones* "Final Burial" 12-11; **1976** *Cannon* "Quasar Kill" 2-4; *Waltons* "The Comeback" 10-7; *Most Wanted* "The Torch" 12-18; **1977** *Charlie's Angels* "Angels on Ice" 9-21; **1978** *Charlie's Angels* "Angels in the Stretch" 12-20.

TELEFILMS

1970 *The Intruders* 11-10 NBC; **1974** *The FBI Story: The FBI Versus Alvin Karpis, Public Enemy Number One* 11-8 CBS; **1979** *Louis L'Amour's "The Sacketts"* 5-15, 5-16 NBC; **1980** *Rage* 9-25 NBC; **1981** *The Big Black Pill* 1-29 NBC; **1982** *Deadly Encounter* 12-18 CBS; **1983** *Women of San Quentin* 10-23 NBC.

Nancy Gates

An RKO starlet of the forties, Nancy had several featured roles in undistinguished fifties films. She began appearing on television in 1953 and was in numerous fifties productions: *Pepsi Cola Playhouse* (3), *General Electric Theater* (3), *Schlitz Playhouse of Stars* (2), *Alfred Hitchcock Presents* (2), *Loretta Young Show* (2), *Damon Runyan Theater* (2), *The Millionaire*, *Wagon Train* and *Maverick*.

Nancy worked in guest roles until the late sixties. In 1960 she had given birth to twin daughters and left acting to spend more time with her family, which also included two sons.

GUEST CREDITS

1959 *77 Sunset Strip* "The Girl Who Couldn't Remember" 1-23; *Maverick* "Passage to Fort Doom" 3-8; *Millionaire* "Millionaire Marcia Forrest" 3-25; *Riverboat* "Payment in Full" 9-13; *Men into Space* "First Woman on the Moon" 12-16; **1960** *Bourbon Street Beat* "Kill with Kindness" 1-4; *Lineup* "Prince of Penmen" 1-6; *Hawaiian Eye* "Then There Were Three" 1-27; *Laramie* "Death Wish" 2-2; *Wichita Town* "The Legend of Tom Horn" 3-30; **1961** *Hong Kong* "Murder by Proxy" 3-1; *Zane Grey Theater* "Storm Over Eden" 5-4; *Detectives* "A Barrel Full of Monkeys" 10-27; *Tales of Wells Fargo* "Jeremiah" 11-11; *Adventures in Paradise* "The Fires of Kanau" 11-19; *Bus Stop* "Accessory By Consent" 11-19; **1962** *New Breed* "Wings for a Plush Horse "2-20; *Gunsmoke* "The Prisoner" 5-19; *Wagon Train* "The Shiloh Degnan Story" 11-7; *Lloyd Bridges Show* "The Sound of the Angels" 12-18; **1963** *Lloyd Bridges Show* "Waltz of the Two Commuters" 4-16; **1964** *Wagon Train* "The Grover Allen Story" 2-3; *Perry Mason* "The Case of the Woeful Widower" 3-26; *Virginian* "Portrait of a Widow"12-9; **1965** *Burke's Law* "Who Killed the Jackpot?" 4-21; *Perry Mason* "The Case of the Candy Queen" 9-26; *Rawhide* "Clash at Broken Bluff" 11-2; *Loner* "The House Rule at Mrs. Wayne's" 11-6; *Amos Burke, Secret Agent* "The Man's Men" 12-8; **1966** *Bonanza* "Brother's Keeper" 3-6; **1967** *Danny Thomas Hour* "The Scene" 9-25; **1969** *Mod Squad* "An Eye for an Eye" 10-7.

Tom Geas

After a 1962 television debut Tom worked mainly in crime dramas, with multiple appearances on *Mission: Impossible* and *Adam-12*.

GUEST CREDITS

1962 *Perry Mason* "The Case of the Fickle Filly" 12-13; **1968** *Mission: Impossible* "The Contender" 10-6, 10-13; **1969** *Mannix* "Memory: Zero" 11-22; **1970** *Mission: Impossible* "Chico" 1-25; *Adam-12* "Log 144-Bank Robbery" 4-11; *Adam-12* "Log Twenty-Five-Indians" 11-28; **1971** *Mannix* "The Color of Murder" 2-27; *The D. A.* "The People vs. Drake" 9-17; *Mission: Impossible* "The Tram" 10-2; *O'Hara, U. S. Treasury* "Operation: Deadhead" 11-12; **1972** *Ironside* "A Man Named Arno" 3-9; *The FBI* "Dark Journey" 3-12; **1973** *Madigan* "Illusion in Terror" 10-23; **1974** *Barnaby Jones* "Friends till Death" 2-17; *Adam-12* "Sunburn" 2-19; **1975** *Bronk* "Betrayal" 12-14; **1976** *Blue Knight* "A Slower Beat" 3-3; **1977** *Rockford Files* "Requiem for a Funny Box" 11-4; **1982** *Simon and Simon* "Earth vs. Stacy" 2-9.

TELEFILMS

1969 *The Silent Gun* 12-16 ABC; **1971** *The D. A.: Conspiracy to Kill* 1-11 NBC.

Frank Gerstle

(born 1915; died 1970)

Onscreen from 1951, Frank Gerstle was typecast as policemen and detectives, in films and on television. Much of his large screen work was in B-films, but in later years, he appeared in *The Silencers, Bullitt* and *I Love You, Alice B. Toklas*.

GUEST CREDITS

1959 *Wyatt Earp* "Wyatt's Decision" 9-22; *Millionaire* "Millionaire Mitchell Gunther" 12-2; *Man and the Challenge* "Man without Fear" 12-19; **1960** *Bat Masterson* "Mr. Fourpaws" 2-18; *Colt .45* "Attack" 5-4; **1961** *Wanted: Dead or Alive* "Baa-Baa" 1-4; *Rawhide* "Incident of the Broken Word" 1-

20; *Wagon Train* "The Jed Polke Story" 3-1; 77 *Sunset Strip* "Common Denominator" 4-14; *Perry Mason* "The Case of the Traveling Treasure" 11-4; **1962** *Perry Mason* "The Case of the Hateful Hero" 10-18; **1963** *Laramie* "No Place to Run" 2-5; **1964** *Perry Mason* "The Case of the Woeful Widower" 3-26; **1967** *Bonanza* "False Witness" 10-22; **1968** *Ironside* "Force of Arms" 1-4; **1969** *Lancer* "Blind Man's Bluff" 9-23.

TELEFILM

1970 *San Francisco International* 9-29 NBC.

Elaine Giftos

(born 1945, Pittsfield, Mass.)

A shapely seventies/eighties actress, Elaine became a regular on *The Interns* (1970-71), less than a year after her television debut. Subsequently, she made 3 appearances on *Love, American Style* and guested on *The Partridge Family* 4 times. Much of her later work was on crime series.

During the mid-eighties she worked in guest roles on *Knight Rider, Murder, She Wrote, Blacke's Magic* and *What a Country!*.

GUEST CREDITS

1970 *Bonanza* "The Lady and the Mark" 2-1; 1971 *Cade's County* "Safe Deposit" 10-3; *Ironside* "Murder Impromptu" 11-2; 1972 *Adam-12* "Lost and Found" 10-4; *Banyon* "The Lady Killer" 12-8; *Cool Million* "The Million Dollar Misunderstanding" 12-20; 1973 *Marcus Welby, M.D.* "The Problem with Charlie" 1-30; *Chase* "The Garbage Man" 11-27; 1974 *New Perry Mason* "The Case of the Tortured Titan" 1-13; *Kolchak: The Night Stalker* "Matchemonedo" 12-13; 1975 *Marcus Welby, M.D.* "Save the Last Dance for Me" 2-18; *Cannon* "To Still the Voice" 12-31; 1976 *Hawaii Five-0* "The Last of the Great Paperhangers" 11-4; 1977 *Hawaii Five-0* "The Friends of Joey Kaliman" 10-13; 1978 *Six Million Dollar Man* "A Date with Danger" 2-20, 2-27; 1979 *Quincy, M.E.* "Hot Ice" 10-18; 1980 *Hawaii Five-0* "episode 264" 3-8; 1982 *Trapper John, M.D.* "Ladies in Waiting" 1-31; 1982 *Magnum, P.I.* "Mixed Doubles" 12-2; 1983 *Matt Houston* "The Centerfold Murders" 9-30.

TELEFILMS

1975 *The Secret Night Caller* 2-18 NBC; 1977

Stonestreet: Who Killed the Centerfold Model? 1-16 NBC; 1979 *Breaking Up Is Hard to Do* 9-5, 9-7 ABC; 1981 *Through the Magic Pyramid* 12-6, 12-13 NBC; 1982 *Games Mother Never Taught You* 11-27 CBS.

Sam Gilman

(born 1915, Salem, Mass.; died December 3, 1985)

A powerful stage presence propelled Sam Gilman into a friendship with Marlon Brando. He toured with Brando in *Arms and the Man* and later appeared in 6 Brando films, beginning with *Desiree* in 1954. Other significant film credits included *One-Eyed Jacks, PT-109, The Young Lions, The Missouri Breaks* and *Every Which Way But Loose.*

Excellent in western roles, Sam earned a television series regular role on *Shane* (1966).

GUEST CREDITS

1960 *Troubleshooter* "Incident at Rain Mountain" 2-16; *Rifleman* "Heller" 2-23; *Untouchables* "The Waxey Gordon Story" 11-10; *Surfside 6* "The

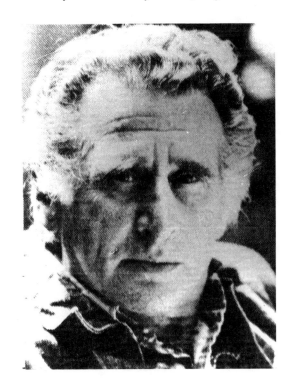

Frightened Canary" 12-12; **1961** *Surfside 6* "License to Steal" 2-6; *Roaring 20's* "Lucky Charm" 2-18; *Thriller* "Yours Truly, Jack the Ripper" 4-11; **1962** *Cain's Hundred* "Blues for a Junkman" 2-20; *Tales of Wells Fargo* "Vignette of a Sinner" 6-2; **1963** *Sam Benedict* "Green Room, Gray Morning" 1-19; **1964** *Ben Casey* "For a Just Man Falleth Seven Times" 4-15; **1966** *Gunsmoke* "Snap Decision" 9-17; **1967** *Felony Squad* "The Desperate Silence" 2-13; *Gunsmoke* "Noose of Gold" 3-4; *Fugitive* "Death of a Very Small Killer" 3-21; *Dragnet* "The Big Pyramid" 11-30; *Gunsmoke* "Rope Fever" 12-4; *Judd, for the Defense* "The Living Victim" 12-15; *Guns of Will Sonnett* "The Secret of Hangtown Mine" 12-22; **1968** *Star Trek* "Spectre of the Gun" 10-25; *Mannix* "In Need of a Friend" 11-23; **1975** *Waltons* "The Emergence" 11-6; **1978** *Little House on the Prairie* "The Rivals" 1-9.

TELEFILMS

1974 *The Morning After* 2-13 ABC; *The Tribe* 12-11 ABC.

Harold Gould
(born Harold V. Goldstein, December 10, 1923,

Schenectady, New York)

One of the most gifted players of the television era, Harold Gould has been featured in every genre from adventure, crime, western and sci-fi to sitcoms. He has appeared in over 400 television episodes, 25 films and over 50 stage plays.

After World War II service in the U. S. Army, he earned a Masters and Ph. D. from Cornell University and taught speech and drama for ten years, at Cornell and at U.C.L.A. In 1960 he decided to become an actor, debuting in films and on television in 1961. During the sixties he displayed fine comic timing and flair on TV shows like *The Jack Benny Program* (3), *Dennis the Menace, Hazel, Get Smart, Hogan's Heroes* (2), *The Flying Nun* (2) and *I Dream of Jeannie.* He became a series regular on *The Long Hot Summer* (1965-66) and *He and She* (1967-68).

During the seventies he had one of his best known roles as the father of the title character in *Rhoda* (1974-78), earning an Emmy for the role in 1974. In 1978 he co-starred with Stefanie Powers in a brief detective series called *Feather and Father.*

The eighties found him in series regular roles in three abbreviated series: *Park Place* (1981), *Foot in the Door* (1983) and *Under One Roof* (1985). During 1990 he had a starring role in *Singer and Sons.* Other featured work during the eighties included guest roles on *St. Elsewhere, Golden Girls, Trapper John, M.D., Scarecrow and Mrs. King,* and *L. A. Law.* He also co-starred with Katherine Hepburn in an excellent 1986 telefilm, *Mrs. Delafield Wants to Marry.* Gould earned a Cable Ace Award for work on *Ray Bradbury Theater.*

Harold has truly become one of America's acting treasures.

GUEST CREDITS

1961 *Cain's Hundred* "Markdown on a Man" 10-11; *Follow the Sun* "Another Part of the Jungle" 10-29; **1962** *Route 66* "Go Read the River" 3-16; *Virginian* "The Accomplice" 12-19; **1963** *Empire* "Stopover on the Way to the Moon" 1-1; *Lieutenant* "The Two-Star Giant" 10-5; *Route 66* "The Stone Guest" 11-8; *Twilight Zone* "Probe Seven, Over and Out" 11-29; **1964** *Twilight Zone* "The Bewitchin'

Pool" 6-19; *Virginian* "The Brazos Kid" 10-21; *Gunsmoke* "Doctor's Wife" 10-24; *Man from UNCLE* "The Double Affair" 11-17; *Virginian* "All Nice and Legal" 11-25; **1965** *Dr. Kildare* "Please Let My Baby Live"1-28; *12 O'Clock High* "The Threat" 3-19; *Virginian* "Farewell to Honesty" 3-24; *Fugitive* "Wings of an Angel" 9-14; *Virginian* "Day of the Scorpion" 9-22; *The FBI* "Slow March Up a Steep Hill" 10-10; *Convoy* "No More Souvenirs" 11-26; **1966** *The FBI* "The Man Who Went Mad by Mistake" 3-6; *Green Hornet* "May the Best Man Lose" 12-23; **1967** *The FBI* "The Courier" 1-15; *Invaders* "The Experiment" 1-17; *Fugitive* "Concrete Evidence" 1-24; *Run for Your Life* "The Assassin" 2-27; *Felony Squad* "The Savage Streets" 4-3; *Big Valley* "Cage of Eagles" 4-24; *Wild Wild West* "The Night of the Bubbling Death" 9-8; *Judd, for the Defense* "Shadow of a Killer" 10-6; *Invaders* "The Trial" 10-10; *Garrison's Gorillas* "Friendly Enemies" 11-21; **1968** *The FBI* "The Daughter" 1-4; *Daniel Boone* "The Imposter" 1-18; *Big Valley* "The Challenge" 3-18; *Judd, for the Defense* "Weep the Hunter Home" 11-8; *Lancer* "The Last Train for Charlie Poe" 11-26; *Wild Wild West* "The Night of the Avaricious Actuary" 12-6; *The FBI* "The Butcher" 12-8; **1969** *Big Valley* "The Royal Road" 3-3; *Mission: Impossible* "The Code" 9-28; **1970** *Lancer* ""Dream of Falcons" 4-7; *High Chaparral* "A Good Sound Profit" 10-30; **1971** *The FBI* "The Stalking Horse" 1-10; *Cannon* "A Lonely Place to Die" 11-16; *Mod Squad* "The Loser" 11-30; **1972** *The FBI* "The Test" 2-20; *Delphi Bureau* "The Man Upstairs/The Man Downstairs Project" 10-26; *Mannix* "One Step to Midnight" 11-12; *Hawaii Five-0* "V for Vashon" 11-14, 11-21, 11-28; *Streets of San Francisco* "The Takers" 12-2; **1973** *Cannon* "The Prisoners" 2-21; *Ironside* "The Armageddon Gang" 10-11; **1974** *Chase* "Joe Don Ducks" 1-16; *Streets of San Francisco* "Death and the Favored Few" 3-14; *Gunsmoke* "The Guns of Cibola Blanca" 9-23, 9-30; *Police Story* "Fathers and Sons" 10-1; *Petrocelli* "Death in High Places" 10-23; *Petrocelli* "Mirror, Mirror on the Wall" 11-6; **1975** *Cannon* "Tomorrow Ends at Noon" 3-19; *Hawaii Five-0* "The Case Against McGarrett "10-17; *Rookies* "Measure of Mercy" 10-28; **1976** *Medical Story* "The Quality of Mercy" 1-28; *Police Story* "Eamon Kinsella Royce" 2-20;

1977 *Police Story* "The Blue Fog" 2-1; *Hallmark Hall of Fame* "Have I Got a Christmas for You" 12-16; **1979** *Rockford Files* "Never Send a Boy King to Do a Man's Job" 3-3; **1979** *Lou Grant* episode 10-29; **1981** *Charlie's Angels* "He Married An Angel" 1-31.

TELEFILMS

1971 *Ransom for a Dead Man* 3-11; *A Death of Innocence* 11-26 CBS; **1973** *Murdock's Gang* 3-20 CBS; **1975** *Medical Story* 9-4 NBC; **1976** *How to Break Up a Happy Divorce* 10-6 NBC; *Never Con a Killer* 12-6 ABC; **1979** *Better Late Than Never* 10-17 NBC; *The Eleventh Victim* 11-6 CBS; *Aunt Mary* 12-5 CBS; *The Man in the Santa Claus Suit* 12-23 NBC; **1980** *Kenny Rogers as the Gambler* 4-8 CBS; *Moviola: The Scarlett O'Hara War* 5-19 NBC; *Moviola: The Silent Lover* 5-20 NBC; *King Crab* 6-15 ABC; **1981** *Born to Be Sold* 11-2 NBC; **1983** *Kenny Rogers as the Gambler: The Adventure Continues* 11-28, 11-29 CBS.

Coleen Gray

(born Doris Jensen, October 23, 1922, Staplelhurst, Nebraska)

After graduating from Hamline University, with honors, Coleen was signed to a 20th Century Fox contract after she had done Midwest stage experience. She made her screen debut in 1945 in *State Fair*, beginning a film career that extended to the early seventies, with numerous roles in westerns and crime movies. She came to television in 1951, with many of her roles in the same genres as her films.

She was a series regular in *Window on Mainstreet* in 1961-62 and later was a cast member on two soaps, *Bright Promise* and *Days of Our Lives*.

GUEST CREDITS

1959 *Markham* "Paris Encounter" 5-16; **1960** *Maverick* "Substitute Gun" 4-2; *Deputy* "A Time to Sow" 4-23; *Perry Mason* "The Case of the Wandering Widow" 10-22; *General Electric Theater* "Learn

to Say Goodbye" 12-4; **1961** *Lawman* "Mark of Cain" 3-26; *Tall Man* "The Woman" 10-28; *Bus Stop* "Jaws of Darkness" 12-31; **1962** *Perry Mason* "The Case of the Glamerous Ghost" 2-3; *Alfred Hitchcock Present* "The Opportunity" 5-22; *Rawhide* "The Devil and the Deep Blue Sea" 9-28; *Wide Country* "A Devil in the Chute" 11-8; *77 Sunset Strip* "The Floating Man" 11-9; **1964** *Perry Mason* "The Case of the Fifty Millionth Frenchman" 12-20; *Kraft Suspense Theatre* "The Threatening Eye" 3-12; **1965** *Branded* "Seward's Folly" 10-17; **1966** *Perry Mason* "The Case of the Fanciful Frail" 3-29; **1967** *Run for Your Life* "A Choice of Evils" 4-3; **1968** *Ironside* "The Challenge" 2-8; **1969** *Name of the Game* "Blind Man's Bluff" 10-3; **1970** *Adam-12* "Log Fifty Five-Missing Child" 10-31; **1971** *The FBI* "The Eye of the Needle" 1-24; *Bold Ones: The Doctors* "An Absence of Lonliness" 1-24; *Mannix* "The Man Outside" 11-24; **1972** *Sixth Sense* "Whisper of Evil" 4-8; **1974** *McCloud* "The Gang That Stole Manhattan" 10-13; **1975** *McCloud* "Return to the Alamo" 3-30; **1977** *McCloud* "London Bridges" 3-6.

TELEFILMS

1971 *Ellery Queen: Don't Look Behind You* 11-19 CBS; **1979** *The Best Place to Be* 5-27, 5-28 NBC.

Gilbert Green

(born 1915; died 1984)

Gilbert made his film debut during 1961, in *By Love Possessed,* after a lengthy stage career. His last film was *Norma Rae,* in 1979. Green's television career extended from 1960 to 1982.

GUEST CREDITS

1960 *Detectives* "Cop on Trial" 11-4; **1962** *Gunsmoke* "Durham Bull" 3-31; *Empire* "Ballard Number One" 10-2; *Untouchables* "The Pea" 10-23; **1963** *Virginian* "the Judgment" 1-16; *Untouchables* "Globe of Death" 2-5; **1964** *Alfred Hitchcock Hour* "The Sign of Satan" 5-8; *Perry Mason* "The Case of the Latent Lover" 12-3; *Rawhide* "No Dogs or Drovers" 12-18 ; **1966** *Blue Light* "The Secret War" 3-2; **1968** *Rat Patrol* "The Fatal Reunion Raid" 1-15; *Star Trek* "Patterns of Force" 2-16; *Judd, for the Defense* "Transplant" 10-4; **1969** *Big Valley* "Danger Road" 4-21; *Mannix* "The Sound of Darkness" 12-6; **1970** *Medical Center* "Runaway" 1-21; **1972** *Ironside*

"The Savage Sentry" 9-21; **1975** *Starsky and Hutch* "Snow Storm"10-1; *Matt Helm* "Murder on Ice" 10-25; **1976** *Police Woman* "Wednesday's Child" 2-3; *McCloud* "Bonnie and McCloud" 10-24; *Baretta* "Crazy Annie" 11-24; **1977** *Streets of San Francisco* "Interlude" 4-28; *Rockford Files* "Requiem for a Funny Box" 11-4; **1978** *Charlie's Angels* "Mother Goose Is Running for His Life" 2-15; *Rockford Files* "A Three Day Affair with a Thirty Day Escrow" 11-10; **1979** *Charlie's Angels* "An Angel Called Rosemary" 5-2; *Rockford Files* "Just a Couple Guys" 12-14; **1981** *Quincy, M.E.* "Scream to the Skies" 2-11; **1982** *Magnum, P.I.* "Almost Home" 12-9.

TELEFILMS

1970 *The Psychiatrist: God Bless the Children* 12-4 NBC; **1973** *Honor thy Father* 3-1 CBS; **1975** *Starsky and Hutch* 4-30 ABC.

Virginia Gregg

(born 1917, Harrisburg, Illinois; died September 15, 1986)

Virginia moved from her native Illinois to California at age six. A musician, she played bass violin with the Pasadena Symphony, and with The Singing Strings, on the CBS and Mutual Radio Networks.

At Mutual, she began doing emceeing and some commentaries, and this evolved into small parts. Her remarkable vocal range helped her gain a reputation as one of radio's greatest voices. She was featured on radio shows like *One Man's Family, Dr. Kildare, Lum and Abner* and *Have Gun-Will Travel*, often playing multiple characters on a single show.

Virginia became a member of the outstanding cast of the *Gunsmoke* radio show in 1952, working in countless episodes until it left the air in 1962. The television version of *Gunsmoke* used her talents in 8 episodes from 1958.

She worked in all manner of guest roles during the sixties; in 1967 she became a part of Jack Webb's "stock company", doing 13 episodes of *Dragnet* and 5 episodes of *Adam-12*. When telefilms came into vogue she appeared on 17 of these vehicles.

Her wonderful talent and versatility permitted her to slip easily into all types of character roles, and few actresses of the television era could match her skill and contributions. Virginia died of lung cancer on September 15, 1986, survived by three sons.

GUEST CREDITS

1959 *Goodyear Theater* "Success Story" 2-16; *Rawhide* "Incident of the Misplaced Indians" 5-1; *Wanted: Dead or Alive* "The Healing Woman" 9-12; *Phillip Marlowe* "The Ugly Duckling" 10-6; **1960** *Man from Blackhawk* "The Last Days of Jesse Turnbull" 4-1; *Broncho* "Winterkill" 5-31; *Deputy* "Bitter Root" 11-5; **1961** *Rebel* "Paperback Hero" 1-29; *Bat Masterson* "A Lesson in Violence" 2-23; *Gunsmoke* "Minnie" 4-15; *Thriller* "Mr. George" 5-9; *Gunsmoke* "The Imposter" 5-13; *Hawaiian Eye* "Satan City" 9-27; *Perry Mason* "The Case of the Pathetic Patient"10-28; **1962** *Ben Casey* "An Uncommonly Innocent Killing" 3-7; *Have Gun-Will Travel* "Don't Shoot the Piano Player" 3-10; *Lawman* "Clooty Hunter" 3-11; *General Electric Theater*

"My Dark Days" 3-18; *Hawaiian Eye* "Koko Kate" 6-13; *Gunsmoke* "The Search" 9-15; *77 Sunset Strip* "The Raiders" 11-2; *Gunsmoke* "Phoebe Strunk" 11-10; *Going My Way* "A Matter of Principle" 11-21; *Hawaiian Eye* "Shannon Mallory" 12-18; **1963** *Eleventh Hour* "Which Man Will Die?" 1-2; *Twilight Zone* "Jess-Belle" 2-14; *Empire* "A House in Order" 3-5; *Rawhide* "Incident of the Comanchero" 3-22; *Alfred Hitchcock Hour* "An Hour Away from Home" 9-27; *Breaking Point* "There Are the Hip and There Are the Square" 10-14; *Temple Houston* "Jubilee" 11-14; *77 Sunset Strip* "Deposit with Caution" 11-29; **1964** *Twilight Zone* "Masks" 3-20; *Rawhide* episode 4-2; *Breaking Point* "Confounding Her Astronomers" 4-6; *Kraft Suspense Theatre* "The Rubrioz Ring" 5-28; *Wagon Train* "The John Gillman Story" 10-4; *Bonanza* "Logan's Treasure" 10-18; *Alfred Hitchcock Hour* "Consider Her Ways" 12-28; **1965** *Alfred Hitchcock Hour* "Thou Still Unravished Bride" 3-22; *Fugitive* "A.P.B." 4-6; *Legend of Jesse James* "Three Men from Now" 9-13; *Perry Mason* "The Case of the Silent Six" 11-21; *Perry Mason* "The Case of the Velvet Claws" 12-5; **1966** *Ben Casey* "In Case of Emergency, Cry Havoc" 1-3; *Run for Your Life* "Meantime We Shall Express Our Darker Purpose" 1-10; *Ben Casey* "For San Diego, You Need a Different Bus" 1-17; *Ben Casey* "Fun and Games and Other Tragic Things" 1-31; *Gunsmoke* "Sanctuary" 2-26; *Girl from UNCLE* "The Danish Blue Affair" 10-25; **1967** *Big Valley* "The Stallion" 1-30; *Dragnet* "The Big Candy Store" 3-9; *Dragnet* "The Big Jade" 3-23; *Guns of Will Sonnett* "A Son for a Son" 10-20; *Dragnet* "The Big Pyramid" 11-30; **1968** *Dragnet* "The Big Clan" 2-8; *Dragnet* "The Big Gambler" 3-21; *Judd, for the Defense* "The Name of the Game Is Acquittal" 10-18; *Outcasts* "Take Your Lover in the Ring" 10-28; *Dragnet* "Robbery-DR-15" 11-7; *Dragnet* "Public Affairs-DR-14" 11-28; *Mod Squad* "Twinkle, Twinkle Little Starlet" 12-17; **1969** *Gunsmoke* "The Twisted Heritage" 1-6; *Mod Squad* "A Hint of Darkness, A Hint of Light" 2-11; *Dragnet* "Juvenile-Dr-35; *Dragnet* "Personnel-The Shooting" 9-18; *Dragnet* "Homicide-The Student" 9-25; *Mannix* "Color Her Missing" 10-4; *Ironside* "Eye of the Hurricane" 10-9; **1970** *Adam-12* "Log 54-Impersonation" 2-7; *Dragnet* "Missing Persons-The Body" 3-

5; *Dragnet* "I.A.D.-The Receipt" 3-26; *Dragnet* "Burglary-Baseball" 4-9; *Adam-12* "Log 75-Have a Nice Weekend" 11-7; **1971** *Mannix* "The Color of Murder" 2-27; *Mod Squad* "Welcome to Our City" 3-2; *Interns* "The Choice" 3-26; *O'Hara, U. S. Treasury* "Operation: Crystal Springs" 12-3; **1972** *Emergency* episode 1-29; *Adam-12* "Dirt Duel" 9-13; *Sixth Sense* "Gallows in the Wind" 12-16; **1973** *Cannon* "He Who Digs a Grave" 9-12; *Adam-12* "Capture" 11-14; **1974** *Chase* "Right to an Attorney" 1-8; *Cannon* "Bobby Loved Me" 2-27; *Ironside* "The Lost Cotillion" 10-31; *Kolchak: The Night Stalker* "The Spanish Moss Murders" 12-6; **1975** *Streets of San Francisco* "Letters from the Grave" 1-6; *Rockford Files* "Roundabout" 3-7; *Adam-12* "Something Worth Dying For" 3-13, 3-20; *Six Million Dollar Man* "The Return of the Bionic Woman, Part II" 9-21; **1976** *Streets of San Francisco* "The Honorable Profession" 1-15; **1977** *Police Woman* "The Buttercup Killer" 1-13; *Streets of San Francisco* "Hang Tough" 2-17; **1978** *Project UFO* "Sighting 4013" 6-4; **1980** *Charlie's Angels* "Of Ghosts and Angels" 1-2.

TELEFILMS

1968 *Prescription: Murder* 2-20 NBC; **1969** *Dragnet* 1-27 NBC; **1970** *The D. A.: Conspiracy to Kill* 1-11 NBC; *Along Came a Spider* 2-3 ABC; *Quarantined* 2-24 ABC; *The Other Man* 10-19 NBC; *Crowhaven Farm* 11-24 ABC; **1972** *Emergency!* 1-15 NBC; *All My Darling Daughers* 1 11-22 ABC; **1973** *The Stranger* 2-26 NBC; *Chase* 3-24 NBC; **1975** *Attack on Terror: The FBI vs. the Ku Klux Klan* 2-20, 2-21 CBS; *You Lie So Deep, My Love* 2-25 ABC; **1977** *Man from Atlantis* 3-4 NBC; **1978** *Little Women* 10-2, 10-3 NBC; **1981** *Evita Peron* 2-23, 2-24 NBC; **1982** *Forbidden Love* 10-18 CBS.

James Griffith

(born February 13, 1919, Los Angeles, Calif.)

Following two tours of duty with The U. S. Marines, James made a film debut in 1944. He really hit his stride in films by 1948, appearing in 50 movies by 1960, the majority being westerns.

He began his television career in 1953, and it was accelerated with the advent of TV western series. Virtually every significant western series used his talents in guest roles and he found time to appear on series like *Perry Mason, The Fugitive* and *Medical Center.* His only regular role was on *Sheriff of Cochise* (1959-60).

This fine veteran was seen as late as 1982 in a *Little House on the Prairie* episode. His contributions to the western genre, films as well as television, were exceptional.

GUEST CREDITS

1959 *Steve Canyon* "The Prisoner" 1-22; *Restless Gun* "Dead Man's Hand" 3-16; *Texan* "No Way Out" 6-15; *Wagon Train* "The Esteban Zamora Story" 10-21; **1960** *Rawhide* "Incident of the Devil and His Due" 1-22; *Bonanza* "Silent Thunder" 12-12; **1961** *Laramie* "Cactus Lady" 2-21; *Checkmate* "One for the Book" 3-18; *Cheyenne* "The Frightened Town" 3-20; *Rawhide* "Incident in the Middle of Nowhere" 4-7; *Tall Man* "A Kind of Courage" 4-8; *Thriller* "Parasite Mansion" 4-25; *Wagon Train* "The Duke Shannon Story" 4-26; *Lawless Years* "The Jonathan Willis Story" 9-8; *Perry Mason* "The Case of the Posthumous Painter" 11-11; **1962** *Thriller* "The Storm" 1-22; *Bronco* "The Last Letter" 2-5; *Have Gun-Will Travel* "The Waiting Room" 2-

25; *Tall Man* "Trial by Fury" 4-14; *Empire* "A Place to Put a Life" 10-9; *Laramie* "Double Eagles" 11-20; **1963** *G. E. True* "The Moonshiners" 2-24; *Ben Casey* "Suffer the Little Children" 2-25; *Gunsmoke* "Quint's Indian" 3-2; *Have Gun-Will Travel* "The Savages" 3-10; *Untouchables* "Torpedo" 5-7; *Cheyenne* "Man Alone" 10-15; *Rawhide* "Incident of the Prophecy" 11-21; *Great Adventure* "Wild Bill Hickok-The Legend and the Man" 11-22; **1964** *Wagon Train* "The Geneva Balfour Story" 1-20; *Gunsmoke* "The Bassops" 2-22; *Perry Mason* "The Case of the Fatal Fetish" 3-4; *Fugitive* "The Homecoming" 4-7; *Daniel Boone* episode 11-5; *Slattery's People* "Question: What Is the Name of the Game?" 11-9; *Wagon Train* "The Nancy Styles Story" 11-22; **1965** *Rogues* "Bow to a Master" 2-7; *Man from Shenandoah* "Obion-1866" 10-25; *Laredo* "The Pride of the Rangers" 12-16; **1966** *Honey West* "It's Earlier Than You Think" 1-21; *Virginian* "The Gentle Tamers" 1-24; *Man from UNCLE* "The Take Me to Your Leader Affair" 12-30; **1967** *Iron Horse* "Welcome for the General" 1-2; *Daniel Boone* "The Necklace" 3-9; *Bonanza* "The Conquistadors" 10-1; **1968** *Gunsmoke* "The Gunrunners" 2-5; *Lancer* "The Heart of Pony Alice" 12-17; **1969** *Guns of Will Sonnett* "Time Is the Rider" 1-10; *Lancer* "Jelly Hoskins' American Dream" 11-11; *Mod Squad* "The Death of Wild Bill Hannachek" 11-25; **1971** *Medical Center* "Heel of the Tyrant" 11-18; *Kolchak: The Night Stalker* "Bad Medicine" 11-29; **1975** *Six Million Dollar Man* "Taneha" 2-2; *Little House on the Prairie* "To See the World" 3-5; *Kojak* "A House of Prayer, a Den of Thieves" 12-7; **1976** *Streets of San Francisco* "The Drop" 10-28; **1982** *Little House on the Prairie* "A Faraway Cry" 3-8.

TELEFILMS

1969 *Seven in Darkness* 9-23 ABC; **1970** *Dial Hot Line* 3-8 ABC; **1974** *Hitchhike* 2-23 ABC; **1975** *Babe* 10-23 CBS; **1976** *Flood!* 11-24 NBC; **1978** *Desperate Women* 10-25 NBC; **1980** *The Legend of Sleepy Hollow* 10-31 NBC; **1981** *The Adventures of Huckleberry Finn* 7-9 NBC.

Simone Griffith
(born April 14, Savannah, Georgia)

Beautiful Simone Griffith came to television in a 1974 telefilm. After some guest work she became a regular in two early eighties TV series: *Ladie's Man* (1980-81) and *Amanda's* (1983). During the mid eighties she guested on *Riptide, Magnum, P.I., Crazy Like a Fox* and *T. J. Hooker*.

GUEST CREDITS

1977 *Six Million Dollar Man* "Dark Side of the Moon" 11-6, 11-13; **1978** *Quincy, M.E.* "Ashes to Ashes" 2-10; *Incredible Hulk* "The Hulk Breaks Las Vegas" 4-21; *American Girls* "The Beautiful People Jungle" 9-30; **1979** *Hawaii Five-0* "A Very Personal Affair" 3-15; *White Shadow* "Links" 1-22; **1980** *Hart to Hart* "Cruise at Your Own Risk" 4-8; **1981** *Greatest American Hero* "Reseda Rose" 4-15; *Nero Wolfe* "Sweet Revenge" 4-28; *Today's FBI* "Career Move" 12-27; **1982** *Bret Maverick* "Faith, Hope and Charity" 4-13, 4-20; *Gavilan* "A Drop in the Ocean" 12-7; **1983** *Hart to Hart* "Love Game" 11-8; *T. J. Hooker* "Undercover Affair" 12-10.

TELEFILMS

1974 *Only with Married Men* 12-4 ABC; **1975** *Starsky and Hutch* 4-30 ABC; **1979** *Mandrake* 1-24

NBC; **1980** *Fighting Back* 12-7 ABC.

Ed Grover
(born 1932)

After stage experience Ed Grover came to films in *Serpico* (1973). He became a regular on television's *Baretta* (1975-78), playing a police lieutenant. Following *Baretta,* he began TV guest work and was quite busy during the 1979-83 period. *Quincy, M.E.* used his talents in 5 episodes.

GUEST CREDITS

1978 *Quincy, M.E.* "Even Odds" 11-9; **1979** *Quincy, M.E.* "A Question of Death" 1-4; *Lou Grant* "Home" 2-26; *Hart to Hart* "Hit Jennifer Hart" 9-29; *Quincy, M.E.* "Hot Ice" 10-18; *Kate Loves a Mystery* "Off the Record" 11-1; **1980** *CHiPs* "Jailbirds" 1-5; *Charlie's Angels* "One Love…Two Angels" 4-30, 5-7; *Eischied* "The Buddy System" 7-29; **1981** *Magnum, P.I.* "No Need to Know" 1-8; *Quincy, M.E.* "Dear Mummy" 1-21; *Magnum, P.I.* "The Curse" 2-19; *Strike Force* "Night Nurse" 12-18; **1982** *Greatest American Hero* "Plague" 1-6; *Quincy, M.E.* "To Clear the Air" 2-17; **1983** *Matt Houston* episodes 4-3, 4-10; *A-Team* "One More Time" 4-12; *Quincy, M.E.* "An Act of Violence" 4-27.

TELEFILMS

1975 *Strike Force* 4-12 NBC; **1979** *High Midnight* 11-27 CBS; **1980** *A Rumor War* 9-24 CBS; **1982** *Games Mother Never Taught You* 11-27 CBS.

Moses Gunn

(born October 2, 1929, St. Louis, Missouri; died 1995)

Moses attended Tennessee State University prior to beginning a stage career in 1962; he made a film debut in 1964. Entering television in 1969, he became one of the most recognized, and most respected, black actors in television. During his TV career he had series regular roles on four series: *The Cowboys* (1974), *Good Times* (1977), *The Contender* (1980) and *Father Murphy* (1981-82).

During his distinguished career Gunn was nominated for a Tony Award, and won an Obie, as Best Actor in 1975. He died of complications from asthma at his home in Guilford, Conn. in 1995.

GUEST CREDITS

1969 *The FBI* "Eye of the Storm" 1-5; **1971** *Hawaii Five-0* "Nine, Ten, You're Dead" 11-30; **1972** *McCloud* "A Little Plot, a Tranquil Valley" 1-12; **1973** *Kung Fu* "The Stone" 4-12; *Assignment: Vienna* "Soldier of Fortune" 6-9; **1975** *Movin' On* "...To Be in Carolina" 10-13; **1977** *Switch* "Whatever Happened to Carol Harmony?" 4-3; *Quincy, M.E.* "A Blow to the Heart" 9-23; *Little House on the Prairie* "The Fighter" 11-21; **1978** *Vegas* "Lost Women" 11-22; *Little House on the Prairie* "Blind Journey" 11-27, 12-4; **1979** *Little House on the Prairie* "Barn Burner" 2-19; *Salvage 1* "Operation Breakout" 4-2; **1981** *Little House on the Prairie* "Make a Joyful Noise" 1-26.

TELEFILMS

1970 *Carter's Army* 1-27 ABC; **1971** *The Sheriff* 3-30 ABC; **1972** *Haunts of the Very Rich* 2-20 ABC; **1973** *Moving Target* 5-22 ABC; **1974** *Legacy of Blood* 3-12 ABC; **1976** *Law of the Land* 4-29 NBC.

Ross Hagen

(born 1938)

Husky Ross Hagen was well suited to the numerous action roles that he played in both films and television. He debuted in both mediums in 1966, becoming a series regular on *Daktari* in 1968-69.

By 1976 he had left acting for independent writing, producing and directing, returning only for a 1982 guest shot on *Bret Maverick*.

GUEST CREDITS

1966 *Shane* "The Great Invasion" 12-17, 12-24; *T.H.E. Cat* "The Ring of Anasis" 12-30; **1967** *Gunsmoke* "Muley" 1-21; *Fugitive* "The Savage Street" 3-14; *Invaders* "Panic" 4-11; *Wild Wild West* "The Night of the Iron Fist' 12-8; **1968** *Guns of Will Sonnett* "What's in a Name?"1-5; *The FBI* "Ring of

Steel" 2-4; *The FBI* "The Messenger" 3-17; *Gunsmoke* "Slocum" 10-28; **1969** *Outcasts* "The Thin Edge" 2-17; *Lancer* "Juniper's Camp" 3-11; **1970** *Lancer* "The Lion and the Lamb" 2-3; *Bonanza* "The Gold Mine" 3-8; *Mannix* "Sunburst" 11-14; *The FBI* "Incident in the Desert" 12-20; **1971** *Gunsmoke* "Pike" 3-1, 3-8; *O'Hara, U. S. Treasury* "Operation: Bandera" 9-24; *Mannix* "A Button for General D" 11-17; **1972** *Longstreet* "Anatomy of a Mayday" 2-3; **1973** *Mission: Impossible* "Speed" 2-16; *Rookies* "The Wheel of Death" 2-19; *Cannon* "Murder bly Proxy" 10-10; **1982** *Bret Maverick* "The Not So Magnificent Six" 3-2.

TELEFILM

1971 *Cannon* 3-26 CBS.

Alan Hale, Jr.

(born March 8, 1918, Los Angeles, Calif.; died January 2, 1990)

When Alan Hale, Jr. died of cancer of the thymus on

January 2, 1990, he left not only a wife and four children but a legion of co-workers and fans who loved his gentle and affectionate manner.   The son of noted character actor, Alan Hale, Sr. (1892-1950), Alan, Jr. made his first film in 1933 as a teen-ager, with the next movie not coming until he appeared in *I Wanted Wings* (1940). His screen career ultimately totaled 82 movies, including World War II films *Dive Bomber, Wake Island* and *Eagle Squadron.*

Entering television in 1951, he appeared as a regular on the spy series *Biff Baker, U.S.A.* ((1952-53). This was followed by a starring role on *Casey Jones* (1958). After numerous guest roles, especially on western series, he gained the role of his life. In September of 1964 he became "The Skipper" on *Gilligan's Island*, a role that lasted until 1967 and one that endeared him to generations of children (and adults). Despite severe panning by critics, *Gilligan's Island* has endured as one of the most popular sitcoms of all time and continues in reruns in countless markets today.

In 1969 he appeared as a regular on a brief sitcom, *The Good Guys.* Later, he was the voice of "The Skipper" on cartoon versions of Gilligan, *The New Adventures of Gilligan* (1974-77) and *Gilligan's Planet* (1982-83). He reprised his role in three *Gilligan's Island* telefilms in 1978, 1979 and 1981.

Alan did a good deal of guest work in the mid eighties on *Murder, She Wrote, Magnum, P.I., Blacke's Magic, Crazy Like a Fox, ALF, Growing Pains* and *Law and Harry McGraw.* Members of the *Gilligan's Island* cast made numerous public appearances together over the years until shortly before Alan's death.

GUEST CREDITS

1959 *Bat Masterson* "A Personal Matter" 1-28; *Restless Gun* "Incident at Bluefield" 3-30; *Colt .45* "The Saga of Sam Bass" 5-17; *Bronco* "Bodyguard" 10-20; *Texan* "Dangerous Ground" 12-14; *Texan* "End of Track" 12-21; **1960** *Man from Blackhawk* "The Three Thousand Dollar Policy" 1-22; *Texan* "Buried Treasure" 2-8; *Texan* "Captive Crew" 2-22; *Texan* "Showdown" 2-29; *Alaskans* "Partners" 1-13; *M Squad* "Two Days for Willy" 5-17; *Johnny Ringo*

Rawhide "Incident of The Woman Trap" 1-26; *Rawhide* "The Bosses' Brothers" 2-2; *Follow the Sun* "The Irresistible Miss Bullfinch" 2-18; *Maverick* "The Troubled Heir" 4-1; **1963** *Route 66* "Narcissus on an Old Red Fire Engine" 12-12; **1966** *Gunsmoke* "Champion of the World" 12-24; **1967** *Hondo* "Hondo and the Death Drive" 12-1; **1968** *Daktari* "A Man's Man" 11-20; **1969** *Wild Wild West* "The Night of the Sabatini Death" 2-7; *Land of the Giants* "Our Man O'Reilly" 12-28; **1971** *Alias Smith and Jones* "The Girl in Boxcar Number Three" 2-11; **1971** *Marcus Welby, M.D.* "In My Father's House" 9-28; **1972** *O'Hara, U. S. Treasury* "Operation: Moonshine" 12-17; **1973** *McMillan and Wife* "The Fine Art of Staying Alive" 3-11; **1982** *Simon and Simon* "Rough Rider Rides Again" 11-18; **1983** *Matt Houston* "The Yacht Club Murders" 1-16.

Alan Hale, Jr., in his role as The Skipper appears overjoyed, while his "little buddy" Gilligan (Bob Denver) looks perplexed. Syndicated reruns have made *Gilligan's Island* one of the most popular sitcoms   in TV history.

TELEFILMS

"Reputation for Murder" 6-12; *Maverick* "Arizona Black Maria" 10-9; *Cheyenne* "Road to Three Graves" 10-31; **1961** *Outlaws* "The Waiting Game" 1-19; *Adventures in Paradise* "Captain Butcher" 2-20; *Acapulco* "The Gentleman from Brazil" 3-16; *Hawaiian Eye* "Dragon Road" 4-5; *Gunsmoke* "Minnie" 4-15; *Adventures in Paradise* "The Serpent" 4-17; *General Electric Theater* "Louise and the Horseless Buggy" 4-30; *Whispering Smith* "The Idol" 9-18; **1962** *Bronco* "A Sure Thing" 1-22;

1978 *Rescue from Gilligan's Island* 10-14, 10-15 NBC; **1979** *The Castaways on Gilligan's Island* 5-3 NBC; **1981** *The Harlem Globetrotters on Gilligan's Island* 5-15 NBC.

Neil Hamilton
(born September 9, 1899, Lynn, Mass.; died September 24, 1984)

Neil Hamilton began his film career in the era of silents, in 1918, a career of well over 100 movies (most prior to 1950). He was very active in television's early days, intermittently hosting *Hollywood Screen Test* (1948-53) and appearing as a regular on *That Wonderful Guy* (1950) and *The Frances Langford-Don Ameche Show* (1951-52).

As the fifties progressed, he performed in productions of *The U.S. Steel Hour, Best of Broadway, Kraft Theatre* and *Perry Mason*. His greatest television fame was to come in 1966-68 during his stint as Commissioner Gordon on *Batman*; his character introduced him to an entire new generation of fans.

GUEST CREDITS

1959 *Maverick* "The Rivals" 1-25; *Zorro* "Spark of Revenge" 2-19; *77 Sunset Strip* "The Hong Kong Caper" 3-20; *Line-Up* "The Chloroform Murder Case" 5-22; *Colt .45* "The Pirate" 5-31; *Perry Mason* "The Case of the Dubious Bridegroom" 6-13; *Perry Mason* "The Case of the Golden Fraud" 11-21; **1960** *Bourbon Street Beat* "Knock on Any Tombstone" 1-25; *Bourbon Street Beat* "The House of Ledezan" 2-22; *Tightrope* "The Penthouse Story" 4-19; *Man From Blackhawk* "The Lady in Yellow" 6-17; **1961** *77 Sunset Strip* "The Hamlet Caper" 1-6; *Aquanauts* "The Defective Tank Adventure" 2-22; *Perry Mason* "The Case of the Difficult Detour" 3-25; *Follow the Sun* "Conspiracy of Silence" 12-10; **1962** *Bus Stop* "Cry to Heaven" 1-14; *Hawaiian Eye* "The Meeting at Molokai" 3-21; *77 Sunset Strip* "Leap, My Lovely" 10-19; **1963** *Perry Mason* "The Case of the Constant Doyle" 1-31; **1964** *Outer Limits* "The Invisibles" 2-3; *Outer Limits* "The Bellero Shield" 2-10; *Perry Mason* "The Case of the Drifting Dropout" 4-7; *Perry Mason* "The Case of the Betrayed Bride" 10-22; **1965** *Kraft Suspense Theatre* "In Darkness Waiting" 1-14, 1-21.

Ben Hammer

(born 1925, Brooklyn, New York)

Following World War II service with The U. S. Army, Ben completed his education, obtaining a B.A. Degree at Brooklyn College in 1948. He began acting and toured in 1950-51, with a Broadway debut coming in 1955.

He began working on television in 1961 with a few sixties guest shots and made a film debut in 1970. Ben worked often on television during the

seventies, alternating between playing heavies and cops on crime dramas. He also did stints on soaps *The Guiding Light* and *The Young and the Restless*.

GUEST CREDITS

1961 *87th Precinct* "Line of Duty" 10-23; *Thriller* "Dialogues with Death: Friend of the Dead" 12-4; **1966** *Mission: Impossible* "Elena" 12-10; **1967** *Dragnet* "The Big Magazine" 12-7; **1969** *Bonanza* "My Friend, My Enemy" 1-12; **1970** *Young Lawyers* "At the Edge of Night" 11-16; **1971** *Owen Marshall, Counselor at Law* "Voice from a Nightmare" 12-16; **1973** *Jigsaw* "Girl on the Run" 2-24; *Police Story* "Ten Year Honeymoon" 10-23; **1974** *Mannix* "A Small Favor for an Old Friend" 11-10; *Police Story* "Smack" 12-6; **1975** *Kojak* "Close Cover Before Killing" 1-5; *Petrocelli* "A Fallen Idol" 1-22; *Six Million Dollar Man* "The Return of the Robot Maker" 1-26; *Police Story* "The Man in the Shadows" 2-25; *Streets of San Francisco* "Labyrinth" 2-27; *The Law* "Prior Consent" 3-26; *Six Million Dollar Man* "The White Lightning War" 11-23; **1976** *Barbary Coast* "Mary Had More Than a Little Lamb" 1-2; *Matt Helm* "Die Once, Die Twice" 1-3; *Kojak* "A Grave Too Soon" 3-7; **1978** *Charlie's Angels* "Angel on High" 9-27; **1979** *Quincy, M.E.* "Nowhere to Run" 11-8; **1981** *Incredible Hulk* "Bring Me the Head of the Hulk" 1-9.

TELEFILMS

1973 *The Marcus-Nelson Murders* 3-8 CBS; **1974** *The Execution of Private Slovik* 3-13 NBC; **1976** *Griffin and Phoenix: A Love Story* 2-27 ABC; *Street Killing* 9-12 ABC; *Victory at Entebbe* 12-13; **1981** *Cagney and Lacey* 10-18 CBS; *Advice to the Lovelorn* 11-30 NBC; **1983** *Confessions of a Married Man* 1-31 ABC.

Don Hanmer

(born 1919)

Don was extremely active during the early days of television, from 1950, in shows like *Lights Out* (2), *The Web* (2), *Suspense*, *Chevrolet Tele-Theatre*,

Armstrong Circle Theater, *U.S. Steel Hour*, *Danger* and *Justice*. His dramatic skills and everyman appearance enabled him to slip in and out of all types of characterizations, and his talents remained in demand for over 30 years.

GUEST CREDITS

1961 *Cain's Hundred* "The Fixer" 12-12; **1962** *Tall Man* "An Hour to Die" 2-17; *Target: The Corruptors* "The Wrecker" 3-2; **1963** *Alcoa Premiere* "The Glass Palace" 1-17; *Ben Casey* "Lullaby for Billy Dignam" 5-6; **1965** *Fugitive* "When the Wind Blows" 12-28; **1966** *Virginian* "Legacy of Hate" 9-14; *Gunsmoke* "Gunfighter, R.I.P" 10-27; **1967** *Mission: Impossible* "The Astrologer" 12-3; *Judd, for the Defense* "The Living Victim" 12-15; **1968** *Cimarron Strip* "Knife in the Darkness" 1-25; *Mannix* "Another Final Exit" 2-10; *Judd, for the Defense* "The Name of the Game Is Acquittal" 10-18; *Adam-12* "And You Want to Get Married" 10-26; *Gunsmoke* "Railroaded" 11-25; **1969** *Outsider* "Take the Key and Lock Him Up" 2-12; **1970** *Young Lawyers* "Are You Running with Me, Jimmy?" 11-23;

1971 *Dan August* "The Law" 2-4; *Bold Ones: The Doctors* "Broken Melody" 9-21; 1972 *Cannon* "That Was No Lady" 10-4; *Mannix* "A Puzzle for One" 11-26; 1973 *McCloud* "Showdown at the End of the World" 1-7; *Owen Marshall, Counselor at Law* "Seed of Doubt" 1-24; *Ironside* "A Game of Showdown" 3-22; *Cannon* "Dead Lady's Tears" 11-7; *McCloud* "Solid Gold Swingers" 12-2; 1974 *Emergency* episode 2-16; *Banacek* "Fly Me if You Can Find Me" 2-19; *Kung Fu* "The Cenotaph" 4-4, 4-11; *McCloud* "Barefoot Girls on Bleeker Street" 9-22; *Kojak* "Slay Ride" 10-13; 1975 *Waltons* "The Emergence" 11-6; *Harry O* "Portrait of a Murder" 11-20; 1976 *Jigsaw John* "Sand Trap" 2-9; *Blue Knight* "Mariachi" 2-11; *City of Angels* "The House on Orange Grove Avenue" 3-16.

TELEFILMS

1975 *The Blue Knight* 5-9 CBS; 1980 *The Hustler of Muscle Beach* 5-16 ABC; 1981 *Hellinger's Law* 3-10 CBS.

Dean Harens

(born 1921)

Dean had a film debut in 1944, making three movies within two years, but didn't appear in another until 21 years later, in 1967. He began his television career in 1949, sometimes appearing with his wife, actress June Dayton. Harens appeared in numerous fifties live dramas like *Studio One* (3), *Alcoa Hour, NBC Presents* (2), *Lights Out* (2), *The Web, Danger* and *Lux Video Theatre*.

The sixties were a busy period of guest roles on TV series. Dean had a recurring role on *The FBI*, appearing as Agent Durant in 6 episodes (1967-69). He also did a stint on *General Hospital* (1965).

GUEST CREDITS

1959 *Perry Mason* "The Case of the Calendar Girl" 4-18; *Perry Mason* "The Case of Paul Drake's Dilemna" 11-14; *Man and the Challenge* "Jungle Survival" 12-5; *Black Saddle* "Change of Venue" 12-11; *Bat Masterson* "The Canvas and the Cane" 12-17; 1960 *Perry Mason* "The Case of the Wandering Widow" 10-22; 1961 *Hong Kong* "Night Cry" 1-25; 1964 *Breaking Point* "A Little Anger Is a Good Thing" 1-6; *Ben Casey* "Dress My Doll Pretty" 3-18; 1965 *Man from UNCLE* "The Mad, Mad Tea Party" 2-1; *Perry Mason* "The Case of the Fatal Fortune" 9-19; 1967 *The FBI* "The Courier" 1-15; *Iron Horse* "Volcano Wagon" 1-16; *Felony Squad* "The Strangler" 1-30; *Invaders* "The Storm" 4-4; *Run for Your Life* "The Company of Scoundrels" 10-17; *The FBI* "Line of Fire" 11-26; *Judd, for the Defense* "The Living Victim" 12-15; 1968 *The FBI* "Ring of Steel" 2-4; *The FBI* "The Enemies" 11-3; 1969 *The FBI* "Conspiracy of Silence" 3-2; *The FBI* "Moment of Truth" 3-30; 1970 *Mannix* "Medal for a Hero" 1-3; 1971 *Dan August* "Prognosis: Homicide" 4-1; 1972 *Mission: Impossible* "Committed" 1-22; *Longstreet* "Please Leave the Wreck for Others to Enjoy" 1-27; *Smith Family* "Homecoming" 5-31; 1973 *Mannix* "Little Girl Lost" 10-7; *Owen Marshall, Counselor at Law* "'N' Is for Nightmare" 10-17; 1974 *Magician* "The Illusion of the Curious Counterfeit" 1-14, 1-21; *Barnaby Jones* "The Platinum Connection" 1-20; *Petrocelli* "A Covenant with Evil" 12-18; 1975 *Archer* "The Body Beautiful" 2-13; *Barnaby Jones* "Doomed Alibi" 3-11; 1977 *Wonder Woman* "The Last of the Two Dollar Bills" 1-8.

TELEFILMS

1969 *The D. A.: Murder One* 12-8 NBC; **1971** *Paper Man* 11-12 CBS.

John Harmon
(born 1917; died 1982)

A character actor, in films since 1939, John appeared in over 80 movies, often in small parts, but his bald head and smallish eyes were familiar to fans of both cinema and television. In television from the early fifties, John labored in relative obscurity, as did many character actors. His ability to slip readily into any type of everyday citizen roles kept him very busy.

In some TV western guest shots he played sly villains, but he could just have readily played a barber, a bartender or a concerned townsman. Much of John's TV guest work was on westerns, especially on *The Rifleman* (8), but he also had multiple appearances on *The Fugitive, The Twilight Zone, Star Trek* and *Perry Mason*.

GUEST CREDITS

1959 *Rifleman* "The Trade" 3-10; *Maverick* "Two Tickets to Ten Strike" 3-15; *Rifleman* "One Went to Denver" 3-17; *Wanted: Dead or Alive* "Double Fee" 3-21; *Rifleman* "The Mindreader" 6-30; *Johnny Ringo* "The Hunters" 10-29; *Perry Mason* "The Case of the Startled Stallion" 10-31; *Johnny Ringo* "Ghost Coach" 11-12; *Black Saddle* "Murdock" 11-13; *Rifleman* "The Spiked Rifle" 11-24; *Bonanza* "The Hanging Posse" 11-28; *Rifleman* "The Legacy" 12-8; **1960** *Rifleman* "The Visitors" 1-26; *Rifleman* "Shotgun Man" 4-12; *Wanted: Dead or Alive* "Death, Divided by Three" 4-23; *Texan* "Bad Man" 6-20; **1961** *Untouchables* "The Organization" 1-26; *Rawhide* "Incident of the Promised Land" 2-3; *Gunsmoke* "Potshot" 3-11; *Bonanza* "Cut-Throat Junction" 3-18; *Whispering Smith* "The Quest" 6-26; *Perry Mason* "The Case of the Left-Handed Liar" 11-25; *Rifleman* "Long Gun from Tucson" 12-11; **1962** *Laramie* "The Replacement" 3-27; *Twilight Zone* "The Dummy" 5-4; *Bonanza* "A Hot Day for a Hanging" 10-14; **1963** *Have Gun-Will Travel* "Cage at McNaab" 2-16; *Twilight Zone* "Of Late I Think of Cliffordsville" 4-11; *Wagon Train* "The Cassie Vance Story" 12-23; **1964** *Perry Mason* "The Case of the Capering Camera" 1-16; *Fugitive* "Come Watch Me Die" 1-21; *Travels of Jaimie McPheeters* "Day of the Haunted Trail" 1-26; *Fugitive* "Tug of War" 10-27; **1965** *Big Valley* "Boots with My Father's Name" 9-29; **1966** *Laredo* "Meanwhile Back at the Reservation" 2-10; *Fugitive* "Death Is the Door Prize" 9-20; *Laredo* "Finnegan" 10-21; *Wild Wild West* "The Night of the Infernal Machine" 12-23; **1967** *Big Valley* "Boy into Man" 1-16; *Felony Squad* "Night of the Shark" 1-16, 1-23; *Star Trek* "City on the Edge of Forever" 4-6; *Big Valley* "Four Days to Furnace Hill" 12-4; **1968** *Star Trek* "A Piece of the Action" 1-12; **1969** *Lancer* "The Lion and the Lamb" 2-3; *Adam 12* "Log Fifty Four-Impersonation" 2-7; **1971** *O'Hara, U. S. Treasury* "Operation: Offset" 10-22.

Stacy Harris
(born 1918, Big Timber, Quebec, Canada; died March 13, 1973)

In films from 1951, Stacy co-starred in the 1952 and 1953 summer replacement series, *Doorway to Danger.* He later starred in a syndicated cop series,

N.O.P.D. (New Orleans Police Department) in 1956. During the final season of *The Life and Legend of Wyatt Earp*, Stacy had yet another series regular role (1960-61).

Stacy worked in guest roles throughout much of the sixties (becoming one of Jack Webb's stock company members), then earned a recurring role on *O'Hara, U. S. Treasury*, appearing as David Janssen's boss, Ben Hazzard.

GUEST CREDITS

1959 *Richard Diamond* episode 5-31; *Black Saddle* "The Long Rider" 10-16; *Phillip Marlowe* "Bum Rap" 11-17; *Tightrope* "Cold Kill" 12-15; *Texan* "Rough Road to Payday" 12-28; **1960** *Man with a Camera* "Touch Off" 1-11; *Bonanza* "House Divided" 1-16; **1961** *Outlaws* "The Sooner" 4-27; *Perry Mason* "The Case of the Crying Comedian" 10-14; *Alfred Hitchcock* "Old Pro" 11-28; **1962** *Casey* "Pack Up All My Cares and Woes" 12-17; **1963** *G.E. True* "OSI" 1-20; *Bonanza* "Twilight Town" 10-13; **1965** *Slattery's People* "Of Damon, Pythias, and Sleeping Dogs" 11-12; *Daniel Boone* "Perilous Journey "12-16; *Honey West* "Invitation to Limbo" 12-17; *Laredo* "A Medal for Reese" 12-30; **1966** *I Spy* "One Thousand Fine" 4-27; **1967** *Tarzan* "The Golden Runaway" 2-2; *Dragnet* "The Big Badge Racket" 9-28; **1968** *Dragnet* "Public Affairs-DR-07" 9-19; **1969** *Adam-12* "Jimmy Eisley's Dealing Smack" 1-11; *Dragnet* "Auto Courtroom" 11-20; **1970** *Dragnet* "Narco-Pillmaker" 2-19; *Dragnet*

"Forgery-The Rangers" 11-20; *Mannix* "Time Out of Mind" 10-3; *Adam-12* "Log Eighty-Five'Sign of the Twins" 12-26; **1971** *Bearcats!* episode 12-2; **1972** *Longstreet* "Through Shattering Glass" 2-24; *Sixth Sense* "With This Ring, I Thee Kill" 3-4.

TELEFILMS

1968 *Companions in Nightmare* 11-23 NBC; **1971** *The D. A.: Conspiracy to Kill* 1-11 NBC; *Vanished* 3-8, 3-9 NBC; *O'Hara, U. S. Treasury: Operation Cobra* 4-2 CBS.

Christina Hart

On television often during the seventies, Christina played countess teen-ager roles during that era, usually on crime dramas. She continued her career well into the eighties.

GUEST CREDITS

1972 *Ironside* "Five Days in the Death of Sergeant Brown" 9-14; *Bold Ones: The Doctors* "Broken Melody" 9-19; **1974** *Rookies* "Death at 6:00 a.m." 10-17; *Petrocelli* "An Act of Love" 11-13; **1976** *Bert D'Angelo* "What Kind of Cop Are You?" 6-12; *Charlie's Angels* "Angels in Chains" 10-20; *Barnaby Jones* "Renegade's Child" 12-23; **1977** *Fantastic*

Journey "An Act of Love" 3-24; *Six Million Dollar Man* "The Ghostly Teletype" 5-l5; *Streets of San Francisco* "Time Out" 6-16; *Hawaii Five-0* "Shake Hands with the Man on the Moon" 11-10; **1978** *Barnaby Jones* "Deadly Sanctuary" l0-l2; **1979** *Incredible Hulk* "Vendetta Road" 5-25; *Operation: Runaway* "Breaking Point" 7-3l; **1980** *B. J. and the Bear* "Bear Bondage" 2-2; **1982** *CHiPs* "Alarmed" 2-l4; *Simon and Simon* "Sometimes Dreams Come True" l2-2.

TELEFILMS

1974 *Can Ellen Be Saved?"* 2-5 ABC; **1975** *The Daughters of Joshua Cabe Return* l-28 ABC; *The Runaway Barge* 3-24 NBC; **1976** *Helter Skelter* 4-l, 4-2; **1980** *The Night the City Screamed* l2-l2 ABC; **1981** *The Sophisticated Gents* 9-29, 9-30 NBC; **1982** *Hear No Evil* 11-20 CBS.

Dee Hartford

(born 1927)

A well-known fashion model prior to her l952 film debut, Dee married famed director Howard Hawks and gave up her acting career. Following a l959 divorce, she returned to modeling and resumed her acting career in 1962, concluding it in 1969.

GUEST CREDITS

1962 *Alfred Hitchcock Hour* "Day of Reckoning" 11-22; **1963** *Perry Mason* "The Case of the Accosted Accountant" l-9; *Gunsmoke* "Ash" 2-l6; **1964** *Outer Limits* "The Invisibles" 2-3; *Twilight Zone* "The Bewitchin' Pool" 6-l9; *Perry Mason* "The Case of the Missing Button" 9-24; **1966** *Girl from UNCLE* "The Montori Device Affair" l0-11; *Time Tunnel* "The Revenge of the Gods" l0-2l; *Lost in Space* "The Android Machine" l0-26; **1967** *Lost in Space* "Revolt of the Androids" 3-8; **1968** *Lost in Space* "Space Beauty" 3-l4; **1969** *Land of the Giants* "Target: Earth" 3-2.

Paul Hartman

(born March l, l904, San Francisco, Calif.; died October 2, l973)

Originally onstage and vaudeville with his wife Grace (l907-55), they appeared as "The Dancing Hartmans". A film career, beginning in l937, included roles in *Inherit the Wind, Soldier in the Rain, How to Succeed in Business without Really Trying* and *The Reluctant Astronaut.*

He first appeared on television during l948 in a *Philco Television Playhouse* production. Paul and wife Grace starred in a l949 sitcom, called appropriately, *The Hartmans.* He did some quality dramatic TV during the fifties, in shows like *Kraft Theatre* (5), *Studio One* (2), *Producer's Showcase* and *Goodyear Playhouse.* He also had a starring role in another sitcom, *Pride of the Family* (l953-54).

In l967-68 Paul became handyman Emmett Clark on *The Andy Griffith Show* and continued the role on *Mayberry, R.F.D.* during l968-7l. He also had a recurring role on *Petticoat Junction*, appearing as Bert Smedley in l968. His final TV appearance was in a l972 special, *Of Thee I Sing.*

GUEST CREDITS

1960 *Alfred Hitchcock Presents* "Not Running the Type" 2-7; *Ford Star Time* "Incident at a Corner" 4-5; *Thriller* "Girl with a Secret" 11-15; **1961**

Naked City "Bullets Cost Too Much" 1-4; *Twilight Zone* "Back There" 1-13; *Hallmark Hall of Fame* "Time Remembered" 2-7; *Alfred Hitchcock Presents* "Gratitude" 4-25; *Checkmate* "The Thrill Seekers" 5-27; *Naked City* "The Day the Island Almost Sank" 6-14; *Have Gun-Will Travel* "The Brothers" 11-25; **1962** *Adventures in Paradise* "Once There Was a Princess" 1-14; *Ben Casey* "Behold a Pale Horse" 2-26; *Alfred Hitchcock Presents* "Burglar Proof" 2-27; *Defenders* "Along Came a Spider" 5-5; **1963** *Alfred Hitchcock Hour* "Death of a Cop" 5-24; *Greatest Show on Earth* "Leaves in the Wind" 11-26; **1964** *Alfred Hitchcock Hour* "The Magic Shop" 1-10; **1965** *For the People* "Guilt Shall Not Escape Nor Innocence Suffer" 2-14; **1966** *Legend of Jesse James* "A Real Tough Town" 1-24; **1967** *Bob Hope Chrysler Theater* "To Sleep, Perchance to Dream" 5-10.

Edmond Hashim
(born 1932; died July 2, 1974)

Edmond acted in the first of his 7 films in 1956. He began working in television during the late fifties, often cast as Hispanics. He appeared on 6 *Gunsmoke* episodes and was in 3 *Alfred Hitchcock Presents* productions.

By the late sixties Edmond had tired of acting

and went into what became a very successful women's clothing business. He died on July 2, 1974, survived by his wife and parents.

GUEST CREDITS

1959 *Richard Diamond* episode 6-21; **1961** *Hong Kong* "The Survivor" 1-18; *Checkmate* "A Matter of Conscience" 2-18; *Alfred Hitchcock Presents* "Gratitude" 4-25; *Alfred Hitchcock Presents* "Gratitude" 4-25; *Alfred Hitchcock Presents* "Keep Me Company" 11-7; **1963** *New Loretta Young Show* "Interesting Jeopardy" 3-4; **1965** *Bob Hope Chrysler Theater* "In Any Language" 3-12; **1966** *Gunsmoke* "The Brothers" 3-12; *Perry Mason* "The Case of the Unwelcome Well" 4-3; *Gunsmoke* "The Hanging" 12-31; **1967** *Gunsmoke* "The Wreckers" 9-11; *Wild Wild West* "The Night of the Montezuma Hordes" 10-27; *Run for Your Life* "The Mustafa Embrace" 12-6; **1968** *Gunsmoke* "The Victim" 1-1; *Mission: Impossible* "Trial by Fury" 3-10; **1969** *Gunsmoke* "Time of

the Jackals" 1-13; *Gunsmoke* "Charlie Noon" 11-3.

Signe Hasso
(born Signe Larrson, August 15, 1918, Sweden)

Signe acted in her first film in 1933 under the name of Signe Larrson. She came to the U. S. from her native Sweden in 1941 and was a beautiful

leading lady for a time before evolving into character roles. Signe returned to Sweden several times during the fifties for films and stage work.

She began her television career in 1952, working in guest roles until the late seventies.

GUEST CREDITS

1962 *Checkmate* "An Assassin Arrives, Andante" 2-21; *Route 66* "A Feat of Strength" 5-18; *Kraft Mystery Theater* "Dead on Nine" 7-4; *Route 66* "One Tiger to a Hill" 9-21; *Alcoa Premiere* "The Contenders" 12-6; **1963** *Bonanza* "A Stranger Passed This Way" 3-3; **1964** *Outer Limits* "Production and Decay of Strange Particles" 4-20; **1966** *Green Hornet* "Programmed for Death" 9-23; *T.H.E. Cat* "Sandman" 9-23; **1967** *Bob Hope Chrysler Theater* "Code Name: Heraclitus 1.4" 11-11; *Road West* "Fair Ladies of France" 2-27; *Girl from UNCLE* "The Samurai Affair" 3-28; *Cornonet Blue* "The Assassin" 6-12; **1971** *Interns* episode 1-29; *Cannon* "The Girl in the Electric Coffin" 10-26; **1972** *Ghost Story* "Half Death" 11-3; **1974** *Streets of San Francisco* "Chapel of the Damned" 1-17; *Hawkins* "Murder on the 13th Floor" 2-5; **1976** *Ellery Queen* "The Adventure of the Black Falcon" 1-4; *City of Angels* "Palm Springs Answer" 3-23; **1978** *Starsky and Hutch* "A Body Worth Guarding" 1-25; **1981** *Magnum, P.I.* "The Sixth Position" 12-17; *Darkroom*

"Makeup" 12-18; **1982** *Quincy, M.E.* "Stolen Tears" 3-17; **1983** *Hart to Hart* "Too Close to Hart" 5-3.

TELEFILMS

1973 *The Magician* 3-17 NBC; *Sherlock Holmes in New York* 10-18 NBC; **1981** *Evita Peron* 2-23, 2-24 NBC.

Allison Hayes

(born March 6, 1930, Charlestown, West Virginia; died February 27, 1977)

Perhaps best known for her starring role in the sci-fi cult film, *Attack of the Fifty-Foot Woman*, beautiful Allison Hayes was onscreen from 1954. She appeared in fifties and sixties guest roles on television, and was a series regular on *Acapulco* (1961); she was also an early cast member on the soap *General Hospital*, during 1963.

Allison died at age 37, in 1977, of blood poisoning.

GUEST CREDITS

1959 *Rough Riders* "An Eye for an Eye" 1-15; *Bat Masterson* "The Secret Is Death" 5-27; *Markham* "Vendetta in Venice" 6-27; *Tombstone*

Territory "Red Terror of Tombstone" l0-9; **1960** *Bat Masterson* "Deadly Diamonds" 2-11; *Men into Space* "Moon Cloud" 2-17; *Perry Mason* "The Case of the Singing Skirt" 3-12; *Bat Masterson* "The Reluctant Witness" 3-31; *Dante's Inferno* "San Quentin Quill" 11-14; **1962** *Perry Mason* "The Case of the Captain's Coins" 1-13; *77 Sunset Strip* "The Paralled Caper" 2-23; *Kraft Mystery Theater* "Change of Heart" 9-12; **1965** *Perry Mason* "The Case of the Deadly Debt" 4-1; *Perry Mason* "The Case of the Laughing Lady" 9-12; **1967** *Iron Horse* "Death by Triangulation" 3-20.

Margaret "Maggie" Hayes

(born December 5, l924, Baltimore, Maryland; died January 26, 1977)

Signed to a Paramount contract as Dana Dale, Margaret "Maggie" Hayes made her first film in l940. She was briefly married to the late actor Lief Erickson in l942. On Broadway and in films of the forties, she began working as Margaret Hayes. Her films included *The Blackboard Jungle, The Glass Key* and *Omar Khayyam.*

She came to television in 1950 and became a repertory player on *Robert Montgomery Presents* during 1952-53. During the 1953-58 period she appeared on *Schlitz Playhouse of Stars, Armstrong Circle Theater, Hallmark Hall of Fame, Producer's Showcase, Climax* (2), *Playhouse 90, Zane Grey Theater* (3), *General Electric Theater, Cheyenne* and *The Life and Legend of Wyatt Earp* (3).

After numerous early sixties guest appearances she wound down her television career with a stint on the soap *Flame in the Wind* (*A Time for Us*) during 1964-65.

In her later years she owned and operated Maggie Hayes Jewelry Botique in Palm Beach, Florida, gaining a national reputation as a jewelry designer. She died in l977, survived by a son and an actress daughter, Pamela Brooks Swope.

GUEST CREDITS

1959 *Desilu Playhouse* "Comeback" 3-2; *Goodyear Theater* "Light in the Fruit Closet" 4-27; *Bourbon Street Beat* "The Mourning Cloak" l0-12; **1960** *Markham* "The Sitting Duck" 5-5; *Perry Mason* "The Case of the Ominous Outcast" 5-21; *Chevy Mystery Show* "I Know What I've Done" 7-24; *Perry Mason* "The Case of the Clumsy Clown" 11-5; **1961** *Rawhide* "Incident of the Night on the Town" 6-2; *Bonanza* "The Countess" 11-19; **1962** *New Breed* "Policemen Die Alone" 1-30, 2-6; *77 Sunset Strip* "Twice Dead" 3-2; *Breck's Golden Showcase* "Tonight in Samarkand" 3-24; *Target: The Corruptors* "The Blind Goddess" 4-20; **1963** *Perry Mason* "The Case of the Reluctant Model" l0-31; **1964** *Defenders* "Blacklist" 1-18; *Flipper* episode l2-12.

Ron Hayes

(born February 26, l932, San Francisco, California)

After a 1957 television debut, Ron Hayes became one of television's busiest actors during the sixties decade. He did countless guest shots and was a regular on *The Everglades* (1961), *The Rounders* (1966-67) and *Lassie* (1972-73). His lanky frame and sober taciturn manner were reminiscent of Gary Cooper; the majority of his TV guest roles were in western series.

Most of the top rated western series used his talents extensively, with *Gunsmoke* (9), *Wagon Train*

(6) and *Bonanza* (6) leading the way. Ron exuded a quiet strength that made him quite believable as settlers, ranchers, cowboys and peace officers. Continuing to work well into the eighties, Ron played a sheriff during 1986 on the soap *General Hospital*.

GUEST CREDITS

1959 *Texan* "The Ringer" 2-16; *Maverick* "Passage to Ft. Doom" 4-3; *Tombstone Territory* "Day of Amnesty" 4-3; *Rawhide* "Incident at the Haunted Hills" 11-6; *Wanted: Dead or Alive* "Reckless" 11-7; **1960** *Hotel de Paree* "Sundance Goes to Kill" 1-22; *Gunsmoke* "Moo Raid" 2-13; *Wichita Town* "Afternoon in Town" 2-17; *Bonanza* "Desert Justice" 2-20; *Texan* "Showdown" 2-29; *Bat Masterson* "The Reluctant Witness" 3-31; *Deputy* "Marked for Bounty" 4-2; *Wagon Train* "Trial for Murder" 4-27, 5-4; *Bat Masterson* "The Rage of Princess Ann" 10-20; *Tales of Wells Fargo* "Run for the River" 11-7; **1961** *Rifleman* "Six Years and a Day" 1-3; *Klondike* "Sitka Madonna" 2-6; *Wagon Train* "The Beth Pearson Story" 2-22; *Bonanza* "The Rescue" 2-25; *Wagon Train* "The Jed Pike Story" 3-1; *Gunsmoke* "Harriet" 3-4; *Gunsmoke* "Old Faces" 3-18; *Acapulco* episode 3-27; *Bat Masterson* "The Fatal Garment" 5-25; *Wagon Train* "The Bettina May Story" 12-20; **1962** *Mystery Theater* "Chez Rouge" 8-8; *Gunsmoke* "Jenny" 10-

13; *Laramie* "Shadow of the Past" 10-16; *Rawhide* "Incident of the Four Horsemen" 10-26; **1963** *Laramie* "Protective Custody" 1-15; *Alcoa Premiere* "Jeeny Ray" 3-14; *Gunsmoke* "I Call Him Wonder" 3-23; *Bonanza* "Mirror of a Man" 3-31; *Temple Houston* episode 11-28; *Kraft Suspense Theatre* "The Long Lost List of Edward Smalley" 12-12; *Wagon Train* "The Story of Cain" 12-16; *Virginian* "Siege" 12-18; **1964** *Wagon Train* "The Duncan McIvor Story" 3-9; *Destry* "Blood Brother-in-Law" 4-17; *Kraft Suspense Theatre* "A Lion Amongst Us" 10-22; **1965** *Outer Limits* "The Probe" 1-16; *Gunsmoke* "South Wind" 11-27; **1966** *Bonanza* "The Bridegroom" 12-4; **1967** *Invaders* "Valley of the Shadow" 9-26; *Bonanza* "Night of Reckoning" 10-15; **1968** *High Chaparral* "Threshold of Courage" 3-31; *Ironside* "Desperate Encounter" 10-24; **1969** *High Chaparral* "A Fella Named Kilroy" 3-7; *Bonanza* "Emily" 3-23; *Mod Squad* "Keep the Faith, Baby" 3-25; *Name of the Game* "The Prisoner Within" 11-14; **1970** *Gunsmoke* "The Judas Gun" 1-19; *Mod Squad* "A Is for Annie" 10-13; *Gunsmoke* "Snow Train I, II" 10-19, 10-26; **1971** *Hawaii Five-0* "The Odd Lot Caper" 1-30; *Cannon* "Press Pass to the Slammer" 3-14; **1976** *Bionic Woman* "The Jailing of Jaimie" 5-12; *Baretta* "Dear Tony" 11-10; *Bionic Woman* "Sister Jaimie" 11-24; **1979** *Barnaby Jones* "Target for a Wedding" 4-12; **1983** *A-Team* "Children of Jamestown" 1-30.

TELEFILMS

1978 *Standing Tall* 1-28 NBC; *Happily Ever After* 9-5 CBS.

Susan Seaforth Hayes (a.k.a. Susan Seaforth)

(born 1943)

Susan began her acting career as a teenager, with her film debut in 1957 at age 14. She began guesting on television in 1961, and in 1963 had her first soap role, in a brief stint on *General Hospital*. She followed this with a role on *The Young Marrieds* (1964-66). More guest roles followed before she gained the role that made her a soap opera legend.

In 1968 she began starring as Julie Olson on *Days of Our Lives*, a role that earned her top recognition as an actress, and that saw her fall in love with, and marry, her leading man, Bill Hayes. In 1976 the couple graced the cover of *Time* magazine, with an accompanying article proclaiming *Days of Our Lives* as America's best soap.

Susan was nominated for Emmys in her *Days of Our Lives* role in 1974, 1976 and 1978. After 16 great years, she left the serial in 1984 (returned 1990-94), and moved to a lengthy role on *The Young and the Restless* (1984-89). She is recognized as one of the best actresses to grace daytime television.

GUEST CREDITS

1961 *Surfside 6* "The Empty Houses" 10-16; **1962** *Surfside 6* "Find Leroy Burdette" 2-19; *Hawaiian Eye* "Blackmail in Satin" 2-28; *77 Sunset Strip* "Flight from Escondito" 5-18; **1963** *Hawaiian Eye* "The Long Way Home" 2-19; **1965** *Man from UNCLE* "The Four Steps Affair" 2-22; *The FBI* "The Insolents" 10-17; *12 0'Clock High* "The Jones Boys" 12-6; **1966** *12 0"Clock High* "A Distant Cry"

10-7; **1967** *Fugitive* "There Goes the Ball Game" 2-7; *The FBI* "The Traitor" 10-15; **1968** *Dragnet* "The Big Starlet" 2-1; *Dragnet* "The Big Investigation" 3-14; *Felony Squad* "The Fatal Hours" 11-29; *Wild Wild West* "The Night of Miguelito's Revenge" 12-13; **1971** *Adam-12* "Log Sixteen-Child in Danger" 3-4; **1972** *Ironside* "Unreasonable Facsimile" 1-6.

Wayne Heffley

(born 1927)

After stage experience Wayne Heffley began an undistinguished film career in 1959. He worked in television guest roles from 1959 well into the eighties. Heffley also performed in numerous telefilms and was in *Days of Our Lives* (1988-93).

GUEST CREDITS

1959 *Rough Riders* "Deadfall" 5-21; *Colt .45* "Amnesty" 5-24; **1960** *Wanted: Dead or Alive* "The Partners" 2-6; *Hotel de Paree* "Hard Luck for Sundance" 2-19; **1961** *Twilight Zone* "The Odessey of Flight 33" 3-24; *Perry Mason* "The Case of the Pathetic Patient" 10-28; **1962** *Virginian* "It Tolls for Thee" 11-21; **1963** *Ben Casey* "Little Drops of Water, Little Grains of Sand" 10-30; **1964** *Twilight Zone* "Black Leather Jackets" 1-31; **1965** *Voyage to the*

Bottom of the Sea "The Monster from Outer Space" 12-19; **1966** *Voyage to the Bottom of the Sea* "Deadly Creature Below" 1-9; *Voyage to the Bottom of the Sea* "Menfish" 3-6; *Bonanza* "Home from the Sea" 5-1; **1967** *Invaders* "Valley of the Shadow" 9-26; *Wild Wild West* "The Night of the Iron Fist" 12-8; **1969** *Lancer* "The Fix-It Man" 2-11; **1971** *O'Hara, U. S. Treasury* "Operation: Time Fuse" 10-15; *O'Hara, U. S. Treasury* "Operation: Moonshine" 12-17; **1973** *New Adventures of Perry Mason* "The Case of Horoscope Homicide" 9-16; *Emergency* episode 10-20; **1974** *Little House on the Prairie* "The Voice of Tinker Jones" 12-4; **1975** *Little House on the Prairie* "Child of Pain" 2-12; *Little House on the Prairie* "Money Crop" 2-19; **1978** *Barnaby Jones* "Deadly Sanctuary" 10-12.

TELEFILMS

1976 *Widow* 1-22 NBC; **1977** *The Amazing Howard Hughes* 4-13, 4-14 CBS; *Danger in Paradise* 5-12 NBC; *Alexander: The Other Side of Dawn* 5-16 NBC; *Billy: Portrait of a Street Kid* 9-12 CBS; 1978 *Crisis in Sun Valley* 3-29 NBC; *The Critical List* 9-11, 9-12 NBC; *Ishi: The Last of His Tribe* 12-20 NBC; **1979** *Mind Over Murder* 10-23 CBS; **1980** *Nightside* 6-8 ABC; **1981** *Fly Away Home* 9-18 ABC; **1982** *Victims* 1-11 NBC; *Johnny Belinda* 10-19 CBS.

"Glass Flowers Never Drop Petals" 3-23; *Combat* "The Glory Among Men" 4-21; *Kraft Television Theatre* "Operation Grief" 10-8; *Mr. Novak* "Born of Kings and Angels" 12-1; *Doctors and Nurses* "Rites of Spring" 12-8; **1965** *Perry Mason* "The Case of the Cheating Chancellor" 10-3; **1967** *Ironside* "The Very Cool Hot Car" 11-30.

Peter Helm

A youthful sixties television actor, Peter disappeared from the medium by 1968.

GUEST CREDITS

1961 *87th Precinct* "The Very Hard Sell" 12-4; **1962** *Alcoa Premiere* "The Man with the Shine on His Shoes" 2-20; *New Breed* "Edge of Violence" 3-27; *Checkmate* "Rendevous in Washington" 5-9; *Naked City* "Dust Devil on a Quiet Street" 11-28; **1963** *Eleventh Hour* "The Wings of Morning" 3-20; *Stoney Burke* "A Girl Named Amy" 4-29; *Fugitive* "Smoke Screen" 10-29; **1964** *Mr. Novak* "The Private Life of Douglas Morgan, Jr." 1-28; *Breaking Point*

Percy Helton

(born 1894; died September 11, 1971)

Percy began acting with his father at the tender age of two. He later worked with David Belasco for five years, and with George M. Cohan for three years, while in his childhood and early youth. Entering The U. S. Army during World War I, he served in France. He returned to Broadway after his military service and soon began appearing in silent films.

Appearing in over 200 films, Percy had a personna unlike any other actor. His voice had a whispering quality and his body was almost gnome-like. Percy's film credits included *Miracle on 34th*

Street, Call Northside 777, My Friend Irma, Cyrano de Bergarac, Fancy Pants, Call Me Madam, The Robe, 20,000 Leagues Under the Sea, A Star Is Born, White Christmas, Jailhouse Rock, The Music Man, Hush...Hush Sweet Charlotte, Funny Girl and Butch Cassidy and the Sundance Kid.

His television guest roles were heavily sprinkled with appearances on western series, and he also had a recurring role on *The Beverly Hillbillies* (1968-71). *Batman, Get Smart* and *Petticoat Junction* also used his unique talents.

GUEST CREDITS

1959 *Lineup* "The Drugstore Cowboy Case" 5-15; *Johnny Ringo* "Cully" 10-8; *Lawman* "Shadow Witness" 11-15; *Gunsmoke* "Thick n' Thin" 12-26; **1960** *Wanted: Dead or Alive* "Tolliver Bender" 2-13; *Law of the Plainsman* "Dangerous Barriers" 3-10; *Texan* "The Guilty and the Innocent" 3-28; *Colt .45* "Martial Law" 5-17; *Maverick* "Bolt from the Blue" 11-27; **1961** *Alfred Hitchcock Presents* "The Horse-player" 3-14; *Perry Mason* "The Case of the Torrid Tapestry" 4-22; *Rawhide* "Incident of the Wager on Payday" 6-16; *Laramie* "Siege at Jubilee" 10-10; *Perry Mason* "The Case of the Pathetic Patient" 10-28; **1964** *Gunsmoke* "Trip West" 5-2; *Twilight Zone* "Mr. Garrity and the Graves" 5-8; **1966** *Gunsmoke*

"The Raid" 1-22, 1-29; **1967** *Bonanza* "The Unseen Wound" 1-29; *Green Hornet* "Bad Bet on a 459 Silent" 2-3; *Girl from UNCLE* "The Furnace Flats Affair" 2-21; *Cimarron Strip* "The Legend of Jud Starr" 9-14; *Virginian* "Execution at Triste" 12-13; **1968** *Cimarron Strip* "The Greeners" 3-7; *Land of the Giants* "Ghost Town" 9-29; *Wild Wild West* "The Night of Miguelito's Revenge" 12-13; **1971** *Mission: Impossible* "The Missile" 1-16.

Douglas Henderson

(born 1918; died 1978)

In films from 1944, Douglas was a frequent guest on television dramatic series, especially on *Perry Mason* (5) and *Mannix* (4). He had a recurring role on *Wild Wild West*, appearing as Colonel Richmond.

Henderson was seen in numerous fifties guest shots, dating back to an appearance on *Superman* in 1954. He was often cast as authority figures, especially army officers and police officials, in both films and television.

GUEST CREDITS

1959 *Perry Mason* "The Case of the Artful Dodger" 12-12; **1960** *Perry Mason* "The Case of the Clumsy Clown" 11-5; **1962** *Perry Mason* "The Case

of the Poison Pen Pal" 2-10; **1963** *Perry Mason* "The Case of the Elusive Element" 4-11; *Outer Limits* "Architects of Fear" 9-30; **1964** *Outer Limits* "The Chamelion" 4-27; *Outer Limits* "Behold, Eck!" 10-3; **1965** *Kraft Suspense Theatre* "Won't It Ever Be Morning?" 5-18; *Bonanza* "Five Sundowns to Sunup" 12-15; **1966** *The FBI* "The Sacrifice" 1-16; *The FBI* "The Divided Man" 3-20; *Perry Mason* "The Case of the Crafty Kidnapper" 5-15; **1967** *The FBI* "A Question of Guilt" 1-22; *Invaders* "Quantity Unknown" 3-7; *Wild Wild West* "The Night of the Falcon" 11-10; *Invaders* "The Captive" 11-28; *Wild Wild West* "The Night of the Turncoat" 12-1; **1968** *Mannix* "The Falling Star" 1-6; *Wild Wild West* "The Night of the Underground Terror" 1-19; *Mannix* "The Girl in the Frame" 3-16; *Wild Wild West* "The Night of Miguelito's Revenge" 12-13; **1969** *Wild Wild West* "The Night of the Diva" 3-7; *Wild Wild West* "The Night of the Plague" 4-4; **1970** *Young Lawyers* "The Alienation Kick" 10-12; *Mannix* "The Mouse That Died" 10-17; **1971** *Longstreet* "A World of Perfect Complicity" 9-23; *Mannix* "Days Beyond Recall" 10-20; **1972** *Mission: Impossible* "The Bride" 1-1; *Streets of San Francisco* "Whose Little Boy Are You?" 10-14; *Mission: Impossible* "Movie" 11-4; *Ghost Story* "Time of Terror" 12-22; **1973** *Circle of Fear* "Graveyard Shift" 2-16; **1976** *Bronk* "Vengeance" 2-22.

Alex Henteloff

(born 1945, Los Angeles, California)

A chubby character actor, Alex made his first television appearance in 1966. He became a series regular that same year on *Pistols 'N' Petticoats*. Another series regular slot on *The Young Rebels* (1970-71) was followed by a sitcom role during 1973 in *Pins and Needles*. His final series role came on *The Betty White Show* during 1977-78.

Alex was a frequent guest on *Barney Miller*, making 6 appearances from 1975 to 1982. Later eighties guest shots included work on *Night Court* (3), *Dynasty, St. Elsewhere, Knight Rider, Hill Street Blues, Cover Up, The Last Precinct* and *Scarecrow and Mrs. King*.

GUEST CREDITS

1966 *I Spy* "My Mother the Spy" 3-30; **1971** *Ironside* "Class of '57" 12-16; **1972** *McCloud* "Fifth Man in a String Quartet" 2-2; **1973** *Barnaby Jones* "Murder at Malibu" 4-29; **1974** *Mannix* "Walk on the Blind Side" 10-13; *Apple's Way* "The Outsider" 12-15; **1975** *Barnaby Jones* "Poisoned Pigeon" 3-25; *Cannon* "Search and Destroy" 4-2; *Barnaby Jones* "The Alpha-Bravo War" 10-31; **1976** *Streets of San Francisco* "Runaway" 4-29; *Charlie's Angels* "Night of the Strangler" 10-13; **1977** *Black Sheep Squadron* "Last Mission Over Sangai" 2-8; *Barnaby Jones* "Anatomy of Fear" 2-17; **1979** *Quincy, M.E.* "House of No Return" 1-11; *Man Called Sloane* "The Venus Microbe" 10-27; *Vegas* "Dan Tanna Is Dead" 11-21; **1980** *Barnaby Jones* "Deadline for Murder" 3-27; *Lou Grant* "Goop" 11-24; **1981** *Strike Force* "The Hollow Man" 12-25; **1982** *Simon and Simon* "Matchmakers" 3-9; *Trapper John, M.D.* "Russians and Roses" 12-19; **1983** *Matt Houston* "The Visitors" 2-27; *Hart to Hart* "As the Harts Turn" 3-1; *Knot's Landing* episode 3-3; *Simon and Simon* "Caught Between the Devil and the Deep Blue Sea" 11-10.

TELEFILMS

1973 *Partners in Crime* 3-24 NBC; **1975** *The Last Survivors* 3-4 NBC; *The Invisible Man* 5-6 NBC;

The First 36 Hours of Dr. Durant 5-13 ABC; **1977** *Code Name: Diamond Head* 5-3 NBC; **1978** *The New Adventures of Heidi* 12-13 NBC; **1982** *Victims* 1-11 CBS; **1983** *The Red Light Sting* 4-5 CBS.

Pepe Hern (a.k.a. Pepe Hernandez)
(born 1927, Spain)

A veteran of 50 films (from 1948) and numerous television appearances, Pepe was virtually always cast in Hispanic roles. He graduated from B films to roles in significant movies during the sixties, in *The Magnificent Seven, Madigan, Change of Habit, Joe Kidd* and *Papillon*.

His acting career extended well into the eighties, touching five decades.

GUEST CREDITS

1959 *Rawhide* "Incident at Spanish Rock" 12-18; **1961** *Rifleman* "The Vaqueros" 10-2; **1962** *Thriller* "The Bride Who Died Twice" 3-19; *Rifleman* "Waste" 10-1, 10-8; **1963** *Fugitive* "Smoke Screen" 10-29; *Gunsmoke* "Extradition" 12-7; 12-14; **1964** *Bonanza* "The Campaneros" 4-19; **1965** *Big Valley* "The Way to Kill a Killer" 11-24; **1966** *I Spy* "Turkish Delight" 2-9; *Big Valley* "The Death Merchant" 2-23; *Big Valley* "Legend of a General" 9-19; 9-26;

Run for Your Life "The Sex Object" 10-17; **1969** *Mod Squad* "The Healer"12-9; *Bonanza* "El Jefe" 11-15; **1971** *O'Hara, U. S. Treasury* "Operation: Payoff" 12-10; **1974** *Adam-12* "Training Wheels" 2-5; **1980** *Quincy, M. E.* "The Hope of Elkwood" 12-3.

TELEFILM

1967 *Stranger on the Run* 10-31 NBC.

Irene Hervey
(born July 11, 1910, Los Angeles, Calif.)

The mother of noted singer Jack Jones, Irene Hervey made her film debut in 1930, with many of her 50 movies being light comedies.

She came to television in 1952, with fifties credits on *Fireside Theater* (3), *Matinee Theater* (2), *Studio '57* (2), *Lux Video Theater* and *Studio One*. Irene guested often during the early sixties prior to a series regular role on *Honey West* (1965-66). She worked infrequently thereafter, as she wound down a lengthy acting career.

Hervey last appeared in a syndicated 1981 telefilm called *Goliath Awaits*.

GUEST CREDITS

1959 *Playhouse 90* "A Quiet Game of Cards" 1-29; *Richard Diamond* episode 2-15; **1960** *Perry Mason* "The Case of the Black-Eyed Blonde" 2-13; *Bourbon Street Beat* "False Identity" 5-23; *Markham* episode 6-9; *Thriller* "The Watcher" 11-1; **1961** *Peter Gunn* "Blind Item" 1-23; *Shirley Temple Theater* "The Princess and the Goblins" 3-19; *Surfside 6* "Little Mister Kelly" 5-1; *Perry Mason* "The Case of the Jealous Journalist" 9-2; *Hawaiian Eye* "Two for the Money" 12-6; **1962** *Target: The Corruptors* "One for the Road" 1-12; *Follow the Sun* "The Last of the Big Spenders" 1-14; *Straightaway* "The Drag Strip" 1-24; *Hawaiian Eye* "The Last Samurai" 4-25; *77 Sunset Strip* "Framework for a Badge" 6-1; *Wide Country* "Our Ernie Kills People" 11-1; *Dr. Kildare* "An Ancient Office" 12-6; **1963** *Hawaiian Eye* "Kupkio Kid" 1-8; *Perry Mason* "The Case of the Lawful Lazarus" 3-14; *Eleventh Hour*

Irene Hervey (left), shakes hands with Chief Ironside, played by Raymond Burr, in a flashback episode of NBC's *Ironside*. Barbara Anderson looks on in the center.

"The Wings of Morning" 3-20; *Hawaiian Eye* "Two for the Money" 5-28; **1964** *Twilight Zone* "Black Leather Jackets" 1-31; *Burke's Law* "Who Killed April?" 1-31; **1968** *Mod Squad* "A Quiet Weekend in the Country" 12-3.

Alan Hewitt

(born January 15, 1915, New York City; died November 7, 1986)

In films from 1959, Alan was also a theater director. He was a member of Disney's "stock company", appearing in numerous comedy films like *The Absent-Minded Professor, Son of Flubber* and *The Monkey's Uncle*.

Following a 1954 TV debut, Alan worked in guest roles until he became a regular on *My Favorite Martian* (1964-66). More guest work followed until

retirement in 1978.

GUEST CREDITS

1959 *Alfred Hitchcock Presents* "Invitation to an Accident" 6-21; *Perry Mason* "The Case of the Golden Fraud" 11-21; **1960** *Barbara Stanwyck Show* "No One" 12-26; **1961** *Defenders* "The Point Shaver" 2-3; *Perry Mason* "The Case of the Wintry Wife" 2-18; *New Breed* "The Torch" 3-6; *Maverick* "Triple Indemnity" 3-19; *Saints and Sinners* "A Shame for a Diamond Wedding" 11-26; *Perry Mason* "The Case of the Brazen Request" 12-2; **1962** *Maverick* "One of Our Trains Is Missing" 4-22; **1963** *Defenders* "The Hour Before Doomsday" 2-9; *Defenders* "The Man Who Was" 10-29; **1965** *Perry Mason* "The Case of the Fatal Fetish" 3-4; *Voyage to the Bottom of the Sea* "And Five of Us Are Left" 10-3; *Slattery's People* "The Hero" 11-5; *Dr. Kildare* "Fathers and Daughters" 11-22; *Dr. Kildare* "A Gift of Love" 11-23; *Dr. Kildare* "The Tent-Dwellers" 11-29; *Dr. Kildare* "Going Home" 11-30; **1967** *Daktari* episode 1-24; *Wild Wild* West "The Night of the Colonel's Ghost" 3-10; *Lost in Space* "The Phantom Family" 3-29; *Judd, for the Defense* "A Civil Case of Murder" 9-22; *Iron Horse* "Wild Track" 12-16; **1968** *Felony Squad* "Man on Fire" 3-4; *Ironside* "The Laying on of Hands" 12-10.

TELEFILMS

1969 *Wake Me When the War Is Over* 10-14 ABC; *The D. A.: Murder One* 12-8 NBC; **1975** *The*

Legend of Lizzie Borden 2-l0 ABC; **1977** *Tail Gunner Joe* 2-6 NBC.

Marcel Hillaire

(born Erwin Hiller, Cologne, Germany, April 23, 1908, died January 1, 1988)

Marcel's film debut came in 1954, in *Sabrina*, and he began his television career in 1952. He appeared in countless film and TV roles, alternating between suave and furtive French characters.   He was also delightful in comic roles, in films like *McHale's Navy, Take Her, She's Mine* and *Monkeys, Go Home!*

GUEST CREDITS

1959 *Markham* "The Mutation" l0-17; **1960** *Peter Gunn* "A Slight Touch of Homicide" 4-11; *Twilight Zone* "A Most Unusual Camera" 12-16; **1961** *Adventures in Paradise* "Beachhead" 6-l2; *Dick Powell Show* "A Swiss Affair" 12-12; **1962** *77 Sunset Strip* "The Gemolist Caper" 5-11; *Thriller* "Guilliotine"9-25; **1963** *Twilight Zone* "The New Exhibit" 4-4; *77 Sunset Strip* "Our Man in Switzerland" 5-24; **1964** *Rogues* "The Personal Touch" 9-13; *Combat* "A Rare Vintage" 12-8; *Rogues* "The Computer Goes West" 12-13; **1965** *Man from*

UNCLE "The See-Paris-and-Die Affair" 3-l; *Rogues* "The Pigeons of Paris" 3-7; *Kraft Suspense Theatre* "Rapture at 240" 4-l5; *I Spy* "Chrysanthemum" l0-6; *Man from UNCLE* "The Virtue Affair" 12-3; **1966** *Girl from UNCLE* "The Dog Gone Affair" 9-13; *Time Tunnel* "Devil's Island" 11-11; **1967** *Girl from UNCLE* "The Petit Prix Affair" 3-3; *Bob Hope Chrysler Theater* "Wipeout" 4-26; *Lost in Space* "The Condemned of Space" 3-6; *Daniel Boone* "The Fleeing Nuns" l0-24; **1970** *Mission: Impossible* "The Falcon" l-4, 1-11, 1-18; *McCloud* "Our Man in Paris" l0-2l; **1972** *McCloud* "The Barefoot Stewardess Caper" 12-3; **1977** *Rosetti and Ryan* "Ms. Bluebeard" l0-27.

TELEFILMS

1968 *Now You See It, Now You Don't* 11-11

NBC; **1976** *Frances Gary Powers: The True Story of the U-2 Incident* 9-29 NBC; **1978** *Keefer* 3-16 ABC; *Beggerman, Thief* 11-26, 11-27 ABC.

John Hillerman

(born December 20, l932, Denison, Texas)

Educated at the University of Texas, John joined the U. S. Air Force (1953-57) and joined a community theatre group during his service. After his

discharge, he studied at the American Theatre Wing, did summer stock and some off-Boadway work.

In 1969, he moved to Hollywood and debuted in a telefilm, *The Great Man's Whiskers* (which didn't air until 1973). During 1972 he had a good role in the film *What's Up Doc?*, directed by his good friend Peter Bogdanovich. By 1973 he began to do TV series guest roles, and appeared in films like *High Plains Drifter* and *Paper Moon*, followed by 1974 films *Blazing Saddles* and *Chinatown*.

During 1976 he had a featured role on *Ellery Queen*, developing the very corrrect and dapper appearance that served him so well later. In 1977-78 he was a regular on *The Betty White Show*, further developing the acerbic personna.

In 1980 he was cast in the role of a lifetime, that of Jonathan Quale Higgins, major domo of the estate housing *Magnum, P.I.* The show ran until 1988 and Hillerman's pompous and pretentious character playing against the totally informal Magnum provided a continuing conflict that had a great deal to do with the show's lengthy run. And Hillerman was rewarded with an Emmy in 1987 as Outstanding Supporting Actor.

GUEST CREDITS

1973 *Mannix* "Silent Target" 10-28; **1974** *Kojak* "The Only Way Out" 5-18; **1975** *Mannix* "Search for a Dead Man" 4-6; **1976** *Hawaii Five-0* "Man on Fire" 10-21; *Serpico* "Rapid Fire" 12-10; *New, Original Wonder Woman* "Wonder Woman vs. Gargantua" 12-18; **1977** *Delvecchio* "Licensed to Kill" 2-13; **1978** *Little House on the Prairie* "Harriet's Happenings" 10-30; **1980** *Young Maverick* "Makin' Tracks" 1-9; *Hart to Hart* "Cruise at Your Own Risk" 4-8; *Ten Speed and Brown Shoe* "Diamonds Aren't Forever" 6-27; *Lou Grant* "Pack" 10-27; **1982** *Simon and Simon* "Emeralds Are Not a Girl's Best Friend" 10-7.

TELEFILMS

1971 *Sweet, Sweet Rachel* 10-2 ABC; **1973** *The Great Man's Whiskers* 2-13 NBC; **1974** *The Last Angry Man* 4-16 ABC; *The Law* 10-22 NBC; **1976** *The Invasion of Johnson County* 7-31 NBC; **1977** *Relentless* 9-14 CBS; *Kill Me If You Can* 9-25 NBC; **1978** *A Guide for the Married Man* 10-13 ABC; *Betrayal* 11-13 NBC; **1980** *Marathon* 1-30 CBS; *Battles: The Murder That Wouldn't Die* 3-9 NBC; **1982** *Little Gloria...Happy at Last* 10-24, 10-25 NBC.

Joseph Hindy

(born 1939)

A solid stage background led Joe Hindy to his screen debut in 1969. He began guest roles in TV crime dramas in 1971 and worked for a time on the soap *Another World*.

GUEST CREDITS

1971 *Sarge* "A Terminal Case of Vengeance" 9-21; *The FBI* "End of a Hero" 11-21; **1972** *Mannix* "Cry Pigeon" 1-26; **1973** *Gunsmoke* "This Golden Land" 3-5; *Kojak* "Knockover" 11-14; *Toma* "Frame-up" 11-15; **1974** *Hawkins* "Murder in the Slave Trade" 1-22; *Toma* "Pound of Flesh" 4-19; *Gunsmoke* "Matt Dillon Must Die" 9-9; **1975**

Mannix "Man in a Trap" 1-12; *Rookies* "Death Lady" 10-21; *Baretta* "Sharper Than a Serpent's Tooth" 12-17; **1976** *Kojak* "A Wind from Corsica" 1-18; *Streets of San Francisco* "The Drop" 10-28; **1977** *Kojak* "Monkey on a String" 2-15; **1978** *Rockford Files* "Local Man Eaten by Newspaper" 12-8; *Eddie Capra Mysteries* "Murder Plays a Hand" 12-22; **1979** *Kate Loves a Mystery* "The Valley Strangler" 11-8.

TELEFILMS

1975 *Crossfire* 3-24 NBC; **1979** *The Return of Charlie Chan* 7-17 NBC.

Mitzi Hoag

(born 1932)

Following stage experience, Mitzi made her film debut in 1963. Primarily a television actress, she has been featured in two series regular roles: *Here Come the Brides* (1968-70) and *We'll Get By* (1975).

GUEST CREDITS

1963 *Gunsmoke* "Tall Chester" 4-20; **1967** *Gunsmoke* "Baker's Dozen" 12-25; **1970** *Interns* episode 12-11; **1971** *Alias Smith and Jones* "Stagecoach Seven" 3-11; *Smith Family* "No Place to Hide" 4-28; **1972** *Owen Marshall, Counselor at Law* "Shine a Light on Me" 2-3; *Bonanza* "Stallion" 11-14; **1973** *Mod Squad* "Scion of Death" 2-8; **1974** *Chopper One* "The Boy Who Cried Wolf" 2-7; **1975** *Medical Story* "The Right to Die" 9-11; *Rookies* "Reading, Writing and Angel Dust" 9-16; **1976** *S.W.A.T.* "Officer Luca, You're Dead" 4-3; *1977* *Police Story* "The Malflores" 1-25; *Little House on the Prairie* "The Election" 3-21; **1978** *Incredible Hulk* "Life and Death" 5-12; *Waltons* "The Calling" 9-28; *Harry O* "Second Sight" 11-7; **1979** *Rockford Files* "The Battle Ax and the Exploding Cigar" 1-12.

TELEFILMS

1968 *Hawaii Five-0* 9-20 CBS; **1973** *The Bait* 3-13 ABC; **1974** *Hit Lady* 10-8 ABC; **1977** *The Girl in the Empty Grave* 9-20 NBC; *Deadly Game* 12-3 NBC; **1981** *Murder in Texas* 5-3, 5-4 NBC; *The Five of Me* 5-12 CBS.

Mitzi Hoag

Victor Holchak

A television actor of the seventies, Victor was active in guest roles from 1970 thru 1977. He also worked for a time on the soap *Days of Our Lives*, during 1971 and 1974-75.

GUEST CREDITS

1970 *Gunsmoke* "The Scavengers" 11-16; **1971** *The FBI* "The Natural" 3-14; *Dan August* "Days of Rage" 3-25; *Mod Squad* "Cricket" 9-21; *Ironside* "Dear Fran" 11-9; **1972** *Gunsmoke* "One for the Road" 1-24; *The FBI* "The Jug-Marker" 12-10; **1974** *Barnaby Jones* "Foul Play" 3-31; **1976** *Cannon* "Blood Lines" 2-25; *City of Angels* "Match Point" 5-18; *Police Woman* "Tennis Bum" 11-30; **1977** *Hardy Boys/Nancy Drew Mysteries* "The Creature Came on Sunday" 10-30.

TELEFILM

1980 *Power* 1-14, 1-15 NBC.

Jonathan Hole

(born 1904)

Onstage, and in films from 1924, Jonathan also did numerous radio shows and became a television performer during the fifties. His only TV series regular role came in 1950 in *Stud's Place*, but he guested often in the fifties and sixties.

He was often cast in westerns as townspeople or pioneers, in series like *Rawhide* (4) and *Maverick* (3). He could adopt a worried personna that was well-cast as harried hotel desk clerks. His last

credited role was in a 1974 episode of *Kung Fu*.

GUEST CREDITS

1959 *Maverick* "A Rope of Pearls" 1-4; *Millionaire* "Millionaire Terrance Costigan" 1-14; *Wanted: Dead or Alive* "The Spur" 1-17; *Peter Gunn* "Scuba" 2-16; *Bat Masterson* "Incident in Leadville" 3-18; *Trackdown* "The Eyes of Jerry Kelso" 4-22; *Cheyenne* "The Fine Art of Murder" 5-24; *Perry Mason* "The Case of the Spanish Cross" 5-30; *M Squad* "The Dangerous Game" 6-5; *Maverick* "A Fellow's Brother" 11-22; *Fury* "The Fort" 12-12; **1960** *Maverick* "Greenbacks, Unlimited" 3-13; *Rawhide* "Incident of the Stargazer" 4-1; **1961** *Rawhide* "The Wager on Payday" 6-16; *Detectives* "One Lucky Break" 11-3; **1962** *Rawhide* "Grandmother's Money" 2-23; *G.E. True* "The Amateurs" 12-30; **1963** *Virginian* "A Distant Fury" 3-20; **1964** *Rawhide* "Incident of the Rusty Shotgun" 1-9; *Perry Mason* "The Case of the Scandalous Sculptor" 10-8; *Bonanza* "A Man to Admire" 12-6; **1965** *Burke's Law* "Who Killed Mr. Colby in Lady's Lingerie?" 5-3; *Amos Burke, Secret Agent* "Steam Heat" 9-29; *Ben Casey* "When Givers Prove Unkind" 11-22; **1966** *Laredo* "Above the Law" 1-13; **1969** *Name of the Game* "The Third Choice" 3-7; *Mod Squad* "Captain Greer, Call Surgery" 4-1; **1974** *Kung Fu* "The Vanishing Image" 12-2.

TELEFILMS

1970 *The Over-the-Hill Gang Rides Again* 11-17 ABC; **1972** *Call Her Mom* 2-15 ABC.

Rex Holman

(born 1935)

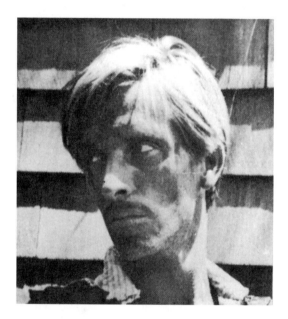

Usually the appearance of lean and sinister-looking Rex Holman on television's western series meant gunfire was imminent, for he was one of the era's meanest villains. *Gunsmoke* worked him in 13 episodes and many other western series made use of his talents. But he appeared in numerous other non-western series from *Star Trek* to *Mission: Impossible* to *The Man from UNCLE* (3).

GUEST CREDITS

1959 *Millionaire* "Millionaire Sergeant Matthew Brogan" 11-25; **1960** *Deputy* "The Choice" 6-25; *Gunsmoke* "Small Water" 9-24; *One Step Beyond* "The Return" 10-11; *Thriller* "Girl with a Secret" 11-15; *Gunsmoke* "No Chip" 12-3; *Tall Man* "Tiger Eye" 12-17; **1961** *Wagon Train* "The Earl Packer Story" 1-4; *Lawman* "The Inheritance" 3-5; *Twilight Zone* "The Passerby" 10-6; *Ben Casey* "My

Good Friend Krikor" 11-27; **1962** *Alcoa Premiere* "Pattern of Guilt" 1-9; *Tales of Wells Fargo* "Who Lives By the Gun" 3-24; *Combat* "Lost Sheep, Lost Shepard" 10-16; *Rifleman* "Death Never Rides Alone" 10-29; **1963** *Bonanza* "The Last Haircut" 2-3; *Have Gun-Will Travel* "Two Plus One" 4-6; **1964** *Gunsmoke* "Comanches Is Soft" 3-7; *Outer Limits* "Demon with a Glass Hand" 10-24; *Man from UNCLE* "The Terbuf Affair" 12-29; **1965** *Gunsmoke* "Malachi" 11-13; *Laredo* "Which Way Did They Go?" 11-18; **1966** *Man from UNCLE* "The Dippy Blonde Affair" 1-7; *Big Valley* "Hazard" 3-9; *Legend of Jesse James* "1863" 3-28; *Road West* "This Savage Land" 9-12, 9-19; *Laredo* "The Legend of Midas Mantee" 9-16; *Iron Horse* "High Devil" 9-26; *Monroes* "The Hunter" 10-26; *Gunsmoke* "The Whispering Tree" 11-12; *Big Valley* "Last Stage to Salt Flats" 12-5; **1967** *Road West* "The Insider" 2-13; *Man from UNCLE* "The Hula Doll Affair" 2-17; *Cimarron Strip* "Journey to a Hanging" 9-7; *Guns of Will Sonnett* episode 9-8; *Gunsmoke* "The Wreckers" 9-11; *Daniel Boone* "The King's Shilling" 11-2; *Iron Horse* "Six Hours to Sky High" 11-25; *Guns of Will Sonnett* "Find a Sonnett, Kill a Sonnett" 12-8; **1968** *Cowboy in Africa* episode 1-29; *High Chaparral* "Threshold of Courage" 3-31; *Gunsmoke* "Zavala" 10-7; *Guns of Will Sonnett* "Chapter and Verse" 10-11; *Star Trek* "Spectre of the Gun" 10-25; *Daniel Boone* "The Return of the Sidewinder" 12-12; **1969** *Gunsmoke* "The Long Night" 2-17; *Lancer* "Child of Rock and Sunlight" 4-1; *Outcasts* "How Tall Is Blood?" 5-5; *Mod Squad* "My Name Is Manolette" 9-30; *Then Came Bronson* "All the World and God" 11-3; *Gunsmoke* "Ring of Darkness" 12-1; *Land of the Giants* "A Place Called Earth" 12-7; **1970** *Lancer* "The Buscaderos" 3-17; *Gunsmoke* "Luke" 11-2; **1971** *Mission: Impossible* "Kitara" 2-20; *Gunsmoke* "Waste" 9-27, 10-4; *Bearcats!* episode 10-7; **1972** *Mannix* "Scapegoat" 3-1; *Nichols* episode 3-7; *Streets of San Francisco* "The Thirty Years Pin" 9-23; *Gunsmoke* "Sarah" 10-16; **1973** *Mod Squad* "And One for My Baby" 3-1; *Kung Fu* "The Jong" 11-1; **1974** *Rookies* "The Authentic Death of Bill Stomper" 1-14; *Gunsmoke* "The Town Tamers" 1-28; *Chase* "Vacation for a President" 2-6; **1975** *S.W.A.T.* "Dealers in Death" 9-27; **1976** *Blue Knight* "The Pink Dragon" 3-24; **1980**

Vegas "Casualty of War" 1-16.

TELEFILMS

1972 *The Bounty Man* 10-31 ABC; **1979** *The Legend of the Golden Gun* 4-10 NBC.

Robert Hooks
(born April 18, 1937, Washington, D. C.)

A strong stage background brought Robert Hooks to a 1965 television debut in a *Profiles in Courage* episode. He made his film debut in 1966 and appeared in *Hurry Sundown* the following year. 1967 also marked the year that he began

Robert Hooks (center) is flanked by *N.Y.P.D.* co-stars Frank Converse (left) and Jack Warden. Hooks established his acting credentials in the 1967-69 ABC series.

his best known television role in *N.Y.P.D.* (1967-69). In 1968 he founded and became Executive Director of the Negro Ensemble Company in New York City.

Following the success of his *N.Y.P.D.* role, Robert virtually left films for television guest roles and appearances in telefilms and miniseries. In recent years, Robert has produced and directed, and his acting work has diminished. In the later eighties he did guest shots on *T. J. Hooker*, *J. J. Starbuck* and *A Different World*. During 1988 he starred on the series *Super Carrier*.

GUEST CREDITS

1969 *Mannix* "Last Rites for Miss Emma" 3-8; *The FBI* "The Silent Partner" 10-12; *Then Came Bronson* "A Long Trip to Yesterday" 12-10; **1970** *Bold Ones: The Doctors* "Killer on the Loose" 10-11; *Man and the City* "Run for Daylight" 11-17; **1973** *Rookies* "The Deadly Cage" 9-24; *McMillan*

and Wife "The Devil You Say?" 10-21; *Marcus Welby, M.D.* "Nguyen" 11-27; **1974** *Streets of San Francisco* "Rampage" 2-28; *The FBI* "Deadly Ambition" 3-17; **1975** *Police Story* "The Cut Man Caper" 10-28; *Petrocelli* "Too Many Alibis" 12-24; **1979** *Time Express* "Rodeo" 5-10; **1980** *Trapper John, M.D.* "Big Bomb" 1-6; **1982** *Quincy, M.E.* "Bitter Pill" 1-6; *Cassie and Company* "Golden Silence" 1-29; *Devlin Connection* episode 12-18; **1983** *Hart to Hart* "Bahama Bound Harts" 2-22; *Hardcastle and McCormick* "Man in a Glass House" 9-25; *Hotel* "Choices" 10-5.

TELEFILMS

1970 *Carter's Army* 1-27 ABC; **1971** *Vanished* 3-8, 3-9 NBC; *The Cable Car Murder* 11-19 CBS; **1972** *Two for the Money* 2-26 ABC; **1973** *Trapped* 11-24 ABC; **1976** *The Killer Who Wouldn't Die* 4-4 ABC; **1978** *To Kill a Cop* 4-10, 4-11 NBC.

Bo Hopkins
(born February 2, 1942, Greenville, South Carolina)

Bo spent two years in the U. S. Army, then studied drama with Stella Adler in New York. He developed a natural "good ol' boy" personna that has stood him well over his lengthy career. After a 1967 television debut there were numerous guest roles before he became a regular on a brief 1974 series, *Doc Elliot*. He gained major exposure with a major role on *Dynasty* during 1981, and in a return to the series in 1987.

Among his numerous eighties guest shots were appearances on *A-Team, Hotel, Finder of Lost Loves, Murder, She Wrote, Fall Guy, Scarecrow and Mrs. King, Crazy Like a Fox* and *The New Mike Hammer*.

His film career, beginning in 1967, included roles in *The Wild Bunch, The Bridge at Remagen, Monte Walsh, The Culpepper Cattle Company, American Graffiti*, and *Midnight Express*.

GUEST CREDITS

1967 *Virginian* "Johnny Moon" 10-11; *Gunsmoke* "Hard Luck Henry" 10-23; *Wild Wild West* "Night of the Iron Fist" 12-8; **1968** *Judd, for the Defense* "No Law Against Murder" 1-19; *Guns of Will Sonnett* "Guilt" 11-29; **1969** *Mod Squad* "A Seat in the Window" 4-15; *Bonanza* "The Witness" 9-21; **1970** *Mod Squad* "A Far Away Place So Near" 11-17; **1972** *Ironside* "And Then There Was One" 1-20; *Nichols* "Sleight of Hand" 2-1; **1973** *Hawaii Five-0* "One Big Happy Family" 10-2; **1974** *Manhunter* "Death on the Run" 10-2; *Rookies* "Death at 6:00 a.m." 10-7; **1975** *Barnaby Jones* "Flight to Danger" 11-7; **1976** *Jigsaw John* "Promise to Kill" 2-2; **1978** *Rockford Files* "The Jersey Bounce" 10-6; *Rockford Files* "Local Man Eaten by Newspaper" 12-8; **1979** *Rockford Files* "The Return of the Black Shadow" 2-17; *Supertrain* "Superstar" 3-14; *Charlie's Angels* "Love Boat Angels" 9-12; **1983** *Matt Houston* "The Beverly Hills Social Club" 3-13.

TELEFILMS

1973 *Doc Elliot* 3-5 ABC; **1975** *The Court Martial of Lt. Calley* 1-12 ABC; *The Runaway Barge* 3-24 NBC; *The Kansas City Massacre* 9-19 ABC; **1976** *Charlie's Angels* 3-21 ABC; *Dawn: Portrait of a Teenage Runaway* 9-27 NBC; **1978** *Thaddeus Rose and Eddie* 2-24 CBS; *Having Babies* 3-21 ABC; *Crisis in Sun Valley* 3-29 NBC; **1979** *Last Ride of the Dalton Gang* 11-20 NBC; *Beggarman, Thief* 11-26 ABC; **1980** *The Plutonium Incident* 3-11 CBS; *Casino* 8-1 CBS; *Rodeo Girl* 9-17 CBS; **1983** *Ghost Dancing* 5-30 ABC.

Charles Horvath
(born 1921; died July 23, 1978)

Charles Horvath began a remarkable career of acting, and being one of Hollywood's premiere stuntmen, in 1946. He doubled stars like Burt Lancaster, Jeff Chandler and Audie Murphy, beginning frequent western outlaw character roles in 1950. There were roles for Horvath in *Vera Cruz, Around the World in Eighty Days, Spartacus* and *Cat Ballou*

Yukon Affair" l2-24; **1966** *Laredo* "The Calico Kid" l-6; *Laredo* "That's Noway, Thataway" l-20; *I Spy* "Turkish Delight" 2-9; *Man from UNCLE* " The Batcave Affair" 4-l; *Big Valley* "Last Train to the Fair" 4-27; **1967** *Wild Wild West* "The Night of the Gypsy Peril" l-20; *Iron Horse* "Banner with the Strange Device" 2-6; *Iron Horse* "Grapes of Grass Valley" l0-2l; *I Spy* "Red Sash of Courage" l0-30; *High Chaparral* "The Firing Wall" l2-3l; **1968** *Lost in Space* "Fugitives in Space" l-3l; *Mission: Impossible* "The Phoenix" 3-3; **1969** *High Chaparral* "Shadow of the Wind" l-l0; *Mod Squad* "Captain Greer, Call Surgery" 4-l; **1975** *Rockford Files* "Chicken Little Is a Little Chicken" ll-l4; **1977** *Police Woman* "The Buttercup Killer" l2-l3.

TELEFILM

1971 *The Desperate Mission* l2-3 NBC.

among his nearly fifty film credits.

While in the U. S. Marines he developed a reputation as a Judo expert, and later trained Elvis Presley in the art. His menacing appearance created castings as a villain on most of his television western and sci-fi series guest roles. A veteran Hollywood stuntman, H. Wills, declared that "Charles has become a figure of monumental influence, whose gifts, personal and professional, can scarcely be exaggerated".

Charles died in l978, survived by a wife, a son and two daughers.

GUEST CREDITS

1959 *Black Saddle* "Client: McQueen" l-24; *Texan* "The Man Hater" 6-22; *Texan* "The Telegraph Story" l0-26; *Bonanza* "The Truckee Strip" 11-2l; *Lineup* "The Chinatown Story" l2-9; **1960** *Twilight Zone* "The Big Tall Wish" 4-8; *Black Saddle* "End of the Line" 5-6; *Peter Gunn* "Send a Thief" 5-l6; *Westerner* "Jeff" 9-30; *Lawman* "Samson the Great" 11-20; **1961** *Wagon Train* "The Christopher Hale Story" 3-15; *Bonanza* "Thunderhead Swindle" 4-29; *Outlaws* "Chalk's Lot" l0-5; **1962** *Tall Man* "Trial by Fury" 4-l4; *Ben Casey* "An Uncommonly Innocent Killing" 5-7; **1965** *Wild Wild West* "The Night of the Glowing Corpse" l0-29; *Man from UNCLE* "The

Susan Howard
(born January 28, l946, Marshall, Texas)

Educated at the University of Texas, Susan made her television debut in 1967. She did several late sixties guest shots on *I Dream of Jeannie* (3) and *The Flying Nun* (2). After numerous sci-fi and detective series guest roles she landed a featured regular role on *Petrocelli* (1974-76).

After additional guest work, Donna moved into a wonderful long-running role on *Dallas*, appearing as Donna Krebs (1979-87). She is currently appearing on a series of commercials for the oil industry.

GUEST CREDITS

1967 *Iron Horse* "Appointment with an Epitaph" 2-13; *Iron Horse* "The Return of Hode Avery" 11-4; **1968** *Tarzan* "Trina" 4-5; *Star Trek* "Day of the Dove" 11-1; *1969* *Outcasts* "The Candidate" 1-27; *Ironside* "A Matter of Love and Death" 4-3; *Bonanza* "The Medal" 10-26; *Land of the Giants* "Collectors' Item" 11-2; *Mannix* "Who Killed Me?" 12-13; **1970** *Immortal* "Legacy" 10-15; **1971** *Mannix* "Round Trip to Nowhere" 1-2; *The FBI* "Center of Peril" 1-17; **1972** *Mission: Impossible* "Committed" 1-2; **1973** *Bold Ones: The Doctors* "Teriminal Career" 1-2; *Griff* "The Framing of Billy the Kid" 9-29; **1976** *City of Angels* "The House on Orange Grove Avenue" 2-16; *Rockford Files* "Feeding Frenzy" 10-15; **1977** *Most Wanted* "Ms. Murder" 1-8; *Barnaby Jones* "Yesterday's Terror" 10-13; **1978** *Paper Chase* "Kingsfield's Daughter" 11-28; **1979** *Julie Farr, M.D.* episode 6-12; *Vegas* "Classic Connection" 12-19.

TELEFILMS

1973 *Savage* 3-31 NBC; **1974** *Indict and Convict* 1-6 ABC; **1977** *Killer on Board* 10-10 NBC; **1978** *Superdome* 1-9 ABC; **1979** *Power Man* 5-11 ABC.

Clark Howat

(born 1917)

Clark began a stage career in 1939, and had a film debut in 1949, with only *Airport* and *Billy Jack* as significant films. However, he has made hundreds of television appearances, dating from the early

fifties. He was a member of Jack Webb's "stock company" appearing in 11 *Dragnet* episodes, and on *Adam-12* and *O'Hara, U. S. Treasury*.

GUEST CREDITS

1959 *One Step Beyond* "Emergency Only" 2-3; *Millionaire* "Millionaire Tom Hampton" 11-28; **1960** *Wyatt Earp* "The Posse" 5-10; **1961** *Perry Mason* "The Case of the Misguided Missile" 5-6; **1962** *Detectives* "Never the Twain" 2-23; **1964** *Perry Mason* "The Case of the Fifty Millionth Frenchman" 2-20; *Man from UNCLE* "The Dove Affair" 12-25; **1965** *Perry Mason* "The Case of the Twelfth Wildcat" 10-31; **1967** *Dragnet* "The Big LSD" 1-12; *Dragnet* "The Big Bank Examiners" 2-23; *Dragnet* "The Big Fur Robbery" 3-16; *Dragnet* "The Big Jade" 3-23; *Dragnet* "The Big Blank" 10-19; *Dragnet* "The Big Senior Citizen" 10-26; *Judd, for the Defense* "To Love and Stand Mute" 12-8; **1968** *Dragnet* "The Big Clan" 2-8; *Dragnet* "The Big Problem" 3-28; *Dragnet* "Training-DR-18" 11-21; **1969** *Dragnet* "Homicide-The Student" 9-25; *Dragnet* "Bunco-$9,000" 12-11; **1971** *O'Hara, U. S. Treasury* "Operation: Stolen Bonds" 10-1; *Adam-12* "Day Watch" 11-24; **1972** *Man and the City* "Diagnosis: Corruption" 1-5; *O'Hara, U. S. Treasury* "Operation: Mr. Felix" 2-18; **1974** *Marcus Welby, M.D.* "Each Day a Miracle" 1-22; **1975** *Mobile One* "The Bank Job" 10-3; *Rockford Files* "The Mayor's

Committee from Deer Lick Falls" 11-25.

TELEFILM

1971 *Vanished* 3-8, 3-9 NBC.

David Hurst

(born 1925)

An Austrian character actor, David got his start on British stage and screen. He worked sporadically on American television from 1960 into the early eighties.

GUEST CREDITS

1960 *Dow Hour of Great Mysteries* "The Dachet Diamonds" 9-20; **1965** *Man from UNCLE* "The Brain Killer Affair" 3-8; **1966** *Hawk* "The Longleat Chronicles" 9-15; *Girl from UNCLE* "The Mata Hari Affair" 10-4; **1967** *Mannix* "The Many Deaths of Saint Christopher" 10-7; *Mission: Impossible* "The Astrologer" 12-3; **1968** *Man from UNCLE* "The Seven Wonders of the World Affair" 1-8, 1-15; *Run for Your Life* "The Exchange" 3-27; **1969** *Mission: Impossible* "The Test Case" 1-19; *Star Trek* "The Mark of Gideon" 1-17; **1970** *Mod Squad* "The Exile" 2-3; *The FBI* "The Traitor" 9-27; **1976**

Serpico "The Indian" 10-8; **1977** *McCloud* "The Moscow Connection" 1-23; **1978** *Quincy, M.E.* "Dead or Alive" 11-16; **1980** *Charlie's Angels* "Angel in Hiding" 11-30.

TELEFILMS

1979 *Nero Wolfe* 12-19 ABC; **1981** *Skokie* 11-17 CBS.

Josephine Hutchinson

(born October 12, 1904, Seattle, Washington)

Josephine Hutchinson made her silent film debut in 1917 at age 13, a screen career that saw her evolve through being a leading lady of the thirties into an energetic matron of the fifties and sixties. Among her films were roles in *Ruby Gentry, North by Northwest, Baby, the Rain Must Fall* and *Nevada Smith*.

She had numerous fifties television series credits, including *Pepsi Cola Playhouse, 20th Century Fox Hour, Schlitz Playhouse of Stars* and *Perry Mason*. Her work on TV continued into the mid- seventies.

GUEST CREDITS

1959 *Perry Mason* "The Case of the Spanish Cross" 5-20; *Gunsmoke* "Johnny Red" 10-3; **1960** *Lineup* "Prince of Penmen" 1-6; *Wagon Train* "The Tom Tuckett Story" 3-2; *Rifleman* "The Prodigal" 4-26; *Deputy* "Mother and Son" 10-29; **1961** *Checkmate* "A Matter of Conscience" 2-18; *General Electric Theater* "A Possibility of Oil" 2-19; *Perry Mason* "The Case of the Barefaced Witness" 3-18; *Tales of Wells Fargo* "Lady Trouble" 4-24; *Dick Powell Show* "Up Jumped the Devil" 11-28; **1962** *New Breed* "Mr. Weltschlmerz" 2-13; *Rawhide* "Grandma's Money" 2-23; *Perry Mason* "The Case of the Mystified Miner" 2-24; *Law and Mr. Jones* "The Boy Who Said No" 4-26; *Twilight Zone* "I Sing the Body Electric" 5-18; **1963** *General Electric Theater* "The Black-Robed Ghost" 3-10; *Kraft Suspense Theatre* "The Machine That Played God" 12-5; **1964** *Burke's Law* "Who Killed the Eleventh

In a 1962 episode of *The Twilight Zone,* Josephine Hutchinson (second from left), played a robotic surrogate mother. The children in "I Sing the Body Electric" were, from left, Angela Cartwright, Dana Dillaway and Charles Herbert (CBS).

Best-Dressed Woman in the World?" 4-24; *Dr. Kildare* "The Last Leaves on the Tree" 10-15; **1967** *Gunsmoke* "Ladies from St. Louis" 3-25; **1968** *Name of the Game* "Nightmare" 10-18; **1969** *Then Came Bronson* "All the World and God" 12-3; *The FBI* "The Doll Courier" 12-21; **1970** *Bold Ones: The Doctors* "If I Can't Sing, I'll Listen" 1-18; *The FBI* "Time Bomb" 10-25; *Bonanza* "The Love Child" 11-8; **1971** *Mod Squad* "A Short Course in War" 1-5; *Mannix* "Dark So Early, Dark So Long" 9-15; *Longstreet* "A World of Perfect Complicity" 9-23; **1972** *Sixth Sense* "And Scream by the Light of the Moon, the Moon" 11-25; **1974** *Little House on the*

Prairie "If I Should Wake Before I Die" 10-23.

TELEFILMS

1968 *Shadow Over Elveron* 3-5 NBC; **1971** *Travis Logan, D. A.* 3-11 CBS; *The Homecoming* "12-19 CBS.

Wilfred Hyde-White

(born May 12, 1903, Bourton-on-the-Water, England; died May 6, 1991)

A magician before winning a scholarship to R.A.D.A., Wilfred had his first film role in 1922. Wilfred often played smooth gentlemen with devious intent; in more recent times he played sly oldsters. His 50-plus film career included over 120 screen roles. He served in the British Army during World War II.

In television from 1953, his first series regular role was in *Peyton Place* (1967), playing the family scion. He starred in an abbreviated 1979 sitcom called *The Associates* and also had a featured role during 1981 on *Buck Rogers in the 25th Century.*

Wilfred died in 1991 of congestive heart failure, survived by his wife, two sons, a daughter and four grandchildren.

GUEST CREDITS

1961 *Route 66* "An Absence of Tears" 3-3; **1962** *Ben Casey* "Monument to an Aged Hunter" 3-19; **1963** *Twilight Zone* "Passage to Lady Anne" 5-9; **1964** *Ben Casey* "Evidence of Things Not Seen" 4-22; **1965** *Ben Casey* "When Givers Prove Unkind" 11-22; *Ben Casey* "The Man from Quasilla" 11-29;

Ben Casey "Why Did the Day Go Backwards?" 12-6; **1966** *Bob Hope Chrysler Theater* "Wind Fever" 3-2; **1967** *Mission: Impossible* "Echo of Yesterday" 12-10; **1968** *Daniel Boone* "Then Who Will Hang from the Yardarm if Willy Gets Away?" 2-8; **1969** *Name of the Game* "The Suntan Mob" 2-7; *It Takes a Thief* "To Lure a Man" 12-18; **1970** *Paris 7000* "Ordeal" 2-26; **1972** *Most Deadly Game* "I Said the Sparrow" 11-22; *Columbo* "Dagger of the Mind" 11-26; **1975** *Get Christie Love!* "Last Salute to the Commodore" 5-2; **1978** *Battlestar Galactica* "Saga of a Star World" 9-17; **1979** *Vegas* "A Way to Live" 5-2.

TELEFILMS

1968 *The Sunshine Patriot* 12-16 NBC; **1969** *Fear No Evil* 3-3 NBC; *Run a Crooked Mile* 11-18 ABC; **1970** *Ritual of Evil* 2-23 NBC; **1973** *A Brand New Life* 2-20 ABC; **1976** *The Great Houdinis* 10-9 ABC; **1980** *Scout's Honor* 9-30 NBC; *Father Damien: The Leper Priest* 10-27 NBC; **1982** *The Letter* 5-3 ABC.

Eugene Iglesias

A husky Mexican-American actor of the sixties, Eugene appeared in some of the better series of the era, until 1969.

GUEST CREDITS

1960 *Rebel* "Don Gringo" 11-20; **1961** *Outlaws* "Rape of Red Sky" 2-23; *Peter Gunn* "Cry Love, Cry Murder" 3-17; *Rebel* "The Uncourageous" 5-7; *One Step Beyond* "Blood Flower"5-16; **1962** *Cain's Hundred* "Savage in Darkness" 3-27; *Rawhide* "The Reunion" 4-6; **1965** *Bonanza* "Woman of Fire" 1-17; **1966** *Fugitive* "Stroke of Genius" 2-1; *Fugitive* "Last Oasis" 9-13; *Wild Wild West* "The Night of the Poisonous Posey" 10-28; **1967** *Hondo* "The Rebel

Hat" 12-29; **1969** *Wild Wild West* "The Night of the Pistoleros" 3-21.

Margie Impert

(born June 4, 1945, Horseheads, New York)

A seventies/eighties television actress, Margie gained her first experience on the soap *Another World* during the early seventies. She began guest work in 1975 and was a regular on the short-lived adventure series, *Spencer's Pilots* (1976). Additional guest work preceded another series regular slot on *Maggie* (1981-82).

During the mid- eighties Margie guested on *Magnum, P.I.* (2) and *Highway to Heaven* (2).

GUEST CREDITS

1975 *Six Million Dollar Man* "The Bionic Woman" 3-17, 3-23; *Doctor's Hospital* "Sleepless and Pale Eyelids" 9-24; *Cannon* "The Iceman" 10-1; **1977** *Rosetti and Ryan* episode 9-22; *Rockford Files* "Forced Retirement" 12-9; **1979** *Barnaby Jones* "Echo of a Distant Battle" 1-11; *Incredible Hulk* "Behind the Wheel" 11-9; **1980** *Lou Grant* episode 2-18; **1981** *Palmerstown, U. S. A.* "Scandal" 3-24; **1982** *Magnum, P.I.* "Mr. White Death" 11-18; **1983** *Trauma Center* "Breakthrough" 10-13.

TELEFILM

1979 *Crisis in Mid-Air* 2-13 CBS.

Dean Jagger

(born November 7, 1903, Lima, Ohio; died February 5, 1991.)

A splendid character actor, Dean studied at Wabash University before moving to vaudeville and Broadway. Following a 1928 film debut, he appeared in 80 theatrical films, including an Academy Award winning role in *12 O'Clock High* (1949). His other films of note were *The Robe, Elmer Gantry* and *Firecreek*.

Dean came to television in 1948, appearing in an early *Studio One* production. Fifties credits included *Lux Video Theatre, Schlitz Playhouse of*

Stars, *Studio '57, Zane Grey Theater* and *Playhouse 90*. Early sixties guest roles were followed by a featured role on *Mr. Novak* (1963-65).

After a number of seventies guest roles, Dean earned an Emmy in 1980 for Best Performance in a Religious Program, for *This Is the Life* "Independence and '76". This fine talent died in 1991 of complications of flu, survived by his wife, a daughter and two stepsons.

GUEST CREDITS

1959 *Loretta Young Show* "Speed from the East" 2-1; **1961** *Twilight Zone* "Static" 3-10; **1962** *General Electric Theater* "Mister Doc" 4-29; **1963** *Alfred Hitchcock Hour* "The Star Juror" 3-15; **1966** *The FBI* "The Assassin" 10-9; *Fugitive* "Right in the Middle of the Season" 11-29; **1970** *Storefront Lawyers* "A Man's Castle" 9-16; *Name of the Game* "Little Bear Died Running" 11-6; **1971** *Bonanza* "Shadow of a Hero" 2-21; **1972** *Columbo* "The Most Crucial Game" 11-5; *Kung Fu* "Dark Angel" 11-11; **1973** *Alias Smith and Jones* "Only Three to a Bed" 1-13; *Medical Center* episode 1-17; *Delphi Bureau*

"The Terror Broker Project" 3-17; *Shaft* "The Executioners" 10-9; **1976** *Harry O* "The Mysterious Case of Lester and Dr. Fong" 3-18; **1977** *Hunter* "The Costa Rica Connection" 4-22; **1979** *Waltons* "Founder's Day" 3-22; **1980** *Hallmark Hall of Fame* "Gideon's Trumpet" 4-30.

TELEFILM

1970 *The Brotherhood of the Bell* 9-17 CBS; **1971** *Incident in San Francisco* 2-28 ABC; **1972** *The Glass House* 3-4 CBS; *The Delphi Bureau* 3-6 ABC; **1973** *The Stranger* 2-26 NBC; **1974** *The Hanged Man* 3-13 ABC.

Clifton James
(born May 29, 1923, New York City)

Following 5 years in The U. S. Army during World War II, Clifton attended the University of Oregon and studied at Actor's Studio. From a 1954 film debut in *On the Waterfront* to later screen efforts like *Cool Hand Luke, Will Penny, The Reivers, Silver Streak* and *The Bad News Bears in Breaking Training*, he created a consistent personna: a rotund cigar-chomping and blustery menace. He played a redneck sheriff in two James Bond films: *Live and Let Die* and *Man with the Golden Gun*.

His television appearances were somewhat sporadic, but he is probably best remembered as the sadistic police lieutenant in *City of Angels* (1976). He was also a regular on the sitcom, *Lewis and Clark* (1981-82).

GUEST CREDITS

1961 *Cain's Hundred* "Comeback" 11-7; **1963** *Nurses* "Strike" 10-24; **1965** *Gunsmoke* "The Lady" 3-27; *Slattery's People* "Rally Round Your Own Flag, Mister" 10-15; **1966** *Gunsmoke* "The Wrong Man" 10-29; *Virginian* "Linda" 11-30; **1967** *Cimarron Strip* "Till the End of Night" 11-16; **1968** *Bonanza* "The Real People of Muddy Creek" 10-6; *Mannix* "A Copy of Murder" 11-2; **1969** *Ironside* "Rundown on a Bum Rap" 1-30; **1970** *Gunsmoke* "Snow Train I, II" 10-19, 10-26; **1971** *Bonanza* "Winter Kill" 3-28; **1974** *Six Million Dollar Man* "The Deadly Replay" 11-22; **1980** *Quincy, M.E.* "Last Rights" 9-16; **1983** *A-Team* "Pros and Cons" 2-8; *A-Team* "The White Ballot" 12-6.

TELEFILMS

1975 *The Runaway Barge* 3-24 NBC; *Friendly Persuasion* 5-18 ABC; *The Deadly Tower* 10-18 NBC; **1979** *Hart to Hart* 9-25 ABC; *Undercover with the KKK* 10-23 NBC; **1980** *Guyana Tragedy: The Story of Jim Jones* 4-15, 4-16 CBS.

Renne Jarrett
(born January 28, 1946, Brooklyn, New York)

A child actor in the mid-fifties soap, *Portia Faces Life* (1954-55), a grown-up Renne reentered television in 1969 and appeared on the soap *The Edge of Night* for a time in 1970. She gained a starring role on an abbreviated sitcom, *Nancy* (1970-71). She also got back to her soap roots, with stints on *Somerset* and on *Love of Life*.

During the later seventies, she guested on a number of TV crime series, and did a couple of guest shots on *Archie Bunker's Place*. In the mid-eighties, a mature Renne was seen on *Finder of Lost Loves* and *Hotel*.

GUEST CREDITS

1969 *Then Came Bronson* "Sybil" 12-31; **1970** *Mod Squad* "The King of Empty Cups" 1-20; *High Chaparral* "The Lieutenant" 2-27; *Medical Center* "The Combatants" 3-18; **1974** *Streets of San Francisco* "I Ain't Marchin' Anymore" 10-10; *Barnaby Jones* "Death on Deposit" 12-3; **1975** *Petrocelli* "Once Upon a Victim" 1-29; *Barnaby Jones* "A Taste for Murder" 12-4; **1976** *Joe Forrester* "Act of Violence" 1-13; *Ellery Queen* "The Adventure of the Tyrant of Tin Pan Alley" 3-7; *Bert D'Angelo, Superstar* "Flanagan's Fleet" 4-24; *City of Angels* "Match Point" 5-18; **1977** *Barnaby Jones* "A Simple Case of Terror" 2-3; *Most Wanted* "The Parasite" 2-26; *Quincy, M.E.* "Hit and Run at Danny's" 3-11; **1979** *Barnaby Jones* "Child of Love, Child of Vengeance" 3-15, 3-22.

TELEFILMS

1971 *In Search of America* 3-23 ABC; **1973** *Cat Creature* 2-11 CBS; **1974** *The Family Kovack* 4-5 CBS; **1975** *The First 36 Hours of Dr. Durant* 5-13 ABC; **1976** *The New Daughters of Joshua Cabe* 5-29 ABC; **1979** *When Hell Was in Session* 10-8 NBC.

Georgann Johnson
(born August 15, 1926, Decorah, Iowa)

A well respected actress for decades, Georgann's introduction to television was as a regular on *Mr. Peepers* (1952-55). Other fifties work included *Studio One* (2), *U.S. Steel Hour* and *Alfred Hitchcock Presents*. After 1967 she was absent from TV guest roles until 1981, but she had prominent roles on soaps *Somerset* and *As the World Turns*.

In 1985 Georgann worked in a series regular role for the first time in 40 years, in *Our Family Honor*. She was also a regular on *The Trials of Rosie O'Neill* (1990-91). Georgann is the widow of actor-director Stanley Prager (1917-72) and is the mother of actress Sally Prager.

GUEST CREDITS

1959 *Goodyear Theater* "Christabel" 6-8; **1960** *One Step Beyond* "Rendezvous" 12-27; **1962** *Dr. Kildare* "Guest Appearance" 10-25; **1963** *Defenders*

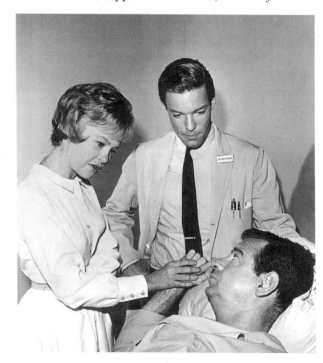

Georgann Johnson ministers to Walter Matthau with Richard Chamberlain looking on . The scene was from a 1964 episode of *Dr. Kildare* (NBC) called "Man Is a Rock".

"A Book for Burning" 3-30; **1964** *Defenders* "The Secret" 2-8; *Nurses* "The Warrior" 6-18; *Dr. Kildare* "Man Is a Rock" 9-24; *Slattery's People* "Is Laura the Name of the Game?" 11-9; **1965** *Fugitive* "When the Wind Blows" 12-28; **1967** *Fugitive* "Run the Man Down" 1-3; **1981** *Lou Grant* "Home Town" 11-23; **1982** *Quincy, M.E.* "The Flight of the Nightengale" 3-3; *Code Red* "No Escape" 3-21; **1983** *Cutter to Houston* "Race for Life" 10-22; *Hart to Hart* "Highland Fling" 11-29.

TELEFILM

1983 *The Day After* 11-20 ABC.

John Dennis Johnston

A frequent eighties television villain, John Dennis Johnston had his only series regular role on the abbreviated 1979 series, *Dear Detective*. He excels at rural and redneck roles, and was recently seen in a featured role in a 1996 telefilm, *Ruby Ridge: An American Tragedy*.

GUEST CREDITS

1971 *Adam-12* "Log 115-Gang War" 1-9; **1976** *Bronk* "The Deadlier Sex" 1-18; *Charlie's Angels* "Hellride" 9-22; **1977** *Police Woman* "The Killer Cowboys" 2-8; *Nashville 99* "episode 4-8; *Rockford Files* "The Battle of Canoga Park" 9-30; **1980** *Charlie's Angels* "An Angel's Trail" 2-27; **1981** *Hill Street Blues* "Blood Money" 11-5; **1982** *Strike Force* "The Outcast" 1-8; *Little House on the Prairie* "He Was Only Twelve" 5-3; *Bret Maverick* "The Hildago Thing" 5-4; *Powers of Matthew Star* episode 11-12; *Bring 'Em Back Alive* "Thirty Hours" 11-16; **1983** *A-Team* "Bad Day at Black Rock" 2-22; *Rousters* "Eye Witness Blues" 12-20.

TELEFILMS

1976 *I Want to Keep My Baby!* 11-19 CBS; **1978** *Kiss Meets the Phantom of the Park* 10-28 NBC; *Steel Cowboy* 12-6 NBC; *The Jordan Chance* 12-12 CBS; **1982** *The Ambush Murders* 1-5 CBS; *The*

Executioner's Song 11-28, 11-29 NBC.

I. Stanford Jolley

(born 1900; died December 6, 1978)

I. Stanford Jolley had the widest possible variety of acting, beginning in stock and vaudeville, thence to Broadway, then radio, films and television. After a 1937 film debut he appeared in nearly 500 movies. He began playing heavies in western films and spent much of the balance of his career in that type of role.

The advent of television brought him a great deal of work, especially in the western series genre. His son is motion picture art director Stan Jolley.

GUEST CREDITS

1960 *Perry Mason* "The Case of the Wayward Wife" 1-23; **1962** *Maverick* "Poker Face" 1-7; **1963** *Rawhide* "The Peddler" 1-19; *Rifleman* "Hostages to Fortune" 3-4; *Rawhide* "Incident of the Pale Rider" 3-15; *Virginian* "Runaway Home" 4-24; *Wagon Train* "The Myra Marshall Story" 10-21; *Gunsmoke* "Carter Caper" 11-16; *Wagon Train* "The Fenton Canaby Story" 12-30; **1964** *Fugitive* "Search in a Windy City" 2-4; *Rawhide* "Incident at Zebulon" 3-5; *Wagon Train* "The Ben Engel Story" 3-16; *Bonanza* "Return to Honor" 3-22; **1965** *Gunsmoke* "The Hostage" 12-4; **1967** *Gunsmoke* "Prairie

Wolfer" 11-13; *High Chaparral* "The Widow from Red Rock" 11-26; **1968** *Cimarron Strip* "The Judgment" 1-4; *Gunsmoke* "Lyle's Kid" 9-23; **1969** *Gunsmoke* "The Reprisal" 2-10; *Gunsmoke* "The Devil's Outpost" 9-22; **1970** *Gunsmoke* "Morgan" 3-2; *Gunsmoke* "The Witness" 11-23.

TELEFILM

1976 *The Macahans* 1-19 CBS.

L.Q. Jones

(born Justus E. McQueen, 1927, Beaumont, Texas)

Educated at Lamar Junior College and the University of Texas, L. Q. (then Justus McQueen), became a Lt. Commander during service with the U. S. Navy. He made his film debut in 1954 in *Battle Cry* and later appeared in *Love Me Tender, The Naked and the Dead, Torpedo Run, The Young Lions, Major Dundee, The Wild Bunch, The Ballad of Cable Hogue* and *Lone Wolf McQuade*.

His television career began with a 1955-56 regular role on *Cheyenne*. From that point on he was a staple on TV westerns in guest starring roles. During 1964-67 he had a recurring role on *The*

Virginian, appearing as Belden, a ranch hand. In the sixties and seventies he also operated a very successful production company called LQ/Jaf.

With the seventies demise of western series, he turned to playing heavies on crime series. True to his western heritage he did 6 eighties guest shots on *The Yellow Rose* and was in a 1988 western telefilm, *Red River*.

GUEST CREDITS

1959 *Black Saddle* "Client: Banke" 4-11; *Tightrope* "The Frame" 9-22; **1960** *Johnny Ringo* "Four Came Quietly" 1-28; *Rebel* "The Earl of Durango" 6-12; *Rebel* "Explosion" 11-27; **1961** *Detectives* "Kinfolk" 1-20; *Wyatt Earp* "Casey and the Clowns" 2-21; *Americans* "The Coward" 5-8; *Laramie* "The Replacement" 3-27; *Lawman* "The Bride" 4-1; **1962** *Ben Casey* "The Fireman Who Raised Rabbits" 11-28; *Wagon Train* "Charlie Wooster—Outlaw" 2-20; **1963** *Route 66* "Shall Forfeit His Dog and Ten Shillings to the King" 2-22; *Empire* "The Convention" 5-14; *Rawhide* "Incident at El Crucero" 10-10; *Gunsmoke* "Tobe" 10-19; *Virginian* "Run Quiet" 11-13; **1964** *Rawhide* "Incident at Gila Flats" 1-30; *Virginian* "First to Thine Own Self" 2-12; *Rawhide* "The Race" 9-25; *Virginian* "Big Image…Little Man" 10-28; *Virginian* "The Girl from Yesterday" 11-11; *Gunsmoke* "Jonah

Hutchinson" 12-5; *Virginian* "Portrait of a Widow" 12-9; **1965** *Slattery's People* "How Do You Fall in Love with a Town?" 1-22; *Virginian* "Old Cowboy" 3-31; **1966** *Man Called Shenandoah* "Rope's End" 1-17; *Big Valley* "By Force and Violence" 3-30; *Bob Hope Chrysler Theater* "The Faceless Man" 5-4; **1967** *Big Valley* "Court-Martial" 3-6; *Big Valley* "Showdown in Limbo" 3-27; *Virginian* "Lady of the House" 4-5; *Big Valley* "Ambush" 9-18; *Cimarron Strip* "The Battleground" 9-28; *Cimarron Strip* "The Search" 11-9; *Hondo* "Hondo and the Death Drive" 12-1; **1968** *Big Valley* "Fall of a Hero" 2-5; **1969** *Hawaii Five-0* "King of the Hill" 1-8; *Gunsmoke* "The Good Samaritans" 3-10; *Lancer* "Blind Man's Bluff" 9-23; **1970** *Gunsmoke* "Albert" 2-9; *Gunsmoke* "The Gun" 11-9; **1971** *Alias Smith and Jones* "Stagecoach Seven" 3-11; *The FBI* "Dynasty of Hate" 10-10; *Cannon* "Fool's Gold" 10-19; *Cade's County* "Delegate at Large" 11-21; **1972** *Gunsmoke* "Tara" 1-17; *Delphi Bureau* "The Man Upstairs/The Man Downstairs Project" 10-26; *Bold Ones: The Doctors* "A Purge of Madness" 12-5; *Alias Smith and Jones* 'McGuffin" 12-9; **1973** *Ironside* "The Caller" 1-25; *Kung Fu* "An Eye for an Eye" 1-25; *Assignment: Vienna* "A Deadly Shade of Green" 1-27; *Cannon* "The Perfect Alibi" 10-31; **1974** *Magician* "The Illusion of the Curious Counterfeit" 1-14, 1-21; **1975** *Kung Fu* "The Last Raid" 4-5; **1975** *Matt Helm* "Deadly Breed" 11-8; **1976** *Movin' On* "The Big Switch" 1-20; *Charlie's Angels* "Bullseye" 12-1; **1977** *McCloud* "The Moscow Connection" 1-23; **1978** *CHiPs* "Rustling" 1-12; *Charlie's Angels* "Angels in the Backfield" 1-25; *Columbo* "The Consirators" 5-13; **1979** *Incredible Hulk* "Jake" 11-2; *Charlie's Angels* "Angel Hunt" 11-2; **1980** *Vegas* "The Lido Girls" 2-6; *Charlie's Angels* "An Angel's Trail" 2-27; **1981** *Walking Tall* "The Hit Man" 2-7; *Riker* "Honkeytonk" 3-14; *Fall Guy* "Colt's Outlaws" 11-10; **1983** *Yellow Rose* "Divided We Fall" 10-8; *Yellow Rose* "When Honor Dies" 10-22; *Yellow Rose* "A Question of Love" 12-10.

TELEFILMS

1972 *The Bravos* 1-9 ABC; *Fireball Forward* 3-5 ABC; **1974** *Mrs. Sundance* 1-15 ABC; *Manhunter* 2-26 CBS; *The Strange and Deadly Occurance* 9-

24 NBC; **1975** *Attack on Terror: The FBI vs. the Ku Klux Klan* 2-20, 2-21 CBS; **1976** *Banjo Hackett: Roamin' Free* 5-30 NBC; **1978** *Standing Tall* 1-21 NBC; **1979** *The Sacketts* 5-15, 5-16 CBS.

William Jordan
(born October 13, Milan, Indiana)

Following a 1964 film debut, there were few large screen roles for William Jordan, but he carved a niche on television, as a guest star and as co-star of two series: *Project UFO* (1978-79) and *Beyond Westworld* (1980).

GUEST CREDITS

1968 *High Chaparral* "The Buffalo Soldiers" 11-22; **1972** *Mannix* "Lost Sunday" 12-3; *Sixth Sense* "Five Widows Weeping" 12-9; **1973** *Griff* "The Framing of Billy the Kid" 9-29; *Magician* "Lady in a Trap" 11-27; *Streets of San Francisco* "Winterkill" 12-13; **1974** *New Perry Mason* "The Case of the Violent Valley" 1-20; *Rockford Files* "Exit Prentiss Carr" 10-4; *Streets of San Francisco* "Cry Help" 11-7; **1975** *Cannon* "Man in the Middle" 10-29; *Barbary Coast* "Arson and Old Lace" 11-14; **1976** *Rockford Files* "The Italian Bird Fiasco" 2-13;

Victor Jory (center), is flanked by Mike Connors and Vera Miles in a 1969 episode of *Mannix* (CBS). The episode, "Return to Summer Grove", had Jory playing the father of the title character.

Hallmark Hall of Fame "The Disappearance of Aimee" 11-17; **1977** *Rockford Files* "The Becker Connection" 2-11.

TELEFILMS

1973 *A Call to Danger* 2-27 CBS; **1975** *The Kansas City Massacre* 9-19 ABC; **1977** *Lucan* 5-22 ABC; *The Night They Took Miss Beautiful* 10-24 NBC; **1979** *Friendly Fire* 4-22 ABC.

Victor Jory

(born November 28, 1902, Dawson City, Canada; died February 11, 1982)

After studying at Pasadena Playhouse in 1918 while still in his teens, Victor spent the next 12 years in traveling theatre. He debuted on Broadway and in the first of over 120 films in 1930. He became a familiar heavy, especially in western movies. Some of his films included *Gone With theWind, The Miracle Worker, Cheyenne Autumn, State Fair, MacKenna's Gold* and *Papillon*.

Victor came to television in 1950, appearing on shows like *Studio One* (3), *Schlitz Playhouse of Stars* (2), and *Hallmark Hall of Fame* productions of "Moby Dick" and "Johnny Belinda". Also there was work on *General Electric Theater, Omnibus, Kraft Television Theatre* (4) and *Playhouse 90* (2). He was a regular on *King's Row* (1955-56) and *Manhunt* (1959-60).

His talent remained in strong demand throughout the sixties and seventies in numerous TV guest roles. His last work was as narrator of a periodic 1978-81 series, *Greatest Heroes of the Bible*. He died of a heart attack in his Santa Monica apartment in 1982.

GUEST CREDITS

1959 *Wanted: Dead or Alive* "The Legend" 3-7; *U.S. Steel Hour* "Night of Betrayal" 3-25; *Playhouse 90* "Diary of a Nurse" 5-7; *Rawhide* "Incident of the Dry Drive" 5-22; **1962** *New Breed* "Cross the Little Line 1-9; *Dr. Kildare* "Oh, My Daughter" 1-25; *New Breed* "Policemen Die Alone" 1-30, 2-6; *Untouchables* "Element of Danger" 3-22; *87th Precinct* "Dawns an Evil Day" 4-23; *Rawhide* "Gold Fever" 5-4; *Empire* "Ride to a Fall" 10-16; *Hawaiian Eye* "They'll Be Some Changes Made" 10-16; **1963** *Wide Country* "Step Over the Sky" 1-10; *Alfred Hitchcock Hour* "Death of a Cop" 5-24; *Temple Houston* "The Twisted Rope" 9-19; **1964** *Great Adventure* "The Testing of Sam Houston" 1-31; *Suspense* "I, Bradford Charles" 4-8; *Virginian* "Dark Challenge" 9-23; *Alfred Hitchcock Hour* "Change of Address" 10-12; *Burke's Law* "Who Killed Lenore Wingfield?" 11-4; **1965** *Gunsmoke* "Chief Joseph" 1-30; *Kraft Suspense Theatre* "That Time in Havana" 2-11; **1966** *Bonanza* "Ride the Wind" 1-16; 1-24; *I Spy* "Return to Glory" 2-23; *Loner* "The Burden of the Badge" 3-5; *Virginian* "The Return of Golden Tom" 3-9; *Legend of Jesse James* "Things Don't Just Happen" 3-14; *Green Hornet* "The Frog Is a Deadly Weapon" 10-7; *Iron Horse* "Price at the Bottom of the Barrel" 10-10; **1967** *Road West* "Beyond the Hill" 1-16; *Time Tunnel* "Pirates of Deadman's Island" 2-17; *Virginian* "Melanie" 2-22; *Voyage to the Bottom of the Sea* "Fires of Death" 9-15; *Virginian* "A Bad Place to Die" 11-8; *Ironside* "Past Is Prologue" 12-7; **1968** *High Chaparral* "The Peace Maker" 3-3; *Name of the Game* "Witness" 9-27; **1969** *Virginian* "Fox, Hound and Widow McCloud" 4-2; *Mannix* "Return to Summer Grove" 10-11; **1971** *Mannix* "Wine from These Grapes" 10-6; *Longstreet* "So, Who's Fred Hornbeck?" 12-3; **1972** *Banacek* "No Sign of the Cross" 10-11; **1973** *Circle of Fear* "The Phantom of Herald Square" 3-30; **1974** *Nakia* "The Non-Person" 9-21; *Kung Fu* "The Cry of

the Night Beast" 10-19; *Kolchak: The Night Stalker* "Bad Medicine" 11-29; *Nakia* "The Fire Dancer" 12-28; **1975** *Marcus Welby, M.D.* "Tomorrow May Never Come" 9-9; **1977** *Tales of the Unexpected* "The Mask of Adonis" 2-9; **1978** *Rockford Files* "The Attractive Nuisance" 1-6; **1980** *Young Maverick* "Makin' Tracks" 1-9.

TELEFILMS

1976 *Perilous Voyage* 7-29 NBC; **1978** *Devil Dog: The Hound of Hell* 10-31 CBS; **1980** *Power* 1-14, 1-15 NBC.

Lenore Kasdorf

(born 1948)

A pretty seventies/eighties television actress, Lenore Kasdorf worked steadily in the medium after her 1972 debut. Following a number of prime-time guest roles, she moved over to the soap *The Guiding Light* for a lengthy run (1975-81). She also did a turn on *Days of Our Lives* in 1983, and later, was on *Santa Barbara*.

Lenore was a busy guest star during the mid and late eighties on *Murder, She Wrote* (2), *Knight Rider, A-Team, Riptide, Matlock, Highway to Heaven* and *Jake and the Fatman*. In 1989 she began a recurring role on *Coach*.

GUEST CREDITS

1971 *Night Gallery* "The
Class of '99" 9-22; **1972** *The
FBI* "Escape to Nowhere" 3-l9;
Sixth Sense "Dear Joan, We're
Going to Scare You to Death"
9-30; **1973** *Search* "Moment of
Madness" 3-l4; *Streets of San
Francisco* "Betrayed" 9-20;
Magician "The Vanishing
Lady" l0-9; **1974** *Barnaby Jones*
"Gold Record for Murder" 2-l0;
Chase "Hot Beef" 2-l3;
Barnaby Jones "A Gathering of
Thieves" 9-l0; *Kolchak: The
Night Stalker* "Firefall" 11-8;
Six Million Dollar Man "Act of
Piracy" 11-29; **1983** *Magnum,
P.I.* "Smaller Than Life" l0-l3;
T. J. Hooker "The Trial" 11-l8.

TELEFILMS

1974 *Manhunter* 2-26
CBS; *Big Rose* 3-26 CBS; *The
FBI Story: The FBI versus
Alvin Karpis, Public Enemy
Number One* 11-8 CBS.

Kurt Kasznar (right) expresses strong emotion in his co-starring role in the l968-70 series, *Land of the Giants* (ABC). Stefan Arngrim looks on.

Kurt Kasznar

(born August l2, l9l3, Vienna, Austria; died August
6, l979)

Bombastic Kurt Kasznar had his film debut in
l924 and came to the U. S. in l936. After a good
deal of stage work, he made his first American film
in l95l. He came to television in l954, with eventual
fifties credits on *Philco Television Playhouse,
Studio One, Kraft Television Theatre, Schlitz
Playhouse of Stars, Studio '57, Suspicion,
Goodyear Playhouse* and *DuPont Show of the
Month.*

After mixing film roles and television guest
appearances during much of the sixties, Kurt earned
his best known TV role, as the Commander in *Land
of the Giants* (1968-70). His seventies TV work was
infrequent as he slowed his acting schedule.

GUEST CREDITS

1959 *Desilu Playhouse* "Chez Rouge" 2-16;
Adventures in Paradise "The Black Pearl" 10-12;
1961 *Naked City* "The Hot Minerva" 11-29; **1963**
Naked City "On the Battlefield, Everything Is
Important" 3-27; *Alcoa Premiere* "This Will Kill
You" 4-11; **1964** *The Reporter* "Hideout" 10-2; **1965**
Trials of O'Brien "How Do You Get to Carnegie
Hall?" 11-l3; **1966** *Girl from UNCLE* "The Dog-

Gone Affair" 9-13; *Run for Your Life* "The Man Who Had No Enemies" 11-21; **1967** *Bob Hope Chrysler Theater* "Code Name: Heraclitus 1.4" 1-11; *I Spy* "The Trouble with Temple" 1-25; *Man from UNCLE* "The Napoleon's Tomb Affair" 1-27; *Run for Your Life* "The Inhuman Predicament" 9-20; **1968** *It Takes a Thief* "A Thief Is a Thief Is a Thief" 1-9; **1970** *Men from Shiloh* "Crooked Corner" 10-28; **1971** *Name of the Game* "A Sister from Napoli" 1-8; **1972** *Search* "The Bullet" 12-20; **1977** *Wonder Woman* "Judgment from Outer Space" 1-15, 1-17; *Young Dan'l Boone* "The Game" 10-10.

TELEFILMS

1968 *The Smugglers* 12-24 NBC; **1971** *Once Upon a Dead Man* 9-17 NBC; **1972** *The Snoop Sisters* 12-18 NBC; **1978** *Suddenly Love* 12-4 NBC.

Stacy Keach, Sr.

(born 1914)

Perhaps better known as a drama coach, Stacy is father to actors Stacy, Jr. and James. Many of his TV guest roles sere as authority figures and he had a recurring role on *Get Smart* (1966-67) as Professor Carlson.

GUEST CREDITS

1959 *Maverick* "The Lass with the Poisonous Air" 11-1; **1960** *Deputy* "The Return of Simon Fry" 2-13; **1961** *Maverick* "Family Pride" 1-8; *Cheyenne* "Lone Patrol" 4-10; **1962** *Roaring 20's* "The People People Marry" 1-20; **1964** *Perry Mason* "the Case of the Frightened Fisherman" 2-27; **1965** *Perry Mason* "The Case of the Cheating Chancellor" 10-3; **1971** *Mannix* "The Glass Trap" 11-3; **1973** *Adam-12* "The West Valley Division" 10-3; *Mannix* "Sing a Song of Murder" 11-11; **1974** *Marcus Welby, M.D.* "No Charity for the MacAllisters" 1-15; *Harry 0* "The Admiral's Lady" 9-19; **1975** *Rockford Files* "The Girl in the Bay City Boy's Club" 12-19; **1976** *Baretta* "Don't Kill the Sparrow" 1-12; **1978** *Project UFO* "Sighting 4007: The Forest City Incident" 4-9; **1979** *Incredible Hulk* "The Disciple" 3-16; **1981** *Buck Rogers* "Mark of the Saurian" 2-5; *Flamingo Road* "Trapped" 3-3.

TELEFILMS

1971 *Vanished* 3-8, 3-9 NBC; *Once Upon a Dead Man* 9-17 NBC; **1972** *The Heist* 11-29 ABC; **1975** *The Desperate Miles* 3-5 ABC; **1976** *Kingston: The Power Play* 9-15 NBC; **1977** *It Happened at Lakewood Manor* 12-2 ABC; **1978** *Little Mo* 9-5 NBC; *The Clone Master* 9-14 NBC; *Harold Robbins "The Pirate"* 11-21, 11-22 CBS; **1980** *The $5.20 an Hour Dream* 1-26 CBS; *Portrait of a Rebel: Margaret Sanger* 4-22 CBS.

Steven Keats

(born 1945, New York City; died May 8, 1994)

Steven received training at Yale Drama School before his film and television debuts in 1973. Readily recognized by his Bronx accent and gap-toothed smile, most of his early roles were in detective series, usually as criminals. He had a starring role in the 1977 miniseries, *Seventh Avenue*.

His film roles included parts in *Death Wish, The Gumball Rally* and *Black Sunday*. Steven was found dead in May of 1994 in his Manhattan apartment, an

appar ent suicide. He was survived by two sons and two daughters.

GUEST CREDITS

1973 *Griff* "Isolate and Destroy" 12-22; **1974** *Streets of San Francisco* "Rampage" 2-28; *Kojak* "Therapy in Dynamite" 4-10; *Streets of San Francisco* "One Chance to Live" 10-17; *Rookies* "The Old Neighborhood" 11-25; *Cannon* "The Prisoner" 12-11; **1975** *Get Christie Love!* "Our Lady in London" 1-29; *Rockford Files* "Just by Accident" 2-28; *Rookies* "Hostage" 9-23; *Bronk* "Bargain in Blood" 11-16; *Matt Helm* "Murder on the Run" 12-13; *Starsky and Hutch* "Shootout" 12-17; **1976** *S.W.A.T.* "Deadly Weapons" 2-21; *Barnaby Jones* "Blood Vengeance" 10-7; **1983** *Quincy, M.E.* "Whatever Happened to Morris Perlmuter?" 5-4; *Yellow Rose* "Divided We Fall" 10-8; *T. J. Hooker* episode 11-12; *Simon and Simon* "The Bare Facts" 11-17.

TELEFILMS

1974 *The Story of Pretty Boy Floyd* 5-7 NBC; **1975** *The Dream Makers* 1-7 NBC; *Promise Him Anything...*5-14 ABC; **1977** *The Last Dinosaur* 2-11 ABC; **1978** *Zuma Beach* 9-27 NBC; **1979** *Mysterious Island of Beautiful Women* 12-1; **1980** *The Ivory*

Ape 4-18 ABC; **1981** *For Ladies Only* 1-9 NBC; **1982** *The Executioner's Song* 11-28, 11-29 NBC.

Linda Kelsey

(born July 28, 1946, Minneapolis, Minnesota)

A University of Michigan graduate, Linda came to television in 1973, working in guest roles until 1977 when she was cast as reporter Billy Newman on *Lou Grant* (1977-82). After that plum role, she did telefilms and guested on *Murder, She Wrote* (2), *St. Elsewhere, Blacke's Magic* and *Twilight Zone*.

In 1988 she became a regular on an abbreviated series called *Day by Day*; the series did return later in the year and ran until summer of 1989.

GUEST CREDITS

1973 *Wide World of Mystery* "The Picture of Dorian Gray" 4-23, 4-24; **1974** *Wide World of Mystery* "Sorority Kill" 3-5; *Emergency* episode 3-30; *Rockford Files* "The Dexter Crisis" 11-15; *Barnaby Jones* "Dark Homecoming" 11-19; **1975** *Harry O* "Mayday" 10-25; **1976** *Starsky and Hutch* "The Hostages" 1-7; *Bert D'Angelo, Superstar* "A Noise in the Street" 3-27; *Most Wanted* "The Slaver" 10-23; *Barnaby Jones* "Voice in the Night" 12-2; **1977** *Tales of the Unexpected* "The Mask of

Adonis" 2-9; *Quincy, M.E.* "The Thigh Bone's Connected to the Knee Bone" 2-11; *Streets of San Francisco* "Let's Pretend We're Strangers" 5-19; *Westside Medical* "Tears for a $2 Wine" 7-28.

TELEFILMS

1977 *Eleanor and Franklin: The White House Years* 3-13 ABC; *Something for Joey* 4-6 CBS; **1978** *Having Babies* 3-21 ABC; **1980** *A Perfect Match* 10-5 CBS.

Douglas Kennedy (a.k.a. Keith Douglas)
(born September 4, 1915, New York City; died 1973)

Douglas was educated at Fairfield Academy and Amhearst College. From 1940, he was a staple leading man of B films and westerns. His career was interrupted by World War II service, as a Major in the Signal Corps, working with Army Intelligence.

Many of his television roles were in western series, either as lawmen or "brains heavies". He starred in a syndicated 1955 series called *Steve Donovan, Western Marshall*.

GUEST CREDITS

1959 *Restless Gun* "Shadow of a Gunfighter" 1-

12; *One Step Beyond* "Twelve Hours to Live" 2-17; *Restless Gun* "Lady by Law" 5-11; *Lineup* "The Drugstore Cowgirl Case" 5-15; *Colt .45* "Law West of the Pecos" 6-7; *Maverick* "Easy Mark" 11-15; *Texan* "Border Incident" 12-7; **1960** *Perry Mason* "The Case of the Wary Wildcatter" 2-20; *Gunsmoke* "Speak Me Fair" 5-7; *Gunsmoke* "Cherry Red" 6-11; **1962** *Perry Mason* "The Case of the Poison Pen Pal" 2-10; **1965** *Outer Limits* "The Brain of Colonel Barham" 1-2; *Perry Mason* "The Case of the Fatal Fetish" 3-4; *Bonanza* "A Natural Wizard" 12-12; **1966** *Gunsmoke* "Prime of Life" 5-7; **1967** *Bonanza* "Second Chance" 9-17; *Virginian* "Paid in Full" 11-22; **1972** *O'Hara, U. S. Treasury* "Operation: Good Citizen" 3-3.

Lincoln Kilpatrick
(born February 12, 1932, St. Louis, Missouri)

Lincoln made his film debut in 1958 and entered television in 1962. He became a regular on *The Leslie Uggams Show* in 1969, did guest work, and then had a high profile regular role on *Matt Houston* (1983-85). Lincoln also had a series regular role on *Frank's Place* (1987-88).

GUEST CREDITS

1962 *Naked City* "The Sweetly Smiling Face of Truth" 4-25; **1963** *Naked City* "Golden Lads and Girls" 5-22; **1968** *N.Y.P.D.* "The Golden Fleece" 11-26; **1969** *Medical Center* 'The Last Ten Yards" 9-24; *Then Came Bronson* "All the World and God" 12-3; **1970** *Ironside* "Too Many Victims" 11-12; *Bold Ones: The Doctors* "In Dreams They Run" 12-13; **1971** *Bold Ones: The Senator* "A Single Blow of the Sword" 2-28; **1972** *Medical Center* "Deadlock" 2-16; *Ironside* "Five Days in the Death of Sgt. Brown" 9-14; *McCloud* "The Barefoot Stewardess Caper" 12-3; **1974** *Six Million Dollar Man* "Little Orphan Airplane" 2-22; *Police Story* "Chief" 3-19; *Mannix* "Walk on the Blind Side" 10-13; **1975** *Harry O* "Shades" 10-2; *Baretta* "The Fire Man" 10-8; **1978** *Kojak* "Mouse" 1-21; **1980** *Buck Rogers* "Space Vampire" 1-3; **1982** *Greatest American Hero* "A Chicken in Every Pot" 2-17; *Lou Grant* "Victims" 8-

30; *Devlin Connection* "Claudine" 12-11; **1983** *Hill Street Blues* episode 2-10.

TELEFILMS

1970 *The Mask of Sheba* 3-9 NBC; **1976** *Just Another Old Sweet Song* 9-14 CBS; **1978** *Dr. Scorpion* 2-24 CBS.

Missing Melody" 9-30; **1962** *Surfside 6* "Squeeze Play" 5-14; *77 Sunset Strip* "Nightmare" 6-22; **1963** *77 Sunset Strip* "Terror in Silence" 1-25; **1967** *Dragnet* "The Big Kids" 5-4; **1975** *Medical Center* "One Last Rebellion" 11-24.

TELEFILM

1968 *Prescription: Murder* 2-2- NBC.

Andrea King

(born 1918)

For several years Andrea King gave every evidence of attaining stardom (from 1944) with films like *God Is My Co-Pilot, Ride the Pink Horse, My Wild Irish Rose* and *The Lemon Drop Kid*. However, the birth of a child and a happy marriage took precedence over her career and she satified herself with periodic television guest roles.

GUEST CREDITS

1959 *Maverick* "Two Tickets to Ten Strike" 3-15; *Perry Mason* "The Case of the Bewildered Doctor" 4-4; *Alaskans* episode 10-18; **1960** *Cheyenne* "The Lawman" 5-23; *Alaskans* "The Devil Made Five" 6-19; *Perry Mason* "The Case of the Singular Double" 10-8; **1961** *Perry Mason* "The Case of the

Bruce Kirby

(born Bruno Quidaciola, April 28, 1928, New York)

A solid television character actor, Bruce became familiar to viewers in his first series regular role in the 1961-63 sitcom, *Car 54, Where Are You?* His sixties TV guest roles were limited, but he worked often during the seventies. He was a regular in two sitcoms during the decade: *Holmes and Yoyo* (1976) and *Turnabout* (1979). He also had a recurring role on *Columbo*, appearing in six episodes.

During the eighties he was a regular in a police series, *Shannon* (1981-82) and in *Anything But Love* (1989). He is the father of actor Bruce Kirby, Jr. (now known as Bruno Kirby). Continuing to work in the present, Bruce guested in a 1996 episode of *Murder, She Wrote*.

GUEST CREDITS

1965 *Defenders* "Death on Wheels" 1-28; **1968** *Bonanza* "Child" 9-22; **1969** *Judd, for the Defense* "The Poisoned Tree" 1-24; *Mission: Impossible* "The Amnesiac" 12-28; **1970** *Ironside* "The Happy Dreams of Hollow Men" 10-1; **1971** *Longstreet* "The Way of the Intercepting Fist" 9-16; **1972** *McCloud* "A Little Plot, a Tranquil Valley" 1-12; *Marcus Welby, M.D.* "We'll Walk Out of Here Together" 9-26; *Banacek* "Project Phoenix" 9-27; **1973** *McCloud* "Showdown at the End of the World" 1-7; *Columbo* "Lovely, But Lethal" 9-23; *New Perry Mason* "The Case of the Wistful Widower" 10-7; *Kojak* "Requiem for a Cop" 11-28; *Medical Center* "Deadly Game" 12-10; **1974** *Toma* "Stillwater-492" 2-8; *Rockford Files* "The Big Ripoff" 10-25; *Columbo* "By the Dawn's Early Light" 10-27; **1975** *Streets of San Francisco* "Ten Dollar Murder" 1-30; *Columbo* "A Deadly State of Mind" 4-27; *Harry O* "Mayday" 10-23; *Rockford Files* "The Real Easy Red Dog" 10-31; *Columbo* "Identity Crisis" 11-2; *Kojak* "Money Back Guarantee" 12-7; **1976** *Columbo* "Last Salute to the Commodore" 5-2; *Kojak* "Out of the Shadow" 10-

17; **1978** *Rockford Files* "The Paper Palace" 1-20; *Columbo* "Make Me a Perfect Murder" 2-28; *Eddie Capra Mysteries* "How Do I Kill Thee?" 9-21; **1979** *Eischied* "Who Is the Missing Woman?" 11-30; **1980** *Vegas* "Golden Gate Cop Killer" 3-19; **1982** *Code Red* "Trial by Fire" 2-28; *Lou Grant* episode 8-30; *Remington Steele* "Steele Trap" 12-10; **1983** *Hill Street Blues* episode 1-27.

TELEFILMS

1970 *The Other Man* 10-19 NBC; **1971** *Thief* 10-9 ABC; **1973** *The Marcus-Nelson Murders* 3-8 CBS; **1975** *Man on the Outside* 6-29 ABC; *Conspiracy of Terror* 12-29 NBC; **1981** *The Other Victim* 11-4 CBS.

Werner Klemperer

(born March 23, 1920, Cologne, Germany)

The son of the late and famed symphony conductor, Otto Klemperer, father and son fled to America when the Nazis came to power in 1933. Young Werner was a talanted pianist but went into

Hogans' Heroes **(CBS) featured Werner Klemperer, at right, in an Emmy-winning performance as Colonel Klink. The 1965-71 series also starred John Banner (left) and Bob Crane. The series has been tremendously popular in syndication.**

theatre after World War II service with the U. S. Army Special Services. After some struggling years, he gained Broadway roles with Tallulah Bankhead and Charles Laughton.

Werner made his film debut in 1956, eventually appearing in *Judgment at Nurenberg, Ship of Fools, The Wicked Dreams of Paula Schultz* and *Youngblood Hawke.*

Klemperer also began his television career in 1956, with early roles in *Alfred Hitchcock Presents, Maverick, Gunsmoke* and *Perry Mason.* After guest work incorporating roles both sinister and comedic, he landed a role that fit his talents like a glove. On September 17, 1965 he became Colonel Wilhelm Klink on *Hogan's Heroes,* a role that earned him Emmys in 1968 and 1969 as the series ran until 1971. Much of the show's success was due to his portrayal of the blundering, naïve prison camp commander.

GUEST CREDITS

1959 *Steve Canyon* "Iron Curtain" 3-5; *One Step Beyond* "Haunted U-Boat" 5-12; *Troubleshooters* "Tunnel to Yesterday" 12-4; **1960** *Alaskans* "Gold Fever" 1-17; *Perry Mason* "The Case of the Two-Faced Turnabout" 2-14; *Overland Trail* "Vigilantes of Montana" 4-3; *Alcoa Theater* "The Observer" 4-18; **1961** *Islanders* "The Pearls of Ratu" 3-19; **1962** *G.E. True* "Man in a Suitcase" 11-18; *77 Sunset Strip* "Escape to Freedom" 2-22; *Dakotas* "Trial at Grand Forks" 3-25; **1964** *Man from UNCLE* "The Project Strigas Affair" 11-24; *Voyage to the Bottom of the Sea* "The Blizzard Makers" 12-7; **1966** *Lost in Space* "All That Glitters" 4-3; **1972** *Night Gallery* "The Funeral" 1-5; **1973** *McMillan and Wife* "The Devil, You Say" 10-21; **1976** *McMillan and Wife* "All Bets Off" 12-5; **1983** *Matt Houston* episode 1-9.

TELEFILMS

1972 *Assignment: Munich* 4-30 ABC; **1977** *The Rhineman Exchange* 3-10 NBC.

Robert Knapp
(born 1924)

After a film debut in 1952 and several minor film roles, Robert Knapp became more recognizable through television guest roles. *Gunsmoke* used his talents in 6 episodes (1962-1971) and he appeared on 5 episodes of *Dragnet.* He disappeared from acting in the early seventies.

Robert was a regular on the syndicated *Blue Angels* (1960), and worked for a time on the soap *Days of Our Lives,* appearing as Ben Olsen.

GUEST CREDITS

1959 *Perry Mason* "The Case of the Caretaker's Cat" 3-7; **1960** *Black Saddle* "Means to an End" 1-29; *Rifleman* "A Time for Singing" 3-8; *Aquanauts* "The Cavediggers" 12-7; **1962** *Gunsmoke* "Cody's Code" 1-20; **1963** *Perry Mason* "The Case of the Bluffing Blast" 1-10; *Gunsmoke* "Old York" 5-4; *Perry Mason* "The Case of the Drowsy Mosquito" 10-17; *Ben Casey* "It Is Getting Dark…And We Are Lost" 12-18; **1965** *Run for Your Life* "The Girl Next Door Is a Spy" 9-20; **1966** *Gunsmoke* "The Hanging" 12-31; **1967** *Dragnet* "The Big LSD" 1-12; *Dragnet* "The Big Bank Examiners" 2-23; *Invaders* "The Saucer" 9-12; *Dragnet* "The Big High" 11-12; *Dragnet* "The Big Magazine" 11-7; **1969** *Gunsmoke* "Time of the Jackals" 1-13; **1970** *Adam-12* "Log-104-The Bomb" 3-14; *Gunsmoke* "Chato" 9-14; **1971** *Gunsmoke* "Mirage" 1-11.

Don Knight

(born 1933)

Don began his acting career in 1942 on the British stage at the tender age of 11. His first film was in 1967, shortly after he debuted on American television. He was an effective villain in TV crime series, and was a regular on *The Immortal* (1970-71), appearing as Fletcher, hired to pursue the hero for the basis of his immortality.

Don is a fine dialectician and also an ordained minister.

GUEST CREDITS

1966 *Time Tunnel* "Rendevous with Yesterday" 9-9; **1967** *Voyage to the Bottom of the Sea* "The Heat Monster" 1-15; **1968** *Tarzan* "Rendevous for Revenge" 3-15; *It Takes a Thief* "A Matter of Royal Larceny" 4-23; *Big Valley* "In Silent Battle" 9-23; *Outsider* "As Cold As Ashes" 10-16; **1969** *Mannix* "Harlequin's Gold" 1-31; **1970** *Mission: Impossible* "Lover's Knot" 2-22; *Lancer* "Lifeline" 5-19; **1971** *Bonanza* "Blind Hunch" 11-21; **1972** *Columbo* "Etude in Black" 9-17; *McCloud* "The Barefoot Stewardess Caper" 12-3; *Bonanza* "The Bucket Dog" 12-19; **1973** *Banacek* "The Three Million Dollar Piracy" 11-21; **1974** *Shaft* "The Capricorn Murders" 1-29; *Cannon* "Triangle of Terror" 3-13; *Little House on the Prairie* "The 100 Mile Walk" 9-

18; *Movin' On* "Antiques" 12-26; **1975** *Barnaby Jones* "A Taste for Murder" 12-4; **1976** *Kojak* "A Grave Too Soon" 3-7; *Bert D'Angelo, Superstar* "What Kind of a Cop Are You?" 6-12; **1977** *Fantastic Journey* "Vortex" 2-3; *Switch* "Thirty Thousand Witnesses" 12-26; **1978** *Charlie's Angels* "Mother Goose Is Running for His Life" 2-15; **1980** *Charlie's Angels* "Island Angels" 12-14.

TELEFILMS

1971 *The Birdmen* 9-8 ABC; **1973** *Murcock's Gang* 3-20 CBS; *Hitched* 3-31 NBC; **1977** *Code Name: Diamond Head* 5-3 NBC; **1980** *The Plutonium Incident* 3-11 CBS.

Martin Kosleck

(born 1904, Russia; died January 16, 1994)

Martin began his stage career in Germany and made his first film there in 1930. He came to Hollywood in 1933 and supported himself as a portrait artist while awaiting a film break. He began acting regularly in 1939 and was quite busy in the following decade in war and horror films. He was often cast as nazi officers or German soldiers, and played Hitler's henchman Goebbels several times.

Martin entered television in 1952 and had fifties credits on *Motorola TV Hour, Studio One, Appoint-*

ment with Adventure and *Suspense*. In addition to sixties/seventies dramatic series guest shots, he appeared in several sitcoms: *Get Smart, Batman, Love, American Style* and *Sanford and Son*.

GUEST CREDITS

1962 *Thriller* "Waxworks" 1-8; **1963** *Saints and Sinners* "New Lead Berlin" 1-28; **1965** *Outer Limits* "The Brain of Colonel Barham" 1-2; *Rogues* "Run for the Money" 2-14; *Kraft Suspense Theatre* "The Easter Breach" 5-13; **1966** *Girl from UNCLE* "The Horns-of-the-Dilemna Affair" 10-18; *The FBI* "List for a Firing Squad" 12-18; **1967** *Man from UNCLE* "The Cap and Gown Affair" 4-14; *Man from UNCLE* "The Test Tube Affair" 9-18; *The FBI* "Blueprint for Betrayal" 12-3; **1968** *Garrison's Gorillas* "Time Bomb" 3-12; *It Takes a Thief* "Sour Note" 10-1; **1969** *Mission: Impossible* "The Bunker" 3-2, 3-9; *Wild Wild West* "The Night of the Diva" 3-7; *It Takes a Thief* "The Second Time Around" 12-4; **1971** *Night Gallery* "The Devil Is Not Mocked" 10-27; **1972** *O'Hara, U. S. Treasury* "Operation: Dorais" 2-4.

TELEFILMS

1969 *Wake Me When the War Is Over* 10-14 ABC; **1971** *Longstreet* 2-23 ABC.

Paul Koslo

(born 1944, Vancouver, British Columbia, Canada)

Paul studied Shakespeare at Canada's National Theater School. He began his American acting career in New York in the rock musical *Hair*.

Following a film debut in 1970, Paul was frequently cast as alienated young drifters or violent hoods. He continued his role as a heavy in the miniseries *Roots: The Next Generations*. Paul was very active during the eighties, in both TV guest appearances and telefilms. His film credits included work in *Joe Kidd, Mr. Majestyk* and *Rooster Cogburn*.

GUEST CREDITS

1971 *Mission: Impossible* ""Double Dead" 2-12; *Bearcats!* episode 9-16; *Longstreet* "The Shape of Nightmares" 11-28; **1972** *Ironside* "His Fiddlers Three" 3-2; **1974** *Manhunter* "The Baby-Faced Killers" 9-25; *Cannon* "A Killing in the Family" 11-6; **1975** *Petrocelli* "The Mark of Cain" 9-17; *Police Woman* "The Score" 9-19; *Switch* "The Man Who Couldn't Lose" 10-14; *Rookies* "Death Lady" 10-21; **1976** *Rockford Files* "The Family Hour" 10-8; *Police Story* "Two Frogs on a Mongoose" 10-12; **1977** *Barnaby Jones* "Anatomy of Fear" 3-3; *Most Wanted* "The Dutchman" 8-20; **1978** *David Cassidy, Man Undercover* "Deadly Convoy" 11-23; **1979** *Rockford Files* "The Return of the Black Shadow" 2-17; *CHiPs* "Ride the Whirlwind" 3-10; **1981** *Hart to Hart* "Murder in the Saddle" 2-24; *Nero Wolfe* "Blue Ribbon Murder" 5-5; *Today's FBI* "The Fugitive" 11-29; **1982** *Strike Force* "The Outcast" 1-8; *Cassie and Company* "The Dark Side of the Moon" 2-19; *Bret Maverick* "A Night at the Red Ox" 2-23; **1983** *A-Team* "Pros and Cons" 2-8.

TELEFILMS

1971 *The Birdmen* 9-18 ABC; **1972** *The Daughters of Joshua Cabe* 9-13 ABC; **1976** *Scott Free* 10-13 NBC; **1979** *Louis L'mour's "The Sacketts"* 5-15, 5-16 NBC; **1980** *Rape and Marriage: The Rideout Case* 10-30 CBS; **1981** *Inmates: A Love Story* 2-3

ABC; **1983** *Kenny Rogers As the Gambler: The Adventure Continues* 11-28, 11-29 CBS.

Yaphet Kotto
(born November 15, 1937, New York City)

Very active in films, television and the stage, Yaphet usually portrays tough and hard-boiled individuals, often in authority roles. He came to television in 1966, appearing in several western/frontier series oriented guest roles.

In 1983-84 he appeared as a regular on *For Love and Honor*. Much of the balance of his eighties work was in telefilms.

His film career, beginning in 1964, included roles in *Five Card Stud, The Thomas Crown Affair, Alien, Brubaker, Eye of the Tiger* and *Midnight Run*.

GUEST CREDITS

1966 *Big Valley* "Iron Box" 11-28; **1967** *Cowboy in Africa* "Incident at Derati Wells" 9-25; *Tarzan* "Thief Catcher" 9-29; *Big Valley* "The Buffalo Man" 12-25; **1968** *Bonanza* "The Child" 9-22; *Daniel Boone* "The Big, Black and Out There" 11-14; *High Chaparral* "The Buffalo Soldiers" 11-22; **1969** *Hawaii Five-0* "King of the Hill" 1-8; *Mannix*

"Death in a Minor Key" 2-8; *Daniel Boone* "Jonah" 2-13; **1970** *Name of the Game* "The Time Is Now" 11-16; *Gunsmoke* "The Scavengers" 11-16; **1971** *Night Gallery* "The Messiah on Mott Street" 12-15; **1975** *Doctor's Hospital* "Knives of Chance" 10-1; **1983** *A-Team* "The Out-of-Towners" 3-22.

TELEFILMS

1970 *Night Chase* 11-20 CBS; **1977** *Raid on Entebbe* 1-9 NBC; **1980** *Rage* 9-25 NBC; **1983** *Women of San Quentin* 10-23 NBC; *Happy* 10-26 CBS.

Nancy Kovack (a.k.a. Nancy Mehta)
(born 1935, Flint, Michigan)

The daughter of a General Motors exucutive, brainy Nancy has an extremely high I.Q. of 158. She entered the University of Michigan at age 15, graduating at a youthful 19. She worked nights during college as a radio disc jockey. Later, she worked on Dave Garroway's *Today Show*, as one of the early "Today Girls".

She made a Broadway debut in 1958. Her first film, *Strangers When We Meet*, came in 1960 and she began a busy television career in 1963. She was a frequent guest on *Bewitched* with 4 appearances. Fascinated with Middle-Eastern cultures, she moved to Iran for 2 1/2 years.

On July 19, 1969 she married the world renowed classical conductor Zubin Mehta, and worked in television rather infrequently thereafter. She was nominated for an Emmy for her excellent work in a 1969 episode of *Mannix*.

GUEST CREDITS

1963 *Perry Mason* "The Case of the Badgered Brother" 12-9; *Kraft Suspense Theatre* "The Name of the Game" 12-26; **1964** *Burke's Law* "Who Killed Who IV?" 4-3; *Alfred Hitchcock Hour* "Second Verdict" 5-29; *12 O'Clock High* "Appointment at Liege" 10-20; *Bob Hope Chrysler Theater* "Parties to the Crime" 11-27; *Voyage to the Bottom of the Sea* "Hail to the Chief" 12-28; **1965** *Burke's Law*

"Who Killed the Man on the White Horse?" 2-17; *Man from UNCLE* "The Brain Killer Affair" 3-8; *Honey West* "The Great Lady" 12-10; **1966** *Perry Mason* "The Case of the Golfer's Gambit" 1-30; *The FBI* "Flight to Harbin" 2-27; *Man from UNCLE* "The King of Diamonds Affair" 3-11; **1967** *Star Trek* "A Private Little War" 2-2; *I Spy* "Apollo" 11-20; *Invaders* "Task Force" 12-26; **1968** *The FBI* "Wind It Up and It Betrays You" 9-22; *It Takes a Thief* "One Night on Soledad" 9-24; **1969** *Name of the Game* "Swingers Only" 1-10; *Mannix* "To Kill a Butcherbird" 2-1; *It Takes a Thief* "38-23-36" 4-8; **1972** *Mannix* "Sing a Song of Murder" 11-11; **1975** *Invisible Man* "The Klae Dynasty" 12-8; **1976** *Bronk* "Long time Dying" 2-1; *Cannon* "Blood Lines" 2-25.

TELEFILM

1975 *Ellery Queen: Too Many Suspects* 3-23 NBC.

Martin Kove
(born March 6, 1947, Brooklyn, New York)

After a 1971 film debut Martin began appearing on television in 1974. His face became familiar to TV audiences as the Gaelic man in Irish Spring soap commercials. Usually appearing in action roles, the rugged appearing Kove had a leading role in the 1977 series, *Code R*. Following it's demise, he moved into a sitcom role in *We've Got Each Other* (1977-78).

The eighties brough stronger series success, for his role in *Cagney and Lacey* ran from 1982 until the series left the air in 1988. He had a starring role in the short-lived 1989 series, *Hard Time on Planet Earth*. Later eighties guest shots were infrequent, with appearances only on *Murder, She Wrote* and *Twilight Zone*.

GUEST CREDITS

1974 *Toma* "Joey the Weep" 3-22; *Gunsmoke* "In Performance of Duty" 11-18; **1975** *Switch* "The Deadly Missiles Caper" 10-7; *Three for the Road* episode 10-26; *Rookies* "Measure of Mercy" 10-28;

1976 *City of Angels* "The November Plan" 2-3, 2-10, 2-17; *Petrocelli* "Six Strings of Guilt" 2-25; *Kojak* "Law Dance" 10-10; *Streets of San Francisco* "The Drop" 10-28; **1977** *Rockford Files* "Dirty Money, Black Light" 4-1; *Nancy Drew Mysteries* "The Mystery of the Solid Gold Kicker" 5-22; **1978** *Incredible Hulk* "Final Round" 3-10; *Barnaby Jones* "Nest of Scorpions" 10-26; **1979** *Starsky and Hutch* "Birds of a Feather" 1-30; *Quincy, M.E.* "Death's Challenge" 3-29; *Barnaby Jones* "Girl on the Road" 10-25; *Man Called Sloane* "Lady Bug" 12-8; **1981** *Freebie and the Bean* "Highway Robbery" 1-17.

TELEFILMS

1974 *The Spy Who Returned from the Dead* 1-8 ABC; **1976** *Kingston: The Power Play* 9-15 NBC; **1980** *Trouble in High Timber Country* 6-27 ABC; **1982** *Cry for Strangers* 12-11.

Taylor Lacher

In television from 1971, with series regular roles on *Cade's County* (1971-72), *Nakia* (1974) and *Joe Forrester* (1975-76), husky Taylor Lacher was in demand for guest roles and telefilms well into the eighties.

He made a film debut in 1972 in *Santee*, was in *Mr. Majestyk* and *The Final Chapter-Walking Tall*, but found most of his work as heavies on television, with a few rural lawmen roles thrown in.

GUEST CREDITS

1973 *Mod Squad* "Run, Lincoln, Run" 1-4; **1974** *Police Story* "Countdown" 1-15, 1-22; *Chopper One* "Ambush" 2-28; **1975** *S.W.A.T.* "The Killing Ground" 2-24; **1976** *City of Angels* "The Bloodshot Eye" 5-11; *Charlie's Angels* "Angels on Wheels" 12-22; **1977** *Police Story* "Hard Rock Brown" 2-15; *Charlie's Angels* "Angels on the Air" 11-9; **1978** *Starsky and Hutch* "Satan's Witches" 2-8; *Rockford Files* "Heartaches of a Fool" 9-22; **1979** *CHiPs* "Wheeling" 12-9; **1980** *Eischied* "Powder Burn" 1-20; *Stone* "Case No. Ho-894287: Homicide" 1-28; *Quincy, M.E.* "Raid!" 1-31; **1981** *CHiPs* "Forty Tons of Trouble" 1-11; *Incredible Hulk* "Wax Museum" 2-13; *Incredible Hulk* "Danny" 5-15; *Simon and Simon* "A Recipe for Disaster" 12-22; **1982** *Father Murphy* "Will's Surprise" 1-12; *Today's FBI* "Deep Cover" 2-7; *T. J. Hooker* "The Mumbler" 12-4; **1983** *Manimal* "Night of the Beast" 12-10.

TELEFILMS

1973 *The Police Story* 3-20 NBC; **1974** *Nakia* 4-17 ABC; **1975** *Attack on Terror: The FBI Versus the Ku Klux Klan* 2-20, 2-21 CBS; **1977** *The Deadly Triangle* 5-19 NBC; *The Hunted Lady* 11-28 NBC; **1978** *Crisis in Sun Valley* 3-29 NBC; **1979** *The Return of the Mod Squad* 5-18 ABC; **1980** *The Return of Frank Cannon* 11-1 CBS; **1981** *Don't Look Back* 5-31 ABC; **1982** *Cry for the Strangers* 12-11 CBS.

Diane Ladd
(born Rose Diane Ladner, November 29, 1932, Meridian, Miss.)

Territory" 1-13; *Shane* "The Distant Bell" 1-10; *Big Valley* "Boy Into Man" 1-16; **1967** *Gunsmoke* "Noose of Gold" 3-11; **1968** *Ironside* "Robert Phillips vs. the Man" 10-10; *Then Came Bronson* "Old Tigers Never Die—They Just Run Away" 11-5; **1975** *Movin' On* "General Delivery, Raleigh" 11-4; **1976** *City of Angels* "The November Plan" 2-3, 2-10, 2-17; **1977** *Police Story* "Stigma" 11-9.

TELEFILMS

1973 *The Devil's Daughter* 1-9 ABC; **1978** *Thaddeus Rose and Eddie* 2-24 CBS; **1979** *Willa* 3-17 CBS; **1980** *Guyana Tragedy: The Story of Jim Jones* 4-15 CBS; **1982** *Desperate Lives* 3-3 CBS; **1983** *Grace Kelly* 2-21 ABC.

Judson Laire

(born August 3, 1902, New York City; died July 5, 1979)

A television pioneer in the truest sense, Judson acted in a 1940 NBC experimental production of *Julius Caesar*, and followed it with four more major roles in similar productions the same year. He starred in the sitcom, *I Remember Mama* (1949-57).

Diane came to television in 1956 from the New York stage, with a film debut in 1961. By 1963 she was working regularly in TV guest roles.

In 1974 Diane received an Academy Award Nomination for her role as Flo in the film, *Alice Doesn't Live Here Anymore*. She later played a character in the TV version of *Alice* (1980-81). Her sporadic eighties TV appearances were mostly in telefilms, with guest shots on *The Love Boat, Father Dowling Mysteries* and *Heartland*.

She and ex-husband, Bruce Dern, are parents of talented young actress, Laura Dern. Diane and Laura appeared together in a 1996 telefilm, *Ruby Ridge: An American Tragedy*.

GUEST CREDITS

1959 *Naked City* "The Canvas Bullet" 6-16; **1963** *Wide Country* "Memory of a Filly" 1-3; *Wide Country* "Stepover the Sky" 1-10; *77 Sunset Strip* "The Left Field Caper" 4-26; *Perry Mason* "The Case of the Shifty Shoebox" 10-10; **1964** *Fugitive* "Come Watch Me Die" 1-21; *Gunsmoke* "Blue Heaven" 9-26; **1966** *Daniel Boone* "Seminole

During the fifties, Judson made 8 appearances on the excellent live drama, *Studio One*. In 1959 he began a season on the soap *Young Dr. Malone*. During the early sixties he began a round of guest appearances, with 8 episode credits in the recurring role of a judge on *The Defenders*: he also had 4 appearances on *The Nurses*.

In 1965 he accepted a role on the soap, *The Nurses*, which ran for two years. At it's conclusion he moved over to a new soap called *Love Is a Many Splendored Thing*, a featured role that ran for six years (1967-73).

GUEST CREDITS

1961 *Defenders* "The Treadmill" 11-25; **1962** *Route 66* "To Walk with the Serpent" 1-5; *Defenders* "The Search" 1-20; *Defenders* "The Benefactors" 4-28; *Defenders* "The Voices of Death" 9-15; *Stoney Burke* "Child of Luxury" 10-15; *Ben Casey* "Degacy from a Stranger" 10-22; **1963** *Nurses* "Night Sounds" 1-24; *Defenders* "The Weeping Baboon" 9-28; *Nurses* "Show Just Cause Why You Should Weep" 10-3; *Nurses* "Strike" 10-24; *Dr. Kildare* "The Exploiters" 10-31; **1964** *Kraft Suspense Theatre* "Leviathan Five" 1-30; *Nurses* "Nurse Is a Feminine Noun" 2-13; **1965** *Defenders* "Death on Wheels" 1-28; *Defenders* "Nobody Asks What Side You're On" 3-11.

Paul Langton

(born April 17, 1913, Salt Lake City, Utah; died April 15, 1980)

Onscreen from 1943, Paul Langton was initially a leading man in war epics like *Thirty Seconds Over Tokyo, They Were Expendable* and *To Hell and Back*. With the advent of television he began doing character roles and stayed busy from 1951 to 1964 when he got the role of his career.

At that time, he became Leslie Harrington on *Peyton Place*, a role that lasted for four years and that familiarized him to many of America's television viewers.

GUEST CREDITS

1959 *Markham* episode 1-16; *Millionaire* "Millionaire Henry Banning" 4-1; *Rough Riders* "Forty-Five Calibre Vow" 5-14; *Perry Mason* "The Case of the Bartered Bikini" 12-5; *Gunsmoke* "Tag, You're It" 12-19; **1960** *Law of the Plainsman* 'Cavern of the Wind" 4-21; *Rawhide* "Incident of the Silent Web" 6-3; *Bat Masterson* "Debt of Honor" 9-29; *Perry Mason* "The Case of the Wandering Widow" 10-22; **1961** *Adventures in Paradise* "Angel of Death" 3-6; *Roaring 20's* "War with the Night Hawkers" 3-11; *Perry Mason* "The Case of the Cowardly Lion" 4-8; *Follow the Sun* "The Woman Who Never Was" 10-15; *Cheyenne* "The Young Fugutives" 10-23; **1962** *Bus Stop* "Summer Lightning" 1-7; *Perry Mason* "The Case of the Counterfeit Crank" 4-28; *Alcoa Premiere* "A Place to Hide" 5-22; *Untouchables* "The Floyd Gibbons Story" 12-11; **1963** *Virginian* "Say Goodbye to All That" 1-23; *Fugitive* "Fatso" 11-19.

John Larkin

(born April 11, 1912, Oakland, Calif.; died January 29, 1965)

While attending Rockhurst College in Kansas City, Missouri, John became interested in acting. He began working in local radio as an announcer; in 1937 he moved to Chicago for network soap opera roles.

Following World War II service in The Signal Corps, he began working in radio in New York. During the late forties he became radio's *Perry Mason*, remaining in the role until the mid fifties. In 1955 he began a well-known role as Mike Karr on the soap *The Edge of Night* (1955-61).

1962 brought a featured series regular role on *Saints and Sinners*, a series that expired in January of 1963. He then guested until he became Maj. General Crowe in 1964, on a hit series, *12 O'Clock High*. John died of a heart attack during the first season of that series, in January of 1965.

GUEST CREDITS

1962 *New Breed* "Hail, Hail, the Gang's All Here" 4-24; *Detectives* "The Walls Have Eyes" 4-27; *Perry Mason* "the Case of the Counterfeit Crank" 4-28; *Detectives* "The Saturday Edition" 5-18; **1963** *Gunsmoke* "Louie Pheeters" 1-5; *Dick Powell Show* "Tissue of Hate" 2-26; *Untouchables* "The Butcher's Boy" 3-12; *Perry Mason* "The Case of the Greek Goddess" 4-18; *Alfred Hitchcock Hour* "Dear Uncle George" 5-10; *Perry Mason* "The Case of the Reluctant Model" 10-31; *Fugitive* "Ticket to Alaska" 11-12; **1964** *Breaking Point* "Better Than a Dead Lion" 1-20; *Alfred Hitchcock Hour* "The Evil of Adelaide Winters" 2-7; *Perry Mason* "The Case of the Betrayed Bride" 10-22; *Kraft Suspense Theatre* "The Wine-Dark Sea" 12-31.

Wesley Lau

(born 1921, Sheboygan, Wisconsin; died August 30, 1984)

Wesley first appeared on television in a 1953 *Studio One* production. In 1961 he earned a four year regular role on *Perry Mason*, appearing as Lt. Anderson. He was also a regular on *Time Tunnel* during 1966-67. He subsequently mixed occasional guest roles with script writing.

GUEST CREDITS

1959 *Gunsmoke* "Young Love" 1-3; *Peter Gunn* "Breakout" 3-30; *One Step Beyond* "The Haunted U-Boat" 5-12; *Gunsmoke* "Miguel's Daughter" 11-28; **1960** *One Step Beyond* "The Mask" 3-1; *Chevy Mystery Show* "Trial by Fury" 8-7; *Gunsmoke* "The Blacksmith" 9-17; *Peter Gunn* "The Death Frame" 11-7; *Wyatt Earp* "He's My Brother" 11-29; *Law and Mr. Jones* "Christmas Is a Legal Holiday" 12-23; **1961** *Twilight Zone* "Twenty Two" 2-10; **1962** *Twilight Zone* "The Fugitive" 3-9; **1965** *Big Valley* "Earthquake" 11-10; *Combat* "Soldier of Fortune" 11-23; **1966** *Laredo* "Callico Kid" 1-6; **1967** *Laredo* "The Seventh Day" 1-6; *Run for Your Life* "A Choice of Evils" 4-3; **1968** *Land of the Giants* "The Creed" 12-1; **1969** *Mod Squad* "Willlie Poor Boy" 11-18; **1970** *Mission: Impossible* "My Friend, My Enemy" 10-25; **1971** *Mission: Impossible* "Double Dead" 2-12; *Mod*

Squad "The Poisoned Mina" 11-2; **1972** *Cannon* "Hear No Evil" 11-29; **1973** *Chase* "Gang War" 9-18; **1974** *Magicican* "Shattered Image" 1-8; **1975** *Six Million Dollar Man* "Lost Love" 1-17.

TELEFILMS

1971 *The Cable Car Murders* 11-19 CBS; **1972** *No Place to Run* 9-19 NBC; **1973** *Incident on a Dark Street* 1-13 NBC; *Call to Danger* 2-27 CBS; **1974** *Cry Panic* 2-6 ABC; **1981** *Jacqueline Susann's "Valley of the Dolls"* 10-19, 10-21 CBS.

S. John Launer

(born 1919)

In films from 1955, S. John Launer came to television in 1956 and gained a regular role in a 1957-58 series called *Court of Last Resort*, which featured seven criminal law experts. Perhaps that series experience helped him into his best-known role. In 1959 he moved into a recurring role as a judge on *Perry Mason*, a part that ran until 1966. He guested in numerous other series, usually as professionals or officials: doctors, lawyers, judges, senators, and police officials.

GUEST CREDITS

1959 *Perry Mason* "The Case of the Glittering Goldfish" 1-17; *Perry Mason* "The Case of the Howling Dog" 4-11; *Restless Gun* "Lady by Law" 5-11; *Perry Mason* "The Case of the Lame Canary" 6-27; *Perry Mason* "The Case of the Dodging Domino" 10-25; *Perry Mason* "The Case of the Golden Fraud" 11-21; *Perry Mason* "The Case of the Lucky Legs" 12-19; **1960** *Twilight Zone* "Third from the Sun" 1-8; *Perry Mason* "The Case of the Prudent Prosecutor" 1-30; *Perry Mason* "The Case of the Nimble Nephew" 4-23; *Perry Mason* "The Case of the Ill-Fated Faker" 10-1; *Perry Mason* "the Case of the Loquacious Liar" 12-3; **1961** *Perry Mason* "The Case of the Envious Editor" 1-7; *Hawaiian Eye* "Services Rendered" 1-18; *Perry Mason* "The Case of the Difficult Detour" 3-25; *Perry Mason* "The Case of the Meddling Medium" 10-21; *Perry Mason*

"The Case of the Posthumous Painter" 11-11; *Perry Mason* "The Case of the Injured Innocent" 11-18; **1962** *Perry Mason* "The Case of the Tarnished Trademark" 1-20; *Perry Mason* "The Case of the Melancholy Marksman" 3-24; *Perry Mason* "The Case of the Counterfeit Crank" 4-28; *Alcoa Premiere* "The Boy Who Wasn't Wanted" 6-5; *Kraft Mystery Theatre* "Night Panic" 7-18; **1963** *Stoney Burke* "Gold Plated Maverick" 1-7; *Twilight Zone* "In Praise of Pip" 9-27; *Alfred Hitchcock Hour* "Starring the Defense" 11-15; **1964** *Perry Mason* "The Case of the Ugly Duckling" 5-21; *Slattery's People* "Question: What Are You Doing Out There, Waldo?" 10-19; **1965** *Perry Mason* "The Case of the Frustrated Folk Singer" 1-7; *Perry Mason* "The Case of the Thermal Thief" 1-14; *Perry Mason* "The Case of the Telltale Tap" 2-4; *Slattery's People* "What Time Is the Next Bandwagon?" 4-9; *Kraft Suspense Theatre* "Rapture at 240" 4-15; *The FBI* "Slow March Up a Steep Hill" 10-10; *Perry Mason* "The Case of the Baffling Bug" 12-12; **1966** *Perry Mason* "The Case of the Vanishing Victim" 1-23; **1967** *Dragnet* "The Big Masked Bandits" 2-16; *Dragnet* "The Big Shooting Board" 9-21; **1968** *The FBI* "The Tunnel" 4-21; **1969** *The FBI* "Eye of the Storm" 1-5; *Dragnet* "The Joy Riders" 2-13; *Big Valley* "Danger Road" 4-21; **1970** *Mod Squad* "The Long Road Home" 9-22; **1971** *Marcus Welby, M.D.* "Cynthia" 2-23; **1972** *Cade's County* "One Small Acceptable Death" 1-16; *Sixth Sense* "Witch, Witch Burning

Bright" 3-11; *Rookies* "To Taste of Terror" 11-20; *Mod Squad* "Sanctuary" 12-21; **1974** *Harry O* "Guardian of the Gates" 9-26; *Marcus Welby, M.D.* "To Father a Child" 10-1; **1975** *Petrocelli* "Terror by the Book" 12-10.

TELEFILMS

1974 *Trapped Beneath the Sea* 10-22 ABC; **1977** *The Amazing Howard Hughes* 4-13, 4-14; *The Girl Called Hatter Fox* 10-12 CBS; **1978** *A Question of Love* 11-26 NBC; **1980** *All God's Children* 4-28 ABC; *Rage* 9-25 NBC; *The Last Song* 10-23 CBS; *Scared Straight! Another Story* 11-6 CBS; **1981** *Inmates: A Love Story* 2-13 ABC; **1983** *MADD: Mothers Against Drunk Driving* 3-14 NBC; *Dempsey* 9-28 CBS.

Harry Lauter

(born January 19, 1925, White Plains, New York)

Harry's father was an artist and musician and his mother a writer, so it was only natural that he was inclined to the arts. He made a film debut in 1948 and appeared in nearly 100 films, mostly "B" adventure and westerns, and 3 cliff-hanger episodic serials.

During the fifties Harry was a regular on the syndicated television series *Waterfront* (1953-56) and co-starred on the Saturday morning series *Tales of the Texas Rangers* (1958-59). He continued his frequent TV appearances during the sixties, especially on westerns, guesting 8 times each on *Gunsmoke* and *Rawhide*.

A renowed painter, he has owned several art galleries, featuring his own work and that of other artists.

GUEST CREDITS

1959 *Millionaire* "Millionaire William Courtney" 1-7; *Rawhide* "Incident of the Widowed Dove" 1-30; *Maverick* "Saga of Waco Williams" 2-15; *National Velvet* "The Rogue Horse" 3-5; *Colt .45* "The Sanctuary" 5-10; *Texan* "The Smiling Loser" 5-11; *Rawhide* "Incident of the Haunted Hills" 11-6;

1960 *Gunsmoke* "Big Tom" 1-9; *Cheyenne* "Riot at Arroyo Seco" 2-1; *Men into Space* episode 2-10; *Gunsmoke* "The Lady Killer" 4-23; *Gunsmoke* "Say Uncle" 10-1; **1961** *Laramie* "Run of the Hunted" 4-4; *Rawhide* "Incident of the Painted Lady" 5-12; *Gunsmoke* "All That" 10-28; *Maverick* "Three Queens Full" 11-12; *77 Sunset Strip* "The Missing Daddy Caper" 11-17; *Rawhide* "The Blue Sky" 12-8; *Laramie* "The Killer Legend" 12-12; **1962** *Rifleman* "The Bullet" 2-25; *Tales of Wells Fargo* "To Kill a Town" 3-31; *Laramie* "Fall into Darkness" 4-17; *Rawhide* "The Devil and the Deep Blue" 5-11; **1963** *Rawhide* "Incident of the Clown" 3-29; *Perry Mason* "The Case of the Potted Planter" 5-9; *Temple Houston* "Thunder Gap" 11-21; *Rawhide* "Incident at Confidence Creek" 11-28; *Gunsmoke* "Ex-Con" 11-30; **1964** *Rawhide* "Incident at Gila Flats" 1-30; **1965** *Slattery's People* "What's New in Timbuctoo?" 3-19; *Gunsmoke* "Honey Pot" 5-15; *Wild Wild West* "The Night of the Double Edged Knife" 11-12; **1966** *Green Hornet* "Eat, Drink and Be Dead" 10-14; *Voyage to the Bottom of the Sea* "Deadly Waters" 10-30; **1967** *Time Tunnel* "Billy the Kid" 2-10; *Virginian* "The Lady from Wichita" 9-27; *Dragnet* "The Big Badge Racket" 9-28; *Tarzan* "The Blue Stone of Heaven" 10-6, 10-13; *Cimarron Strip* "The Search" 11-9; *Tarzan* "Mountains of the Moon" 11-24, 12-1; *Gunsmoke* "Baker's Dozen" 12-25; **1968** *Wild Wild West* "The Night of the Headless Woman" 1-5; *Cimarron Strip* "The Greeners" 3-7; *Guns of Will Sonnett* "A Town in Terror" 2-7, 2-14; *Big*

Valley "Lightfoot" 2-17; *Mannix* "The Silent Cry" 9-28; **1970** *Adam-12* "Log 114-The Hero" 3-28; *Ironside* "The Happy Dreams of Hollow Men" 10-1; **1972** *Cade's County* "Slay Ride" 1-30, 2-6; *Mission: Impossible* "Two Thousand" 9-23; **1973** *Chase* "The Winning Ticket Is a Loser" 10-2; **1974** *Chopper One* "Deadly Carrier" 3-28; *Manhunter* "Terror from the Skies" 10-16; **1976** *Blue Knight* "The Creeper" 1-28.

Marc Lawrence
(born Max Goldsmith, Bronx, New York, 1910)

Few actors have played more violent gangsters than Marc Lawrence; his hollow-cheeks and pitted complexion, set off by narrow eyes, gave him a menacing look. From 1933 well into the eighties, Marc has played the most nefarious types in both American and Italian films. His film credits include roles in *This Gun for Hire, Dillinger, Key Largo, The Man with the Golden Gun* and *Marathon Man.*

His television roles, from *The Untouchables* to *Mannix*, usually found him cast as gangster chieftans. Educated at CCNY, and with New York stage experience prior to coming to Hollywood, Marc is also a producer, director and writer.

GUEST CREDITS

1959 *Playhouse 90* "For Whom the Bell Tolls" 3-12; **1960** *Detectives* "Life in the Balance" 1-1; *Troubleshooters* "High Steel" 1-15; *Untouchables* "Star Witness" 1-21; *Zane Grey Theater* "Killer Instinct" 3-7; *Bronco* "Tangled Trail" 5-3; *Rifleman* "Trail of Hate" 9-27; *Detectives* "The Other Side" 12-2; **1961** *Deputy* "The Hard Decision" 1-28; *Whispering Smith* "Death at Even Money" 7-10; *Untouchables* "The Genna Brothers" 11-2; **1962** *Detectives* "Three Blind Mice" 3-30, 4-6; **1963** *Untouchables* "Blues for a Gone Goose" 1-29; **1964** *Bob Hope Chrysler Theater* "The Timothy Heist" 10-30; **1969** *Mannix* "The Nowhere Victim" 11-29; **1970** *Bonanza* "Caution, Easter Bunny Crossing" 3-29; **1971** *Mannix* "Overkill" 3-13; **1974** *Mannix* "A Fine Day for Dying" 10-6; *McCloud* "The Gang That Stole Manhattan" 10-13; **1975** *Switch* "Kiss of Death" 11-25; **1976** *Rookies* "Journey to Oblivion" 3-30;

Baretta "Street Edition" 10-13; **1979** *Wonder Woman* "Going, Going, Gone" 1-12.

TELEFILMS

1973 *Honor Thy Father* 3-1 CBS; **1982** *Terror at Alcatraz* 7-4 NBC.

Linda Lawson
(born January 11, 1936, Ann Arbor, Michigan)

Linda Lawson used her series regular role on *Adventures in Paradise* (1959-60) as a springboard to numerous early sixties guest roles. During 1962-63 she had another regular slot on a short-lived sitcom, *Don't Call Me Charlie*. Thereafter, she resumed guesting until she disappeared from television in 1966.

GUEST CREDITS

1959 *Millionaire* "Millionaire Sergeant Matthew Brian" 11-25; **1960** *77 Sunset Strip* "Ten Cents a Dance" 1-29; *Colt .45* "Impasse" 1-31; *Alfred Hitchcock Presents* "I Can Take Care of Myself" 5-15; *Wagon Train* "Princess of a Lost Tribe" 11-2; *Hawaiian Eye* "Girl on a String" 11-16; *Bonanza* "The Trail Gang" 11-26; **1961** *Rifleman* "Assault" 3-21; *Perry Mason* "The Case of the Injured Innocent" 11-18; *Malibu Run* "The Jeremiah Adventure" 3-1;

1964 *Alfred Hitchcock Hour* "The World's Oldest Motive" 11-12; *Bonanza* "To Own the World" 4-18; **1965** *Ben Casey* "What to Her Is Plato?" 4-18; *Ben Casey* "Francini? Who Is Francini?" 10-25; *Ben Casey* "Then I, and You, and All of Us Fall Down" 11-1; *Ben Casey* "No More Cried the Rooster: There Will Be Truth" 11-8; *Ben Casey* "The Importance of Being 65937" 11-15; *Ben Casey* "When Givers Prove Unkind" 11-22; *Ben Casey* "Why Did the Day Go Backwards?" 12-6; *Ben Casey* "You Wanna Know What Really Goes On in a Hospital?" 12-20; *Ben Casey* "If You Play Your Cards Right, You Too Can Be a Loser" 12-27; **1966** *Virginian* "Chaff in the Wind" 1-26.

Peter Leeds

(born 1918)

Peter made his screen debut in 1941 and began appearing on television during the fifties. He landed a series regular role on *Pete and Gladys* during 1960-62. A good friend of Bob Hope, Peter accompanied him on many of his Christmas tours to entertain troops around the world.

Peter's TV career extended well into the eighties.

GUEST CREDITS

1959 *Trackdown* "Terror" 2-4; *Trackdown* "The Threat" 3-4; *Trackdown* "Stranger in Town" 3-25; *Perry Mason* "The Case of the Artful Dodger" 12-12; **1960** *Loretta Young Show* "The Seducer" 11-6; **1961** *Hawaiian Eye* "The Pretty People" 5-10; *87th Precinct* "Lady Killer" 10-9; *77 Sunset Strip* "The Laurel Canyon Caper" 11-17; **1962** *Hawaiian Eye* "Cricket's Millionaire" 2-7; *77 Sunset Strip* "Ghost of a Memory" 4-20; *General Electric Theater* "The Unstoppable Gray Fox" 5-6; *Wide Country* "The Girl in the Sunshine Smile" 11-15; **1963** *Perry Mason* "The Case of the Velvet Claws" 3-21; *Alfred Hitchcock Hour* "A Home Away from Home" 9-27; **1964** *Rawhide* "Incident of the Swindlers" 2-20; *Breaking Point* "Confounding Her Astronomers" 4-6; **1965** *Honey West* "Invitation to Limbo" 12-17; *Honey West* "A Nice Little Till to Tap" 12-31; **1966** *Monroes* "Ride with Terror" 9-21; **1967** *Mannix* "Warning: Live Blueberries" 10-28; **1968** *Mod Squad* "Find Tara Chapman" 11-19; **1969** *Hawaii Five-0* "The Big Kahuna" 3-19; **1970** *Land of the Giants* "Pay the Piper" 1-11; **1972** *Adam-12* "The Parole Violater" 1-26; *Mission: Impossible* "The

Deal" 9-30; **1974** *Hawaii Five-0* "Killer at Sea" 2-19; **1975** *Kolchak: The Night Stalker* "The Trevi Collection" 1-24; **1977** *Police Woman* "Ambition" 12-28.

TELEFILM

1981 *Senior Trip!* 12-30 CBS.

Lance LeGault

(born 1940)

A multi-talented actor of French-Cajun descent, Lance LeGault began his early career as a dancer-stuntman and stand-in for Elvis Presley. The possessor of a distinctive deep voice, he is also a singer. After a handful of sixties films Lance devoted his energies to television, beginning in 1973.

The seventies brought Lance a number of guest roles, but he did his most recognizable work during the eighties. In 1981 he began a recurring role on *Magnum, P.I.*, as a Naval Intelligence Officer, and sometimes nemesis of Magnum's, in eight episodes (1981-88). He was also the mysterious industrial tycoon Logan Rhinewood on *Dynasty* during 1981-82.

In 1981 he began a semi-regular role on *The A-Team*, appearing as Colonel Roderick Decker in 17 episodes (1983-85). Mid and late eighties guest roles included work on *Automan, Airwolf* (2), *Simon and Simon* (2), *Blacke's Magic, MacGyver* and *Murder, She Wrote*. He was a regular on *Werewolf* during 1987-88.

GUEST CREDITS

1974 *Gunsmoke* "A Town in Chains" 9-16; *Police Woman* "Requiem for Bored Housewives" 11-29; **1975** *Rockford Files* "Claire" 1-31; *Petrocelli* "A Night of Terror" 4-2; *Barbary Coast* "Jesse Who?" 4-2; *Police Woman* "Farewell, Mary Jane" 11-4; **1977** *Police Woman* "Bondage" 3-1; *Logan's Run* "Judas Goat" 12-19; *Rockford Files* "A Deadly Maze" 12-23; **1978** *Incredible Hulk* "The Antowick Horror" 9-29; *New Adventures of Wonder Woman* "Hot Wheels" 9-29; *Battlestar Galactica* "The Lost Warrior" 10-8; **1981** *Buck Rogers* "Time of the Hawk"

1-15; *Magnum, P.I.* "Missing in Action" 2-5; *Walking Tall* episode 4-18; *Magnum, P.I.* "Memories are Forever" 11-5; *Dynasty* "Chapter XXI" 12-16; **1982** *Dynasty* "Chapter XXIV" 1-27; *McClain's Law* "Use of Deadly Force" 2-19; *Simon and Simon* "Tanks for the Memories" 3-16; *Dynasty* "Chapter XXXI" 3-24; *Dynasty* "Chapter XXXII" 4-7; *Magnum, P.I.* "Did You See the Sunrise?" 9-30; *Voyagers* "Old Hickory and the Pirate" 11-28; **1983** *T. J. Hooker* "The Hostages" 3-5; *A-Team* "When You Comin' Home, Range Rider?" 10-25; *A-Team* "Labor Pains" 11-8; *A-Team* "There's Always a Catch" 11-15; *A-Team* "White Ballot" 12-6.

TELEFILMS

1973 *Pioneer Woman* 12-19 ABC; **1974** *This Is the West That Was* 12-17 NBC; **1978** *Nowhere to Run* 1-16 NBC; *Donner Pass: The Road to Survival* 10-24 NBC; **1979** *Captain America* 1-19 CBS; **1980** *wer* 1-14, 1-15; *Kenny Rogers as the Gambler* 4-8 CBS; *Reward* 5-23 ABC.

Kay Lenz (a.k.a. Kaye Ann Kemper)

(born March 4, 1953, Los Angeles, Calif.)

After making numerous commercials and appearing in teen television shows, Kay made her television debut at the Pasadena Playhouse at age 13. She debuted on network television in 1966 on the

Cannon "The Avenger" 10-30; **1975** *Petrocelli* "Face of Evil" 12-17; **1976** *Jigsaw John* "Eclipse" 3-29.

TELEFILMS

1972 *The Weekend Nun* 12-20 ABC; **1973** *A Summer Without Boys* 12-2 ABC; **1974** *Unwed Father* 2-27 ABC; *The Underground Man* 5-6 NBC; *The FBI Story: The FBI vs. Alvin Karpis, Public Enemy Number One* 11-8 CBS; **1975** *Journey from Darkness* 2-25 NBC; **1978** *The Initiation of Sarah* 2-6 ABC; **1979** *The Seeding of Sarah Burns* 4-7 CBS; **1980** *Escape* 2-20 CBS; *The Hustler of Muscle Beach* 5-16 ABC.

Tammy Grimes Show, but really hit her stride in TV work during 1972-73, in guest roles and telefilms.

She made her first film, *Breezy*, in 1973 (with William Holden). In 1975, at age 22, she received an Emmy as Best Actress in a Daytime Drama Special for Heart in Hiding. After appearing in the miniseries *Rich Man-Poor Man-Book I*, she became a regular on *Rich Man-Poor Man-Book II*.

During the post 1983 period, a busy Kay guested on *Hotel, Simon and Simon* (4), *Hill Street Blues, Magnum, P.I., Cagney and Lacey, The Fall Guy, Matt Houston, Finder of Lost Loves, Murder, She Wrote, MacGyver, Riptide, Hunter, Starman, Moonlighting, Hotel, Midnight Caller* (2) and *Houston Knights*.

In 1989 she received her second Emmy, as Outstanding Guest Actress in a Drama Series for an episode of *Midnight Caller*, "After It Happened". Kay was married to actor David Cassidy.

GUEST CREDITS

1969 *Monroes* "Teach Tigers to Purr" 3-8; **1972** *Ironside* "Cold, Hard Cash" 12-14; **1973** *Owen Marshall, Couselor at Law* "A Girl Named Tham" 3-14; *Streets of San Francisco* "Harem" 10-25; *Hallmark Hall of Fame* "Lisa, Bright and Dark" 11-28; **1974** *Gunsmoke* "The Foundling" 2-11; *Medical Center* "The Conspirators" 3-11; *Kodiak* "Death Chase" 9-20; *McCloud* "The Barefoot Girls on Bleeker Street" 9-22; *Nakia* "The Hostage" 10-12;

Rick Lenz

(born November 21, 1939, Springfield, Illinois)

A tall and lanky actor, Rick made his film debut during 1969 in *Cactus Flower*. He also made his television entry that year in a *Green Acres* episode. His only TV series regular role was in *Hec Ramsey* (1972-74).

Rick worked in guest roles fairly steadily throughout the seventies and eighties. In the mid and later eighties he guested on *Automan, Airwolf, Magnum, P.I., Simon and Simon, Murder, She Wrote* and *Law and Harry McGraw*.

GUEST CREDITS

1972 *Ironside* "Achilles' Heel" 2-17; *Marcus Welby, M.D.* "Don and Denise" 10-31; **1973** *Circle of Fear* "Spare Parts" 2-23; *Owen Marshall, Counselor at Law* "N Is for Nightmare" 10-17; **1975** *Wide World of Mystery* "Violence in Blue" 2-3; *Six Million Dollar Man* "The Return of the Bionic Woman" 9-14, 9-21; *Police Woman* "Pattern for Evil" 10-3; *Kate McShane* "Publish or Perish" 10-22; **1976** *Six Million Dollar Man* "Welcome Home, Jaime (Part 1)" 1-11; *Bionic Woman* "Welcome Home, Jaime (Part 2)" 1-21; **1977** *McMillan* "Dark Sunrise" 1-2; *Streets of San Francisco* "One Last Trick" 1-6; **1980** *Vegas* "The Black Cat Killer" 11-12; **1982** *T. J. Hooker* "God Bless the Child" 3-27; *Lou Grant* "Blacklist" 4-5; **1983** *Simon and Simon* "Pirate's Key" 1-20; *Masquerade* "Diamonds" 12-22.

TELEFILMS

1971 *Owen Marshall, Counselor at Law* 9-12 ABC; **1981** *Elvis and the Beauty Queen* 3-1 NBC; **1981** *Advice to the Lovelorn* 11-30 NBC.

Fred Lerner

A noted stuntman, stunt coordinator-second unit director, Fred turned to part-time acting in a 1960 *Rawhide* episode. He didn't receive additional guest roles until 1971, then did them periodically, well into the eighties.

He made a film debut in 1967 in *The President's Analyist*; he also appeared in *Dirty Harry* and *The Sterile Cockoo*.

GUEST CREDITS

1960 *Rawhide* "Incident of the Sharpshooter" 2-26; **1971** *Immortal* "Sanctuary" 1-7; **1973** *Kung Fu* "The Spirit Helper" 11-8; **1974** *Kung Fu* episode 1-17; *Rockford Files* "The Kirkhoff Case" 9-13; *Six Million Dollar Man* "The Seven Million Dollar Man "11-1; **1975** *Gunsmoke* "Hard Labor" 2-24; *Rockford Files* "Roundabout" 3-7; **1977** *Quincy, M.E.* "A Dead Man's Truth" 9-3; *Rockford Files* "The Birds, the

Bees and T. T. Flowers" 11-21, 11-28; **1978** *Wonder Woman* "The Girl from Ilandia" 4-7; *Spiderman* "The Captive Tower" 9-5; **1979** *Rockford Files* "Nice Guys Finish Last" 11-16; **1982** *Dynasty* episode 4-14; *Knight Rider* "Forget Me Not" 12-17; **1983** *A-Team* "Children of Jamestown" 1-30.

TELEFILMS

1977 *Murder in Peyton Place* 10-3 NBC; *Killer On Board* 10-10 NBC; **1978** *The New Adventures of Heidi* 12-13 NBC; **1979** *Silent Victory: The Kitty O'Neil Story* 2-24 CBS; *Samurai* 4-30 ABC.

Michael Lerner

(born 1937, Brooklyn, New York)

After obtaining a Master's Degree in English Drama from U.C.L.A., Michael studied for two years at the London Academy of Dramatic Art (LADA), then began acting at the American Conservatory Theatre in San Francisco.

From his debut in a 1969 telefilm, the majority of Michael's work has been in television. Frequently cast as dishonest businessmen or small time hoods, Michael has made deceit and treachery his twin hallmarks and has created a distinct persona.

He might well have been called "the king of telefilms" for he had performed in 20 of them by 1983.

GUEST CREDITS

1971 *Ironside* "The Professionals" 9-28; **1972** *Banacek* "Let's Hear It for a Living Legend" 9-13; *Bold Ones: The Doctors* "Is This Operation Necessary?" 9-26; *Night Gallery* "You Can Come Up Now, Mrs. Millikan" 11-2; *Streets of San Francisco* "The Takers" 12-2; **1973** *Emergency* episode 2-17; *New Adventures of Perry Mason* "The Case of the Furious Father" 11-11; **1974** *Chase* "Remote Control" 2-27; **1975** *Starsky and Hutch* "Texas Longhorn" 9-17; **1976** *Jigsaw John* "Too Much, Too Soon" 2-16; *Harry O* "Victim" 3-4; *Police Woman* "Tennis Bum" 11-30; *Rockford Files* "Piece Work" 12-10; **1978** *Kojak* "The Halls of Terror" 2-18; *Wonder Woman* "One of Our Teen Idols Is Missing" 9-22; **1980** *Barnaby Jones* "Run to Death" 1-3; *Vegas* "The Andreas Connection" 12-24; **1982** *Today's FBI* "Serpent in the Garden" 2-14; *Hart to Hart* "Blue and Broken-Harted" 2-23; **1983** *Hill Street Blues* "Spotlight on Rico" 4-28; *Hill Street Blues* "A Hill of Beans" 5-2.

TELEFILMS

1969 *Three's a Crowd* 12-2 ABC; *Daughter of the Mind* 12-9 ABC; **1971** *Marriage: Year One* 10-15 NBC; *What's a Nice Girl Like You...?* 12-18 ABC; **1974** *The Rockford Files* 3-24 NBC; *Reflections of a Murder* 11-24 ABC; **1975** *The Dream Makers* 1-7 NBC; *Sarah T-Portrait of a Teen Age Alcoholic* 2-11 NBC; *A Cry for Help* 2-12 ABC; *Starsky and Hutch* 4-30 ABC; **1976** *Dark Victory* 2-5 NBC; *F. Scott Fitzgerald in Hollywood* 5-16 ABC; *Scott Free* 10-13 NBC; **1977** *Killer on Board* 10-10 NBC; **1978** *A Love Affair: The Eleanor and Lou Gehrig Story* 1-15 NBC; *Ruby and Oswald* 2-8 CBS; *Vegas* 4-25 ABC; **1979** *Hart to Hart* 9-25 ABC; **1980** *Gridlock* 10-2 NBC; **1983** *Rita Hayworth: The Love Goddess* 11-2 CBS.

Len Lesser

(born 1922)

A sinister look typecast Len Lesser into adversarial and criminal roles early in his rather prolific acting career. Following a 1955 film debut, Len had roles in some excellent movies: *Lust for Life, The Brothers Karamazov, Some Came Running, Birdman of Alcatraz, Papillon* and *The Outlaw Josey Wales.*

From the mid-fifties to the mid-eighties Len created a gallery of bad-guys in numerous television dramatic series guest roles, and also found time to practice his villainy on sitcoms like *Get Smart.*

GUEST CREDITS

1959 *M Squad* "Death Threat" 3-13; *Peter*

Gunn "The Family Affair" 5-4; *Man and the Challenge* "The Visitors" 12-26; **1960** *Hotel de Paree* "Hard Luck for Sundance" 2-19; **1961** *Hong Kong* "Lesson in Fear" 1-11; *Investigators* "In a Mirror, Darkly" 11-16; **1962** *Follow the Sun* "Chicago Style"1-7; **1964** *Outer Limits* "The Invisibles" 2-3; **1965** *Bob Hope Chrysler Theater* "Escape into Jeopardy" 5-28; *Wild Wild West* "The Night of the Casual Killer" 10-15; *Ben Casey* "Then I, and You, and All of Us Fall Down" 11-1; **1966** *Laredo* "A Very Small Assignment" 3-17; **1969** *Land of the Giants* "Brainwash" 1-12; **1970** *Bonanza* "Caution, Easter Bunny Crossing" 3-29; **1972** *Bonanza* "Heritage of Anger" 9-19; *Delphi Bureau* "The White Plague Project"11-16; **1974** *Medical Center* "Three on a Tightrope" 11-25; **1975** *Rockford Files* "Say Goodbye to Jennifer" 2-7; **1976** *Switch* "Maggie's Hero" 12-14; **1977** *Nancy Drew Mysteries* "The Mystery of the Diamond Triangle" 2-20; **1978** *Quincy, M.E.* "The Last Six Hours"9-21; **1983** *Hardcastle and McCormick* "Man in a Glass House" 9-25.

TELEFILMS

1967 *How I Spent My Summer Vacation* 1-7 NBC; **1974** *It's Good to Be Alive* 2-22 CBS; **1975** *The Big Ripoff* 3-11 NBC; **1977** *Spider- Man* 9-14 CBS; **1978** *Someone's Watching Me* 11-29 NBC.

Suzanne Lloyd
(born Toronto, Canada)

Canadian-born Suzanne Lloyd grew up in Pasadena, California. She became an actress when she, on a lark, went for an audition for *Stage Door* in Glendale and won the lead role. During the 1959-63 period she was one of television's most sought-after guest actresses.

Suzanne Lloyd, in her role as a gypsy, finds something amusing in this scene from a 1959 *Gunsmoke* (CBS) episode called "Target". James Arness, as Matt Dillon, obviously doesn't share the feeling.

She continued her film career through 1968, then left acting.

GUEST CREDITS

1959 *Rawhide* "Incident at Alabaster Plain" 1-16; *Gunsmoke* "Target" 9-5; *One Step Beyond* "Ordeal on Locust Street" 9-22; *Tightrope* "The Thousand Dollar Bill" 10-13; *Bourbon Street Beat* "Torch Song for Trumpet" 10-19; *Troubleshooters* "Lower Depths" 10-2; *Law of the Plainsman* "The Hostiles" 10-22; *Twilight Zone* "Perchance to

Dream" 11-27; *77 Sunset Strip* "The Widow and the Web" 11-27; *Maverick* "Trooper Maverick" 11-29; *Laramie* "The Gitanos" 12-27; *Millionaire* "Millionaire Timothy Mackail" 12-30; **1960** *Colt .45* "Under False Pretenses" 1-10; *Bourbon Street Beat* "Green Hell" 3-4; *Overland Trail* "Westbound Stage" 3-6; *Bat Masterson* "Thee Bullets for Bat" 3-24; *Lawman* "Girl from Grantsville" 4-10; *Law of the Plainsman* "Jeb's Daughter" 4-14; *77 Sunset Strip* "Stranger Than Fiction" 4-22;

Anne Lockhart plays a newswoman in a 1977 episode of Barnaby Jones (CBS). The late Robert Reed is at left, interviewing Buddy Ebsen in his title role as *Barnaby Jones*.

Markham "Escorts a la Carte" 6-16; *Wrangler* "Affair at the Trading Post" 8-18; *Hawaiian Eye* "The Blue Goddess" 10-19; *Wyatt Earp* "Johnny Ringo's Girl" 12-13; *Sugarfoot* "Welcome Enemy" 12-26; **1961** *Bonanza* "The Bride" 1-28; *Maverick* "Last Stop: Oblivion" 2-12; *Gunsmoke* "Harriett" 3-4; *Perry Mason* "The Case of the Difficult Detour" 3-25; *Tales of Wells Fargo* "Casket 7.3" 9-30; **1962** *Checkmate* "Ride a Wild Horse" 4-4; *Thriller* "The Specialists" 4-30; **1963** *Laramie* "Edge of Evil" 4-2.

Anne Lockhart

(born 1953)

The daughter of actress June Lockhart, Anne made a few appearances with her mother during the latter's years of starring in *Lassie* (1958-64), but really didn't begin her acting career until she was

grown, in 1972. She had numerous seventies guest roles and became a regular on *Battlestar Galactica* in 1978-79.

Anne had a busy eighties period, with nearly 40 guest appearances. Her work in the post-1983 period included guest shots on *Airwolf* (2), *T. J. Hooker, Automan, Murder, She Wrote* (2), *Simon and Simon* (2), *New Love American Style* (4) and *The Highwayman.*

GUEST CREDITS

1972 *Cannon* "A Deadly Quiet Town" 2-15; *Sixth Sense* "Dear Joan, We're Going to Scare You to Death" 9-30; **1973** *Hallmark Hall of Fame* "Lisa, Bright and Dark" 11-28; **1974** *Sierra* episode 9-19; *Get Christie Love!* "Bullet from the Grave" 11-20; **1977** *Barnaby Jones* "Death Beat" 9-15; *Hardy Boys Mysteries* "Mystery of the African Safari" 10-16;

1978 *Emergency* episode 1-7; *Police Story* "A Chance to Live" 5-28; *Hardy Boys Mysteries* "The Last Kiss of Summer" 10-1, 10-8; *Project UFO* "Sighting 4020: The Believe It or Not Incident" 10-19; *Eddie Capra Mysteries* "Breakout to Murder" 12-1; **1979** *B. J. and the Bear* "Pogo Lil" 10-20; *CHiPs* "Return of the Supercycle" 10-27; *Incredible Hulk* "Captive Night" 12-21; **1980** *Buck Rogers* "A Dream of Jennifer" 2-14; *Hagen* "Hear No Evil" 3-29; **1981** *Magnum, P.I.* "Lest We Forget" 2-12; *Incredible Hulk* "The Phenom" 10-16; *Darkroom* "Exit Line" 12-25; **1982** *Fall Guy* "Snow Job" 3-3; *Knight Rider* "Good Day at White Rock" 10-8; *Magnum, P.I.* "Flashback"11-4; *Tales of the Gold Monkey* "The Lady and the Tiger" 12-8; *Voyagers* "Merry Christmas, Bogg" 12-19; **1983** *Simon and Simon* "What's in a Gnome?" 2-24; *Knight Rider* "Return to Cadiz" 10-30; *Fall Guy* "Inside, Outside" 11-16.

TELEFILM

1973 *Magician* 3-17 NBC.

Richard Loo

(born 1903, Hawaii; died 1983)

One of the first memories of Richard Loo, to many film-goers, was his role as Japanese fighter ace "Tokyo Joe", in the 1945 movie, *God Is My Co-Pilot*, and Loo yelling "Now you die, Yankee dog" as he gets the hero in his gunsights during an aerial gunfight. A wonderful actor of Chinese descent, Richard often played Japanese officers during World War II films.

His film career eventually included roles in *Love Is a Many Splendored Thing, Around the World in Eighty Days, Battle Hymn* and *The Sand Pebbles*. He began his television acting career in 1953 and worked often until the late seventies in castings as Orientals. He did 5 guest appearances on *Kung Fu*.

GUEST CREDITS

1961 *Hong Kong* "Suitable for Framing" 1-4; *Hong Kong* "The Jade Empress" 4-12; *Follow the Sun* "The Woman Who Never Was" 10-15; *Bonanza* "Day of the Dragon" 12-3; **1963** *Hawaiian Eye* "Two Too Many" 1-29; *Dakotas* "The Chooser of the Slain" 4-22; *Outer Limits* "Three Hundred Days of the Dragon" 9-23; *Wagon Train* "The Widow O'Rourke Story" 10-7; **1965** *I Spy* "So Long Patrick Henry" 9-15; *Honey West* "The Owl and the Eye" 9-24; *Voyage to the Bottom of the Sea* "Time Bomb" 9-26; *Amos Burke, Secret Agent* "Deadlier Than the Male" 11-17; **1966** *Wild Wild West* "The Night the Dragon Screamed" 1-14; *Man from UNCLE* "The Indian Affairs Affair" 4-15; **1968** *Hawaii Five-0* "The 24 Karat Kill" 11-14; *It Takes a Thief* "A Case of Red Turnips" 11-26; **1969** *It Takes a Thief* "Payoff in the Piazza" 11-13; **1970** *It Takes a Thief* "Project 'X'"3-23; **1972** *Sixth Sense* "With This Ring, I Thee Kill" 3-4; *Delphi Bureau* "The Deadly Errand Project" 10-5; **1973** *Kung Fu* "Blood Brothers" 1-8; *Kung Fu* "The Tong" 11-5; **1974** *Owen Marshall, Counselor at Law* "The Attacker" 1-26; *Kung Fu* "Arrogant Dragon" 3-14; *Kung Fu* "The Devil's Champion" 11-1; *Kung Fu* "Besieged: Cannon at the Gate" 11-22; **1976** *Quest* "Welcome to America, Jade Snow" 11-24; **1977** *Police Story* "The Blue Fog" 2-1; *Hardy Boys Mysteries* "The Mystery of Jade Kwan Yin" 5-15.

TELEFILMS

1969 *Marcus Welby, M.D.* 3-26 ABC; **1972** *Kun Fu* 2-22 ABC.

Lynn Loring

(born 1945)

Lynn Loring literally grew up on television, beginning a ten year role on *Search for Tomorrow* as a six year old (1951-61). She had a simultaneous role in 1953-53 on a sitcom, *The Jean Carroll Show* (1953-54). During 1962-63 she was a regular on another sitcom, *Fair Exchange*.

She worked on *The FBI* during it's first season (1965-66) as the daughter of Inspector Erskine (Efrem Zimbalist, Jr.), then guested until she appeared for a year on the daytime soap, *Return to Peyton Place*, in 1973-74.

Married to noted actor Roy Thinnes, Lynn has become an executive at Aaron Spelling Productions and a successful film producer.

GUEST CREDITS

1961 *Defenders* "Young Lovers" 10-14; *Bus Stop* "The Runaways" 12-24; **1962** *Target: The Corruptors* "Fortress of Dispair"2-16; **1963** *Eleventh Hour* "The Wings of Morning" 3-20; *Gunsmoke* "Pa Hack's Brood" 12-28; **1964** *Alfred Hitchcock Hour* "Behind a Locked Door" 3-27; *Defenders* "Die Laughing" 4-11; *Greatest Show on Earth* "You're All Right, Ivy" 4-28; *Perry Mason* "The Case of the Paper Bullet" 10-1; *Daniel Boone* "Tekaurtha

McLeod" 10-1; *Mr. Novak* "Born of Kings and Angela" 12-1; *Alfred Hitchcock Hour* "Memo from Purgatory" 12-21; **1965** *Big Valley* "Judgment in Heaven" 12-22; **1966** *Amos Burke, Secret Agent* "Terror in a Tiny Town" 1-5, 1-12; *Wild Wild West* "Night of the Flaming Ghost" 2-4; *Man Called Shenandoah* "Run and Hide" 2-14; *Bonanza* "Something Hurt, Something Wild" 9-11; **1967** *Man from UNCLE* "The Deadly Smorgasbord Affair" 1-13; *Bob Hope Chrysler Theater* "Dead Wrong" 4-5; *Man from UNCLE* "The Test Tube Killer" 9-18; **1968** *Lancer* "Foley" 10-15; **1970** *Lancer* "Shadow of a Dead Man" 1-6; *Mod Squad* "The Deadly Sin" 2-24; **1971** *Young Lawyers* "Legal Maneuver" 1-20; **1972** *Mod Squad* "Shockwave" 1-25; *Ghost Story* "Touch of Madness" 12-8; **1974** *Police Woman* "Flowers of Evil" 11-8.

TELEFILMS

1971 *Black Noon* 11-5 CBS; **1973** *The Horror at 37,000 Feet* 2-13 CBS; **1975** *The Desperate Miles* 3-5 ABC; *The Kansas City Massacre* 9-19 ABC.

Jon Lormer

(born 1905; died May 3, 1985)

Jon moved into an acting career after years of

producing plays in New York. His characters were usually scowling and irritable, but he parlayed them into over 30 years of film and television roles. He had a recurring role on *Perry Mason*, appearing as the coroner in 9 episodes.

GUEST CREDITS

1959 *Perry Mason* "The Case of the Jaded Joker" 2-21; *Perry Mason* "The Case of the Stuttering Bishop" 3-14; *Wanted: Dead or Alive* "Railroaded" 3-14; **1960** *Perry Mason* "The Case of the Frantic Flyer" 1-9; *Gunsmoke* "Jailbait Janet" 2-27; *Twilight Zone* "Execution" 4-1; *Perry Mason* "The Case of the Clumsy Clown" 11-5; *Rebel* "The Legacy" 1-13; **1961** *Twilight Zone* "Dust" 1-6; *Perry Mason* "The Case of the Renegade Referee" 2-9; **1962** *Perry Mason* "The Case of the Glamerous Ghost" 2-3; *Twilight Zone* "The Last Rites of Jeff Myrtlebank" 2-23; *Perry Mason* "The Case of the Melancholy Marksman" 3-24; *Perry Mason* "The Case of the Hateful Hero" 10-18; **1963** *Twilight Zone* "Jess-Belle" 2-14; *Virginian* "Vengeance Is the Spur" 2-27; *Perry Mason* "The Case of the Elusive Element" 4-11; *Ben Casey* "Hang No Hats or Dreams" 5-13; **1964** *Empire* "Nobody Dies on Saturday" 4-26; *Bonanza* "The Scapegoat" 10-25; *Fugitive* "Tug of War" 10-27; **1965** *Ben Casey* "Journeys End in Lover's Meeting" 4-19; *Fugitive* "End of the Line" 12-21; **1967** *Big Valley* "The Stallion" 1-30; *Star Trek* "The Return of the Archons" 2-9; *Invaders* "Valley of the Shadow" 9-26; *Daniel Boone* "The Renegade" 9-28; *Voyage to the Bottom of the Sea* "Fatal Cargo" 11-5; **1968** *Run for Your Life* "One Bad Turn" 1-10; *Bonanza* "The Thirteenth Man" 1-21; *Mission: Impossible* "The Counterfeiter" 2-4; *Lancer* "Blood Rock" 10-1; *Star Trek* "For the Sky Is Hollow and I Have Touched the Sky" 11-8; **1969** *Wild Wild West* "The Night of the Spanish Curse" 1-3; *Mission: Impossible* "Nicole" 3-30; **1970** *Medical Center* "The V. D. Story" 3-25; *Gunsmoke* "McCabe" 11-30; **1971** *Adam-12* "Log-175-Con Artists" 1-2; *Young Lawyers* "Down at the House of Truth, Visiting" 3-3; *Alias Smith and Jones* "Jailbreak at Junction City" 9-30; *Gunsmoke* "New Doctor" 10-11; *Gunsmoke* "Trafton" 10-25; *Alias Smith and Jones* "The Biggest Game in the West"

11-13; **1972** *Gunsmoke* "Alias Festus Haggin" 3-6; **1974** *Toma* "Stillwater…492" 2-1; *Harry O* "Gertrude" 9-12; *Planet of the Apes* "The Legacy" 10-11; **1975** *Waltons* "The Triumph" 12-11; **1979** *Incredible Hulk* "Haunted" 2-23; *Little House on the Prairie* "The Preacher Takes a Wife" 10-22.

TELEFILMS

1973 *Frankenstein* 1-16, 1-17 ABC; **1974** *The Gun and the Pulpit* 4-3 ABC; **1975** *Conspiracy of Terror* 12-29 NBC; **1979** *The Golden Gate Murders* 10-3 CBS.

George Loros

(born 1944)

A particular favorite on *The Rockford Files* with 6 episode credits, George was primarily a late seventies/eighties television actor. Following some stage experience, he debuted in a brief film career in 1968. His strongest roles were castings as violent criminals on TV detective series.

GUEST CREDITS

1975 *Baretta* "He'll Never See Daylight Again" 1-17; *Kojak* "Two-Four-Six for Two Hundred" 2-23; *Starsky and Hutch* "Texas Longhorn" 9-17; **1976** *Harry O* "Hostage" 2-19; *Bronk* "Vengeance" 2-22; *Delvecchio* "Good Cop" 10-10; **1977** *Starsky and Hutch* "Psychic" 1-15; *Rockford Files* "To Serve and Protect" 3-11, 3-18; *Baretta* "Carla" 3-16; *Rockford Files* "The Dog and Pony Show" 10-21; **1978** *Baretta* "The Snake Chaser" 5-11; **1979** *Rockford Files* "The Man Who Saw Alligators" 2-10; *Incredible Hulk* "The Disciple" 3-16; *Rockford Files* "Only Rock 'n' Roll Will Never Die" 10-19, 10-26; **1981** *Charlie's Angels* "Moonshinin' Angels" 1-24; *Whiz Kids* "Fatal Error" 10-12; *Greatest American Hero* "Classical Gas" 12-2.

TELEFILMS

1975 *Force Five* 3-28 CBS; *Death Scream* 9-26 ABC; **1978** *The New Maverick* 9-3 ABC; **1983** *Policewoman Centerfold* 10-17 NBC.

Donald Losby

(born 1951)

A fine juvenile actor of the late fifties and sixties, Donald Losby made a film debut in *Raintree County* at age 6. His acting career lasted until 1968 when he reached his late teens.

Fans of *The Fugitive* will well remember Donald's skillful performance in a 1964 episode, "Cry Uncle". He was well-cast in that role of an orphaned youngster whose anguish caused him to lash out at the world.

GUEST CREDITS

1961 *Twilight Zone* "Mr. Dingle, the Strong" 3-3; **1962** *Bonanza* "The Jackknife" 2-18; *Adventures in Paradise* "The Secret Place" 2-25; *Eleventh Hour* "Of Roses and Nightengales and Other Lovely Things" 11-7; *Wide Country* "A Devil in the Chute" 11-8; *Rawhide* "Incident at Quevara" 12-14; **1963** *Wagon Train* "The Michael McGoo Story" 3-20; *Fugitive* "Fear in a Desert City" 9-17; **1964** *Temple Houston* episode 4-2; *Daniel Boone* "The Family

Fluellen" 10-15; *Fugitive* "Cry Uncle" 12-1; **1965** *Ben Casey* "When I Am Grown to Man's Estate" 2-8; *Gunsmoke* "The Pariah" 4-17; *Lost in Space* "Return from Outer Space" 12-29; **1966** *Blue Light* "How to Kill a Toy Soldier" 4-13; *Gunsmoke* "The Whispering Tree" 11-12.

Tom Lowell

(born 1941)

Tom Lowell played a variety of youthful television roles during the sixties, highlighted by a regular slot on *Combat* (1963-64). His films (from 1962), included *The Manchurian Candidate, The Carpetbaggers, The Gnome-Mobile* and *Escape from the Planet of the Apes*. He disappeared from acting by 1981.

GUEST CREDITS

1962 *Twilight Zone* "The Changing of the Guard" 6-1; *Perry Mason* "The Case of the Lurid Letter" 12-6; **1963** *Alfred Hitchcock Hour* "Death and the Joyful Woman" 4-12; *Gunsmoke* "Kate Heller" 9-28; **1964** *Gunsmoke* "Homecoming" 5-23; *Perry Mason* "The Case of the Careless Kidnapper" 10-30; **1966** *Bonanza* "Ride the Wind" 1-16, 1-23; *Felony Squad* "Flame Out" 10-17; **1967** *The FBI*

GUEST CREDITS

1968 *N.Y.P.D.* "Naked in the Streets" l0-1; **1970** *Bold Ones: The Senator* "The Continual Roar of Musketry" 11-22, 11-29; **1971** *Dan August* "Dead Witness to a Killing" 1-28; *Bonanza* "Shadow of a Hero" 2-21; **1972** *Mission: Impossible* "Image" 1-15; **1974** *The FBI* "Diamond Run" 3-10; *Wide World of Mystery* "Murder Impossible" 3-26; *Harry O* "Mortal Sin" l0-3; *Rookies* "Vendetta" 11-18; *Barnaby Jones* "Time to Kill" 11-26; **1976** *City of Angels* "The November Plan" 2-3, 2-l0, 2-17; **1978** *Columbo* "Make Me a Perfect Murder" 2-25; **1979** *Barnaby Jones* "Echo of a Distant Battle" 1-11.

TELEFILMS

1972 *Delphi Bureau* 3-6 ABC; **1974** *Death Sentence* l0-2 ABC; *Panic on the 5:22* 11-20 CBS; **1975** *Winner Takes All* 3-3 NBC; **1980** *The Mating Season* 12-30 CBS.

"The Satellite" 4-2; *Invaders* "Dark Outpost" l0-24; **1968** *Daniel Boone* "The Patriot" 12-5; **1973** *The FBI* "The Loper Gambit" 4-l; **1979** *Quincy, M.E.* "Murder by S.O.P." 11-29.

TELEFILM

1980 *The Aliens Are Coming* 3-20 NBC.

Laurence Luckinbill

(born November 2l, 1934, Little Rock, Arkansas
    Educated at The University of Arkansas and Catholic University of America, Laurence served in The U. S. Army Chemical Corps. in l956. He worked onstage prior to his television debut in the soap, *The Secret Storm* (1967-68). Another soap role, in *Where the Heart Is* (1970-7l), came soon thereafter. During 1970 he was honored as Best Actor by the New York Drama Critics Poll. In 1971-72 he gained a starring role in *The Delphi Bureau*, perhaps his best known work.

    After *Delphi Bureau*, he worked in seventies guest roles and telefilms, with his only eighties guest work in *Murder, She Wrote* (2) and *Hotel*.

    During 1987 he did a one-man show on PBS, *Lyndon Johnson*. Married to actress Luci Arnaz, he co-produced a recent TV tribute to Lucy and Desi.

William "Bill" Lucking
(born June 17, Vicksburg, Michigan)

A strapping and rugged-appearing supporting actor, Bill Lucking first appeared on television in 1968, making a film debut the following year. Effective as a heavy, he also had numerous authority roles.

The eighties provided three series regular roles, in *Shannon* (1981-82), *The A-Team* (1983-84) and in *Jessie* (1984). His film career included roles in *Oklahoma Crude*, *10*, and *Stripes*.

GUEST CREDITS

1968 *Mission: Impossible* "Mercenaries" 11-27; **1969** *Lancer* "Juniper's Camp" 3-11; **1970** *High Chaparral* "A Matter of Vengeance" 11-27; *Bonanza* "The Imposters" 12-13; **1971** *Name of the Game* "A Sister from Napoli" 1-8; **1974** *Chopper One* "Ambush" 2-28; *Gunsmoke* "Matt Dillon Must Die" 9-9; *Mannix* "Desert Sun" 12-1; **1975** *S.W.A.T.* "The Killing Ground" 2-24; *Police Woman* "Blaze of Glory" 11-11; *Rockford Files* "Pastoria Prime Pick" 11-28; *Waltons* "The Intruders" 12-18; **1976** *Westside Medical* "Risks" 6-30; *Westside Medical* "Deep Blue Sea" 9-14; *Barnaby Jones* "Final Ransom" 11-11; *Black Sheep Squadron* "New Georgie On My Mind" 11-30; **1977** *Delvecchio* "One Little Indian" 1-

30; **1978** *Charlie's Angels* "Hours of Desperation" 1-11; *Incredible Hulk* "The Antowok Horror" 9-29; **1979** *Hart to Hart* "Jonathan Hart, Jr. "10-6; **1980** *Vegas* "Consortium" 2-27; *Incredible Hulk* "Darkside" 12-5; **1981** *Lou Grant* "Campesinos" 3-16; *Vegas* "Out of Sight" 3-18; *Riker* "Gun Run" 3-28; *CHiPs* "Moonlight" 10-18; **1982** *Greatest American Hero* "It's All Downhill from Here" 3-3; *Tales of the Gold Monkey* "Legends Are Forever" 10-20; *Tales of the Gold Monkey* "Honor Thy Brother" 11-24; *Knight Rider* "A Plush Ride" 12-10; **1983** *Magnum, P.I.* "Two Birds of a Feather" 3-17; *Hill Street Blues* episode 11-3; *Simon and Simon* "Caught Between the Devil and the Deep Blue Sea" 11-10.

TELEFILMS

1971 *Ellery Queen: Don't Look Behind You* 11-19 NBC; **1972** *Blood Sport* 12-5 ABC; **1975** *Force Five* 3-28 CBS; **1976** *Mallory: Circumstantial Evidence* 2-8 NBC; **1977** *Danger in Paradise* 5-12 NBC; *San Pedro Bums* 5-13 ABC; **1978** *Dr. Scorpion* 2-24 ABC; *Happily Ever After* 9-5 CBS; **1979** *Captain America II* 11-23, 11-24; **1980** *Power* 1-14, 1-15 NBC; *The Last Song* 10-23 CBS; **1983** *M.A.D.D.: Mothers Against Drunk Driving* 3-14 NBC.

Paul Lukather
(born 1936)

Paul's stage and film career began in 1957; he eventually appeared in films like *Fate Is the Hunter* and *Alvarez Kelly*. Television provided steady work for Paul, from 1959 through the seventies, mainly in action-oriented roles. He had a memorable role in a 1966 episode of *Perry Mason*, starring as a boxer falsely accused of murder. During 1969-71, he appeared on the soap *Bright Promise*.

From a theatrical family, Paul is the son of production manager Lee Lukather, is the brother of assistant director Bill Lukather and the father of singer Suzanne Lukather.

GUEST CREDITS

1959 *M Squad* "The Dangerous Game" 6-5;
1960 *Rawhide* "The Incident of the Murder Steer" 5-13; *Bonanza* "Breed of Violence" 11-5; 1961 *Bat Masterson* "End of the Line" 1-26; 1964 *Fugitive* "Man in a Chariot" 9-15; 1965 *Outer Limits* "The Brain of Col. Barham" 1-2; *12 O'Clock High* "The Albatross" 1-15; *Man from UNCLE* "The Secret Scepter Affair" 2-8; *Bob Hope Chrysler Theater* "A Time for Killing" 4-30; *Ben Casey* "A Horse Named Stavinsky" 5-17; 1966 *Fugitive* "Echo of a Nightmare" 1-25; *Perry Mason* "The Case of the Misguided Model" 4-24; *Fugitive* "Approach with Care" 11-16; *12 O'Clock High* "The High Graveyard" 12-30; 1967 *Mission: Impossible* "The Trial" 1-28; *Invaders* "Moonshot" 4-18; *The FBI* "False Witness" 12-10; 1968 *The FBI* "The Widow" 12-29; 1969 *Mission: Impossible* "The Bunker" 3-2, 3-9; *Mod Squad* "A Place to Run, a Place to Hide" 12-2; 1973 *Mannix* "The Girl in the Polka Dot Dress" 9-16; 1975 *Adam-12* "Pot Shot" 1-14; *Cannon* "Missing at FL 307?" 2-5; *Barnaby Jones* "The Lonely Victims" 1-8; 1977 *Starsky and Hutch* "Fatal Charm" 9-24.

TELEFILMS

1970 *The House on Greenapple Road* 1-11 ABC; 1979 *The Ordeal of Patty Hearst* 3-4 ABC; *Mind over Matter* 10-23 CBS.

James Lydon

(born May 30, 1923, Harrington Park, New Jersey)
    Best known as Henry Aldrich in 9 films of the forties, James moved on to adult roles in movies and had series regular roles on two fifties television sitcoms: *So This Is Hollywood* (1955) and *Love That Jill* (1958). He mixed occasional guest shots with producing and directing, and worked behind the cameras on TV hits like *Wagon Train* and *M*A*S*H*.

GUEST CREDITS

1959 *Wanted: Dead or Alive* "Twelve Hours to Crazy Horse" 11-21; *77 Sunset Strip* "Secret Island" 12-4; *Wagon Train* "The Vittorio Bottecelli Story" 12-16; 1960 *Hotel de Paree* "Sundance and the Barren Soil" 5-20; *Wagon Train* "The Jeremy Dow Story" 12-28; 1961 *Twilight Zone* "Back There" 1-13; *Wanted: Dead or Alive* "Dead Reckoning" 3-22; *Wyatt Earp* "Until Proven Guilty" 4-11; *Stagecoach West* "The Raider" 5-9; *Whispering Smith* "The Devil's Share" 5-22; *Checkmate* "Kill the Sound" 11-15; 1962 *Wagon Train* "The Dr. Denker Story" 1-31; 1968 *The FBI* "Act of Violence" 1-21; *Gunsmoke* "First People" 2-19; 1970 *The FBI* "The Traitor" 9-27; 1971 *Cade's County* "Requiem for Miss Madrid" 12-12; 1972 *Adam-12* "Adoption" 2-2; 1974 *Adam-12* "Suspect Number One" 10-29; *Rockford Files* "Find

Me If You Can" 11-1; *Six Million Dollar Man* "Straight On 'Til Morning" 11-8; *Rockford Files* "Joey Blue Eyes" 1-30; **1982** *Greatest American Hero* "A Train of Thought" 1-13.

TELEFILMS

1975 *Ellery Queen* 3-23 NBC; **1976** *The New Daughters of Joshua Cabe* 5-29 ABC; **1977** *Peter Lundy and the Medicine Hat Stallion* 11-6 NBC.

Hal Lynch

A folksinger and television actor, Hal Lynch has also done some stage work and four films. He was

married to actress Joyce Van Patten.

Most of Hal's TV work was in action-oriented roles; a brief film career began in 1966.

GUEST CREDITS

1965 *Fugitive* "All the Scared Rabbits" 10-26; *Gunsmoke* "The Bounty Hunter" 10-30; *Amos Burke, Secret Agent* "Peace, It's a Gasser" 11-3; **1966** *The FBI* "Quantico" 1-30; *Perry Mason* "The Case of the Unwelcome Well" 4-3; *Big Valley* "The Midas Man" 4-13; *Big Valley* "Last Train to the Fair" 4-27; *Shane* "The Great Invasion" 12-17; **1967** *Gunsmoke* "Mis-

taken Identity" 3-18; *Custer* "Blazing Arrows" 11-29; **1968** *The FBI* "Region of Peril" 2-25; *Bonanza* "Commitment at Angelus" 4-7; *Bonanza* "The Real People of Muddy Creek" 10-6; *Big Valley* "The Jonah" 11-11; **1969** *Mod Squad* "Peace Now, Arly Blau" 4-8; **1970** *The FBI* "The Dollar" 2-22; *Dan August* "The Soldier" 12-2; **1971** *Interns* "The Choice" 3-26; **1973** *Emergency* episode 11-10.

Richard Lynch

(born April 29, 1936, Brooklyn, New York)

Richard started acting on the New York stage after a tour of duty with the U. S. Marines. He made a film debut in 1973 and came to television in 1975, quickly typecast as a cold-eyed and often sadistic killer. He was also quite effective in sci-fi roles as can be seen below.

During the eighties he had two series regular roles, in *Galactica 1980* (1980) and *The Phoenix* (1982). His skills were in strong demand throughout the eighties for guest roles, and he worked on *Fall Guy, Blue Thunder, Automan, Matt Houston, A-Team, Riptide, MacGruder and Loud, Scarecrow and Mrs. King, Airwolf, Last Precinct, One a Hero, Law and Harry McGraw* and *Werewolf*.

Richard received the Mercury Award from the Academy of Science Fiction and Fantasy for his work in the 1982 film *The Sword and the Sorcerer*.

GUEST CREDITS

1976 *Bronk* "Target: Unknown" 2-8; *Switch* "The Twelfth Commandment" 9-28; *Serpico* "Every Man Pays His Dues" 10-29; **1977** *Police Woman* "Solitaire" 2-22; *Streets of San Francisco* "Time Out" 6-16; **1978** *Bionic Woman* "Out of Body" 3-4; *Starsky and Hutch* "Quadromania" 5-10; *Battlestar Galactica* "The Gun on Ice Planet Zero" 10-22, 10-29; **1979** *Vegas* "Yours Truly, Jack the Ripper" 1-10; *Starsky and Hutch* "Starsky vs. Hutch" 5-8; *Barnaby Jones* "Nightmare in Hawaii" 9-27; *Buck Rogers* "Vegas in Space" 10-4; *Man Called Sloane* "Masquerade of Terror" 10-13; *Charlie's Angels* "Angels on the Street" 11-7; **1980** *Buck Rogers* "A Blast for Buck" 1-17; **1981** *Vegas* "Dead Ringer" 4-

29; **1982** *McClain's Law* "Sign of the Beast" 1-22, 1-29; **1983** *Fall Guy* "Pleasure Isle" 10-5; *Manimal* "Illusion" 10-14; *T. J. Hooker* "Carnal Express" 12-31.

TELEFILMS

1972 *Jigsaw* 3-26 ABC; **1975** *Starsky and Hutch* 4-30 ABC; **1977** *Roger and Harry* 5-2 ABC; *Good Against Evil* 5-22 NBC; *Dog and Cat* 7-22 ABC; **1979** *Vampire* 10-7 ABC; **1980** *Alcatraz: The Whole Shocking Story* 11-5, 11-6; **1981** *Sizzle* 11-29 ABC; **1983** *White Water Rebels* 1-8 CBS; *The Last Ninja* 7-7 ABC.

Gene Lyons

(born 1923, Pittsburgh, Pa.; died July 8, 1974)

A strong Broadway career propelled Gene Lyons into a great deal of fifties live television (from 1952), in shows like *Philco Playhouse* (4), *Goodyear Theater* (3), *Studio One* (2), *Kraft Television Theatre* (7), *The Web, U.S. Steel Hour* and *Armstrong Circle Theater*.

In the early and mid sixties Gene did a considerable amount of guesting prior to settling into a long running regular role (1967-74), appearing as the police commissioner on *Ironside*. He died July 8,

1974 at age 51; his obituary did not state the cause of death.

GUEST CREDITS

1960 *Twilight Zone* "King Nine Will Not Return" 9-30; *Untouchables* "A Seat on the Fence" 11-24; *One Step Beyond* "Tonight at 12:17" 12-6; *Gunsmoke* "Brother Love" 12-31; **1961** *Hong Kong* "Murder by Proxy" 3-1; *Americans* "The Bounty Jumpers" 4-7; **1962** *Stoney Burke* "The Mob Riders" 10-29; **1963** *Alfred Hitchcock Hour* "What Really Happened" 1-11; *Virginian* "If You Have Tears" 2-13; *Great Adventure* "Six Wagons to Sea" 10-18; *Fugitive* "Ticket to Alaska" 11-12; **1964** *Alfred Hitchcock Hour* "The Evil of Adelaide Winters" 2-7; *Great Adventure* "Plague" 2-28; *Gunsmoke* "Bently" 4-11; *Fugitive* "Man in a Chariot" 9-15; *Alfred Hitchcock Hour* "Consider Her Ways" 12-28; **1965** *Slattery's People* "Question: How Long Is the Shadow of a Man?" 1-1; *Bob Hope Chrysler Theater* "Perilous Times" 3-14; *Slattery's People* "Color Him Red" 11-26; *Perry Mason* "The Case of the Wrathful Wraith" 11-7; **1966** *I Spy* "Crusade to Limbo" 3-23; **1967** *The FBI* "The Courier" 1-15; *Star*

Trek "A Taste of Armageddon" 2-23; *Invaders* "The Enemy" 10-3; **1968** *Invaders* "The Pursued" 3-19; **1972** *The FBI* "Escape to Nowhere" 3-19.

TELEFILM

1967 *Ironside* 3-28 NBC.

Robert F. Lyons

(born 1940)

Robert F. Lyons grew up in Albany, New York and studied acting at the American Academy of Dramatic Arts (AADA). He began his television career in 1966; his youthful and innocent-looking appearance belied frequent castings as vicious criminals. He made his screen debut in 1969 as a rapist and killer.

Extremely busy on television from 1967 until the mid eighties, he has increasingly turned from television to film roles, in offerings like *Death Wish II, Murphy's Law* and *Platoon Leader*.

GUEST CREDITS

1966 *The FBI* "Flight to Harbin" 2-27; **1967** *Cornonet Blue* "A Charade for Murder" 7-24; *Gunsmoke* "Major Glory" 10-30; **1968** *Judd, for the*

Defense "The Sound of the Plastic Axe" 10-25; **1969** *Name of the Game* "The Suntan Mob" 2-7; *Land of the Giants* "The Chase" 4-20; **1970** *Medical Center* 'Ghetto Clinic" 10-21; *Young Lawyers* "At the Edge of Night" 11-16; *Ironside* "Backfire" 12-3; **1971** *Night Gallery* "Midnight Never Ends" 11-3; *Sarge* "A Party to a Crime" 12-28; *Medical Center* "Shock!" 12-29; **1972** *Assignment: Vienna* "Queen's Gambit" 11-9; **1973** *The FBI* "The Loper Gambit" 4-1; *New Perry Mason* "The Case of the Perilous Pen" 12-30; *Petrocelli* "Face of Evil" 12-17; **1976** *Serpico* "Country Boy" 9-24; **1979** *Incredible Hulk* "The Quiet Room" 5-11; **1980** *Quincy, M.E.* "A Matter of Principle" 11-12; **1981** *CHiPs* "The Poachers" 6-21; *CHiPs* "Suicide Stunt" 10-25; *Falcon Crest* "In His Father's House" 12-4; **1982** *Fall Guy* "Soldiers of Fortune" 2-10; *McClain's Law* "What Patrick Doesn't Know" 2-12; *Voyager* "All Fall Down" 2-27; **1983** *A-Team* "A Nice Place to Visit" 5-10; *Matt Houston* episode 9-16.

TELEFILMS

1972 *The Rookies* 3-7 ABC; **1974** *The Disappearance of Flight 412* 10-1 NBC; **1977** *The Strange Possession of Mrs. Oliver* 2-28 NBC; **1978** *The Ghost of Flight 401* 2-18 NBC; **1979** *Death Car on the Freeway* 9-25 CBS; **1980** *Waikiki* 4-21 ABC; **1981** *Miracle on Ice* 3-1 ABC; *Dark Night of the Scarecrow* 10-24 ABC.

James MacArthur

(born December 8, 1937, Los Angeles, Calif.)

James was adopted by playwright Charles MacArthur and famed actress Helen Hayes and grew up in a theatrical atmosphere. He debuted at age 8 in a summer stock production, and came to television in 1955 at age 17.

Educated at Harvard, James made his film debut in 1957, then starred in a quartet of Disney films: *The Light in the Forest, Third Man on the Mountain, Kidnapped* and *Swiss Family Robinson*. He had a prominent role in the 1965 war epic, *The Battle of the Bulge*, and appeared in *Hang 'Em High* (1967).

After numerous television guest appearances, including fifties productions of Studio One (2), he gained a plum role on *Hawaii Five-0* in September of 1968. He remained in the role of detective Danny Williams until 1979. Perhaps tired of hearing Jack Lord command "Book him, Danno—murder one!", MacArthur left the series for "better things". They didn't materialize, and his acting career was wrapped up by the mid-eighties.

GUEST CREDITS

1959 *Desilu Playhouse* "The Innocent Assassin" 3-16; **1961** *Untouchables* "Death for Sale" 4-27; *Bus Stop* "And the Pursuit of Evil" 12-17; **1962** *Wagon Train* "The Dick Pederson Story" 1-10; *Dick Powell Show* "The Court Martial of Captain Wycliff" 12-11; **1963** *Sam Benedict* "Some Fires Die Slowly" 2-16; *Great Adventure* "The Hunley" 9-27; *Arrest and Trial* "The Shield Is for Hiding Behind" 10-6; *Burke's Law* "Who Killed the Kind Doctor?" 11-29; *Eleventh Hour* "La Belle Indifference" 12-18; **1964** *Great Adventure* "Rodger Young" 1-24; *Alfred Hitchcock Hour* "Behind the Locked Door"

3-27; **1965** *Virginian* "Jennifer" 11-3; **1966** *Branded* "A Destiny Which Makes Us Brothers" 1-23; *12 O'Clock High* "The Outsider" 1-31; *Gunsmoke* "The Harvest" 3-26; **1967** *Combat* "Encounter" 1-31; *Hondo* "Hondo and the Mad Dog" 10-27; *Tarzan* "Pride of the Lioness" 11-17; *Bonanza* "Check Rein" 12-3; **1979** *Time Express* "Doctor's Wife" 4-26; **1981** *Vegas* "Heist" 2-25; *Walking Tall* episode 3-31.

TELEFILMS

1980 *Alcatraz: The Whole Shocking Story* 11-5, 11-6 NBC; **1983** *The Night the Bridge Fell Down* 2-28 NBC.

Charles Macauley

(born 1927)

Onstage from 1952, Charles debuted in films in 1962 and began making an impact on television during the late sixties. He was virtually always cast in the role of strong authority figures. A close friend of the late Raymond Burr, Charles appeared as the District Attorney in several of the last *Perry Mason* telefilms during the late eighties and early nineties.

GUEST CREDITS

1961 *Rifleman* "Sheer Terror" 10-16; **1963** *Combat* "Ambush" 12-3; **1967** *Star Trek* "The Return of the Archons" 2-9; *Star Trek* "Wolf in the Fold" 12-22; **1968** *It Takes a Thief* "Birds of a Feather" 3-19; *Wild Wild West* "The Night of the Fire and Brimstone" 11-22; **1969** *Ironside* "The Prophecy" 2-6; **1970** *Mission: Impossible* "Lover's Knot" 2-22; **1971** *Dan August* "The Assassin" 4-8; **1972** *Night Gallery* "The Funeral" 1-5; *Columbo* "Etude in Black" 9-17; *Owen Marshall, Counselor at Law* "Hour of Judgment" 10-5; *The FBI* "The Franklin Papers" 10-8; **1973** *Griff* "Prey" 10-27; *Cannon* "The Limping Man" 11-14; **1974** *Columbo* "Mind Over Mayhem" 2-10; *Movin' On* "The Time of His Life" 9-12; **1975** *Barnaby Jones* "Jeopardy for Two" 4-1; *Barbary Coast* "Funny Money" 9-8; *Kate McShane* "Conspiracy of Silence" 10-29; *Starsky and Hutch* "The Bait" 11-5; *Bronk* "Crackback" 11-30; *Ellery Queen* "The Adventure of the Pharoah's Curse" 12-11; *Family Holvak* "Crisis" 12-21; **1977** *Wonder Woman* "Formula 407" 1-22; *Barnaby Jones* "Yesterday's Terror" 10-13; **1978** *Black Sheep Squadron* "Wolves in the Sheep Pen" 1-4; **1980** *Barnaby Jones* "The Killing Point" 1-17; **1983** *Tales of the Gold Monkey* "God Save the Queen" 1-19.

TELEFILMS

1971 *Ransom for a Dead Man* 3-1 NBC; **1974** *A Case of Rape* 2-20 NBC; **1975** *The Big Ripoff* 3-11 NBC; **1976** *The Return of the World's Greatest Detective* 6-16 NBC; *Frances Gary Powers: The True Story of the U-2 Incident* 9-29 NBC; **1977** *Tail Gunner Joe* 2-6 NBC; **1978** *The Winds of Kitty Hawk* 12-17 NBC; **1981** *The Munsters' Revenge* 2-27 NBC.

Diane McBain

(born 1941)

Diane made her television debut during 1959 and did her first film in 1960. Under a Warner Bros. Contract, she spent the early sixties working in their related television series: *77 Sunset Strip, Hawaiian Eye, Bourbon Street Beat* and *Surfside 6.*

She was a regular on the latter series during 1960-62.

Subsequently she worked in various TV guest roles until 1970. Semi-retired from acting during the seventies, she worked on a regular role on the soap *Days of Our Lives* during 1982. Later eighties guest shots included appearances on *Airwolf, Crazy Like a Fox* and *Knight Rider.* She also appeared on the soap *General Hospital* during 1988.

GUEST CREDITS

1959 *Maverick* "Passage to Fort Doom" 3-8; *77 Sunset Strip* "Six Superior Skirts" 10-16; **1960** *77 Sunset Strip* "The Starlet" 2-26; *Alaskans* "Behind the Moon" 3-6; *Bourbon Street Beat* "The Missing Queen" 3-14; *Sugarfoot* "Return to Boot Hill" 3-15; *Bourbon Street Beat* "Wall of Silence" 3-28; *77 Sunset Strip* "Fraternity of Fear" 5-6; *Lawman* "The Judge" 5-15; *Bourbon Street Beat* "Ferry to Algiers" 6-6; **1962** *77 Sunset Strip* "Leap, My Lovely" 10-19; *Hawaiian Eye* "Pursuit of a Lady" 12-11; **1963** *Hawaiian Eye* "Pretty Pigeon" 1-

22; *77 Sunset Strip* "Nine to Five" 3-8; *77 Sunset Strip* "5" 9-27; **1964** *Burke's Law* "Who Killed Mary Kelso?" 2-28; *Arrest and Trial* "Tigers Are for Jungles" 3-22; *Burke's Law* "Who Killed Mr. Cartwheel?" l0-2l; *Burke's Law* "Who Killed the Tall One in the Middle?"11-25; **1965** *Kraft Suspense Theatre* "Double Jeopardy" 1-8; *Wild Wild West* "Night of a Thousand Eyes" l0-22; *Man from UNCLE* "The Deadly Toys Affair" 11-12; **1967** *Wild Wild West* "Night of the Vicious Valentine" 2-l0; **1970** *Land of the Giants* "Panic" l-25; **1975** *Barbary Coast* "Sauce for the Goose" l0-20; **1976** *Marcus Welby, M.D.* "The Highest Mountain" 2-l7, 2-24; **1979** *Charlie's Angels* "Disco Angels" 1-3l; *Hawaii Five-0* "Though the Heavens Fell" l0-18; **1980** *Hawaii Five-0* "The Moroville Covenant" 3-29; **1981** *Charlie's Angels* "Angels on the Line" 2-l4; *Dallas* episode 1-15;**1983** *Matt Houston* "The Rock and a Hard Place" 1-2.

TELEFILM

1978 *Donner Pass: The Road to Survival* l0-24 NBC.

Amanda McBroom

(born Burbank, Calif.)

The daughter of an actor, David Bruce, and a drama coach mother, Amanda is a multi-talented actress-lyricist-composer-singer. She studied theater at the University of Texas and made her stage debut at the Dallas State Fair Music Hall. Entering television in 1973, Amanda guested in a number of detective series episodes through 1985.

However, her greatest fame came from her Grammy-winning song, *The Rose*, which she composed in only 15 minutes. The song was the theme for a 1979 20th Century Fox film of the same name; it also won a Golden Globe as Best Song of the Year.

Amanda was featured in a 1989 NBC special called *From the Heart*.

GUEST CREDITS

1973 *Medical Center* "Broken Image" 9-24;

Magician "The Vanishing Lady" l0-9; *Cannon* "Dead Lady's Tears" 11-7; **1974** *Police Story* "Captain Hook" 12-3; **1975** *Gunsmoke* "Brides and Grooms" 2-l0; *Joe Forrester* "Bus Station" 9-23; **1976** *Hawaii Five-0* "Loose Ends" 1-8; *Jigsaw John* "Death of the Party" 3-22; *Hawaii Five-0* "Tour de Force-Man Abroad" l0-28; *Hawaii Five-0* "Heads, You're Dead" 11-11; **1977** *Hawaii Five-0* "Dealer's Choice: Blackmail" 2-3; *Charlie's Angels* "Angel in Love" l0-26; **1978** *Starsky and Hutch* "Discomania" 9-12; **1979** *Lou Grant* "Convention" 3-l2; *Big Shamus, Little Shamus* episode 1 9-29; **1980** *Hart to Hart* "Death Set" 5-l3; **1982** *Powers of Matthew Star* "Experiment" 12-l0; **1983** *Remington Steele* "Steele in Circulation" 4-12.

TELEFILMS

James McCallion

(born September 27, l9l8, Glasgow, Scotland)

In films from l953, James appeared in noted epics like *Vera Cruz, North by Northwest, PT-*l09 and *Coogan's Bluff*. Married to the late actress Nora Marlowe (19l5-77), he worked in numerous sixties and seventies guest roles.

His only series regular role came during l960-62 in *National Velvet*, with James playing the handyman.

GUEST CREDITS

1963 *Outer Limits* "Man with the Power" 10-7; **1965** *Fugitive* "End of the Line" 12-21; **1966** *Fugitive* "The Evil Men Do" 12-27; **1967** *Girl from UNCLE* "Samurai Affair" 3-28; *Fugitive* "Shattered Silence" 4-11; *Invaders* "The Trial" 10-10; **1968** *Adam-12* "Log Seventy-Two" 11-9; *Gunsmoke* "Railroaded" 11-25; **1969** *Mission: Impossible* "Nicole" 3-30; *Ironside* "Beyond a Shadow" 12-11; *Mannix* "Missing: Sun and Sky" 12-20; **1970** *The FBI* "Conspiracy of Corruption" 1-11; **1971** *Night Gallery* "Diary" 11-10; **1972** *Banyon* "Meal Ticket" 10-13; **1973** *Cannon* "The Prisoners" 2-21; *Barnaby Jones* "Death Leap" 9-23; *Cannon* "Arena of Fear" 12-19; **1974** *Ironside* "A Taste of Ashes" 2-14; **1975** *Harry O* "Silent Kill" 2-6; *Mobile One* episode 9 12-1; **1976** *Streets of San Francisco* "Judgment Day" 2-19.

TELEFILMS

1972 *Adventures of Nick Carter* 2-20 NBC; **1973** *Crime Club* 3-6 CBS; *Letters from Three Lovers* 10-3 ABC; **1974** *The Strange and Deadly Occurance* 9-24 NBC.

Mercedes McCambridge

(born March 17, 1918, Joliet, Illinois)
Debuting on television on an experimental

episode in 1945, Mercedes came back to TV in the soap *One Man's Family* in 1949-50. During 1949 she had lept to prominence in her film debut, winning an Academy Award for her brilliant work in *All the King's Men*. She received another Oscar Nomination in 1956 for *Giant*.

The fifties were a busy time for her television work, appearing in *Studio One* (3), *Lux Video Theatre* (2), *Climax*, *Front Row Center* (2) and *Wagon Train*, in addition to the credits listed below. She also was a regular on the series *Wire Service* (1956-57). Much of her work was in tough, hard-bitten roles. More recent TV roles included a guest appearance during 1988 on *Cagney and Lacey*.

She has written a biography, titled *The Two of Us* (1960).

GUEST CREDITS

1959 *Schlitz Playhouse of Stars* "On the Brink" 2-27; *Rawhide* "Incident of the Curious Street" 4-10; *Riverboat* "Jessie Quinn" 12-6; **1960** *Overland Trail* "Sour Annie" 5-8; *Rawhide* "Incident of the Captive" 12-60; *Bonanza* "The Lady from Baltimore" 1-14; *Rawhide* "The Greedy Town" 2-16; **1963** *Dakotas* "Trouble at Trench Creek" 1-28; **1964** *Nurses* "Credo" 1-9; *Defenders* "The Man Who" 10-29; *Dr. Kildare* "Rome Will Never Leave

You" 11-12, 11-19; **1965** *Rawhide* "Hostage for Hanging" 10-19; **1966** *Lost in Space* "The Space Cropper" 3-30; **1970** *Bonanza* "The Law and Billy Burgess" 2-15; *Medical Center* "A Matter of Tomorrow" 2-25; **1971** *Name of the Game* "A Capital Affair" 2-12; *Gunsmoke* "The Lost" 9-13; **1978** *Charlie's Angels* "Angels in the Springtime" 10-11; **1980** *Hagen* "More Deadly Poison" 4-24; **1981** *Magnum, P.I.* "Don't Say Goodbye" 3-26.

Patty McCormick registers strong apprehension in a 1975 episode of *Cannon* (CBS) called "Coffin Corner". Gary Lockwood shares her concern at left.

TELEFILMS

1972 *Killer by Night* 1-7 CBS; *Two for the Money* 2-26 ABC; **1973** *The Girls of Huntington House* 2-14 ABC; *The President's Plane Is Missing* 10-23 ABC; **1975** *Who Is the Black Dahlia* 3-1 NBC; **1979** *The Sacketts* 5-15, 5-16 NBC.

Patricia "Patty" McCormick

(born August 21, 1945, Brooklyn, New York)

Patty McCormick was a child model at age 4 and made her film debut in 1951 at age 6. A year later, she began her television career on a *Kraft Television Theatre* episode. In 1956 she was propelled to last fame as the murderous child in *The Bad Seed*, a role that earned her an Academy Award Nomination.

The fifties were a busy period in Patty's television career, with series regular roles on *Mama* (1953-56) and *Peck's Bad Girl* (1959). She also appeared on *Armstrong Circle Theater* (2), General Electric Theater, *Kraft Theatre* (3), *Goodyear Theater*, *DuPont Theater*, *Matinee Theater* (2), *Climax* and *Playhouse 90* (5).

With prime-time guest work interspersed, Patty turned to soap roles on *Young Doctor Malone* (1962), *The Best of Everything* (1970) and *As the World Turns* (1975-76). She left acting for a time during the sixties, but returned to a busy seventies schedule, culminated by a series regular role on a sitcom, *The Ropers* (1979-80).

Her later eighties guest appearances included work on *Hotel*, *Remington Steele*, *Murder, She Wrote* (2), *Law and Harry McGraw* and *Head of the Class*.

GUEST CREDITS

1959 *Playhouse 90* "Project Immortality" 6-11; *U.S. Steel Hour* "Rachel's Summer" 10-7; *One Step Beyond* "Make Me Not a Witch" 12-22; **1960** *Chevy Mystery Show* "Summer Hero" 6-12; *Route 66*

"Black November" 10-7; **1962** *New Breed* "Thousands and Thousands of Miles" 4-17; *Rawhide* "Incident of the Wolves" 11-16; **1963** *Rawhide* "Incident at Paradise" 10-24; **1968** *Wild Wild West* "Night of the Death Masks" 1-28; **1969** *Lancer* "Child of Rock and Sunshine" 4-1; **1972** *O'Hara, U. S. Treasury* "Operation: Dorais" 2-4; **1973** *Emergency* episode 5-19; **1974** *Police Story* "Chain of Command" 1-8; *Streets of San Francisco* "Blockade" 1-24; *Barnaby Jones* "Image in a Cracked Mirror" 3-24; *Marcus Welby, M.D.* "The Brittle Warrior" 9-10; *Manhunter* "The Truck Murders" 11-6; **1975** *Cannon* "Coffin Corner" 1-15; *Mobile One* "Life Preserver" 9-19; **1981** *Dallas* "The Prodigal" 12-18; **1982** *Dallas* "Anniversary" 2-12; *Magnum, P.I.* "Foiled Again" 11-11.

TELEFILM

1983 *Night Partners* 10-11 CBS.

Ruth McDevitt

(born September 13, 1895, Coldwater, Michigan; died 1976)

A wonderful character actress, Ruth is best remembered as a television performer in several series regular roles, and on soaps. She frequently played snoopy neighbors or gentle and kindly older ladies.

Her first television exposure came in the 1949 DuMont soap (first daytime, then evening), *A Woman to Remember*. She followed that with a stint on *Mr. Peepers* (1953-55) and soaps *Young Doctor Malone* (1958-61) and *The Doctors* (1964-65). A 1966-67 sitcom, *Pistols and Petticoats*, offered Ruth a featured role.

She began the seventies as a regular on the 1970 summer replacement show, *The Everly Brothers*, and captured a role on another soap, *Bright Promise* (1971-72). Just prior to her death in 1976, Ruth had a very visible role on *Kolchak: The Night Stalker* (1975-76).

GUEST CREDITS

1961 *Naked City* "Bridge Party" 12-27; **1962** *Dr. Kildare* "Gravida One" 9-27; **1963** *Nurses* "Night Shift" 9-27; **1964** *Alfred Hitchcock Hour* "The Cadaver" 1-17; *Alfred Hitchcock Hour* "The Gentleman Caller" 4-10; **1969** *Mannix* "Merry-Go-Round for Murder" 4-5; **1973** *Mannix* "A Matter of Principle" 1-14; *Streets of San Francisco* "Winterkill" 12-13; **1974** *Kojak* "Deliver Us Some Evil" 2-13; *Little House on the Prairie* "If I Should Wake Before I Die" 10-23; *Gunsmoke* "The Tarnished Badge" 11-11; *Marcus Welby, M.D.* "Child of Silence" 12-3; *Rookies* "Blue Christmas" 12-16; **1975** *Ellery Queen* "The Adventure of the Twelfth Express" 10-9; *Medical Center* "Two Against Death" 11-17.

TELEFILMS

1971 *In Search of America* 3-23 ABC; **1972** *The Couple Takes a Wife* 12-5; **1973** *The Girl Most Likely To...* 11-6 ABC; **1974** *Skyway to Death* 1-19 ABC; *Winter Kill* 4-15 ABC; **1975** *The Abduction of Saint Anne* 1-21 ABC; *My Father's House* 6-1 ABC; *Man on the Outside* 6-29 ABC; **1976** *One of My Wives Is Missing* 3-5 ABC.

Biff McGuire

(born Willliam J. McGuire, October 25, 1926, New Haven, Conn.)

Biff was educated at Massachusetts State and at Shrivenham University in England. A strong television presence during the fifties, he had credits on *Studio One* (3), *Armstrong Circle Theater* (4), *U.S. Steel Hour* (5), *Alfred Hitchcock Presents* (4), *The Web* (2), *Justice* (2), *Kraft Theatre* (4) and *Goodyear Playhouse*.

His sixties work on TV was rather limited, but he worked regularly from the mid seventies, capped by a co-starring role on *Gibbsville* (1976). Biff was married to actress Jeannie Carson.

GUEST CREDITS

1959 *U.S. Steel Hour* "Wish on the Moon" 7-29; **1960** *Diagnosis Unknown* "The Parasite" 9-13; **1962** *Defenders* "The Tarnished Cross" 3-17; **1963** *Defenders* "The Seal of Confession" 11-30; **1974** *Gunsmoke* "The Fourth Victim" 11-4; **1975** *Kate McShane* "Murder Comes in Little Pills" 10-1; *Barnaby Jones* "The Orchid Killer" 10-3; *Matt Helm* "The Game of the Century" 10-18; **1976** *Rookies* "Journey to Oblivion" 3-16; *Family* episode 9-28; *Kojak* "Law Dance" 10-10; **1977** *Police Story* "Spitfire" 1-11; *Starsky and Hutch* "The Velvet Jungle" 3-5; *Hawaii Five-0* "See How She Runs" 3-31; *Hallmark Hall of Fame* "The Court Martial of George Armstrong Custer" 12-1;

1978 *Family* episode 5-16; *Barnaby Jones* "A Frame for Murder" 11-16; **1979** *Paper Chase* "Scavenger Hunt" 4-24; *Police Story* "A Cry for Justice" 5-23.

TELEFILMS

1975 *The Turning Point of Jim Malloy* 4-12 NBC; **1976** *Law and Order* 5-6 NBC; *Kingston: The Power Play* 9-15 NBC; **1977** *Roger and Harry* 5-2 ABC; *In the Matter of Karen Ann Quinlan* 9-26 NBC; **1978** *The Gift of the Magi* 12-21 NBC.

Michael McGuire (a.k.a. Maguire)

(born 1936)

After extensive stage work, Michael appeared often in television guest roles, from 1973 through the remainder of the seventies. He worked in several eighties telefilms and was a regular during 1988 on the soap *Loving*.

GUEST CREDITS

1973 *Kojak* "Conspiracy of Fear" 12-19; **1974** *Mannix* "A Night Full of Darkness" 1-27; *Harry O* "Gertrude" 9-12; *Columbo* "A Friend in Deed" 12-29; **1975** *Streets of San Francisco* "Labyrinth" 2-27; *The Law* "Prior Consent" 3-26; *Cannon* "The Star" 12-10; **1976** *Harry O* "Mister Five and Dime"

l-8; *Kojak* "Deadly Innocence" 2-8; *Hawaii Five-0* "Assault on the Palace" l0-7; *Most Wanted* "The Torch" l2-l8; **1977** *Police Story* "The Blue Fog" 2-l; *Kingston: Confidential* "Shadow Game" 3-23; **1978** *Police Story* "No Margin for Error" 4-30; **1979** *Rockford Files* "A Material Difference" 2-24.

TELEFILMS

1974 *Larry* 4-23 CBS; *The Gun* 11-l3 ABC; **1976** *The Keegans* 5-3 CBS; **1977** *The Hunted Lady* 11-28; **1978** *The Great Wallendas* 2-l2 NBC; *Home to Stay* 5-2 CBS: **1979** *Like Normal People* 4-l3 ABC; *Sanctuary of Fear* 4-23 NBC; **1980** *The Ordeal of Dr. Mudd* 3-25 CBS; *The Long Days of Summer* 5-23 ABC; *Blinded by the Light* l2-l6 CBS.

Bill McKinney

(born l931)

From his film debut in l967, Bill McKinney was typecast as red-necked ruffians. His film credits included *Junior Bonner, Deliverance, Thunderbolt and Lightfoot, The Outlaw Josey Wales, The Shootist, Bronco Billy, Any Which Way You Can* and *Heart Like a Wheel.*

His only TV series regular role was on the short-lived l975 series, *The Family Holvak.* His

guest appearances continued throughout the eighties in shows like *Houston Knights, Falcon Crest, Beauty and the Beast* and *Murder, She Wrote.*

GUEST CREDITS

1970 *Bold Ones: The Doctors* "This Will Really Kill You" 9-20; *McCloud* "The Concrete Corral" 9-30; **1971** *Alias Smith and Jones* "Return to Devil's Hole" 2-25; *Alias Smith and Jones* "The Man Who Murdered Himself" 3-l8; **1972** *Alias Smith and Jones* "The Biggest Game in the West" 2-3; **1973** *Ironside* "All About Andrea" 2-22; **1974** *Mannix* "Rage to Kill" 2-24; *Columbo* "Swan Song" 3-3; **1975** *Manhunter* "Day of Execution" l-l5; *Baretta* "Woman in the Harbor" l-3l; *Baretta* "The Glory Game" 9-l7; *Bronk* "Wheel of Death" 9-28; **1978** *Starsky and Hutch* "The Trap" 2-l; **1980** *Galactica 1980* "Space Croppers" 4-27; **1981** *Bret Maverick* "The Lazy Ace" l2-l; **1983** *A-Team* "Holiday in the Hills" 3-22; *Mississippi* epidose 9-27.

TELEFILMS

1971 *Alias Smith and Jones* l-l5 ABC; **1974** *The Execution of Private Slovik* 3-l3; *The Underground Man* 5-6 NBC; *The Healers* 5-22 NBC; *The Strange and Deadly Occurance* 9-24 NBC; *The Godchild* 11-26 ABC; *This Is the West That Was* l2-l7 NBC; **1975** *Strange New World* 7-l3 ABC; **1977** *Christmas Miracle in Caulfield, U.S.A.* l2-26 NBC.

David Macklin

A fine juvenile actor of the sixties, David's work was primarily on television, with a few scattered film roles from l962. He was a series on two brief sixties series, *Harris Against the World* (l964-65) and *Tammy* (l965-66).

By 1974 his acting career was over and he became an acting teacher.

GUEST CREDITS

1962 *Target: The Corruptors* "The Malignant Hearts" 3-23; **1963** *Stoney Burke* "Kincaid" 4-22; *Mr. Novak* "X Is the Unknown Factor" 10-15; *Twilight Zone* "Ring-A-Ding Girl" 12-27; **1964** *Eleventh Hour* "Does My Mother Have to Know?" 4-1; *Perry Mason* "The Case of the Missing Button" 9-24; **1965** *Mr. Novak* "Enter a Strange Animal" 1-19; *Fugitive* "Scapegoat" 2-2; *Perry Mason* "The Case of the Silent Six" 11-21; *The FBI* "How to Murder an Iron Horse" 12-12; **1966** *12 O'Clock High* "Falling Star" 1-3; *Blue Light* "Traitor's Blood" 2-3; *The FBI* "The Price of Death" 9-18; *Virginian* "Dead-Eye Dick" 11-9; **1967** *Iron Horse* "Welcome for the General" 1-2; *Fugitive* "The Savage Street" 3-14; *The FBI* "By Force and Violence" 10-22, 10-29; *Guns of Will Sonnett* "The Turkey Shoot" 11-24; **1968** *Ironside* "Trip to Hashburg" 3-21; *Felony Squad* "Jury of One" 10-4; *Bold Ones: The Lawyers* "The Sound of Anger" 12-10; **1969** *Lancer* "Welcome to Genesis" 11-18; **1970** *The FBI* "The Savage Wilderness" 10-18; **1973** *Cannon* "Deadly Heritage" 3-21.

TELEFILM

1968 *The Sound of Anger* 12-10 NBC.

Murray MacLeod

Murray first appeared on television during 1964, with a film debut following in 1968. He was a series regular on *Karen* (part of the *90 Bristol Court* trilogy) during 1964-65 before moving into guest work. Murray is also a gifted composer.

GUEST CREDITS

1967 *Man from UNCLE* "The Cap and Gown Affair" 4-14; *Run for Your Life* "Three Passengers for the Luisitania" 9-27; **1968** *Name of the Game* "Witness" 9-27; *Virginian* "Death Wait" 1-15; *Mod Squad* "Flight Five Doesn't Answer" 1-31; *Ironside* "Moonlight Means Money" 2-27; *Mod Squad* "The Death of Wild Bill Hannachek" 11-25; **1970** *Medical Center* "Undercurrent" 9-23; **1971** *Room 222* "If It's Not Here, Where Is It?" 5-24; *Longstreet* "One in the Reality Column" 9-30; *Mod Squad* "The Poisoned Mina" 11-2; **1972** *Cannon* "Blood on the Vine" 1-18; *Adam-12* "Who Won?" 3-1; *Bonanza* "Ambush at Rio Lobo" 10-24; *Cannon* "Child of Fear" 11-15; **1973** *Adam-12*

"O'Brien's Stand" 1-3; *Mod Squad* "Don't Kill My Child" 1-18; *Columbo* "A Stitch in Crime" 2-11; *Kung Fu* "A Praying Mantis Kills" 3-22; **1974** *Marcus Welby, M.D.* "A Full Life" 1-8; *Police Woman* "Shoefly" 12-20; **1976** *Rockford Files* "Where's Houston?" 2-20; **1977** *Switch* "The Hemline Heist" 2-27; **1981** *Incredible Hulk* "Bring Me the Head of the Hulk" 1-9.

TELEFILMS

1974 *Death Sentence* 10-2 ABC; **1975** *Who Is the Black Dahlia?* 3-1 NBC; *Conspiracy of Terror* 12-29 NBC; **1976** *Law of the Land* 4-29 NBC; **1982** *Moonlight* 9-14 CBS.

Pam McMyler kisses a disheveled James Drury in a 1969 episode of *The Virginian* (NBC). The episode was called "A Flash of Darkness".

Pam McMyler

(born 1946)

Pam made her television debut in 1964 and began working in films the following year. Often cast as troubled teens or anguished young ladies, Pam worked well into the eighties.

GUEST CREDITS

1964 *Man from UNCLE* "The Neptune Affair" 12-8; **1966** *Ben Casey* "Smile, Baby, Smile, It's Only Twenty Dols of Pain" 1-24; **1969** *Dragnet* "D.O.D.-DR-27" 1-23; *Adam-12* "I'm Still a Cop" 2-22; *Ironside* "A Matter of Love and Death" 4-3; *Virginian* "A Flash of Darkness" 9-24; *Ironside* "Stolen on Demand" 12-25; **1970** *Paris 7000* "Beyond Reproach" 1-22; *The FBI* "Summer Terror" 2-8; *Ironside* "No Game for Amateurs" 9-24; *Matt Lincoln* "Doc" 11-12; *Marcus Welby, M.D.* "Sounding Brass" 12-1; **1971** *Dan August* "Days of Rage" 3-25; *The D. A.* "The People vs. Drake" 9-17; *Medical Center* "The Albatross" 11-3; *Smith Family* "Ambush" 11-10; **1972** *Bold Ones: The Lawyers* "The Long Morning After" 1-9, 1-16; **1973** *Emergency* episode 9-22; *Mannix* "Desert Run" 10-21; **1974** *Marcus Welby, M.D.* "No Charity for the MacAllisters" 1-15; **1981** *Waltons* "The Whirlwind" 1-22; *Waltons* "The Tempest" 2-5.

TELEFILMS

1980 *The $5.20 an Hour Dream* 1-26 CBS; *Children of Divorce* 11-24 NBC.

Sandy McPeak

Highly visible during the eighties, Sandy McPeak alternated between authority and villainous roles. He was a regular on *Blue Thunder*

(1984), *Wildside* (1985) and *Nasty Boys* (1990)-all in authority roles. He also did a late eighties stint on the soap *Days of Our Lives* (1989).

Sandy was also a heavy contributor to telefilms during 1977-83, with 15 credits.

GUEST CREDITS

1977 *Big Hawaii* "Graduation Eve" 10-26; **1978** *Baretta* "Barney" 4-6; *Incredible Hulk* "A Child in Need" 10-20; **1979** *Charlie's Angels* "Love Boat Angels" 9-12; *Paris* "Decisions" 12-18; **1981** *Incredible Hulk* "Bring Me the Head of the Hulk" 1-8; *CHiPs* "Hawk and the Hunter" 4-5; *Hill Street Blues* "Hearts and Minds" 10-29; *Hill Street Blues* "Blood Money" 11-5; *Hill Street Blues* "The Last White Man on East Ferry Avenue" 11-19; *Quincy, M.E.* "Dead Stop" 12-31; **1982** *Bret Maverick* "The Ballad of Bret Maverick" 2-16; *Simon and Simon* "Tanks for the Memories" 3-16; *Lou Grant* episode 4-19; **1983** *Knight Rider* "Short Notice" 5-6; **1983** *Trauma Center* "No Easy Days" 10-6.

TELEFILMS

1977 *Pine Canyon Is Burning* 5-18 NBC; *Delta County, U.S.A.* 5-20 ABC; *Having Babies II* 10-28 ABC; *Tarantulas: The Deadly Cargo* 12-28 CBS; **1978** *Ruby and Oswald* 2-8 CBS; *The Two-Five* 4-14 ABC; **1979** *Disaster on the Coastliner* 10-28

ABC; *Mysterious Island of Beautiful Women* 12-1 CBS; **1980** *Belle Star* 4-2 CBS; *A Rumor of War* 9-24, 9-25 CBS; *Fighting Back* 12-7 ABC; *Blinded by the Light* 12-16 CBS; **1981** *No Place to Hide* 3-4 CBS; *Scruples* 5-22 ABC; **1983** *Kentucky Woman* 1-11 CBS.

Tyler McVey

(born 1912)

A veteran of over 1,000 radio broadcasts, Tyler made his film debut in *The Day the Earth Stood Still* (1951). Films of note included From *Here to Eternity, That Touch of Mink, Dead Heat on a Merry-Go-Round, Patton* and *Hello Dolly*.

He worked often in guest roles on TV westerns during the late fifties and early sixties, and had a recurring role on *Men into Space* (1959-60).

GUEST CREDITS

1959 *Rough Riders* "The Double Dealers" 3-19; *Restless Gun* "The Pawn" 4-6; *M Squad* "The Crush Out" 4-10; *Gunsmoke* "The Choice" 5-9; *Alfred Hitchcock Presents* "Human Interest Story" 5-28; *Wanted: Dead or Alive* "The Empty Cell" 10-17; *Wagon Train* "The Cappy Darin Story" 11-11; *Rebel* "Dark Secret" 11-22; **1960** *Law of the*

Plainsman "The Imposter" 2-4; *Gunsmoke* "Moo Moo Raid" 2-l3; *Colt .45* "Absent without Leave" 4-l9; *Man and the Challenge* "The Dropper" 4-23; *Wagon Train* "The Trial for Murder" 4-27, 5-4; *Wyatt Earp* "Shoot to Kill" l0-l8; *Klondike* "Sure Thing, Men" 11-28; *Perry Mason* "The Case of the Ill-Fated Fakir" l0-l; *Deputy* "Day of Fear" l2-l7; **1961** *Rawhide* "Rio Salado" 9-29; **1962** *Ben Casey* "Victory Wears a Cruel Smile" 2-l2; *National Velvet* "The Clown" 4-2; *Alfred Hitchcock Hour* "Hangover" l2-6; **1963** *Redigo* "Hostage Hero Riding" l2-l0; **1964** *Alfred Hitchcock Hour* "A Matter of Murder" 4-3; **1965** *Wild Wild West* "The Night of the Double-Edged Knife" 11-l2; **1969** *Wild Wild West* "The Night of the Plague" 4-4.

TELEFILM

1974 *Sidekicks* 3-2l CBS.

Peter Mamakos

(born 1918)

Following a 1938 stage debut, Peter Mamakos went on to become one of America's most prolific screen and television character actors. He had more than 90 films (from 1949) and his television credits exceeded 200. Among his films were roles in *The Ten Commandments* and *The Searchers*.

He was active in television from 1952 and specialized in all types of Mediterraneans: Greeks, Italians, North Africans, and Middle-Easterners. Many of his films were of the swash-buckling sea epic type. Television roles aslo tended to be of the adventure or detective genres.

GUEST CREDITS

1959 *Richard Diamond* episode 3-l2; *Wyatt Earp* "The Actress" 4-l4; *Wyatt Earp* "The Posse" 5-l0; *Texan* "South of the Border" 5-11; *Lawless Years* "The Lion and the Music" 5-2l; *Markham* "On the Other Side of the Wall" 8-l5; *Bourbon Street Beat* "The Golden Beetle" l2-l4; **1960** *Rawhide* "Incident of the Devil and His Due" l-22; *Deputy* "The Return of Simon Fry" 2-l3; *Islanders* "Five O'Clock Friday" l0-2; *Roaring 20's* "Vendetta on Bleeker Street" 11-5; **1961** *Untouchables* "The Nick Moses Story" 2-22; *Checkmate* "Dance of Death" 4-22; *Rawhide* "Incident of the Running Man" 5-5; *Peter Gunn* "A Bullet for the Boy" 5-29; **1962** *Perry Mason* "The Case of the Stand-In Sister" 11-l5; **1963** *Virginian* "The Final Hour" 5-l; **1964** *Fugitive* "Somebody to Remember" 3-24; *Voyage to the Bottom of the Sea* "The City Beneath the Sea" 9-2l; **1965** *Amos Burke, Secret Agent* "Balance of Terror" 9-l5; *Daniel Boone* episode 9-23; *Convoy* "Lady on the Rock" l0-l5; **1966** *Perry Mason* "The Case of the Sausalito Sunrise" 2-l3; *Girl from UNCLE* "The Horns of the Dilemna Affair" l0-l8; *Daniel Boone* "The Matchmaker" l0-27; *Bob Hope Chrysler* Theater "Storm Crossing" l2-7; **1967** *Ironside* "Backfire" 11-2; **1969** *Land of the Giants* "Target: Earth" l2-7; **1970** *Mod Squad* "A Town Called Sincere" l-27; *Daniel Boone* "Run for the Money" 2-l7; **1971** *Night Gallery* "The Hand of Borgus Weems" 9-l5; *Cannon* "Flight Plan" l2-28; **1973** *Mission: Impossible* "The Pendulum" 2-23; **1975** *Kojak* "Queen of the Gypsies" l-l9.

TELEFILM

1973 *I Love a Mystery* 2-27 NBC.

Ric Mancini

(born 1933)

From the New York stage, Ric made a film debut in 1968, coming to television in 1970. Stockily built, with broad features, he divided his roles between cops and bad guys during the seventies, his most active period on television. He also guested on sitcoms like *The Bob Newhart* Show (2).

Ric continued to work in television throughout the eighties; he became a member of the cast of the soap *General Hospital* during 1989.

GUEST CREDITS

1970 *McCloud* "Horse Stealing on Fifth Avenue" 9-23; **1973** *Police Story* "Man on a Rack" 12-11; **1975** *Police Story* "The Witness" 3-11; *Police Story* "Officer Needs Help" 9-9; *Rockford Files* "The Deep Blue Sleep" 10-10; *Rookies* "Reign of Terror" 10-14; *Police Story* "The Test of Brotherhood" 11-14; **1976** *Charlie's Angels* "Hellride" 9-22; *Starsky and Hutch* "Iron Mike" 12-18; **1977** *Most Wanted* "The White Collar Killer" 1-1; *Rockford Files* "There's One in Every Port" 1-7; *Baretta* "Not on Our Block" 2-9; *Delvecchio* "Requiem for a Loser" 3-6; *Quincy, M.E.* "Touch of Death" 11-28; **1978** *Kojak* "May the Horse Be With You" 2-25; **1979** *Lou Grant* "Denial" 1-1; *Kaz* "A

Piece of Cake" 3-7.

TELEFILMS

1974 *Thursday's Game* 4-14 ABC; **1977** *Green Eyes* 1-3 ABC; **1978** *To Kill a Cop* 4-10, 4-11 NBC; **1979** *The Ordeal of Patty Hearst* 3-4 ABC; **1983** *Mickey Spillane's Mike Hammer: Murder Me, Murder You* 4-9 CBS.

Ralph Manza

(born December 1, 1921, San Francisco, Calif.)

Raph was in pre-med at the University of California at Berkeley when the acting bug bit him. After stage work, he broke into films in 1957 and had his first television series regular role in 1959, in *The D. A.'s Man*. He was an early member of the cast of the soap *General Hospital*, during 1963.

He worked in guest roles throughout the sixties and had his most visible role in 1972-74, appearing in a featured role as Jay, the chauffeur, on *Banacek*. After that stint, he was a series regular in three sitcoms: *A.E.S. Hudson Street* (1978), *Mama Malone* (1984) and *Newhart* (1985). Ralph continues, during the nineties, to make an occasional film appearance.

GUEST CREDITS

1961 *Perry Mason* "The Case of theCowardly Lion" 4-8; *Outlaws* "The Little Colonel" 5-18; **1962** *Ben Casey* "To a Grand and Natural Finale" 3-12; *Twilight Zone* "The Dummy" 5-4; *New Breed* "The Sea Witch" 10-23; **1963** *Perry Mason* "The Case of the Bluffing Blast" 1-10; *Virginian* "If You Have Tears" 2-13; **1964** *Perry Mason* "The Case of the Wednesday Woman" 1-2; *Perry Mason* "The Case of the Scandalous Sculptor" 10-8; **1965** *Laredo* "Jinx" 12-2; **1966** *Laredo* "No Bugles, One Drum" 2-24; **1967** *Dragnet* "The Big Explosion" 1-19; **1968** *Gunsmoke* "Deadman's Law" 1-8; **1970** *Adam-12* "Log-124-Airport" 2-28; *High Chaparral* "Only the Bad Come to Sonora" 10-2; **1976** *Serpico* "Prime Evil" 11-19; **1981** *Nero Wolfe* "Might As Well Be Dead" 2-13; *Greatest American Hero* "The Two Hundred Mile an Hour Fastball" 11-4; **1983** *Little House on the Prairie* "Once Upon a Time" 1-24; *Hart to Hart* "Too Close to Hart" 5-3.

Andrea Marchovicchi is a murder suspect in *Smile, Jenny, You're Dead* (ABC), a 1974 telefilm pilot for *Harry O*. David Janssen is Harry Orwell, a private investigator looking into a friend's murder.

TELEFILMS

1968 *The Smugglers* 12-24 NBC; **1972** *Banacek: Detour to Nowhere* 3-20 NBC; **1975** *A Cry for Help* 2-12 ABC; **1977** *Terraces* 6-27 NBC; **1978** *Perfect Gentlemen* 3-14 CBS; **1979** *Samurai* 4-30 ABC.

Andrea Marcovicci
(born November 18, 1948, New York City)

Primarily a television actress, Andrea got her TV career well started with a 1967-73 stint on the soap *Love Is a Many Splendered Thing*. A lead role on the telefilm *Cry Rape* in 1973 made an impact on evening audiences. She then moved into a lengthy series of guest roles. Fans of *Taxi* will remember her as the neurotic who has a fling with the Louie (Danny DeVito) character.

During the mid and late eighties she appeared on *Trapper John, M.D.* (2) and *Murder, She Wrote*.

GUEST CREDITS

1974 *Medical Center* "Center of Peril" 9-23; *Kojak* "Cross Your Heart and Hope to Die" 12-1; **1975** *Mannix* "Bird of Prey" 3-2, 3-9; **1976** *Baretta* "Street Edition" 10-13; **1977** *Kojak* "Once More from Birdland" 10-30; **1981** *Hill Street Blues* "Film at Eleven" 2-7; *Hill Street Blues* "Choice Cut" 2-14; *Hill Street Blues* "Up in Arms" 2-21; *Hill Street Blues* "Your Kind, My Kind, Humankind" 2-28; *Magnum, P.I.* "Don't Say Goodbye" 3-26; *Incredible Hulk* "Two Godmothers" 11-13; *Magnum, P.I.* "The Sixth Position" 12-17; **1982** *Phoenix* "One of Them"

4-2; *Voyagers* "Cleo and the Babe" 10-17.

TELEFILMS

1973 *Cry Rape* 11-27 CBS; **1974** *Smile, Jenny, You're Dead* 2-3 ABC; **1979** *Some Kind of Miracle* 1-3 CBS; *Vacation in Hell* 5-21 ABC; **1983** *Packin' It In* 2-7 CBS.

Theodore "Theo" Marcuse
(born 1920, died November 27, 1967)

From 1959 to his death in 1967, Theodore "Theo" Marcuse was probably television's most used and abused heavy. He played characters of various nationalities, most having evil intent. In television from 1950, he crafted a whole repetiore of villainous personnas. Theo also directed Shakespeare: *Richard II, Antony and Cleopatra* and *Oedipus Rex*.

He died on the Hollywood Freeway on November 27, 1967, when his car hit a truck.

GUEST CREDITS

1959 *Perry Mason* "The Case of the Shattered Dream" 1-3; *Have Gun-Will Travel* "The Return of the Lady" 2-21; *Alaskans* "The Golden Fleece" 11-

29; **1960** *Lineup* "Seven Sinners" 1-20; *Islanders* "Five O'Clock Friday" 10-2; *Dow Hour of Great Mysteries* "The Great Impersonation" 11-15; *Dan Raven* "Japanese Sand Bag" 11-18; *Roaring 20's* "Layoff Charlie" 12-17; **1961** *Thriller* "Man in a Cage" 1-17; *Dante's Inferno* "Dante's Fickle Fate" 2-6; *77 Sunset Strip* "Tiger by the Tail" 3-3; *Shirley Temple Theatre* "Two for the Road" 7-16; *Untouchables* "City without a Name" 12-14; **1962** *Thriller* "Man in a Cage" 1-17; *Twilight Zone* "To Serve Man" 3-2; *Twilight Zone* "The Trade-Ins" 4-20; *77 Sunset Strip* "The Catspaw Caper" 11-16; *New Loretta Young Show* "Decision at Midnight" 12-10; **1964** *Outer Limits* "Fun and Games" 3-30; *Voyage to the Bottom of the Sea* "Eleven Days to Zero" 9-14; **1965** *Amos Burke, Secret Agent* "Balance of Terror" 9-15; *Man from UNCLE* "The Re-Collector's Affair" 10-22; *Laredo* "The Heroes of San Gill" 12-23; **1966** *I Spy* "My Mother, the Spy" 3-30; *Man from UNCLE* "The Minus X Affair" 4-8; *Wild Wild West* "The Night of the Sudden Plague" 4-22; *Wild Wild West* "The Night of the Bottomless Pit" 11-4; *Time Tunnel* "Devil's Island" 11-11; *T.H.E. Cat* "The Cat Who Lost His Voice" 12-23; **1967** *Invaders* "The Leeches" 1-31; *Man from UNCLE* "The Pieces of Eight Affair" 2-24; *Star Trek* "Cat's Paw" 10-27; **1968** *Wild Wild West* "The Night of the Headless Woman" 1-5; *Daniel Boone* "Fort New Madrid" 2-8.

Stuart Margolin
(born January 31, 1940, Davenport, Iowa)

A television writer, director and excellent character actor, Stuart Margolin is one of Hollywood's most verstaile and talented individuals. At age 20 he had his own play produced off-Broadway. He began making sitcom appearances on television in 1962, with dramatic series guest shots beginning in 1963.

A series regular role on *Occasional Wife* (1966-67) led to a long running role (1969-73) on *Love, American Style*, as one of the "blackout" segment regulars. During 1971 he joined James Garner in the short-lived western series, *Nichols*, but the experience paid dividends, for in January of 1975 he made

his first visit to *The Rockford Files* as "Angel" Martin; he became a regular during the following season.

His excellent portrayal of Rockford's shifty and conniving former prison cellmate earned him Emmy Awards in 1979 and 1980 as Best Supporting Actor in a Drama Series. He has written and directed telefilms and continued to act; in 1995 and 1996 he appeared in Rockford telefilms, resurrecting the Angel character.

GUEST CREDITS

1963 *Lieutenant* "A Very Private Affair" 10-12; *Burke's Law* "Who Killed Sweet Betsy?" 11-1; **1964** *Channing* "A Rich, Famous Folk Singer Like Me" 1-8; *Bob Hope Chrysler Theater* "A Wind of Hurricane Force" 2-7; *Fugitive* "End Game" 4-24; *Ben Casey* "Who Shall Beat the Drums?" 9-28; **1965** *Alfred Hitchcock Hour* "The Monkey's Paw: A Retelling" 4-19; *Branded* "A Taste of Poison" 5-2; **1966** *Blue Light* "The Deserters" 4-20; **1968** *It Takes a Thief* "Magnificent Thief" 1-9; *Virginian* "Jed" 1-20; *The FBI* "The Homecoming" 2-11; *It Takes a*

Thief "The Lay of the Land" 4-30; **1969** *It Takes a Thief* "The Great Chess Gambit" 4-15; *Land of the Giants* "The Mechanical Man" 9-21; **1973** *Gunsmoke* "Homecoming" 1-8; *Cannon* "Press Pass to the Slammer" 3-14; **1974** *Gunsmoke* "A Family of Killers" 1-14; **1983** *Fall Guy* "The Molly Sue" 3-2; *Magnum, P.I.* "Legacy from a Friend" 3-10; *Magnum, P.I.* "By Its Cover" 3-31.

TELEFILMS

1970 *The Intruders* 11-10 NBC; **1974** *The California Kid* 9-25 ABC; *This Is the West That Was* 12-17 NBC; **1976** *Lannigan's Rabbi* 6-16 NBC; **1983** *A Killer in the Family* 10-30 NBC.

Steven Marlo

Once a double and stand-in for Marlon Brando, Steve made his film debut in 1958, first appearing on television in 1959. He continued to do TV guest roles and telefilms well into the eighties.

GUEST CREDITS

1959 *Rifleman* "The Patsy" 9-29; *Johnny Staccato* "Poet's Touch" 11-19; **1960** *Johnny Ringo*

"Soft Cargo" 5-5; **1961** *Hong Kong* "Double Jeopardy" 2-1; **1962** *Rifleman* "The Assailants" 11-12; *Rifleman* "The Anvil Chorus" 12-17; **1964** *Ben Casey* "For Jimmy, the Best of Everything" 10-19; **1965** *Ben Casey* "Fancini, Who Is Francini?" 10-25; *Ben Casey* "Why Did the Day Go Backwards?" 12-6; **1966** *Combat* "The Bankroll" 12-13; **1967** *Mission: Impossible* "Snowball in Hell" 2-18; **1968** *Mannix* "License to Kill, Limit Three" 1-13; *Mission: Impossible* "The Condemned" 1-28; *Garrison's Gorillas* "War and Crime" 2-13; **1969** *Land of the Giants* "Return of the Inido" 3-16; *Land of the Giants* "The Mechanical Man" 9-21; *Land of the Giants* "Deadly Pawn" 10-12; **1972** *Sarge* "Napoleon Never Wanted to Be a Cop" 1-11; **1975** *Columbo* "Playback" 3-2.

TELEFILMS

1973 *Voyage of the Yes* 1-16 CBS; *The Strangler* 2-26 NBC; **1974** *The Hanged Man* 3-31 ABC; **1975** *Adventures of the Queen* 2-14 CBS; *Sky Heist* 5-26 NBC; **1976** *Mayday at 40,000 Feet* 11-12 CBS; **1979** *Hanging by a Thread* 5-8, 5-9 NBC; **1983** *The Night the Bridge Fell Down* 2-28 NBC.

Hugh Marlowe

(born January 30, 1911, Philadelphia, Pa.; died May 2, 1982)

Hugh worked at the Pasadena Playhouse until his film debut in 1936; he ultimately appeared in *12 O'Clock High, Elmer Gantry, Birdman of Alcatraz* and *Twelve Days in May*. A radio role as Ellery Queen led to a 1954 television series starring role in *The Adventures of Ellery Queen*.

He had fifties television credits on *Studio One* (2), *Schlitz Playhouse of Stars* (2), *General Electric Theater* and *U.S. Steel Hour*. There was a good deal of sixties guest work, especially on *Perry Mason* (5). In 1970 he joined the cast of *Another World*, as Jim Matthews, and continued in the role until his death of a heart attack in 1982. He was survived by his wife, actress Rosemary Tory, and three sons.

GUEST CREDITS

1959 *Perry Mason* "The Case of the Fraudulent Photo" 2-7; *Alfred Hitchcock Presents* "Touche" 6-14; **1960** *Rawhide* "Incident of the Champagne Bottles" 3-18; *Perry Mason* "The Case of the Slandered Submarine" 5-14; *Michael Shayne* "The Poison Pen Club" 11-25; **1961** *Alfred Hitchcock Presents* "Services Rendered" 12-12; *Perry Mason* "The Case of the Borrowed Baby" 4-14; *Tales of Wells Fargo* "The Wayfarer" 5-19; *Law and Mr. Jones* "Poor Eddie's Dead" 7-12; *Alfred Hitchcock Hour* "Day of Reckoning" 11-12; **1963** *Dick Powell Show* "The Third Side of the Coin" 3-26; *Perry Mason* "The Case of the Nervous Nephew" 9-26; **1964** *Arrest and Trial* "An Echo of Conscience" 1-26; *Virginian* "The Intruders" 3-4; *Perry Mason* "The Case of the Sleepy Slayer" 10-15; **1965** *Perry Mason* "The Case of the Hasty Honeymooner" 10-24; **1966** *Virginian* "Trail to Ashley Mountain" 11-2; *Voyage to the Bottom of the Sea* "Thing from Inner Space" 11-6; **1968** *Man from UNCLE* "The Seven Wonders of the World Affair" 1-8, 1-15; *Judd, for the Defense* "Murder on a Square Hole" 3-1.

Kenneth Mars

(born 1936, Chicago, Illinois)

Primarily a television actor/comedian, bulky Kenneth Mars initially appeared on television in a 1963 episode of *Car 54, Where Are You?* He became

a regular on three seventies variety shows and had a regular role on a 1967-68 sitcom, *He and She*.

During the seventies he played villains on several TV crime series guest shots as a counterpoint to comedy guest appearances on *Love, American Style* (4), *That Girl*, *Barney Miller* and *Alice*.

Kenneth was very active in eighties guest roles with work on *Simon and Simon* (2), *Call to Glory*, *Murder, She Wrote*, *Remington Steele*, *Twilight Zone*, *Hardcastle and McCormick* (2), *The Last Precinct* and *Head of the Class*.

GUEST CREDITS

1965 *Trials of O'Brien* "Never Bet on Anything That Talks" 10-9; **1967** *Gunsmoke* "Fandango" 2-18; **1969** *Room 222* "Clothes Make the Boy" 12-3; **1971** *McMillan and Wife* "Murder by the Barrel" 9-29; **1972** *McMillan and Wife* "Cop of the Year" 11-19; **1973** *Ironside* "Ollinger's Last Case" 1-4; *Hawkins* "Murder in Hollywood" 10-2; **1974** *Harry O* "Coinage of the Realm" 10-10; **1975** *Barnaby Jones* "Double Vengeance" 10-17; *Police Woman* "Cold Wind" 10-17; *Harry O* "Tender Killing Care" 10-30; **1977** *Black Sheep Squadron* "Five the Hard Way" 2-1; *Police Woman* "Bondage" 3-1; *Columbo* "The Bye-Bye High I.Q. Murder Case" 5-2; **1978** *Project UFO* "Sighting 4005: The Medicine Bow Incident" 3-26; **1979** *Supertrain* "Queen's the Impossible

Knight" 2-21; **1980** *Barnaby Jones* "Killin' Cousin" 4-30; *Hart to Hart* "Murder Is Man's Best Friend" 12-9; **1981** *Magnum, P.I.* "The Woman on the Beach" 10-22; **1982** *Simon and Simon* "The Dead Letter File" 1-5; *Trapper John, M.D.* "The Good Life" 11-28; **1983** *Mississippi* episode 11-1.

TELEFILMS

1972 *Second Chance* 2-8 ABC; **1973** *Guess Who's Sleeping in My Bed?* 10-31 ABC; **1975** *Someone I Touched* 2-26 ABC; *The New Original Wonder Woman* 11-7 ABC; **1979** *Before and After* 10-5 ABC; **1983** *The Rules of Marriage* 5-10, 5-11 CBS.

Maurice Marsac
(born March 23, 1920, La Croix, France)

In American films since 1944, Maurice appeared in 50 movies, ranging from *The Razor's Edge* to *Herbie Rides Again*. He worked in some excellent fifties television anthologies like *Studio One* and *Alfred Hitchcock Presents*.

Maurice did TV guest roles intermittently from the sixties into the mid eighties, playing French citizens and partisans in a number of war series episodes.

GUEST CREDITS

1959 *Markham* "The Searing Flame" 4-7; **1960** *One Step Beyond* "The Peter Hurkos Story" 4-19, 4-26; *One Step Beyond* "The Lonely Room" 5-31; **1965** *Daniel Boone* "Cain's Birthday" 4-1, 4-8; *Combat* "Odyssey" 4-20; *Combat* "Finest Hour" 12-21; **1966** *Run for Your Life* "Who's Minding the Fleshpot?" 3-7; **1967** *Combat* "The Masquers" 2-14; *Garrison's Gorillas* "The Great Theft" 10-10; **1968** *Garrison's Gorillas* "Ride of Terror" 1-30; *Garrison's Gorillas* "The War Diamonds" 3-5; *Daniel Boone* "The Fleeing Nuns" 10-24; **1970** *McCloud* "Our Man in Paris" 10-21; **1971** *Mannix* "The Crime That Wasn't" 1-30; *Mission: Impossible* "Double Dead" 2-12; *O'Hara, U.S. Treasury* "Operation: Dorais" 2-4; **1973** *Search* "A Honeymoon to Kill" 1-10; **1974** *Columbo* "Publish or Perish" 1-13; *Chase* "Joe Don Ducks" 1-16; *McCloud* "The Concrete Jungle Caper" 11-24; *Barnaby Jones* "Time to Kill" 11-26; *Kolchak: The Night Stalker* "The Spanish Moss Murders" 12-6; **1975** *Get Christie Love!* "From Paris with Love" 3-5; **1977** *Barnaby Jones* "The Damocles Gun" 10-20; *Rockford Files* "Irving the Explainer" 11-18; **1982** *Hart to Hart* "The Hart of a Murder" 2-16.

TELEFILMS

1977 *Cover Girls* 5-18 NBC; **1981** *Jacqueline Bouvier Kennedy* 10-14 ABC; **1982** *Bare Essence* 10-4, 10-5 CBS.

Don Marshall
(born May 2, 1936, San Diego, California)

Don made a film debut in 1962 in *The Interns*, moving to television guest roles in 1965. In 1968 he became a regular on *Land of the Giants*, his best known television role.

GUEST CREDITS

1965 *Rogues* "Diamond Studded Pie" 1-31; *Bob Hope Chrysler Theater* "The War and Eric Kurtz" 3-

5; *Alfred Hitchcock Hour* "Night Fever" 5-3; *Bob Hope Chrysler Theater* "The Admiral" 12-29; **1966** *Daktari* episodes 1-18, 1-25; *Mission: Impossible* "The Ransom" 11-5; *12 O'Clock High* "Graveyard" 12-30; **1967** *Star Trek* "The Galileo Seven" 1-5; *Dragnet* "The Big Shooting" 3-30; *Tarzan* "The Fanatics" 10-27; *Ironside* "Backfire" 11-2; **1968** *Dragnet* "Community Relations-DR-10" 10-3; **1975** *Police Story* "The Execution" 2-18; **1976** *Bionic Woman* "The Vega Influence" 12-1; **1977** *Hardy Boys* "The Strange Fate of Flight 608" 11-6; **1978** *Incredible Hulk* "The Hulk Breaks Las Vegas" 4-21; *Incredible Hulk* "Mystery Man" 3-2, 3-9.

TELEFILMS

1971 *The Reluctant Heroes* 11-23 ABC; **1977** *Benny and Barney: Las Vegas Undercover* 1-9 NBC; **1978** *Rescue from Gilligan's Island* 10-14, 10-21 NBC; **1979** *The Suicide's Wife* 11-7 CBS.

E. G. Marshall
(born June 18, 1910, Owatonna, Minnesota)

One of America's truly distinguished actors, E. G. was educated at Carlton College and the University of Minnesota. He made his film debut in 1945, with eventual roles in *Call Northside 777, The Caine Mutiny, 12 Angry Men, Town Without Pity, The Silver Chalice, Is Paris Burning?, The Bridge at Remagen* and *Tora! Tora! Tora!*

He came to television early, in 1949, and was a stalwart on live television. He appeared on *Studio One* (5), *Actor's Studio* (2), *Kraft Television Theatre* (12), *Philco Television Playhouse* (11), *Goodyear Playhouse* (5), *Armstrong Circle Theater* (3), *Playhouse 90* (2), *Hallmark Hall of Fame* (3) and a special "The Sacco-Vanzetti Story" (1960).

From 1961 to 1965 he starred on *The Defenders* as attorney Lawrence Preston, winning Emmy Awards for the role in 1962 and 1963. He later took a co-starring role on *The Bold Ones: The Doctors* from 1969 to 1973.

By the mid eighties he had semi-retired, working only in occasional theatrical movies and telefilms. He makes a few appearances in the current time frame when he finds something particularly appealing. E. G. has acted as host and narrator for countless television specials.

E. G. Marshall, standing, played attorney Lawrence Preston in *The Defenders* (CBS), a role that earned him two Emmys. In this 1965 episode, "Death on Wheels", he defends Leslie Nielsen (seated). The late Nancy Wickwire is in the background.

1969 *Hallmark Hall of Fame* "The Littlest Angel" 12-6; **1970** *Paris 7000* "Beyond Reproach" 1-22; **1970** *Men from Shiloh* "Lady at the Bar" 11-4; **1971** *Men from Shiloh* "Nan Allen" 1-6; *Night Gallery* "A Death in the Family" 9-22; **1972** *Ironside* "Five Days in the Death of Sergeant Brown" 9-14; **1982** *Phoenix* "In Search of Mira" 3-26; *Nurse* "Father" 4-23; *Falcon Crest* "The Challenge" 10-1; **1983** *Falcon Crest* "Broken Promises" 1-21.

GUEST CREDITS

1959 *Playhouse 90* "A Quiet Game of Cards" 1-29; *Desilu Playhouse* "Man in Orbit" 5-11; *Playhouse 90* "Made in Japan" 3-5; **1960** *Moment of Fear* "The Third Party" 8-12; *Route 66* "Three Sides" 11-18; *Islanders* "Forbidden Cargo" 11-27; **1961** *Rawhide* "Incident of the Broken Word" 1-20; *DuPont Show of the Month* "The Night of the Storm" 3-21; **1964** *Suspense* "I, Dan Krolick" 5-6;

TELEFILMS

1966 *The Poppy Is Also a Flower* 4-22 ABC; **1970** *A Clear and Present Danger* 3-21 NBC; **1971** *Vanished* 3-8, 3-9 NBC; *The City* 5-17 ABC; *Ellery Queen: Don't Look Behind You* 11-19 NBC; **1972** *Pursuit* 12-12 ABC; **1973** *Money to Burn* 10-27 ABC; **1975** *The Abduction of Saint Anne* 1-21 ABC; **1979** *Vampire* 10-7 ABC; *Disaster on the Coastliner* 4-26 ABC; **1982** *Eleanor, First Lady of the World* 5-12

Joan Marshall

(born 1934, Evanston, Illinois)

After a 1958 television debut, Joan Marshall gained recognition as a regular in a syndicated 1959 adventure series, *Bold Venture*. Thereafter, she guested on many of the prominent sixties TV series before leaving acting in 1967.

GUEST CREDITS

1960 *M Squad* "Needle in a Haystack" 2-23; *Men into Space* episode 4-6; *Lawman* "The Lady Belle" 5-1; *Hawaiian Eye* "White Pigeon Ticket" 10-26; **1961** *Michael Shayne* "Murder 'Round My Wrist" 1-20; *Broncho* "The Invaders" 1-23; *Tales of Wells Fargo* "The Barefoot Bandit" 1-30; *Maverick* "Substitute Gun" 4-2; *Dante's Inferno* "The Sesame Key" 4-3; *Broncho* "Stage to the Sky" 4-24; *Roaring 20's* "Right Off the Boat" 5-13, 5-20; *Surfside 6* "Who Is Sylvia?" 2-12; **1962** *Hawaiian Eye* "The Missile Rogue" 1-3; *Twilight Zone* "Dead Man's Shoes" 1-19; *Gunsmoke* "Wagon Girls" 4-7; *77 Sunset Strip* "Pattern for a Bomb" 5-21; **1966** *Dr. Kildare* "The Art of Taking a Powder" 3-14; *Dr. Kildare* "Read the Book, Then See the Picture" 3-15; **1967** *Star Trek* "Court Martial" 2-2; *I Spy* "Casanova from Canarsie" 3-29.

Joan Marshall (right) has the drop on Warren Stevens in this 1962 episode of *The Twilight Zone* called "Dead Man's Shoes".

During the early eighties Sarah appeared in several telefilms, a miniseries (*Scruples*) and some guest shots.

GUEST CREDITS

1960 *Ford Startime* "Dear Arthur" 3-22; *Dow Hour of Great Mysteries* "The Cat and the Canary" 9-27; *Hong Kong* "Colonel Cat" 11-16; **1961** *Thriller* "The Poisoner" 1-10; *U.S. Steel Hour* "Double-Edged Sword" 7-26; *Thriller* "God Grant That She Lye Stille" 10-23; *Target: The Corruptors* "Quicksand" 12-29; *Perry Mason* "The Case of the Roving River" 12-30; **1962** *Twilight Zone* "Little Girl Lost" 3-16; *Alfred Hitchcock Presents* "The Twelve Hour Caper" 5-29; **1963** *Nurses* "A Difference of Years" 1-

Sarah Marshall

(born 1933, London, England)

The daughter of noted British actor Herbert Marshall, Sarah made a television debut in 1953. She appeared in a number of sixties guest roles, but was largely absent the medium during the seventies. She was a regular on a short-lived 1979 sitcom, *Miss Winslow and Son*.

3; **1964** *DuPont Show of the Month* "The Gambling Heart" 2-23; *Rogues* "Fringe Benefits" 11-22; **1965** *12 O'Clock High* "End of the Line" 3-12; *Fugitive* "Middle of a Heat Wave" 9-21; *Daniel Boone* "Cry of Gold" 11-4; **1966** *I Spy* "Little Boy Lost" 12-14; **1967** *Wild Wild West* "Night of the Hangman" 10-20; *Star Trek* "The Deadly Years" 12-8; **1968** *The FBI* "The Phone Call" 2-18; **1972** *Medical Center* episode 9-9; **1983** *Hart to Hart* "As the Harts Turn" 3-1.

TELEFILMS

1981 *The Bunker* 1-27 CBS; *The People vs. Jean Harris* 5-7, 5-8 NBC; **1982** *The Letter* 5-3 ABC.

Arlene Martel

(born April 14)

With almond eyes and high cheek bones, Arlene Martel had a rather exotic look, and played some unusual roles. She was rather shapely and could be sexy when her roles required. She came to television in 1964 and left the medium in 1975 after one of her best roles, on *Gunsmoke*.

GUEST CREDITS

1964 *Outer Limits* "Demon with a Glass Hand"

10-17; *Man from UNCLE* "The King of Knaves Affair" 12-22; **1966** *Perry Mason* "The Case of the Deadly Ringer" 4-17; *Fugitive* "The Blessings of Liberty" 12-20; *Iron Horse* "Hellcat" 12-26; **1967** *Star Trek* "Amok Time" 9-15; *Wild Wild West* "The Night of the Circus of Death" 11-3; **1969** *It Takes a Thief* "Guess Who's Coming to Rio?" 1-7; **1970** *Mission: Impossible* "Terror' 2-15; *Mannix* "Murder Revisited" 3-7; **1971** *McCloud* "The Disposal Man" 12-29; **1972** *McCloud* "A Little Plot, a Tranquil Valley" 1-12; *Columbo* "The Greenhouse Jungle" 10-15; **1973** *Mannix* "The Danford File" 3-11; *Delphi Bureau* "The Terror Broker Project" 3-17; *Banacek* "The Three Million Dollar Piracy" 11-21; *Columbo* "Double Exposure" 12-16; **1974** *Six Million Dollar Man* "The Last of the Fourth of July" 3-29; *Rookies* "Vendetta" 11-18; *Petrocelli* "A Very Lonely Lady" 11-27; *Columbo* "A Friend in Deed" 12-29; **1975** *Gunsmoke* "The Squaw" 1-6.

TELEFILMS

1972 *The Adventures of Nick Carter* 2-20 ABC; **1974** *Indict and Convict* 1-6 ABC; **1975** *Conspiracy of Terror* 12-29 NBC.

Andra Martin

(born July 15, 1935, Rockford, Illinois)

Andra Martin's television career was compressed into a four year span (1958-61), but her petite lovliness enhanced the adventure and western series that she appeared in. She had a co-starring role in the Clint Walker western, *Yellowstone Kelly*, and appeared with James Garner in the war film, *Up Periscope*.

Andra and actor Ty Hardin were married for a time.

GUEST CREDITS

1959 *Maverick* "Gun Shy" 1-11; *77 Sunset Strip* "Lovely Alibi" 2-20; *Bronco* "Borrowed Glory" 2-24; *Colt .45* "Sanctuary" 5-10; *Lawman* "The Huntress" 5-10; **1960** *77 Sunset Strip* "Return to San Dede" 3-18; *Alaskans* "The Last Bullet" 3-27; *Colt .45* "Absent Without Leave" 4-19; *Hawaiian Eye* "Little Blalah" 5-18; *Alaskans* "White Vengeance" 6-5; *Bourbon Street Beat* "Teresa" 7-4; *Maverick* "Hadley's Hunters" 9-25; *Hawaiian Eye* " Sea Fire" 10-5; *Roaring 20's* "Vendetta on Beecker Street" 11-5; *Maverick* "Thunder from the North" 11-13; *Surfside 6* "Girl in the Galleon" 12-19; **1961** *Perry*

Mason "The Case of the Waylaid Wolf" 2-4; *Wagon Train* "The Don Alvarado Story" 6-21; **1962** *Roaring 20's* "Footlights" 1-13.

Pepper Martin

(born 1936, Canada)

A powerful physique and a stern countenance created frequent castings as a heavy for Pepper Martin. Following a 1968 film debut he appeared in tough-guy roles in films like *The Wrecking Crew, Walking Tall* and *The Longest Yard*.

Pepper was an oft-seen heavy in seventies crime series, with multiple appearances on *Police Woman* (6), *City of Angels* (5), *Rockford Files* (4) and *Police Story* (3).

GUEST CREDITS

1968 *Mod Squad* "My, What a Pretty Bus" 10-8; **1971** *Mission: Impossible* "The Tram" 10-2; **1973** *Police Story* "The Ten Year Honeymoon" 10-25; **1974** *Police Story* "Chief" 3-19; *Police Story* "Robbery: Forty Eight Hours" 9-24; *Police Woman* "The Stalking of Joey Marr" 11-22; **1975** *Police Woman* "The Loner" 3-14; *Rookies* "Death Lady" 10-21; *Matt Helm* "Deadly Breed" 11-8; **1976** *Police Woman* "Angela" 1-27; *City of Angels* "The November Plan"

2-3, 2-10, 2-17; *Rockford Files* "Foul on the First Play" 3-12; *City of Angels* "The Castle of Dreams" 4-20; *City of Angels* "Match Point" 5-18; *Police Woman* "Brain Wash" 11-16; **1977** *Police Woman* "Shark" 2-15; *Rockford Files* "Just Another Polish Wedding" 2-18; **1978** *Rockford Files* "The Competitive Edge" 2-10; *Police Woman* "Sweet Kathleen" 3-15; *Incredible Hulk* "Killer Instinct" 11-10; *Hawaii Five-0* "The Miracle Man" 11-23; **1979** *Rockford Files* "Never Send a Boy King to Do a Man's Job" 3-3; **1983** *Hardcastle and McCormick* "Man in a Glass House" 9-25.

TELEFILMS

1970 *The Love War* 3-10 ABC; *The Over-the-Hill Gang Rides Again* 11-17 ABC; **1971** *The Feminist and the Fuzz* 1-26 ABC; **1975** *The Secret Night Caller* 2-18 NBC; *Murder on Flight 502* 11-21 ABC.

Todd Martin

(born 1927, Brooklyn, New York)

Born of German and Norwegian parents, Todd began acting in school plays, in grammar school, junior high and high school. After spending 18 months in the U. S. Navy, he attended Adelphi University in Garden City, New York, graduating with a B. A. in Speech and Dramatic Arts. Following college theatrical productions, and graduation, he moved to summer stock and appeared off-Broadway.

Todd then spent 6 years with Americana Corporation, becoming their Northeastern Sales Director of School and Military Divisions. He began film work in 1960, with eventual U. S. credits on *The Longest Day, The Battle of the Bulge*, and *The Hindenburg*. A linguist fluent in French and Spanish, with knowledge of German and Italian, he appeared in 12 French films and 8 Spanish films during the 1960-65 period.

From 1966, he was very active in television, especially on *Mission: Impossible* (4), *Police Story* (5) and *Streets of San Francisco* (3). He had a recurring role on *Bold Ones: The Lawyers*, appearing as the Deputy D. A.

GUEST CREDITS

1966 *Blue Light* "How to Kill a Toy Soldier" 4-13; *Mission: Impossible* "A Spool There Was" 3-17; **1967** *Cowboy in Africa* "Little Boy Lost" 11-27; **1969** *Bonanza* "The Deserter" 3-16; *Bold Ones: The Lawyers* "A Game of Chance" 9-21; **1970** *High Chaparral* "New Hostess in Town" 3-20; **1971** *Mission: Impossible* "Takeover" 1-2; *Bold Ones: The Lawyers* "The Price of Justice" 2-21; *Mission: Impossible* "The Merchant" 3-17; *Bold Ones: The Lawyers* "The Invasion of Kevin Ireland" 9-26; *The FBI* "The Last Job" 9-26; *Bold Ones: The Lawyers* "By Reason of Insanity" 11-28; **1972** *Mannix* "The Sound of Murder" 1-12; *Mission: Impossible* "Bag Woman" 1-29; *Alias Smith and Jones* "Bushwhack" 10-21; **1973** *Adam-12* "The Beast" 1-31; *Streets of San Francisco* "Going Home" 10-11; **1974** *Police Story* "Cop in the Middle" 1-29; *Toma* "The Accused" 5-10; *Police Story* "A Dangerous Age" 9-10; *Rockford Files* "The Countess" 9-27; *Police Story* "Wolf" 11-19; *Streets of San Francisco* "The Twenty Five Calibre Plague" 12-12; **1975** *Streets of San Francisco* "No Place to Hide" 9-25; *Starsky and Hutch* "Death Notice" 10-15; *Switch* "Death by Resurrection" 12-2; **1976** *Police Story* "Spanish Class" 1-2; *Baretta* "The Dippers" 2-25; *Six Million Dollar Man* "H+2+0=Death" 10-24; **1977** *Police Story* "Spitfire" 1-11; *Columbo* "The Bye-Bye Sky High I.Q. Murder

Case" 5-22; **1979** *Rockford Files* "Never Send a Boy King to Do a Man's Job" 3-3; **1983** *Automan* "The Great Pretender" 12-29.

TELEFILMS

1971 *Thief* 10-29 NBC; **1972** *Haunts of the Very Rich* 9-20 ABC; **1973** *Drive Hard, Drive Fast* 9-11 NBC; **1975** *Barbary Coast* 5-4 ABC; *The Return of Joe Forrester* 5-6 NBC; **1977** *Cover Girls* 5-18 NBC; **1983** *Cave-In!* 6-19 NBC.

Tim Matheson

(born December 31, 1947, Glendale, Calif.)

Tim began his television career while a teenager, as a regular on *Window on Mainstreet* (1961-62). He became a Hanna-Barbera voice artist, providing the cartoon voices of *Johnny Quest* (1964-65), Jace on *Space Ghost* (1966-68) and Samson on *Samson and Goliath* (1967-68).

During 1969-70 he became a regular on *The Virginian*, and played a similar role on *Bonanza* during it's final season in 1972-73. Following some guest work, he co-starred in a short-lived series, *The Quest*, in 1976.

The eighties brought co-starring roles in two

series: *Tucker's Witch* (1982-83) and *Just in Time* (1988). Tim's youthful voice is heard regularly on reruns of the sixties Hanna-Barbera cartoons that have remained popular for over 25 years.

GUEST CREDITS

1969 *Adam-12* "Grand Theft Horse" 1-18; **1970** *Bracken's World* "The Country Boy" 12-18; **1971** *Matt Lincoln* "Karen" 1-7; *Room 222* "The Long Honeymoon" 1-27; *The D. A.* "The People vs. Slovik" 10-22; *Bold Ones: The Lawyers* "By Reason of Insanity" 11-28; *Night Gallery* "Logoda's Heads" 12-29; **1973** *Owen Marshall, Counselor at Law* "Why Is a Crooked Letter" 2-7; *Medical Center* "Impasse" 10-1; *Kung Fu* "The Soldier" 11-29; **1974** *Owen Marshall, Counselor at Law* "A Killer with a Badge" 2-9; *Magician* "The Illusion of the Fatal Arrow" 3-4; *Police Story* "Fingerprint" 3-12; **1976** *Jigsaw John* "Thicker Than Blood" 2-23; **1977** *Hawaii Five-0* "Deadly Doubles" 11-17; **1978** *Black Sheep Squadron* "Wolves in the Sheep Pen" 1-4.

TELEFILMS

1971 *Owen Marshall, Counselor* at Law 9-12 ABC; *Lock, Stock and Barrel* 9-24 NBC; **1973** *Hitched* 3-31 NBC; **1974** *Remember When* 3-23 NBC; **1975** *The Last Day* 2-15 NBC; *The Runaway Barge* 3-24 NBC; **1976** *The Quest* 5-13 NBC; **1977** *Mary White* 11-18 ABC; **1983** *Listen to Your Heart* 1-4 CBS.

Carmen Mathews

(born 1918)

Carmen began a stage career in 1943, debuting in films during 1960 in *Butterfield 8*. Primarily a television actress, Carmen's talents were in strong demand in the fifties decade, from 1951. She appeared on *Kraft Televsion Theatre* (6), *Goodyear Playhouse* (2), *Alfred Hitchcock Presents* (7), *Armstrong Circle Theater* (3), *U.S. Steel Hour* (2), *Omnibus*, *Playhouse 90* and *Hallmark Hall of Fame*.

She worked less as the sixties progressed, and

was seen infrequently during the seventies. Her eighties work included a *Kate and Allie* guest shot and a 1985 episode of the syndicated *Tales of the Darkside*.

GUEST CREDITS

1959 *Alfred Hitchcock Presents* "The Impossible Dream" 4-19; *General Electric Theater* "The Indian Giver" 5-19; *Ford Startime* "My Three Angels" 12-8; **1960** *Naked City* "Killer with a Kiss" 11-16; **1961** *General Electric Theater* "The Drop-Out" 1-29; *Twilight Zone* "Static" 3-10; **1962** *Alfred Hitchcock Presents* "The Kerry Blue" 4-17; *Ben Casey* "And Eve Wore a Veil of Tears" 4-23; *New Breed* "Wherefore Art Thou, Romeo?" 5-15; **1964** *Fugitive* "World's End" 9-22; **1965** *Dr. Kildare* "My Name Is Lisa and I Am Lost" 1-21; **1968** *The FBI* "The Hero" 12-22; **1971** *Alias Smith and Jones* "Six Strangers at Apache Springs" 10-28; **1972** *Cannon* "Cain's Mark" 3-7; **1975** *Ellery Queen* "The Adventure of the Mad Tea Party" 10-30.

TELEFILMS

1971 *Sam Hill: Who Killed the Mysterious Mr. Foster?* 2-1 NBC; *Death Takes a Holiday* 10-23 ABC; *They Call It Murder* 12-17 NBC; **1972** *Streets of San Francisco* 9-16 ABC; **1976** *Window* 1-22 NBC; **1977** *Charlie Cobb: Nice Night for a Hanging* 6-9 NBC.

Charles Maxwell

(born 1925)

Charles Maxwell first became visible to television audiences on a brief 1950 sitcom, *The Hank McCune Show*, one of the first shows to use a laugh track. During 1953-56 he had a recurring role as Special Agent Joe Carey on the spy drama, *I Led Three Lives*.

During the later fifties Charles began appearing on numerous TV western series, usually riding with the outlaws. With the exception of several episodes of the syndicated *Sea Hunt*, virtually all of Charles' early sixties guest appearances were on western series, with *Bonanza* using him on 7 episodes.

Toward the end of his television career he branched out to series like *Mission: Impossible* (2) and *Star Trek*.

GUEST CREDITS

1959 *Rough Riders* "The Double Dealers" 3-19; *Texan* "Blood Money" 4-20; *Bat Masterson* "Double Showdown" 5-6; *Gunsmoke* "The Choice" 5-9; *Restless Gun* "The Cavis Boy" 6-1; *Texan* "The Sheriff of Boot Hill" 6-8; *Maverick* "A Fellow's Brother" 11-22; **1960** *Maverick* "The Resurrection of Joe November" 2-28; *Zane Grey Theatre* "Seed of Evil" 4-7; *77 Sunset Strip* "Spark of Freedom" 5-13; *Texan* "The Invisible Noose" 5-16; *Rawhide* "Inci-

dent of the Silent Web" 6-3; *Men into Space* "Mystery Satellite" 9-7; *Bonanza* "The Hopefuls" 10-8; **1961** *Rebel* "Burying Sammy Hart" 3-5; *Bat Masterson* "Dead Man's Claim" 5-4; **1962** *Rawhide* "The Long Count" 1-5; *Bonanza* "The Guilty" 2-25; **1963** *Laramie* "Naked Steel" 1-1; *Rifleman* "The Sixteenth Cousin" 1-26; **1964** *Bonanza* "A Dime's Worth of Glory" 11-1; **1965** *Gunsmoke* "Honey Pot" 5-15; **1966** *Mission: Impossible* "Operation Rogosh" 10-1; *Tarzan* "The Prisoner" 10-7; *Bonanza* "Credit for a Kill" 10-23; **1967** *Rat Patrol* "The One Who Got Away Raid" 1-7; *Big Valley* "Joaquin" 9-11; *Iron Horse* "Five Days to Washiba" 10-7; *Bonanza* "Check Rein" 12-3; **1968** *High Chaparral* "Threshold of Courage" 3-31; *Bonanza* "Child" 9-22; *Star Trek* "Spectre of the Gun" 10-25; *High Chaparral* "The Buffalo Soldiers" 11-22; *Mission: Impossible* "The Play" 12-8; **1969** *Gunsmoke* "Time of the Jackals" 1-13; *Bonanza* "Company of Forgotten Men" 2-2; **1971** *High Chapparal* "Sangre" 2-26; *Bonanza* "Blind Hunch" 11-21.

Patricia Medina

(born July 19, 1921, Liverpool, England)

Stunningly beautiful Patricia Medina made her film debut in 1937, and did her share of costume dramas: *The Three Musketeers, Siren of Baghdad, Pirates of Tripoli* and *The Foxes of Harrow*. In 1960 she married the late actor Joseph Cotton (1906-94) and they had one of Hollywood's longest and happiest marriages, often performing together in dinner theatre productions.

Patricia came to television in 1953, working occasionally during the fifties in *Ford Theater* (2), *Climax* and *Lux Video Theater*. By 1959 she had begun to appear more frequently in guest roles, but slowed the pace in the mid sixties. Thereafter, she was seen infrequently on television or in films.

GUEST CREDITS

1959 *Zorro* "The Gay Caballero" 1-22; *Zorro* "Zorro vs. Cupid" 2-5; *General Electric Theater* "The Last Lesson" 2-8; *Zorro* "The Legend of Zorro" 2-12; *Have Gun-Will Travel* "Return of the

Lady" 2-21; *Adventures in Paradise* "The Black Pearl" 10-12; *Rawhide* "Incident at Jacob's Well" 10-16; *General Electric Theater* "Absalom, My Son" 12-6; *Black Saddle* "Change of Venue" 12-11; **1960** *Bonanza* "The Spanish Grant" 2-6; *Rebel* "Fair Game" 3-27; *Riverboat* "Night of the Faceless Man" 3-28; *Ford Star Time* "The Young Juggler" 3-29; *Hotel de Paree* "Sundance and the Black Widow" 4-1; *Rebel* "The Earl of Durango" 6-12; *Dante's Inferno* "The Feline Traveler" 10-17; **1961** *Rawhide* "Incident of the Boomerang" 3-24; *Thriller* "The Devil's Ticket" 4-18; *Whispering Smith* "The Hemp Reeger Case" 7-17; *Thriller* "The Premature Burial" 10-2; *Cain's Hundred* "Blue Water, White Beach" 10-3; **1963** *Have Gun-Will Travel* "Unforgiving Minute" 1-26; *Kraft Mystery Theatre* "Man Without a Witness" 9-25; **1964** *Burke's Law* "Who Killed Don Pablo?" 5-1; *Rogues* "Two of a Kind" 11-8; *Alfred Hitchcock Hour* "See the Monkey Dance" 11-9; **1965** *Man from UNCLE* "The Foxes and Hounds Affair" 10-8; **1966** *Branded* "Yellow for Courage" 2-20; **1970** *Name of the Game* "Man of the People" 3-6; *Men from Shiloh* "Nightmare at New Life" 11-18; **1971** *Mannix* "Cold Trail" 9-22.

Jan Merlin

(born 1924, New York City)

Jan decided to make acting his profession while serving in The U. S. Navy during World War II. He wrote a play that was performed aboard his ship, and later in Tokyo. After discharge from service, Jan returned to New York and enrolled at the Neighborhood Playhouse School of Theatre.

Following graduation, he played stock engagements on the Atlantic seaboard, eventually making his Broadway debut in *Mr. Roberts*. He entered television early on, in the 1950-52 children's series, *Tom Corbett, Space Cadet*, and made his film debut in 1955 in *Six Bridges to Cross*.

Jan had a co-starring role in the 1958-59 western series, *The Roughriders*. Thereafter, he worked frequently in guest roles in all types of series. He polished his writing skills and earned an Emmy in 1975 for his fine work on the soap *Another World*.

Concentrating on writing, Jan allowed his acting career to languish, returning in two mid-eighties telefilms.

GUEST CREDITS

1959 *Lawless Years* "The Nick Joseph Story" 4-16; **1960** *Islanders* "Hostage Island" 11-6; *Bat Masterson* "Last Stop to Austin" 12-1; **1961** *Tall Man* "First Blood" 1-7; *Laramie* "Stolen Tribute" 1-31; *Whispering Smith* "The Blind Gun" 5-8; *Perry Mason* "The Case of the Jealous Journalist" 6-24;

1962 *Outlaws* "The Verdict" 1-18; *Bonanza* "The Ride" 1-21; *Tales of Wells Fargo* "End of a Minor God" 4-7; *Laramie* "Trial by Fire" 4-10; *Laramie* "Among the Missing" 9-25; **1963** *Laramie* "The Fugitive" 2-12; **1964** *Lieutenant* "Blue Water, Green Flag" 2-15; *Virginian* "Ryker" 9-16; *Gunsmoke* "Blue Heaven" 9-26; *Voyage to the Bottom of the Sea* "No Way Out" 11-30; *Man from UNCLE* "The King of Knaves Affair" 12-22; **1965** *Kraft Suspense Theatre* "In Darkness Waiting" 1-21; *Voyage to the Bottom of the Sea* "The X Factor" 12-5; **1966** *Long Hot Summer* "The Intruders" 2-2; *Combat* "One Day at a Time" 3-22; *12 O'Clock High* "Massacre" 9-16; *12 O'Clock High* "Practice to Deceive" 10-14; *Tarzan* "The Prodigal Puma" 10-21; *Combat* "Headcount" 11-1; *Jerico* "Two for the Road" 11-10, 11-17; *Fugitive* "The Blessings of Liberty" 12-20; **1967** *Voyage to the Bottom of the Sea* "Death from the Past" 1-8; *Time Tunnel* "Visitors from the Stars "1-13; **1968** *Garrison's Gorillas* "The Frame-Up" 2-27; *The FBI* "Blood Tie" 11-9; **1969** *Mission: Impossible* "Robot" 11-30; **1970** *Mannix* "A Chance at the Roses" 1-17; **1971** *Mission: Impossible* "The Merchant" 2-13; **1972** *Cade's County* "Dead Past" 2-13; **1974** *The FBI* "The Lost Man" 3-24; *Little House on the Prairie* "Town Party, Country Party" 10-30; **1975** *Baretta* "If You Can't Pay the Price" 2-7; **1976** *Switch* "Quicker Than the Eye" 11-9; **1977** *Tales of the Unexpected* "You're Not Alone" 9-17.

Art Metrano

(born September 22, 1936, Brooklyn, New York)

After earning a B. A. at The College of Pacific, Art studied drama with Stella Adler. He gained early television exposure on *The Tonight Show* as a goofy magician, and followed with several appearances on *Laugh-In*. He made 4 guest appearances on *Bewitched* (1968-70) and started guesting on TV crime shows, often as a villain.

In 1970 he became a regular on the brief *Tim Conway Comedy Hour*, and had series regular slots on *The Chicago Teddy Bears* (1971), *Amy Prentiss* (1974-75), *Movin' On* (1975-76) and *Loves Me, Loves Me Not* (1977). During the eighties, Art was a regular on two abbreviated sitcoms, *Joanie Loves*

Chachi (1982-83) and *Tough Cookies* (1986).
    Later eighties guest shots included *Punky Brewster, The A-Team, The Last Precinct* and *Cagney and Lacey.*

GUEST CREDITS

    1968 *Mod Squad* "You Can't Tell the Players without a Programmer" 10-29; **1969** *Mannix* "Death Run" 1-4; *Adam-12* "Log 142-As High As You Are" 12-20; **1973** *Kojak* "One for the Morgue" 11-7; **1974** *Toma* "Joey the Weep" 3-22; **1975** *Kolchak: The Night Stalker* "Chopper" 1-31; **1976** *Police Story* "Open City" 3-12; *Starsky and Hutch* "Nightlight" 10-23; **1977** *Streets of San Francisco* "Monkey Is Back" 1-13; *Police Story* "Hard Rock Brown" 2-15; *Charlie's Angels* "Angels in Paradise" 9-14; *Baretta* "The Runaways" 12-16; **1978** *Incredible Hulk* "Stop the Presses" 11-24; *Wonder Woman* "Skateboard Whiz" 11-24; **1979** *Kaz* "The Stalking Man" 2-7; **1981** *Today's FBI* "Charlestown Chase" 11-8.

TELEFILMS

    1969 *Then Came Bronson* 3-24 CBS; *In Name Only* 11-25 ABC; **1976** *Brinks: The Great Robbery* 3-26 CBS; **1980** *A Cry for Love* 10-20 NBC.

Joanna Miles

(born 1940)
    Following stage experience, Joanna made her film debut during 1960 in *Butterfield 8*. She also appeared in *Splendor in the Grass* in 1961. In 1964 she was in the original cast of the soap, *A Time for Us*, which ran until 1966. She later did soap stints on *All My Children* and *The Edge of Night*.
    In 1973 she turned in her finest television performance in a telefilm with Katherine Hepburn, *The Glass Menagerie*. Joanna earned an Emmy as Best Supporting Actress in a Drama. That was followed by numerous telefilms and guest roles. She had a memorable role in the spooky 1978 telefilm, *The Dark Secret of Harvest Home*.
    Joanna continued her guest work well into the eighties on shows like *Cagney and Lacey* and *St. Elsewhere*.

GUEST CREDITS

    1973 *Mannix* "Carol Lockwood, Past Tense" 1-28; **1974** *Medical Center* "Dark Warning" 2-1; *Magician* "The Illusion of the Lethal Playthings" 3-18; **1975** *Caribe* "One Second to Doom" 4-14; *Barbary Coast* "Crazy Cats" 9-15; *Kojak* "Target in the Sky" 10-26; **1976** *Petrocelli* "Six Strings of Guilt" 2-26; *Barnaby Jones* "Wipeout" 3-4; **1977** *Most Wanted* "The Dutchman" 8-20; *Rafferty* "The

Epidemic" 10-17; **1978** *Eddie Capra Mysteries* "Murder on the Flip Side" 10-6; **1979** *Kaz* "The Battered Bride" 4-11; *Incredible Hulk* "Vandetta Road" 5-25; *Runaways* "False Images" 8-21; **1982** *Trapper John, M.D.* "Angel of Mercy" 1-17.

TELEFILMS

1973 *The Glass Menagerie* 12-16 ABC; **1974** *Born Innocent* 9-10 NBC; *Aloha Means Goodbye* 10-11 CBS; **1975** *The Trial of Chaplain Jenson* 2-11 ABC; **1977** *Delta County, U.S.A.* 5-20 ABC; **1978** *The Dark Secret of Harvest Home* 1-23, 1-24 NBC; *A Fire in the Sky* 11-26 NBC; **1980** *The Promise of Love* 11-11 CBS.

Diana Millay

(born 1938)

A teenaged Dianna Millay came to television in 1955 and made the first of only 3 films in 1957. She found television to be much more suited to her talents, and from 1960 to 1964, was one of TV's busiest actresses.

Dianna joined the cast of *Dark Shadows* in 1966 and worked throughout its run, until 1971. Exhausted, she left acting at that point.

GUEST CREDITS

1960 *Wyatt Earp* "Shoot to Kill" 10-18; *Stagecoach West* "Red Sand" 11-22; *Maverick* "Dodge City or Bust" 12-11; *Michael Shayne* "Death Selects the Winner" 12-23; **1961** *Perry Mason* "The Case of the Resolute Reformer" 1-14; *Thriller* "Man in a Cage" 1-17; *Rifleman* "The Actress" 1-24; *Dante's Inferno* "Around a Dark Corner" 4-10; *Gunsmoke*

Diana Millay is listening as Paul Stevens (center) makes an appeal in this 1964 episode of *The Man from UNCLE* (NBC) called "The King of Knaves Affair". Series star Robert Vaughn peers from behind the throne.

"Melinda Miles" 6-3; *Whispering Smith* "Dark Circle" 9-4; *Hawaiian Eye* "The Moon of Mindanao" 10-11; *New Breed* "Blood Money" 12-19; **1962** *Laramie* "Justice in a Hurry" 3-20; **1963** *Travels of Jaimie McPheeters* "The Day of the Skinners" 10-20; *Redigo* "Horns of Fate" 11-19; *Temple Houston* "Thunder Gap" 11-21; *Perry Mason* "The Case of the Bouncing Boomerang" 12-12; **1964** *77 Sunset Strip* "Alimony League" 1-10; *Eleventh Hour* "How Do I Say 'I Love You'"1-15; *Virginian* "Rope of Lies" 3-25; *Man from UNCLE* "The King of Knaves Affair" 12-22.

Mark Miller

(born November 20, 1925, Houston, Texas)

In films from 1958, Mark was best known for his television work. He was a regular on the 1954-55 soap, *Portia Faces Life*, then co-starred in a 1960-61 sitcom, *Guestward Ho!* His best-recognized TV work came during 1965-67 in a co-starring role in *Please Don't Eat the Daisies*.

Mark had a recurring role in The *Name of the Game* (1968-71), with an overlapping stint on the soap, *Bright Promise* (1969-72). He also had soap roles on *General Hospital* (1965) and on *Days of Our Lives*.

Miller also wrote for television, including scripts for his series *Please Don't Eat the Daisies*.

GUEST CREDITS

1959 *Gunsmoke* "Wind" 3-21; **1960** *Millionaire* "Millionaire Patricia Collins" 6-8; **1961** *Follow the Sun* "The Hunters" 11-12; **1962** *Alfred Hitchcock Presents* ""Apex" 3-20; *Stoney Burke* "Sidewinder" 11-12; *Hawaiian Eye* "The After Hours Heart" 11-13; **1963** *Twilight Zone* "I Dream of Genie" 3-21; **1967** *Invaders* "The Spores" 10-17; **1972** *Smith Family* "Where There's Smoke" 1-5; *The FBI* "Holiday with Terror" 12-3; *Adam-12* "Gifts and Long Letters" 12-20; **1973** *Marcus Welby, M.D.* "The Other Martin

Loring" 2-20; *Griff* "Death by Prescription" 10-6; *Streets of San Francisco* "No Badge for Benjy" 11-1; *Emergency* episode 12-22; **1974** *Barnaby Jones* "The Deadly Jinx" 1-13; *Waltons* "The Spoiler" 10-31; **1975** *Marcus Welby, M.D.* "Public Streets" 1-21; *Matt Helm* "The Deadly Breed" 11-8; *Streets of San Francisco* "The Cat's Paw" 12-4.

TELEFILMS

1971 *Harpy* 3-12 CBS; **1977** *The Hunted Lady* 11-28 NBC.

Spencer Milligan

Beginning in 1974, Spencer was the star of a live-action Saturday morning television show called *Land of the Lost*. It ran from 1974 until 1976, then returned in 1978 and 1985. Spencer worked intermittently in prime-time guest roles from 1975 until 1981. During 1987 he was a member of the cast of the soap *General Hospital*.

GUEST CREDITS

1975 *Gunsmoke* "Brides and Grooms" 2-10; **1976** *Barbary Coast* "The Dawson Marker" 1-9; **1976** *Bionic Woman* "Fly Jaimie" 5-5; **1977** *McCloud* "London Bridges" 3-6; *Baretta* "Shoes" 10-27;

Bionic Woman "Motorcycle Boogie" 11-5; *Logan's Run* "Judas Goat" 12-19; **1978** *Sword of Justice* "Deadly Fashion" 12-31; **1979** *Quincy, M.E.* "Walk Softly Through the Night" 2-1; **1981** *Father Murphy* "Father Murphy" 11-3; *Quincy, M.E.* "Gentle into That Good Night" 12-16; **1982** *Quincy, M.E.* "Across the Line" 12-8.

TELEFILMS

1976 *The Keegans* 5-3 CBS; **1980** *Alcatraz: The Whole Shocking Story* 11-5, 11-6 NBC; **1981** *Terror Among Us* 1-12 CBS.

Juliet Mills
(born November 21, 1941, London, England)

The daughter of noted English actor, John Mills (and sister of actress Hayley Mills), Juliet appeared as an infant in her first film, in 1942. Her film career was rather limited, but she became well known on American television from her first work in 1965.

Following several late sixties guest shots, Juliet earned a starring role on *Nanny and the Professor* (1970-71). In 1975 she was honored with an Emmy as Best Supporting Actress in a Drama Special for her work in *QB VII*.

During the late seventies/early eighties she became a favorite guest on *The Love Boat* (5) and *Fantasy Island* (3). Later eighties guest work included appearances on *Dynasty* (2), *Murder, She Wrote, Hotel* (2) and *Law and Harry McGraw*.

GUEST CREDITS

1965 *Man from UNCLE* "The Adriatic Express Affair" 12-17; **1966** *12 O'Clock High* "The Slaughter Pen" 1-10; *12 O'Clock High* "Siren Voices" 3-4; *Ben Casey* "Pull the Wool Over Your Eyes: Here Comes the Cold Wind of Truth" 3-14; **1967** *Bob Hope Chrysler Theater* "Don't Wait for Tomorrow" 4-19; *Coronet Blue* "Man Running" 7-17; **1974** *Harry O* "Ballenger's Choice" 10-31; **1975** *Marcus Welby, M.D.* "Public Secrets" 1-21; *Medical Story* "The Right to Die" 9-11; *Hawaii Five-0* "Termination with Extreme Prejudice" 9-26; *Wide World of Mystery* "Demon, Demon: 11-11; *Matt Helm* "Death Rods" 11-15; **1976** *Ellery Queen* "The Adventure of the Hard-Hearted Huckster" 3-21; **1977** *Wonder Woman* "The Queen and the Thief" 10-28; **1978** *Police Woman* "Sixth Sense" 2-8; *Switch* "Coronado Circle" 7-2; **1980** *Hart to Hart* "Downhill to Death" 2-5.

TELEFILMS

1967 *Wings of Fire* 2-14 NBC; **1969** *The Challengers* 3-28 CBS; **1973** *Letters from Three Lovers* 10-3 ABC; *QB VII* 4-29, 4-30 ABC; *Kiss Me Again, Stranger* 5-1 NBC; **1977** *Alexander: The Other Side of Dawn* 5-16 NBC; **1979** *The Cracker Factory* 3-16 ABC.

Mort Mills
(born 1919)

Following a 1952 screen debut, Mort jumped headlong into a very busy television career in 1955. He was especially active in western TV series, appearing as a guest in over 50 episodes.
His strong personna made him ideal as sheriffs and police officers as indicated by series regular roles in the syndicated *Man without a Gun*, playing the

the marshal (1959) and *Dante's Inferno*, playing a police lieutenant (1960-61). He also had a recurring role on *Perry Mason*, appearing in 8 episodes as Lt. Landau (1960-64).

GUEST CREDITS

1959 *Trackdown* "Bad Judgment" 1-28; *Wanted: Dead or Alive* "Railroaded" 3-14; *Gunsmoke* "Murder Warrant" 4-18; *Have Gun-Will Travel* "Hunt the Man Down" 4-25; *Tales of Wells Fargo* "The Bounty Hunter" 6-1; *Markham* "Thirteen Avenue Muerte" 7-7; *Wanted: Dead or Alive* "The Healing Woman" 9-12; *Bat Masterson* "Who'll Buy My Violence?" 11-12; *Man from Blackhawk* "Station Six" 11-13; *Law of the Plainsman* "The Gibbet" 11-26; *Bonanza* "Vendetta" 12-5; *Untouchables* "The Dutch Schultz Story" 12-19; **1960** *Sugarfoot* "Journey to Provision" 1-5; *Wanted: Dead or Alive* "The Most Beautiful Woman" 1-23; *Texan* "Thirty Hours to Kill" 2-1; *Men into Space* episode 3-30; *Tales of Wells Fargo* "The Trading Post" 4-11; *Perry Mason* "The Case of the Slandered Submarine" 5-14; *Johnny Ringo* "Killer, Choose a Card" 6-9; *Bronco* "Apache Treasure" 11-7; *Wyatt Earp* "The Fanatic" 11-22; *Stagecoach West* "By the Deep Six" 12-27; **1961** *Laramie* "Rimrock" 3-21; *Stagecoach West* "The Marker" 6-27; *Lawman* "Owny O'Reilly, Esq." 10-15; *Perry Mason* "The Case of the Pathetic Patient" 10-28; *Laramie* "The Last Journey" 10-31; *Perry Mason* "The Case of the Brazen Request" 12-2; *Bonanza* "The Day of the Dragon" 12-13; **1962** *Perry Mason* "The Case of the Crippled Cougar" 3-3; *Rifleman* "Jealous Man" 3-26; *Bonanza* "The Miracle Worker" 5-20; *Perry Mason* "The Case of the Playboy Pugilist" 10-11; *Perry Mason* "The Case of the Fickle Filly" 12-13; **1963** *Virginian* "Duel at Shiloh" 1-2; *Bonanza* "Song in the Dark" 1-13; *G.E. True* "The Black-Robed Ghost" 3-10; *Perry Mason* "The Case of the Difficult Detour" 9-19; **1964** *Gunsmoke* "Take Her, She's Cheap" 10-31; *Wagon Train* "The Clay Shelby Story" 12-6; **1965** *Kraft Suspense Theatre* "In Darkness Waiting I, II" 1-14, 1-21; *Perry Mason* "The Case of the Golden Venom" 1-21; *Fugitive* "Moonchild" 2-16; *Fugitive* "Conspiracy of Silence" 10-12; *Man Called Shenandoah* "The Locket" 11-22; **1966** *Green Hornet* "Give 'Em Enough Rope" 9-16; *Laredo* "Finnegan" 10-21; *Iron Horse* "Explosion at Way Crossing" 11-21; **1967** *Mission: Impossible* "The Frame" 1-21; *Bonanza* "Joe Cartwright, Detective" 3-5; *Invaders* "Condition: Red" 9-5; *Felony Squad* "The Death Bag" 10-9; *Daniel Boone* "The King's Shilling" 10-19; *Gunsmoke* "Death Train" 11-27; **1968** *Mission: Impossible* "The Seal" 2-11; *Daniel Boone* "Flag of Truce" 11-21; **1969** *Outcasts* "They Shall Rise Up" 1-6; *Guns of Will Sonnett* "A Town in Terror" 2-7, 2-14; *Name of the Game* "A Wrath of Angels" 2-28; *Ironside* "The Machismo Bag" 11-13; *Land of the Giants* "Home Sweet Home" 12-21; **1970** *Mannix* "War of Nerves" 3-14; **1972** *Adam-12* "Ambush" 11-10; **1972** *Mod Squad* "Kill Gently, Sweet Jessie" 1-18; *Mission: Impossible* "Two Thousand" 9-23; *Alias Smith and Jones* "McGuffin" 12-9.

TELEFILMS

1967 *Return of the Gunfighter* 1-29 ABC; **1970** *Breakout* 12-8 NBC.

William Mims

(born 1927)

Initially a stage actor, William Mims began his television career in 1959, with a screen debut following, in 1961. Among his films were roles in *Lonely Are the Brave*, *Paint Your Wagon* and *The Ballad of Cable Hogue*.

Frequently mustachioed, William's only TV series regular role was in *The Long Hot Summer* (1965-66). He also did a stint on the soap *General Hospital*.

GUEST CREDITS

1959 *Rough Riders* "The Wagon Raiders" 6-4; *Have Gun-Will Travel* "Champagne Safari" 12-5; **1960** *Westerner* "School Days" 10-7; **1961** *Bonanza* "The Bride" 1-21; *Perry Mason* "The Case of the Guilty Clients" 6-10; **1962** *Thriller* "An Attractive Family" 1-1; *Lawman* "The Bride" 4-1; *Have Gun-Will Travel* "Trial at Table Rock" 12-15; **1963** *Twilight Zone* "The New Exhibit" 4-4; **1964** *Bonanza* "A Man to Admire" 12-6; **1965** *Wild Wild West* "The Night the Wizard Shook the Earth" 11-15; **1966** *Daniel Boone* "Fifty Rifles" 3-10; *Big Valley* "The Martyr" 10-17; **1967** *Big Valley* "Wagonload of Dreams" 1-2; *Daniel Boone* "The Desperate Raid" 11-16; **1968** *I Spy* "The Spy Business" 4-1; *Outcasts* "The Understanding" 10-14; **1969** *Adam-12* "Jimmy Eisley's Dealing Smack" 1-11; **1970** *Lancer* "Splinter Group" 3-3; *Dan August* "Epitaph for a Swinger" 11-18; **1971** *Gunsmoke* "Pike" 3-8, 3-15; *Night Gallery* "The Hand of Borgus Weems" 9-15; **1972** *Mannix* "Babe in the Woods" 1-5; *Alias Smith and Jones* "Which Way to Crooked Corral" 2-10; *Bonanza* "One Ace Too Many" 4-2; *Rookies* "Dead,

Like a Lost Dream" 9-18; **1973** *Kung Fu* "Alethia" 3-15; *Ironside* "Downhill All the Way" 11-8; **1974** *Kolchak: The Night Stalker* "The Devil's Platform" 11-15; **1975** *Rookies* "Nightmare" 3-17; **1976** *Switch* "The Argonaut Special" 10-12; **1979** *Quincy, M.E.* "Aftermath" 2-7; *.240 Robert* "Models" 9-17.

TELEFILMS

1970 *Breakout* 12-8 NBC; **1973** *Hijack!* 9-26 ABC; **1974** *Fer-de-Lance* 10-18 CBS; **1982** *The Day the Bubble Burst* 2-7 NBC.

Nico Minardos

(born 1930)

Of Greek extraction, Nico played Latinos in most of his television roles, but was occasionally cast as Greeks, Turks or Arabs. Many of his roles found him cast as handsome rogues, castings that kept him busy on TV for two decades.

His screen career, from 1955, was undistinguished, consisting mainly of B films.

GUEST CREDITS

1959 *77 Sunset Strip* "Sing Something Simple" 11-6; *Phillip Marlowe* "Time to Kill" 2-16; *Riverboat* "The Two Faces of Holden Grey" 10-3; *Route 66* "A Lance of Straw" 10-14; **1961** *Rebel* "The Liberators" 1-1; **1962** *Hawaiian Eye* "Year of Grace" 1-24; *87th Precinct* "Killer's Choice" 3-5; *Surfside 6* "The Money Game" 4-9; *77 Sunset Strip* "The Lovely American" 5-4; *Naked City* "The Virtues of Madame Douray" 12-5; **1963** *Redigo* "Prince Among Men" 10-15; **1964** *Channing* "Memory of a Firing Squad" 1-1; **1965** *Rogues* "The Laughing Lady of Luxor" 2-21; *Perry Mason* "The Case of the Sad Sicilian" 3-11; *Amos Burke, Secret Agent* "Nightmare in the Sun" 10-20; *Ben Casey* "The Man from Quasilia" 11-29; *Branded* "Romany Roundup" 12-5, 12-12; **1966** *Big Valley* "The Martyr" 10-17; *Mission: Impossible* "Odds on Evil" 10-22; **1967** *Run for Your Life* "Who's Che Guevara?" 9-13; *Hondo* "The Savage" 10-6; **1968** *The FBI* "The Predators" 4-7; *Outcasts* "The Understanding" 10-14;

Nico Minardos (right), series star Raymond Burr (left) and regular Elizabeth Baur show concern in a 1972 episode of *Ironside* (NBC). The episode was called "A Man Called Arno".

1970 *Mod Squad* "The Exile" 2-3; *Immortal* "Queen's Gambit" 11-12; *Mission: Impossible* "Squeeze Play" 12-12; **1971** *Ironside* "Escape" 2-11; *Alias Smith and Jones* "Journey from San Juan" 4-8; *O'Hara, U. S. Treasury* "Operation: Heroin" 10-29; *Alias Smith and Jones* "The Miracle at Santa Maria" 12-30; **1972** *Marcus Welby, M.D.* "All the Pretty People" 1-25; *Ironside* "A Man Named Arno" 3-9; *Cool Million* "The Adduction of Bayard Barnes" 12-6; *Medical Center* "No Way Out" 12-27; **1973** *Jigsaw* "Kiss the Dream Goodbye" 2-19; *Barnaby Jones* "The Loose Connection" 3-18; **1977** *Hardy Boys/Nancy Drew Mysteries* "Nancy Drew's Love Match" 11-20.

TELEFILMS

1970 *The Challengers* 2-20 CBS; **1971** *Sarge: The Badge or the Cross* 2-22 NBC; *River of Mystery* 10-1 NBC.

George Mitchell

(born February 21, 1905, Larchmont, New York; died January 8, 1972)

George did not decide to become an actor until, at age 35, he married actress Katherine Squire. After stage experience he made his film debut in 1955 in *The Phoenix City Story*. Among his later films were roles in *Birdman of Alcatraz, Twilight of Honor, The Unsinkable Molly Brown, Nevada Smith, The Flim Flam Man* and *The Andromedia Strain*.

From the late fifties through the mid sixties George was in strong demand for television guest roles in all types of series. He died in his sleep in 1972, while in Washington, D. C. during rehearsal for a play.

GUEST CREDITS

1959 *Californians* "A Turn in the Trail" 1-20; *Gunsmoke* "Annie Oakley" 10-24; *Law of the Plainsman* "The Gibbet" 11-26; **1960** *Perry Mason* "The Case of the Bashful Burro" 3-26; *Twilight Zone* "Execution" 4-1; *Alfred Hitchcock Presents* "Forty Detectives Later" 4-24; *Gunsmoke* "Distant Drummer" 11-19; *Have Gun-Will Travel* "The Prisoner" 12-17; **1961** *Americans* "Half Moon Road" 2-27; *National Velvet* "Epidemic" 3-5; *Cain's Hundred* "Markdown on a Man" 10-10; *Alfred Hitchcock Presents* "Portrait Without a Face" 12-25; *Bonanza* "Land Grab" 12-31; **1962** *Laramie* "Justice in a Hurry" 3-20; *Ben Casey* "Among Others, a Girl

Named Abilene" 4-2; *Stoney Burke* "Fight Night" 10-8; *Stoney Burke* "A Matter of Pride" 11-5; *Stoney Burke* "Cousin Eunice" 12-24; **1963** *Twilight Zone* "Jess-Belle" 2-14; *Sam Benedict* "Some Fires Die Slowly" 2-16; *Fugitive* "The Witch" 9-24; *Twilight Zone* "The Ring-a-Ding Girl" 12-27; **1964** *Fugitive* "Devil's Carnival" 12-22; **1965** *Alfred Hitchcock Hour* "Wally the Beard" 3-1; *Voyage to the Bottom of the Sea* "Secret of the Loch" 4-5; **1966** *Virginian* "Morgan Starr" 2-9; *Time Tunnel* "Massacre" 10-28; **1969** *Land of the Giants* "Six Hours to Live" 9-28.

Laurie Mitchell

(born 1936)

From 1956 until 1971 beautiful Laurie Mitchell graced the small screen in a number of television guest roles. She was especially effective in western series appearances.

GUEST CREDITS

1959 *Markham* "The Father" 10-31; *Millionaire* "Millionaire Tom Hampton" 11-18; *Wanted: Dead or Alive* "Chain Gang" 12-12; *M Squad* "One of Our Armored Cars Is Missing" 12-18; **1960** *Man from Blackhawk* "El Patron" 2-5; *Bourbon Street Beat* "Twice Betrayed" 4-4; *Wagon Train* "The Shad

Bennington Story" 6-22; **1961** *Hawaiian Eye* "A Touch of Velvet" 1-11; *Perry Mason* "The Case of the Waylaid Wolf" 2-4; *Maverick* "Triple Indemnity" 3-19; *Investigators* "New Sound for the Blues" 10-19; *Rawhide* "The Prairie Elephant" 11-17; **1962** *Broncho* "Moment of Doubt" 4-2; **1964** *Bonanza* "King of the Mountain" 2-23; *Wagon Train* "The Pearlie Garnet Story" 2-24; **1965** *Alfred Hitchcock Hour* "Night Fever" 5-3; **1966** *Laredo* "Above the

Law" 1-13; *Virginian* "Girl on Glass Mountain" 2-23; **1971** *Bold Ones: The Doctors* "An Absence of Lonliness" 1-24.

Donald Moffatt

(born December 26, 1930, Plymouth, England)

Trained at the Royal Academy of Dramatic Arts (RADA), Donald made a film debut in 1956, and came to American television in 1960. Stage work occupied most of his sixties efforts, and he was nominated for two Tony Awards during 1967. He returned to television in 1969 and has worked often

in the medium since. A number of guest roles were spliced around two abbreviated seventies series regular roles in *The New Land* (1974), and *Logan's Run* (1977-78).

His eighties guest credits included work on *Murder, She Wrote, Dallas* (2) and *Buck James* (3). He also appeared in 9 telefilms during the decade.

GUEST CREDITS

1960 *U.S. Steel Hour* "You Can't Have Everything" 1-27; **1963** *Defenders* "The Colossus" 4-13; **1970** *High Chaparral* "The Lieutenant" 2-17; *Hawaii Five-0* "And a Time to Die" 9-16; *Young Rebels* "The Age of Independence" 11-15; **1971** *Mission: Impossible* "Mindbend" 10-9; *Bonanza* "Face of Fear" 11-14; *Night Gallery* "Pickman's Model" 12-1; **1972** *Ironside* "Shadow Soldiers" 12-21; **1973** *Mannix* "All the Dead Were Strangers" 12-16; *Snoop Sisters* "Corpse and Robbers" 12-19; **1974** *Gunsmoke* "The Foundling" 2-11; *Ironside* "Close to the Heart" 2-28; **1975** *Six Million Dollar Man* "The Bionic Criminal" 11-9; **1977** *Waltons* "John's Crossroads" 1-20; *Code R* episode 2-11; *Family* episode 3-8; **1979** *Family* episode 1-4.

TELEFILMS

1971 *The Devil and Miss Sarah* 12-4 ABC; **1976** *The Call of the Wild* 5-22 NBC; **1977** *Eleanor and*

Franklin: The White House Years 3-13 ABC; *Exo-Man* 6-18 NBC; *The Last Hurrah* 11-16 NBC; *Mary White* 11-18 ABC; **1978** *Sergeant Matlovich vs. the U. S. Air Force* 8-21 NBC; *The Gift of Love* 12-8 ABC; **1979** *Strangers: The Story of a Mother and Daughter* 5-13 CBS; *Ebony, Ivory and Jade* 8-3 CBS; *Mrs. R's Daughter* 9-19 NBC; **1980** *The Long Days of Summer* 5-23 ABC; **1983** *Who Will Love My Children?* 2-14 ABC; *Through Naked Eyes* 12-11 ABC.

Victor Mohica

(born 1933)

Usually cast in Hispanic or American Indian roles, Vic did much of his television work during the seventies, starting in 1972. Husky and muscular, he was well-suited for action roles. His career extended into the eighties, working in additional guest roles and telefilms.

He also appeared for a time on soaps *The Young and the Restless* and *General Hospital* (1994).

GUEST CREDITS

1972 *McCloud* "The New Mexican Connection" 10-1; **1973** *Faraday and Company* "Say Hello to a Dead Man" 9-26; *Streets of San Francisco* "For the

Love of God" 9-27; **1974** *The FBI* "Vendetta" 4-7;
Rookies "A Test of Courage" 12-2; **1975** *Cannon*
"Lady on the Run" 3-5; *Caribe* "Assault on the
Calavera" 5-12; *Six Million Dollar Man* "The Song
and Dance Spy" 10-5; *Cannon* "The Melted Man"
11-12; **1976** *Doctor's Hospital* "And Hear a Sudden
Cry" 1-6; *Blue Knight* "A Fashionable Connection"
1-7; *Police Story* "The Long Ball" 2-13; *Bert
D'Angelo, Superstar* "The Book of Fear" 3-20; **1977**
Fantastic Journey "An Act of Love" 3-24; **1980**
Barnaby Jones "Killer without a Name" 2-14; **1983**
Hardcastle and McCormick "Flying Down to Rio"
12-4.

TELEFILMS

1972 *Banacek: Detour to Nowhere* 3-20 NBC;
1973 *Brock's Last Case* 3-5 NBC; **1974** *Little House
on the Prairie* 3-30 NBC; **1975** *The Abduction of
Saint Anne* 1-21 ABC; *Ellery Queen: Too Many
Suspects* 3-23 NBC; **1976** *The Macahans* 1-19 ABC;
Mallory: Circumstantial Evidence 12-13 NBC;
Victory at Entebbe 12-13 ABC; **1977** *Return of the
Incredible Hulk* 11-28 CBS; **1978** *The Deerslayer*
12-18 NBC; **1980** *Stunts Unlimited* 1-4 ABC; **1981**
California Gold Rush 7-30 NBC.

Lee Harcourt Montgomery

(born 1961, Winnipeg, Manitoba, Canada)
    The brother of actress Belinda J. Montgomery,
Lee H. Montgomery was one of television's most-
seen juvenile actors of the early seventies. He made
both screen and TV debuts in 1971.
    A grown-up Lee starred in a 1983 telefilm,
Happy Endings.

GUEST CREDITS

1971 *Marcus Welby, M.D.* "A Woman's Place" 2-
2; *Man and the City* "Hands of Love" 9-15; *Mod
Squad* "Cricket" 9-21; *Longstreet* "Wednesday's
Child" 11-11; *Medical Center* "Conspiracy" 12-8;
1972 *The FBI* "Escape to Nowhere" 3-19; *Marcus
Welby, M.D.* "Jason Be Nimble, Jason Be Quick" 11-
28; **1973** *Ironside* "Downhill All the Way" 11-8;

Medical Center "Child of Violence" 11-12; **1974**
Columbo "Mind Over Mayhem" 2-10; *Kojak* "The
Only Way Out" 5-8; *Adam-12* "Camp" 9-24; 10-1;
Streets of San Francisco "The Twenty-Five Calibre
Plague" 12-12; **1975** *Emergency* episode 1-11;
Ironside "If a Body See a Body" 1-23; *Griff* "Man
on the Outside" 6-29; *Petrocelli* "Chain of Com-
mand" 10-8.

TELEFILMS

1971 *The Harness* 11-12 CBS; **1973** *Female
Artillery* 1-17 ABC; *Runaway!* 9-29 ABC; **1974** *A
Cry in the Wilderness* 3-26 ABC; **1975** *Man on the
Outside* 6-29 ABC; **1979** *True Grit (A Further
Adventure)* 5-19 ABC; **1983** *Happy Endings* 12-26
NBC.

Ralph Moody

(born 1888; died 1971)
    A performer on radio for many years, Ralph
appeared on the *Gunsmoke* radio show frequently,
usually playing various oldtimers. He was very
active on television from the mid fifties, often
appearing as old settlers and townsmen on TV
westerns. He continued to work in guest roles until
1970, with a telefilm in 1971.
    His film work ran the gamut from westerns to

comedies, and included *Road to Bali, Going Steady, Red Mountain, The Story of Ruth* and *The Big Fisherman*.

GUEST CREDITS

1959 *Have Gun-Will Travel* "The Monster of Moon Ridge" 2-28; *Rawhide* "Incident at Chubasco" 4-3; *Perry Mason* "The Case of the Calendar Girl" 4-18; *Gunsmoke* "Cheyenne" 6-13; *Black Saddle* "Murdock" 11-13; *Perry Mason* "The Case of Paul Drake's Dilemna" 11-14; *Law of the Plainsman* "The Dude" 12-3; **1960** *Rifleman* "The Spoiler" 2-16; *Wagon Train* "The Tom Tuckett Story" 3-3; *Gunsmoke* "The Bobsy Twins" 5-21; *Rifleman* "The Hangman" 5-31; **1961** *Rifleman* "Six Years and a Day" 1-3; *Rifleman* "The Actress" 1-24; *Klondike* "The Man Who Owned Skagway" 1-30; *Rifleman* "Dark Day at North Fork" 3-7; *Rifleman* "The Mescalero Curse" 4-18; **1962** *Twilight Zone* "The Last Rites of Jeff Myrtlebank" 2-23; *Thriller* "The Lethal Ladies" 3-16; *Gunsmoke* "Old Comrade" 12-29; **1963** *Ben Casey* "Father Was an Intern" 4-1; **1964** *Gunsmoke* "Friend" 1-25; *Bonanza* "The Saga of Muley Jones" 3-29; **1965** *Wild Wild West* "The Night of the Howling Light" 12-17; **1967** *Dragnet* "The Big Hammer" 3-2; *Man from UNCLE* "The Maze Affair" 12-18; *The FBI* "Legend of John Rim" 12-31; **1969** *Adam-12* "Log 103-A Sound Like Thunder" 11-1; **1970** *Dragnet* "Burglary-Helpful

Woman" 1-22; *Dragnet* "D.H.Q.-The Victims" 4-16; *Night Gallery* "The Little Black Bag" 12-23.

TELEFILM

1971 *The Impatient Heart* 10-8 NBC.

Read Morgan

(born 1931)

Tall and husky, Read played numerous action roles in both films and television. He was a particular favorite on Gunsmoke, appearing in 10 episodes. Read had one series regular role, on *The Deputy* (1960-61).

GUEST CREDITS

1959 *Gunsmoke* "Passive Resistance" 1-17; *Steve Canyon* "The Fight" 2-5; *Tales of Wells Fargo* "Little Man" 5-18; *Markham* "Forty-Two on a Rope" 7-11; *Deputy* "Powderkeg" 10-10; *Twilight Zone* "What You Need" 12-25; **1960** *Alfred Hitchcock Presents* "Hitchhike" 2-21; *Hotel de Paree* "Sundance and the Useless" 3-14; *Adventures in Paradise* "Beached" 5-2; *Westerner* "Dos Pinos" 11-4; **1961** *Whispering Smith* "Double Edge" 8-7; *Alcoa Premiere* "The Fugitive Eye" 10-17; **1963** *Alfred*

Hitchcock Hour "Death of a Cop" 5-24; *Wagon Train* "The Myra Marshall Story" 10-21; **1964** *Outer Limits* "Fun and Games" 3-30; *Outer Limits* "I, Robot" 11-14; **1965** *Fugitive* "Nicest Fella You'd Ever Want to Meet" 1-19; *Bonanza* "The Ballerina" 1-24; *Gunsmoke* "Dry Road to Nowhere" 4-3; **1967** *Custer* "Spirit Women" 12-13; **1968** *Tarzan* "Alex the Great" 3-22; **1970** *Gunsmoke* "Morgan" 3-2; *Immortal* "White Elephants Don't Grow on Trees" 10-1; *Gunsmoke* "Sam McTavish, M.D." 10-5; *Gunsmoke* "Sergeant Holly" 12-14; **1971** *Virginian* "Nan Allen" 1-6; *Alias Smith and Jones* "The Day They Hanged Kid Curry" 9-16; *Gunsmoke* "The Legend" 10-18; *McMillan and Wife* "The Easter Sunday Murder Case" 10-20; **1972** *Gunsmoke* "ThePredators" 1-31; *Gunsmoke* "The River" 9-11, 9-18; *Gunsmoke* "Milligan" 11-6; *Sixth Sense* "Five Widows Weeping" 12-9; **1973** *Gunsmoke* "The Boy and the Sinner" 10-1; *Mannix* "A Matter of the Heart" 11-4; **1974** *Gunsmoke* "Trail of Bloodshed" 3-4; **1975** *Police Story* "War Games" 3-4; *Police Woman* "Blaze of Glory" 11-11; **1977** *Tales of the Unexpected* "The Nomads" 2-23; *Barnaby Jones* "Circle of Treachery" 3-3; *Charlie's Angels* "Circus of Terror" 10-19.

TELEFILMS

1967 *Return of the Gunfighter* 1-29 ABC; **1973** *Jarrett* 3-17 CBS; **1974** *Hurricane* 9-10 ABC; *Punch and Jody* 11-26 NBC; **1975** *A Shadow in the Streets* 1-28 NBC; *Crossfire* 3-24 NBC; **1976** *Helter Skelter* 4-1, 4-2 CBS; *Mary Jane Harper Cried Last Night* 10-5 CBS; **1978** *Crash* 10-29 ABC; **1979** *The Billion Dollar Threat* 4-15; ABC; **1980** *Power* 1-14, 1-15 NBC.

Byron Morrow

(born September 8, Chicago, Illinois)

Prematurely gray, Byron Morrow was one of television's busiest actors during the entire sixties/seventies period, with frequent castings as authority figures. He made film and television debuts in 1959, with subsequent movie roles in *The Best of Everything, Captain Newman, M.D., Torn Curtain* and *The Wrecking Crew.*

His TV series regular roles were in *The New Breed* (1961-62) and *Executive Suite* (1976-77). He also had a prominent role in the 1983 miniseries, *The Winds of War.*

GUEST CREDITS

1959 *Markham* "The Cruelist Thief" 6-30; **1960** *Man and the Challenge* "The Storm" 1-2; *Men into Space* episode 1-27; *Twilight Zone* "People Are Alike All Over" 3-25; *Millionaire* "Millionaire Peter Longmen" 5-25; *Peter Gunn* "Dream Big, Dream Deadly" 12-12; *Perry Mason* "The Case of the Larcenous Lady" 12-17; **1961** *Untouchables* "The Organization" 1-26; *Loretta Young Show* "Quiet Desperation" 2-5; *Untouchables* "The Antidote" 3-9; *Rawhide* "The Incident of the Painted Lady" 5-12; **1962** *Rawhide* "The Bosses' Daugthers" 2-2; *Virginian* "The Accomplice" 12-19; **1963** *Redigo* "Lady War Bonnet" 9-24; *Great Adventure* "The Man Who Stole New York City" 12-13; **1964** *Wagon Train* "The Jed Whitmore Story" 1-13; **1965** *Kraft Suspense Theatre* "In Darkness Waiting" 1-21; *Fugitive* "The Old Man Picked a Lemon" 4-13; *Kentucky Jones* episode 4-13; *Lost in Space* "The Reluctant Stowaway" 9-15; *Perry Mason* "The Case of the Impetuous Imp" 10-10; *Ben Casey* "Because of the Needle, the Haystack Was Lost" 10-11; *Perry Mason* "The Case of the Wrathful Wraith" 11-7; *I Spy* "No Exchange on Damaged Merchandise" 11-10; **1966**

Honey West "Stay Gypsy, Stay" 2-25; *Man Called Shenandoah* "The Death of Matthew Eldredge" 3-21; *12 O'Clock High* "Gauntlet of Fire" 9-9; **1967** *Invaders* "The Ivy Curtain" 3-21; *Star Trek* "Amok Time" 9-15; *Ironside* "Dead Man's Tale" 9-28; *Dragnet* "The Big Pyramid" 11-30; **1968** *Lost in Space* "The Time Merchant" 1-17; *Mannix* "Comes Up Rose" 10-5; *Star Trek* "For the World Is Hollow and I Have Touched the Sky" 11-8; *Bonanza* "The Sound of Drums" 11-17; **1969** *Big Valley* "Top of the Stairs" 1-6; *Lancer* "The Black McGloins" 1-21; *It Takes a Thief* "Boom at the Top" 2-25; **1970** *Mod Squad* "The Exile" 2-3; *Mission: Impossible* "The Killer" 9-19 **1971** *Bearcats!* episode 11-25; **1972** *Waltons* "The Star" 10-6; *Marcus Welby, M.D.* "House of Mirrors" 10-10; *Waltons* episode 10-20; *Owen Marshall, Counselor at Law* "Starting Over Again" 12-7; *Owen Marshall, Counselor at Law* "Sigh No More, Lady" 12-21; *McMillan and Wife* "An Elementary Case of Murder" 12-31; **1973** *Search* "Suffer My Child" 3-28; *Barnaby Jones* "A Little Glory, a Little Death" 4-29; *Owen Marshall, Counselor at Law* "A Lesson in Loving" 9-12; **1974** *Ironside* "For the Love of God" 1-3; *Owen Marshall, Counselor at Law* "The Attacker" 1-26; *Police Story* "Glamour Boy" 10-29; *Columbo* "A Friend in Deed" 12-29; **1975** *Kolchak: The Night Stalker* "The Primal Scream" 1-17; *Cannon* "The Set-Up" 2-12; *Caribe* "Vanished" 2-24; *S.W.A.T.* "Blind Man's Bluff" 5-19; *Police Story* "A Community of Victims" 9-23; *Rockford Files* "The Girl in the Bay City Boy's Club" 12-19; **1976** *Blue Knight* "A Fashionable Connection" 1-7; *Hunter* "The Lysemko Syndrome" 3-4; *McNaughton's Daughter* "Love Is a Four-Letter Word" 3-24; *Bionic Woman* "Kill Oscar" 11-3; **1977** *Rockford Files* "There's One in Every Port" 1-7; *Rockford Files* "Kill the Messenger" 10-27; *Rockford Files* "Irving the Explainer" 11-18; **1979** *Rockford Files* "Trouble in Paradise Cove" 9-28; *Quincy, M.E.* "Mode of Death" 11-1; **1981** *Greatest American Hero* "Don't Mess Around with Him" 10-18; **1982** *Bret Maverick* "Dateline: Sweetwater" 1-12.

TELEFILMS

1969 *Night Gallery* 11-8 NBC; **1970** *The Challenge* 2-10 ABC; **1972** *Man on a String* 2-18

CBS; *The Adventures of Nick Carter* 2-20 CBS; **1974** *Panic on the 5:22* 11-20 ABC; **1975** *The Turning Point of Jim Malloy* 4-12 NBC; *Babe* 10-13 CBS; **1977** *Little Ladies of the Night* 1-16 ABC; *The Girl in the Empty Grave* 9-20 NBC; *In the Matter of Karen Ann Quinlan* 9-26 NBC; *Don't Push, I'll Charge When I'm Ready* 12-18 NBC; **1978** *The Ghost of Flight 401* 2-18 NBC; **1979** *The Golden Gate Murders* 10-3 CBS; **1980** *Power* 1-14, 1-15 NBC; **1981** *Jacqueline Susann's "Valley of the Dolls"* 10-19, 10-20; **1982** *Bare Essence* 10-4, 10-5 CBS.

Jeff Morrow

(born January 13, 1913, New York City; died December 26, 1993)

With a screen debut in 1953, Jeff ultimately appeared in films like *The Robe, Sign of the Pagan, Captain Lightfoot* and *The Story of Ruth*. His best known role in television was a starring role on *Union Pacific* (1958-59).

Guest roles followed *Union Pacific* until he gained a regular slot on *Temperatures Rising* (1973-74).

GUEST CREDITS

1959 *Markham* "Crash in the Desert" 8-18; **1960** *Wagon Train* "The Clayton Tucker Story" 2-10;

Billy Mumy (second from left), is overwhelmed by a kidnap attempt from Ronald Long (left), as Jonathan Harris looks on helplessly. The Robot steers in a 1967 episode of *Lost in Space* (CBS) called "Space Mutiny".

Twilight Zone "Eligy" 2-19; *Chevy Mystery Show* "Murder by the Book" 9-4; *Deputy* "The Jason Harris Story" 10-8; **1961** *Bonanza* "The Honor of Cochise" 10-1; **1962** *Cheyenne* "The Idol" 1-29; *Perry Mason* "The Case of the Ancient Romeo" 5-12; *Tales of Wells Fargo* "Vignette of a Sinner" 6-2; *Perry Mason* "The Case of the Dodging Domino" 10-25; **1963** *Virginian* "The Man Who Couldn't Die" 1-30; *Rifleman* "The End of the Hunt" 2-18; *Perry Mason* "The Case of the Festive Falcon" 11-28; **1966** *Iron Horse* "No Wedding Bells for Tony" 11-7; *Daniel Boone* "The Symbol" 12-29; **1968** *Daniel Boone* "Faith's Way" 4-4; **1968** *Name of the Game* "The Protector" 11-15.

Billy Mumy

(born 1954)

A child actor of the sixties, Billy made film and television debuts in 1960. He had several strong performances on *The Twilight Zone* and other dramatic series, and guested on sitcoms like *The Munsters, I Dream of Jeannie* and *Bewitched* (2). From 1965 to 1968 he appeared as Will Robinson on *Lost in Space*, and with Zachary Smith and "The Robot", became the focus of most of the episodes.

After adulthood Billy worked infrequently on television, although he gained a series regular role on an abbreviated 1975 sitcom, *Sunshine*. After *Lost in Space*, Billy entered, and completed, high school and studied music for two years at Santa Monica College. He has subsequently performed in several rock bands, and has written for television (and later, for comic books).

The multi-talented Mumy has written songs for the rock group America, and produced two of them. He last acted on television in several episodes of *Superboy* in 1988. Billy and fellow *Lost in Space* cast members have recently hosted a special on the Sci-Fi Network, celebrating the television and film hits of Irwin Allen.

GUEST CREDITS

1960 *Loretta Young Show* "My Own Master" 12-18; **1961** *Loretta Young Show* "The Lie" 1-22; *Twilight Zone* "Long Distance Call" 3-31; *Alfred Hitchcock Presents* "Bang, You're Dead" 10-17; *Twilight Zone* "It's a Good Life" 11-3; *General Electric Theater* "A Friendly Tribe" 12-31; **1962** *Alfred Hitchcock Presents* "The Door without a Key" 1-16; *Dr. Kildare* "The Bronc Buster" 3-1; *Alfred Hitchcock Hour* "House Guest" 11-8; **1963** *Twilight Zone* "In Praise of Pip" 9-27; **1964** *Fugitive* "Home Is the Hunted" 1-7; *Eleventh Hour* "Sunday Father" 1-8; **1965** *Virginian* "The Old Cowboy" 3-31; **1969** *Lancer* "The Kid" 10-7.

TELEFILMS

1973 *Sunshine* 11-9 CBS; **1974** *The Rockford Files* 3-27 NBC; **1977** *The Sunshine Christsmas* 12-12 NBC.

Charles Napier

(born 1935)

Charles got his start in Russ Meyers' flicks, then came to mainstream films in 1969. He has been doing television work since 1968, including an unusual 1969 episode of *Star Trek* in which he sings.

Napier was a regular on the short-lived 1977 series, *Oregon Trail*, and on a 1986-87 western series called *The Outlaws*. Contemporary film fans will remember him for roles on *The Blues Brothers*, *Rambo-First Blood, Part II* and *The Silence of the Lambs*.

GUEST CREDITS

1968 *Mission: Impossible* "The Play" 12-8; **1969** *Star Trek* "The Way to Eden" 2-21; **1971** *Mission: Impossible* "Run for the Money" 12-11; **1972** *Mission: Impossible* "Cocaine" 10-21; **1975** *Starsky and Hutch* "Texas Longhorn" 9-17; *Kojak* "My Brother, My Enemy" 9-21; *Baretta* "Double Image" 10-15; **1976** *Delvecchio* "Hot Spell" 11-14; **1977** *Rockford Files* "New Life, Old Dragons" 2-25; **1978** *Starsky and Hutch* "Satan's Witches" 2-8; **1979** *Incredible Hulk* "The Slam" 10-19; **1981** *Walking Tall*

"The Protectors of the People" 1-24; *Concrete Cowboys* "El Dorado" 2-7, 2-14; *Incredible Hulk* "Triangle"11-13; **1982** *Strike Force* "Deadly Chemicals" 3-26; *Simon and Simon* "Mike and Pat" 10-14; *CHiPs* "Something Special" 11-21; **1983** *Tales of the Gold Monkey* "High Stakes Lady" 1-26; *A-Team* "Labor Pains" 11-8.

TELEFILMS

1977 *Ransom for Alice!* 6-2 NBC; **1978** *Big Bob Johnson and His Fantastic Speed Circus* 6-2 NBC; **1980** *Gridlock* 10-2 NBC.

Barry Nelson

(born Robert Neilson, April 20, 1920, Oakland, Calif.)

Barry made a film debut in 1941 and worked often in Broadway plays and musicals. He came to television in 1948 and had 5 appearances on *Suspense* and 3 on *Starlight Theater* before earning a starring role on *The Hunter* (1952). During 1953-55, he co-starred with Joan Caulfield in the sitcom, *My Favorite Husband*. Later fifties guest credits included work on *Schlitz Playhouse of Stars, Lux Playhouse* and *Climax*.

He continued his TV guest work well into the eighties. Later eighties work included appearances

on *Fantasy Island, Murder, She Wrote* and *J. J. Starbuck*.

His forty-plus year film career included *Bataan, Winged Victory, Airport* and *The Shining*.

GUEST CREDITS

1959 *Alfred Hitchcock Presents* "The Waxwork" 4-12; **1960** *June Allyson Show* "Threat of Evil" 2-15; *U.S. Steel Hour* "A Time to Decide" 11-2; **1963** *DuPont Show of the Month* "The Bachelor Game" 9-29; **1964** *Bob Hope Chrysler Theater* "Wake Up Darling" 2-21; *Alfred Hitchcock Hour* "Anyone for Murder?" 3-13; *Greatest Show on Earth* "There Are No Problems, Only Opportunites" 4-21; *Twilight Zone* "Stopover in a Quiet Town" 4-24; *Dr. Kildare* "Maybe Love Will Save My Apartment" 10-1; *Kraft Suspense Theatre* "One Tiger to a Hill" 12-3; *Alfred Hitchcock Hour* "Misadventure" 12-17; **1969** *Name of the Game* "Break Out to a Fast Buck" 3-14; *The FBI* "Tug-of-War" 12-28; **1971** *Longstreet* "Spell Legacy Like Death" 10-21; **1972** *Owen Marshall, Counselor at Law* "A Piece of God" 12-14; **1973** *Circle of Fear* "Doorway to Death" 1-26; *Cannon*

"The Seventh Grave" 2-28; **1978** *Kaz* "A Case of Class" 10-1; *David Cassidy, Man Undercover* "Rx for Dying" 12-21; **1979** *Salvage l* "Golden Orbit" 3-12; **1981** *Nero Wolfe* "Sweet Revenge" 4-28; *Dallas* "Little Boy Lost" 10-30; *Dallas* "Waterloo at South Fork" 12-11; *Dallas* "The Prodigal" 12-18; **1982** *Magnum, P.I.* "Double Jeopardy" 2-25.

TELEFILMS

1967 *The Borgia Stick* 2-25 NBC; **1969** *Seven in Darkness* 9-23 ABC; **1972** *Climb an Angry Mountain* 12-23 NBC; **1974** *Ring Once for Death* 4-22 ABC.

Claudette Nevins

Claudette made her television debut in 1964, but was relatively inactive in the medium until she became a regular on Andy Griffith's abbreviated 1970-71 series, *The Headmaster*. During the balance of the seventies she made a number of guest appearances on crime series. Often cast as assertive

women, she was also effective in sitcom guest shots, on *The Bob Newhart Show*, *The Mary Tyler Moore Show*, *Three's Company* and *One Day at a Time* (2). She was a regular on two forgettable, and very brief, late seventies series.

Her later eighties guest work included appearances on *The Mississippi*, *Hardcastle and McCormick* and *Just in Time*.

GUEST CREDIITS

1964 *Doctors and Nurses* "Once Bitten" 9-22; **1965** *Defenders* "The Prosecutor" 4-29; **1972** *The FBI* "The Engineer" 10-29; **1973** *Police Story* "Requiem for an Informer" 10-9; **1974** *Barnaby Jones* "Image in a Cracked Mirror" 3-10; *Petrocelli* "An Act of Love" 11-13; **1975** *Archer* "The Arsonist" 2-6; *Harry O* "Street Games" 3-13; *Harry O* "Reflections" 11-9; **1976** *Switch* "The Lady from Lichtenstein" 11-23, 11-30; **1977** *Rockford Files* "Trouble in Chapter 17" 9-23; *Lou Grant* "Hen House" 10-11; *Rafferty* "Will to Live" 11-7; **1978** *Switch* "Formula for Murder" 8-20; *Barnaby Jones* "Memory of a Nightmare" 12-14; **1979** *Mrs. Columbo* "Caviar with Everything" 3-22; **1980** *Barnaby Jones* "Run to Death" 1-3; **1981** *Hart to Hart* "A Couple of Harts" 10-13; *CHiPs* "Concourse d'Elegance" 12-13; **1982** *Cassie and Company* "Gorky's Army" 2-19; *Magnum, P.I.* "Mixed Doubles" 12-2.

TELEFILMS

1977 *The Possessed* 5-1 NBC; **1978** *More Than Friends* 10-20 ABC; **1982** *Take Your Best Shot* 10-12 CBS; *Don't Go to Sleep* 12-10 ABC.

Stuart Nisbit

(born 1934)

A veteran of over 150 television shows, Stuart got his acting start onstage in 1952. He began guest work on television in 1961 and worked in all types of roles, typically townsmen or professionals. He was a member of Jack Webb's stock company, appearing in 7 episodes of *Dragnet* and *Adam-12*.

Stuart appeared in a number of significant films:

The Quick and the Dead, The Graduate, In the Heat of the Night, The Sting, Thunderbolt and Lightfoot, Earthquake, The Eiger Sanction, Midway and *Smokey and the Bandit.*

GUEST CREDITS

1961 *Bonanza* "The Dream Riders" 5-20; *Ben Casey* "To the Pure" 10-2; **1962** *Checkmate* "Remembrance of Crimes Past" 2-28; *Virginian* "It Tolls for Thee" 11-21; **1963** *Twilight Zone* "In Praise of Pip" 9-27; **1964** *Ben Casey* "A Thousand Word Are Mute" 11-9; **1965** *Fugitive* "Landscape with Running Figures" 11-16; **1966** *Laredo* "That's Noway, Thataway" 1-20; *Laredo* "A Very Small Assignment" 3-17; *Dr. Kildare* "Travel a Crooked Road" 3-22; *Man from UNCLE* "The Round Table Affair" 3-25; *Fugitive* "The 2130" 3-29; *Dr. Kildare* "Something Old, Something New" 5-16; *Road West* "Pariah" 12-5; **1967** *Fugitive* "Run the Man Down" 1-3; *Man from UNCLE* "The When in Rome Affair" 3-7; *Dragnet* "The Big Hit-and-Run Driver" 4-6; *Invaders* "The Condemned" 5-9; *Judd, for the Defense* "The Other Face of the Law" 9-22; *Ironside* "Dead Man's Tale" 9-28; *Mission: Impossible* "The Council" 11-19, 11-26; *Dragnet* "The Big Magazine" 12-7; *Iron Horse* "Wild Track" 12-16; *Virginian* "A Small Taste of Justice" 12-20; **1968** *Dragnet* "The Big Amateur Cop" 1-25; *Dragnet* "The Big Gambler" 3-21; *Dragnet* "Homicide-DR-06" 10-24; **1969**

Dragnet "Juvenile-DR-32" 3-27; *Dragnet* "Juvenile-DR-35" 4-3; **1970** *Bonanza* "It's a Small World" 1-4; *Bonanza* "Danger Road" 1-11; *Bonanza* "The Night Virginia City Died" 9-13; **1971** *Mannix* "Round Trip to Nowhere" 1-2; *Name of the Game* "L.A.-2017" 1-15; *Bonanza* "Winterkill" 3-28; **1972** *Columbo* "Short Fuse" 1-19; *Adam-12* "The Late Baby" 9-20; *Night Gallery* "Spectre in Tap Shoes" 10-29; *Night Gallery* "You Can Come Up Now, Mrs. Milliken" 11-12; **1973** *McMillan and Wife* "The Fine Art of Staying Alive" 3-11; *Columbo* "The Most Dangerous Match" 4-4; **1974** *Adam-12* "The Sweet Smell" 1-9; *Barnaby Jones* "The Challenge" 9-24; *Rockford Files* "This Case Is Closed" 10-18; *Police Story* "Glamour Boy" 10-29; **1975** *Manhunter* "Man in a Cage" 1-22; *McCloud* "Sharks" 2-23; *Lucas Tanner* episode 3-12; *Barnaby Jones* "The Price of Terror" 10-10; *Mobile One* "The Crusader" 11-3; **1976** *City of Angels* "The Bloodshot Eye" 5-11; **1977** *McMillan and Wife* "Dark Surprise" 1-2; *Most Wanted* "The Death Dealer" 8-12; **1980** *Quincy, M.E.* "Diplomatic Immunity" 1-17; **1981** *Quincy, M.E.* "Scream to the Skies" 2-11; **1983** *Hardcastle and McCormick* "Goin' Nowhere Fast" 10-9.

Arnie and *The Bob Crane Show*. In 1976 she became a part of the quality cast of *Executive Suite*.

After a couple of miniseries (*Rhinemann Exchange* and *Testimony of Two Men*), and several guest roles, she earned her second series regular slot, on *Strike Force* (1981-82).

TELEFILMS

1969 *The Whole World is Watching* 3-11 ABC; *The Silent Gun* 12-16 ABC; **1971** *Marriage: Year One* 10-15 NBC; **1972** *The Judge and Jake Wyler* 12-2 NBC; **1973** *Outrage!* 11-28 ABC; **1974** *Heatwave!* 1-26 ABC; *It's Good to Be Alive* 2-22 CBS; **1975** *The Missing Are Deadly* 1-8 ABC; *Medical Story* 9-4 NBC; **1976** *Brink's: The Great Robbery* 3-26 NBC; **1977** *Black Market Baby* 10-7 ABC; **1979** *The Night Rider* 5-11 ABC; *High Midnight* 11-27 CBS.

GUEST CREDITS

1975 *Columbo* "Playback" 3-2; **1977** *McMillan* "Have You Heard About Vanessa?" 4-24; **1978** *James at 16* episode 2-9; **1979** *Rockford Files* "Never Send a Boy King to Do a Man's Job" 3-3; *Mrs. Columbo* "Caviar with Everything" 3-22; *Eischied* "Do They Really Need to Die?" 11-9; *Buck Rogers* "Cruise Ship to the Stars" 12-27; **1980** *Buck Rogers* "A Blast for Buck" 1-17; *Stone* "But Can She Type?" 1-21; **1982** *Hart to Hart* "In the Hart of the Night" 11-30; *Casablanca* "Why Am I Killing?" 4-10; *T. J. Hooker* "Carnal Express" 10-3; *Matt Houston* "Butterfly" 11-18.

Tricia Noble

(born February 3, 1946, Sydney, Australia)

A beautiful and shapely Australian actress, Tricia made her film debut in 1965. She first appeared on television in 1972 in a guest role on *The Courtship of Eddie's Father*. She also did guest shots on sitcoms like *The Mary Tyler Moore Show*,

TELEFILMS

1975 *One of Our Own* 5-5 NBC; **1978** *The Courage and the Passion* 5-27 NBC; **1979** *The Wild Wild West Revisited* 5-9 CBS.

Kathleen "Kathy" Nolan
(born September 27, 1933, St. Louis, Missouri)

Best known on television as the pretty young wife of Richard Crenna on *The Real McCoys* (1957-62), Kathleen first came to television in 1953 and immediately gained a regular role on a sitcom called *Jaimie* (1953-54). Her role on *The Real McCoys* was the highlight of her career, but she also had a co-starring role on *Broadside* (1964-65). All of her work thereafter was in guest roles.

She became President of The Screen Actors' Guild in 1975, and was reelected in 1977.

GUEST CREDITS

1962 *Gunsmoke* "Call Me Dodie" 9-22; *Saints and Sinners* "The Man on the Rim" 10-1; *Alfred Hitchcock Hour* 11-1; **1963** *Untouchables* "Blues for a Gone Goose" 1-29; *Lloyd Bridges Show* "The Rising of the Moon" 2-19; *Ben Casey* "Who Killed Cynthia Royal?" 12-13; **1964** *Gunsmoke* "Comanches Is Safe" 3-7; *Alfred Hitchcock Hour* "Beast in View" 3-20; *Breaking Point* "Confounding Her Astronomers" 4-6; **1966** *Big Valley* "Into the Widow's Web" 3-22; **1967** *Custer* "The Breakout" 11-1; **1971** *Name of the Game* "Seek and Destroy" 2-5; **1973** *Bold Ones: The Doctors* "And Other Things I May Not See" 5-4; *Gunsmoke* "Susan Was Evil"

12-3; **1974** *Kolckak: The Night Stalker* "Vampire" 10-4; **1976** *Bionic Woman* "Sister Jaimie" 11-24; **1977** *Rockford Files* "New Life, Old Dragons" 2-25; **1979** *Charlie's Angels* "Angels on Skies" 2-7; **1981** *Quincy, M.E.* "Sugar and Spice" 4-1; *Incredible Hulk* "Two Godmothers" 10-9; **1982** *Magnum, P.I.* "Double Jeopardy" 2-25.

TELEFILMS

1981 *Jacqueline Susann's "Valley of the Dolls"* 1-19, 1-20 CBS.

Maidie Norman
(born 1912)

Maidie had her screen debut in 1948 and began working in television during the fifties. She did numerous sixties/seventies guest shots and was a regular on the soap *Days of Our Lives*. Her lengthy acting career extended well into the eighties.

GUEST CREDITS

1960 *Alfred Hitchcock Presents* "Mrs. Bixby and the Colonel's Cat" 9-27; **1962** *Perry Mason* "The Case of the Mystified Miner" 2-24; **1963** *Wide Country* "Speckle Bird" 1-31; *Ben Casey* "Allie" 10-

2; **1967** *Ironside* "Backfire" 11-2; *Dragnet* "The Big Dog" 11-23; **1968** *Dragnet* "The Big Problem" 3-28; **1970** *Storefront Lawyers* episode 10-28; *Mannix* "The World Between" 11-7; **1971** *Mannix* "The Glass Trap" 11-3; **1973** *Adam-12* "Capture" 11-14; *Griff* "Hammerlock" 12-15; *Love Story* "A Glow of Dying Embers" 12-26; **1974** *Marcus Welby, M.D.* "Each Day a Miracle" 1-22; *Streets of San Francisco* "Jacob's boy" 10-24; **1975** *Kolchak: The Night Stalker* "Mr. Ring" 1-20; *Harry O* "Shades" 10-2; **1976** *Bronk* "Death with Honor" 3-21; *Baretta* "Can't Win for Losin'" 12-15; **1977** *Little House on the Prairie* "The Wisdom of Solomon" 3-7; **1979** *Barnaby Jones* "Girl on the Road" 10-25; **1981** *White Shadow* episode 2-2.

TELEFILMS

1972 *Say Goodbye Maggie Cole* 9-27 ABC; **1973** *A Dream for Christmas* 12-14 ABC; **1981** *Thornwell* 1-21 CBS; **1982** *Bare Essence* 10-4, 10-5 CBS; **1983** *Secrets of a Mother and Daughter* 10-4 CBS.

Phillip Ober

(born 1902, Ft. Payne, Alabama; died September 13, 1982)

A Broadway stage actor for 20 years before he came to Hollywood in 1950, Phillip went on to appear in numerous films like *The Magnificent Yankee, Come Back, Little Sheba, From Here to Eternity, Ten North Frederick, Torpedo Run, Elmer Gantry, The Ugly American* and *The Ghost and Mr. Chicken.*

Married for a time to actress Vivian Vance, Phillip was active on television from 1954 to 1965. In 1965-66 he became a regular on *I Dream of Jeannie.* Thereafter, he entered the U. S. Diplomatic Service, becoming a consolar agent in Puerto Vallarta, Mexico for the balance of his life.

GUEST CREDITS

1960 *Man and the Challenge* "Early Warning" 5-28; **1961** *Perry Mason* "The Case of the Fickle Fortune" 1-21; *Checkmate* "Juan Moreno's Body" 11-18; *Investigators* "The Dead End Man" 12-28; *Perry Mason* "The Case of the Roving River" 12-31; **1962** *Alfred Hitchcock Presents* "Burglar Proof" 2-27; *Thriller* "Till Death Do Us Part" 3-12; *General Electric Theater* "Hercule Poirot" 4-1; *Alfred Hitchcock Hour* "I Saw the Whole Thing" 10-11; **1963** *Sam Benedict* "Run Softly, Oh Softly" 1-26; *Temple Houston* episode 11-28; **1964** *Eleventh Hour* "You're So Smart, Why Can't You Be Good?" 1-22; *Twilight Zone* "Spur of the Moment" 2-21; *Perry Mason* "the Case of the Tandem Target" 5-14; **1965** *Iron Horse* "Broken Gun" 10-17; *Honey West* "The Princess and the Paupers" 10-29.

Joan O'Brien

A pretty blonde actress of the early sixties, Joan got her television start as a singer on *The Bob Crosby Show* (1953-57). She also appeared on *The Liberace Show* during 1958.

GUEST CREDITS

1959 *Bat Masterson* "Bullet from Broken Arrow" 1-21; *M Squad* "The Takeover" 2-7; *Bat Masterson* "Shakedown at St. Joe" 10-29; **1960**

Perry Mason "The Case of the Singing Skirt" 3-12; *Alaskans* "Kangaroo Court" 5-8; *Deputy* "Meet Sergeant Tasker" 10-1; *Islanders* "The Terrified Blonde" 10-16; *Bat Masterson* "High Card Loses" 11-10; *Wagon Train* "The Candy O'Hara Story" 12-7; **1961** *Cheyenne* "Incident at Dawson Flats" 1-9; *Adventures in Paradise* "Wild Mangoes" 5-8; *Whispering Smith* "The Idol" 9-18; *Surfside 6* "Jonathan Wembley Is Missing" 11-13; **1962** *Tall Man* "The Impatient Brides" 2-3; *Follow the Sun* "Annie Beeler's Place" 2-11; *Bus Stop* "The Ordeal of Kevin McBride" 2-25; *Rawhide* "The Pitchwagon" 3-2; **1964** *Lieutenant* "Man with an Edge" 3-21.

Soon Teck Oh

(born 1943, Korea)

Without question, Soon Teck Oh played more Oriental roles than any actor on television during the 1965-1990 period, and he did them extremely well. He made his television debut in 1966, and did the first of a handful of films in 1967.

He appeared in 6 *Hawaii Five-O* episodes, plus the 1968 pilot, did 4 *M*A*S*H* episodes and appeared on *Magnum, P.I.* 5 times. His busy guest schedule continued from the mid eighties in episodes of *The Fall Guy, Matt Houston* (2), *Airwolf* (3), *T. J. Hooker* (2), *Hill Street Blues* (2), *Dynasty* and *McGyver*. The quality of his work will rank him among the finest Oriental-American actors of the TV generation.

GUEST CREDITS

1969 *Hawaii Five-0* "Face of the Dragon" 1-22; *Hawaii Five-0* "Sweet Terror" 11-5; *It Takes a Thief* "Payoff in the Piazza" 11-13; **1971** *Ironside* "Joss Sticks and Wedding Bells" 10-26; *Hawaii Five-0* "Wednesday, Ladies Free" 12-14; **1972** *Hawaii Five-O* "The Clock Struck Twelve" 10-10; **1973** *Kung Fu* "Sun and Cloud Shadow" 2-22; **1974** *Magician* "The Illusion of the Lost Dragon" 2-18; **1977** *Black Sheep Squadron* "Poor Little Lambs" 2-2; *Logan's Run* "Crypt" 11-7; *Black Sheep Squadron* "Divine Wind" 12-14; **1978** *Hawaii Five-0* "The Silk Trap" 2-9; **1979** *Hawaii Five-0* "Image of Fear" 11-8; **1980** *Charlie's Angels* "Angels of the Deep" 12-7; **1981** *Charlie's Angels* "Waikiki Angels" 1-4; *Trapper John, M.D.* "The Albatross" 5-10; *Magnum, P.I.* "Memories Are Forever" 11-5; **1982** *Cassie and Company* "There Went the Bride" 7-20; **1982** *Tales of the Gold*

Monkey "Honor Thy Brother" 11-24; *Quincy, M.E.* "Sword of Honor, Blade of Death" 12-15; **1983** *Greatest American Hero* "30 Seconds Over Little Tokyo" 2-3; *Magnum, P.I.* "Birds of a Feather" 3-17; *Hart to Hart* "Year of the Dog" 12-13.

TELEFILMS

1968 *Hawaii Five-0* 9-20 CBS; **1971** *The Reluctant Heroes* 11-23 ABC; **1974** *Epicac* 5-1 NBC; *Judge Dee and the Monastery Murders* 12-29 ABC; **1979** *Stunt Seven* 5-30 CBS; *The Return of Charlie Chan* 7-17 ABC; **1982** *The Letter* 5-3 ABC; **1983** *Girls of the White Orchid* 11-28 NBC.

Jenny O'Hara
(born Febraury 24, Sonoma, Calif.)

A busy television actress, from 1975, Jenny has been featured as a series regular on three sitcoms. She appeared on *The Facts of Life* (1979), *Highcliff Manor* (1979) and *My Sister Sam* (1986-88).

Jenny also appear on a prime-time soap, *Secrets of Midland Heights*, in 1980-81. Later eighties guest work included episodes of *Trapper John, M.D., St. Elsewhere, Scarecrow and Mrs. King* and *Murphy Brown*.

GUEST CREDITS

1975 *Wide World of Mystery* "Rock-a-Die Baby" 3-21; *Streets of San Francisco* "Dead Air" 11-13; *Rockford Files* "The Reincarnation of Angie" 12-5; **1976** *Barnaby Jones* "The Lonely Victims" 1-8; *Charlie's Angels* "Hellride" 9-22; *Barnaby Jones* "Final Reunion" 11-11; *Police Story* "The Jar" 12-14, 12-21; **1977** *Westside Medical* "King Solomon's Kid" 4-7; *Tales of the Unexpected* "You're Not Alone" 8-17; *Kojak* "Laid Out" 10-16; *Barnaby Jones* "The Devil's Handmaiden" 12-1; **1979** *Barnaby Jones* "Echo of a Distant Battle" 1-11; *CHiPs* "The Matchmakers" 1-27; **1980** *Family* "Smarts" 6-18; **1981** *CHiPs* "New Guy in Town" 3-15; *Simon and Simon* "Trapadoors" 12-8; *McClain's Law* "Let the Victims Beware" 12-11; **1982** *Bret Maverick* "The Mayflower Women's Historical Society" 2-2; *Quincy, M.E.* "Deadly Protection" 5-5; **1983** *Remington Steele* "Steele in the News" 3-4; *Mississippi* episode 10-11.

TELEFILMS

1976 *Brink's: The Great Robbery* 3-26 NBC; *Return of the World's Greatest Detective* 6-16 NBC; **1977** *Good Against Evil* 5-22 NBC; *The Hunted Lady* 11-28 NBC; **1978** *A Fire in the Sky* 11-26 NBC; **1979** *Letters from Frank* 11-22 CBS; **1980** *Blinded by the Light* 12-16 CBS; **1983** *Another Woman's Child* 1-19 CBS.

Susan Oliver
(born Charlotte Gercke, Febrary 13, 1937, New York City; died May 10, 1990)

Few actresses have attained an equal amount of fame outside the acting realm, but Susan Oliver came close. During the sixties, her skill as an aviator nearly eclipsed her remarkable performing career.

Born in New York City, Susan's father, George Gercke, was with the U. S. Information Agency. She grew up in Tokyo and attended International College there. Susan was musically talented, playing both guitar and piano. She enrolled in, and graduated from, Neighborhood Playhouse School of Theater in New York City, and Swarthmore College.

She made a stage debut in Jose Quintero's Circle in the Square Theatre, in *La Ronde*. She came to television in a 1955 *Goodyear Playhouse* production, and began to make an impact on the medium in shows like *Kaiser Aluminum Hour, U.S. Steel Hour, Matinee Theater, Wagon Train, Climax* and *Kraft Theatre*.

During the period chronicled in this book, 1959-83, Susan was one of Hollywood's busiest guest actresses , in all manner of dramatic series roles, and found time to appear in sitcoms like *The Andy Griffith Show, Gomer Pyle, U.S.M.C.* and *Love, American Style*.

She frequently played vulnerable young women, with her large and clear blue eyes conveying this quality in large measure. In real-life, Susan was anything but vulnerable, being fiercely independent in an era long before Women's Lib. She became an accomplished flyer, and had a close call in a 1966 crash in Santa Paula, California.

The following year she flew a single engine Aero Commander 200 across the Atlantic Ocean from New York to Denmark, winning the "Pilot of the Year Award" from the Association of Executive Pilots. She also won the Powder Puff Derby in 1967. She planned to fly from New York to Moscow, and would have been the first woman to fly into the U.S.S.R. Regretably, she was denied permission to do so. In 1983 Susan wrote a book about her flying experiences, called *Odyssey*.

In later years, Susan wound down her acting in favor of directing; she had directorial credits on hit series like *M*A*S*H* and *Trapper John, M.D.* In 1975-76 she was a member of the cast on the soap *Days of Our Lives*. During the later eighties she guested on *Magnum, P.I., Murder, She Wrote* (2), *Spenser: For Hire, Simon and Simon* and *Our House*.

Susan's remarkable life ended on May 10, 1990, when she succumbed to cancer.

GUEST CREDITS

1959 *Playhouse 90* "A Trip to Paradise" 3-26; *Millionaire* "Millionaire Phillip Burnell" 10-7;

Lineup "Run to the City" 11-11; *Alcoa Theater* "The Long House on Avenue A" 12-14; **1960** *Bonanza* "The Outcast" 1-9; *Playhouse 90* "A Dream of Treason" 1-21; *June Allyson Show* "The Blue Goose" 3-21; *Twilight Zone* "People Are Alike All Over" 3-25; *Wanted: Dead or Alive* "The Pariah" 3-26; *Wagon Train* "The Maggie Hamilton Story" 4-6; *Adventures in Paradise* "Whip Fight" 5-9; *Wrangler* "Incident at Bar M" 8-4; *Deputy* "The Deadly Breed" 9-24; *Wagon Train* "The Cathy Eckhardt Story" 11-9; *Zane Grey Theater* "Knife of Hate" 12-8; *Barbara Stanwyck Theater* "No One" 12-26; **1961** *Thriller* "Choose a Victim" 1-24; *Untouchables* "The Organization" 1-26; *Michael Shayne* "The Heiress" 2-3; *Aquanauts* "The Storm Adventure" 2-8; *Rawhide* "Incident of His Brother's Keeper" 3-31; *Americans* "The Gun" 4-3; *Naked City* "A Memory of Crying" 4-12; *Zane Grey Theater* "Image of a Drawn Sword" 5-11; *Adventure in Paradise* "Hill of Ghosts" 5-15; *Checkmate* "The Thrill Seeker" 5-27; *Route 66* "Welcome to Amnity" 6-9; *Dick Powell Show* "Somebody's Waiting" 11-7; *Breck Golden Showcase* "The Picture of Dorian Gray" 12-6; **1962** *Laramie* "Shadows in the Dusk" 1-16; *Cain's Hun-*

dred "The Cost of Living" 3-20; *Checkmate* "So Beats My Plastic Heart" 4-11; *Route 66* "Between Hello and Goodbye" 5-11; *Alfred Hitchcock Hour* "Annabel" 11-1; **1963** *Rawhide* "Incident at Spider Rock" 1-18; *Wagon Train* "The Lily Legend Story" 2-13; *Dick Powell Show* "Thunder in a Forgotten Town" 3-5; *Route 66* "Fifty Miles from Home" 3-22; *77 Sunset Strip* "Your Fortune for Penny" 5-31; *Nurses* "No Score" 9-26; *Fugitive* "Never Wave Goodbye" 10-8, 10-15; *Dr. Kildare* "The Eleventh Commandment" 11-14; *Burke's Law* "Who Killed the Kind Doctor?" 11-29; **1964** *Defenders* "The Hidden Fury" 3-28; *Destry* "One Hundred Bibles" 5-8; **1965** *Rogues* "Money Is for Burning" 1-3; *Ben Casey* "Pas de Deux" 1-18; *Man from UNCLE* "The Bow-Wow Affair" 2-15; *Virginian* "A Little Learning" 9-29; *The FBI* "Courage of a Conviction" 11-7; *Dr. Kildare* "Perfect Is Hard to Be" 12-27; *Dr. Kildare* "Duet for One Hand" 12-28; **1966** *Man Called Shenandoah* "Rope's End" 1-17; *I Spy* "One Thousand Fine" 4-27; *Star Trek* "Menagerie" 11-17, 11-24; **1967** *Tarzan* "The Day the Earth Trembled" 1-13; *Invaders* "The Ivy Curtain" 3-21; *T.H.E. Cat* "Twenty-One and Out" 3-24; *Wild Wild West* "The Night Dr. Loveless Died" 9-29; *Virginian* "A Small Taste of Justice" 12-20; **1968** *Invaders* "Inquisition" 3-26; *Virginian* "The Storm Gate" 11-13; *Name of the Game* "The White Birch" 11-29; *Outsider* "The Land of the Fox" 12-18; **1969** *Big Valley* "Alias Nellie Hanley" 2-24; *Mannix* "The Odds Against Donald Jordan" 3-1; **1970** *Men from Shiloh* "Hannah" 12-30; **1971** *Name of the Game* "Seek and Destroy" 2-5; *Dan August* "Prognosis: Homicide" 4-1; *Alias Smith and Jones* "Journey from San Juan" 4-8; *The D. A.* "The People vs. Whitehead" 12-17; *Longstreet* "The Long Way Home" 12-30; **1972** *Sarge* "An Accident Waiting to Happen" 1-4; *Night Gallery* "The Tune in Dan's Café" 1-5; *Gunsmoke* "Eleven Dollars" 10-30; **1973** *Cannon* "Moving Target" 1-31; *Circle of Fear* "Spare Parts" 2-23; *Medical Center* "Visions of Doom" 4-18; *The FBI* "Fatal Reunion" 11-4; *Magician* "Ovation for Murder" 11-6; **1974** *Barnaby Jones* "Friends Till Death" 2-17; *Wide World of Mystery* "Death in Space" 6-17; *Petrocelli* "Edge of Evil" 10-2; **1975** *Manhunter* "Death Watch" 2-12; **1977** *Streets of San Francisco* "Hang Tough" 2-17; **1980** *Dallas* "Fourth

Son" 12-12; **1981** *Dallas* "End of the Road" 1-16, 1-23.

TELEFILMS

1970 *Carter's Army* 1-27 ABC; **1971** *Do You Take This Stranger?* 1-18 NBC; **1976** *Amelia Earhart* 10-25 NBC; **1982** *Tomorrow's Child* 3-22 ABC.

Tricia O'Neil

(born 1945)

Tricia made her film debut in 1972, but quickly found her niche in television. She became a regular on a 1974-75 daytime serial called *How to Survive a Marriage*. She worked often from 1975 through 1983, in guest roles and several telefilms.

After 1983 Tricia made guest appearances on *The A-Team*, *Murder, She Wrote* (3), *Airwolf*, *Riptide*, *Scarecrow and Mrs. King*, *Blacke's Magic*, *MacGyver*, *Hunter* and *Simon and Simon*.

GUEST CREDITS

1976 *Ellery Queen* "The Adventure of the Wary Witness" 1-25; *Serpico* "The Indian" 10-8; **1977** *Delvecchio* "A Madness Within" 2-20, 2-27; **1978**

Columbo "How to Dial a Murder" 4-15; *Eddie Capra Mysteries* "Who Killed Lloyd Wesley Gordon?" 9-29; *Hawaii Five-0* "The Bark and the Bite" 9-28; **1979** *Hawaii Five-0* "Labyrinth" 12-25; **1981** *Fall Guy* "Charlie" 10-6; **1982** *Hart to Hart* "The Harts Strike Out" 5-4; *Powers of Matthew Star* "Mother" 11-26; *Voyagers* "Old Hickory and the Pirate" 11-28; **1983** *Simon and Simon* "It's Only a Game" 2-3; *A-Team* "Black Day at Bad Rock" 2-22; *Mississippi* episode 9-27; *Fall Guy* "The Last Drive" 10-26; *Whiz Kids* "Deadly Access" 10-26; *Hardcastle and McCormick* "Once Again with Vigorish" 10-30.

TELEFILMS

1977 *Charlie Cobb: Nice Night for a Hanging* 6-9 NBC; *Mary Jane Harper Cried Last Night* 10-5 CBS; **1978** *Are You in the House Alone?* 9-20 CBS; **1979** *The Kid from Left Field* 9-30 NBC; **1980** *Brave New World* 3-7 NBC; **1981** *Jacqueline Susann's "Valley of the Dolls"* 10-19, 10-20 CBS.

Dick O'Neill

(born August 29, 1928)

In films from 1958, Dick didn't appear on television until 1974. He had two TV series regular roles during the seventies: *Rosetti and Ryan* (1977) and *Kaz* (1978-79).

During 1983-87 he became a semi-regular on *Cagney and Lacey*, appearing as Cagney's alcoholic father. He also had regular roles on two very abbreviated sitcoms, *Empire* (1984) and *Better Days* (1986). He did later eighties guesting on *Simon and Simon* and *Murder, She Wrote*.

Dick appeared in guest roles on a number of sitcoms throughout the seventies and eighties: *Barney Miller* (2), *M*A*S*H* (3), *Rhoda, Three's Company, One Day at a Time* (2), *Diff'rent Strokes, Cheers* and *Growing Pains*.

GUEST CREDITS

1974 *Get Christie Love!* "Pawn Ticket for Murder" 10-2; **1975** *Kojak* "Two-Four-Six for Two

Hundred" 2-23; *The Law* "Prior Consent" 3-26; **1976** *Bronk* "Jailbreak" 2-15; *Baretta* "Death on the Run" 3-17; **1979** *CHiPs* "Drive, Lady, Drive" 11-10; **1981** *Shannon* "Gotham Swan Song" 11-11; **1982** *Cagney and Lacey* "Pop Used to Work Chinatown" 4-1; *Trapper John, M.D.* "John's Other Life" 5-2; **1983** *Magnum, P.I.* "I Do?" 2-17; *St. Elsewhere* "Monday, Tuesday, Sven's Day" 2-22; *St. Elsewhere* "Remission" 3-1; *Rousters* "Finder's Keepers" 10-22.

TELEFILMS

1975 *Hustling* 2-22 ABC; *The UFO Incident* 10-20 NBC; **1976** *The Entertainer* 3-10 NBC; *Woman of the Year* 7-28 CBS; **1977** *Rosetti and Ryan: Men Who Love Women* 5-19 NBC; *It Happened One Christmas* 12-11 ABC; **1978** *Perfect Gentlemen* 3-14 CBS; **1980** *Comeback Kid* 4-11 ABC.

Alan Oppenheimer

(born April 23, 1930, New York City)

Alan began a stage career in 1954, coming to television in 1964. He worked for a decade in guest roles on TV prior to his best-known roles as the bionic scientist, Dr. Rudy Wells, on *The Six Million Dollar Man* (1974-75). He was also a regular on an abbreviated sitcom called *Big Eddie*(1975) and on

Eischied (1979-80).

An excellent voice artist, Alan did cartoon voices for *Inch High Private Eye, Valley of the Dinosaurs, Mighty Mouse, Flash Gordon, The Smurfs, Tarzan: Lord of the Jungle* and *The Tom and Jerry/Grapeape/Mumbly Show*.

GUEST CREDITS

1964 *Defenders* "Mind Over Murder" 5-16; **1966** *I Spy* "A Gift from Alexander" 10-12; *Felony Squad* "Flame Out" 10-17; **1968** *Mod Squad* "Twinkle, Twinkle Little Starlet" 12-17; **1969** *Outsider* "A Bowl of Cherie" 1-29; *Lancer* "The Great Humbug" 3-4; *Ironside* "Stolen on Demand" 12-25; **1970** *High Chaparral* "The Badge" 12-18; **1971** *Bonanza* "Customs of the Country" 2-6; *Mannix* "A Gathering of Ghosts" 2-6; *McCloud* "Encounter with Aries" 10-21; *Mod Squad* "Feet of Clay" 12-14; **1972** *Marcus Welby, M.D.* "Unto the Next Generation" 12-5; **1973** *Chase* "One for You, Two for Me" 10-9; **1974** *Petrocelli* "An Act of Love" 11-13; **1975** *Mannix* "A Ransom for Yesterday" 2-9; *Medical Center* "The Fourth Center-the Fourth Sex" 9-8, 9-15; *S.W.A.T.* "Silent Night, Deadly Night" 12-13; **1976** *Gemini Man* "Smithereens" 9-23; **1979** *Vegas* "Touch of Death" 3-14; **1980** *Lou Grant* "Libel" 12-8; **1982** *Hart to Hart* "Blue and Broken-Harted" 2-23; *Knight Rider* "Deadly Maneuvers" 10-1; **1983** *St.*

Elsewhere episode 3-22; *Hotel* "Blackout" 9-28.

TELEFILMS

1973 *What Are Best Friends For?* 12-18 ABC; **1974** *Death Sentence* 10-2 ABC; **1976** *Helter Skelter* 4-1, 4-2 CBS; **1977** *Tail Gunner Joe* 2-6 NBC; **1978** *The Ghost of Flight 401* 2-18 NBC; **1982** *Divorce Wars* 3-1 ABC; **1983** *Memorial Day* 11-27 CBS.

Felice Orlandi

(born 1925)

Felice made a film debut in 1955, typecast almost immediately as mob figures and criminals in the majority of his movies, which included *Never Love a Stranger, Bullitt*, and *They Shoot Horses, Don't They?* His television roles followed the same sort of casting, and seventies crime series utilized him often.

GUEST CREDITS

1963 *Naked City* "Howard Running Bear Is a Turtle" 4-3; **1968** *Gunsmoke* "The Jackals" 2-12; **1970** *Mission: Impossible* "The Crane" 3-8; *The FBI* "Antennae of Death" 11-29; **1971** *Storefront Lawyers* "Hostage" 2-24; *Mission: Impossible* "The Tram"

10-2; *Sarge* "Silent Target" 11-9; **1972** *Cade's County* "Blackout" 3-26; *Streets of San Francisco* "Timelock" 11-11; **1973** *McMillan and Wife* "The Fine Art of Staying Alive" 3-11; **1974** *Barnaby Jones* "Programmed for Killing" 1-27; *Mannix* "Trap for a Pigeon" 3-24; *Hawaii Five-0* "A Hawaiian Nightmare" 9-17; *Petrocelli* "A Life for a Life" 10-9; **1975** *Streets of San Francisco* "Labyrinth" 2-27; *Police Story* "Company Man" 12-19; **1977** *Bionic Woman* "The Over-the-Hill Spy" 12-17; **1983** *Powers of Matthew Star* episode 2-25.

Burly Gregg Palmer (right) listens to Don Gordon in this scene from a 1956 film called *Revolt at Fort Laramie* (United Artists Corporation). Palmer appeared in countless western films and TV western series guest appearances.

TELEFILMS

1973 *Honor Thy Father* 3-1 CBS; **1974** *The Girl on the Late, Late Show* 4-1 NBC; **1980** *Fugitive Family* 10-1 CBS.

Gregg Palmer (a.k.a. Palmer Lee)

(born January 25, 1927, San Francisco, Calif.)

Rugged Gregg Palmer was featured in numerous western and adventure films from his screen debut in 1951. His television roles were of the same genres; he was one of *Gunsmoke's* favorite guest stars, with 15 episode credits over a 12 year period. He continued to work into the eighties in the 1982 miniseries, *The Blue and the Gray.*

Gregg had a featured role on the 1966-67 sitcom *Run, Buddy, Run.*

GUEST CREDITS

1959 *Have Gun-Will Travel* "The Misguided Father" 2-27; *Have Gun-Will Travel* "The Fight at Adobe Wells" 3-12; *Tales of Wells Fargo* "The Warrior's Return" 9-21; **1960** *Gunsmoke* "Big Tom" 1-9; *Millionaire* "Millionaire Jessica Marsh" 3-16; *Deputy* "Trail of Darkness" 6-4; *Surfside 6* "High Tide" 10-10; *Lawman* "Old Stefano" 12-25; **1961** *Tall Man* "A Gun Is for Killing" 1-14; *Wyatt Earp* "Doc Holliday Faces Death" 1-17; *Wyatt Earp* "The Law Must Be Fair" 5-2; *Wyatt Earp* "Gunfight at O. K. Corral" 6-20; *Tales of Wells Fargo* "Death Rattle" 10-21; **1962** *77 Sunset Strip* "Framework for a Badge" 6-1; *Laramie* "The Long Road Back" 10-23; *Gunsmoke* "Phoebe Strunk" 11-10; *Have Gun-Will Travel* "Trial at Table Rock" 12-15; **1963** *Gunsmoke* "Blind Man's Bluff" 2-23; *Laramie* "Badge of Glory" 5-7; *Gunsmoke* "the Odyssey of Jubal Tanner" 5-18; **1964** *Bonanza* "Return to Honor" 3-22; **1965** *Gunsmoke* "Eliab's Alm" 2-27; *Run for*

Your Life "Never Pick Up a Stranger" 10-11; *Gunsmoke* "The Bounty Hunter" 10-30; *Laredo* "The Golden Trail" 11-4; *Gunsmoke* "The Pretender" 11-20; *Gunsmoke* "South Wind" 11-27; *Branded* "$10,000 for Durango" 11-28; *Wild Wild West* "The Night of the Human Trigger" 12-3; **1966** *Legend of Jesse James* "A Real Rough Town" 1-24; *Gunsmoke* "Which Dr." 3-19; **1967** *Tarzan* "Cap'n Jai" 1-20; *Cimarron Strip* "Journey to a Hanging" 9-7; *Cimarron Strip* "The Deputy" 12-21; **1968** *Gunsmoke* "The Victim" 1-1; *Tarzan* "Trek to Terror" 2-2; *Mission: Impossible* "The Town" 2-18; *Gunsmoke* "The Hide Cutters" 9-30; *Star Trek* "The Spectre of the Gun" 10-25; *Wild Wild West* "The Night of the Gruesome Games" 10-25; *Gunsmoke* "Abelia" 11-18; **1970** *Gunsmoke* "The Cage" 3-23; *Gunsmoke* "Sergeant Holly" 12-14; **1971** *Cannon* "Scream of Silence" 10-12; **1972** *Gunsmoke* "Alias Festus Haggin" 3-6; **1977** *Quincy, M.E.* "A Good Smack in the Mouth" 4-15.

TELEFILMS

1971 *Mongo's Back In Town* 12-10 CBS; **1976** *The New Daughters of Joshua Cabe* 5-29 ABC; **1978** *Go West, Young Girl!* 4-27 ABC; *True Grit* 5-19 ABC; **1979** *Beggarman Thief* 11-26, 11-27 NBC.

Lew Palter

During the 1968-85 period, character actor Lew Palter was seen in a number of smallish television guest roles. He is a well known theatre director in the Los Angeles area.

GUEST CREDITS

1968 *It Takes a Thief* "A Very Warm Reception" 2-6; *Gunsmoke* "Lyle's Kid" 9-23; **1969** *Mission: Impossible* "The Numbers Game" 10-5; **1970** *High Chaparral* "Mi Casa, Su Casa" 2-20; **1971** *McCloud* "The Disposal Man" 12-29; **1972** *The FBI* "A Game of Chess" 11-5; **1973** *McCloud* "Showdown at the End of the World" 1-7; **1974** *Ironside* "For the Love of God" 1-3; *Griff* "Fugitive from Fear" 1-5; *Columbo* "Publish or Perish" 1-13; *Kojak* "Before

the Devil Knows" 2-27; *Six Million Dollar Man* "Eyewitness to Murder" 3-8; **1975** *McMillan and Wife* "Love, Honor and Swindle" 2-16; *Doctor's Hospital* "My Cup Runneth Over" 11-12; **1976** *Bionic Woman* "In This Corner, Jaimie Summers" 9-29; **1977** *McCloud* "The Moscow Connection" 1-23; **1981** *Waltons* "The Revel" 6-4; **1983** *A-Team* "A Small and Deadly War" 2-15.

TELEFILMS

1972 *Lieutenant Schuster's Wife* 10-11 ABC; **1976** *Richie Brockelman: Missing 24 Hours* 10-27 NBC; **1977** *Stonestreet: Who Killed the Centerfold Model?* 1-16 NBC; **1982** *The Rules of Marriage* 5-10, 5-11 CBS.

Lara Parker

(born 1942)

Best remembered as the evil and scheming witch Angelique on *Dark Shadows* (1968-71), Lara subsequently turned to guest appearances throughout the seventies and eighties.

Later eighties guest work included episodes of *Highway to Heaven* and *The Highwayman*. She also did a stint on the soap *Capitol*.

GUEST CREDITS

TELEFILMS

1973 *My Darling Daughters* 11-6 ABC; **1974**
The Chadwick Family 4-17 ABC; **1975** *Adventures
of the Queen* 2-14 CBS; **1977** *The Incredible Hulk*
11-4 CBS; **1980** *Desperate Voyage* 11-29 CBS; **1982**
Rooster 8-19 ABC.

Andrew Parks

(born 1951)
The son of actors Betty Garrett and Larry Parks
(1914-1979), Andrew made his film debut in 1968
while still in his teens. After 3 films he switched to
television, staying busy on seventies crime drama
guest roles, usually playing delinquient teens.

GUEST CREDITS

1972 *The FBI* "The Engineer" 10-29; **1973**
Barnaby Jones "The Murdering Class" 3-4; **1974**
Hawkins "Murder on the Thirteenth Floor"2-5;
Cannon "The Cure That Kills" 2-20; *Rookies*
"Rolling Thunder" 2-25; **1975** *Cannnon* "The
Iceman" 10-1; *Police Woman* "Above and Beyond"
10-31; **1976** *Barnaby Jones* "Dead Heat" 1-1; *Kojak*
"Justice Deferred" 2-15; *Joe Forrester* "Pressure
Point" 3-22; **1978** *Barnaby Jones* "The Scapegoat" 1-

1968 *N.Y.P.D.* "The Love Hustle" 12-31; **1972**
Kung Fu "King of the Mountain" 10-14; **1973** *Medi-
cal Center* "The Guilty" 9-10; *Kojak* "Dark Sunday"
12-12; **1974** *Owen Marshall, Counselor at Law*
"Etude for a Kidnapper" 1-2; *Six Million Dollar
Man* "The Deadly Replay" 11-22; **1975** *Police
Woman* "Sidewinder" 1-17; *Rockford Files* "Sleight
of Hand" 1-17; *Kolchak: The Night Stalker* "The
Trevi Collection" 1-24; *Mobile One* "The Informant"
9-12; **1976** *Switch* "The Case of the Purloined Case"
3-2; *City of Angels* "The House on Orange Grove
Avenue" 3-16; *Kojak* "Out of the Shadows" 10-17;
1977 *Switch* "Eye Witness" 1-23; *Switch* "Go for
Broke" 12-12; **1978** *Hawaii Five-0* "A Big Aloha" 1-
12; *Baretta* "The Stone Conspiracy" 2-23; *Quincy,
M.E.* "Double Death" 3-3; **1979** *Sword of Justice*
"Blackjack" 7-11; **1980** *Barnaby Jones* "The Price of
Anger" 1-10; *Hawaii Five-0* "Bird in Hand" 3-22;
Hagen "Trauma" 4-5; *Galactica 1980* "The Night the
Cyclons Landed" 4-13, 4-20; **1981** *Jessica Novak*
"Man on the Street" 11-26; **1983** *Remington Steele*
"Steele Threads" 12-13.

5; **1979** *Hart to Hart* "With This Gun I Thee Wed" 12-4.

TELEFILMS

1975 *Attack on Terror: The FBI Versus the Ku Klux Klan* 2-20, 2-21 CBS; **1982** *The Kid from Nowhere* 1-4 NBC; *Country Gold* 11-23 CBS.

Michael Pataki

(born January 16, 1938, Youngstown, Ohio)

Michael made his film debut in 1958, in *Ten North Frederick*. He became a frequent guest star on television, especially on crime and sci-fi series. During 1974-75 he tried comedy in a sitcom called *Paul Sand in Friends and Lovers*.

He was a series regular again in 1975's *Get Christie Love!*, and on *The Amazing Spider-Man* (1978-79), in both cases playing police officers. Pataki entered the eighties as a regular on the very abbreviated sitcom, *Phyl and Mikhy*. He continued to do occasional guest work and telefilms well into the eighties.

GUEST CREDITS

1961 *Twilight Zone* "A Quality of Mercy" 12-29; **1967** *Felony Squad* "Breakout" 2-6; *Run for Your Life* "Better World Next Time" 4-17; *Mission: Impossible* "The Psychic" 4-22; *Star Trek* "The Trouble with Tribbles" 12-29; **1968** *Mannix* "The Girl in the Frame" 3-16; **1972** *Cade's County* "The Brothers" 1-23; *Bonanza* "Frenzy" 1-30; *Sixth Sense* "Face of Ice" 4-22; *Rookies* "The Rabbits on the Runway" 12-25; **1973** *Cannon* "To Ride a Tiger" 2-14; *Search* "The Packagers" 4-11; *Columbo* "Etude in Black" 9-17; **1974** *Kung Fu* "The Cenotaph" 4-4, 4-11; *Amy Prentiss* "The Desperate World of Jane Doe" 12-22; **1975** *Invisible Man* "The Fine Art of Diplomacy" 9-15; **1976** *Harry O* "Mr. Five and Dime" 1-8; *Baretta* "The Blood Bond" 2-18; *Ellery Queen* "The Adventure of the Judas Tree" 2-1; *McCloud* "The Day New York Turned Blue" 2-22; **1977** *Nancy Drew Mysteries* "The Mystery of the Solid Gold Kicker" 5-22; *Little House on the*

Prairie "To Run and Hide" 10-31; **1979** *Little House on the Prairie* "The Family Tree" 10-1; *Eischied* "The Dancer" 11-23; *Man Called Sloane* "Architect of Evil" 12-15; **1980** *Charlie's Angels* "Three for the Money" 3-12; **1981** *Nero Wolfe* "Sweet Revenge" 4-28; **1982** *T. J. Hooker* "The Witness" 4-10.

TELEFILMS

1971 *They Call It Murder* 12-17 NBC; **1976** *The Call of the Wild* 5-22 NBC; **1977** *Benny & Barney: Las Vegas Undercover* 1-9 NBC; *Spider-Man* 9-14 CBS; **1978** *Superdome* 1-9 ABC; *Ruby and Oswald* 2-8 CBS; *When Everyday Was the Fourth of July* 3-12 NBC; *Harold Robbins' "The Pirate"* 11-21, 11-22 CBS; **1979** *Samurai* 4-30 ABC; *Survival of Danz* 5-29 CBS; *Marciano* 10-21 ABC; *Disaster on the Coastliner* 10-28 ABC; **1980** *High Noon, Part II-The Return of Will Kane* 11-15 CBS; **1982** *Terror at Alcatraz* 7-4 NBC; **1983** *Cowboy* 4-30 CBS.

Michael Pate

(born 1920, Sydney, Australia)

After starring in Australian-made films from 1941, Michael Pate came to America in 1951, and appeared in *Julius Caesar, Something of Value, Sergeants Three, PT-109, McClintock!, Major Dundee* and *The Singing Nun*. He became a familiar face on television, especially on TV western series.

In 1967 he finished work as a regular on the TV series *Hondo* and moved back to Australia as a producer and writer of films and television series.

GUEST CREDITS

1959 *Rawhide* "Incident of the Power and the Plow" 2-13; *Rifleman* "The Second Witness" 3-3; *Gunsmoke* "Renegade White" 4-11; *Gunsmoke* "Blue Horse" 6-6; **1960** *Rifleman* "The Visitors" 1-26; *Law of the Plainsman* "Common Ground" 2-11; *Islanders* "Operation Dollar Sign" 10-30; *Rawhide* "Incident at Superstition Prairie" 12-2; **1962** *Thriller* "Trio for Terror" 3-14; *Rawhide* "Incident of the Boomerang" 3-24; *Tall Man* "The Legend and the Gun" 4-4; *Roaring 20's* "The Fifth Pin" 4-8; *Acapulco* "Blood Money" 4-10; *Rifleman* "The Mescalera Curse" 4-18; *Have Gun-Will Travel* "The Race" 10-28; *Frontier Circus* "The Shaggy Kings" 12-7; **1962** *Laramie* "Day of the Savage" 3-13; *77 Sunset Strip* "The Pet Shop Caper" 4-6; *Perry Mason* "The Case of the Skeleton's Closet" 5-5; **1963** *Virginian* "Man of Violence" 12-25; **1964** *Alfred Hitchcock Hour* "The McGregor Affair" 11-23; *Voyage to the Bottom of the Sea* "Long Live the King" 12-21; **1965** *Alfred Hitchcock Hour* "Thou Still Unravished Bride" 3-22; *Voyage to the Bottom of the Sea* "The Traitor" 4-19; **1966** *Man from UNCLE* "The Foreign Legion Affair" 2-18; *Time Tunnel* "The Last Patrol" 10-7; *Wild Wild West* "The Night of the

Infernal Machine" 12-23; **1967** *Time Tunnel* "The Walls of Jerico" 1-27; *Tarzan* "Tiger, Tiger" 9-15; *Mission: Impossible* "Trek" 9-17; **1968** *Voyage to the Bottom of the Sea* "Flaming Ice" 3-3.

TELEFILM

1967 *Return of the Gunfighter* 1-29 ABC.

Lee Paul

(born 1939)

A huge 6 foot 5 inch 230 pounder, Lee Paul began a stage career in 1960, moving to films and television in 1969. Among his films were *Ben, The Sting* and *Island at the Top of the World*. His hulking appearance made him an ideal villain in TV crime dramas.

GUEST CREDITS

1969 *Hawaii Five-0* "Not That Much Different" 3-5; **1971** *Mission: Impossible* "The Invasion" 11-13; **1972** *Hawaii Five-0* "Skinhead" 1-25; *Ironside* "Bubble, Bubble, Toil and Murder" 2-3; *Mission: Impossible* "The Deal" 9-30; **1973** *Hec Ramsey* "The Mystery of Chalk Hill" 2-18; *Cannon* "Memo from a Dead Man" 9-19; *Kung Fu* "The Chalice" 10-11; **1974** *Mannix* "Game Plan" 9-29; **1975** *Police Woman*

"Nothing Left to Lose" 2-14; *Police Woman* "The Purge" 11-25; **1976** *Bronk* "Jackson Blue" 1-25; **1977** *Police Woman* "Shark" 2-15; **1979** *Quincy, M.E.* "A Small Cirle of Friends" 1-18; **1981** *Nero Wolfe* "To Catch a Dead Man" 2-20.

TELEFILMS

1974 *Scream of the Wolf* 1-16 ABC; *Get Christie Love!* L-22 ABC; *The Underground Man* 5-6 NBC; **1975** *Target Risk* 1-6 NBC; *Force Five* 3-28 CBS; **1979** *The Golden Gate Murders* 10-3 CBS; **1980** *Kenny Rogers as the Gambler* 4-8 CBS; *The Children of An Lac* 10-9 CBS; **1983** *Kenny Rogers as the Gambler: The Adventure Continues* 11-28, 11-29 CBS.

Morgan Paull

(born 1944)

Morgan made his film debut in 1964's *Ensign Pulver*, and eventually appeared in *Patton, Twilight's Last Gleaming, Norma Rae, Fade to Black* and *Blade Runner*. His credited television work occured between 1973 and 1980.

GUEST CREDITS

1973 *Ironside* "All About Andrea" 2-22; *Emergency* episode 3-10; **1974** *Gunsmoke* "A Family of Killers" 1-14; *Petrocelli* "Edge of Evil" 10-2; **1975** *Gunsmoke* "The Squaw" 1-6; *Cannon* "The Investigator" 2-26; *Waltons* "The Emergence" 11-6; *Blue Knight* "Two to Make Deadly" 12-17; **1976** *Bronk* "Death with Honor" 3-21; *McCloud* "The Moscow Connection" 1-23; *Fantastic Journey* "Dream of Conquest" 3-10; **1978** *Black Sheep Squadron* "Ten'll Get You Five" 1-18; *Kaz* "Kaz and the Kid" 12-17; **1979** *Quincy, M.E.* "Walk Softly Through the Night" 2-1; **1980** *Beyond Westworld* "Westworld Destroyed" 3-5.

TELEFILMS

1972 *Fireball Forward* 3-5 ABC; **1975** *Stowaway to the Moon* 1-10 CBS; *The Kansas City Massacre* 9-19 ABC; **1976** *Kiss Me, Kill Me* 5-8 ABC; **1979** *Stunt Seven* 5-30 CBS; **1980** *Belle Starr*.

E.J. Peaker

(born Edra Jeanne Peaker, 1942)

E. J. began a television career in 1964, with several sitcom guest appearances (*Occasional Wife, Flying Nun, Good Morning World*) preceding a sitcom regular slot on *That's Life* (1968-69). In 1969 she made the first of 7 appearances on *Love, American Style*; that show gave her cheerful and bouncy style a good platform and she is probably best remembered for those scintillating roles. The balance of the seventies were given over to guest appearances on detective and sci-fi series.

She virtually disappeared from television by the mid-eighties, with only a 1987 *CBS Schoolbreak Special* credit.

GUEST CREDITS

1964 *Route 66* "Is It True There Are Pixies at the Bottom of Landfair Lake?" 1-10; **1971** *Night Gallery* "A Matter of Semantics" 11-10; *Cade's County* "Requiem for Miss Madrid" 12-12; **1972** *Banyon* "The Clay Clarinet" 10-27; **1974** *Police*

Woman "Requiem for Bored Housewives" 11-29; **1975** *Get Christie Love!* "My Son, the Murderer" 2-12; *Rockford Files* "Just By Accident" 2-28; **1976** *Barnaby Jones* "The Lonely Victims" 1-8; *Movin' On* "Living It Up" 2-3; *Most Wanted* "The Two Dollar Kidnappers" 11-6; *Streets of San Francisco* "In Case of Madness" 12-23; **1977** *Quincy, M.E.* "Sullied Be Thy Name" 5-6; *Six Million Dollar Man* "Danny's Inferno" 11-23; **1978** *Wonder Woman* "Screaming Javelin" 1-20; *Charlie's Angels* "Winning Is for Losers" 10-18; **1981** *Greatest American Hero* "Reseda Rose" 4-15.

TELEFILMS

1969 *Three's A Crowd* 12-2 ABC; **1972** *Getting Away from It All* 1-18 ABC.

Ed Peck

Stern-faced Ed Peck has been in television since his featured role in the 1951-52 adventure series, *Major Dell Conway of the Flying Tigers.* His guest appearances lessened during the seventies, but he was a regular on two abbreviated sitcoms: *The Super* (1972) and *Semi-Tough* (1980). His smooth but gruff voice lent itself to a recurring role on *Happy Days*, appearing as Officer Kirk.

GUEST CREDITS

1961 *Have Gun-Will Travel* "The Gospel Singers" 10-21; *General Electric Theater* "Call to Danger" 12-10; **1962** *Dakotas* "Crisis at High Bank" 2-11; *Alcoa Premiere* "The Boy Who Wasn't Wanted" 6-5; *Gunsmoke* "Quint Asper Comes Home" 9-29; *Lloyd Bridges Show* "Little Boy, Big Bridge" 11-27; **1963** *Redigo* "Papa San" 11-12; **1964** *Gunsmoke* "Old Man" 10-10; *Daniel Boone* "Mountain of the Dead" 12-17; **1965** *The FBI* "Image in a Crooked Mirror" 9-26; *Loner* "The Kingdom of McComb" 10-9; *Convoy* "Admiral Do-Right" 11-5; *Long Hot Summer* "The Desperate Innocent" 11-11; *Wild Wild West* "The Night of the Double-Edged Knife" 11-12; **1966** *Combat* "Ask Me No Questions" 2-8; *Loner* "Pick Me Another Time to Die" 2-26; **1967** *Star Trek* "Tomorrow Is Yesterday" 1-26; *Invaders* "Labyrinth" 11-21; **1969** *High Chaparral* "No Irish Need Apply" 1-17; *Outcasts* "Hung for a Lamb" 3-10; **1970** *Land of the Giants* "Doomsday" 2-15; *Bracken's World* "A Preview in Samarkand" 10-16; **1971** *McCloud* "Top of the World, Ma?" 11-3; *O'Hara, U. S. Treasury* "Operation: Hijack" 11-26; **1975** *Police Story* "The Cutting Edge" 9-16; *Cannon* "The Wrong Medicine" 9-24; **1977** *Police Story* "The Six Foot Stretch" 3-22; *Rosetti and Ryan* "The Ten-Second Client" 10-13.

TELEFILMS

1971 *O'Hara, U. S. Treasury-Operation: Cobra* 4-2 CBS; *Thief* 10-9 ABC; **1972** *Jigsaw* 3-26 ABC; **1974** *Roll, Freddy, Roll* 12-17 ABC; **1975** *The Big Ripoff* 3-11 NBC; **1980** *Swan Song* 2-8 ABC.

Larry Pennell

(born 1928)

To fans of *The Beverly Hillbillies*, Larry Pennell will forever be Jethoe's "screenstar idol" Dash Riprock; that hilarous recurring role lasted from 1965 to 1969. He is also remembered for a co-starring role in the syndicated series *Ripcord* (1961-62).

Larry debuted in films during 1955 in *Seven Angry Men* and began receiving television roles in the late fifties. Rugged appearing, he did numerous western and adventure series guest roles.

He made a cameo appearance in a 1993 TV reunion of *The Beverly Hillbillies*.

GUEST CREDITS

1959 *Millionaire* "Millionaire Larry Maxwell" 3-2; *Have Gun-Will Travel* "Commanche" 5-16; **1960** *Alaskans* "Kangaroo Court" 5-8; *Aquanauts* episode 9-14; *Klondike* "Sure Thing, Men" 11-28; **1961** *Outlaws* "The Daltons Must Die" 1-26, 2-2; *Thriller* "Last Date" 4-4; **1964** *Outer Limits* "The Mutant" 3-16; *Mr. Broadway* "Bad Little Rich Girl" 12-5; **1965** *Kraft Suspense Theatre* "The Green Felt Jungle" 4-1; *Branded* "I Killed Jason McCord" 10-3; **1966** *Blue Light* "Sacrifice" 2-23; **1967** *Big Valley* "Price of Victory" 2-13; *Custer* "To the Death" 9-27; *Cimarron Strip* episode 12-21; **1968** *Gunsmoke* "Mr. Sam'l" 2-26; *Dragnet* "Police Commission-DR-13" 10-17; **1969** *Land of the Giants* "Six Hours to Live" 9-28; *Mannix* "Return to Summer Grove" 10-11; **1970** *Mission: Impossible* "Homecoming" 10-10; **1971** *Mannix* "Round Trip to Nowhere" 1-2; *O'Hara, U. S. Treasury* "Operation: Spread" 11-5; *McMillan and Wife* "Death Is a Seven Point Spread" 12-8; **1972** *O"Hara, U. S. Treasury* "Operation: Good Citizen" 3-3; **1973** *Streets of San Francisco* "A Wrongful Death" 9-13; *Banacek* "No Stone Unturned" 10-3; **1974** *Owen Marshall, Counselor at Law* "A Foreigner Among Us" 2-2; *Gunsmoke* "Trail of Bloodshed" 3-4; *Rookies* "An Ugly Way to Die" 9-9; *McMillan and Wife* "Buried Alive" 11-10; **1977** *Little House on the Prairie* "Gold Country" 4-4.

TELEFILMS

1971 *City Beneath the Sea* 1-25 NBC; **1976** *Helter Skelter* 4-1, 4-2 CBS; **1979** *Elvis* 2-11 ABC; **1980** *Marilyn: The Untold Story* 9-28 ABC; **1983** *The Night the Bridge Fell Down* 2-28 NBC.

Joseph Perry

(born 1931)

Tough-guy roles were frequent for rugged and gruff Joe Perry, but he displayed his versatility in a two year stint as a regular on the 1969-71 *Bill Cosby Show*. Joe came to television in 1956 and worked steadily though the seventies.

GUEST CREDITS

1959 *Richard Diamond* episode 3-8; *Wanted: Dead or Alive* "The Conquerers" 5-2; *Have Gun-Will Travel* "The Black Handkerchief" 11-14; **1960**

Killing in the Family" 11-6; *Waltons* "The Marathon" 11-7; **1976** *Police Story* "Spanish Class" 1-2; *Kojak* "Deadly Innocence" 2-8; *Most Wanted* "The Slaver" 10-23; *Serpico* "The Serbian Connection" 12-24; **1977** *Police Woman* "Do You Still Beat Your Wife" 10-25; **1978** *Quincy, M.E.* "The Heart of the Matter" 3-3; *Police Story* "A Chance to Live" 5-28; **1979** *Rockford Files* "The Man Who Saw Alligators" 2-10; *Quincy, M.E.* "An Ounce of Prevention" 3-22.

TELEFILMS

1971 *Travis Logan, D. A.* 3-11 CBS; **1972** *Fireball Forward* 3-5 ABC; **1973** *Shirts/Skins* 10-9 ABC; **1974** *Heatwave!* L-26 ABC; **1974** *Panic on the 5:22* 11-20 ABC.

Deputy "Queen Bea" 2-20; *Twilight Zone* "Nightmare As a Child" 4-29; *Law of the Plainsman* "Trojan Horse" 5-5; *Gunsmoke* "The Deserter" 6-4; **1961** *Follow the Sun* "Journey into Darkness" 10-8; *Untouchables* "Jigsaw" 11-21; *87ᵗʰ Precinct* "The Heckler" 12-18; **1962** *Twilight Zone* "The Gift" 4-27; *Ben Casey* "Preferably the Less-Used Arm" 4-30; **1963** *Gunsmoke* "The Cousin" 2-2; *Rawhide* "Incident of the Geisha" 12-19; **1964** *Ben Casey* "The Wild Waltzing World" 12-14; **1965** *Fugitive* "Fun and Games and Party Favors" 1-26; *Fugitive* "Wings of an Angel" 9-14; **1966** *Fugitive* "Not with a Whimper" 1-4; *The FBI* "Special Delivery" 1-23; *Felony Squad* "Flame-Out" 10-27; **1967** *Iron Horse* "Execution" 3-13; *Invaders* "Panic" 4-11; **1968** *Wild Wild West* "The Night of the Undead" 2-2; *Daniel Boone* episode 2-29; *Lancer* "Foley" 10-15; **1969** *Lancer* "The Great Humbug" 3-4; **1970** *Lancer* "The Buscaderos" 3-17; **1971** *Room 222* "The Last Full Moon"2-10; *Sarge* "Silent Target" 11-9; *Mannix* "Cat's Paw" 12-8; *Bold Ones: The Lawyers* "Justice Is a Sometimes Thing" 12-12; **1972** *The FBI* "Escape to Nowhere" 3-19; *Owen Marshall, Counselor at Law* "The Trouble with Ralph" 10-19; *Streets of San Francisco* "Tower Beyond Tragedy" 10-28; *Banyon* "Dead End" 11-3; *Magician* "The Man Who Lost Himself" 12-11; **1973** *Rookies* "Sound of Silence" 12-17; *Griff* "Isolate and Destroy" 12-22; **1974** *Police Story* "Fathers and Sons" 10-1; *Rookies* "Judgment" 10-28; *Cannon* "A

Eugene Peterson

Entering television in 1970, Eugene Peterson has a recurring role on *Medical Center* from 1970 to 1975. His distinguished-looking silver hair often created castings as professionals or crooked businessmen. He was a frequent guest star on *Barnaby Jones* with 5 appearances.

His film career, from 1973, included roles in *Breezy, MacArthur* and the 1981 remake of *The Postman Always Rings Twice.*

GUEST CREDITS

1970 *Medical Center* "The Combatants" 3-18; *Medical Center* "Undercurrent" 9-23; **1971** *Medical Center* "The Albatross" 11-3; **1972** *Mannix* "Portrait of a Hero" 10-15; *The FBI* "Dark Christmas" 12-24; **1973** *Cannon* "Come Watch Me Die" 10-24; **1974** *Barnaby Jones* "Conspiracy of Terror" 10-1; **1975** *Caribe* "School for Killers" 4-7; *Cannon* "The Wrong Medicine" 9-24; *Barnaby Jones* "Double Vengeance" 10-17; *Medical Center* "Two Against Death" 11-17; *Rockford Files* "The Reincarnation of Angie" 12-5; **1976** *Bronk* "The Deadlier Sex" 1-18; *Barnaby Jones* "Deadly Reunion" 2-12; *City of Angels* "The Castle of Dreams" 4-20; *Bionic Woman* "Kill Oscar" 10-27, 11-3; **1977** *Kingston: Confidential* "Eight Columns Across the Top" 3-30; *Most Wanted* "The Driver" 3-14; *Rockford Files* "Hotel of Fear" 10-2; **1978** *Barnaby Jones* "The Picture Pirates" 12-21; **1980** *Barnaby Jones* "Run to Death" 1-3; **1981** *Greatest American Hero* "The Best Desk Scenario" 5-13; **1982** *Greatest American Hero* "There's Just No Accounting…" 3-24.

TELEFILMS

1970 *She's Dressed to Kill* 12-10 NBC; **1973** *Crime Club* 3-6 CBS; **1974** *The Law* 10-22 NBC; **1978** *The Critical List* 9-11, 9-12 NBC; **1980** *Mother and Daughter: The Loving War* 1-25 ABC.

Jo Ann Pflug

(born May 2, 1940, Atlanta, Georgia)

Three significant things happened in Jo Ann's career during 1966: she made a television debut on *The Tonight Show*, made a film debut in *Cyborg* and had her first TV guest role, on *The Beverly Hillbillies*. From 1967, her voice was used for three seasons as "The Invisible Girl" on a Saturday morning cartoon show called *The Fantastic Four*. Her best-remembered film role came in 1970 when she played Lt. Dish on *M*A*S*H*.

In 1972 Jo Ann married TV game show host Chuck Woolery. She worked steadily during the

seventies, in telefilms and guest shots, and became co-host of *Candid Camera* in 1976, with Allen Funt. Jo Ann was a member of the *Operation Petticoat* cast in it's last season, 1978-79.

Following several Love Boat guest shots she had a featured role on *The Fall Guy* during 1981-82, appearing as "Big Jack". One more series regular role remained, on the daytime soap, *Rituals* (1989). Mid-eighties guest appearances included *The Love Boat, Knight Rider* and *Matt Houston* and *The New Love American Style*.

GUEST CREDITS

1967 *Big Valley* "Down Shadow Street" 1-23; **1970** *Bracken's World* "One, Two, Three…Cry" 3-27; **1972** *Search* "Moonrock" 10-4; *Banyon* "Time to Kill" 11-10; *McCloud* "The Barefoot Stewardess Caper" 12-3; **1973** *Alias Smith and Jones* "Only Three to a Bed" 1-13; *Delphi Bureau* "The Self-Destruct Caper" 12-3; **1975** *Adam-12* "Dana Hall" 4-29; **1977** *Quincy, M.E.* "Snake Eyes" 2-4; **1978** *Quincy, M.E.* "The Trick of Death" 9-28; **1979** *Quincy, M.E.* "A Small Circle of Friends" 1-18; *Vegas* "Redhanded" 9-19; *Charlie's Angels* "Angels on Campus" 11-28.

TELEFILMS

1969 *They Call It Murder* 3-13 NBC; **1971** *A Step Out of Line* 2-26 CBS; **1973** *The Night Stalker* l-l6 ABC; **1974** *Scream of the Wolf* 5-6 NBC; **1980** *The Day the Women Got Even* 12-4 NBC.

Lee Philips
(born Brooklyn, New York)

Signed to a 20ᵗʰ Century Fox contract, Lee came to the screen in 1957, doing films like *Peyton Place* and *The Hunters*. His handsome good looks helped make him a popular television guest star during the early sixties, but he developed quickly as a director and was rarely seen in front of the camera after 1965. Lee has also been a prolific writer for television.

Among his directorial credits were episodes of *The Andy Griffith Show, The Dick Van Dyke Show, The Waltons, Longstreet, The Rookies* and countless telefilms.

GUEST CREDITS

1960 *One Step Beyond* "Delia" 5-3; *U.S. Steel Hour* "The Girl Who Knew Too Much" 4-20; **1961** *Untouchables* "Augie 'The Banker' Cimino" 2-9; *Alfred Hitchcock Presents* "Deathmate" 4-18; *Target: The Corruptors* "Bite of a Tiger" 11-3; *Follow the Sun* "The Hunters" 11-12; *77 Sunset Strip* "The Deadly Solo" 12-1; **1962** *Surfside 6* "A Piece of

Tommy Minor" 3-19; *Defenders* "Reunion with Death" 4-1; *Alfred Hitchcock Hour* "The Black Curtain" 11-15; **1963** *Twilight Zone* "Passage on the Lady Anne" 5-9; *Outer Limits* "The Galaxy Being" 9-16; *Fugitive* "Never Say Goodbye" 10-8, 10-15; *Route 66* "The Stone Guest" 11-8; **1964** *Route 66* "Who In His Right Mind Needs a Nice Girl?" 2-7; *Dr. Kildare* "The Child Between" 3-4; *Twilight Zone* "Queen of the Nile" 3-6; **1965** *Perry Mason* "The Case of the Golden Venon" 1-21; *Combat* "A Walk with an Eagle" 3-2; *Perry Mason* "The Case of the Fatal Fortune" 9-19; **1970** *Dan August* "Passing Fair" 12-30.

William Edward "Bill" Phipps
(born 1923)

William Phipps debuted onscreen in 1947, ultimately appearing in over 50 films, mostly westerns, but as varied as *Julius Caesar, War of the Worlds* and *Lust for Life*. His adaptability to the western genre is reflected in his best known TV work (from 1952), in a recurring role on *The Life and Times of Wyatt Earp*, appearing as "Curley Bill" Brocius (1959-61).

Phipps did numerous TV guest roles on TV westerns, or rural series like *The Waltons* (4). He was a regular on *Sara* (1976), *Time Express* (1979) and *Boone* (1983-84).

GUEST CREDITS

1959 *Wanted: Dead or Alive* "The Corner" 2-21; *Gunsmoke* "The Coward" 3-7; *M Squad* "The Crush Out" 4-10; *Wyatt Earp* "Little Gray Home in the West" 5-5; *Rifleman* "The Money Gun" 5-12; *Wanted: Dead or Alive* "Breakout" 9-26; *Gunsmoke* "Odd Man Out" 11-21; *Wyatt Earp* "The Clanton's Family Row" 12-8; **1960** *Wyatt Earp* "Let's Hang Curley Bill" 1-26; *Twilight Zone* "The Purple Testament" 2-12; *Wyatt Earp* "Wyatt's Bitterest Enemy" 6-7; **1961** *Wanted: Dead or Alive* "Triple Vise" 2-27; *Wyatt Earp* "Until Proven Guilty" 4-11; *Wyatt Earp* "The Law Must Be Fair" 5-2; *Wyatt Earp* "Requeim for Old Man Clanton" 5-23; *Wyatt Earp* "Just Before the Battle" 6-13; *Wyatt Earp* "The

Outlaws Cry Murder" 6-27; **1962** *Thriller* "Man of Mystery" 4-2; *Perry Mason* "The Case of the Hateful Hero" 10-18; *Virginian* "Impasse" 11-14; *Gunsmoke* "The Prisoner" 11-16; *Alfred Hitchcock Hour* "Hangover" 12-6; **1963** *Gunsmoke* "Carter Caper" 11-16; **1965** *Ben Casey* "Where Does the Boomerang Go?" 1-11; *Combat* "The Old Men" 12-16; *Laredo* "The Heroes of San Gill" 12-23; **1967** *Wild Wild West* "The Night of the Falcon" 11-10; **1968** *Cimarron Strip* "Knife in the Darkness" 1-25; *Virginian* "The Orchard" 10-2; *Mod Squad* "The Price of Terror" 11-26; **1969** *Mannix* "Missing: Sun and Sky" 12-20; **1975** *Waltons* "The Prophecy" 10-2; *Baretta* "And Down Will Come Baby" 11-19; *Rockford Files* "The Girl in the Bay City Boys' Club" 12-19; **1976** *Police Woman* "The Melting Point of Ice" 1-6; *City of Angels* "The Bloodshot Eye" 5-11; *Rockford Files* "Feeding Frenzy" 10-15; **1977** *Waltons* "John's Crossroads" 1-20; *Oregon Trail* "The Water Hole" 9-28; *Charlie's Angels* "Angels on Horseback" 12-21; *Waltons* "The Celebration" 12-22; **1980** *Waltons* "The Medal" 2-28.

TELEFILMS

1970 *The Intruders* 11-10 NBC; **1976** *Eleanor and Franklin* 1-11, 1-12

ABC; **1977** *The Trial of Lee Harvey Oswald* 9-30, 10-2 ABC; **1980** *Bogie* 3-4 CBS; **1983** *I Want to Live* 5-9 ABC.

Slim Pickens

(born Louis Lindley, June 29, 1919, Kingsburg, Calif.; died December 8, 1983)

Leaving home to join the rodeo circuit at age 12, Louis Lindley was told to expect "slim pickens" economically, and he later adopted that as a stage name. By the late thirties he had become one of rodeo's finest clowns; he continued the dangerous job into the forties, incurring countless injuries.

His drawling voice and lanky appearance made him a natural for western films, and he moved over to acting, making a film debut in 1950. Among his 80 films were roles in *One-Eyed Jacks, Dr. Strangelove* (featured role), *Major Dundee, In Harm's Way, The Flim Flam Man, Will Penny, The Ballad of Cable Hogue, The Apple Dumpling Gang* and *Tom Horn*.

He entered television in 1954 and was particularly effective in TV western series guest roles. Slim was a regular on *The Outlaws* (1961-62), *Custer* (1967), *B. J. and the Bear* (1979) and *Filthy Rich* (1982). He served as co-host of a variety show, *Nashville Palace* in 1981-82 and appeared often on

Hee Haw. A truly unique performer, Pickens contributed richly to television and films.

GUEST CREDITS

1960 *Overland Trail* "Sour Annie" 5-8; *Riverboat* "River Champion" 10-10; *Westerner* "Line Camp" 12-9; *Americans* "On to Richmond" 2-13; **1961** *Surfside 6* "Ghost of a Chance" 3-6; *Americans* "The Escape" 3-13; *Americans* "The Invaders" 3-27; *Alfred Hitchcock Presents* "Final Arrangement" 6-20; **1962** *Route 66* "A Long Piece of Mischief" 1-19; *Tall Man* "The Black Robe" 5-5; *Wide Country* "Tears on a Painted Face" 11-29; *Wagon Train* "The Eve Stanhope Story" 12-5; *Wide Country* "Memory of a Filly" 12-5; **1963** *Wide Country* "Don't Cry for Johnny Devlin" 1-24; *Bonanza* "Half a Rogue" 1-27; *Wide Country* "Speckle Bird" 1-31; *Wide Country* "The Man Who Runs Away" 2-7; *Virginian* "Run Quiet" 11-13; **1964** *Gunsmoke* "Friend" 2-1; *Alfred Hitchcock Hour* "The Jar" 2-14; *Bonanza* "King of the Mountain" 2-23; *Man from UNCLE* "The Iowa Scuba Affair" 9-29; *Fugitive* "Nemesis" 10-4; *Virginian* "Image, Little Man" 10-28; *Rawhide* "The Backshooter" 11-27; **1966** *Gunsmoke* "Sweet Billy, Singer of Songs" 1-15; *Daniel Boone* "The Deserter" 1-20; *Legend of Jesse James* "Wanted: Dead Only" 5-2; *Daniel Boone* "Dan'l Boone Shot a Ba'r" 9-15; **1967** *Run for Your Life* "A Very Small Injustice" 3-13; *Cimarron Strip* "Fool's Gold" 1-11; **1968** *Gunsmoke* "Blood Money" 1-15; *Bonanza* "Catch as Catch Can" 10-27; **1969** *Mannix* "Only Giants Can Play" 1-18; *Ironside* "Goodbye to Yesterday" 9-25; **1970** *Name of the Game* "Little Bear Died Running" 11-6; *Gunsmoke* "The Scavengers" 11-16; **1971** *Alias Smith and Jones* "Exit from Wickenberg" 1-28; *Men from Shiloh* "The Angus Killer" 2-10; *Alias Smith and Jones* "The Day They Hanged Kid Curry" 9-16; **1972** *Gunsmoke* "The River" 9-11, 9-18; *Alias Smith and Jones* "The Strange Fate of Conrad Meyer Zulick" 12-2; **1973** *Hawaii Five-0* "One Big Happy Family" 10-2; **1974** *Kung Fu* "Empty Pages of a Dead Book" 1-10; **1975** *Baretta* "When Dues Come Down" 11-12; **1976** *McMillan and Wife* "Greed" 2-15; **1977** *Switch* "Butterfly Mourning" 2-6; *Baretta* "Big Band Charlie" 3-30; **1978** *Vegas* "Yes, My Darling Daughter" 10-25.

TELEFILMS

1971 *Sam Hill: Who Killed the Mysterious Mr. Foster?* 2-1 NBC; *Desperate Mission* 12-3 ABC; *The Devil and Miss Sarah* 12-4 ABC; **1972** *Rolling Man* 10-4 ABC; **1973** *Hitched* 3-31 NBC; **1974** *Twice in a Lifetime* 3-16 NBC; *The Gun and the Pulpit* 4-3 ABC; **1975** *Babe* 10-23 CBS; **1976** *Banjo Hackett: Roamin' Free* 9-1 NBC; **1979** *The Sacketts* 5-16 NBC; *Undercover with the KKK* 10-23 NBC; **1980** *Swan Song* 2-8 ABC; **1981** *The House Possessed* 2-6 ABC; *Charlie and the Great Balloon Race* 7-12 NBC; *Nashville Grab* 10-18 NBC.

Stack Pierce

Stack made film and television debuts in 1972, but found more work in television with frequent roles throughout the seventies, on crime and sci-fi guest roles. He continued his TV work into the eighties, especially in telefilms.

GUEST CREDITS

1972 *Mission: Impossible* "Hit" 11-11; **1973** *Mannix* "Search in the Dark" 11-25; **1974** *The FBI* "Diamond Run" 3-10; **1975** *Rookies* "The Hunting Ground" 1-20; *Switch* "The Old Diamond Game" 9-

23; *Bronk* "Wheel of Death" 9-28; **1976** *Joe Forrester* "Fire Power" 1-16; *Bronk* "Jackson Blue" 1-25; *Six Million Dollar Man* "The Bionic Badge" 2-22; *Blue Knight* "A Slower Beat" 3-3; **1977** *Bionic Woman* "Doomsday Is Tomorrow" 1-19, 1-26; *Switch* "Butterfly Mourning" 2-6; **1978** *Wonder Woman* "Light-Fingered Lady" 1-6; **1979** *Starsky and Hutch* "Ballad for a Blue Lady" 1-23; *Quincy, M.E.* "Dark Angel" 2-15; *Incredible Hulk* "Brain Child" 10-5; *Quincy, M.E.* "Sweet Land of Liberty" 10-25; *Incredible Hulk* "Prometheus" 11-7, 11-14.

TELEFILMS

1973 *Jarrett* 3-17 NBC; **1974** *The Healers* 5-22 NBC; **1976** *Louis Armstrong-Chicago Style* 1-25 ABC; *Kiss Me, Kill Me* 5-8 ABC; **1979** *Flesh and Blood* 10-14, 10-16 CBS; **1980** *Alcatraz: The Whole Shocking Story* 11-5, 11-6 NBC; **1981** *Charlie and the Great Balloon Race* 7-12 NBC; **1983** *V* 5-1, 5-2 NBC.

Priscilla Pointer

(born May 18, New York City)

Onstage from the late fifties, Priscilla is the mother of actress Amy Irving, and later married noted character actor Robert F. Simon. She began guesting on television in 1970 and appeared periodically through much of the eighties.

Her finest and most visible role was on *Dallas*, as Rebecca Wentworth (1981-83). She was also a semi-regular on *Call to Glory* (1984-85).

GUEST CREDITS

1970 *High Chaparral* "Matter of Vengeance" 11-27; **1971** *McCloud* "Someone's Out to Get Jennie" 11-24; **1974** *Rockford Files* "Profit and Loss" 12-20, 12-27; **1975** *Kojak* "Elegy in an Asphalt Graveyard" 2-2; *Cannon* "Search and Destroy" 4-2; *City of Angels* "The Losers" 4-6; *Kate McShane* "The Best Possible Defense" 9-10; *Cannon* "The Wrong Medicine" 9-24; **1976** *Barnaby Jones* "Deadly Reunion" 2-12; *Harry O* "Hostage" 2-19; **1978** *Quincy, M.E.* "Dead or Alive" 11-16; **1980**

Stone "Deep Sleeper" 1-14; **1981** *Lou Grant* "Depression" 4-13; **1983** *Quincy, M.E.* "Quincy's Wedding" 2-16, 2-23.

TELEFILMS

1971 *Death Takes a Holiday* 10-23 ABC; *The Failing of Raymond* 11-27 ABC; **1975** *The Big Ripoff* 3-11 NBC; **1976** *The Keegans* 5-3 CBS; **1977** *Eleanor and Franklin: The White House Years* 3-13 ABC; *The 3,000 Mile Chase* 6-16 NBC; *A Killing Affair* 9-21 CBS; *Mary Jane Harper Cried Last Night* 10-5 CBS; **1981** *The Archer—Fugitive from the Empire* 4-12 NBC; **1982** *The Gift of Life* 3-16 CBS; *Mysterious Two* 5-31 NBC.

Laurie Prange

Ash blonde Laurie Prange was primarily a seventies/eighties television actress, her delicate beauty often menaced by the bad guys in crime series guest roles. She had one of her finest and best-acted roles in a 1971 *Gunsmoke* episode, playing a "wild child".

During the mid-eighties she guested on *Hardcastle and McCormick* and *Highway to Heaven*.

GUEST CREDITS

1970 *Name of the Game* "So Long, Baby, and Amen" 9-18; *Medical Center* "Death Grip" 11-4; **1971** *Marcus Welby, M.D.* "The Windfall" 3-23; *Gunsmoke* "The Lost" 9-13; *Man and the City* "A Very Special Gift" 10-6; *Night Gallery* "Brenda" 11-3; **1973** *Waltons* "The Fire" 1-11; **1974** *Chopper One* "Strain of Innocence" 1-24; **1975** *Manhunter* "The Wrong Man" 2-5; *Baretta* "And Down Will Come Baby" 11-19; **1976** *Charlie's Angels* "Consenting Adults" 12-8; **1977** *Hawaii Five-0* "Elegy in a Rain Forest" 1-27; *Switch* "The Four Horsemen" 2-13; *Black Sheep Squadron* "WASP's" 3-1; *Barnaby Jones* "The Inside Man" 5-12; *Incredible Hulk* "A Death in the Family" 11-28; *Barnaby Jones* "Prisoner of Deceit" 12-15; **1979** *How the West Was Won* "The Confederate; **1980** *Incredible Hulk* "Prometheus" 11-7, 11-14; **1982** *McClain's Law* "Sign of the Beast" 1-29; **1982** *Cagney and Lacey* episode 11-22; **1983** *T. J. Hooker* "The Return" 10-1; *Mississippi* episode 10-11.

TELEFILMS

1974 *Trapped Beneath the Sea* 10-22 ABC; **1977** *Ransom for Alice* 6-2 NBC; **1978** *The Dark Secret of Harvest Home* 1-23, 1-24 NBC.

Judson Pratt

(born 1916)

In films from 1955, Judson Pratt began making television guest appearances in 1954, had a series regular role on *Union Pacific* during 1958, and found a continuing demand for his work throughout the sixties/seventies era.

GUEST CREDITS

1959 *Lawless Years* "The Big Grocery Store" 10-8; **1960** *Man from Blackhawk* "Drawing Account" 2-12; *Bourbon Street Beat* "Twice Betrayed" 4-4; *Thriller* "Mark of the Hand" 10-4; *Dan Raven* "Tinge of Red" 12-16; **1961** *Bronco* "Manitoba Manhunt" 4-3; *Americans* "The Sentry" 4-10; *Bonanza* "Thunderhead Swindle" 4-29; *Cain's Hundred* "Crime and Commitment" 9-19; *Adventures in Paradise* "The Assassins" 11-26; **1962** *Rawhide* "The Reunion" 4-6; *Saints and Sinners* "A Servant in the House of My Party" 11-5; *Virginian* "Riff-Raff" 11-7; **1963** *Rawhide* "Incident of the Gallows Tree" 2-22; *Gunsmoke* "Blind Man's Bluff" 2-23; **1964** *Fugitive* "Come Watch Me Die" 1-21; *Daniel Boone* "Family Fluellen" 10-15; **1965** *Slattery's People* "How Impregnable Is a Magic Tower?" 10-1; **1966** *Daniel Boone* "Seminole Territory" 1-13; *Perry Mason* "The Case of the Twice Told Twist" 2-27; **1967** *Iron Horse* "Wild Track" 12-16;

Virginian "A Small Taste of Justice" 12-20; **1969**
Guns of Will Sonnett "One Angry Juror" 3-7; **1971**
O'Hara, U. S. Treasury "Operation: Spread" 11-5;
1972 *Cannon* "Treasure of San Ignaciz" 1-11;
Mission: Impossible "Hit" 11-11; **1973** *Rookies*
"Justice for Jill Danko" 10-22; **1975** *Police Story*
"The Witness" 3-11; **1976** *S.W.A.T.* "Officer Luca,
You're Dead" 4-3; *Charlie's Angels* "The Killing
Kind" 11-3; *Switch* "Maggie's Hero" 12-14; **1977**
Police Story "One of Our Cops Is Crazy" 3-1;
Quincy, M.E. "The Hero Syndrome" 11-18; **1978**
Incredible Hulk "Stop the Presses" 11-24; **1979**
Quincy, M.E. "Even Odds" 1-4.

TELEFILMS

1972 *The Weekend Nun* 12-20 ABC; **1973**
Runaway! 9-29 ABC; **1979** *The Ordeal of Patty
Hearst* 3-4 ABC.

Denver Pyle

(born May 11, 1920, Bethune, Colorad0)

Following World War II service, in which he had
four ships torpedoed from under him, Denver began
a film career in 1947. Among his 80 plus films were
roles in *The Alamo, The Man Who Shot Liberty
Valance, Shenandoah, The Great Race, Bonnie and
Clyde, Five Card Stud* and *Escape to Witch Mountain.*

He made a television debut in 1951 in a *Cisco
Kid* episode, ultimately appearing in over 80 TV
western series episodes, including 8 on *The Life and
Legend of Wyatt Earp* and 12 on *Gunsmoke*. In 1963
he appeared on *The Andy Griffith* Show in the first
of 4 episodes as the patriarch of the hilarious
Darling family. His comedic ability earned him
series regular roles on two sixties sitcoms: *Tammy*
(1965-66) and *The Doris Day Show* (1968-70).

During 1977-78 he narrated and co-starred in
The Life and Times of Grizzly Adams. His best
roles was just ahead, for in 1979 he began a long-
running role as Uncle Jesse on *The Dukes of
Hazzard* (1979-85). In 1986 he reprised his Briscoe
Darling role in a telefilm, *Return to Mayberry*.

GUEST CREDITS

1959 *Have Gun-Will Travel* "The Wager" 1-3;
Wyatt Earp "A Good Man" 1-6; *Gunsmoke* "Mike
Blocker" 2-28; *Bat Masterson* "Marked Deck" 3-11;
Restless Gun "The Pawn" 4-6; *Texan* "No Place to
Stop" 6-1; *Texan* "Sheriff of Boot Hill" 6-8; *Deputy*
"Shadow of the Noose" 10-3; *Rifleman* "Bloodlines"
10-6; *Tales of Wells Fargo* "Double Reverse" 10-19;
Texan "The Telegraph Story" 10-26; *Rifleman* "The
Legacy" 12-8; **1960** *Law of the Plainsman* "The
Matriarch" 2-18; *Texan* "The Guilty and the Inno-
cent" 3-28; *Hotel de Paree* "Sundance and the Long
Trek" 4-22; *Overland Trail* "The Baron Comes
Back" 5-15; *Perry Mason* "The Case of the Ominous
Outcast" 5-21; *Rifleman* "The Hangman" 5-31; *Man
from Blackhawk* "The Man Who Owned Everything"
6-3; *Have Gun-Will Travel* "Ransom" 6-4; *Tall Man*
"Garrett and the Kid" 9-10; *Have Gun-Will Travel*
"The Calf" 10-15; *Gunsmoke* "The Wake" 11-5;
Wyatt Earp "The Perfect Crime" 12-6; *Stagecoach
West* "Three Wise Men" 12-20; **1961** *Maverick*
"Family Pride" 1-8; *Bat Masterson* "End of the
Line" 1-26; *Deputy* "The Example" 3-25; *Checkmate*
"Jungle Castle" 4-1; *Rifleman* "The Clarence Debs
Story" 4-4; *Route 66* "The Newborn" 5-5; *Cheyenne*
"Winchester Quarantine" 9-25; *National Velvet* "The
Tramp" 10-23; *Rifleman* "The Decision" 11-6;

Detectives "Beyond a Reasonable Doubt" 11-17; *Perry Mason* "The Case of the Renegade Referee" 12-9; **1962** *Route 66* "A Long Piece of Mischief" 1-19; *Thriller* "The Hollow Watcher" 2-12; *Ben Casey* "Among Others, a Girl Named Abilene" 4-2; *Empire* "The Day the Empire Stood Still" 9-25; *Cheyenne* "Sweet Sam" 10-8; *Bonanza* "A Hot Day for a Hanging" 10-14; *Gunsmoke* "Us Haggens"12-8; **1963** *Laramie* "Vengeance" 1-8; *Virginian* "Vengeance Is the Spur" 2-27; *Gunsmoke* "Jubal Tanner" 5-18; *Bonanza* "The Boss" 5-19; *Bonanza* "Little Man—Ten Feet Tall" 5-26; *Channing* "Dragon in the Den" 10-23; *Rawhide* "Incident of the Rawhiders" 11-14; **1964** *Dr. Kildare* "A Willing Suspension of Disbelief" 1-9; *Twilight Zone* "Black Leather Jackets" 1-31; *Temple Houston* "The Case for William Gotch" 2-6; *Gunsmoke* "No Hands" 2-8; *Great Adventure* "The Special Courgage of Captain Pratt" 2-14; *Bonanza* "Bullet for a Bride" 2-16; *Lieutenant* "The War Called Peace" 4-11; *Gunsmoke* "The Violators" 10-17; *Mr. Novak* "Johnny Rides the Pony—1, 2, 3" 12-15; **1965** *Gunsmoke* "Deputy Festus" 1-6; *Slattery's People* "Question: What Did You Do Today, Mr. Slattery?" 1-15; **1966** *Gunsmoke* "By Lien" 4-9; *Perry Mason* "The Case of the Final Fade-Out" 5-22; *Gunsmoke* "The Gold Takers" 9-24; **1967** *Gunsmoke* "Mad Dog" 1-4; *High Chaparral* "A Hanging Offense" 11-12; *Hondo* "Hondo and the Hanging Town" 12-8; *Cimarron Strip* "The Last Wolf" 12-14; *Gunsmoke* "Baker's Dozen" 12-25; **1968** *Guns of Will Sonnett* "The Warriors" 3-1; *Bonanza* "The Passing of a King" 10-13; **1972** *Waltons* "The Reunion" 12-14; **1973** *Gunsmoke* "Shadler" 1-15; *Kung Fu* "The Ancient Warrior" 5-3; *Streets of San Francisco* "Winterkill" 12-13; **1974** *Cannon* "Duel in the Desert" 1-16; *New Perry Mason* "The Case of the Violent Valley" 1-20; *Kung Fu* "Cross Ties" 2-21; *Manhunter* "The Baby-Faced Killers" 9-25; **1975** *Family Holvak* "Remembrance of a Guest" 9-28; **1976** *Petrocelli* "Blood Money" 2-11; **1979** *How the West Was Won* "The Enemy" 2-5.

TELEFILMS

1973 *Hitched* 3-31 NBC; **1974** *Sidekicks* 3-21 CBS; *Murder or Mercy?* 4-19 ABC; **1975** *Murder Among Friends* 5-20 NBC.

John S. Ragin
(born May 5, 1929, Irvington, New Jersey)

John obtained a scholarship to Rutgers, then transferred to Carnegie Tech where he earned rave notices as *Hamlet*. A fine Shakespearean actor, John appeared in *The Winter's Tale* and *Macbeth* in the New York Shakespearean Festival, and The American Shakespearean Festival (Stratford, Conn.), in which he appeared in *Anthony and Cleopatra, The Tempest* and *A Midsummer Night's Dream*.

After a discouraging period of little progress, John made army training films for a time. He began an aggressive campaign to break into films or television, landing a lucrative Shell Oil commercial and a role in the film, *I Love You, Alice B. Toklas*. A short lived role as the father on *Sons and Daughters* followed (1974).

A friendship with producer Glen Larson led to

his "career" role as cornoner Dr. Robert J. Aston when Larson created *Quincy, M.E.* (1976-83). Ragin's excellent portrayal as the tough supervisor of the lead character contributed significantly to the success of the series.

GUEST CREDITS

1960 *Alfred Hitchcock Presents* "Insomnia" 5-8; **1966** *Blue Light* "The Last Man" 1-12; *Blue Light* "Sacrifice" 2-23; *Felony Squad* "Flame Out" 10-17; **1967** *Invaders* "The Condemned" 5-9; *Invaders* "The Ransom" 12-12; **1969** *Bold Ones: The Lawyers* "A Game of Chance" 9-21; *Bold Ones: The Doctors* "Crisis" 12-7; **1970** *Mission: Impossible* "Flight" 10-17; *Mission: Impossible* "Hunted" 11-21; **1971** *Night Gallery* "They're Tearing Down Tim Riley's Bar" 1-20; *Bold Ones: The Doctors* "An Absence of Lonliness" 1-24; *Storefront Lawyers* "Hostage" 2-24; *Storefront Lawyers* "The Truth, the Whole Truth—and Anything Else That Works" 3-3; *Storefront Lawyers* "Yesterday Is But a Dream" 3-31; *Bold Ones: The Lawyers* "The Invasion of Kevin Ireland" 9-26; *The FBI* "The Last Job" 9-26; **1972** *Ironside* "Programmed for Panic" 9-28; *Alias Smith and Jones* "Six Strangers at Apache Springs" 10-28; *Cool Million* "The Million-Dollar Misunderstanding" 12-20; *The FBI* "The Edge of Desperation" 12-31; **1973** *Barnaby Jones* "Echo of a Murder" 9-30; **1974** *Magician* "The Stainless Steel Lady" 1-28; *The FBI* "The Animal" 2-17; *Six Million Dollar Man* "Athena One" 3-15; **1975** *Rookies* "Solomon's Dilemna" 1-27; *Switch* "The James Caan Con" 9-9; *Barnaby Jones* "Theatre of Fear" 9-26; **1976** *Harry O* "Book of Changes" 1-15; *Jigsaw John* "Sand Trap" 2-9; *City of Angels* "A Sudden Silence" 4-13.

TELEFILMS

1969 *The Whole World Is Watching* 3-11 NBC; *The Lonely Profession* 10-21 NBC; **1971** *The Forgotten Man* 9-14 ABC; **1974** *Killer Bees* 2-26 ABC; *Senior Year* 3-22 CBS; **1975** *Delancy Street: The Crisis Within* 4-19 NBC; **1977** *The Amazing Howard Hughes* 4-13, 4-14 CBS; **1978** *The Islander* 9-16 CBS.

Gene Raymond
(born Raymond Guion, August 13, 1908, New York City)

The husband of singer and movie star Jeanette McDonald, Gene Raymond was a child stage actor, subsequently making a film debut in 1931. He came to television in 1950 and appeared in fifties productions of *Schlitz Playhouse of Stars* (2), *Matinee Theater* (4), *Lux Video Theater* (2), *Ford Theater* and *Climax* (2). He served as host of *Fireside Theatre* (1953-55), *Hollywood Summer Theatre* (1956) and *TV Reader's Digest* (1956).

Gene then worked in television guest roles until 1975, with time out for a short-lived series regular role in *Paris 7000* (1970).

GUEST CREDITS

1959 *U.S. Steel Hour* "Big Doc's Girl" 11-4; **1960** *Johnny Ringo* "Poster Incident" 1-14; **1961** *Barbara Stanwyck Theater* "Big Career" 2-13; *U.S. Steel Hour* "The Shame of Paula Marsten" 4-19; *U.S. Steel Hour* "The Haven" 6-28; **1962** *Sam Benedict* "Hannigan" 9-15; **1963** *Dick Powell Show* "The Old Man and the City" 4-23; *Defenders* "The Brother Killers" 5-25; *Channing* "Dragon in the Den" 10-23; *Outer Limits* "The Borderland" 12-16; **1964** *Burke's Law* "Who Killed My Girl?" 4-17;

Defenders "The Non-Violent" 6-6; *Reporters* "He Stuck in His Thumb" 10-30; **1965** *Man from UNCLE* "The Secret Sceptor Affair" 2-8; **1966** *Laredo* "The Land Slickers" 10-14; **1967** *Girl from UNCLE* "The Fountain of Youth Affair" 2-7; *Judd, for the Defense* "The Death of a Flower Girl" 11-3; *Hondo* "Hondo and the Sudden Town" 11-17; **1968** *Ironside* "Desperate Encounter" 10-24; **1969** *Bold Ones: The Doctors* "To Save a Life"9-14; *Name of the Game* "High Card" 12-5; *Name of the Game* "The Power" 12-12; **1970** *Interns* "The Price of Life" 10-30; *The FBI* "The Inheritors" 12-27; **1971** *The D. A.* "The People vs. Barrington" 11-12; **1975** *Invisible Man* "Man of Influence" 9-22.

TELEFILM

1964 *The Hanged Man* 11-18 NBC.

Paula Raymond

(born Paula Raymond Wright, November 23, 1921, San Francisco, Calif.)

The daughter of a noted San Francisco attorney, beautiful Paula Raymond trained in ballet at age 8 and also studied voice and piano. She was a law student before moving into little theater.

Paula became a model in Hollywood and was eventually placed under contract to Paramount, making a film debut in 1948.

She came to television in 1949, with early appearances on *Fireside Theater* (3), *Ford Theater* and *Schlitz Playhouse of Stars*. From 1959, until she left television in 1964, Paula was one of Hollywood's busiest guest stars, with *Perry Mason* using her talents in 5 episodes.

GUEST CREDITS

1959 *Perry Mason* "The Case of the Borrowed Brunette" 1-10; *Schlitz Playhouse of Stars* "Practically Strangers" 1-30; *One Step Beyond* "Emergency Only" 2-3; *Rough Riders* "The Double Dealers" 3-19; *Bat Masterson* "A Matter of Honor" 4-29; *Markham* "Vendetta in Venice" 6-27; *Man and the Challenge* "Maximum Capacity" 9-19; *Texan* "Cattle Drive" 9-28; *Hawaiian Eye* "Waikiki Widow" 10-14; *Perry Mason* "The Case of the Garrulous Gambler" 10-17; *77 Sunset Strip* "Clay Pidgeon" 10-23; *General Electric Theater* "Signs of Love" 11-8; *Wyatt Earp* "The Paymaster" 12-1; **1960** *Deputy* "Backfire" 1-2; *Bat Masterson* "Mr. Fourpaws" 2-18; *Bourbon Street Beat* "The House of Ledizon" 2-22; *Cheyenne* "Home Is the Brave" 3-14; *Have Gun-Will Travel* "Lady with a Gun" 4-9; *Tightrope* "Borderline" 5-17; *M Squad* "Open Season" 5-31; *Untouchables* "Mark of Caine" 11-17; *Bat Masterson* "The Last of the Night Riders" 11-24; *Aquanauts* "The Cave Divers" 12-7; **1961** *Hawaiian Eye* "The Manabi Figurine" 2-1; *Michael Shayne* "Four Lethal Ladies" 2-17; *77 Sunset Strip* "A Face in the Window" 2-24; *Law and Mr. Jones* "The Concert" 3-10; *Perry Mason* "The Case of the Torrid Tapestry" 4-22; *Surfside 6* "The Bhoyo and the Blonde" 5-15; *Maverick* "The Golden Fleecing" 10-8; **1962** *Hawaiian Eye* "Year of Grace" 1-24; *New Breed* "The Deadlier Sex" 3-20; *Perry Mason* "The Case of the Angry Astronaut" 4-7; *Rawhide* "House of the Hunter" 4-20; *Hawaiian Eye* "Rx Cricket" 5-2; **1964** *Perry Mason* "The Case of the Capering Camera" 1-16; *Temple Houston* "Miss Katherina" 4-2; *Man from UNCLE* "The Double Affair" 11-17.

John Rayner

(born 1934)

Primarily a stage actor, John's television and film appearances were rather infrequent. He had only two credits on the big screen, *Countdown* (1968) and *Trackdown* (1976).

GUEST CREDITS

1965 *I Spy* "Tatia" 11-17; **1966** *Perry Mason* "The Case of the Fanciful Frail" 3-27; *Big Valley* "The River Monarch" 4-6; **1967** *Bonanza* "Judgment at Red Creek" 2-26; *Invaders* "The Trial" 10-10; **1968** *The FBI* "The Daughter" 1-14; *Adam-12* "Log 111" 12-7; *Adam-12* "Log 122" 12-21; **1970** *Paris 7000* "No Place to Hide" 1-29; *Mission: Impossible* "Gitano" 2-1; **1974** *Chase* "Right to an Attorney" 1-8; *Adam-12* "L. A. International" 3-12; **1975** *Kung Fu* "The Brothers Cain" 3-1; **1976** *Marcus Welby, M.D.* "Vanity Case: Aspects of Love" 4-27, 5-4, 5-11; **1979** *Quincy, M.E.* "Walk Softly Through the Night" 2-1.

TELEFILMS

1973 *The President's Plane Is Missing* 10-23 ABC; **1976** *Kingston: The Power Play* 9-15 NBC.

Marge Redmond

(born 1926, Lakewood, Ohio)

A cheerful redhead, Marge began performing as a stage actress in 1944. She did a good deal of mid sixties guest work and was a regular in two sitcoms of that era: *The Double Life of Henry Phyfe* (1966) and *The Flying Nun* (1967-70).

Marge was married to the late Jack Weston.

GUEST CREDITS

1962 *Ben Casey* "Imagine a Long Bright Corridor" 1-15; **1963** *Twilight Zone* "The Bard" 5-23; **1964** *Fugitive* "When the Bough Breaks" 10-6; **1965** *Dr. Kildare* "Please Let My Baby Live" 1-28; *Slattery's People* "What Time Do We Hang the Good Samaritan?" 2-19; *Perry Mason* "The Case of the Mischevious Doll" 5-13; **1966** *I Spy* "Trial by Treehouse" 10-19; *Bob Hope Chrysler Theater* "The Fatal Mistake" 11-30; **1970** *The FBI* "Escape to Terror" 10-4; **1972** *Sixth Sense* "Coffin, Coffin in the Sky" 9-23; **1974** *Six Million Dollar Man* "Little Orphan Airplane" 2-22; *Streets of San Francisco* "Cry Help" 11-7; **1975** *Lucas Tanner* "Those Who

Cannot, Teach" 1-22; **1976** *McCloud* "The Day New York Turned Blue" 2-22; *Barnaby Jones* "The Stalking Horse" 3-18; **1979** *Rockford Files* "The Battle Ax and the Exploding Cigar" 1-12; **1982** *Quincy, M.E.* "Dying for a Drink" 11-3.

TELEFILM

1973 *A Brand New Life* 2-20 ABC.

Pat Renella

(born 1933)

Pat began his film career in 1961, subsequently appearing in *A Gathering of Eagles* and *Bullitt*. He was a regular on *The Phil Silvers Show* (1963-64), and began receiving TV guest credits in 1967, appearing throughout the seventies. Most of his castings were as various kinds of criminals.

GUEST CREDITS

1967 *Combat* "Gadjo" 1-17; **1970** *Mannix* "Bang, Bang, You're Dead" 11-28; **1972** *Mannix* "Cry Pigeon" 1-26; **1973** *Streets of San Francisco* "No Badge for Benjy" 11-1; *Toma* "The Cain Connection" 11-1; *Cannon* "Arena of Fear" 12-19; **1974**

Mannix "A Question of Murder" 3-10; *Planet of the Apes* "The Gladiators" 9-20; *Ironside* "Set-Up: Danger!" 10-24; *Planet of the Apes* "The Deception" 11-1; **1975** *Mannix* "The Empty Tower" 2-16; *Police Woman* "Above and Beyond" 10-31; *Bronk* "The Fifth Victim" 10-26; **1976** *S.W.A.T.* "Deadly Weapons" 2-21; **1978** *Rockford Files* "Local Man Eaten by Newspaper" 12-8; **1979** *Quincy, M.E.* "No Way to Treat a Flower" 9-20.

TELEFILMS

1974 *The Rockford Files* 3-27 NBC; **1978** *Three on a Date* 2-17 ABC.

Alan Rich

(born 1927)

After lengthy stage experience, Alan made a film debut in 1973, with television guest roles beginning in 1975. He was often cast in authority roles, especially judges, and had numerous eighties guest shots and telefilms.

GUEST CREDITS

1975 *Kojak* "A Question of Answers" 9-14; *Harry O* "Tender Killing Care" 10-30; **1976** *Rockford Files* "The Hammer of 'C' Block" 1-9; *Delvecchio*

"Numbers" 12-5; **1977** *Hawaii Five-0* "Practical Jokes Can Kill You" 5-5; **1978** *Kojak* "Chain of Custody" 1-28; *Little House on the Prairie* "The Inheritance" 2-6; *Baretta* "Just for Laughs" 2-9; **1980** *CHiPs* "Jailbirds" 1-5; *Incredible Hulk* "Sideshow" 1-25; **1981** *Magnum, P.I.* "From Moscow to Maui" 10-29; *Today's FBI* "Hostage" 11-1; *Hill Street Blues* "Fruits of the Poisonous Tree" 12-3; **1982** *Hill Street Blues* "Some Like It Hot-Wired" 3-18; **1983** *Hill Street Blues* "A Hill of Beans" 5-6; *Hardcastle and McCormick* "The Crystal Duck" 10-2.

TELEFILMS

1975 *Strike Force* 4-12 NBC; **1976** *Mallory: Circumstantial Evidence* 2-8 NBC; *Scott Free* 10-13 NBC; **1977** *Tail Gunner Joe* 2-6 NBC; *Terraces* 6-27 NBC; *The Hostage Heart* 9-9 CBS; *A Killing Affair* 9-21 CBS; **1978** *The Millionaire* 12-19 CBS; **1980** *Gideon's Trumpet* 4-30 CBS; **1981** *A Gun in the House* 2-11 CBS; *Chicago Story* 3-15 NBC; *The Archer—Fugitive from the Empire* 4-12 NBC; *The Ordeal of Bill Carney* 12-23 CBS.

Mark Roberts

(born 1921)

Mark appeared in an early television drama, *The Front Page*, during 1949-50, followed a 1951 stint on the soap, *Miss Susan*. During 1953-54 he had a prominent role on the daytime soap, *Three Steps to Heaven*, then in 1956, narrated and appeared in another soap, *A Date with Life*.

He co-starred in a 1960 syndicated detective series, *The Brothers Brannigan*. After scattered guest roles, he returned to his soap roots in *Days of Our Lives* and *General Hospital* (1982).

GUEST CREDITS

1959 *Perry Mason* "The Case of the Fraudelent Photo" 2-7; *77 Sunset Strip* "The Canine Caper" 5-15; *Phillip Marlowe* "Ricochet" 12-19; **1960** *One Step Beyond* "The Forests of the Night" 1-19; **1962** *Follow the Sun* "Run, Clown, Run" 4-1; **1963** *Outer Limits*

"The Hundred Days of the Dragon" 9-23; **1964** *Perry Mason* "The Case of the Nautical Knot" 10-29; **1965** *Perry Mason* "The Case of the Golden Girls" 12-19; **1966** *12 O'Clock High* "Fighter Pilot" 11-11; **1967** *Invaders* "Valley of the Shadow" 9-26; *The FBI* "Counter-Stroke" 10-1; **1968** *The FBI* "Region of Peril" 2-25; **1969** *The FBI* "Boomerang" 10-5; **1971** *Dan August* "Prognosis: Homicide" 4-1; **1973** *Barnaby Jones* "Trial Run for Death" 10-14; **1975** *Barnaby Jones* "Doomed Alibi" 3-11; **1978** *Rockford Files* "Heartaches of a Fool" 9-22.

TELEFILMS

1972 *Welcome Home, Johnny Bristol* 1-30 CBS; **1973** *The Affair* 11-20 ABC; **1974** *Tell Me Where It Hurts* 3-12 CBS; *The FBI Story: The FBI Versus Alvin Karpis, Public Enemy Number One* 11-8 CBS; **1976** *Return to Earth* 5-14 ABC.

Bartlett Robinson

(born 1912, New York City; died March 26, 1986)

A radio star during the thirties, Bartlett was radio's original *Perry Mason*. He later appeared in 5 eposides of television's *Perry Mason*. Robinson was a regular on two sixties sitcoms: *Wendy and Me* (1964-65) and *Mona McClusky* (1965-66).

His film career, which began in 1956, included roles in *Battle Hymn, The Spirit of St. Louis, No Time for Sergeants, I Want to Live!, The Fortune Cookie* and *The Wrecking Crew*.

GUEST CREDITS

1959 *Markham* "The Assailant" 1-23; *Perry Mason* "The Case of the Fraudulent Photo" 2-7; *Gunsmoke* "Doc Quits" 2-21; *Richard Diamond* episode 4-12; *Rifleman* "Outlaw's Inheritance" 6-16; *Lawless Years* "The Kid Dropper Story" 7-7; *Lawless Years* "The Ray Baker Story" 8-6; *Lawless Years* "The Prantere Story" 9-3; *Gunsmoke* "The Horse Deal" 9-29; *Johnny Ringo* "The Accused" 10-15; *Men into Space* "Building a Space Station" 10-21; *Richard Diamond* episode 10-26; *Bonanza* "Vendetta" 12-5; **1960** *Fury* "Gymkhama" 1-23; *Untouchables* "Little Egypt" 2-11; *Alfred Hitchcock Presents* "The Hero" 5-1; **1961** *Wyatt Earp* "Billy Buckett Incorporated" 1-3; *Twilight Zone* "Back There" 1-13; *Thriller* "The Devil's Ticket" 4-18; *Alfred Hitchcock Presents* "Final Arrangement" 6-20; *Follow the Sun* "The Highest Wall" 10-1; *Surfside 6* "Witness for the Defense" 10-23; **1962** *Perry Mason* "The Case of the Mystified Miner" 2-24; *New Breed* "Edge of Violence" 3-27; *G.E. True* "Mile Long Shot to Kill" 11-25; *Perry Mason* "The Case of the Fickle Filly" 12-13; **1963** *Laramie* "The

Fugitive" 2-12; *Dakotas* "Trial at Grand Forks" 3-25; **1964** *Alfred Hitchcock Hour* "The Evil of Adelaide Winters" 2-7; *Perry Mason* "The Case of the Frightened Fisherman" 2-27; *Alfred Hitchcock Hour* "The Ordeal of Mrs. Snow" 4-17; **1965** *Amos Burke, Secret Agent* "Operation Long Shadow" 9-22; *Amos Burke, Secret Agent* "The Man's Men" 12-8; **1966** *Perry Mason* "The Case of the Golfer's Gambit" 1-30; **1967** *Bonanza* "Judgment at Red Creek" 2-26; *Guns of Will Sonnett* "The Natural Way" 9-29; *Virginian* "Ah Sing vs. Wyoming" 10-25; **1969** *Mannix* "Killjoy" 1-25; *Mod Squad* "The Healer" 12-9; **1971** *Cannon* "Salinas Jackpot" 9-14; **1976** *Cannon* "Revenge" 1-21.

TELEFILMS

1969 *Trial Run* 1-18 NBC; **1978** *The New Adventures of Heidi* 12-13 NBC.

Jay Robinson

(born 1930)

Few actors have fallen from the heights of fame to the depths of despair more quickly than Jay Robinson. At age 23 he debuted in *The Robe* and received rave reviews. In 1954 he repeated the part of Caligula, in *Demetrius and the Gladiators*, again

to great reviews and success. However, just four years later his world came crashing down with the discovery of methadone in his home. And on the date of his preliminary hearing on drug charges his father dropped dead of a seizure.

Hollywood turned it's back on him and he wandered for years, broke and doing menial jobs, including cleaning cages at a zoo, fry cook and skid-row rooming house manager. Finally, after doing a long delayed 15 month sentence in California, he began the long road back by doing guest roles in television. He was helped by Bette Davis demanding that he be given a role in the film *Bunny O'Hare*.

The road back has been long and slow but he has been clean and sober from 1960, and has transformed his life with the help of a fine wife. He worked in guest roles on television from 1968, appearing in 5 episodes of *Mannix*. During 1988-89 he had a good role on the soap *Days of Our Lives*.

GUEST CREDITS

1968 *Mannix* "Pressure Point" 10-12; *Wild Wild West* "The Night of the Sedgwick Curse" 10-18; *Star Trek* "Elaan of Troyius" 12-20; **1970** *Mannix* "The Search for Darrell Andrews" 2-28; **1971** *Mannix* "Overkill" 3-13; **1972** *Hawaii Five-0* "Cloth of Gold" 2-8; **1973** *Search* "Ends of the Earth" 3-21; **1974** *Mannix* "Trap for a Pigeon" 3-24; *Planet of the Apes* "Tomorrow's Tide" 10-18; *Mannix* "Picture of a Shadow" 11-24; **1975** *Kolchak: The Night Stalker* "Chopper" 1-31; *Waltons* "The Breakdown" 10-16; *Harry O* "Group Terror" 11-13; **1976** *Waltons* "The House" 2-19; **1979** *Buck Rogers* "Planet of the Amazon Women" 11-8; **1983** *Tales of the Gold Monkey* "Last Chance Louie" 3-11.

TELEFILMS

1973 *She Lives* 9-12 ABC; **1982** *Memories Never Die* 12-15 CBS.

Roger Robinson
(born May 2, 1940, Seattle, Washington)
Roger made his film debut in 1971, with his

television guest roles beginning in 1973. He was a particular favorite on *Kojak*, appearing in 6 episodes. A regular on the 1979 sitcom, *Friends*, Roger continued his career well into the eighties.

GUEST CREDITS

1973 *Kojak* "One for the Morgue" 11-7; *Ironside* "The Last Payment" 12-20; **1974** *Kojak* "Marker for a Dead Bookie" 1-16; *The FBI* "Selkirk's War" 1-27; *Kojak* "A Very Deadly Game" 9-29; *Get Christie Love!* "The Longest Fall" 12-11; *Kojak* "Loser Takes All" 12-22; **1975** *Kojak* "The Nicest Guys on the Block" 11-16; **1976** *Kojak* "Bad Dude" 1-25; *Baretta* "Pay or Die" 1-28; **1977** *Baretta* "Pay or Die" 1-28; *Kingston: Confidential* "The Rage at Hannibal" 6-8; **1978** *Quincy, M.E.* "Death by Good Intention" 10-26; **1981** *Incredible Hulk* "Prometheus" 11-7, 11-14; **1983** *Voyager* "All Fall Down" 3-27.

TELEFILMS

1973 *The Marcus-Nelson Murders* 3-8 CBS; **1974** *This Is the West That Was* 12-17 NBC; **1976** *Mallory: Circumstantial Evidence* 2-8 NBC.

Kasey Rogers

(born Missouri)

Raised in California, Kasey was playing piano at The Hollywood Bowl at age 8, and began acting in school plays at Burbank High School. She became a dancer in *The Earl Carroll Show* and was soon signed by MCA, and was given the lead in the film *Special Agent* (1949). Her film work was done under the name of Laura Elliot and included roles in *Sampson and Delilah, A Place in the Sun, Strangers on a Train, Denver and Rio Grande* and *Jamacia Run*.

She guested on *The Lone Ranger* during the early fifties and estimates that she has made over 500 television appearances. During 1964-66 she was Julie Anderson on *Peyton Place*, ultimately doing 252 episodes of the bi and tri-weekly evening soap.

In 1966 Kasey moved into the Louise Tate role on *Bewitched* and remained with it until the show left the air in 1972. Thereafter, her guest roles were infrequent as she concentrated on raising her four sons and teaching acting.

GUEST CREDITS

1959 *Rough Riders* "Death Sentence" 3-12; *Wanted: Dead or Alive* "Railroaded" 3-14; *Perry Mason* "The Case of the Calendar Girl" 4-18; *Restless Gun* "A Trial for Jenny May" 5-25; *M Squad* "Dangerous Game" 6-5; *Colt .45* "Return to El Paso" 6-21; *Wanted: Dead or Alive* "The Matchmaker" 9-19; **1960** *Colt .45* "Strange Encounter" 4-26; *Perry Mason* "The Case of the Irate Inventor" 5-28; *Bat Masterson* "Dakota Showdown" 11-17; *Wanted: Dead or Alive* "Three for One" 12-21; **1961** *Maverick* "The Devil's Necklace" 4-16, 4-23; **1962** *Thriller* "Kill My Love" 3-26; **1970** *Mission: Impossible* "Flip Side" 9-26; **1971** *Bold Ones: The Doctors* "An Absence of Lonliness" 1-24; **1974** *Lucas Tanner* "Echoes" 11-13; *Marcus Welby, M.D.* "The Last Rip-Off" 11-26.

Gilbert Roland

(born Luis Antonio Damasco Alonso, December 11, 1905, Chihuahua, Mexico; died May 15, 1994)

A leading actor from silent film days (some sources give 1919), Gilbert did over 100 Hollywood films like *Around the World in 80 Days, Cheyenne*

Autumn and *Islands in the Stream*. There were also numerous films made in Mexico. In 1943 he joined The U. S. Air Force.

Roland came to television in 1954 in a *Ford Theater* presentation; other fifties work included *Climax, Playhouse 90, Schlitz Playhouse of Stars* and *Wagon Train*. Although his television appearances were limited, his wonderful talent enhanced those roles. He died of cancer in 1988, survived by his second wife, and two children from an earlier marriage to actress Constance Bennett.

GUEST CREDITS

1959 *Desilu Playhouse* "Border Justice" 11-13; **1962** *Dick Powell Show* "Death in a Village" 1-2; *Frontier Circus* "Quick Shuffle" 2-1; **1963** *Alfred Hitchcock Hour* "Death and the Joyful Woman" 4-12; *Greatest Show on Earth* "Don't Look Down, Don't Look Back" 10-8; *Gunsmoke* "Extradition" 12-7, 12-14; **1964** *Fugitive* "Somebody to Remember" 3-24; **1965** *Combat* "The Convict" 2-16; *Bonanza* "The Lonely Runner" 10-10; **1967** *Fugitive* "Savage Street" 3-14; *Garrison's Gorillas* "The Big Con" 9-5; **1969** *The FBI* "The Patriot" 2-2; **1971** *High Chaparral* "The New Lion of Sonata" 2-19; **1972** *Night Gallery* "The Waiting Room" 1-26; *McCloud* "The New Mexican Connection" 10-1; *Medical Center* episode 11-8; **1973** *Kung Fu* "The Chalice" 10-11; **1974** *Barnaby Jones* "Rendevous with Terror" 2-24; **1980** *Hart to Hart* "The Raid" 2-26.

TELEFILMS

1966 *The Poppy Is Also a Flower* 4-22 ABC; **1973** *Incident on a Dark Street* 1-13 NBC; **1974** *The Mark of Zorro* 10-29 ABC; **1979** *The Sacketts* 5-15 NBC.

Richard Romanus

(born February 28, 1943, Barre, Vermont)

A fine guitarist, Richard supported himself through college and part of law school by doing small gigs. He got the acting bug and left law school to study with Lee Strasburg. Romanus made his

screen debut during 1973 in *Mean Streets*.

He hit television in 1970 and continued to do periodic guest roles up to the present, including a prominent role in a 1995 *Rockford Files* telefilm. He was a regular on *Foul Play* (1981) and *Strike Force* (1981-82), playing commissioned police officers on each series, and was in *Days of Our Lives* (1983-85).

GUEST CREDITS

1970 *Mission: Impossible* "Gitano" 2-1; *Mod Squad* "Is There Anyone Left in Santa Paula?" 12-29; **1974** *Kojak* "The Betrayal" 12-15; **1977** *Charlie's Angels* "The Big Tap Out" 1-12; *Starsky and Hutch* "Huggy Bear and Turkey" 2-19; **1978** *Hawaii Five-0* "Small Potatoes" 10-26; *Rockford Files* "A Three-Day Affair with a Thirty Day Escrow" 11-10; **1980** *Tenspeed and Brownshoe* "Savage Says the Most Dangerous Bird is the Jailbird" 3-23; *Hart to Hart* "This Lady Is Murder" 11-25; **1982** *CHiPs* "Speedway Fever" 11-7; *Matt Houston* episode 11-28; **1983** *A-Team* "The Rabbit Who Ate Las Vegas" 3-1; *Hardcastle and McCormick* "The Boxer" 10-23.

TELEFILMS

1970 *Night Chase* 11-20 CBS; **1977** *Night Terror* 2-7 NBC; **1979** *Gold of the Amazon Women* 3-6 CBS.

Caesar Romero

(born February 15, 1907, New York City; died 1992)

Without question, Caesar Romero was one of Hollywood's most personable, durable and likeable stars for decades. Suave and romantic, he appeared in over 110 films, from 1933. Of Cuban extraction, he first appeared on television in 1951 and hosted a 1954 variety show, *Chevrolet Showroom*. During 1954-55 he starred in a syndicated adventure series called *Passport to Danger*. Other fifties work included *Schlitz Playhouse of Stars* (2), *Ford Theater*, *Pepsi Cola Playhouse*, *Climax* (2), *Studio One*, *Wagon Train* (2) and *Zane Grey Theater*.

After a good deal of early sixties guesting, Caesar became the rollicking Joker on *Batman* for 20 episodes, a role that greatly enhanced the campy hit. After *Batman*, he did numerous guest roles, and from 1979 became a favorite on *Fantasy Island* (3) and *The Love Boat* (3).

After 1985 guest appearances on *Magnum, P.I.* and *Murder, She Wrote*, he became a regular on *Falcon Crest* as Peter Stavros (1985-87), playing opposite series lead Jane Wyman.

He did telefilms into the nineties and appeared on countless variety and comedy shows over the years, always with a huge smile and great warmth and wit. Caesar died in 1992 of complications of a blood clot after being hospitalized with pneumonia and severe bronchitis. His passing left a huge void in the medium.

Caesar Romero (top), as The Joker, enlivened 20 episodes of *Batman* (ABC) during 1966-68. He is joined by Frank Gorshin (center) as The Riddler, and by the wonderful Burgess Meridith as The Penguin.

GUEST CREDITS

1959 *Zorro* "The Gay Caballero" 1-22; *Zorro* "Tornado Is Missing" 1-29; *Zorro* "Zorro vs. Cupid" 2-5; *Zorro* "The Legend of Zorro" 2-5; *Texan* "Caballero" 4-13; **1960** *Zane Grey Theater* "The Reckoning" 1-14; *Chevy Mystery Show* "The Suicide Club" 9-18; *Stagecoach West* "A Time to Run" 11-15; **1961** *Zane Grey Theater* "The Man from Everywhere" 4-13; *Stagecoach West* "The Big Gun" 4-25; *DuPont Show of the Month* "The Battle of the Paper Bullets" 10-15; **1962** *Target: The Corruptors* "My Native Land" 3-16; *Follow the Sun* "A Ghost in Her Gazebo" 3-18; *Rawhide* "The Child Woman" 3-23; **1963** *Dick Powell Show* "Charlie's Duet" 3-19; *Rawhide* "Incident at Rio Doloroso" 5-10; *G.E. True* "Five Tickets to Hell" 5-26; *77 Sunset Strip* "5" 10-11; *Burke's Law* "Who Killed Billy Jo?" 11-8; **1964** *Burke's Law* "Who Killed Snooky Martinelli?" 1-10; *Dr. Kildare* "Onions, Garlic and Flowers That

Bloom in the Spring" 2-6; *Burke's Law* "Who Killed Don Pablo?" 5-1; *Burke's Law* "Who Killed Davidian Jones?" 12-30; **1965** *Bonanza* "The Deadliest Game" 2-21; *Branded* "The Mission" 3-14, 3-21, 3-28; *Burke's Law* "Who Killed the Rest?" 3-17; *Man from UNCLE* "The Never-Never Affair" 3-22; *Ben Casey* "Did Your Mother Come from Ireland?" 5-3; *Rawhide* "The Vasquez Woman" 10-26; **1966** *Daniel Boone* "Gabriel" 1-6; **1967** *T.H.E. Cat* "Queen of Diamonds, Knave of Hearts" 1-6; **1969** *Daniel Boone* "The Grand Alliance" 11-13; **1970** *It Takes a Thief* "Beyond a Reasonable Doubt" 3-16; **1971** *Alias Smith and Jones* "The McCreedy Bust" 1-21; *Night Gallery* "A Matter of Semantics" 11-10; **1972** *Alias Smith and Jones* "The McCreedy Bust—Going, Going, Gone" 1-13; *O'Hara, U. S. Treasury* "Operation: Mr. Felix" 2-18; *Mod Squad* "The Connection" 9-14; *Alias Smith and Jones* "The McCreedy Feud" 9-30; **1973** *Chase* "A Bit of Class" 12-11; **1974** *Banacek* "The Vanishing Chalice" 1-15; *Ironside* "The Lost Cotillion" 10-31; **1975** *Medical Center* "The High Cost of Winning" 12-15; **1976** *Ellery Queen* "The Adventure of the Wary Witness" 1-25; **1978** *Vegas* "Lost Women" 11-22; **1980** *Charlie's Angels* "Dancin' Angels" 2-6; **1982** *Matt Houston* "Who Killed Ramona?" 10-31; **1983** *Hart to Hart* "Chamber of Lost Harts" 2-1.

TELEFILMS

1969 *The D. A.: Murder One* 12-8 NBC; **1977** *Don't Push, I'll Charge When I'm Ready* 12-18 NBC.

Don Ross

Don Ross was a semi-regular on *Dragnet* during it's last two seasons (1968-69, 69-70), and was a major part of Jack Webb's stock company of players. His credits are shown for those last two seasons because he played the same character only twice in four years of appearing on the series. Burly appearing, he often played police officers, but did a variety of roles on the series: reporters, criminals, lab. technicians and ordinary citizens.

Don made 5 appearances on *The Fugitive*, with several castings as police officers.

GUEST CREDITS

1961 *One Step Beyond* "The Executioner" 1-3; *Loretta Young Show* "Double Edge" 2-19; *Surfside 6* "One for the Road" 10-2; **1964** *Outer Limits* "The Mice" 1-6; **1965** *Fugitive* "Runner in the Dark" 3-30; *Gunsmoke* "Ten Little Indians" 10-9; *The FBI* "Courage of a Conviction" 11-7; *Fugitive* "Landscape with Running Figures" 11-16, 11-23; **1966** *Fugitive* "This'll Kill You" 1-18; *Fugitive* "Last Oasis" 9-13; *12 O'Clock High* "A Distant Cry" 10-7; *Fugitive* "Approach with Care" 11-15; **1967** *Dragnet* "The Big Bank Examiners" 2-23; *Invaders* "Panic" 4-11; *Gunsmoke* "Major Glory" 10-30; *Dragnet* "The Big Magazine" 12-7; **1968** *Dragnet* "The Big Goodbye" 2-29; *Dragnet* "Public Affairs-DR-07" 9-19; *Dragnet* "Juvenile-DR-05" 9-26; *Dragnet* "Robbery-DR-15" 11-7; *Dragnet* "Public Affairs-DR-12" 11-14; **1969** *Dragnet* "White Community Relations-DR-07" 1-2; *Dragnet* "Homicide-DR-22" 1-9; *Wild Wild West* "The Night of the Winged Terror" 1-17, 1-24; *Dragnet* "Frauds-DR-28" 2-20; *Dragnet* "Burglary-DR-31" 3-6; *Dragnet* "Forgery-DR-33" 3-20; *Dragnet* "Juvenile-DR-35" 4-3; *Dragnet* "Homicide-Cigarette Butt" 10-30; *Dragnet* "D.H.Q.-Missing Persons" 11-13; *Dragnet* "Burglary-Auto Courtroom" 11-20; *Dragnet* "Burglary-Juvenile Genius" 12-4; **1970** *Dragnet* "Missing Hypo" 1-8; *Dragnet* "Burglary-Helpful Woman" 1-22; *Dragnet* "Narco-Pillmaker" 2-19; *Dragnet* "Auto

Theft-Dognapper" 2-26; *Dragnet* "Missing Persons-
The Body" 3-5; **1971** *McMillan and Wife* "Death Is a
Seven Point Spread" 12-8; **1973** *Barnaby Jones*
"Murder at Malibu" 4-29; *Emergency* "The Old
Engine" 9-29; **1974** *Kojak* "Slay Ride" 10-13; **1979**
CHiPs "Drive, Lady, Drive" 11-10.

TELEFILMS

1972 *Emergency!* 1-15 NBC; *The Priest Killer* 9-
14 NBC; *The Streets of San Francisco* 9-16 ABC;
1973 *Poor Devil* 2-14 NBC.

Al Ruscio

(born January 2, 1924, Salem, Mass.)

Following stage experience on the east coast, Al
broke into films in 1946. He began working in
television during the fifties and had numerous early
sixties guest roles, frequently appearing as underworld figures.

After a decade-long absence from television
(1965-74), he worked regularly from 1975 well into
the eighties. He became a regular on *Shannon*
during 1981-82; during 1988 he appeared on the soap
General Hospital.

Married to actress Kate Williamson, four of his
children are involved in the business: an actress
(Elizabeth Ruscio), a film editor, an art director and
an acting teacher-director.

GUEST CREDITS

1959 *Lawless Years* "Lucky Silva" 4-13; *77
Sunset Strip* "Abra-Cadaver" 4-17; *Lawless Years*
"The Story of Cutie Jaffe" 5-7; **1960** *Troubleshoot-
ers* "Senorita" 3-4; *Detectives* "Twelve Hours to
Live" 2-19; *M Squad* "A Kid Up There" 3-22;
Detectives "You Only Die Once" 11-18; **1961** *Thriller*
"Man in a Cage" 1-11; *Islanders* "La Cosa Ven-
detta" 3-26; *Malibu Run* "The Double Adventure" 3-
29; *Peter Gunn* "Voodoo" 6-19; *Lawless Years* "The
Kid Dropper Story" 7-7; *Follow the Sun* "The
Primative Clay" 12-3; **1962** *Target: The Corruptors*
"My Native Land" 3-16; *87ᵗʰ Precinct* "Idol in the
Dust" 4-2; **1963** *Have Gun-Will Travel* "Unforgiving

Minute" 1-26; **1964** *Great Adventure* "The Pirate and
the Patriot" 5-1; *Voyage to the Bottom of the Sea*
"The City Beneath the Sea" 9-21; **1975** *Baretta* "The
Good-Bye Orphan Annie Blues" 9-10; *Six Million
Dollar Man* "Return of the Bionic Woman" 9-14;
Invisible Man "Panic" 10-20; *S.W.A.T.* "The
Swinger" 11-22; **1976** *Kojak* "A Wind from Corsica"
1-18; *Joe Forrester* "Squeeze Play" 2-9; *Rockford
Files* "Foul on the First Play" 3-12; **1977** *Rockford
Files* "The Dog and Pony Show" 10-21; *Kojak* "Cry
for the Kids" 10-23; *Starsky and Hutch* "The
Plague" 11-19, 11-26; **1978** *Incredible Hulk* "Final
Round" 3-10; **1979** *Mrs. Columbo* "A Riddle for
Puppets" 3-15; *Lou Grant* "Skid Row" 4-2; **1981**
Hart to Hart "Murder Is a Drag" 2-3; **1983**
Remington Steele "Love Among the Steele" 11-8.

TELEFILMS

1978 *Ruby and Oswald* 2-8 CBS; **1980** *A Rumor
of War* 9-24, 9-25 CBS; **1981** *People vs. Jean Harris*
5-7, 5-8 NBC; **1982** *Farrell for the People* 10-18
NBC.

Bing Russell

(born 1928)

Retired from acting, today Bing is best-known

as the father of former child actor and contemporary film star, Kurt Russell. Bing got his start in films in 1953, appearing in movies like *Gunfight at the O. K. Corral, Fear Strikes Out, Last Train from Gun Hill, The Magnificent Seven, A Gathering of Eagles, Cheyenne Autumn* and *The Computer Wore Tennis Shoes*.

A former athlete, Bing was a natural for western TV series and worked in the genre from 1956, appearing in most of the hit series of the era. He also appeared in 5 episodes of *The Fugitive*, usually as a cop; son Kurt appeared in two of the episodes with him.

In 1963 he began appearing on *Bonanza* as the local deputy Clem, and this evolved into a recurring role for the remainder of the series run; he became the sheriff during the final years. Bing worked in crime series and telefilms during the mid seventies.

GUEST CREDITS

1959 *Black Saddle* "Client: Robinson" 2-21; *Colt .45* "Dead Aim" 4-12; *Rifleman* "A Matter of Faith" 5-19; *Texan* "The Dishonest Posse" 10-5; *Wanted: Dead or Alive* "Desert Seed" 11-14; *Maverick* "A Fellow's Brother" 11-22; **1960** *Laramie* "Defiance" 4-19; *Tate* "The Reckoning" 8-24; *Rifleman* "Seven" 10-11; *Gunsmoke* "Don Matteo" 10-22; **1961** *Wanted: Dead or Alive* "Triple

Vise" 2-27; *Bronco* "Stage to the Sky" 4-24; *Twilight Zone* "The Arrival" 9-21; *Gunsmoke* "Old Yellow Boots" 10-27; *Laramie* "The Lawless Seven" 12-26; **1962** *Rawhide* "Abilene" 5-18; *Have Gun-Will Travel* "Memories of Monica" 10-27; *Virginian* "Riff Raff" 11-7; **1963** *G.E. True* "Five Tickets to Hell" 3-24; *Bonanza* "Mirror of a Man" 3-31; *Ben Casey* "In the Name of Love, a Small Corruption" 5-27; *Fugitive* "Little Egypt" 12-17; **1964** *Fugitive* "Nemesis" 10-13; **1965** *Fugitive* "Runner in the Dark" 3-30; *Combat* "Odyssey" 4-20; *Fugitive* "Wings of an Angel" 9-14; *Bonanza* "The Other Son" 10-3; **1966** *Big Valley* "Barbary Red" 2-16; *Fugitive* "In a Plain Paper Wrapper" 4-19; *Bonanza* "Horse of a Different Hue" 9-18; *Bonanza* "To Bloom for Thee" 10-16; **1967** *Gunsmoke* "Mail Drop" 1-28; *Bonanza* "Joe Cartwright, Detective" 3-5; *Bonanza* "Napoleon's Children" 4-16; *Big Valley* "Cage of Eagles" 4-24; *Virginian* "The Deadly Past" 9-20; *Bonanza* "The Gentle Ones" 10-29; *Bonanza* "Desperate Passage" 11-5; *Bonanza* "Showdown at Lake Tahoe" 11-19; **1968** *Big Valley* "The Profit and the Lost" 12-2; **1969** *Big Valley* "The Secret" 1-27; *Bonanza* "Emily" 3-23; *Bonanza* "To Stop a War" 10-19; **1970** *Bonanza* "It's a Small World" 1-4; *Bonanza* "Danger Road" 1-11; *Adam-12* "Log 124-Airport" 2-28; *Bonanza* "The Imposters" 12-13; **1971** *Bonanza* "Terror at 2:00" 3-7; *Bonanza* "The Prisoners" 10-17; *O'Hara, U. S. Treasury* "Operation: Crystal Springs" 12-3; *Bonanza* "The Rattlesnake Brigade" 12-5; **1973** *Streets of San Francisco* "Shield of Honor" 11-15; **1974** *Gunsmoke* "The Iron Blood of Courage" 2-18; *Mannix* "Picture of a Shadow" 11-24; **1975** *Streets of San Francisco* "Labyrinth" 2-27; *Petrocelli* "Terror by the Book" 12-10.

TELEFILMS

1971 *Yuma* 3-2 ABC; *A Taste of Evil* 10-12 ABC; **1973** *Satan's School for Girls* 9-19 ABC; *Runaway!* 9-29 ABC; **1974** *A Cry in the Wilderness* 3-26 ABC; *The Sex Symbol* 9-17 ABC; *Death Sentence* 10-2 ABC; **1976** *The New Daughters of Joshua Cabe* 5-29 ABC; *The Loneliest Runner* 12-20 NBC.

Ayn Ruymen (center) expresses dismay, in an episode of *The McLean Stevenson Show* (NBC), while the series star looks flustered. Co-star Barbara Stuart, at left, registers disgust.

Ayn Ruymen

(born July 18, 1947, Brooklyn, New York)

After only one film (1972), Ayn devoted her talents to television. Her TV career ran from 1972 until 1981 when she faded from the medium. She was a regular on *The McLean Stevenson Show*, a 1976-77 sitcom.

GUEST CREDITS

1972 *Medical Center* episode 3-8; **1973** *Owen Marshall, Counselor at Law* "A Lesson in Loving" 9-12; *Streets of San Francisco* "Shield of Honor" 11-15; **1974** *Medical Center* "No Escape" 1-28; *Lucas Tanner* "Look the Other Way" 11-20; **1975** *Baretta* "The Five-and-a-Half Pound Junkie" 1-24; *Cannon* "Tomorrow Ends at Noon" 3-19; *Police Story* "A Community of Victims" 9-23; *Rookies* "Hostage" 9-23; *Petrocelli* "Terror on Wheels" 11-5; **1976** *Harry O* "Hostage" 2-19; **1977** *Hawaii Five-0* "Tounai" 12-22; **1978** *Richie Brockelman* "Escape from Caine Abel" 4-14; *Quincy, M.E.* "Dead or Alive" 11-16.

TELEFILMS

1973 *Go Ask Alice* 1-24 ABC; **1974** *Tell Me Where It Hurts* 3-12 CBS; *Hurricane* 9-10 ABC; **1981** *Our Family Business* 9-20 ABC.

Eddie Ryder

A versatile character actor, Eddie Ryder was at home in comedy or drama. He was a regular on *The Dennis O'Keefe Show* in 1959-60 and spent a season (1961-62) as one of the doctors on *Dr. Kildare*. He did a good deal of guest work, especially on *Mannix* (6 episodes). During 1981 he appeared on the soap *General Hospital* as a cabbie, Slick Jones.

GUEST CREDITS

1960 Tightrope "Achilles and His Heels" 4-5; *Dan Raven* "The Mechanic" 9-30; *Detectives* "Adopted" 11-25; **1961** *Rebel* "The Helping Hand" 4-30; **1962** *Dr. Kildare* "My Brother, the Doctor" 1-4; *Roaring 20's* "The People People Marry" 1-20; *Wide*

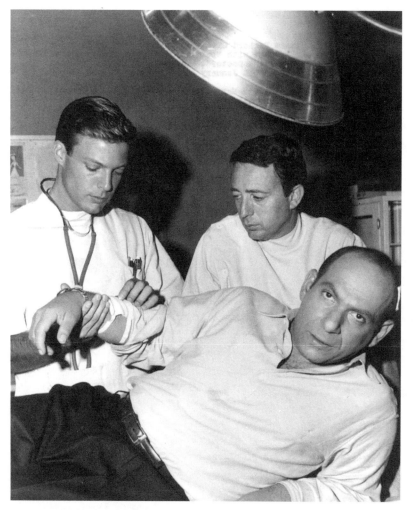

Eddie Ryder (center) looks on, as Richard Chamberlain checks a bandage on the arm of guest Hershel Bernardi (right). The episode, "My Brother, the Doctor", aired on NBC's *Dr. Kildare* in 1962.

Scene Stealers" 10-23; *Mannix* "Search in the Dark" 11-25; **1974** *Mannix* "Picture of a Shadow" 11-24; **1975** *Police Woman* "Target Black" 1-3; **1976** *Waltons* "The Secret" 1-8; *Police Story* "Payment Deferred" 9-21; **1977** *Baretta* "Guns and Brothers" 4-6; **1978** *Rockford Files* "The Empty Frame" 11-3.

TELEFILM

1979 *The Man in the Santa Claus Suit* 12-23 NBC.

Fred Sadoff

(born 1926)

Following a 1952 film debut in *Viva Zapata!*, Fred's film roles were rather sporadic, but included parts in *The Posideon Adventure* (1972) and *Cinderalla Liberty* (1973). He first appeared on television in 1956, and was seen often during the seventies in guest roles, in 12 telefilms and in a miniseries.

Fred has been active as a producer-director of stage plays.

GUEST CREDITS

Country "Who Killed Eddie Gannon?" 10-11; **1964** *Combat!* The Glory Among Men" 4-21; *Voyage to the Bottom of the Sea* "Submarine Sunk Here" 11-16; **1967** *Bonanza* "The Conquisadors" 10-1; **1968** *Mission: Impossible* "The Town" 2-18; **1968** *Mannix* "Delayed Action" 3-2; *Mannix* "Edge of the Knife" 11-9; **1970** *Ironside* "Too Many Victims" 11-12; **1972** *Mission: Impossible* "Casino" 2-19; *Mannix* "Death in the Fifth Gear" 3-8; *Mod Squad* "Corbey" 11-2; *Gunsmoke* "The Brothers" 11-27; **1973** *Mannix* "Carol Lockwood, Past Tense" 1-28; *Streets of San Francisco* "A Room with a View" 2-8; *Barnaby Jones* "Catch Me If You Can" 10-21; *Chase* "The

1966 *Court Martial* "Silence Is the Enemy" 4-8; **1971** *Cade's County* "The Alien Land" 12-19; **1972** *Banyon* "The Clay Clarinet" 10-27; **1973** *Mannix* "The Faces of Murder" 2-4; **1974** *Kojak* "Deliver Us Some Evil" 2-13; *Barnaby Jones* "Friends Till Death" 2-17; *Magician* "The Illusion of the Fatal Arrow" 3-4; *Toma* "Joey the Weep" 3-22; *Harry O* "Gertrude" 9-12; *Rockford Files* "This Case Is Closed" 10-18; *Sons and Daughters* "The Pregnancy" 10-23; *Manhunter* "The Truck Murders" 11-6; **1975** *Rockford Files* "Just by Accident" 2-28; *Baretta* "Walk Like You Talk" 3-14; *Harry O* "A.P.B. Harry Orwell" 11-6; **1976** *Jigsaw John* "Sand Trap" 2-9; *Streets of San Francisco* "Judg-

ment Day" 2-19; *Quincy, M.E.* "Who's Who in Never Land" 10-10; **1977** *Black Sheep Squadron* "Last Mission Over Sangai" 2-8; **1980** *Barnaby Jones* "Murder in the Key C" 2-17; **1983** *Manimal* "Night of the Beast" 12-10.

TELEFILMS

1971 *Incident in San Francisco* 2-28 ABC; *Dead Men Tell No Tales* 12-17 CBS; **1973** *Murdock's Gang* 3-20 CBS; **1974** *The Questor Tapes* 1-23; *The FBI Story: The FBI vs. Alvin Karpis, Public Enemy Number One* 11-8 CBS; **1975** *Someone I Touched* 2-26 ABC; **1976** *Most Wanted* 3-21 ABC; **1977** *Green Eyes* 1-3 ABC; *Alexander: The Other Side of Dawn* 5-16 NBC; **1978** *Betrayal* 11-13 NBC; **1979** *Breaking Up Is Hard to Do* 9-5, 9-7 ABC; **1980** *Moviola: This Year's Blonde* 5-18 NBC; **1981** *Death Ray 2000* 3-5 NBC; *The Star Maker* 5-11, 5-12 NBC.

Robert Sampson

(born 1932)

Robert Sampson debuted in films in 1954 and began a busy television career in the late fifties. He became a favorite performer on Alfred Hitchcock productions with 5 guest appearances. The sixties/seventies era provided numerous guest shots, 8 teleman roles and a series regular slot, on *Bridget*

Loves Bernie (1972-73).

He became a regular on *Falcon Crest* during 1981-82, and also appeared on the soap *Capitol* during the early eighties.

GUEST CREDITS

1959 *Markham* episode 6-9; **1960** *One Step Beyond* "The Death Waltz" 10-4; *Alfred Hitchcock Presents* "The Doubtful Doctor" 10-4; *Alfred Hitchcock Presents* "A Very Moral Theft" 10-11; *Wyatt Earp* "He's My Doctor" 11-29; **1961** *Alfred Hitchcock Presents* "The Changing Heart" 1-3; *Alfred Hitchcock Presents* "A Crime for Mothers" 1-24; **1962** *Tales of Wells Fargo* "Incident at Cross-bow" 2-3; *Alcoa Premiere* "The Jail" 2-6; *Twilight Zone* "Little Girl Lost" 3-16; *Thriller* "Men of Mystery" 4-2; *Virginian* "Woman from White Wing" 9-26; *Bonanza* "The Deserter" 10-21; **1963** *Alfred Hitchcock Hour* "Dear Uncle George" 5-10; **1964** *Outer Limits* "The Mutant" 3-16; *Mr. Novak* "Moment Without Armor" 3-31; *Ben Casey* "A Thousand Words Are Mute" 11-9; **1965** *Voyage to the Bottom of the Sea* "The Enemies" 3-29; **1967** *Star Trek* "A Taste of Armageddon" 2-23; *T.H.E. Cat* "Twenty-One and Out" 3-24; **1968** *I Spy* "Home to Judgment" 1-8; **1969** *Big Valley* "Joshua Watson" 1-20; **1970** *Interns* episode 12-11; *Immortal* "To the Gods Alone" 12-31; **1971** *Mission: Impossible* "The Party"

3-6; *Owen Marshall, Counselor at Law* "Make No Mistake" 10-14; **1972** *Sarge* "An Accident Waiting to Happen" 1-4; *Griff* "Elephant in a Cage" 11-24; *Police Story* "The Big Walk" 12-4; **1974** *Hawkins* "Murder in the Slave Trade" 1-22; *McCloud* "The Colorado Cattle Caper" 2-24; *Police Story* "Smack" 12-6; **1975** *Police Story* "Incident in the Kill Zone" 1-7; *Police Story* "Officer Needs Help" 9-9; *Police Woman* "Above and Beyond" 10-31; **1976** *Police Story* "Odyssey of Death" 1-9, 1-16; *Joe Forrester* "Pressure Point" 3-22; *Most Wanted* "The Wolf Pack Killer" 11-20; **1977** *Hardy Boys/Nancy Drew Mysteries* "Arson and Lace" 4-1; **1979** *Rockford Files* "The Deuce" 1-25; *Wonder Woman* "The Man Who Would Not Die" 8-28; **1980** *Hagen* "The Buddy System" 4-24; **1981** *Strike Force* "Magic Man" 12-11; **1982** *Quincy, M.E.* "The Shadow of Death" 2-24; *Knight Rider* "Just My Bil" 10-24; *Powers of Matthew Star* episode 11-19; **1983** *A-Team* "West Coast Turnaround" 3-22.

TELEFILMS

1969 *Fear No Evil* 3-3 NBC; **1971** *The Priest Killer* 9-14 NBC; **1974** *Thursday's Game* 4-14 ABC; **1975** *Shell Game* 5-9 CBS; **1976** *The Dark Side of Innnocence* 5-20 NBC; *Kingston: The Power Play* 9-15 NBC; **1977** *In the Glitter Palace* 2-27 NBC; **1978** *The Grass Is Always Greener Over the Septic Tank* 10-25 CBS; **1981** *Jacqueline Susann's "Valley of the Dolls"* 10-19, 10-20 CBS.

Hugh Sanders

(born 1912; died 1966)

Onscreen from 1950, the large frame and strong voice of Hugh Sanders created numerous casting as sheriffs and police officers, and he also had his share of bad-guy roles. *The Fugitive* and *Rawhide* each used his talents in 4 episodes.

GUEST CREDITS

1959 *Lawman* "The Runaway" 2-1; *Wanted: Dead or Alive* "Crossroads" 4-11; *Colt .45* "The Man Who Loved Lincoln" 5-3; *Yancy Derringer*

"Outlaw at Liberty" 5-7; *Rawhide* "Incident of the Judas Trap" 6-5; **1960** *Bat Masterson* "Pigeon and Hawk" 1-21; *Rawhide* "Incident of the Sharpshooter" 2-26; *Texan* "Showdown" 2-29; *Perry Mason* "The Case of the Bashful Burro" 3-26; *Perry Mason* "The Case of the Wandering Widow" 10-22; *Klondike* "Halliday's Club" 12-19; **1961** *National Velvet* "Star Wish" 1-8; *Rawhide* "Incident Near the Promised Land" 2-3; *Rawhide* "Incident of the Big Blowout" 2-10; *Whispering Smith* "The Mortal Coil" 7-24; **1962** *Gunsmoke* "Old Dan" 1-27; *Cain's Hundred* "Quick Brown Fox" 5-8; *Laramie* "Shadow of the Past" 10-16; *Going My Way* "Parish Car" 10-17; *Ben Casey* "The Fireman Who Raised Rabbits" 11-26; **1963** *Perry Mason* "The Case of the Golden Oranges" 3-7; *Fugitive* "The Other Side of the Mountain" 10-1; *Bonanza* "Twilight Town" 10-13; *Kraft Suspense Theatre* "Are There Anymore Out There Like You?" 11-7; **1964** *Bonanza* "Alias Joe Cartwright" 1-26; *Bonanza* "Return to Honor" 3-22; *Fugitive* "Ballad for a Ghost" 11-29; **1965** *Fugitive* "A.P.B." 4-6; **1966** *Fugitive* "Echo of a Nightmare" 1-25.

Penny Santon

(born Pierina della Santino, September 2, 1916)

One of television's most familiar and enduring character actresses, Penny Santon, of Italian heritage, started acting at age 2 in presentations of Italian stage in New York. She later worked in radio for many years. Perhaps her most familiar characterization was as a stressed and concerned mother; proprietors of restaurants and boarding houses were also typical castings.

Penny entered films in 1955 and began her television career in 1956. She was a regular on two sitcoms: *Don't Call Me Charlie* (1962-63) and *Roll Out* (1973-74). In 1982-83 she had a featured role on *Matt Houston*, and became a regular on *Life Goes On* in 1989.

GUEST CREDITS

1959 *Markham* "The Searing Flame" 4-7; **1960** *Wyatt Earp* "The Case of Senor Huerto" 2-9; *77 Sunset Strip* "The Antwerp Caper" 12-2; **1961** *Route 66* "Sleep on Four Pillows" 2-24; *Roaring 20's* "The Twelfth Hour" 3-18; *Asphalt Jungle* "The Nine-Twenty Hero" 5-21; **1962** *Roaring 20's* "Footlights" 1-13; *Ben Casey* "Imagine a Long Bright Corridor" 1-15; *Detectives* "The Outsider" 2-16; *Cain's Hundred* "The Cost of Living" 3-20; *77 Sunset Strip* "The Lovely American" 5-4; *77 Sunset Strip* "The Floating Man" 11-9; **1963** *Saints and Sinners* "The Home-Coming Bit" 1-7; *Combat* "The Battle of the

Ropes" 4-2; **1966** *Man from UNCLE* "The Concrete Overcoat Affair" 11-25, 12-2; **1968** *High Chaparral* "A Joyful Noise" 3-24; *Bonanza* "The Sound of Drums" 11-17; **1969** *Outsider* "A Bowl of Cherie" 1-29; *Name of the Game* "Keep the Doctor Away" 2-14; **1970** *Hallmark Hall of Fame* "A Storm in Summer" 2-6; *Matt Lincoln* "Doc" 11-12; **1972** *Streets of San Francisco* "The Year of the Locusts" 12-9; **1973** *Adam-12* "Clear with a Citizen" 1-10, 10-17; *Adam-12* "Van Nuys Division" 10-31; **1974** *Kojak* "Cops in a Cage" 1-2; *Magician* "The Stainless Steel Lady" 1-28; *Chase* "Eighty-Six Proof TNT" 3-20; *Ironside* "What's New with Mark?" 9-26; *Rookies* "Prelude to Vengeance" 11-11; **1975** *Get Christie Love!* "My Son, the Murderer" 2-12; *Doctor's Hospital* "Surgeon, Heal Thyself" 12-17; **1976** *Police Woman* "Generation of Evil" 2-10; *McNaughton's Daughter* "The M.O.M. Principle" 4-7; **1978** *Lou Grant* "Airliner" 1-3; **1979** *Rockford Files* "The Man Who Saw Alligators" 2-10.

TELEFILMS

1969 *Marcus Welby, M.D.* 3-26 ABC; **1971** *The Impatient Heart* 10-8 NBC; **1974** *The Last Angry Man* 4-16 ABC; **1975** *The Legend of Valentino* 11-23 ABC; **1977** *Rosetti and Ryan: Men Who Love Women* 5-19 NBC; **1979** *And Your Name Is Jonah* 1-28 CBS; **1982** *Moonlight* 9-14 ABC; **1983** *When Your Lover Leaves You* 10-31 NBC.

Katherine Leigh Scott

(born January 26, 1943, Robbinsdale, Minnesota)

Of Norwegian parentage, Katherine grew up on a Minnesota farm. After graduation from acting school Katherine went directly to a major role in *Dark Shadows* (1966-71). Following it's run, She moved to Europe and worked onstage and in films.

Returning to the U. S., she began guesting on television and was a regular on an abbreviated 1979 series, *Big Shamus, Little Shamus*. During 1980-82 her voice was used on the *Scooby-Doo and Scrappy-Do* Saturday morning cartoon series.

A busy eighties actress, she worked in guest roles in *Hardcastle and McCormick, Call to Glory,*

Kathryn Leigh Scott is trying to explain her point of view to an obviously angry Tom Sellick. The scene occured in a 1981 episode of *Magnum, P.I.* (CBS) called "Black Orchid".

Cagney and Lacey, The A-Team, Hotel, Knott's Landing, Jake and the Fat Man, Paradise, Matlock and several episodes of *Dallas*. She began her own publishing company, Pomegranate Press, initially offering *My Scrapbook Memories of Dark Shadows*, which heightened the huge cult following of Dark Shadows. Scott has expanded to publishing numerous entertainment industry books.

GUEST CREDITS

1978 *Baretta* "The Dream" 5-4; *Switch* "Blue

Crusaders Reunion" 7-9; *Hawaii Five-0* "My Friend, the Enemy" 8-3; **1979** *Little House on the Prairie* "Blind Man's Bluff" 1-15; *Quincy, M.E.* "A Small Circle of Friends" 1-18; *Incredible Hulk* "A Solitary Place" 1-24; **1981** *Dynasty* episode 6 2-2; *Magnum, P.I.* "The Black Orchid" 4-2; *Shannon* "Neither a Borrower" 11-18; **1982** *Shannon* "John's Awakening" 4-7; *Quest* "His Majesty, I Presume" 11-12; **1983** *Tales of the Gold Monkey* "God Save the Queen" 1-19; *Renegades* "The Big Time" 3-18.

TELEFILM

1974 *Turn of the Screw* 4-15, 4-16 ABC.

Ken Scott

(born 1933)

Ken made two films in 1943 as a child actor, but didn't appear onscreen again until he work during 1957 on *The Three Faces of Eve*. Other film credits included *Beloved Infidel, The Bravados, Desire in the Dust, The Second Time Around* and *Fantastic Voyage*.

His television work was infrequent until the 1968-78 time span when he appeared in a number of TV crime series episodes, especially in a recurring role on *McCloud* (10).

GUEST CREDITS

1962 *Tales of Wells Fargo* "Hometown Detour" 2-17; **1965** *Gunsmoke* "Circus Trick" 2-6; **1966** *Laredo* "Oh Careless Love" 12-23; **1968** *The FBI* "The Mercenary" 4-8; **1970** *McCloud* "Horse Stealing on Fifth Avenue" 9-23; *McCloud* "The Concrete Corral" 9-30; *McCloud* "Walk in the Dark" 10-14; *McCloud* "Our Man in Paris" 10-21; **1971** *Dan August* "Prognosis: Homicide" 4-1; *Mission: Impossible* "Encounter" 10-30; *Alias*

Smith and Jones "Dreadful Sorry Clementine" 11-18; **1972** *Cannon* "Sky Above, Death Below" 9-20; *Mission: Impossible* "The Puppet" 12-22; **1974** *McCloud* "This Must Be the Alamo" 3-24; **1975** *Barnaby Jones* "Poisoned Pigeon" 3-25; *McCloud* "Return to the Alamo" 3-30; *McCloud* "Park Avenue Pirates" 9-21; *McCloud* "Three Guns for New York" 11-23; **1976** *McCloud* "The Day New York Turned Blue" 2-22; **1977** *McCloud* "McCloud Meets Dracula" 4-17; **1978** *Hardy Boys/Nancy Drew Mysteries* "Death Surf" 3-12; *Charlie's Angels* "Antique Angels" 5-10; **1981** *Hart to Hart* "The Murder of Jonathan Hart" 4-28; **1982** *Fall Guy* "License to Kill" 1-13, 1-20.

TELEFILM

1977 *The Amazing Howard Hughes* 4-13, 4-14 CBS.

Vito Scotti

(born January 26, 1918, San Francisco, Calif.; died June 5, 1996)

In films since 1948, Vito usually played Italian characters, in films like *Von Ryan's Express* and *The Godfather*, and he excelled in comedies like *Herbie Rides Again* and *Herbie Goes Bananas*. He carried the comic aspect in TV sitcom guest appearances as

he did in two visits to *Gilligan's Island*.

His comedic gift brought him sitcom roles in *Mama Rosa* (1950), *Life with Luigi* (1953), *The Flying Nun* (1968-69), *To Rome with Love* (1969-71) and *Barefoot in the Park* (1970-71). Some of his numerous guest roles in drama series also had a comic tinge.

GUEST CREDITS

1959 *Texan* "The Ringer" 2-16; *Steve Canyon* "The Robbery" 2-19; *Californians* "Deadly Tintype" 3-31; *Perry Mason* "The Case of the Howling Dog" 4-11; *Tales of Wells Fargo* "Young Jim Hardie" 9-7; *Wagon Train* "The St. Nicholas Story" 12-23; **1960** *Twilight Zone* "Mr. Bevis" 6-3; *Cheyenne* "Counterfeit Gun" 10-10; **1961** *Tales of Wells Fargo* "The Hand That Shook the Hand" 2-6; *Loretta Young Show* "The Golden Cord" 2-12; *Bonanza* "Thunderhead Swindle" 4-29; *Frontier Circus* "The Depths of Fear" 10-5; *Bonanza* "The Lonely House" 10-15; *Tales of Wells Fargo* "Mr. Mute" 11-4; *Investigators* "De Luca" 11-23; **1962** *Bronco* "The Last Letter" 3-5; *Target: The Corruptors* "The Blind Goddess" 4-20; *Twilight Zone* "The Gift" 4-27; *Rifleman* "Waste" 10-1, 10-8; **1963** *Going My Way* "Cornelius, Come Home" 3-6; *Wide Country* "Farewell to Margarita" 3-21; *G.E. True* "The Tenth Mona Lisa" 3-31; *Rifleman* "Which Way'd They Go?" 4-1; *Bob Hope Chrysler Theater* "Four Kings" 11-1; *Breaking*

Point "The Gnu, Now Almost Extinct" l2-l6; **1964** *Kraft Suspense Theatre* "Knight's Gambit" 3-26; **l965** *Man from UNCLE* "The Yellow Scarf Affair" l-25; *Virginian* "Nobility of Kings" 11-l0; *Gunsmoke* "The Hostage" 12-4; **1966** *Wild Wild West* "The Night of the Infernal Machine" 12-23; **1967** *Girl from UNCLE* "The Doublegate Affair" l-31; *Man from UNCLE* "The Matterhorn Affair" 3-31; *Gunsmoke* "The Pillagers" 11-6; **1968** *Daniel Boone* "The Ballad of Sidewinder and Cherokee" 4-25; **1969** *Gunsmoke* "Danny" l0-13; *Ironside* "The Machismo Bag" 11-13; **1970** *Gunsmoke* "Sergeant Holly" 12-l4; **l97l** *McMillan and Wife* "Murder by the Barrel" 9-29; **1972** *McMillan and Wife* "Cop of the Year" 11-l9; **1973** *Columbo* "Any Old Port in a Storm" l0-7; *Columbo* "Candidate for Crime" 11-4; **1974** *Columbo* "Swan Song" 3-3; *Columbo* "Negative Reaction" l0-6; *Get Christie Love!* "Highway to Murder" l0-30; *Get Christie Love!* "Fatal Damage" 11-6; *Adam-l2* "Alcohol" l2-l0; **1975** *McCoy* "Bless the Big Fish" l0-5; *Columbo* "Identity Crisis" 11-2; *Mobile One* "The Listening Year" 12-22; **1976** *Bionic Woman* "Fly, Jaimie, Fly" 5-5; *Bionic Woman* "Assault on a Princess" l0-6; **1977** *Police Woman* "Silky Chamberlain" 9-28; *CHiPs* "Highway Robbery" 12-l; **1980** *Charlie's Angels* "Home Sweet Angels" l-30; *Hawaii Five-0* "Woe to Wo Fat" 4-5; *Vegas* "Sudden Death" 11-l9; *CHiPs* "Journey to a Spacecraft" 2-6.

TELEFILMS

1974 *Twice in a Lifetime* 3-16 NBC; *Adventures of the Queen* 2-l4 CBS; **1975** *The Big Ripoff* 3-11 NBC.

James Seay

(born l9l4)

A leading man in B-Films of the forties and fifties, James also had roles in major movies like *Northwest Mounted Police, Eagle Squadron, Miracle on 34th Street, Vera Cruz, Whatever Happened to Baby Jane?* and *The Green Berets.* He worked in television from l953 and by the sixties was doing mainly smaller character parts.

James had a recurring role on *The Life and*

Times of Wyatt Earp (1960-6l), appearing a judge.

GUEST CREDITS

1959 *Cimarron City* "A Legacy for Ozzie Harper" l-l0; *Trackdown* "The Vote" 5-6; *Meet McGraw* "The Diamond" 9-l5; *Perry Mason* "The Case of the Spurious Sister" l0-3; **1960** *Wyatt Earp* "Let's Hang Curley Bill" l-26; *Wyatt Earp* "The Arizona Lottery" 2-l6; *Rebel* "The Captive of Temblor" 4-l0; *Wyatt Earp* "The Court vs. Doc Holliday" 4-26; *Wyatt Earp* "The Toughest Judge in Arizona" 5-24; *Wyatt Earp* "My Enemy, John Behan" 5-3l; *Wyatt Earp* "Shoot to Kill" l0-l8; *Thriller* "Girl with a Secret" 11-l5; *Wyatt Earp* "He's My Brother" 11-29; **l96l** *Wyatt Earp* "Horse Thief" l-l0; *Wyatt Earp* "Terror in the Desert" l-24; *Wyatt Earp* "Old Slanders Never Die" l-3l; *Wyatt Earp* "Until Proven Guilty" 4-11; *Surfside 6* "Vengeance Is Bitter" 4-24; *Wyatt Earp* "Hiding Behind a Star" 5-23; *Tall Man* "Death or Taxes" 5-27; *Wyatt Earp* "Wyatt's Brothers Join In" 6-6; *Wyatt Earp* "Gunfight at O. K. Corral" 6-20; **1963** *Twilight Zone* "In His Image" l-3; *77 Sunset Strip* "Terror in

Silence" 1-25; *Fugitive* "Smoke Screen" 10-29; **1964** *Gunsmoke* "Owney Tupper Had a Daughter" 4-4; *Fugitive* "Dark Corner" 11-10; **1965** *Laredo* "Three's Company" 10-14; **1966** *Fugitive* "Right in the Middle of the Season" 11-29; **1967** *I Spy* "Cops and Robbers" 4-12; *Invaders* "The Watchers" 9-19.

Charles Seel
(born 1898, New York City; died 1980)

Charles Seel played in vaudeville and on the radio before beginning a film career in 1949. He was in a number of memorable films: *The Man with the Golden Arm, Dark at the Top of the Stairs, Please Don't Eat the Daisies, The Man Who Shot Liberty Valance, Cheyenne Autumn, The Great Race, Mister Buddwing, Winning* and *Westworld.*

He often played older townspeople and is well remembered for his recurring roles, as Barney the telegraph operator on *Gunsmoke*, and as Mr. Krinkle on *Dennis the Menace.* Charles was a series regular on *The Road West* (1966-67).

GUEST CREDITS

1959 *Rifleman* "The Boarding House" 2-24; *One Step Beyond* "The Open Window" 11-3; **1960** *Wichita Town* "The Long Night" 1-20; *Wagon Train*

"The Coulter Craven Story" 11-23; **1961** *One Step Beyond* "Dead Man's Tale" 1-17; *Gunsmoke* "Stolen Horses" 4-8; **1962** *Twilight Zone* "The Hunt" 1-26; *Laramie* "The Sunday Shoot" 11-13; **1963** *Gunsmoke* "Panacea Sykes" 4-13; *Alfred Hitchcock Hour* "You'll Be the Death of Me" 10-18; *Gunsmoke* "Quint's Trail" 11-9; **1965** *Man from UNCLE* "The Deadly Affair" 1-11; *Ben Casey* "Three Li'l Lambs" 3-29; *Gunsmoke* "The Storm" 9-25; *Gunsmoke* "The Bounty Hunter" 10-30; *Gunsmoke* "The Hostage" 12-4; **1967** *Gunsmoke* "The Wreckers" 9-11; *Man from UNCLE* "The Pieces of Eight Affair" 10-18; *Cimarron Strip* "The Search" 11-9; **1968** *Star Trek* "Spectre of the Gun" 10-25; **1969** *Gunsmoke* "Mannon" 1-20; *Then Came Bronson* "All the World and God" 12-3; **1970** *Gunsmoke* "Celia" 2-23; *Gunsmoke* "Morgan" 3-2; *Adam-12* "Log 134-Child Stealer" 4-4; **1972** *Marcus Welby, M.D.* "Is It Soon That I am Done For?" 2-8; **1974** *Gunsmoke* "Disciple" 4-1; *Apple's Way* "The Still Life" 12-22.

TELEFILM

1971 *The Priest Killer* 9-14 NBC.

Eric Server
Eric worked for a time on the soap *General*

Hospital during the early seventies, then turned his attention to prime-time work. He did numerous guest roles prior to providing voice work on *Buck Rogers in the 25th Century* (1979-80). In 1981 he joined the cast of *B. J. and the Bear*.

He guested often in crime dramas during the mid eighties, working in series like *Simon and Simon*, *Riptide* and *Automan*.

GUEST CREDITS

1972 *Mission: Impossible* "Movie" 11-4; **1973** *Police Story* "Dangerous Games" 10-2; **1974** *Chase* "Thirty-Five Dollars Will Fly You to the Moon" 1-23; *Emergency* episode 2-16; *Kung Fu* "Cross Ties" 2-21; *Medical Center* "The Faces of Peril" 9-23; *Kolchak: The Night Stalker* "Horror in the Heights" 12-20; **1975** *Rockford Files* "Counter Gambit" 1-24; *Rockford Files* "The Farnsworth Stratagem" 9-19; *Harry O* "Lester Two" 9-25; *Kate McShane* "Accounts Receivable" 10-8; **1976** *Rockford Files* "The Italian Bird Fiasco" 2-13; *Quest* "Shanklin" 10-13; *Black Sheep Squadron* "Presumed Dead" 10-26; **1977** *Switch* "Fade Out" 10-14; **1978** *Incredible Hulk* "Ricky" 10-6; *Battlestar Gallactica* "The Magnificent Warriors" 11-12; **1979** *Lou Grant* "Sweep" 1-22; *240 Robert* "Out of Sight" 10-15; *Man Called Sloane* "Architect of Evil" 12-15; **1980** *Incredible Hulk* "A Rock and a Hard Place" 2-29; **1981** *Greatest American Hero* "The Best Desk Scenario" 5-13; *Jessica Novak* "Man on the Street" 11-26; **1983** *Knight Rider* "A Nice Indecent Little Town" 2-18; *Simon and Simon* "Betty Grable Flies Again" 12-8.

TELEFILMS

1975 *The UFO Incident* 10-20 NBC; **1976** *Dark Victory* 2-5 NBC; *Wanted: The Sundance Woman* 10-1 NBC; **1977** *The City* 1-12 NBC; *The Incredible Hulk* 11-4 CBS; *The Hunted Lady* 11-28 NBC; **1978** *Dr. Scorpion* 2-24 ABC; **1980** *The Night the City Screamed* 12-14 ABC; **1983** *Shooting Stars* 7-28 ABC.

Pilar Seurat

(born Rita Hernandez, July 25, 1938, Manila, Phillipines)

Pilar is of Phillipine, French, Scottish, Spanish and Chinese descent. Her father was a Phillipine national and an officer in the U. S. Army Intelligence Corps. He fought in the hills as a guerilla after war against Japan broke out in 1941, and after the Phillipines fell into Japanese hands. Pilar's mother fled with her, a sister and an older brother to back islands in the Phillipines, staying on the run throughout the war, fearful that her father's identity would be disclosed.

Pilar was seven when the war ended and the family was reunited in the U. S. She took singing, dancing and drama lessons and obtained a role in the road company of *The King and I*, with Gisele MacKenzie and Cameron Mitchell. After work in *Ken Murray's Blackouts of 1958-59*, Pilar moved into a busy career of television guest roles that continued until 1972.

Married to actor-writer Don Devlin, Pilar was usually cast in ethnic roles from Polynesian to French to Mexican to Native Americans. She frequently played idealistic young women, dedicated to various noble causes.

GUEST CREDITS

1960 *Maverick* "The White Widow" 1-24; **1961** *Checkmate* "Terror from the East" 1-7; *Islanders*

"The Strange Courtship of Danny Koo"2-l9; *New Breed* "Prime Target" l0-l0; **1962** *Naked City* "The Contract" 1-24; *Adventures in Paradise* "Blueprint for Paradise" 4-l; *Naked City* "Without Stick or Sword" 3-28; **1963** *Stoney Burke* "Weapons Man" 4-8; *Alfred Hitchcock Hour* "You'll Be the Death of Me" l0-l0; *Lieutenant* "A Troubled Image" 11-l6; **1964** *Ben Casey* "The Sound of One Hand Clapping" 2-l9; *Temple Houston* episode 2-27; *Burke's Law* "Who Killed the Richest Man in the World?" 11-11; **1965** *Daniel Boone* "Daughter of the Devil" 4-l5; *I Spy* "Carry Me Back to Old Tsing-Tao" 9-29; *Slattery's People* "How Impregnable Is a Magic Tower?" l0-l; *Voyage to the Bottom of the Sea* "The Silent Saboteurs" 11-2l; *The FBI* "All the Streets Are Silent" 11-28; **1966** *Wild Wild West* "The Night the Dragon Screamed" l-l4; *Virginian* "Long Ride to Wind River" l-l9; *Fugitive* "Wine Is a Traitor" 11-l; *The FBI* "Collision Course" 11-l3; *Man from UNCLE* "The Abominable Snowman Affair" l2-9; **1967** *The FBI* "Flood Verdict" l0-8; *High Chaparral* "The Terrorist" l2-l7; *Star Trek* "Wolf in the Fold" l2-22; **1969** *The FBI* "The Catalyst" 2-23; *Mannix* "To Catch a Rabbit" 4-l2; *Then Came Bronson* "Against a Cold Blank Wall" l2-24; **1970** *The FBI* "Diamond Millstone" l-l8; *Hawaii Five-O* "Nightmare Road" l-l8; *Mod Squad* "A Far Away Place So Near" 11-l7; *1971 O'Hara, U. S. Treasury* "Operation: Bandera" 9-24; **1972** *Bonanza* "Customs of the Country" 2-6.

TELEFILM

1971 *A Death of Innocence* 11-26 CBS.

Anne Seymour

(born Anne Eckert, September 11, 1909;died December 8, 1988)

After Anne Seymour received stage training at American Laboratory Theatre School, she had an extensive radio career during the thirties and forties, claiming over 5,000 radio episodes. She intersperced 20 years of stage work with her radio career before her screen debut in *All The King's Men* in 1949. She usually played strong ladies and

created some wonderful character parts. Her screen career was highlighted with roles in *Desire Under the Elms, Sunrise at Campobello, Misty, Good Neighbor Sam, How to Succeed in Business Without Really Trying* and *Fitzwilly.*

Television work included a stint as a repertory player on *Robert Montgomery Presents* (1954), and series regular roles on *Empire* (1962-63) and *The Tim Conway Show* (1970). Anne worked well into the eighties with a 1984 stint on the soap *General Hospital.*

GUEST CREDITS

1959 *Gunsmoke* "Kitty's Injury" 9-l9; *Peter Gunn* "Terror on the Campus" l2-2l; **1960** *Dow Hour of Great Mysteries* "The Burning Court" 4-24; *Chevy Mystery Show* "Dark Possession" 6-l9; *Chevy Mystery Show* "I Know What I'd Have Done" 7-24; *Gunsmoke* "The Wake" l2-l0; **1961** *Hawaiian Eye* "The Kapua of Coconut Bay" l0-4; *Bus Stop* "The Resurrection of Annie Ahearne" l0-l5; *Adventures in Paradise* "The Pretender" 11-l2; **1962** *Naked City* "One of the Most Important Men in the World" l-3l; **1963** *Perry Mason* "The Case of the Festive Falcon" 11-28; **1964** *Perry Mason* "The Case of the Bullied Bowler" 11-5; **1965** *Run for Your Life* "Make Angels Weep" l2-l3; **1966** *Bob Hope Chrysler Theater* "The Sister and the Savage" 4-6; **1969** *Land of the Giants*

"Six Hours to Live" 9-28; **1970** *Medical Center* "The V. D. Story" 3-25; **1972** *Cade's County* "Slay Ride" 1-30; 2-6; **1973** *Banyon* "Time Lapse" 1-12; **1974** *Ironside* "A Taste of Ashes" 2-14; *Harry O* "Second Sight" 11-7; **1975** *Kung Fu* "The Last Raid" 4-5; **1976** *Police Story* "Firebird" 2-6.

TELEFILMS

1973 *Tenafly* 2-12 NBC; **1974** *A Cry in the Wilderness* 3-26 ABC; *A Tree Grows in Brooklyn* 3-27 NBC; **1975** *The Last Survivors* 3-4 NBC; **1976** *Dawn: Portrait of a Runaway* 9-27 NBC; **1977** *James at 15* 9-5 NBC; **1979** *The Miracle Worker* 10-14 NBC; **1980** *Angel on My Shoulder* 5-11 ABC; **1981** *Charlie and the Great Balloon Race* 7-12 NBC; **1982** *Life of the Party: The Story of Beatrice* 9-29 CBS.

Joshua Shelley

Character actor Joshua Shelley came to television and films in 1949 and, during 1951, was a regular on a variety show called *Holiday Hotel*. He became a director and was absent from in front of the cameras for many years until he returned to acting in 1973, especially television.

Shelley worked into the eighties in television

guest roles and was a series regular on *B. J. and the Bear* during 1979-80.

GUEST CREDITS

1973 *McMillan and Wife* "The Devil, You Say" 10-21; **1974** *McCloud* "Barefoot Girls on Bleeker Sreet" 9-22; *Police Story* "Explosion" 12-3; **1975** *McMillan and Wife* "Love, Honor and Swindle" 2-16; *Switch* "The Man Who Couldn't Lose" 10-14; *Harry O* "The Acolyte" 10-16; *Police Story* "Face for a Shadow" 11-7; *Ellery Queen* "The Adventure of Veronica's Veils" 11-13; **1976** *Joe Forrester* "An Act of Violence" 1-13; *Blue Knight* "Bull's Eye" 9-22; *Delvecchio* "Requiem for a Loser" 3-6; *Baretta* "Think Mink" 3-9; *Quincy, M.E.* "The Hot Dog Murder" 4-22; *Kojak* "Once More From Birdland" 10-30; **1978** *Baretta* "Hot Horse" 1-4; **1981** *Hart to Hart* "Ex-Wives Are Murder" 1-20; *Incredible Hulk* "Patterns" 5-22; **1982** *Cassie and Company* "The Golden Silence" 1-29; *Nurse* "The Clown Prince Is Indisposed" 4-30; **1983** *Remington Steele* "Steele Threads" 12-19.

TELEFILMS

1973 *Firehouse* 1-2 ABC; *The Marcus-Nelson Murders* 3-8 CBS; **1978** *Ring of Passion* 2-4 NBC.

Paul Shenar

(born February 12, 1936; died October 11, 1989)
Paul Shenar began his acting career off-Broadway in 1962 after serving in The U. S. Air Force during 1954-57. He came to television in 1974 and starred in two seventies telefilms: *The Night That Panicked America* (1975) and *Ziegfield: The Man and His Women* (1978). And he became a popular voice-over artist for TV commercials.

His later eighties guest roles included appearances on *Spenser: For Hire* and *Dynasty*. Paul died of AIDS on October 11, 1989.

GUEST CREDITS

1974 *Columbo* "Publish or Perish" 1-13; *Owen*

Marshall, Counselor at Law "House of Friends" 1-19; *Mannix* "The Dark Hours" 1-20; **1975** *Kojak* "Night of the Piraeus" 1-26; *Petrocelli* "Death in Small Doses" 3-27; *Invisible Man* "Barnard Wants Out" 10-6; **1976** *Hawaii Five-0* "A Killer Grows Wines" 2-5; *Bionic Woman* "The Ghost Murder" 5-26; *Wonder Woman* "The Feminine Mystique" 11-6, 11-8; **1977** *Hawaii Five-0* "See How She Runs" 3-31; *Logan's Run* "Man Out of Time" 10-17; **1980** *Hart to Hart* "Night Horrors" 1-22; **1982** *Today's FBI* "Kidnap" 4-19; **1983** *Scarecrow and Mrs. King* "Service Above and Beyond"11-7.

TELEFILMS

1974 *The Execution of Private Slovik* 3-13 NBC; **1975** *The Night That Panicked America* 10-31 ABC; **1976** *The Keegans* 5-3 CBS; *Gemini Man* 5-10 NBC; **1977** *The Hostage Heart* 9-9 CBS; **1978** *The Courage and the Passion* 5-27 CBS; *Ziegfeld: The Man and His Women* 5-28 NBC; *Suddenly, Love* 12-4 NBC.

Jan Shepard

(born 1932)

Jan Shepard's television career extended from

1950 through 1973. She was a regular on *Captain Midnight* (1954-56) and appeared on fifties series like *Science Fiction Theatre* and *Inner Sanctum*. And she was a regular on the daytime soap *Clear Horizon* during 1960.

Jan was very effective in portraying determined and dedicated frontier women in numerous TV western series appearances, including 4 episodes of *Gunsmoke* and *The Virginian*, and 3 each on *Rawhide* and *Laramie*.

GUEST CREDITS

1959 *Rawhide* "Incident with an Executioner" 1-23; *Trackdown* "Terror" 2-4; *Rin Tin Tin* "Apache Stampede" 3-20; *Markham* "A Grave and Present Danger" 9-20; *Man and the Challenge* "White Out" 11-14; **1960** *Wanted: Dead or Alive* "Mental Lapse" 1-2; *Rawhide* "Incident at Sulphur Creek" 3-11; *Phillip Marlowe* "Last Call for Murder" 3-22; **1961** *Dante's Inferno* "Dial D for Dante" 1-16; *Gunsmoke* "Tall Trapper" 1-21; *Rawhide* "Incident at the Top of the World" 1-27; *Bat Masterson* "Bullwhacker's Bounty" 2-16; *Gunslinger* "Rampage" 3-16; *Gunsmoke* "Old Faces" 3-18; *Stagecoach West* "The Raider" 5-9; *Laramie* "Badge of the Outsider" 5-23; *Cain's Hundred* "King of the Mountain" 10-24; *Laramie* "The Jailbreakers" 12-19; **1962** *Lawman* "Change of Venue" 2-11; *Perry Mason* "The Case of

the Capricious Corpse" 10-4; *Laramie* "Bad Blood" 12-4; **1963** *G.E. True* "Gertie the Great" 4-14; *Perry Mason* "The Case of the Deadly Verdict" 10-3; **1964** *Gunsmoke* "Friend" 1-25; *Perry Mason* "The Case of the Paper Bullets" 10-1; **1965** *Virginian* "The Brothers" 9-15; *Perry Mason* "The Case of the Runaway Racer" 11-14; *Convoy* "No More Souvenirs" 12-3; *Long Hot Summer* "Return of the Quicks" 12-16; **1966** *Virginian* "Harvest of Strangers" 2-16; *Virginian* "Long Journey Home" 12-14; **1967** *Road West* "No Sancturary" 2-6; *Gunsmoke* "Noose of Gold" 3-4; *Ironside* "The Taker" 10-12; *High Chaparral* "Sudden Country" 11-5; *The FBI* "Line of Fire" 11-26; **1968** *Mannix* "Another Final Exit" 2-10; *The FBI* "The Runaways" 10-13; *High Chaparral* "Our Lady of Guadalupe" 12-20; **1969** *Virginian* "Stopover" 1-8; *Land of the Giants* "Shell Game" 4-13; **1970** *Then Came Bronson* "The Gleam of the Eagle Eye" 1-21; *Marcus Welby, M.D.* "The Labyrinth" 11-10; **1972** *Longstreet* "Survival Times Two" 1-13; *Rookies* "Code 261" 11-5.

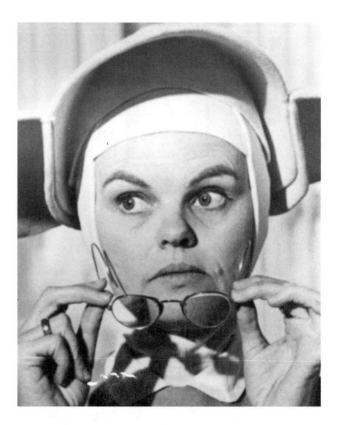

Madeleine Sherwood

(born Madeleine Thornton, November 13, 1922, Montreal, Canada)

Madeleine attended Yale Drama School and studied acting at Montreal Repertory Theater and at Actor's Studio. She made her film debut in *Baby Doll* (1956) and also appeared in *Cat on a Hot Tin Roof, Parrish, Sweet Bird of Youth, Hurry Sundown* and *Pendulum*.

Sherwood came to television in 1952 in a *Philco Television Playhouse* production and later appeared on *Studio One*. Following sixties guest work she played Mother Superior on *The Flying Nun* for three seasons (1967-70). During the seventies she worked on soaps *The Secret Storm* and *The Guiding Light*. This fine veteran character actress worked intermittently on television until the late eighties.

GUEST CREDITS

1961 *Alfred Hitchcock Presents* "Make My Death Bed" 6-27; **1962** *Naked City* "The One Marked Hot Gives Cold" 3-21; **1963** *Nurses* "The Perfect Nurse" 2-28; *Naked City* "S.S. American Dream" 5-8; *Fugitive* "The Witch" 9-24; **1964** *Fugitive* "Devil's Carnival" 12-22; **1965** *Ben Casey* "When I Am Grown to Man's Estate" 2-8; **1969** *Outcasts* "The Candidates" 1-27; **1970** *Name of the Game* "The Garden" 1-30; *Bonanza* "For a Young Lady" 12-27; **1972** *Owen Marshall, Counselor at Law* "The First Day of Your Life" 11-30; **1973** *Toma* "Crime Without Victim" 10-18.

Pamela Susan Shoop

(born June 7, 1947, Hollywood, California)

The daughter of actress Julie Bishop, Pamela began a spasmodic film career in 1969 while in her teens, but quickly established a herself on television, beginning in 1970 and extending through the eighties. She was a featured regular on the soap *Return to Peyton Place* (1972-73), playing the lead role of Allison MacKenzie.

Post-1983 guest credits included work on *Masquerade, Scarecrow and Mrs. King, Knight

Rider, Murder, She Wrote, Simon and Simon (2), *Law and Harry McGraw* and *The Highwayman*.

GUEST CREDITS

1970 *Interns* "Mondays Can Be Fatal" 11-27; **1972** *The FBI* "The Corruptor" 2-27; *Rookies* "The Bear That Didn't Get Up" 10-23; *Mannix* "To Kill a Memory" 10-29; *Mod Squad* "Crime Club" 11-23; **1973** *Emergency* "That Time of Year" 10-23; **1976** *Switch* "Before the Holocaust" 2-17; *New, Original Wonder Woman* "The Feminine Mystique" 11-6, 11-8; **1977** *Code R* episode 4-15; **1978** *Incredible Hulk* "Terror in Times Square" 3-31; *Kaz* "A Fine Romance" 12-3; **1979** *Buck Rogers* "Vegas in Space" 10-24; *B. J. and the Bear* "Silent Night, Unholy Night" 12-15; *CHiPs* "Christmas Watch" 12-15; **1980** *Hawaii Five-0* "School of Assassins" 1-1; *Vegas* "The Private Eye Connection" 1-2; *Buck Rogers* "A Blast for Buck" 1-17; *Galactica 1980* "Galactica Discovers Earth" 1-27, 2-3, 2-10; *Magnum, P.I.* "Please Don't Eat the Snow in Hawaii" 12-11; **1981** *B. J. and the Bear* "The Fast and the Furious" 1-20, 1-27; *Fall Guy* "The Meek Shall Inherit Rhonda" 11-4; **1982** *Fall Guy* "Bail and Bond" 10-27; **1983** *Tales of the Gold Monkey* "Force of Habit" 2-2.

TELEFILM

1979 *The Dallas Cowboy Cheerleaders* 1-14 ABC.

Charles Siebert

(born March 9, 1938, Kenosha, Wisconsin)

Educated at Marquette University, Charles began his acting career onstage, in both the U. S. and in England. His television started in soap operas, first on *Search for Tomorrow* (1967-71), followed by a stint on *As the World Turns*.

Charles began guesting on prime-time television in 1975 and became a regular on *The Blue Knight* (1976). He also had a recurring role on *One Day at a Time* (1976-78) and was a regular on an abbreviated sitcom, *Husbands and Lovers* (1978). He began his most visible role as Dr. Riverside on *Trapper John, M.D.* in 1979 and stayed with it for the series' run (1979-86).

Siebert had one additional series regular role, on *Mancuso, FBI* during 1989-90.

GUEST CREDITS

1975 *Rockford Files* "The Reincarnation of Angie" 12-5; **1976** *Harry O* "Mister Five and Dime" 1-8; *Barnaby Jones* "The Fatal Dive" 10-28; *Kojak* "By Silence Betrayed" 11-14; **1977** *Police Woman*

"Shark" 2-15; *Rockford Files* "New Life, Old Dragons" 2-25; *Dog and Cat* "Dead Dog and Cat" 3-12; *Most Wanted* "The People Mover" 4-25; **1978** *Barnaby Jones* "The Coronado Triangle" 3-2; *Barnaby Jones* "Stages of Fear" 11-23; *Dallas* "Julie's Murder" 2-2, 2-9; *Operation: Runaway* "Forty-Eight Hours to Live" 8-28.

TELEFILMS

1976 *Panache* 5-15 ABC; **1977** *Tail Gunner Joe* 2-6 NBC; *Murder in Peyton Place* 10-3 NBC; *Tarantulas: The Deadly Cargo* 12-28 CBS; **1978** *Nowhere to Run* 1-16 NBC; *Wild and Wooley* 2-20 ABC; **1979** *The Seeding of Sarah Burns* 4-7 CBS; *The Miracle Worker* 10-14 NBC; *Topper* 11-9 ABC; **1980** *A Cry for Love* 10-20 NBC.

Mark Slade

(born 1939, Salem, Mass.)

Mark made a film debut in 1960 in *Splendor in the Grass* and appeared in *Voyage to the Bottom of the Sea* the following year. He came to television in 1964 and became a regular on *The Wackiest Ship in the Army* during 1965-66. He gained his most visible role on *The High Chaparral*, as Billy Blue Cannon (1967-70).

Slade had one other regular role, on a short lived and syndicated adventure series, *Salty* (1974). Thereafter, he did occasional guest roles and telefilms into the eighties.

GUEST CREDITS

1964 *Perry Mason* "The Case of the Careless Kidnapper" 4-30; *Rawhide* "The Enormous Fist" 10-2; *Alfred Hitchcock Hour* "Memo from Purgatory" 12-21; **1965** *Mr. Novak* "Beat the Plowshare, Edge the Sword" 1-26; **1966** *Bonanza* "A Real Nice, Friendly Little Town" 11-27; **1967** *Wild Wild West* "The Night of the Gyspy Peril" 1-20; **1972** *Rookies* "Dead, Like a Lost Dream" 9-18; *Mod Squad* "Crime Club" 11-23; **1973** *Rookies* "Code 261" 11-5; **1975** *Rookies* "Cliffy" 3-3; *Bronk* "There's Gonna Be a War" 12-21; **1978** *Project UFO* "Sighting 4020-The Believe It or

Not Incident" 10-19; **1979** *CHiPs* "High Octane" 10-6; *Paris* "Friends and Enemies" 10-20; **1981** *Charlie's Angels* "Chorus Line Angels" 2-21; **1982** *CHiPs* "Tight Fit" 10-17.

TELEFILMS

1973 *Message to My Daughter* 12-12 ABC; **1979** *The Return of the Mod Squad* 5-18 ABC; **1980** *Waikiki* 4-21 ABC.

Richard X. Slattery

(born 1925, New York City)

A New York City policeman for 12 years before turning to acting in 1958, burly Richard X. Slattery was typecast as take-charge types, i.e. military officers and police officials. Following a 1960 film debut, he moved into television guest and series regular roles and became highly visible on the medium. He was a favorite guest on *Bewitched*, with 6 appearances.

Slattery was a regular on 4 TV series: *The*

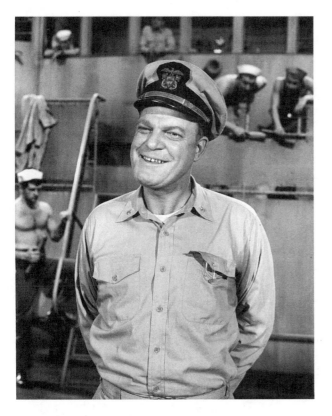

Gallant Men (1962-63), *Mr. Roberts* (1965-66), *Switch* (1976-77) and *C.P.O. Sharkey* (1977-78). He had a prominent roles on the 1983 miniseries *The Winds of War*, appearing as Admiral William "Bull" Halsey.

GUEST CREDITS

1960 *Naked City* "A Hole in the City" 2-1; **1962** *Bus Stop* "Door without a Key" 3-4; *77 Sunset Strip* "The Long Shot Caper" 3-23; *77 Sunset Strip* "The Gemologist Caper" 5-11; **1963** *Rawhide* "Incident of the Iron Bull" 10-3; *Great Adventure* "Six Wagons to Sea" 10-18; **1964** *Eleventh Hour* "A Full Moon Every Night" 3-4; *Alfred Hitchcock Hour* "Anyone for Murder?" 3-31; *Temple Houston* episode 4-2; *Kraft Suspense Theatre* "The Kamchatka Incident" 11-12; **1965** *Rawhide* "Blood Harvest" 2-12; *Kraft Suspense Theatre* "Connery's Hands" 7-1; **1967** *Road West* "Reap the Whirlwind" 1-9; *Daniel Boone* "The Williamsburg Cannon" 1-12, 1-19; *Iron Horse* "The Bridge at Forty Mile" 1-23; *Green Hornet* "Ace in the Hole" 2-3; *Invaders* "Moon Shot" 4-18; *Cimarron Strip* episode 10-12; *Bonanza* "Six Black

Horses" 11-26; **1968** *The FBI* "The Predators" 4-7; **1969** *High Chaparral* "Stinky Flanagan" 2-21; *Lancer* "The Knot" 3-18; *Lancer* "The Kid" 10-7; **1970** *Lancer* "Dream of Falcons" 4-7; *Bold Ones: The Doctors* "The Will Really Kill You" 9-20; **1972** *Room 222* "Suing Means Saying You're Sorry" 2-4; *Owen Marshall, Counselor at Law* "Five Will Get You Six" 10-26; **1974** *Chopper One* "Chopper One" 1-17; *Cannon* "The Cure That Kills" 2-20; *Police Story* "Love, Mabel" 11-26; *Ironside* "Fall of an Angel" 12-19; **1975** *Kojak* "Close Cover Before Killing" 1-5; *Invisible Man* "Panic" 10-20.

TELEFILMS

1968 *Now You See It, Now You Don't* 11-11 NBC; **1974** *Wonder Woman* 3-12 ABC; **1975** *Adventures of the Queen* 2-14; CBS; **1976** *Louis Armstrong-Chicago Style* 1-25 ABC.

Sandra "Sandy" Smith

After major roles in soaps *The Guiding Light* (1962), and *Our Private World* (1965), Sandra turned to prime-time guest work and a series regular role on *The Interns* (1970-71).

GUEST CREDITS

1966 *Iron Horse* "Through Ticket to Gunsight" 11-28; *Virginian* "TheStrange Quest of Claire Bingham" 4-12; *Run for Your Life* "The Frozen Image" 10-4; *Mannix* "Huntdown" 11-18; **1968** *Big Valley* "Days of Wrath" 1-8; *Wild Wild West* "Night of the Vipers" 1-21; *Gunsmoke* "Mr. Sam'l" 2-26; *Gunsmoke* "The Miracle Man" 12-2; *Hawaii Five-0* "No Blue Skies" 12-5; **1969** *Star Trek* "Turnabout Intruder" 6-3; *Bold Ones: The Lawyers* "A Game of Chance" 9-21; **1970** *The FBI* "Deadly Reunion" 1-25; **1972** *Columbo* "The Greenhouse Jungle" 10-15; *Gunsmoke* "Tatum" 11-13; **1973** *Hawaii Five-0* "Here Today…Gone Tonight" 1-23; *Ironside* "All Honorable Men" 3-8; **1974** *Nakia* "The Non-Person" 9-21; **1975** *Rockford Files* "Resurrection in Black and White" 11-7; **1977** *Starsky and Hutch* "Starsky's Lady" 2-12.

TELEFILM

1966 *Scalplock* 4-10 ABC.

Abraham Sofaer

(born October 1, 1886, Burma; died December 21, 1988)

Initially a stage actor in England, Abraham came to America in 1921 and made a film debut in 1931. He appeared in a number of film epics like *Quo Vadis?*, *Omar Khayyam, King of Kings, Taras Bulba* and *The Greatest Story Ever Told*. Of Jewish and Burmese extraction, he worked in radio as well as films and appeared in fifties television productions.

He was a busy fifties TV guest actor, playing all types of ethnic roles, often sinister characters. Abraham was 102 years old when he died in 1988.

GUEST CREDITS

1960 *Perry Mason* "The Case of the Crying Cherub" 4-9; *Riverboat* "The Long Trail" 4-4; *Twilight Zone* "The Mighty Casey" 6-17; *Thriller* "The Prediction" 11-22; *Adventures in Paradise* "Incident in Suva" 12-26; **1961** *Alfred Hitchcock Presents* "The Changing Heart" 1-3; *Ben Casey* "My Good Friend Krikor" 11-27; *General Electric Theater* "The Other Wise Man" 12-24; **1962** *Naked City* "The Contract" 1-24; *Alfred Hitchcock Presents* "Don't Look Behind You" 9-27; *Dr. Kildare* "The Visitors" 10-11; **1964** *Alfred Hitchcock Hour* "Beyond the City of Death" 1-24; *Outer Limits* "Demon with a Glass Hand" 10-24; **1965** *Bob Hope Chrysler Theater* "Terror Island" 2-26; *Man from UNCLE* "The Brain-Killer Affair" 3-8; *Daniel Boone* "The Thanksgiving Story" 11-25; **1966** *Star Trek* "Charlie X" 9-15; *Time Tunnel* "Revenge of the Gods" 10-21; *Mission: Impossible* "Elena" 12-10; **1967** *Time Tunnel* "The Wall of Jerico" 1-27; *Felony Squad* "Let Him Die" 9-11; **1968** *Lost in Space* "The Flaming Planet" 2-21; *Girl from UNCLE* "The Prisoner of Zalamar Affair" 9-20; *Star Trek* "Spectre of the Gun" 10-25; **1972** *Search* "Operation Iceman" 10-25; **1974** *Kolchak: The Night Stalker* "Horror in the Heights" 12-20.

Paul Sorensen

(born 1926)

Character actor Paul Sorensen received stage training at Pasadena Playhouse in 1947. He came to television in 1952 and has done hundreds of TV appearances. He made his film debut in 1956, eventually appearing in *Battle Hymn, Flower Drum*

Song, The Greatest Story Ever Told, I Love You, Alice B. Toklas and *Escape to Witch Mountain*.

Western series guest roles were a significant part of Paul's TV career, with appearances in over 20 episodes of that genre from 1959. He usually played strong and forceful types, on either side of the law.

GUEST CREDITS

1959 *Have Gun-Will Travel* "Maggie O'Banion" 4-24; *Black Saddle* "End of the Line" 5-6; *Have Gun-Will Travel* "The Gold Toad" 11-21; **1960** *Johnny Ringo* "Die Twice" 1-21; *Law of the Plainsman* "Amnesty" 4-7; *Zane Grey Theater* "A Gun for Willie" 10-6; *Rifleman* "Seven" 10-11; *Westerner* "The Painting" 12-30; **1962** *Ben Casey* "Pack Up all My Cares and Woes" 12-17; **1963** *Rifleman* "The Sixteenth Cousin" 1-28; *Virginian* "Vengeance Is the Spur" 2-27; *Ben Casey* "The Last Splintered Spoke on the Old Burlesque Wheel" 12-25; **1964** *Outer Limits* "Behold, Eck!" 10-3; **1965** *Big Valley* "The Guilt of Matt Bentell" 12-8; *Big Valley* "The Brawlers" 12-15; **1966** *Honey West* "It's Earlier Than You Think" 1-21; *Perry Mason* "The Case of the Scarlet Scandal" 2-20; *Fugitive* "A Taste for Tomorrow" 4-12; *Big Valley* "Target" 10-31; *Big Valley* "Barbary Red" 12-16; **1967** *Big Valley* "Wagonload of Dreams" 1-2; *Jerico* "The Big Brass Conra Band" 1-12; *Mission: Imposssible* "The Traitor" 4-15; *Fugitive* "The Judgment" 8-22; *Cimarron Strip* "Whitey" 10-

19; *Big Valley* "Explosion" 11-20; *Guns of Will Sonnett* "The Turkey Shoot" 11-24; **1969** *Land of the Giants* "The Bounty Hunter" 1-19; *Mod Squad* "My Name Is Manolette" 9-30; **1970** *High Chaparral* "The Long Shadow" 1-2; *Name of the Game* "The War Merchants" 10-30; **1972** *McMillan and Wife* "An Elementary Case of Murder" 3-1; *Streets of San Francisco* "Forty Five Minutes from Home" 10-7; *Gunsmoke* "The Drummer" 10-9; *McMillan and Wife* "Terror Times Two" 12-13; **1973** *McMillan and Wife* "The Fine Art of Staying Alive" 3-11; *Barnaby Jones* "Sing a Song of Murder" 4-1; *Gunsmoke* "The Widow and the Rogue" 10-29; **1974** *Police Story* "A Dangerous Age" 9-10; *Mannix* "Death Has No Face" 10-27; *Gunsmoke* "The Fourth Victim" 11-4; **1975** *Police Story* "Headhunter" 1-14; *Marcus Welby, M.D.* "Unindicted Wife" 2-25; *S.W.A.T.* "Pressure Cooker" 3-17; **1976** *Blue Knight* "To Kill a Tank" 3-10; *Police Story* "Payment Deferred" 9-21; **1978** *Rockford Files* "The Attractive Nuisance" 1-6; *Police Story* "A Chance to Live" 5-28; **1979** *Salvage 1* "Hard Water" 1-4, 1-11; *Kaz* "Kazinsky vs. Bennett" 1-31.

TELEFILM

1980 *Flamingo Road* 5-12 NBC.

Olan Soulé

(born February 28, 1909, La Harpe, Illinois; died February 1, 1994)

The reed-thin Olan began performing in tent shows in 1926, moving to radio in Chicago during 1933. For eleven years he was a featured player on a radio soap *Bachelor's Children*. He moved to Hollywood in 1947, with a film debut in 1949, the first of over 100 film appearances, including roles in *North by Northwest, Days of Wine and Roses* and *The Towering Inferno*.

In 1954 Olan captured a regular slot on *Captain Midnight*, a children's show that ran until 1956. During the fifties he made guest appearances on *Schlitz Playhouse of Stars, Studio One* and *I Love Lucy*.

He became a regular on *My Three Sons* during

1961-63, and did guest appearances on sitcoms like *The Andy Griffith Show* (5), *Petticoat Junction*, and *Mr. Ed. Arnie* offered another sitcom regular role in 1970-71.

Olan estimated that he had appeared in over 200 television shows and 7,000 radio shows. He died of lung cancer in his daugher's home in Corona, Calif., just a few days short of his 85th birthday.

GUEST CREDITS

1959 *Perry Mason* "The Case of the Glittering Goldfish" 1-17; *Wanted: Dead or Alive* "Eager Man" 2-28; *Wanted: Dead or Alive* "The Kovack Affair" 3-28; *One Step Beyond* "The Navigator" 4-14; *Wanted: Dead or Alive* "Amos Carter" 5-9; *Wanted: Dead or Alive* "The Hostage" 10-10; **1960** *One Step Beyond* "Earthquake" 1-12; *Johnny Ringo* "Poster Incident" 1-14; *Detectives* "My Brother's Keepers" 1-22; *Wagon Train* "The Larry Hanify Story" 1-27; *Rawhide* "Incident of the Sharpshooter" 2-26; *Johnny Ringo* "Shoot the Moon" 6-2; *Twilight Zone* "The Man in the Bottle" 10-7; *Wanted: Dead or Alive* "To the Victor" 11-9; *Loretta Young Show* "No Margin for Error" 11-13; *One Step Beyond* "Legacy of Love" 12-20; **1961** *Maverick* "Family Pride" 1-8; *Bonanza* "Vengeance" 2-11; *Rawhide* "Incident in the Middle of Nowhere" 4-7; *Have Gun-Will Travel* "The Road" 5-27; *Rawhide* "Incident of the Fear in the Streets" 6-23; *New Breed* "Death of a Ghost" 10-17; *Laramie* "The Fatal Step" 10-24; *New Breed* "Till Death Do Us Part" 11-7; **1962** *Perry Mason* "The Case of the Shapely Shadow" 1-6; *Alcoa Premiere* "Mr. Easy" 2-13; *Tales of Wells Fargo* "To Kill a Town" 3-31; *Have Gun-Will Travel* "Hobson's Choice" 4-7; *Have Gun-Will Travel* "Taylor's Woman" 9-22; *Alfred Hitchcock Hour* " Ride the Nightmare" 11-29; **1964** *Twilight Zone* "Caesar and Me" 4-10; **1965** *Bonanza* "The Flapjack Contest" 1-3; *Big Valley* "The Brawlers" 12-15; *Gunsmoke* "The Avengers" 12-18; **1966** *Fugitive* "Stroke of Genius" 2-1; *The FBI* "The Defector" 3-27; *The FBI* "Ordeal" 11-6; **1967** *Dragnet* "The Big LSD" 1-12; *Dragnet* "The Big Hit-and-Run Driver" 4-6; *Dragnet* "The Big Bullet" 5-11; *Bonanza* "Second Chance" 9-17; *Bonanza* "The Conquistadors" 10-1; **1968** *Bonanza* "The Thirteenth Man" 1-21; *Cimarron Strip* "The Greeners" 3-7; **1969** *The FBI* "The Eye of the Storm" 1-5; *Gunsmoke* "The Mark of Cain" 2-3; *Big Valley* "Danger Road" 4-21; *Dragnet* "Personnel-The Big Shooting" 9-18; *Dragnet* "D.H.Q.-Medical" 10-9; *Dragnet* "Burglary-Auto Courtroom" 11-20; *Land of the Giants* "Comeback" 11-23; **1970** *Dragnet* "Missing Persons-The Body" 3-5; **1972** *Cannon* "The Endangered Species" 12-12; **1973** *Mission: Impossible* "Imitation" 3-30; **1974** *Chase* "Right to an Attorney" 1-8; *Adam-12* "The Sweet Smell…" 1-9; **1975** *Harry O* "Elegy for a Cop" 2-27; **1978** *Project UFO* "Sighting 4002-The Believe It or Not Incident" 10-20; *Eddie Capra Mysteries* "The Two Million Dollar Stowaway" 12-8; **1979** *Battlestar Gallactica* "War of the Gods" 1-14, 1-21; *Project UFO* "Sighting 4026" 7-26.

TELEFILMS

1970 *House on Greenapple Road* 1-11 ABC; **1971** *The D. A.: Conspiracy to Kill* 1-11 NBC; **1973** *The Six Million Dollar Man* 3-7 ABC; **1975** *The Legend of Lizzie Borden* 2-10 ABC; **1981** *Code Red* 9-20 ABC.

Arthur Space

(born 1908, New Brunswick, New Jersey; died January 13, 1983)

Acting in high school plays propelled Arthur Space into summer stock and eventually to Broadway. Out of acting during the depression, Space went to Hollywood and made his film debut in 1941. Among his 150 film credits were roles in *Random Harvest, Thirty Seconds Over Tokyo, Wing and a Prayer, Leave Her to Heaven, Black Beauty, The Paleface, The Spirit of St. Louis, Twilight for the Gods, A Summer Place, The Shakiest Gun in the West* and *Herbie Rides Again*.

Arthur worked in television from the early fifties until 1980. He had a recurring role on *Lassie* from 1954 to 1964, appearing as Doc Weaver; he also had a series regular role on *National Velvet* (1960-62). Space was one of Hollywood's most enduring character actors, a recognizable face for 40 years.

GUEST CREDITS

1959 *Wanted: Dead or Alive* "The Corner" 2-21; *Phillip Marlowe* "Bum Wrap" 11-17; **1960** *Have Gun-Will Travel* "The Night the Town Died" 2-6; *Colt .45* "Arizona Anderson" 2-14; *Rifleman* "The Grasshopper" 3-1; *M Squad* "Dead Parents Don't Talk" 5-3; *Colt .45* "The Trespasser" 6-21; **1962** *Broncho* "The Last Letter" 3-5; **1964** *Wagon Train* "The Last Circle-Up" 4-27; *Perry Mason* "The Case of the Paper Bullets" 10-1; **1965** *Wild Wild West* "The Night of the Double-Edged Knife" 11-12; *Big Valley*

"The Man from Nowhere" 11-14; **1967** *Wild Wild West* "The Night of the Tottering Tontine" 1-6; *Voyage to the Bottom of the Sea* "Destroy Seaview" 3-19; **1968** *Wild Wild West* "The Night of the Sedgewick Curse" 10-18; **1970** *Young Lawyers* "A Simple Thing Called Justice" 9-28; **1971** *Cade's County* "Company Town" 9-26; **1975** *Six Million Dollar Man* "Look Alike" 2-23; *Baretta* "Barney" 4-6; **1980** *Charlie's Angels* "Home Sweet Homes" 1-30.

Laurette Spang

(born 1951)

Primarily a seventies television actress, Laurette Spang broke into the medium in 1972 and worked diligently in guest roles and telefilms. An engaging smile and huge eyes also earned her guest work on sitcoms like *Happy Days* (3), *The Dukes of Hazzard* and *Three's Company*, plus a couple of cruises on *The Love Boat*. During 1978-79 she was a series regular on *Battlestar Galactica*.

Married to actor John McCook, one of her later

guest roles was on a 1984 episode of *Magnum, P.I.*, appearing in tandem with her husband on the show.

GUEST CREDITS

1972 *Emergency* episode 12-2; **1973** *Alias Smith and Jones* "Only Three to a Bed" 1-13; *Emergency* episode 2-29; *Marcus Welby, M.D.* "The Panic Path" 9-11; *Chase* "Foul Up" 9-25; *Adam-12* "Venice Division" 10-10; *Streets of San Francisco* "Harem" 10-25; *Owen Marshall, Counselor at Law* "Second Victim" 12-19; **1974** *Six Million Dollar Man* "Survival of the Fittest" 1-25; **1976** *Gemini Man* "Run, Sam, Run" 10-28; *Charlie's Angels* "Consenting Adults" 12-8; **1978** *Lou Grant* "Spies" 2-27; *Project UFO* "Sighting 4015: The Underwater Incident" 9-21; **1979** *B. J. and the Bear* "Snow White and the Seven Lady Truckers" 9-29, 10-6; **1980** *Barnaby Jones* "The Final Victim" 3-6; **1980** *Today's FBI* "Spy" 1-10.

TELEFILMS

1972 *Short Walk to Daylight* 10-24 ABC; **1973** *Runaway* 9-29 ABC; **1975** *Sunshine* 4-3 NBC; **1982** *The Day the Bubble Burst* 2-7 NBC.

Joan Staley

(born 1940, Minneapolis, Minnesota)

A sixties television actress, Joan was quite busy in the medium from 1960 through 1965, in numerous guest roles and series regular roles. She was a regular on *The Beachcomber* (1960-61), *The Lively Ones* (1962), *77 Sunset Strip* (1963-64) and *Broadside* (1964-65).

Her only significant film role was as Don Knotts' romantic interest in *The Ghost and Mr. Chicken* (1966).

GUEST CREDITS

1959 *Lawless Years* "The Miles Miller Story" 6-30; **1960** *Perry Mason* "The Case of the Gallant Grifter" 2-6; *Bonanza* "The Stranger" 2-27; *Hawaiian Eye* "Girl on a String" 11-16; **1961** *77 Sunset Strip* "Once Upon a Caper" 2-10; *Checkmate* "A Matter of Conscience" 2-18; *Asphalt Jungle* "The Professor" 5-28; *Dick Powell Show* "Who Killed Julie Greer?" 9-22; *Untouchables* "Hammerlock" 12-12; **1962** *Alcoa Premiere* "All My Clients Are Innocent" 4-17; *87th Precinct* "Girl in the Case" 4-30; *Hawaiian Eye* "Location Shooting" 5-9; *Perry Mason* "The Case of the Lonely Eloper" 5-22; **1963** *Dick Powell Show* "Colossus" 3-12; *Stoney Burke* "Kelly's Place" 4-15; **1965** *Kraft Suspense Theatre* "Kill Me Only on July 20th" 6-17; *Laredo* "Anybody Here Seen Billy?" 10-21; *Perry Mason* "The Case of the Double Entry Mind" 12-26; **1967** *Mission: Impossible* "The Council" 11-19, 11-26; **1969** *Adam-12* "Tell Him He Pushed a Little Too Hard" 3-29.

Harry Dean Stanton

(born 1926, Kentucky)

In films from 1956, Harry Dean Stanton was frequently cast as threatening rurals or various types of criminals. His films included *Pork Chop Hill, How the West Was Won, Cool Hand Luke, Dillinger,*

The Godfather, Part II, The Missouri Breaks, Alien, The Rose, Escape from New York and *Pretty in Pink*.

Most of his television work was in guest roles, from 1959-69, primarily in TV westerns, and usually as heavies. His film career took off and he was rarely seen on TV after 1970.

GUEST CREDITS

1959 *Have Gun-Will Travel* "Treasure Trail" 1-24; *Rifleman* "Tension" 10-27; *Rawhide* "Incident at the Buffalo Smokehouse" 10-30; **1961** *Gunsmoke* "Love Thy Neighbor" 1-28; *Laramie* "Cactus Lady" 2-21; *Law and Mr. Jones* "The Enemy" 4-28; *Gunsmoke* "Old Yellow Boots" 10-7; **1962** *Laramie* "The Confederate Express" 1-30; *Have Gun-Will Travel* "The Waiting Room" 2-24; *Gunsmoke* "The Boys" 5-26; *Rawhide* "Incident of the Lost Women" 11-2; **1963** *Laramie* "The Betrayers" 1-22; *Bonanza* "The Way of Aaron" 3-10; *Empire* "Breakout" 4-16; *Rawhide* "Incident of the Prophecy" 11-21; **1964** *Gunsmoke* "Comanches Is Soft" 3-7; *Daniel Boone* "A Short Walk to Salem" 11-19; **1965** *Fugitive* "Moon Child" 2-16; **1966** *Big Valley* "By Force and Violence" 3-30; **1967** *Guns of Will Sonnett* "Meeting at Devil's Fork" 10-27; *Cimarron Strip* "Till the End of Night" 11-16; **1968** *High Chaparral* "Gold Is Where You Leave It" 1-21; *Mannix* "Who Will Dig the Graves?" 11-16; *Name of the Game* "Pineapple

Rose" 12-20; **1969** *Adam-12* "So This Little Guy Goes into This Bar, and …" 4-5.

TELEFILMS

1979 *Flatbed Annie & Sweetpie: Lady Truckers* 2-10 CBS; **1983** *I Want to Live* 5-9 ABC.

Karen Steele
(born March 20, 1935, Honolulu, Hawaii)

The daughter of a pineapple company executive, Karen attended convent school in Honolulu before enrolling in Rollins College in Florida where she became a fine tennis player and acted in college plays. Moving to Hollywood, she experienced three lean years before producer Delbert Mann mistook her for another actress and gave her a part in the film *Marty* (1954).

From 1956 to 1970 her blonde loveliness was featured in numerous television guest roles.

GUEST CREDITS

1959 *Hawaiian Eye* "All Expenses Paid" 10-28; **1960** *Alaskans* "Counterblow" 4-24; *Tightrope* "The Horse Runs High" 5-3; *Bourbon Street Beat* "Theresa" 7-4; *77 Sunset Strip* "The Negotiable

Blonde" 10-21; *77 Sunset Strip* "Antwerp Caper" 12-2; **1961** *Surfside 6* "The Impractical Joker" 3-13; *Dante's Inferno* "Friendly Assassin" 3-27; *Follow the Sun* "The Primitive Clay" 12-3; **1962** *Rawhide* "Incident of the Woman Trap" 1-26; *Surfside 6* "Who Is Sylvia?" 2-12; *Naked City* "To Walk Like a Lion" 2-28; **1963** *Empire* "Burnout" 3-19; **1965** *Perry Mason* "The Case of the Fatal Fetish" 3-4; *Bob Hope Chrysler Theater* "The Crime" 9-22; *Long Hot Summer* "The Twisted Image" 10-7, 10-14; *Man Called Shenandoah* "The Reward" 11-29; *Voyage to the Bottom of the Sea* "Levithan" 11-7; **1966** *Star Trek* "Mudd's Women" 10-13; **1967** *T.H.E. Cat* "A Hot Place to Die" 1-13; *Felony Squad* "The Night of the Shark" 1-16, 1-23; **1970** *Mannix* "Harlequin's Gold" 1-31.

Mel Stewart
(born September 19, 1928, Cleveland, Ohio)

Mel made his film debut in 1959 in *Odds Against Tomorrow*, and appeared in *The Hustler* during 1961. He came to television in a guest shot on *Car 54, Where Are You?*, in 1962. Following a couple of guest roles on Julia, he became a semi-regular on *All in the Family* (1972-74). He was a series regular on four short-lived sitcoms: *Roll Out* (1973-74), *On the Rocks* (1975-76), *Tabitha* (1977-78) and *One in a Million* (1980).

In 1981-82 he gained yet another regular role, on *Freebie and the Bean*. From 1983 until 1987 he had his most successful series role, as the section chief on *Scarecrow and Mrs. King*.

GUEST CREDITS

1970 *Marcus Welby, M.D.* "The Soft Phrase of Peace" 1-6; **1972** *Bold Ones: The Doctors* "A Substitute Womb" 10-24; **1974** *Toma* "Funeral for Max Berlin" 2-22; *Harry O* "Gertrude" 9-12; *Harry O* "Balleger's Choice" 10-31; *Lucas Tanner* "Look the Other Way" 11-20; **1975** *Rockford Files* "Charlie Harris at Large" 2-14; *Harry O* "Elegy for a Cop" 2-27; *Police Story* "A Community of Victims" 9-23; **1977** *Hallmark Hall of Fame* "The Last Hurrah" 11-16; **1980** *Stone* "But Can She Type?" 1-21; *Stone* "Case Number HO-894287: Homicide" 1-28; **1981** *Little House on the Prairie* "Make a Joyful Noise" 1-26; *Greatest American Hero* "Saturday on Sunset Boulevard" 4-8.

TELEFILMS

1974 *Punch and Jody* 11-26 NBC; **1975** *The Last Survivors* 3-24 NBC; **1978** *Ring of Passion* 2-4 NBC; *Stone* 8-26 ABC; **1980** *Marriage Is Alive and Well* 1-25 NBC; **1983** *The Kid with the 200 I.Q.* 2-6 CBS; *The Invisible Woman* 2-13 NBC.

Beatrice Straight
(born August 2, 1916, Old Westbury, New York)

Beatrice Straight grew up in England after her parents moved there while she was eleven years of age. She became a fine stage actress and came to television in 1951, with a film debut in 1952. Her screen career peaked with a 1976 Academy Award for her work on *Network*.

She had a busy fifties decade in television with *Studio One* (2), *Armstrong Circle Theater* (2), *U.S. Steel Hour* (2), *Hallmark Hall of Fame*, *Kraft Theatre* (2), *Omnibus* (2) and *Danger*.

Beatrice became a series regular on *Beacon Hill*

(1975) and *King's Crossing* (1982). Her limited eighties guest roles included 3 episodes of *St. Elsewhere* in 1988.

GUEST CREDITS

1959 *Alfred Hitchcock Presents* "Special Delivery" 11-29; **1960** *Alfred Hitchcock Presents* "The Cukoo Clock" 4-17; *Diagnosis: Unknown* "Final Performance" 8-16; **1961** *Route 66* "Most Vanquished, Most Victorious" 4-14; *Dr. Kildare* "For the Living" 11-30; **1962** *Route 66* "Kiss the Maiden All Forlorn" 4-13; *Naked City* "Memory of a Red Trolley Car" 6-13; *Nurses* "The Lady Made of Stone" 11-29; **1963** *Eleventh Hour* "Where Have You Been, Lord Randall, My Son?" 1-9; *Ben Casey* "Rigadoon for Three Pianos" 3-24; *Route 66* "The Cage Around Maria" 7-26; **1965** *Defenders* "Eye Witness" 1-14; **1966** *Mission: Impossible* "Zubrovnik's Ghost" 11-26; **1967** *Felony Squad* "Who'll Take Care of Joey?" 11-20; **1970** *Matt Lincoln* "Doc" 11-12; **1973** *Hallmark Hall of Fame* "The Borrowers" 12-14; **1977** *Andros Targets* "Requiem for a Stolen Child" 3-7; *Wonder Woman* "The Return of Wonder Woman" 9-16.

TELEFILM

1977 *Killer on Board* 10-10 NBC.

Elliott Street

A chubby juvenile actor, much of Elliott's work was on television during the seventies. He had some excellent telefilm roles during the decade.

His TV career continued into the eighties, principally in telefilms and miniseries.

GUEST CREDITS

1971 *Mod Squad* "A Bummer for R. J." 1-19; *Hawaii Five-0* "The Grandstand Play" 3-3, 3-10; *Mod Squad* "Survival" 10-5; **1972** *Cade's County* "The Brothers" 1-23; *Ironside* "Camera…Action…Murder!" 10-26; **1973** *Mod Squad* "Run, Lincoln, Run" 1-4; *Hawaii Five-0* "Draw Me a Killer" 9-18; **1974** *Chase* "Thirty-Five Dollars Will Fly You to the Moon" 1-23; *Rookies* "Judgment" 10-28; *Streets of San Francisco* "Flags of Terror" 10-31; **1975** *S.W.A.T.* "Omega One" 5-12; **1976** *Jigsaw John* "Homicide Is a Fine Art" 5-31; *Serpico* "Dawn of the Furies" 12-17; **1977** *Rockford Files* "The Battle of Canoga Park" 9-30; **1978** *Barnaby Jones* "Terror on a Quiet Afternoon" 2-9.

TELEFILMS

1970 *Dial Hot Line* 3-8 ABC; *The Young Country* 3-17 ABC; **1971** *Paper Man* 11-12 CBS; **1972** *Jigsaw* 3-26 ABC; **1974** *Melvin Purvis: G-*

Man 4-9 ABC; **1975** *The Kansas City Massacre* 9-19 ABC; **1979** *Elvis* 2-11 ABC; *The Last Ride of the Dalton Gang* 11-20 NBC; **1980** *Escape* 12-20 CBS.

Gail Strickland
(born May 18, 1947, Birmingham, Alabama)

Educated at Florida State University, Gail made her Broadway debut in 1973, coming to television the same year on an episode of *The Mary Tyler Moore Show*. She also made a couple of appearances on *The Bob Newhart Show*, numerous crime series guest shots and 10 telefilms en route to her first series regular role.

During 1984-85 she appeared on *Night Court, Family Ties, Hill Street Blues* and *Cagney and Lacey*. She then became a regular on *The Insiders* (1985-86), followed by a stint on the syndicated *What a Country!* (1986-87).

She did *Murder, She Wrote* and *Highway to Heaven* guest roles in 1987 before becoming a prominent member of the cast of *Heartbeat* (1988-89). Gail's films included *Bound for Glory, The Drowning Pool, Norma Rae* and *Uncommon Valor*.

GUEST CREDITS

1974 *Barnaby Jones* "Friends Till Death" 2-17;

Hawaii Five-0 "Killer at Sea" 2-19; *Police Story* "Country Boy" 2-19; *Hawaii Five-0* "How to Steal a Masterpiece" 11-12; **1975** *Harry O* "Silent Kill" 2-6; *Rookies* "The Code Five Affair" 12-9; **1976** *Kojak* "Both Sides of the Law" 2-22; **1977** *Westside Medical* "The Devil and the Deep Blue Sea" 7-14; **1978** *Lou Grant* "Scandal" 2-13; **1981** *Walking Tall* "Deadly Impact" 2-21; *Darkroom* "The Siege of 31 August" 12-11; **1982** *Trapper John, M.D.* "Doctors and Other Strangers" 3-28; *Cagney and Lacey* "Suffer the Children" 4-25; *Hill Street Blues* "Invasion of the Third World Mutant Body Snatchers" 5-13; **1983** *Hardcastle and McCormick* "Flying Down to Rio" 12-4.

TELEFILMS

1978 *The President's Mistress* 2-10 CBS; *Ski Lift to Death* 3-3 CBS; **1979** *One to One* 10-30 CBS; *Letters from Frank* 11-22 CBS; *The Gathering, Part II* 12-17 NBC; **1981** *A Matter of Life and Death* 1-13 CBS; **1982** *My Body, My Child* 4-12 NBC; *Eleanor, the First Lady of the World* 5-12 CBS; **1983** *Starflight: The Plane That Couldn't Land* 2-27 ABC.

Barbara Stuart
(born 1930, Paris, Illinois)

A fine comedic actress, Barbara made her television debut playing the secretary to the lead character on *The Great Gildersleeve* (1955). She then had a prominent role as a neighbor to *Pete and Gladys* in 1960-61. This was followed by a recurring role on *Gomer Pyle, U.S.M.C.*, appearing as Sgt. Carter's girlfriend Bunny. There was also a regular slot on a short-lived 1969 series called *The Queen and I*.

Barbara found time between sixties series regular roles to guest on sitcoms like *The Dick Van Dyke Show, The Andy Griffith Show, The Joey Bishop Show* (2), *Mr. Roberts* (2), *Batman* (2), *Captain Nice, Mr. Terrific* and *The Debbie Reynolds Show*. In the seventies she became a regular on *The McLean Stevenson Show* (1976-77).

During the eighties Barbara guested on *Mama's

Jones "Smile with a Gun" 10-7; **1973** *Circle of Fear* "Spare Parts" 2-23; *Barnaby Jones* "Perchance to Kill" 3-11; *Kung Fu* "The Third Man" 4-26; *Cannon* "The Limping Man" 11-14; **1975** *Rookies* episode 73 10-7; **1979** *Starsky and Hutch* "Birds of a Feather" 1-30; *Trapper John, M.D.* "Flashback" 9-23; **1982** *Code Red* "From One Little Spark" 1-3; *Quincy, M.E.* "Smoke Screen" 1-27.

TELEFILM

1978 *Leave Yesterday Behind* 5-14 ABC.

Randy Stuart (a.k.a. Randi Stuart)

In television from 1952, Randy co-starred in a 1952-53 adventure series, *Biff Baker, U.S.A.* From 1952 until 1956 she was a semi-regular on a syndicated religious show called *This Is the Life*.

During the period 1953-58, Randy appeared on *Lux Video Theatre*, *Schlitz Playhouse of Stars*, *Omnibus*, *Fireside Theater* and *The Millionaire*. She became a regular on *The Life and Legend of Wyatt Earp* during the 1959-60 season. Thereafter, she did guest work before leaving television in 1968. She returned for a single 1976 episode of *Police Woman*.

Family, Hotel and *Simon and Simon*; she also was a member of the cast of a 1985-86 dramatic series, *Our Family Honor*. She was married to actor Dick Gautier.

GUEST CREDITS

1959 *Lawless Years* "The Marie Walters Story" 6-18; *Lawless Years* "The Mark Gorman Story" 6-25; *Lawless Years* "The Billy Boy 'Rockabye' Creel Story" 11-5; *Untouchables* "The George 'Bugs' Moran Story" 11-5; **1960** *Texan* "The Taming of Rio Nada" 1-11; *Texan* "Sixgun Street" 1-18; *Texan* "The Terrified Town" 1-25; *Markham* "The Man from Salzburg" 6-2; *Chevy Mystery Show* "Dead Man's Walk" 7-10; *Kraft Mystery Theatre* "Enough Rope" 7-31; *Tales of Wells Fargo* "All That Glitters" 10-24; **1961** *Peter Gunn* episode 3-20; *Perry Mason* "The Case of the Guilty Clients" 6-10; *Lawless Years* "Ginny" 7-14; *87th Precinct* "Run, Rabbit, Run" 12-25; **1962** *Eleventh Hour* "Eat Little Fishie, Eat" 12-5; **1963** *Sam Benedict* "Run Softly, Oh Softly" 1-26; *Rawhide* "Incident of the Deuces" 12-12; **1967** *Iron Horse* "Sister of Death" 4-3; **1971** *Alias Smith and*

GUEST CREDITS

1960 *Cheyenne* "White Warrior" 2-22; *Bourbon Street Beat* "Neon Nightmare" 3-21; *Bronco* "Twisted Creek" 4-19; *Bronco* "Tangled Trail" 5-3; *Bourbon Street Beat* "Interrupted Wedding" 6-20; *One Step Beyond* "Anniversary of Murder" 9-27; *Cheyenne* "Two Trails to Santa Fe" 11-28; **1961** *Lawman* "The Frame-Up" 1-15; *Roaring 20's* "Two a Day" 2-4; *Bonanza* "The Duke" 3-11; *Maverick* "Benefit of Doubt" 4-9; *Peter Gunn* "Last Resort" 5-15; *Cheyenne* "Retaliation" 11-13; **1962** *Hawaiian Eye* "Lalama Lady" 6-20; *77 Sunset Strip* "The Reluctant Spy" 10-12; **1963** *Hawaiian Eye* "Passport" 4-2; **1967** *Dragnet* "The Big Neighbor" 10-12; **1968** *Dragnet* "Homicide-DR-06" 10-24; **1976** *Police Woman* "Wednesday's Child" 2-3.

Jenny Sullivan

The daughter of the late and renowed actor Barry Sullivan (1912-93), Jenny has carved out a niche of her own. From her televison debut in 1968 she worked regularly in the medium through the mid-eighties. She had one series regular role, on *Me and Maxx* (1980). Her eighties work included appearances on *Highway to Heaven* and in the well-received miniseries *V* (1983) and *V: The Final Battle* (1985).

Jenny is now a skilled theatrical director.

GUEST CREDITS

1968 *Dragnet* "Juvenile DR-08" 9-26; *Wild Wild West* "Night of the Avaricious Actuary" 12-6; **1969** *Adam-12* "Jimmy Eisley's Dealing Smack" 1-11; **1971** *Mod Squad* "Suffer, Little Children" 2-9; *Cannon* "Call Unicorn" 9-28; **1973** *Waltons* "The Deed" 2-8; *Mission: Impossible* "Speed" 2-16; *Ironside* "All About Andrea" 2-22; *Hawaii Five-0* "Murder Is a Taxing Affair" 10-16; *Barnaby Jones* "Divorce-Murderer's Style" 10-28; **1974** *Firehouse* "The Hottest Place in Town" 1-31; **1975** *Movin' On* "Fraud" 1-30; *Cannon* "The Melted Man" 11-12; **1976** *Starsky and Hutch* "Coffin for Starsky" 3-3; *Starsky and Hutch* "Bounty Hunter" 4-21; **1978**

Project UFO "Sighting 4017: The Devilish Lights Incident" 9-28; *Lucan* "Creature from Beyond the Door" 11-27; **1979** *Little House on the Prairie* "Someone Please Love Me" 3-5; *Lou Grant* episode 11-24; **1982** *Falcon Crest* "Kindred Spirits" 1-1; **1983** *Fall Guy* "Just a Small Circle of Friends" 5-4.

TELEFILMS

1975 *Katherine* 10-5 ABC; **1979** *Friendly Fire* 4-22 ABC.

Liam Sullivan

(born May 11, 1923, Jacksonville, Illinois)

One of Liam's early television roles, following a 1950 debut, was in a *Kraft Television Theatre* production of *Romeo and Juliet*. He moved on to guest appearances over four decades and a series regular role on *The Monroes* (1966-67). *Twilight Zone* fans will recall his wonderful portrayal of a young man who pays a terrible price in an attempt to

Center "Edge of Violence" 2-10; **1973** *Mannix* "Sing a Song of Murder" 11-11; **1975** *Harry O* "Group Terror" 11-13; **1976** *Hawaii Five-0* "The Capsule Killing" 2-12; *Starsky and Hutch* "Dancing Their Way into Your Hearts" 11-20; **1977** *Logan's Run* "Crypt" 11-7; **1978** *Battlestar Galactica* "The Gun on Ice Planet Zero" 10-22, 10-29; **1981** *Nero Wolfe* "The Golden Spiders" 1-16; *Code Red* "Dark Fire" 11-15; **1983** *A-Team* "Recipe for Heavy Bread" 9-27.

TELEFILMS

1979 *The Best Place to Be* 5-27, 5-28 NBC; **1981** *The Five of Me* 5-12 CBS; *Isabel's Choice* 12-16 CBS; **1982** *Computerside* 8-1 NBC.

win a bet in an episode called "The Silence".

Liam worked on the soap *General Hospital* during 1988.

GUEST CREDITS

1960 *Cheyenne* "Gold, Glory and Custer" 1-4; *Alfred Hitchcock Presents* "Call 227" 6-5; *Law and Mr. Jones* "The Promise of Life" 11-18; *Have Gun-Will Travel* "The Prisoner" 12-17; **1961** *Bat Masterson* "End of the Line" 1-26; *Perry Mason* "The Case of the Fickle Fortune" 1-21; *Twilight Zone* "The Silence" 4-28; *Perry Mason* "The Case of the Crying Comedian" 10-14; **1962** *Twilight Zone* "The Changing of the Guard" 6-1; *Perry Mason* "The Case of the Unsuitable Uncle" 11-8; **1963** *Untouchables* "Jake Dance" 1-22; **1965** *Man from UNCLE* "The Brain Killer Affair" 3-8; *Rawhide* "The Winter Soldier" 3-12; *Kraft Suspense Theatre* "Nobody Will Ever Know" 3-25; *Fugitive* "All the Scared Rabbits" 10-26; *Voyage to the Bottom of the Sea* "Leviathan" 11-7; *Honey West* "The Flame and the Pussycat" 11-12; **1966** *Bonanza* "A Dublin Lad" 1-2; *Legend of Jesse James* episode 2-10; *Lost in Space* "His Majesty Smith" 3-16; *Virginian* "That Saunders Woman" 3-3; *Gunsmoke* "Quaker Girl" 12-10; **1968** *Dragnet* "The Big Prophet" 1-4; *Star Trek* "Plato's Stepchildren" 11-22; **1970** *Bracken's World* "The Money Men" 1-9; *Adam-12* "Log 173-Shoplift" 5-9; **1971** *Medical*

William Sylvester

(born January 31, 1922, Oakland, Calif.)

William got his acting career start in England, working there from 1946 until 1968. Following his return to the U. S. he was cast in *2001: A Space Odyssey*, subsequently appearing in films like *The Hindenburg* and *Heaven Can Wait*.

He debuted on television in 1969, working well into the eighties. His only series regular role was on *The Gemini Man* (1976), appearing as Intersect director Leonard Driscoll.

GUEST CREDITS

1969 *High Chaparral* "No Bugles, No Women" 3-14; *Marcus Welby, M.D.* "Don't Argue the Miracles" 10-7; *High Chaparral* "The Little Thieves" 12-26; **1970** *Bonanza* "Danger Road" 1-11; **1972** *Bonanza* "The Bucket Dog" 12-19; **1973** *Banacek* "If Max Is So Smart, Why Doesn't He Tell Us Where He Is" 11-7; **1974** *Get Christie Love!* "For the Family Honor" 10-23; **1975** *Harry O* "Silent Kill" 2-6; *Six Million Dollar Man* "Outrage in Balinderry" 4-19; *Harry O* "Anatomy of a Frame" 9-11; *Mobile One* "The Reporter" 10-10; **1976** *Harry O* "The Mysterious Case of Lester and Dr. Fong" 3-18; *Switch* "Death Squad" 4-6; *McCloud* "It Was the Fight Before Christmas" 12-26; **1977** *Quincy, M.E.* "Visitors in Paradise" 2-18; *Six Million Dollar* Man "U-509" 2-20; *Switch* "Three for the Money" 3-6; *Six Million Dollar Man* "Sharks" 9-11, 9-18; **1979** *Quincy, M.E.* "The Eye of the Needle" 4-12; **1982** *Quincy, M.E.* "To Clear the Air" 2-17.

TELEFILMS

1970 *The Challengers* 2-2 CBS; **1973** *Don't Be Afraid of the Dark* 10-10 ABC; **1975** *Guilty or Innocent: The Sam Sheppard Murder Case* 11-17 NBC.

Christopher Tabori

(born August 4, 1952, Los Angeles, Calif.)

The son of Viveca Lindefors and director Don Siegel, Christopher made his screen debut at age 6 (1958), but didn't make his second film until 1968 when he appeared in *Coogan's Bluff*. He also had roles in *Sweet Charity, Making It* and *Dirty Harry*.

His television debut came in 1970 in a *Hallmark Hall of Fame* production. He did numerous guest roles during the seventies, often playing troubled teens in crime dramas. During 1982 he became a regular on *Chicago Story*. Later eighties guest work included appearances on *Trapper John, M.D., Facts of Life, The Fall Guy, Murder, She Wrote* (2), *Twilight Zone, Blacke's Magic, Hunter* and *Tour of Duty*.

GUEST CREDITS

1970 *Hallmark Hall of Fame* "Neither Are We Enemies" 3-13; **1971** *Nichols* "The One-Eyed Mule's Time Has Come" 11-23; **1972** *Medical Story* episode 10-4; **1973** *Owen Marshall, Counselor at Law* "A Lesson in Loving" 9-12; **1974** *Toma* "The Friends of Danny Beecher" 3-29; *Marcus Welby, M.D.* "The Faith of Childish Things" 9-17; *Rookies* "Walk a Tightrope" 10-21; *Cannon* "Flashpoint" 11-13; **1975** *Barnaby Jones* "The Orchid Killer" 10-3; **1976** *Streets of San Francisco* "Most Likely to Succeed" 6-3; *Most Wanted* "Wolf Pack Killer" 11-20; **1979** *Rockford Files* "Only Rock 'n' Roll Will Never Die" 10-19, 10-26; *Trapper John, M.D.* episode 12-9; **1982** *T. J. Hooker* "Terror at the Academy" 11-6; **1983** *Trapper John, M.D.* "Life, Death and Vinnie Duncan" 1-2.

TELEFILMS

1972 *The Glass House* 2-4 CBS; *Family Flight* 10-24 ABC; **1973** *Terror on the Beach* 9-18 CBS; **1974** *QB VII* 4-29 ABC; **1980** *Brave New World* 3-7 NBC; **1981** *The Chicago Story* 3-15 NBC.

Gloria Talbot

(born February 7, 1934, Glendale, Calif.)

Gloria Talbot is about to bash Steve McQueen's head in this scene from a 1959 episode of *Wanted: Dead or Alive* (CBS). The episode was called "Fatal Memory"; Gloria was a frequent guest on western series of the era.

Gloria attended Glendale High in Los Angeles and was named Miss Glendale. While in school she tied for first place in the annual Shakespeare contest at Occidental College. She acted in plays at the Eagle Rock Little Theater and started her own dramatic group. A major breakthrough occured when she had an opportunity to join Charlie Ruggles in *One Fine Day*, playing in Los Angeles and San Francisco.

She graduated from Pasadena Playhouse and began a strong film and television career in 1951. Her films included *We're No Angels* and *All That Heaven Allows*.

In 1955-56 she had her only TV series regular role on *The Life and Times of Wyatt Earp*. Following her last acting job in 1966 Gloria married a dentist and dropped out of the limelight.

GUEST CREDITS

1959 *Rawhide* "Incident of the Calico Gun" 4-24; *Wanted: Dead or Alive* "Fatal Memory" 9-13; **1960** *Riverboat* "Landlubbers" 1-10; *Markham* "The Heiress" 2-4; *Wanted: Dead or Alive* "Tolliver Bender" 2-13; *Bonanza* "Escape to the Ponderosa" 3-5; *Law of the Plainsman* "Stella" 3-31; *Rebel* "Absolution" 4-24; *Bat Masterson* "Barbary Castle" 6-30; *Roaring 20's* "The Velvet Frame" 10-29; *Riverboat* "Devil in Skirts" 11-20; *Wanted: Dead or Alive* "Three for One" 12-21; **1961** *Islanders* "The Twenty Six Paper" 1-8; *Rawhide* "Incident of the Broken Word" 1-20; *Perry Mason* "The Case of the Angry Dead Man" 2-25; *Whispering Smith* "The Grudge" 5-15; *Wyatt Earp* "Hiding Behind a Star" 5-23; *Laramie* "Ladie's Day" 10-3; *Dr. Kildare* "Admitting Service" 11-2; *Rawhide* "The Prairie Elephant" 11-17; *Islanders* "The Old School Tie" 11-20; *Tales of Wells Fargo* "Defiance at the Gate" 11-25; **1962** *General Electric Theater* "The Wall Between" 1-7; *Gunsmoke* "Cody's Code" 1-20; *Broncho* "Rendevous with a Miracle" 2-12; *87th Precinct* "Killer's Choice" 3-5; *Frontier Circus* "Never Won Fair Lady" 4-5; *Wagon Train* "The Frank Carter Story" 5-23; *Untouchables* "The Contract" 5-31; **1963** *Laramie* "Naked Steel" 1-1; *Gunsmoke* "The Cousin" 2-2; *Perry Mason* "The Case of the Elusive Element" 4-11; **1966** *Perry Mason* "The Case of the Unwelcome Well" 4-3.

Clay Tanner

(born 1929)

In films from 1965, Clay played the devil in *Rosemary's Baby*, and appeared in *Hello Dolly!, How to Frame a Figg, Lady Sings the Blues, The Outlaw Josey Wales* and *Final Chapter-Walking Tall*.

His powerful physique created roles on both sides of the law in his TV career from 1963 to 1979.

GUEST CREDITS

1963 *Outer Limits* "Architects of Fear" 9-30; **1965** *Perry Mason* "The Case of the Impetuous Imp" 10-10; **1966** *Bonanza* "Ride the Wind" 1-16, 1-23; *Fugitive* "The 2130" 3-29; **1967** *Fugitive* "The Breaking of the Habit" 1-31; *Big Valley* "Court Martial" 3-6; **1971** *Gunsmoke* "Trafton" 10-25; **1973** *Kung Fu* "The Squaw Man" 10-11; **1974** *Gunsmoke* "The Town Tamers" 1-28; *Harry O* "Gertrude" 9-12; *Kung Fu* "Crossfire" 10-12; **1975** *Harry O* "Elegy for a Cop" 2-27; *Harry O* "APB Harry Orwell" 11-6; **1976** *Starsky and Hutch* "Hostages" 1-7; *Cannon* "Revenge" 1-21; **1977** *Starsky and Hutch* "The Set-Up" 1-22, 1-29.

TELEFILMS

1970 *Night Chase* 11-20 CBS; **1973** *She Lives* 9-12 ABC; **1977** *Nowhere to Hide* 6-5; **1978** *Thaddeus Rose and Eddie* 2-24 CBS; *Big Bob Johnson & His Fantastic Speed Circus* 6-27 NBC; **1979** *Mr. Horn* 2-1, 2-3 CBS.

Mark Tapscott

From 1957 to 1972 Mark worked regularly in television series guest roles, especially in the western genre where he held forth in no less than 25 episodes. From 1972 until 1980 he had a prominent role on the soap *Days of Our Lives* and left prime-time TV, except for a handful of telefilms. Mark also worked on *The Young and the Restless* during the early eighties.

GUEST CREDITS

1959 *Have Gun-Will Travel* "The Man Who Lost" 2-7; *Black Saddle* "Client: Steele" 3-21; *Maverick* "The Strange Journey of Jenny Hill" 3-29; *Tombstone Territory* "Surrender at Sunset" 5-15; *Richard Diamond* "Act of Grace" 10-24; *Maverick* "Trooper Maverick" 11-29; **1961** *Rawhide* "Incident of the Road Back" 2-24; *Maverick* "The Devil's Necklace" 4-16, 4-23; *Rawhide* "Incident of the Wager on Payday" 6-16; *Twilight Zone* "Still Valley"

11-24; *Tall Man* "Legend of Billy" 12-9; **1962** *Tall Man* "The Hunt" 1-27; **1963** *Wagon Train* "The Sam Spicer Story" 10-28; **1965** *Perry Mason* "The Case of the Sausalito Sunrise" 2-13; *Perry Mason* "The Case of the Hasty Honeymooner" 10-24; **1966** *Big Valley* "The Great Safe Robbery" 11-21; **1968** *Big Valley* "Presumed Dead" 10-7; *Bonanza* "The Sound of Drums" 11-17; *Big Valley* "The Profit and the Lost" 12-2; **1969** *Big Valley* "Joshua Watson" 1-20; *Big Valley* "The Battle of Mineral Springs" 3-24; *High Chaparral* "Bad Day for a Bad Man" 10-17; **1970** *Silent Force* "Prosecutor" 9-21; *High Chaparral* "Wind" 10-9; **1971** *Mission: Impossible* "Underwater" 11-16; **1972** *Sixth Sense* "Shadow in the Wall" 4-15; *Mission: Impossible* "Two Thousand" 9-23; *Ghost Story* "Time of Terror" 12-22.

TELEFILMS

1971 *The Neon Ceiling* 2-8 NBC; *Escape* 4-6 ABC; **1971** *Sweet, Sweet Rachel* 10-2 ABC; **1974** *Terror on the 40th Floor* 9-17 NBC; **1981** *The Miracle of Kathy Miller* 10-5 CBS.

Dub Taylor

(Walter Clarence Taylor, 1907; died October 3, 1994)

Appearing in well over 100 films since 1938, Dub Taylor spent much of the forties playing comic sidekicks to Charles Starrett, Tex Ritter and other western stars of the era, often called "Cannonball". He also appeared in many significant films, among them *Mr. Smith Goes to Washington, A Star Is Born, No Time for Sergeants, Sweet Bird of Youth, Spencer's Mountain, Major Dundee, Bonnie and Clyde, Don't Make Waves, The Reivers, A Man Called Horse, The Undefeated, Thunderbolt and Lightfoot* and *Cannonball Run II*. His wide grin and thick southern drawl helped make him a unique personna for over 50 years of performing.

He worked in television from the early fifties and was a regular on *Casey Jones* (1956-58), and later, on *Please Don't Eat the Daisies* (1965-66). He did a number of mid-sixties guest shots, mainly on western series, and during the eighties, turned up on *Hee Haw* fairly often.

Dub's actor son Buck starred on *Gunsmoke* from 1967 to 1975. Dub died of heart failure on October 3, 1994.

GUEST CREDITS

1962 *Twilight Zone* "The Last Rites of Jeff Myrtlebank" 2-23; **1965** *Laredo* "Yahoo" 9-30; *Wild Wild West* "The Night of the Casual Killer" 10-15; *Loner* "The Sheriff of Fetterman's Crossing" 11-13; **1966** *Gunsmoke* "My Father's Guitar" 2-12; *Big Valley* "The Lost Treasure" 9-12; *Monroes* "War Arrow" 11-2; **1967** *Gunsmoke* "Mad Dog" 1-14; *Monroes* "Wild Bull" 2-15; *Gunsmoke* "Nitro I, II" 4-8, 4-15; *Wild Wild West* "The Night of the Running Death" 12-15; **1968** *Guns of Will Sonnett* "Look for the Hound Dog" 1-26; *Big Valley* "Fall of a Hero" 2-5; *Gunsmoke* "Kiowa" 2-16; *Cimarron Strip* "The Greeners" 3-7; *Gunsmoke* "Slocum" 10-21; *Mod Squad* "A Quiet Weekend in the Country" 12-3; **1971** *Hawaii Five-0* "Dear Enemy" 2-17; *Cade's County* "Delegate at Large" 11-21; **1977** *McMillan* "Dark Sunrise" 1-2; **1979** *Salvage 1* "Confederate Gold" 5-28; **1982** *Bret Maverick* "The Hildago Thing" 5-4.

TELEFILMS

1968 *Something for a Lonely Man* 11-26 NBC; **1971** *Sam Hill: Who Killed the Mysterious Mr. Foster?* 2-1 NBC; **1972** *The Delphi Bureau* 3-6

ABC; **1973** *Brock's Last Case* 3-5 NBC; **1974** *Shootout in a One Dog Town* 1-9 ABC; *Honky Tonk* 4-1 NBC; **1975** *The Daughters of Joshua Cabe* 1-28 ABC.

Irene Tedrow

(born August 3, 1910, Denver, Colorado; died March 10, 1995)

The daughter of an attorney, Irene Tedrow graduated from Carnegie-Mellon with a B.A. in Drama. She became one of America's most enduring character actresses, appearing in over 50 films (from 1937), and in countless television episodes dating from 1949. She also had a lengthy radio career, starring as the mother on *Meet Corliss Archer*.

Irene was a regular on two early-day TV sitcoms, *The Ruggles* (1949) and *Meet Corliss Archer* (1952). She also had a recurring role on *Dennis the Menace*, appearing as Mrs. Elkins (1959-63). Additional series regular roles were on a soap, *The Young Marrieds* (1964-65), and on *Mr. Novak* (1965). Her

strong work continued well into the eighties.

She was nominated for two Emmys: as Best Supporting Actress for the 1976 telefilm *Eleanor and Franklin*, and as Best Leading Actress for her guest work in *James at 16* (1978). This wonderful talent died on March 10, 1995 from complications of a massive stroke.

GUEST CREDITS

1959 *Maverick* "Gun-Shy" 1-11; *Texan* "The Peddler" 1-22; *Rawhide* "Incident Below the Brazos" 5-15; *Texan* "Cattle Drive" 9-28; *Twilight Zone* "Walking Distance" 10-30; **1960** *Maverick* "The Cruise of the Cynthia B" 1-10; *One Step Beyond* "The Lovers" 2-16; *Alfred Hitchcock Presents* "The Hero" 5-1; *Perry Mason* "The Case of the Ominous Outcast" 5-21; *Twilight Zone* "The Lateness of the Hour" 12-2; **1962** *Ben Casey* "The Big Trouble with Charlie" 1-29; *Alcoa Premiere* "Mr. Easy" 2-13; **1963** *Perry Mason* "The Case of the Nebulous Nephew" 9-26; *Breaking Point* "Fire and Ice" 9-30; *Greatest Show on Earth* "Lady in Limbo" 12-10; **1965** *Man from UNCLE* "The Deadly Decoy Affair" 1-11; *Fugitive* "Runner in the Dark" 3-30; *Man from UNCLE* "The Arabian Affair" 10-29; **1967** *Invaders* "Nightmare" 2-21; **1971** *Mannix* "A Button for General D" 11-17; **1972** *Adam-12* "If the Shoe Fits" 12-12; **1974** *Rockford Files* "In Pursuit of Carol Thorne" 11-8; *Marcus Welby, M.D.* "The Last Rip Off" 11-26; **1975** *Harry O* "The Last Heir" 1-9; *Streets of San Francisco* "River of Fear" 2-13; **1976** *Charlie's Angels* "Target: Angels" 10-27; **1977** *Quincy, M.E.* "A Question of Time" 10-14; **1978** *Rockford Files* "The House on Willis Avenue" 2-24; *Police Story* "Day of Terror, Night of Fear" 3-4; *Spider-Man* "Night of the Clones" 4-26; **1979** *Paris* "Pawn" 10-13; *Quincy, M.E.* "Mode of Death" 11-1; **1981** *Quincy, M.E.* "Of All Sad Words" 3-11.

TELEFILMS

1974 *Live Again, Die Again* 2-16 ABC; *A Cry in the Wilderness* 3-26 ABC; **1976** *Eleanor and Franklin* 1-11, 1-12 ABC; **1979** *The Two Worlds of Jennie Logan* 10-31 CBS; **1981** *Isabel's Choice* 12-16 CBS; **1983** *The Last Ninja* 7-7 ABC.

Torin Thatcher

(born 1905, India; died 1981)

Originally a British schoolmaster and amateur boxer, Torin was onstage in England from 1928. His wonderful screen career, which consisted of 70 films, included roles in *The Snows of Kilimanjaro, The Robe, Mutiny on the Bounty* and *The Sandpiper.*

Tall and husky, his strong personna made him a very effective guest star in sci-fi and adventure series. He died of cancer in 1981.

GUEST CREDITS

1959 *Alfred Hitchcock Presents* "Relative Value" 3-1; *Wagon Train* "The Steve Campson Story" 5-13; *One Step Beyond* "Doomsday" 10-13; **1960** *Diagnosis: Unknown* "The Red Death" 9-20; **1961** *Thriller* "The Well of Doom" 2-28; *Adventures in Paradise* "Beach Head" 6-12; *Follow the Sun* "A Rage for Justice" 9-17; *Perry Mason* "The Case of the Unwelcome Bride" 12-16; **1963** *Untouchables* "The Giant Killer" 4-9; **1964** *East Side/West Side* "It's War, Man" 2-10; *Great Adventure* "The Night Raiders" 2-21; *Defenders* "May Day! May Day!" 4-18; *Alfred Hitchcock Hour* "Bed of Roses" 5-22; *Slattery's People* "Question: Why the Lonely…Why the Misbegotten?" 9-28; **1965** *Voyage to the Bottom of the Sea* "The Secret of the Loch" 4-5; **1966** *Bob Hope Chrysler Theater* "The Enemy on the Beach"

1-5; *Lost in Space* "The Space Trader" 3-9; *Time Tunnel* "The Crack of Doom" 10-14; **1967** *Star Trek* "Return of the Archons" 2-9; *Gunsmoke* "Fandango" 2-11; *Daniel Boone* "Take the Southbound Stage" 4-6; **1968** *Guns of Will Sonnett* "The Sins of the Father" 2-23; *Mission: Impossible* "The Heir Apparent" 9-29; **1969** *Daniel Boone* "To Slay a Giant" 1-9; *Mission: Impossible* "The Numbers Game" 10-5; **1970** *Land of the Giants* "Nightmare" 1-4; **1971** *Night Gallery* "Lone Survivor" 1-13; **1972** *Search* "Live Men Tell Tales" 10-11; **1975** *Petrocelli* "Death in Small Doses" 3-27.

TELEFILM

1976 *Brenda Starr* 5-8 ABC.

Hillary Thompson (a.k.a. Hillarie Thompson)

(born 1949)

The sister of actors Rex Thompson (1942-) and Victoria Thompson (1952-), Hillary made her film and television debuts in 1968. Her first television guest shots were on sitcoms like *I Dream of Jeannie, Bewitched* and *The Flying Nun.*

She became a series regular on *The Young Rebels* (1970-71), followed by regular slots on *The Manhunter* (1974-75), *Operation Petticoat* (1978-79)

and *Number 96* (1980). Eighties guest roles were on *Automan* and *ALF*.

GUEST CREDITS

1969 *Outcasts* "The Town That Wouldn't" 3-31; *Bonanza* "Hawk" 10-20; **1971** *Matt Lincoln* "Karen" 1-7; *Room 222* "I Hate You Silas Marner" 3-10; **1974** *Hec Ramsey* "Scar Tissue" 3-10; *Harry O* "Reasons to Kill" 12-5, 12-12; **1976** *Barnaby Jones* "Hostage" 1-15; **1977** *Quincy, M.E.* "Visitors in Paradise" 2-18; *Streets of San Francisco* "Dead Lift" 5-5; **1978** *Barnaby Jones* "Nest of Scorpions" 10-26; *Charlie's Angels* "Counterfeit Angels" 1-24; **1979** *Starsky and Hutch* "Targets Without a Badge" 3-11; **1980** *Barnaby Jones* "The Final Victim" 3-6.

TELEFILMS

1974 *Manhunter* 2-26 CBS; **1978** *Cruise Into Terror* 2-3 ABC.

Kelly Thordsen
(born 1915; died January 23, 1978)

Husky Kelly Thordsen was typecast early in his career as sheriffs, policemen and various authority figures for he always projected a strong image. His films (from 1956) included *Desire in the Dust, Sweet Bird of Youth, To Kill a Mockingbird, The Ugly Dachshund* and *The Parallax View*.

In television from 1957, the majority of his work was in guest roles on TV western series. During the seventies he switched to guesting on crime dramas. Kelly died of cancer in 1978, survived by his wife, a daughter and four sons.

GUEST CREDITS

1959 *Californians* "Gold Tooth Charlie" 3-10; *Texan* "A Race for Life" 3-16; *Yancy Derringer* "Five on the Frontier" 4-2; *Yancy Derringer* "Outlaw at Liberty" 5-7; *Yancy Derringer* "Gone But Not Forgotten" 5-28; *Maverick* "Full House" 10-25 ; *Deputy* "The Deal" 12-5; **1960** *Maverick* "The Resurrection of Joe November" 2-28; **1961** *Rifleman* "Closer Than a Brother" 2-21; *Maverick* "The Deadly Image" 3-12; *Rifleman* "The Score Is Even" 4-11; *Laramie* "The Accusers" 11-14; *Perry Mason* "The Case of the Roaring River" 12-30; **1962** *Tall Man* "Girl from Paradise" 1-13; *Law and Mr. Jones* "No News Is Good News" 4-19; *Untouchables* "The Contract" 5-31; *Bonanza* "A Hot Day for a Hanging" 10-14; *Perry Mason* "The Case of the Lurid Letter" 12-6; **1963** *Laramie* "Vengeance" 1-8; *Bonanza* "Five into the Wind" 4-21; *Perry Mason* "The Case of the Decadent Dean" 10-24; *Alfred Hitchcock Hour* "Body in the Barn" 11-22; *Lieutenant* "Tour of Duty" 11-23; *Wagon Train* "The Fenton Canaby Story" 12-30; **1964** *Bonanza* "Enter Thomas Bowers" 4-26; **1965** *Bonanza* "The Search" 2-14; *Gunsmoke* "The Storm" 9-25; *Man Called Shenandoah* "Incident at Dry Creek" 11-15; *Fugitive* "Set Fire to a Strawman" 11-30; **1966** *Virginian* "The Return of Golden Tom" 3-9; *Legend of Jesse James* "Wanted: Dead and Only" 5-2; *Road West* "Ashes and Tallow and One True Love" 10-24; *Big Valley* "The Velvet Trap" 11-7; **1967** *Fugitive* "Breaking of a Habit" 1-31; *Daniel Boone* "The Necklace "3-9; *Time Tunnel* "Town of Terror" 4-7; *Invaders* "The Saucer" 9-12; *Gunsmoke* "The Prodigal" 9-25; *Daniel Boone* "The King's Shilling" 11-2; *Virginian* "Execution at Triste" 12-13; *Bonanza* "The Gold Detector" 12-24; **1968** *High Chaparral* "The Hair Hunter" 3-10; *High*

Chaparral "The Covey" 10-18; *Daniel Boone* "The Bait" 11-7; **1969** *Adam-12* "We Just Can't Walk Away from It" 3-1; **1970** *The FBI* "Deadfall" 3-1; **1971** *Mission: Impossible* "Cat's Paw" 1-9; *Name of the Game* "The Savage Eye" 2-19; *Cannon* "No Pockets in a Shroud" 11-23; **1972** *Nichols* episode 2-29; **1973** *Cannon* "Hard Rock Roller Coaster" 1-3; **1974** *The FBI* "A Piece of the Action" 1-6; *Manhunter* "Death on the Run" 10-2; *Rockford Files* "The Big Ripoff" 10-25; **1976** *Barnaby Jones* "Blood Vengeance" 10-7; **1977** *Switch* "The Hemline Heist" 2-27.

TELEFILMS

1972 *Killer by Night* 1-7 CBS; **1974** *The Day the Earth Moved* 9-18 ABC; *The FBI Story: The FBI vs. Alvin Karpis, Public Enemy Number One* 11-8 CBS.

Russell Thorson

(born 1910; died July 6, 1982)

After thousands of radio shows during the thirties and forties, Russell did the radio version of *One Man's Family* until it became a daytime television soap in 1954. He moved over to the TV version until 1955. Thereafter, he performed in television guest roles for several years; in 1959 he became a regular on *The Detectives, Starring Robert Taylor* (1959-61).

Russell stayed busy on television throughout the sixties in guest roles, primarily on western series. His rich voice and experience enhanced countless TV episodes in his later years, usually playing elders and professionals. In the seventies he made the transition from westerns to detective series in fine fashion.

His films (from 1949) included *Zero Hour, I Want to Live!, The Stalking Moon* and *Hang 'Em High*.

GUEST CREDITS

1959 *Lawman* "The Brand Release" 1-25; *Trackdown* "The Protector" 4-1; *Perry Mason* "The Case of the Petulant Partner" 4-25; *Rawhide* "Inci-

dent of the Thirteenth Man" 10-23; **1960** *Wanted: Dead or Alive* "The Monsters" 1-16; *Man from Blackhawk* "Trial by Combat" 5-27; *Tales of Wells Fargo* "The Wade Place" 11-28; **1961** *Wagon Train* "The Eleanor Culhane Story" 5-17; *Rawhide* "The Gentlemen's Gentleman" 12-15; **1962** *Outlaws* "The Verdict" 1-18; *Dr. Kildare* "A Very Present Help" 4-12; *Ben Casey* "Preferably the Less Used Arm" 4-30; *Tall Man* "The Black Robe" 5-5; *Virginian* "The Devil's Children" 12-5; **1963** *Virginian* "Duel at Shiloh" 1-2; *G.E. True* "Open Season" 1-6; *Ben Casey* "Suffer the Little Children" 2-25; *Empire* "A Home in Order" 3-5; *Virginian* "The Golden Door" 3-13; *Rawhide* "Incident of the Pale Rider" 3-15; *Sam Benedict* "Of Rusted Cannons and Fallen Sparrows" 3-23; *Virginian* "Echo of Another Day" 3-27; *Kraft Suspense Theatre* "Catch Fear by the Throat" 7-10; *Lieutenant* "A Million Miles from Clary" 9-14; *Temple Houston* "The Siege at Thayer's Bluff" 11-7; *Gunsmoke* "Pa Hack's Brood" 12-28; **1964** *Perry Mason* "The Case of the Arrogant Arsonist" 3-5; *Bob Hope Chrysler Theater* "A Case of Armed Robbery" 4-3; **1965** *Gunsmoke* "Song for Dying" 2-13; *Run for Your Life* "Never Pick Up a Stranger" 10-11; **1967** *Judd, for the Defense* "Tempest in a Texas Town" 9-8; *Invaders* "The Enemy" 9-8; **1968** *Cimarron Strip* "The Assassin" 1-11; *Bonanza* "The Real People of Muddy Creek" 10-6; *The FBI* "Nightmare" 1-10; *Lancer* "Jelly" 11-19;

Outsider "Land of the Fox" 12-18; **1969** *Big Valley* "Point and Counterpoint" 5-19; *Lancer* "Blind Man's Bluff" 9-23; **1971** *Mission: Impossible* "Takeover" 1-2; *Mission: Impossible* "Nerves" 12-4; **1972** *Cannon* "A Deadly Quiet Town" 2-15; *Night Gallery* "Spectre in Tap Shoes" 10-29; **1973** *Emergency* episode 12-1; *Magician* "The Man Who Lost Himself" 12-11; **1974** *Cannon* "The Exchange" 10-23; *Manhunter* "The Doomsday Gang" 10-23; **1975** *Barnaby Jones* "The Alpha Bravo War" 10-31; **1976** *Streets of San Francisco* "Clown of Death" 2-26; **1977** *Tales of the Unexpected* "Devil Pack" 2-16; *Barnaby Jones* "Deadly Homecoming" 12-22; **1978** *Rockford Files* "The House on Willis Avenue" 2-24.

TELEFILMS

1968 *Hawaii Five-0* 9-20 CBS; **1970** *Night Slaves* 9-29 ABC; **1971** *Incident in San Francisco* 2-29 ABC; **1974** *Manhunter* 2-26 CBS; **1975** *Guilty or Innocent: The Sam Sheppard Murder Case* 11-17 NBC.

Kenneth Tigar

Kenneth began appearing in television guest roles during 1976 and was a semi-regular on *The Gangster Chronicles: An American Story*. He

appeared in a number of eighties telefilms and was a regular on *Dynasty* during it's final season (1988-89). His most current work was in the final episode of *Murder, She Wrote*, in May of 1996.

GUEST CREDITS

1976 *Wonder Woman* "The Pluto File" 12-25; **1977** *Waltons* "John's Crossroads" 1-20; *Man from Atlantis* "The Death Scouts" 5-7; *Man from Atlantis* "The Killer Spores" 5-17; *Man from Atlantis* "The Disappearances" 6-20; **1978** *Charlie's Angels* "Antique Angels" 5-10; *Kaz* "Verdict in Department Twelve" 9-24; *Rockford Files* "Local Man Eaten by Newspaper" 12-8; *Wonder Woman* "Stolen Faces" 12-15; **1979** *Project UFO* "Sighting 4025" 1-4; *Barnaby Jones* "Fatal Overture" 2-8; *Battlestar Galactica* "Greetings from Earth" 2-25; *Lou Grant* episode 10-15; **1981** *Lou Grant* "Business" 3-23; *CHiPs* "Finders Keepers" 11-29; **1982** *Lou Grant* episode 1-25.

TELEFILMS

1979 *The Golden Gate Murders* 10-3 CBS; **1980** *The Babysitter* 11-28 ABC; **1981** *The Big Black Pill* 1-29 NBC; **1982** *Pray TV* 2-1 ABC; **1983** *Thursday's Child* 2-1 CBS; *Special Bulletin* 3-20 NBC; *Missing Pieces* 5-14 CBS.

Dan Tobin

(born 1909; died November 26, 1982)

Dan was in films from 1938, always having a light comedic touch in his acting. Some of his later films included *The Last Angry Man, Who's Got the Action?, How to Succeed in Business Without Really Trying* and *Herbie Rides Again*.

In television from the early fifties, Dan was a regular in two fifties sitcoms: *I Married Joan* (1954-55) and *My Favorite Husband* (1955). He spent a season as a regular on *Perry Mason*, appearing as restauranteur Terrence Clay. The sixties were a very busy period on TV for Dan as he guested in two dozen episodes. He wrapped up his film and television careers in 1974.

GUEST CREDITS

1959 *Maverick* "The Rivals" 1-25; **1960** *Goodyear Theater* "Capital Gains" 2-1; **1961** *Twilight Zone* "A Penny for Your Thoughts" 2-3; *Maverick* "Diamond Flush" 2-5; *Aquanauts* "The Scavenger Adventure" 5-31; **1962** *Dr. Kildare* "Love Is a Sad Song" 1-3; *87ᵗʰ Precinct* King's Ransom" 2-19; *Saints and Sinners* "Judith Was a Lady" 12-3; **1963** *Gunsmoke* "Panacea Sykes" 4-13; *Burke's Law* "Who Killed Beau Sparrow" 12-27; **1964** *77 Sunset Strip* "Not Such a Simple Knot" 1-17; *Breaking Point* "Shadows of a Starless Night" 3-9; *Perry Mason* "The Case of the Scandalous Sculptor" 10-8; **1965** *Ben Casey* "Pas de Deux" 1-18; *Amos Burke, Secret Agent* "Operation Long Shadow" 9-22; *Bob Hope Chrysler Theater* "March from Camp Tyler" 10-6; **1966** *Wild Wild West* "The Night of the Burning Diamond" 4-8; *Gunsmoke* "Champion of the World" 12-24; **1967** *Felony Squad* "The Pat Hand of Death" 10-30; **1968** *I Spy* "Suitable for Framing" 3-25; *Outcasts* "The Bounty Children" 12-23; **1971** *Matt Lincoln* "Christopher" 1-14; **1973** *The FBI* "The Disinherited" 1-21; *Barnaby Jones* "Sing a Song of Murder" 4-1; *Marcus Welby, M.D.* "For Services Rendered" 9-25.

TELEFILMS

1973 *Letters from Three Lovers* 10-3 ABC; **1974** *Only with Married Men* 12-4 ABC.

Angel Tompkins
(born Decemer 20, 1943, Albany, Calif.)

A stunningly beautiful blonde, Angel Tompkins graced television from 1968 through much of the eighties. She was a regular on *Search* during 1972-73). Later eighties guest work included episodes of *Simon and Simon* (2), *Hardcastle and McCormick*, *T. J. Hooker* and *Amazing Stories*. She also appeared on the soap *General Hospital* during 1985.

GUEST CREDITS

1968 *Wild Wild West* "The Night of the Death Maker" 2-23; **1969** *Dragnet* "Forgery-DR-33" 3-20; *Mannix* "Asleep in the Deep" 11-8; **1970** *Night Gallery* "Room with a View" 12-23; **1971** *Name of the Game* "A Sister from Napoli" 1-8; *The FBI* "The Death Watch" 2-14; *Ironside* "Love, Peace, Brotherhood and Murder" 2-18; *O'Hara, U. S. Treasury*

"Operation: Big Store" 9-17; **1972** *Ironside* "Achilles Heel" 2-17; **1974** *Police Woman* "Anatomy of Two Rapes" 10-11; *McCloud* "The Concrete Jungle Caper" 11-24; **1977** *Kojak* "Case without a File" 12-17; *Charlie's Angels* "Angels on Horseback" 12-21; **1978** *Eddie Capra Mysteries* "And the Sea Shall Give Up Her Dead" 10-20; **1979** *CHiPs* "Destruction Derby" 11-24; **1980** *Eischied* "The Buddy System" 1-27; **1983** *Knight Rider* "Nobody Does It Better" 4-29; *Knight Rider* "Custom KITT" 11-13.

TELEFILMS

1972 *Probe* 2-12 NBC; **1975** *You Lie So Deep, My Love* 2-25 ABC.

Joan Tompkins

(born 1916)

The widow of noted character actor Karl Swenson (1908-78), Joan had a wonderful career in her own right. After a 1954 television debut Joan became a regular on *Sam Benedict* (1962-63) and on *Occasional Wife* (1966-67). In addition to numerous guest roles she also did a stint on the soap *General Hospital*.

GUEST CREDITS

1960 *One Step Beyond* "Where are They?" 12-13; **1961** *Adventures in Paradise* "The Assassins" 11-26; *Bus Stop* "The Runaways" 12-24; **1962** *Straightaway* "Crossroad" 1-31; *Perry Mason* "The Case of the Poison Pen Pal" 2-10; *New Breed* "How Proud the Guilty" 2-27; *Dr. Kildare* "Operation: Lazarus" 5-24; **1963** *Eleventh Hour* "I Feel Like a Rutabaga" 4-24; *Perry Mason* "the Case of the Deadly Verdict" 10-3; **1964** *Lieutenant* "Gone the Sun" 1-18; *Dr. Kildare* "To Walk in Grace" 2-13; *Eleventh Hour* "Does My Mother Have to Know?" 3-18, 3-25; **1965** *Fugitive* "Fun and Games and Party Favors" 1-26; *Dr. Kildare* "No Mother to Guide Them" 2-4; *Slattery's People* "Question: What Time Is the Next Bandwagon?" 4-9; *Dr. Kildare* "Enough La Boheme for Everybody" 10-11; **1967** *Fugitive* "There Goes the Ball Game" 2-7; *Mission: Impossible* "The Seal" 11-5; *Mannix* "Turn Every Stone" 12-9; **1972** *Owen Marshall, Counselor at Law* "Victim in the Shadows" 1-27; *The FBI* "End of a Nightmare" 10-22; *Owen Marshall, Counselor at Law* "A Piece of God" 12-14; **1974** *Manhunter* "The Baby-Faced Killers" 9-24; *Police Woman* "Warning: All Wives" 9-27; **1976** *Little House on the Prairie* "Fred" 11-29; **1977** *Waltons* "The Achievement" 3-17; **1979** *Little House on the Prairie* "Barn Burner" 2-19.

TELEFILMS

1971 *The Harness* 11-12 NBC; **1973** *Set This Town on Fire* 1-8 NBC; *Crime Club* 3-6 CBS; **1978** *The Awakening Land* 2-19 NBC; *The Critical List* 9-11, 9-12 NBC; **1980** *The Night the City Screamed* 12-14 ABC.

Regis Toomey

(born August 13, 1902, Pittsburgh, Pa.; died October 12, 1991)

A 1922 graduate of The University of Pittsburgh, Regis became interested in acting and made a stage debut in 1923. He began a screen career of over 200 movies in 1929, a career that included roles in *Spellbound, Show Boat, Guys and Dolls, The High*

and the Mighty and *Voyage to the Bottom of the Sea*.

He was highly visible in fifties television, appearing in *Four Star Playhouse* (8), *Schlitz Playhouse of Stars* (3), *20th Century Fox Hour* (2), *Loretta Young Show* (5) and *Cheyenne* (2). In addition, he was a regular on *The Mickey Rooney Show* (1954-55) and *Richard Diamond, Private Eye* (1957-58).

During the sixties he was a regular on *Shannon* (1961-62), *Burke's Law* (1963-65) and *Petticoat Junction* (1969-70). He worked in guest roles well into the seventies and appeared on *Making a Living* (1982) as he neared his 80th birthday.

GUEST CREDITS

1959 *Lux Playhouse* "Frederick" 3-20; *Maverick* "Shady Deal at Sunny Acres" 4-5; *Restless Gun* "Hill of Death" 6-22; *Markham* "The Long Haul" 10-10; *Goodyear Theater* "Any Friend of Julie's" 10-19; *Rawhide* "Incident of the Stalking Death" 11-13; *Loretta Young Show* "Ten Men and a Girl" 11-15; **1960** *Tightrope* "Broken Rope" 1-12; *Rawhide* "Incident of the Tinker's Dam" 2-5; *Broncho* "Volunteers from Aberdeen" 2-9; *Loretta Young Show* "The Trial" 3-20; *June Allyson Show* "The Doctor and the Redhead" 4-25; *Man from Blackhawk* "The Lady in Yellow" 6-17; *General*

Electric Theater "The Playoff" 11-20; *Tall Man* "The Beast" 11-26; *Perry Mason* "The Case of the Loquacious Liar" 12-3; *Peter Gunn* "Dream Big, Dream Deadly" 12-12; **1961** *Route 66* "The Quick and the Dead" 1-13; *Sugarfoot* "Shepherd with a Gun" 2-6; **1962** *Cain's Hundred* "Murder by Proxy" 2-26; *Cheyenne* "The Vanishing Breed" 11-19; **1963** *Virginian* "The Judgment" 1-16; *Eleventh Hour* "The Man Who Came Home Late" 5-8; **1965** *Voyage to the Bottom of the Sea* "The Left-Handed Man" 10-24; *Perry Mason* "The Case of the 12th Wildcat" 10-31; **1966** *Legend of Jesse James* "Things Don't Just Happen" 3-14; **1967** *Time Tunnel* "Pirates of Deadman's Island" 2-17; **1972** *Ghost Story* "The Summer House" 10-13; *The FBI* "End of a Nightmare" 10-22; *Jigsaw* "Finder's Fee" 12-21; **1973** *Adam-12* "A Fool and His Money" 2-28; *Police Story* "The Big Walk" 12-4; **1974** *Owen Marshall, Counselor at Law* "The Desertion of Keith Ryder" 3-30.

TELEFILM

1974 *The Phantom of Hollywood* 2-12 CBS.

Harry Townes
(born September 18, 1914, Huntsville, Alabama)

Harry attended The University of Alabama prior to graduating from Columbia University in New York City. The acting bug bit during his under-graduate days and he acted in numerjous little theatre plays. After graduation, he read for, and got the role of The Leprechaun in *Finian's Rainbow*, playing it for two years on Broadway and another in London.

Upon returning to the U. S. he played Mercury in *Amphitryon*. Maurice Evans then wanted him for a revival of *Twelfth Night*, which was followed by a role of a pixie-ish ghost in *Gramercy Ghost*.

Townes rebelled at the typecasting and de-manded broader roles. During 1949 he began an extremely prolific television career. He was a very prominent player in the live television of the fifties, with especially stalwart work in 14 productions of *Kraft Television Theatre* and 5 productions of *Studio One*.

Other fifties work of note included appear-ances on *Suspense, The Web, Danger, Omnibus* (3), *Climax* (4), *Philco Television Playhouse* (2), *Armstrong Circle Theater* (4), *U.S. Steel Hour* (3) and *Playhouse 90* (3).

He made his film debut in a leading role in *Manhunt* (1954) and was featured in a 1958 film production of *The Brothers Karamazov*. His film work was limited thereafter to 10 additional films due to the tremendous demands that countless television roles placed on him. From 1959 to 1970 there were few actors who worked as often in the medium.

Townes exuded power and authority and was frequently cast in roles requiring these qualities. He slowed his pace a bit during the seventies, in some measure due to the increasing demands of his church. In 1974 he was ordained a Full Priest in The Episcopal Church.

During the later eighties Harry wound down a magnificent career on television with 2 guest appear-ances on *Magnum, P.I.* and a recurring role on *Knot's Landing* (1986-88). He has returned to his native Alabama to enjoy his well-earned retirement. The television medium and millions of viewers were indeed fortunate to have enjoyed the remarkable talents of this most gifted actor for four decades.

GUEST CREDITS

1959 *One Step Beyond* "The Bride Possessed" 1-20; *Playhouse 90* "The Dingaling Girl" 2-26; *Rawhide* "Incident of the Town in Terror" 3-6; *Playhouse 90* "The Rank and File" 5-28; *Zane Grey Theater* "Interrogation" 10-1; *Troubleshooters* "Moment of Terror" 10-16; *Gunsmoke* "Tail to the Wind" 10-17; *Men into Space* "Lost Missile" 11-4; *Millionaire* "Millionaire Mitchell Gunther" 12-2; *Playhouse 90* "The Silver Whistle" 12-29; **1960** *Twilight Zone* "The Four of Us Are Dying" 1-1; *Wanted: Dead or Alive* "Mental Lapse" 1-2; *Rebel* "The Death of Gray" 1-3; *Laramie* "Rope of Steel" 2-16; *Detectives* "Twelve Hours to Live" 2-19; *General Electric Theater* 'The Web of Guilt" 3-27; *Deputy* "The Truly Yours" 4-9; *Johnny Ringo* "Judgment Day" 4-14; *Wrangler* "Incident of the Wide Loop" 9-1; *Aquanauts* episode 9-21; *One Step Beyond* "Anniversary of a Murder" 9-27; *Bonanza* "The Mill" 10-1; *Perry Mason* "the Case of the Singular Double" 10-8; *Route 66* "The Strengthening Angels" 11-4; *Armstrong Circle Theater* "The Antique Swindle" 11-9; *Stagecoach West* "Life Sentence" 12-6; *Hong Kong* "Nine Lives" 12-7; *Thriller* "The Cheaters" 12-27; **1961** *Law and Mr. Jones* "Unbury the Dead" 2-3; *Islanders* "to Bell a Cat" 2-5; *Shirley Temple Show* "Onawandeh" 2-12; *Law and Mr. Jones* "Everybody vs. Quayton" 3-17; *Twilight Zone* "Shadow Play" 5-5; *Loretta Young Show* "The Wedding" 5-21; *Thriller* "Dark Legacy" 5-30; *Rawhide* "Incident of the Night on the Town" 6-2; *Route 66* "Blue Murder" 9-29; *Defenders* "Death Across the Counter" 9-30; *Alcoa Premiere* "Moment of Decision" 11-7; *Investigators* "In a Mirror Darkly" 11-16; *Straightaway* "The Sports Car Breed" 12-8; *Outlaws* "Masterpiece" 12-21; *Target: The Corruptors* "The Fix" 12-22; *General Electric Theater* "The Other Wise Man" 12-24; **1962** *Outlaws* "A Day to Kill" 2-22; *Route 66* "Love Is a Skinny Kid" 4-6; *Tall Man* "The Frame" 4-22; *Armstrong Circle Theater* "Anatomy of a Betrayal: Dateline Cuba" 5-9; *U.S. Steel Hour* "Scene of the Crime" 6-27; *U.S. Steel Hour* "Murder on the Agenda" 8-22; *Sam Benedict* "Twenty Aching Years" 10-20; *Bonanza* "The War Comes to Washoe" 11-4; **1963** *Eleventh Hour* "The Wings of Morning" 3-20;

Dakotas "Feud at Snake River" 4-29; *Fugitive* "Fear in a Desert City" 9-17; *Alfred Hitchcock Hour* "A Nice Touch" 10-4; *Gunsmoke* "Tobe" 10-19; *Ben Casey* "Little Drops of Water, Little Grains of Sand" 10-30; *Outer Limits* "O.B.I.T." 11-4; *Great Adventure* "The Treasure Train of Jefferson Davis" 11-15; *Kraft Suspense Theatre* "The Hunt" 12-19; **1964** *Mr. Novak* "The Death of a Teacher" 2-4; *Perry Mason* "The Case of the Woeful Widower" 3-2; *Great Adventure* "The President Vanishes" 3-14; *Suspense* "I, Donald Roberts" 4-29; *Rawhide* "Incident at Seven Fingers" 5-7; *Rawhide* "Incident of the Lost Herd" 10-16; *Fugitive* "Tug of War" 10-17; *Perry Mason* "The Case of a Place Called Midnight" 11-12; **1965** *Kraft Suspense Theatre* "In Darkness Waiting" 1-14; *Dr. Kildare* "My Name Is Lisa and I Am Lost" 1-21; *Fugitive* "Scapegoat" 2-2; *Alfred Hitchcock Hour* "The Photographer and the Undertaker" 3-15; *Mr. Novak* "Tender Twigs" 3-15; *Gunsmoke* "Two Tall Men" 5-8; *Man Called Shenandoah* "The Verdict" 11-1; *Wild Wild West* "The Night of the Double-Edged Knife" 11-12; *Gunsmoke* "Malachi" 11-13; *12 O'Clock High* "Target 802" 12-27; *Fugitive* "When the Wind Blows" 12-28; **1966** *Branded* "The Golden Fleece" 1-2; *The FBI* "The Forests of the Night" 1-2; *Perry Mason* "The Case of the Golfer's Gambit" 1-30; *Dr. Kildare* "A Strange Sort of Accident" 3-29; *Fugitive* "Joshua's Kingdom" 10-18; *Monroes* "The Friendly Enemy" 11-9; **1967** *Wild Wild West* "The Night of the Tottering Tontine" 1-6; *Felony Squad* "The Night of the Shark" 1-16, 1-23; *Star Trek* "Return of the Archons" 2-9; *Felony Squad* "The Counterfeit Cop" 9-18; *Invaders* "Valley of the Shadow" 9-26; *Judd, for the Defense* "Conspiracy" 10-13; *Tarzan* "Mountains of the Moon" 11-24, 12-1; **1968** *Hallmark Hall of Fame* "Elizabeth, the Queen" 1-31; *Big Valley* "The Emperor of Rice" 2-12; *Mod Squad* "A Time to Love-A Time to Cry" 11-12; **1969** *Judd, for the Defense* "Between Dark and Daylight" 2-7; **1970** *Mannix* "The Search for Darrell Andrews" 2-27; *Medical Center* "The Rebel Doctor" 4-14; *Young Lawyers* "The Glass Prison" 11-2; *Immortal* "The Return" 12-17; **1971** *Gunsmoke* "Lijah" 11-8; *Ironside* "Gentle Oaks" 11-25; *O'Hara, U. S. Treasury* "Operation: Payoff" 12-10; **1972** *Night Gallery* "Lindemann's Catch" 1-12; *Cade's County* "Ragged

Edge" 3-5; *Sixth Sense* "Witch, Witch, Burning Bright" 3-11; *Delphi Bureau* "The Deadly Errand Project" 10-5; *Planet of the Apes* "The Interrogation" 11-15; *Mannix* "Lost Sunday" 12-3; **1973** *Emergency* episode 3-10; **1975** *Cannon* "Nightmare" 9-10; *Kate McShane* "Murder Comes in Little Pills" 10-1; *Mobile One* episode 12-15; **1978** *Quincy, M.E.* "Dead or Alive" 11-15; **1979** *Quincy, M.E.* "The Money Plague" 11-15; **1980** *Quincy, M.E.* "Last Day, First Day" 11-19; **1981** *Buck Rogers* "The Guardians" 1-29; *Incredible Hulk* "The First" 3-6, 3-13; **1982** *Falcon Crest* "The Extortionist" 1-15; *Falcon Crest* "Pentulltimate Questions" 4-9; *Quincy, M.E.* "A Ghost of a Chance" 10-6; **1983** *Voyagers!* "The Trial of Phineas Bogg" 1-16; *Simon and Simon* "Pirate's Key" 1-20.

TELEFILMS

1971 *They Call It Murder* 12-17 NBC; **1975** *The Specialists* 1-6 NBC; **1978** *B. J. and the Bear* 10-4 NBC; **1979** *Last Ride of the Dalton Gang* 11-20 NBC; **1980** *Casino* 8-1 ABC.

Les Tremayne
(born April 16, 1913, London, England)

Reared in the U. S., British-born Les Tremayne became a star of radio during the thirties and forties on shows like *Grand Hotel* and *First Nighter*. His mellow voice was ideal for romantic radio roles and his familiar tones helped him to be rated as one of the three most familiar forties voices in America: the other two were Bing Crosby and then President Roosevelt.

Les worked in television during the early years of the medium and was a regular on *One Man's Family* (1950) and on *The Adventures of Ellery Queen* (1958-59). He became a popular guest star during the sixties, with *Perry Mason* using him in 6 episodes.

Les retained a handsome debonair appearance as he aged and his distinctive voice was used during the seventies for Saturday morning children's shows. A working actor well into his seventies, Les appeared on the soap *General Hospital* during 1988.

GUEST CREDITS

1959 *Rin Tin Tin* "Star of India" 1-2; *Texan* "Outpost" 1-19; *Rin Tin Tin* "Major Mockingbird" 1-30; *Rin Tin Tin* "Pillajohn's Progress" 3-6; *Rifleman* "The Challenge" 4-7; *June Allyson Show* "A Summer's Ending" 10-12; **1960** *M Squad* "Let There Be Light" 4-5; *Wagon Train* "The Maggie Hamilton Story" 4-6; *Perry Mason* "The Case of the Madcap Modiste" 4-30; *Alfred Hitchcock Presents* "Mr. Bixby and the Colonel's Coat" 9-27; **1961** *Rawhide* "Incident at the Top of the World" 1-27; *Perry Mason* "The Case of The Angry Dead Man" 2-25; *Alfred Hitchcock Presents* "Death Mate" 4-18; *Whispering Smith* "Safety Valve" 5-29; *Perry Mason* "The Case of the Left-Handed Liar" 11-25; **1962** *New Breed* "The Torch" 3-6; *Alfred Hitchcock Hour* "Day of Reckoning" 11-22; **1964** *Mr. Novak* "The Exile" 1-14; *77 Sunset Strip* "The Target" 1-24; *Perry Mason* "The Case of the Nervous Neighbor" 2-13; *Alfred Hitchcock Hour* "Isabel" 6-5; *Voyage to the Bottom of the Sea* "Turn Back the Clock" 10-26; *Perry Mason* "The Case of the Ruinous Road" 12-31; **1965** *Virginian* "A Slight Case of Charity" 2-10; *Dr. Kildare* "The Time Buyers" 4-8; *Defenders* "A Matter of Law and Disorder" 4-8; **1966** *Perry Mason* "The Case of the Unwelcome Well" 4-3; **1970** *Bonanza* "The Law and Bill Burgess" 2-15.

Ivan Triesault
(born Tallinn, Estonia; died January 3, 1980)

Ivan began his acting career at age 14 in his native Estonia, and continued his studies in London. In 1942 he signed a contract with Warner Brothers

and moved to Hollywood. Typecast as European characters, usually villains, he worked regularly through a long and rewarding career. His films included *Mission to Moscow, Days of Glory, Notorious, Golden Earrings, Five Fingers, The Bad and the Beautiful, Barabbas* and *Von Ryan's Express*.

GUEST CREDITS

1959 *Perry Mason* "The Case of the Shattered Dream" 1-3; *One Step Beyond* "The Dark Room" 2-10; *Markham* "Double Negative" 9-29; **1964** *Voyage to the Bottom of the Sea* "The Price of Doom" 10-12; **1965** *Bob Hope Chrysler Theater* "The Game" 9-15; **1966** *Mission: Impossible* "The Trial" 1-28; *Voyage to the Bottom of the Sea* "The Death Ship" 2-20; *Girl from UNCLE* "The Danish Blue Affair" 10-25; **1967** *Wild Wild West* "The Night of the Surreal McCoy" 3-3; **1968** *It Takes a Thief* "It Takes One to Know One" 1-16; *Garrison's Gorillas* "Time Bomb" 3-12; *Bonanza* "Commitment at Angelous" 4-7; **1969** *Wild Wild West* "The Night of the Cossacks" 3-21.

Tom Troupe

(born 1928)

Onscreen from the late fifties, Tom appeared in *The Big Fisherman, The Devil's Brigade, Che and Sofi* (he wrote the screenplay) and *Kelly's Heroes*.

In television from 1960, Tom was often cast as professionals or sly citizens with criminal intent. Married to actress Carole Cook, he continued to do guest roles well into the eighties.

GUEST CREDITS

1960 *Lawman* "Cornered" 12-11; **1961** *Dr. Kildare* "The Patient" 11-23; **1964** *Ben Casey* "A Falcon's Eye, a Lion's Heart, a Girl's Hand" 2-26; *Fugitive* "Escape into Black" 11-17; **1965** *Man from UNCLE* "The Secret Sceptre Affair" 2-8; *Man from UNCLE* "The Bow-Wow Affair" 2-15; **1966** *Iron Horse* "No Wedding Bells for Tony" 11-7; **1967** *Star Trek* "Arena"1-19; *Mission: Impossible* "Action!" 3-4; *Judd, for the Defense* "To Love and Stand

Mute" 12-8; **1969** *Mannix* "A Question of Midnight" 10-25; **1971** *Dan August* "The Worst Crime" 2-11; *Owen Marshall, Counselor at Law* "Nothing Personal" 11-11; **1972** *Smith Family* episode 4-12; *Rookies* "Dirge for Sunday" 10-30; *McMillan and Wife* "Blues for Sally M" 10-22; *The FBI* "The Jug-Marker" 12-10; **1973** *Streets of San Francisco* "Legion of the Lost" 4-12; *Cannon* "the Perfect Alibi" 10-31; *McMillan and Wife* "Free Fall to Terror" 11-11; *Griff* "Her Name Was Nancy" 12-8; **1974** *Owen Marshall, Counselor at Law* "The Break-In" 3-2; *Ironside* "Trial by Error" 10-3; *Marcus Welby, M.D.* "Child of Silence" 12-3; **1975** *Marcus Welby, M.D.* "Calculated Risk" 11-11; *Streets of San Francisco* "Most Likely to Succeed" 12-19; *Barbary Coast* episode 12-26; **1979** *CHiPs* "Pressure Point" 1-20; **1980** *Quincy, M.E.* "The Final Gift" 3-20; **1982** *Cassie and Company* "A Ring Ain't Always a Circle" 8-20; **1983** *Voyagers!* "Buffalo Bill and Annie Oakley Play the Palace" 1-9.

TELEFILMS

1973 *The Alpha Caper* 10-3 ABC.

Natalie Trundy

(born 1942)

Natalie was a regular at age 12 in an abbreviated 1954 sitcom called *The Marriage*. She Began her film career in 1956 but had to drop out of acting for several years during the sixties after her back was broken in an auto accident.

In 1965 she married producer Arthur Jacobs (1918-1973) and began a comeback in three of his *Planet of the Apes* films, in 1970, 1971 and 1973. She was on location, in *Huckleberry Finn*, when her husband died suddenly. Her TV guest roles were rather scattered, last appearing in 1978.

GUEST CREDITS

1960 *Adventures in Paradise* "The Violent Journey" 3-28; *Thriller* "The Twisted Image" 9-13; **1962** *New Breed* "Echoes of Hate" 4-3; **1963** *Twilight Zone* "Valley of the Shadows" 1-17; *Eleventh Hour* "Advice to the Lovelorn and Shopworn" 1-30; *Perry Mason* "The Case of the Golden Oranges" 3-7; *Alfred Hitchcock Hour* "The Long Silence" 3-22; **1964** *Perry Mason* "The Case of the Tandem Target" 5-14; **1967** *Judd, for the Defense* "To Kill a Madman" 11-24; *Felony Squad* "An Arrangement with Death" 12-11, 12-18; **1970** *Silent Force* "Horse in a White Collar" 11-9; **1978** *Quincy, M.E.* "Matters of Life and Death" 1-20.

TELEFILM

1972 *A Great American Tragedy* 10-18 ABC.

Tom Tully

(born 1908, Durango, Colorado; died April 27, 1982)

After service in the U. S. Navy, Tom became a newspaper reporter, then moved to New York and worked in radio for over 3,000 broadcasts. Several Broadway hits brought him to Hollywood and a film career, beginning in 1938. Included in his films were roles in *I'll Be Seeing You, Ruby Gentry, The Moon Is Blue, The Jazz Singer*, an Academy Award Nominated role in *The Caine Mutiny, Ten North Frederick, The Carpetbaggers, Coogan's Bluff* and *Charlie Varrick*.

He began appearing on television in 1952 and, in 1954, began a lengthy co-starring role (until 1959) on the cop show, *The Lineup*. Tom was in strong demand for sixties guest roles with his tough, no-nonsense persona. A regular on *Shane* in 1966, he retired from acting in 1973 except for a cameo role in a 1981 telefilm.

GUEST CREDITS

1960 *Alfred Hitchcock Presents* "Backward, Turn Backward" 1-31; **1961** *U.S. Steel Hour* "Summer

Rhapsody" 5-3; *Rawhide* " Rio Salado" 9-29; *Tales of Wells Fargo* "Defiant at the Gate" 11-25; **1962** *Empire* "Long Past, Long Remembered" 10-23; **1963** *Untouchables* "A Taste for Pineapple" 5-21; *Burke's Law* "Who Killed Betty Jo?" 11-8; **1964** *Perry Mason* "The Case ofthe Arrogant Arsonist" 3-5; *Perry Mason* "The Case of the Nautical Knot" 10-29; *Virginian* "The Hour of the Tiger" 12-30; **1965** *Rawhide* "Blood Harvest" 2-12; *Bonanza* "The Dilemna" 9-19; *Loner* "Hunt the Man Down" 12-11; *Legend of Jesse James* "The Man Who Killed Jesse" 12-27; **1967** *Guns of Will Sonnett* "The Favor" 11-10; *Bonanza* "The Sure Thing" 11-12; **1969** *Guns of Will Sonnett* "Join the Army" 1-3; *High Chaparral* "The Last Hundred Miles" 1-24; *Mod Squad* "A Place to Run" 12-2; **1972** *Mission: Impossible* "Trapped" 2-26; *Rookies* "Dead, Like a Lost Dream" 9-18; **1973** *Rookies* "Down Home Boy" 11-19.

TELEFILMS

1969 *Any Second Now* 2-11 NBC; **1973** *Hijack* 9-26; **1981** *Madam X* 3-16.

Lurene Tuttle

(born August 29, 1906, Pleasant Lake, Indiana; died 1986)

Educated at USC, Lurene made her film debut in 1941, after a lengthy radio career. She began to appear on television in the early fifties and co-starred in the television version of *Life With Father* (1953-55); she was also a regular on *Father of the Bride* (1961-62).

Lurene did a great deal of guest work on TV drama series of the sixties, and had sitcom appearances on *The Andy Griffith Show* (2), *Hazel, The Munsters, I Dream of Jeannie, My Favorite Martian, The Beverly Hillbillies* and *Petticoat Junction*. The sitcom work served her well for she had a featured regular role on *Julia* (1968-70).

She worked well into the eighties, making guest appearances on *St. Elsewhere* in 1984 and on *Murder, She Wrote* in 1985.

GUEST CREDITS

1959 *Playhouse 90* "The Wings of the Dove" 1-8; *Californians* "The Painted Lady" 1-13; *Lawman* "The Bandit" 5-31; *Perry Mason* "The Case of the Artful Dodger" 12-12; **1960** *Wagon Train* "The Lita Foladaire Story" 1-6; *Bourbon Street Beat* "The Missing Queen" 3-14; *Goodyear Theater* "All in the Family" 3-28; *Michael Shayne* "Die Like a Dog" 10-14; *Perry Mason* "The Case of the Loquacious Liar" 12-3; *Gunsmoke* "Brother Love" 12-31; **1961** *Rawhide* "Incident of the Wager on Payday" 6-16; **1962** *Alcoa Premiere* "Blues for a Hanging" 12-27; **1963** *Perry Mason* "The Case of the Shoplifter's Shoe" 1-3; *Mr. Novak* "The Risk" 10-29; **1965** *Perry Mason* "The Case of the Grinning Gorilla" 4-29; **1966** *Perry Mason* "The Case of the Avenging Angel" 3-13; **1967** *Judd, for the Defense* "The Confessional" 10-20; **1971** *Name of the Game* "The Man Who Killed a Ghost" 1-29; **1972** *Gunsmoke* "Homecoming" 1-8; **1973** *Adam-12* "A Fool and His Money" 2-28; **1974** *Rookies* "Eyewitness" 2-11; **1975** *Mannix* "Chance Meeting" 1-19; *Little House on the Prairie* "The Gift" 12-17; **1976** *Switch* "Ain't Nobody Here Named Barney" 1-13; *Little House on the Prairie* "Going Home" 3-31; **1977** *Police Woman* "Merry Christmas, Waldo" 12-14; **1978** *Charlie's Angels* "The Jade Trap" 3-1; **1980** *Barnaby Jones* "The Killin' Cousin" 4-3; **1981** *Hart to Hart* "Murder Takes A Bow" 5-19; *Trapper John, M.D.* "'Tis the Season" 12-20.

TELEFILMS

1974 *Mrs. Sundance* 1-15 ABC; *Live Again, Die Again* 2-16 ABC; **1976** *Law and Order* 5-6 NBC; **1978** *Crash* 10-29 ABC; **1980** *White Mama* 3-5 CBS; *For the Love of It* 9-26 ABC; **1981** *The Adventures of Huckleberry Finn* 7-9 NBC; *Return of the Beverly Hillbillies* 10-6 CBS; **1983** *Shooting Stars* 7-28 ABC.

Gene Tyburn

Gene made his television debut in 1963, and became a popular guest star, with multiple appearances on *Wild Wild West* (3), *Mission: Impossible* (3) and *Gunsmoke* (2). His screen career was insignificant, with only 3 films from 1969.

GUEST CREDITS

1963 *Rifleman* "The Bullet" 2-25; **1965** *Outer Limits* "The Mice" 1-6; *Gunsmoke* "Outlaw's Woman" 12-11; **1966** *Wild Wild West* "The Night of the Ready-Made Corpse" 11-25; **1967** *Wild Wild West* "The Night of the Falcon" 11-10; **1968** *Wild West* "The Night of the Egyptian Queen" 11-15; **1969** *Bonanza* "Silence at Stillwater" 9-28; **1970** *Mission: Impossible* "Submarine" 1-16; *Mission: Impossible* "The Innocent" 10-3; **1971** *Night Gallery* "The Boy Who Predicted Earthquakes" 9-15; *Mission: Impossible* "The Visitors" 11-27; **1972** *Sixth Sense* "The Heart That Wouldn't Stay Buried" 1-22; *Gunsmoke* "Milligan" 11-6; *Bold Ones: The Doctors* "End Theme" 12-12; **1974** *Ironside* "Close to the Heart" 2-28; *Petrocelli* "Double Negative" 10-30; **1976** *Barbary Coast* "Mary Had More Than a Little" 1-2; *Rockford Files* "The No-Cut Contract" 1-16; *McCloud* "Bonnie and McCloud" 10-24; **1977** *Logan's Run* "The Innocent" 10-10; *Logan's Run* "Man Out of time" 10-17.

TELEFILMS

1974 *Cry Panic* 2-6 ABC; *It's Good To Be Alive* 2-22 CBS; **1975** *Eric* 11-10 NBC; **1979** *Silent Victory: The Kitty O'Neil Story* 2-24 CBS; **1981** *The Star Maker* 5-11, 5-12 NBC; **1982** *Something So Right* 11-30 CBS.

Lee Van Cleef
(born January 9, 1925, Somerville, New Jersey; died December 14, 1989)

Following high school graduation Lee joined The U. S. Navy, serving four years from 1942 until 1946 on subchasers. After the war, and discharge from service, he tried his hand at various occupations before joining a little theater group.

He made a film debut in 1950, but gained lasting fame as one of the killers who awaited Gary Cooper for the deadly showdown in *High Noon* (1952). He would go on to over 70 U. S. films, including roles in *Gunfight at O.K. Corral, The Young Lions, The Man Who Shot Liberty Valance* and *How the West Was Won.*

But greater recognition came from some of his so-called Italian "spaghetti westerns" (1965-76), two of which co-starred Clint Eastwood; *For a Few Dollars More* and *The Good, the Bad and the Ugly.* In some later films of this genre Lee was the hero instead of his usual bad-guy roles.

Lee's piercing eyes and malevolent gaze were an unforgettable part of film and television history. He worked in televison guest roles from 1951 until 1966 when his film career gathered momentum. During 1984 he starred in a TV series about a martial arts expert, *The Master*. He died of a heart attack in 1989, survived by his wife, two sons and a daughter.

GUEST CREDITS

1959 *Rifleman* "The Deadly Wait" 3-24; *Tombstone Territory* "The Hostage" 5-1; *Yancy Derringer* "Outlaw at Liberty" 5-7; *Lawman* "The Conclave" 6-14; *Law of the Plainsman* "Clear Title" 12-17; **1960** *Hotel de Paree* "Sundance and the Man in Room Seven" 2-12; *Untouchables* "The Unhired Assassin" 2-25, 3-3; *Alaskans* "Peril at Caribou Crossing" 2-28; *Black Saddle* "The Cabin" 4-1; *Rifleman* "The Prodigal" 4-26; *Deputy* "Palace of Chance" 5-21; *Gunsmoke* "Old Flame" 5-28; *Mr. Lucky* episode 6-11; *Lawman* "Man on a Mountain" 6-12; *Colt .45* "The Trespasser" 6-21; *77 Sunset Strip* "The Attic" 9-16; *Lawman* "The Return of Owny O'Reilly" 10-16; *Laramie* ".45 Calibre" 11-15; *Bonanza* "The

Blood Line" 12-31; **1961** *Hawaiian Eye* "The Stanhope Brand" 2-22; *Maverick* "Red Dog" 3-5; *Broncho* "Yankee Tornado" 3-13; *Rifleman* "The Clarence Bibs Story" 4-14; *Stagecoach West* "Never Walk Alone" 4-18; *Laramie* "Killer's Odds" 4-25; *Bronco* "Trouble Street" 10-2; *Twilight Zone* "The Grave" 10-27; **1962** *Broncho* "One Evening in Abilene" 3-19; *Cheyenne* "A Man Called Ragan" 4-23; *Cheyenne* "Trouble Street" 5-14; *Rifleman* "Death Never Rides Alone" 10-29; *Have Gun—Will Travel* "The Treasure" 12-29; **1963** *Laramie* "Vengeance" 1-8; *Dakotas* "Thunder in Pleasant Valley" 2-4; *Dick Powell Show* "Colossus" 3-12; *Have Gun—Will Travel* "Face of a Shadow" 4-20; *Laramie* "The Stranger" 4-23; **1964** *Destry* "Destry Had a Little Lamb" 2-21; *Rawhide* "The Enormous Fist" 10-2; *Rawhide* "Piney" 10-9; **1965** *Branded* "The Richest Man in Boot Hill" 10-31; **1966** *Branded* "Call to Glory" 2-27, 3-6, 3-13; *Rawhide* "Quarter Past Eleven" 3-24; *Gunsmoke* "My Father, My Son" 4-23.

TELEFILM

1977 *Nowhere to Hide* 6-5 NBC.

Diana Van Der Vlis

(born 1935)

A fine stage actress, Diana entered film and television work in 1957. Following extensive TV guest work during the sixties, she began a lengthy starring role on the soap *Where the Heart Is* (1969-73). In 1975-76 she had another featured soap role on *Ryan's Hope*.

After her 1957 film debut she appeared in only 4 movies, with *The Swimmer* being the best known.

GUEST CREDITS

1960 *DuPont Show of the Month* "Heaven Can Wait" 11-16; **1961** *Alfred Hitchcock Presents* "Make My Death Bed" 6-27; *Great Ghost Tales* "Room 13" 9-7; **1963** *DuPont Show of the Week* "The Bachelor Game" 9-29; *East Side/West Side* "Something for the Girls" 10-14; *Fugitive* "The Glass Tightrope" 12-

3; **1964** *Route 66* "Child of a Night" 1-3; *Dr. Kildare* "A Hundred Million Tomorrows" 3-12; *Defenders* "The Uncivil War" 6-27; *Mr. Broadway* "Bad Little Rich Girl" 12-5; *Rogues* "The Boston Money Party" 12-6; **1965** *Defenders* "The Silent Killers" 1-21; *12 O'Clock High* "The Lorelei" 1-22; *Fugitive* "Runner in the Dark" 3-30; **1967** *Invaders* "The Leeches" 1-31; *T.H.E. Cat* "Lisa" 3-31; *Man from UNCLE* "The Deep Six Affair" 12-25; **1968** *The FBI* "The Predators" 4-7.

Granville Van Dusen

(born 1944)

After stage experience Granville made his film debut in 1970, but switched to television in 1974, working very steadily thereafter in guest roles, telefilms and a regular role on *Soap* (1980-81).

Some later eighties guest work included *Hotel* (2), *Magnum, P.I., Hill Street Blues, Murder, She Wrote, Moonlighting, Highway to Heaven, Mr. Belvedere, Matlock, Family Ties* and *Buck James*. He was a regular on an abbreviated 1987 sitcom called *Karen* which ran on the FOX network.

GUEST CREDITS

1974 *Harry O* "Coinage of the Realm" 10-10; *Waltons* "The Book" 11-14; **1975** *Baretta* "This Ain't My Bag" 4-30; *Switch* "Stung from Behind" 9-30; **1976** *Harry O* "Past Imperfect" 1-22; **1977** *Bionic Woman* "Biofeedback" 1-12; *Barnaby Jones* "Yesterday's Terror" 10-13; *Kojak* "Tears for All Who Loved Her" 11-20; **1978** *Eddie Capra Mysteries* "Dirge for a Dead Dachsund" 10-29; *Barnaby Jones* "Memory of a Nightmare" 12-14; **1979** *Quincy, M.E.* "A Question of Death" 1-4; *Kaz* "They've Taken Our Daughter" 3-21; *Quincy, M.E.* "Mode of Death" 11-1; *CHiPs* "The Watch Commander" 11-17; **1980** *Paris* "The Price Is Right" 1-1; *Stone* "Deep Sleeper" 1-14.

TELEFILMS

1974 *Dr. Max* 4-4 CBS; **1975** *Someone I*

Touched 2-26 ABC; *The Night That Panicked America* 10-31 ABC; **1976** *James A. Michener's "Dynasty"* 3-13 NBC; **1977** *The War Between the Tates* 6-13 NBC; **1978** *Dr. Scorpion* 2-24 ABC; *Love's Dark Ride* 4-2 NBC; **1979** *Transplant* 4-17 CBS; *High Midnight* 11-27 CBS; **1980** *The Wild and the Free* 11-26 CBS; **1981** *Madam X* 3-16 NBC; **1982** *This Is Kate Bennett* 5-28 ABC; *Bare Essence* 10-4, 10-5 CBS; *Hotline* 10-16 CBS.

Jo Van Fleet (right), hires Mike Connors as her bodyguard in a 1970 episode of *Mannix* (CBS). The episode was called "One for the Lady".

Jo Van Fleet
(born 1919; died June 10, 1996)

After winning a scholarship to Neighborhood Playhouse in New York and appearing in a half-dozen Broadway hits, Jo won an Academy Award in her first film outing, in *East of Eden* (1955). She later appeared in some renowed films like *The Rose Tatoo, I'll Cry Tomorrow, Gunfight at O.K. Corral, Cool Hand Luke, I Love You, Alice B. Toklas!* and *The Gang That Couldn't Shoot Straight.*

Jo made her television debut in 1952 and appeared, during the fifites, on *Philco Television Playhouse* (3), *U.S. Steel Hour, Armstrong Circle Theater, Suspense, Robert Montgomery Presents* and *Alfred Hitchcock Presents* (2). She appeared intermittently in guest roles until 1977.

GUEST CREDITS
1959 *Alcoa Theater* "30 Pieces of Silver" 1-26; *DuPont Show of the Month* "The Human Comedy" 3-28; *General Electric Theater* "Disaster" 11-1; 1961 *DuPont Show of the Month* "The Night of the Storm" 3-21; *Alfred Hitchcock Presents* "Servant Problem" 6-6; *Thriller* "The Remarkable Mrs. Hawk" 12-18; **1962** *Naked City* "The Night the Saints Lost Their Halos" 1-17; *Frontier Circus* "The Courtship" 2-15; **1963** *77 Sunset Strip* "Don't Wait for Me" 11-8; *Route 66* "The Stone Guest" 11-8; **1964** *Kraft Suspense Theatre* "The World I Want" 10-1; **1966** *Virginian* "Legacy of Hate" 9-14; **1967** *Bob Hope Chrysler Theater* "Verdict for Terror" 3-29; **1969** *Wild Wild West* "Night of the Tycoons" 3-28; **1970** *Bonanza* "The Trouble with Amy" 1-25; *Mannix* "One for the Lady" 9-26; *Mod Squad* "A Is for Annie" 10-15; **1971** *Bonanza* "The Stillness Within" 3-14; *Medical Center* episode 11-10; **1973** *Medical Center* "Time of Darkness" 9-17; **1977** *Police Woman* "The Buttercup Killer" 12-13.

TELEFILMS

1972 *The Family Rico* 9-12 CBS; **1973** *Satan's School for Girls* 9-19 ABC.

Richard Venture
(born November 12, 1923, West New York, New Jersey)

A solid stage background propelled Richard into films in 1965, with a soap role in The *Secret Storm* his first television work. He made one guest appearance in 1966, but didn't make another one until 1975. He appeared on the medium rather steadily from that point, with a series regular role on *Street Hawk* (1985), a role in the miniseries, *The Thorn Birds* (1983) and 11 telefilm roles highlighting his eighties work.

In the nineties Richard appeared on the soap *General Hospital* (1991) and was featured in a 1993

sitcom called *The Boys*.

GUEST CREDITS

1966 *Bob Hope Chrysler Theater* "Guilty or Not Guilty" 3-9; **1975** *Harry O* "Lester Two" 9-25; *Starsky and Hutch* "Snowstorm" 10-1; *Police Woman* "Above and Beyond" 10-31; *Kojak* "Out of the Frying Pan…" 11-2; *Cannon* "To Still the Voice" 12-3; **1976** *Rockford Files* "In Hazard" 2-6; *Joe Forrester* "Pressure Point" 3-22; *Jigsaw John* "Runaway" 4-12; **1977** *Rockford Files* "The Birds, The Bees and T. T. Flowers" 1-21, 1-28; *Police Story* "The Malflores" 1-25; *Police Story* "The Blue Fog" 2-1; *Police Story* "Pressure Point" 9-27; *Kojak* "Once More from Birdland" 10-30; **1978** *Starsky and Hutch* "The Action" 1-7; **1979** *Waltons* "The Journal" 10-25; **1980** *Quincy, M.E.* "Diplomatic Immunity" 1-17; **1981** *Walking Tall* episode 3-31; **1983** *The Powers of Matthew Star* episode 3-4.

TELEFILMS

1976 *Helter Skelter* 4-1, 4-2 CBS; **1977** *Johnny, We Hardly Knew Ye* 1-27 NBC; *Danger in Paradise* 5-12 NBC; *A Sensitive, Passionate Man* 6-6 NBC; *Corey: For the People* 6-12 NBC; **1978** *The Dark Secret of Harvest Home* 1-23, 1-24; *Sticking Together* 4-14 ABC; **1979** *The Tenth Month* 9-16 CBS; **1980** *Off the Minnesota Strip* 5-5 ABC; *Rape and*

Marriage: The Rideout Case 10-3 CBS; *Enola Gay* 11-23 NBC; *My Kidnapper, My Love* 12-8 NBC; **1981** *Chicago Story* 3-15 NBC; *The Violation of Sarah McDavid* 5-19 CBS; *The Best Little Girl in the World* 5-11 ABC; **1982** *The Executioner's Song* 11-28, 11-29 NBC; **1983** *Cocaine: One Man's Seduction* 2-27 NBC.

Herb Vigran

(born 1910, Ft. Wayne, Indiana; died November 28, 1986)

A graduate of Indiana University, Herb came to Broadway in 1937 and began a film career of over 50 movies in 1940. In military service from 1943-45, he worked a greaat deal in radio prior to beginning a busy TV career in 1953. His only series regular role came in 1958-59 on *The Ed Wynn Show*.

During 1970-75 Herb had a recurring role on *Gunsmoke*, appearing in 9 episodes as Judge Brooker. He was a member of Jack Webb's "stock company", appearing in several episodes of *Dragnet* and *Adam-12*. His talents were also used on sitcoms like *Bewitched* (4) and *The Beverly Hillbillies*.

Herb died of cancer November 26, 1986.

GUEST CREDITS

1959 *Wanted: Dead or Alive* "Rope Law" l-3; *M Squad* "Murder in C Sharp Major" 10-l6; **1960** *Bonanza* ""San Francisco Holiday" 4-2; *Perry Mason* "The Case of the Slandered Submarine" 9-l4; *Maverick* "Hadley's Hunters" 9-25; *Peter Gunn* "Take Five for Murder" l2-5; *Maverick* "The Bold Fenian Men" l2-18; **1961** *Bonanza* "The Bride" l-21; *Shirley Temple Theatre* "The Princess and the Goblins" 3-l9; *Law and Mr. Jones* "A Very Special Citizen" 3-24; *Maverick* "The Golden Fleecing" 10-8; *Lawman* "The Catalogue Woman" 11-5; **1962** *Surfside 6* "Find Leroy Burdette" 2-l9; *Maverick* "Marshall Maverick" 3-11; **1963** *Virginian* "The Exiles" l-9; **1964** *Fugitive* "Escape into Black" 11-17; **1966** *Bonanza* "A Real Nice, Friendly Little Town" 11-27; **1967** *Dragnet* "The Big Trial" l2-14; **1968** *Dragnet* "The Big Goodbye" 2-29; *Mod Squad* "The Price of Terror" 11-26; *Dragnet* "Public Affairs-DR-l4" 11-28; **1969** *Dragnet* "Frauds-DR-28" 2-20; *Dragnet* "Homicide-The Student" 9-25; *Hawaii Five-0* "Just Lucky, I Guess" 10-15; **1970** *Dragnet* "Homicide-Who Killed Who?" 1-29; *Dragnet* "D.H.Q.-The Victims" 4-l6; *Gunsmoke* "The Witness" 11-23; **1971** *Gunsmoke* "Lijah" 11-8; **1972** *Gunsmoke* "No Tomorrow" l-3; *Gunsmoke* "One for the Road" l-24; *Gunsmoke* "Alias Festus Haggin" 3-6; *Adam-l2* "The Late Baby" 9-20; **1973** *Gunsmoke* "A Quiet Day in Dodge" l-29; *Gunsmoke* "The Deadly Innocent" l2-17; *Adam-l2* "Southwest Division" l2-19; **1974** *Griff* "Fugitive from Fear" l-5; *Gunsmoke* "To Ride a Yellow Horse" 3-18; *Streets of San Francisco* "One Chance to Live" 10-17; *Kolchak: The Night Stalker* "Horror in the Heights" l2-20; **1975** *Gunsmoke* "The Fires of Ignorance" l-27; **1979** *Charlie's Angels* "Angels on Location" l-10.

TELEFILMS

1971 *Vanished* 3-8, 3-9 NBC; **1972** *Emergency!* l-15 NBC; **1973** *Chase* 3-24 NBC; **1975** *Babe* 10-23 CBS; **1976** *The Lonliest Runner* l2-20 NBC; **1977** *Kill Me If You Can* 9-25 NBC; **1982** *I Was a Mail Order Bride* l2-14 CBS.

Robert Viharo

(born l939)

Robert came to the screen in l966 and appeared in *The Valley of the Dolls, Villa Rides* and *I Never Promised You a Rose Garden*. He made his TV debut in l966 and worked well into the eighties. His only series regular role was in *The Survivors* (1969-70).

GUEST CREDITS

1966 *Fugitive* "Devil's Disciples" l2-6; **1967** *Judd, for the Defense* "The Other Face of the Law" 9-22; *Cimarron Strip* "The Battle of Richard Sarafian" 10-l2; **1970** *Most Deadly Game* "Gabrielle" 10-24; *San Francisco International* "Hostage" 11-11; *Mod Squad* "Fever" l2-15; **1972** *Gunsmoke* "The Sodbusters" 11-20; **1973** *Ironside* "A Special Person" l-11; *Police Story* "Line of Fire" l2-18; **1975** *Kojak* "Night of the Piraeus" l-26; **1976** *S.W.A.T.* "Lessons in Fear" l-3l; *Starsky and Hutch* "Running" 2-25; **1977** *Quincy, M.E.* "Holding Pattern" 11-4; *Starsky and Hutch* "The Collector" l2-3; **1978** *Baretta* "The Gadjo" 3-30; **1979** *Quincy, M.E.* "Semper Fidelis" 3-15; **1981** *CHiPs* "Sick

Leave" 6-7; **1983** *Hardcastle and McCormick* "The Black Widow" 10-16.

TELEFILMS

1981 *Evita Peron* 2-23, 2-24 NBC.

June Vincent
(born Dorothy June Smith, 1920, Harrods, Ohio)

Onscreen from 1943, June's best known movie role was a starring appearance in *Black Angel*. She appeared on television from 1953 and, by the sixties, was playing mature ladies of character in a variety of TV series. June appeared on the soap *Bright Promise* during 1969-72. She was in strong demand for television commercials during her middle years.

GUEST CREDITS

1959 *Millionaire* "Millionaire Mitchell Gunther" 12-2; *Perry Mason* "the Case of the Bartered Bikini" 12-5; **1960** *One Step Beyond* "Vanishing Point" 2-23; *Peter Gunn* "Sepi" 12-19; **1961** *Checkmate* "The Human Touch" 1-14; *Perry Mason* "The Case of the Wintry Wife" 2-18; *Loretta Young Show* "When Queens Ride By" 3-12; *Untouchables* "The Lily Dallas Story" 3-16; *Have Gun—Will Travel* "Everyman" 3-25; *Loretta Young Show* "The Best Season" 4-17; **1962** *Hawaiian Eye*

"An Echo of Honor" 4-4; *Tales of Wells Fargo* "Don't Wake a Tiger" 5-18; *Twilight Zone* "I Sing the Body Electric" 5-18; *Route 66* "From an Enchantress Fleeing" 6-1; **1963** *Lieutenant* "A Touching of Hands" 10-26; *Mr. Novak* "Love in the Wrong Season" 12-3; **1964** *Alfred Hitchcock Hour* "The Ordeal of Mrs. Snow" 4-17; *Fugitive* "When the Bow Breaks" 10-6; **1966** *The FBI* "The Chameleon" 1-9; *Voyage to the Bottom of the Sea* "Death Ship" 2-20; *Fugitive* "Death Is the Door Prize" 9-20; *Virginian* "Dead Eye Dick" 11-9.

TELEFILMS

1972 *The Delphi Bureau* 3-6 ABC; *The Streets of San Francisco* 9-16 ABC.

Virginia Vincent
(born 1924)

A familiar and hard-working character actress, Virginia often appeared in either comic or "plain-Jane" roles following her 1953 screen debut. She appeared as a regular in four TV sitcoms: *Meet Millie* (1956), *The Joey Bishop Show* (1961-62), *The Super* (1972) and *Eight Is Enough* (1977-78). In between regular slots she appeared in numerous

sixties/seventies guest roles, including 6 appearances on *Dragnet*.

She continued to appear on television during the eighties, mainly in telefilms.

GUEST CREDITS

1959 *Perry Mason* "The Case of the Shattered Dream" 1-3; *M Squad* "The Star Witness" 2-20; *Millionaire* "Millionaire Charlie Webber" 3-11; *Markham* "On the Other Side of the Wall" 8-15; *Wanted: Dead or Alive* "The Matchmaker" 9-19; *Detectives* "The Long Drive" 12-18; *Untouchables* "The Underground Railway" 12-31; **1960** *Perry Mason* "The Case of the Frantic Flyer" 1-9; **1961** *Peter Gunn* "A Kill and a Half" 2-20; *Aquanauts* "Defective Tank Adventure" 2-22; *Detectives* "Not So Long Ago" 3-10; **1962** *87th Precinct* "King's Ransom" 2-19; *77 Sunset Strip* "Violence for Your Furs" 3-30; *Going My Way* "Not Good Enough for My Sister" 11-14; **1963** *Alfred Hitchcock Hour* "The Paragon" 2-8; *77 Sunset Strip* "Paper Chase" 12-27; **1964** *Fugitive* "Rat in a Corner" 2-18; *Bob Hope Chrysler Theater* "The Game with Glass Pieces" 5-1; **1966** *Honey West* "Like Visions and Omens…and All That Jazz" 2-4; *Virginian* "Legacy of Hate" 9-14; **1967** *Dragnet* "The Big Masked Bandits" 2-16; **1968** *Dragnet* "The Big Gambler" 3-21; *Dragnet* "Homicide-DR-06" 10-24; **1969** *Dragnet* "Juvenile-DR-32" 3-27; *Dragnet* "Burglary-Mister" 10-16; **1970** *Dragnet* "Narco-Missing Hypo" 1-8; *Young Lawyers* "The Two Dollar Thing" 10-5; **1971** *Smith Family* "The Blue Tie" 2-10; *Longstreet* "Wednesday's Child" 11-11; **1972** *Adam-12* "Clinic on Eighteeen Street" 3-13; *Kolchak: The Night Stalker* "Firefall" 11-8; **1975** *Cannon* "Killer on the Hill" 1-29; **1979** *Police Story* "A Cry for Justice" 12-27.

TELEFILMS

1970 *Night Slaves* 9-29 ABC; *The Psychiatrist: God Bless the Children* 12-14 NBC; **1972** *The Stranger in 7A* 11-14 CBS.

George Voskovec

(born June 19, Sazava, Czechoslovakia; died July 1, 1981)

George graduated from Prague's Charles University and co-founded the Liberated Theatre, witing, producing and performing-with his first film in 1926. He came to the U. S. in 1939; during World War II he beamed propaganda into Czechoslovakia.

Voskovec made a Broadway debut in 1945, first working in films and television in 1952. His films included *Twelve Angry Men, Butterfield 8, The Spy Who Came in from the Cold, The Boston Strangler* and *Mr. Buddwing*.

After years of television guest roles George gained series regular roles in *Skag* (1980) and *Nero Wolfe* (1981).

GUEST CREDITS

1959 *Playhouse 90* "The Velvet Alley" 1-22; **1960** *Johnny Staccato* "Swinging Longhair" 3-17; **1961** *Naked City* "The Deadly Guinea Pig" 3-8; **1962** *Naked City* "The Night the Saints Lost Their Halos" 1-17; *Cain's Hundred* "The Manipulator" 1-30; *Hallmark Hall of Fame* "Arsenic and Old Lace" 2-5; *Defenders* "The Hickory Indian" 3-3; *Dr. Kildare* "Something of Importance" 5-3; **1963** *Nurses* "Express Stop from Lennox Avenue" 5-9; *Channing* "A Hall Full of Strangers" 12-25; **1964** *Defenders* "The Secret" 2-8; *Fugitive* "Blood Line" 2-11; *Arrest and Trial* "A Circle of Strangers" 3-8;

DuPont Show of the Week "Hell Walkers" 3-8; **1965** *12 O'Clock High* "We're Not Coming Back" 11-29; **1966** *The FBI* "The Defector" 3-27; *Hallmark Hall of Fame* "Lamp at Midnight" 4-27; *Hawk* "The Hands of Corlin Claybrooke" 12-15; **1967** *Run for Your Life* "Flight from Tirana" 1-9, 1-16; **1968** *I Spy* "The Spy Business" 4-1; **1971** *Mission: Impossible* "Image" 1-15; *Mannix* "Cold Trail" 9-22; **1972** *The FBI* "The Hunters" 1-30; *Streets of San Francisco* "The Year of the Locusts" 3-23; **1973** *Hawaii Five-0* "The Finishing Touch" 11-20; **1976** *Jigsaw John* "Follow the Yellow Brick Road" 3-8; *Switch* "Round Up the Usual Suspects" 3-23.

TELEFILMS

1974 *Nicky's World* 4-19 CBS; *The Nativity* 12-17 ABC; **1980** *Skag* 1-6 NBC.

Gregory Walcott

(born January 13, 1928, Wendell, North Carolina)

A forty year veteran of films and television, Gregory Walcott's North Carolina roots are reflected in his soft southern accent. Born in Wendell, North Carolina, he became a fine high school football player at nearby Wilson, playing on two state championship teams. Following a hitch in The U. S. Army, Greg attended Furman University on a football scholarship (then Bernard Mattox).

He hitchhiked to Hollywood in 1949 to seek an acting career. A stage debut in *The Moon is Blue* propelled him into a film career of 60 movies. Included in that total were roles in *Mr. Roberts, The Outsider, Captain Newman, M.D., Joe Kidd, Prime Cut, The Eiger Sanction, Midway, Thunderbolt and Lightfoot, Every Which Way But Loose* and *Norma Rae*. Under contract to Warner Brothers in 1954-55, he signed with Universal-Revue in 1960-63.

Greg began appearing on television in 1957, with frequent guest appearances on TV western series like *Bonanza* (6), *Rawhide* (4) and *Laramie* (3). His best recognized television role came as Detective Roger Havilland on the well-received *87th Precinct* (1960-61).

After *87th Precinct*, Greg concentrated on films and TV guest roles. He became a lay minister and a renowed speaker in colleges and civic clubs. An honorary Doctor of Laws degree was conferred by Georgetown University (Kentucky) in 1966; he has made numerous college commencement addresses and received a large number of civic honors.

Married since 1954 to a former Miss San Diego runner-up, Barbara Watkins, the couple are parents to Jina, Pamela and Todd.

During the eighties Greg wound down his TV career on *The Fall Guy, Airwolf, Dynasty, Alice, Simon and Simon, Dallas* (2) and *Murder, She Wrote* (2).

Gregory Walcott is living proof that an actor can combine acting, Christianity and a wholesome family life. His acting career was most notable, but his contributions to life and inspiration to others have been much more meaningful.

GUEST CREDITS

1959 *Perry Mason* "The Case of the Howling Dog" 4-11; *Tales of Wells Fargo* "Desert Showdown" 9-14; *Maverick* "Full House" 10-25; *Rifleman* "Tension" 10-27; **1960** *Bat Masterson* "Mr. Fourpaws" 2-18; *Bonanza* "Death at Dawn" 4-30;

Rawhide "Incident in the Garden of Eden" 6-17; *Tall Man* "The Shawl" 10-1; *Wyatt Earp* "The Doctor" 10-4; *Rawhide* "Incident at Paco Tiempo" 12-9; *Tales of Wells Fargo* "Escort to Santa Fe" 12-19; **1961** *Laramie* "Trigger Point" 5-16; *Bat Masterson* "Farmer with a Badge" 5-18; *Deputy* "The Legend of Dixie" 5-20; **1962** *Rawhide* "Incident of the Hunter" 9-28; *Laramie* "The Sunday Shoot" 11-13; **1963** *Bonanza* "Song in the Dark" 1-13; *Laramie* "Protective Custody" 1-15; *Dakotas* "Thunder in Pleasant Valley" 2-4; *Rawhide* "Incident of the Wanderer" 2-27; **1966** *Man Called Shenandoah* "The Death of Matthew Eldridge" 3-21; *Shane* "Day of the Hawk" 10-22; *Big Valley* "The Man from Nowhere" 11-14; **1967** *Bonanza* "Amigo" 2-12; *Daniel Boone* "The Renegade" 9-28; **1969** *Bonanza* "My Friend, My Enemy" 1-12; *Bonanza* "A Darker Shadow" 11-23; **1970** *High Chaparral* "Auld Lang Syne" 4-10; *Bonanza* "Thornton's Account" 11-1; **1971** *Alias Smith and Jones* "Miracle at Santa Maria" 12-30; **1973** *Chase* "One for You, Two for Me" 10-9; *Police Story* "Collision Course" 11-20; **1975** *Mod Squad* "The Prince of Love" 3-23; *Little House on the Prairie* "In the Beginning" 10-1; *Invisible Man* "Go Directly to Jail" 11-3; *Kojak* "No Immunity for Murder" 11-23; **1976** *McCloud* "Bonnie and McCloud" 10-24; **1977** *Six Million Dollar Man* "Sharks" 9-11, 9-18; *Barnaby Jones* "The Mercenaries" 9-22; **1978** *Baretta* "I'll Take You to Lunch" 1-18; **1979** *CHiPs* "The Matchmakers" 1-27; *Vegas* "Demand and Supply" 2-14; **1981** *Simon and Simon* "The Least Dangerous Game" 12-29.

Larry Ward (right) is listening to Jack Elam expound on an episode of *The Dakotas*. The pair co-starred in the series which ran during 1963 on ABC.

Educated at Dennison and Ohio Universities, and trained at The American Theater Wing, Larry Ward was on national tours and appeared off-Broadway and on Broadway. He was a regular on the soap *Brighter Day* from 1954 until 1957, and did live fifties television shows like *Omnibus, Kraft Theatre* and *The U.S. Steel Hour.*

A prolific writer, some of his works were adapted for *Alfred Hitchcock Presents* and *The DuPont Show of the Week.* In 1963 Larry became a co-starring member of the cast of *The Dakotas.* Thereafter, he guested in numerous sixties/seventies TV series. After a distinguished career of writing and acting, Larry passed away on Feburary 16, 1985, survived by his wife, two sons and a daughter.

TELEFILMS

1976 *Gemini Man* 5-10 NBC; *The Quest* 5-13 NBC; **1978** *Donner Pass: The Road to Survival* 6-24 NBC; **1980** *To Race the Wind* 3-12 CBS.

Larry Ward

(born 1925, Columbus, Ohio; died February 16, 1985

GUEST CREDITS

1962 *77 Sunset Strip* "Pattern for a Bomb" 6-8; *Have Gun-Will Travel* "Memoirs of Monica" 10-27; **1963** *Gunsmoke* "Louie Pheeters" 1-5; **1964** *Outer Limits* "Counterweight" 12-26; **1965** *Slattery's People* "Question: When Do We Hang the Good Samaritan?" 2-19; *Loner* "The Flight of the Artic Tern" 10-23; *Fugitive* "When the Wind Blows" 12-

28; **1966** *I Spy* "A Day Called 4 Jaguar" 3-9; *Lost in Space* "All That Glitters" 4-6; *Rat Patrol* "The Chase of Fire Raid" 9-12; *Time Tunnel* "One Way to the Moon" 9-16; *Run for Your Life* "Hang Down Your Head and Laugh" 12-5; *Gunsmoke* "The Hanging" 12-31; **1967** *Invaders* "The Condemned" 5-9; **1968** *Bonanza* "Yonder Man" 12-8; **1969** *Land of the Giants* "Shell Game" 4-13; **1970** *The FBI* "Fatal Imposter" 1-4; **1972** *Mod Squad* "Deal with the Devil" 1-11; **1974** *Get Christie Love!* "Deadly Betrayal" 9-18; *Cannon* "Lady in Red" 10-2; *Manhunter* "Terror from the Skies" 10-16; **1975** *Cannon* "The Melted Man" 11-12; **1978** *Wonder Woman* "Light-Fingered Lady" 1-6.

TELEFILM

1974 *The Gun and the Pulpit* 4-3 ABC.

Harlan Warde

Onscreen from the early forties, in films like *I Wanted Wings* and *Task Force*, Harlan was a familiar character actor in both movies and television (from 1953). Numerous western TV series guest roles led to a semi-regular role on *The Virginian*, as the sheriff (1964-66). He also had a recurring role on *The Rifleman*, appearing in 14 episodes. His television career wound down by 1968, except for one 1979 guest shot.

GUEST CREDITS

1959 *Rough Riders* "The Scavengers" 1-28; *Rifleman* "The Boarding House" 2-24; *Rifleman* "One Went to Dinner" 3-17; *Rifleman* "The Challenge" 4-7; *Rifleman* "The Money Gun" 5-12; *Perry Mason* "The Case of the Spanish Cross" 5-30; *Rifleman* "Outlaw's Inheritance" 6-16; *Rifleman* "Boomerang" 6-23; *M Squad* "Jeopardy by Fire" 10-9; *Man with a Camera* "The Killer" 10-19; *Rifleman* "The Spiked Rifle" 11-24; *Rifleman* "Letter of the Law" 12-1; *Rifleman* "The Survivors" 12-29; **1960** *Rifleman* "The Lariat" 3-29; *Wanted: Dead or Alive* "Payoff at Pinto" 5-21; *Millionaire* "Millionaire Peter Longman" 5-25; *Rifleman* "Trail of Hate" 9-27; *Rifleman* "Dead Cold Cash" 11-22; *One Step Beyond* "Where Are They?" 12-13; **1961** *Wyatt Earp* "Clanton and Cupid" 3-21; *Perry Mason* "The Case of the Duplicate Daughter" 5-20; *87th Precinct* "Lady Killer" 10-9; *Rifleman* "Sheer Terror" 10-16; *Rifleman* "A Friend in Need" 12-25; **1962** *Alcoa Premiere* "Pattern of Guilt" 1-9; *Cain's Hundred* "Take a Number" 1-9; *Rifleman* "The Man from Salinas" 2-12; *Bonanza* "Inger, My Love" 4-15; **1963** *Laramie* "Naked Steel" 1-1; *G.E. True* "Security Risk" 3-3; *Kraft Mystery Theatre* "Pattern of Guilt" 9-18; **1965** *Perry Mason* "The Case of the Thermal Thief" 1-14; *Slattery's People* "What Time Do We Hang the Good Samaritan?" 2-19; *Kraft Suspense Theatre* "Streetcar, Do You Read Me?" 2-25; *Wild Wild West* "The Night of th Sudden Death" 10-8; *Big Valley* "The Odyssey of Jubal Tanner" 10-13; **1966** *Big Valley* "Into the Widow's Web" 3-23; *Fugitive* "The 2130" 3-29; *Fugitive* "Death Is the Door Prize" 9-20; *Big Valley* "Target" 10-31; **1967** *Big Valley* "Wagonload of Dreams" 1-2; *Iron Horse* "Welcome for the General" 1-2; *Fugitive* "The One That Got Away" 1-17; *Big Valley* "The Stallion" 1-30; *Dragnet* "The Big Hit and Run Driver" 4-6; *Invaders* "The Condemned" 5-9; *Big Valley* "Guilty" 10-30; *The FBI* "Overload" 11-12; *Bonanza* "Justice Deferred" 12-17; **1968** *Mannix* "A Copy of Murder" 11-2; **1979** *Rockford Files* "A Different Drummer" 4-13.

1964 *See How They Run* 10-7 NBC; **1970** *The Aquarians* 10-24 NBC; **1971** *Ransom for a Dead Man* 3-1 NBC.

Beverly Washburn

(born 1942)

A fine juvenile actress, Beverly Washburn made a film debut in 1950, coming to television in a 1951 episode of *Superman*. She became a regular on *Professional Father* in 1955, and was a very popular player on fifties shows like *Schlitz Playhouse of Stars* (2), *Four Star Playhouse* (2), *Fireside Theater, Science Fiction Theater, Loretta Young Show* (2), *General Electric Theater* (2), *Wagon Train* (2), *Zane Grey Theater, 20th Century Fox Hour* and *The Texan*.

After some early sixties guest work, she became a regular on *The New Loretta Young Show* during the 1962-63 season. Juvenile film roles included *Shane* and *Old Yeller*. Her television acting was rather infrequent after 1967, but she resurfaced on an episode of *Scarecrow and Mrs. King* in 1984.

GUEST CREDITS

1959 *One Step Beyond* "Premonition" 3-10; **1960** *Texan* "Badman" 6-20; *Law and Mr. Jones* "A Question of Guilt" 12-16; **1961** *Best of the Post* "Martha" 2-18; **1961** *Thriller* "Parasite Mansion" 4-25; **1962** *Target: The Corruptors* "Nobody Gets Hurt" 6-1; **1963** *Hawaiian Eye* "Passport" 4-2; **1964** *77 Sunset Strip* "Lover's Lane" 1-3; *Mr. Novak* "Visions of Sugar Plums" 10-6; **1967** *Star Trek* "The Deadly Years" 12-8; **1973** *Streets of San Francisco* "Most Feared in the Jungle" 12-20; **1974** *Manhunter* "The Ma Gentry Gang" 9-11.

Carlene Watkins

(born June 4, 1952, Hartford, Conn.)

Beautiful blonde Carlene Watkins, reared in Houston, Texas, became a familiar face on television during the late seventies and throughout the eighties. By 1979 she had earned a regular role on *The Empire* segment of *Cliffhanger*. She co-starred in a 1981-82 sitcom, *Best of the West*, and had a starring role in an abbreviated 1983 sitcom called *It's Not Easy*.

She was also aboard in Mary Tyler Moore's unsuccessful sitcom *Mary* (1985-86), and on *The Tortellis* (1987). In 1992 she appeared as Bob Newhart's wife, Kaye McKay, on *Bob*.

Later eighties guest roles included *Hotel, The Love Boat* and a recurring role on *Dear John*.

GUEST CREDITS

1977 *Columbo* "The Bye-Bye Sky High IQ Murder Case" 5-22; *Bionic Woman* "The Bionic Dog" 9-10; *Rockford Files* "Beamer's Last Case" 9-16; **1978** *Quincy, M.E.* "A Night to Raise the Dead" 12-7; **1979** *B. J. and the Bear* "Snow White and the Seven Lady Truckers" 9-29, 10-6; **1980** *B. J. and the Bear* episode 3-1; **1981** *Nero Wolfe* "The Golden Spider" 1-16; **1982** *Remington Steele* "In the Steele of the Night" 12-3; **1983** *Magnum, P.I.* "Basket Case" 2-3; *Magnum, P.I.* "Legacy from a Friend" 3-10; *Magnum, P.I.* "...By It's Cover" 3-31.

TELEFILMS

1978 *The Two-Five* 4-14 ABC; **1978** *Little Women* 10-2, 10-3 NBC.

Quincy, M.E. "Across the Line" 12-8.

TELEFILMS

1970 *The Old Man Who Cried Wolf* 10-13 ABC; **1971** *The Last Child* 10-5 ABC; **1972** *The Strangers in 7A* 11-14 CBS; **1974** *Killdozer* 2-2 ABC; **1975** *Returning Home* 4-29 ABC; **1978** *First You Cry* 11-8 CBS; **1980** *Reward* 5-23 ABC.

James A. Watson, Jr.

(born 1945)

After television and film debuts in 1969, James began to concentrate his efforts in the former medium. He was a repertory player on *Love, American Style* during 1972-74 and had a recurring role on *Quincy, M.E.*, appearing as a prosecutor.

GUEST CREDITS

1969 *Virginian* "Black Jade" 12-31; **1970** *Silent Force* "The Hero" 9-28; **1971** *Medical Center* "Danger Point" 1-27; **1972** *Cannon* "A Long Way Down" 10-25; **1973** *Mod Squad* "Run, Lincoln, Run" 1-4; *Mannix* "Out of the Night" 1-21; **1975** *Mannix* "Edge of the Web" 2-2; *Joe Forrester* "Bus Station" 9-23; *Kojak* "The Nicest Guys on the Block" 11-16; **1976** *Rockford Files* "The Hammer of 'C' Block" 1-9; *Blue Knight* "The Candy Man" 2-4; Police Woman "Task Force: Cop Killer" 3-2, 3-9; **1978** *Quincy, M.E.* "Accomplice to Murder" 2-3; *Quincy, M.E.* "Speed Trap" 10-12; **1979** *Quincy, M.E.* "Walk Softly Through the Night" 2-1; *Quincy, M.E.* "Death's Challenge" 3-29; *Quincy, M.E.* "Nowhere to Run" 11-8; **1981** *Quincy, M.E.* "D.U.I." 12-2; **1982**

Richard Webb

(born 1915; died June 10, 1993)

Richard Webb made a film debut in 1941, and played in forties action movies like *I Wanted Wings, This Gun for Hire* and *The Sands of Iwo Jima*. He came to televison in 1950, doing 5 episodes of *The Web* in the 1950-53 period. He then gained his most famous TV roles, starring in *Captain Midnight* (1954-56). During 1959 he starred in a syndicated series *Border Patrol*.

He worked in television guest roles for the balance of his acting career. An author, he had three books published on psychic phenomenia. In failing health, Richard took his own life on June 10, 1993, survived by two daughters.

GUEST CREDITS

1959 *Maverick* "The White Widow" 1-24; **1960** *Rawhide* "Incident of the Star Gazer" 4-1; *Alaskans* "Calico" 5-22; *Cheyenne* "Two Trails to Santa Fe" 11-28; **1961** *Surfside 6* "The Fat's on the Fire" 1-16; *Rawhide* "Little Fishes" 11-24; **1962** *Cheyenne* "The Bad Penny" 3-12; *Cheyenne* "Wanted for the Murder of Cheyenne Bodie" 12-10; **1963** *Saints and Sinners* "New Lead Berlin" 1-28; *Perry Mason* "The Case of the Velvet Claws" 3-21; *Eleventh Hour* "Oh, You Shouldn't Have Done It" 10-30; *Fugitive* "Terror at High Point" 12-17; **1964** *Breaking Point* "And If Thy Hand Offends Thee" 1-13; *Voyage to the Bottom of the Sea* "No Way Out" 11-30; **1965** *Perry Mason* "The Case of the Impetuous Imp" 10-10; **1966** *Gunsmoke* "Treasure of John Walking Fox" 4-16; *Branded* "Kellie" 4-24; **1967** *Star Trek* "The Court-Martial" 2-2; *Daniel Boone* "The Long Way Home" 2-16; *Gunsmoke* "The Returning" 2-18; *Daniel Boone* "The Secret Code" 12-14; **1968** *I Spy* "Tag, You're It" 1-22; *Guns of Will Sonnett* "The Warriors" 3-1; **1969** *Medical Center* "The Crooked Circle" 10-29; **1970** *Then Came Bronson* "The Gleam of the Eagle Mind" 1-21; *Mod Squad* "The Judas Trap" 12-8; *Smith Family* "Lost Lady" 10-6; *Smith Family* "Father's Day" 10-13; **1974** *Six Million Dollar Man* "Eyewitness to Murder" 3-8; *Chase* "The People Parley" 4-10.

Sheilah Wells

Beautiful Sheilah Wells worked regularly in television from 1965 until 1980, appearing n some of the better series of the era. She was married for a time to the late actor Fred Beir (1927-80).

GUEST CREDITS

1965 *Virginian* "Six Graves at Cripple Creek" 1-27; *Kraft Suspense Theatre* "The Rise and Fall of Eddie Carew" 6-24; *Dr. Kildare* "The Bell in the Schoolhouse Tolls for Thee, Kildare" 9-27; *Dr. Kildare* "Life in the Dance Hall; F-U-N" 9-28; *Dr. Kildare* "Some Doors Are Slamming" 10-5; *Dr. Kildare* "Enough La Boheme for Everybody" 10-11; *Dr. Kildare* "Now, the Mummy" 10-12; *Dr. Kildare* "A Pyrotechnic Display" 10-18; **1966** *Tarzan* "The Ultimate Weapon" 9-16; *Green Hornet* "Crime Wave" 9-20; **1967** *Wild Wild West* "The Night of the Cadre" 3-24; **1968** *Bonanza* "A Girl Named George" 1-14; **1969** *Mod Squad* "Captain Greer, Call Surgery" 4-1; **1971** *Bonanza* "Winter Kill" 3-28; *Dan August* "Prognosis: Homicide" 4-1; *Hawaii Five-0* "Wednesday, Ladies Free" 12-14; **1972** *Owen*

Marshall, Counselor at Law "Shine a Light on Me" 2-13; *Cannon* "The Torch" 2-29; **1975** *Cannon* "The Wrong Medicine" 9-24; *Streets of San Francisco* "Men Will Die" 10-2; **1976** *Six Million Dollar Man* "Love Song for Tonya" 2-15; **1977** *Six Million Dollar Man* "Killer Wind" 10-16; *Quincy, M.E.* "Tissue of Truth" 10-28.

TELEFILMS

1974 *Twice in a Lifetime* 3-16 NBC; **1980** *Moviola: The Scarlett O'Hara War* 5-19 NBC.

James Westerfield

(born 1912, Tennessee; died September 20, 1971)

A huge bald presence in dozens of films, James made a screen debut in 1941. In subsequent years he played a befuddled policeman character in a trio of Disney films: *The Shaggy Dog, The Absent-Minded Professor* and *Son of Flubber*. But he also had roles in critically acclaimed dramatic films like *On the Waterfront, Birdman of Alcatraz* and *True Grit*.

His stage career was outstanding, with Drama Critics Awards in 1948 and 1949 as Best Supporting Actor in Broadway plays. He produced and directed more than fifty musicals in his summer tent in Danbury, Connecticut.

Westerfield had television roles during the live era in quality shows like *Playhouse 90*. The sixties found him in a variety of TV guest roles and a regular slot on *The Travels of Jaimie McPheeters* (1963-64). He died of a heart attack on September 20, 1971.

GUEST CREDITS

1959 *Playhouse 90* "The Blue Men" 1-15; *Richard Diamond* episode 3-15; *Rawhide* "Incident of the Curious Street" 4-10; *Rifleman* "The Woman" 5-5; *Rough Riders* "Forty-Five Calibre Vow" 5-14; *Wanted: Dead or Alive* "The Healing Woman" 9-12; *Tightrope* "The Patsy" 10-13; *Deputy* "Like Father" 10-17; *Alaskans* "Starvation Stampede" 11-1; *Maverick* "The Ghost Soldiers" 11-8; *Rebel* "The Scavengers" 11-8; *Johnny Ringo* "Bound Boy" 12-31; **1960**

Rifleman "The Fourflusher" 5-3; *Law of the Plainsman* "Trojan Horse" 5-5; *Alfred Hitchcock Presents* ""Cell 227" 6-5; *Law and Mr. Jones* "Music to Hurt By" 10-14; *Thriller* "The Watcher" 11-1; *Bonanza* "The Trail Gang" 11-26; **1961** *Untouchables* "The Big Train" 1-5, 1-12; *Law and Mr. Jones* "The Big Gambling Raid" 1-6; *Perry Mason* "The Case of the Irresolute Reformer" 1-14; *Shirley Temple Theatre* "The Return of Long John Silver" 2-19; *Twilight Zone* "Mr. Dingle the Strong" 3-3; *Asphalt Jungle* "The Burglary Ring" 4-2; *Maverick* "The Art Lovers" 10-1; *Straightaway* "Heatwave" 10-27; **1962** *Wide Country* "What Are Friends For?" 10-18; **1963** *Gunsmoke* "Anybody Can Kill a Marshall" 3-9; *Going My Way* "Florence, Come Home" 4-10; *Dakotas* "Feud at Snake River" 4-29; **1964** *Daniel Boone* "A Short Walk to Salem" 11-19; **1966** *Time Tunnel* "The End of the World" 9-23; *Lost in Space* "Space Circus" 10-12; **1967** *Judd, for the Defense* "The Confessional" 10-20; **1968** *Daniel Boone* "The Scrimshaw Ivory Chart" 1-4; *Outcasts* "The Heroes" 11-11; **1969** *Gunsmoke* "The Still" 11-10; **1970** *Bonanza* "The Lady and the Mark" 2-1; **1971** *O'Hara, U. S. Treasury* "Operation: Crystal Springs" 12-3.

TELEFILMS

1966 *Scalplock* 4-10 ABC; **1968** *Now You See Him, Now You Don't* 11-12 NBC; **1969** *Set This Town on Fire* 1-8 NBC.

Ellen Weston

(born April 19, 1939, New York City)

Roles on soaps *The Guiding Light* and *Another World* were Ellen's entree into television, and she was seen often in prime-time series guest roles from 1967 through much of the seventies. She had a featured role on *S.W.A.T.* (1975-76), playing the wife of the lead character.

GUEST CREDITS

1967 *NYPD* "Cruise to Oblivion" 12-26; **1969**

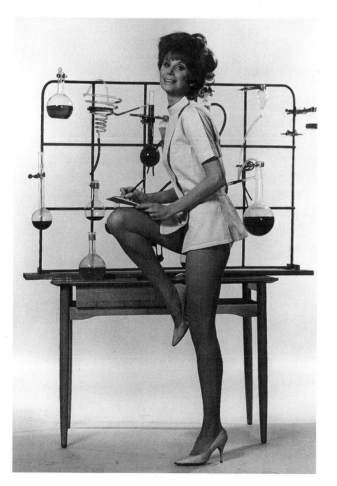

The FBI "The Fraud" 1-12; *The FBI* "Nightmare Road" 9-21; **1970** *Young Lawyers* "The Two-Dollar Thing" 10-5; **1972** *Sixth Sense* "Five Widows Weeping" 12-9; **1974** *Hawkins* "Murder in the Slave Trade" 1-22; *Harry O* "The Admiral's Lady" 9-19; *Kolchak: The Night Stalker* "The Devil's Platform" 11-15; *Barnaby Jones* "Time to Kill" 11-26; **1975** *Cannon* "Killer on the Hill" 1-29; *Caribe* "The Plastic Connection" 2-17; *Ellery Queen* "The Adventure of the Blunt Instrument" 12-18; **1976** *Cannon* "Quasar Kill" 2-4; **1977** *Fantastic Journey* "An Act of Love" 3-24; *Logan's Run* "Crypt" 11-7; **1978** *Lucan* "The Pariah" 3-27; *Wonder Woman* "Disco Devil" 10-20.

TELEFILMS

1973 *Letters from Three Lovers* 10-3 ABC; *Miracle on 34th Street* 12-12 CBS; **1974** *The Questor Tapes* 1-23 NBC; *Smile Jenny, You're Dead* 2-3 ABC; *The Healers* 5-22 NBC; **1975** *The Adventures of the Queen* 2-14 CBS; **1980** *Revenge of the Stepford Wives* 10-12 NBC.

Jack Weston

(born Jack Weinstein, August 21, 1915, Cleveland, Ohio; died May 3, 1996)

This rotund character actor began a stage career in 1934, with his film debut not coming until 1958. His acting career was interrupted during World War II for U. S. Army service; a machine-gunner, he was involved in bitter fighting in Europe.

Jack became a familiar face on fifties television, starting with a childrens' series regular role on *Rod Brown and The Rocket Rangers* (1953-54). The fifties also saw Jack in a *Playhouse 90* production and a *DuPont Show of the Month* version of *Harvey*.

By the sixties he had established his screen personna as a fumbling, usually well-intentioned blunderer. He was a regular on *My Sister Eileen* (1960-61) and *The Hathaways* (1961-62), followed by guesting until 1967. Thereafter his TV appearances were confined to variety shows and telefilms, until 1984 when he became a regular on *The Four Seasons*.

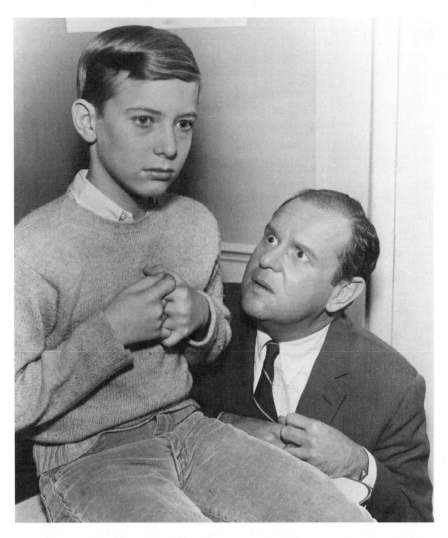

The late Jack Weston shows deep concern at the condition of Floyd Alden in a 1966 episode of *Ben Casey* (ABC). The episode was called "Twenty Six Ways to Spell Heartbreak, A, B, C, D..."

Jack was married to actress Marge Redmond for many years. He died in May of 1996 of the efffects of lyphoma.

GUEST CREDITS

1959 *Rawhide* "Incident at the Buffalo Smokehouse" 10-30; *Untouchables* "The Artichoke King" 12-3; *Playhouse 90* "The Tunnel" 12-10; **1960** *Twilight Zone* "the Monsters Are Due on Main Street" 3-4; *Have Gun-Will Travel* "Lady with a Gun" 4-9; *Markham* "A Cry from the Penthouse" 7-

21; *Alfred Hitchcock Presents* "Forty Detectives Later" 11-3; *Have Gun-Will Travel* "The Poker Fiend" 11-12; *Thriller* "The Cheaters" 12-27; **1961** *Route 66* "Like a Motherless Child" 3-17; *General Electric Theater* "Love Is a Lion's Roar" 3-19; *Lawless Years* "The Kid Dropper Story" 7-7; *Dr. Kildare* "Twenty Four Hours" 9-28; **1962** *Thriller* "Flowers of Evil" 3-5; *Sam Benedict* "A Split Week in San Quentin" 9-15; **1963** *Stoney Burke* "A Matter of Percentage" 1-28; *Twilight Zone* "The Bard" 5-23; *Fugitive* "Fatso" 11-19; **1964** *Burke's Law* "Who Killed Andy Zygmunt?" 3-13; *Bob Hope Chrysler Theater* "The Turncoat" 10-23; **1965** *Burke's Law* "Who Killed the 13th Clown?" 2-24; *Gunsmoke* "The New Society" 5-22; *Bob Hope Chrysler Theater* "Kicks" 10-13; *12 O'Clock High* "Runaway in the Dark" 11-1; **1966** *Ben Casey* "26 Ways to Spell Heartbreak, A, B, C, D..."2-28; *Man from UNCLE* "The Project Deephole Affair" 3-18; *Bob Hope Chrysler Theater* "The Faceless Man" 5-4; **1967** *Bob Hope Chrysler Theater* "Code Name: Heraclitus" 1-4.

TELEFILMS

1966 *Fame Is the Name of the Game* 11-26 NBC; **1968** *Now You See It, Now You Don't* 11-11 NBC; **1973** *I Love a Mystery* 2-17 NBC; **1973** *Deliver Us from Evil* 9-11 ABC.

Jesse White
(born January 3, 1919, Buffalo, New York)

Perhaps better known to television audiences as "The Maytag Repairman" for two decades, Jesse White was a regular during 1953-57 on Ann Southern's sitcom vehicle, *Private Secretary*. His scheming theatrical agent character led to a similar and simultaneous casting on *Make Room for Daddy* (1954-57).

He appeared with Southern again during 1959-61 on *The Ann Southern Show*. Thereafter he worked in guest roles, often with the blustering bombastic personna that he was so closely identified with for much of his career. He was a frequent guest on sitcoms like *The Dick Van Dyke Show, The Andy Griffith Show, Pete and Gladys, The Addams Family, The Munsters, Green Acres, Petticoat Junction, Rango, That Girl* and *Happy Days*.

His film career of over 50 movies began in 1947 and included roles in *Gentlemen's Agreement, Harvey, Marjorie Morningstar, It's a Mad Mad Mad Mad World* and *The Reluctant Astronaut*.

GUEST CREDITS

1959 *Texan* "Private Account" 4-6; *Tightrope* "The Money Fight" 11-17; **1960** *Man with a Camera* "Fragment of Murder" 2-1; *Tightrope* "The Shark" 4-26; **1961** *Law and Mr. Jones* "One for the Money" 2-24; *General Electric Theater* "A Voice on the Phone" 11-19; *Roaring 20's* "Pinky Goes to College" 11-25; *Twilight Zone* "Once Upon a Time" 12-15; **1962** *Hawaiian Eye* "The Missile Rogues" 1-3; *Roaring 20's* "The People People Marry" 1-20; *Adventures in Paradise* "The Quest of Ambrose Feather" 2-11; *Twilight Zone* "Cavender Is Coming" 5-25; **1965** *Kraft Suspense Theatre* "Four into Zero" 2-18; *Perry Mason* "The Case of the Fatal Fortune" 9-19; **1966** *Wild Wild West* "The Night of the Whirring Death" 2-18; **1969** *Hawaii Five-0* "Golden Boy in Black Trunks" 2-12; *Land of the Giants* "Comeback" 11-23; **1971** *Mannix* "Nightshade" 12-29; **1972** *Hallmark Hall of Fame* "Harvey" 3-22; **1975** *Kolchak: The Night Stalker* "Chopper" 1-31.

Grace Lee Whitney
(born April 1, 1930, Ann Arbor, Michigan)

A busy sixties television actress, Grace Lee captured a coveted regular role on *Star Trek*, appearing as yeoman Janice Rand (1966-67). However, excessive weight gain cost her the job and personal

problems overwhelmed her by the end of the decade. She struggled through several difficult years of rock-bottom existence before recovering and finding a solid family life.

GUEST CREDITS

1961 *Michael Shayne* "Four Lethal Ladies" 2-17; *Islanders* "The World Is Her Oyster" 3-12; *Acapulco* episode 3-20; *Michael Shayne* "No Shroud for Shayne" 5-5; *Untouchables* "Line of Fire" 5-14; *Roaring 20's* "Another Time, Another War" 11-4; *77 Sunset Strip* "The Missing Daddy Caper" 11-17; *Detectives* "Hit or Miss" 12-1; *General Electric Theater* "Call to Danger" 12-10; **1962** *77 Sunset Strip* "Penthouse on Skid Row" 1-19; *Gunsmoke* "Reprisal" 3-10; *Rifleman* "The Tin Horn" 3-12; *Bat Masterson* "The Good and the Bad" 3-21; *Surfside 6* "Love Song for a Deadly Redhead" 4-30; *New Breed* "Walk This Street Lightly" 6-5; *Surfside 6* "The Neutral Corner" 6-11; **1963** *77 Sunset Strip* "Falling Stars" 1-4; *Untouchables* "Line of Fire" 5-14; *77 Sunset Strip* "88 Bars" 11-1; **1964** *Outer Limits* "Controlled Experiment" 1-13; *Wagon Train* "The Andrew Elliott Story" 2-10; *Bob Hope Chrysler Theater* "White Snow, Red Ice" 3-13; *Temple Houston* "Do Unto Others, Then Gallop" 3-19; **1967** *Run For Your Life* "The List of Alice McKenna" 1-23; **1968** *Cimarron Strip* "Knife in the Darkness" 1-25; *Mannix* "Another Final Exit" 2-10; *Big Valley* "Run for the Savage" 3-11; *Virginian* "The Mustangers" 12-4; **1969** *Outsider* "The Secret of Marino Bay" 1-15; **1974** *Cannon* "Deadly Trail" 10-16.

TELEFILMS

1983 *The Kid with the 200 I.Q.* 2-6 NBC.

Peter Whitney

(born 1916, Long Branch, New Jersey; died March 30, 1972)

A graduate of Pasadena Playhouse, Peter appeared in both stock and Shakespeare before coming to Hollywood in 1941 under a Warner Brothers contract. In that year he appeared in the

first of his 43 films, which later included roles in *In the Heat of the Night* and *The Ballad of Cable Hogue*. He worked often in fifties television before gaining a co-starring role on *The Rough Riders* (1958-59).

Big and tough looking, Peter worked often in sixties crime, western and adventure series, frequently playing strong adversarial roles. His versatility was evidenced in guest shots on *The Beverly Hillbillies* (3) and *Gilligan's Island*.

Peter died of a heart attack in his Santa Barbara home on March 30, 1972, survived by his wife and 6 children.

GUEST CREDITS

1959 *Gunsmoke* "Kangaroo" 10-10; *Law of the Plainsman* "The Hostiles" 10-22; *Rifleman* "Eddie's Daughter" 11-3; *Hotel de Paree* "A Rope Is for Hanging" 11-6; *Riverboat* "A Night at Trapper's Landing" 11-8; *Johnny Ringo* "Dead Wait" 11-19; *Law of the Plainsman* "The Dude" 12-3; *Fury* "The Vanishing Blacksmith" 12-19; **1960** *Rifleman* "Mail Order Groom" 1-12; *Rifleman* "Heller" 2-23; *Lawman* "The Surface of Truth" 4-17; *Rawhide* "Incident of the Hundred Amulets" 5-6; *Peter Gunn* "The Best Laid Plans" 5-9; *Rawhide* "Incident of the Music Maker" 5-20; *Alaskans* "White Vengeance" 6-5; *Bonanza* "The Mission" 9-17; *Cheyenne* "The Long

Peter Whitney (left), is joined by his co-stars of *The Rough Riders*, Kent Taylor (center) and Jan Merlin. The series aired on ABC during 1958-59.

Rope" 10-3; *Islanders* "The Terrified Blonde" 10-16; *Untouchables* "The Jack 'Legs' Diamond Story" 10-20; *Rifleman* "Strange Town" 10-25; *Adventures in Paradise* "Hangman's Island" 11-21; *Have Gun-Will Travel* "Fogg Bound" 12-3; *Maverick* "Dodge City or Bust" 12-11; **1961** *Rebel* "The Promise" 1-15; *Zane Grey Theater* "The Bible Man" 2-23; *Zane Grey Theater* "The Man from Everywhere" 4-13; *Tales of Wells Fargo* "Something Pretty" 4-17; *Rifleman* "The Queue" 5-16; *Detectives* "Tobey's Place" 9-29; *Gunsmoke* "Harper's Blood" 10-21; *Perry Mason* "The Case of the Pathetic Patient" 10-28; *Lawman* "The Stalker" 10-29; *New Breed* "The Butcher" 11-14; *Rifleman* "Long Gun from Tucson" 12-11; *Dr. Kildare* "Johnny Temple" 12-28; **1962** *Laramie* "The Fortune Hunter" 10-9; *Rifleman* "Lou Mallory" 10-15; *Wagon Train* "The Shiloh Degnan Story" 11-7; *Perry Mason* "The Case of the Stand-In Sister" 11-15; *Rifleman* "Gun Shy" 12-10; **1963** *Untouchables* "Man in the Cooler" 3-5; *Wide Country* "The Quest of Jacob Blaufus" 3-7; *Rifleman* "Which Way'd They Go?" 4-1; *Travels of Jaimie McPheeters* "The

Day of the Skinners" 10-20; *Temple Houston* "Jubilee" 11-14; *Combat* "Thunder from the Hill" 12-17; **1964** *Wagon Train* "The Starks Bluff Story" 4-6; *Virginian* "A Bride for Lars" 4-15; *Rogues* "Death of a Fleming" 10-25; *Daniel Boone* "Pompey" 12-10; **1965** *Gunsmoke* "Run, Sheep, Run" 1-9; *Wagon Train* "The Betsy Blee Story" 3-28; *Virginian* "The Showdown" 4-14; *Perry Mason* "The Case of the Wrongful Writ" 5-6; *Legend of Jesse James* "The Raiders" 10-18; **1967** *The Guns of Will Sonnett* "Of Lasting Summers and Jim Sonnett" 10-6; *Iron Horse* "T Is for Traitor" 12-2; *Big Valley* "Night of the Executioners" 12-11; **1968** *Tarzan* "A Gun for Jai" 2-2; *Bonanza* "Commitment at Angelus" 4-7; **1970** *Mannix* "Harlequin's Gold" 1-31; *San Francisco International* "Crisis" 11-18.

Robert J. Wilke

(born 1914, Cincinnati, Ohio; died March 28, 1989)

Beginning a film career in 1936, Robert J. Wilke went on to appear in over 150 movies, with roles in major films like *From Here to Eternity, Written on the Wind, The Magnificent Seven* and *Spartacus.* And all film buffs will remember him as one of the heavies in *High Noon* who arrive for a showdown with Gary Cooper. Beginning his screen career as a stuntman, Robert appeared as a heavy in countless B-westerns of the forties, as well as in 8 episodic serials.

Television provided Wilke a great deal of work in the late fifties and he began to branch out into roles other than those of a villain. He played a marshal in his only TV series regular role, in *The Legend of Jesse James.*

Bob has left a legacy of snarling, menacing western bad-guys, without question, one of the finest in Hollywood history. He also created many excellent character portrayals in non-western roles.

GUEST CREDITS

1959 *Bonanza* "The Visitors" 1-2; *Rifleman* "The Pet" 1-6; *Have Gun-Will Travel* "The Man Who Lost" 2-7; *Texan* "The Marshal of Yellow Jacket" 3-16; *Wanted: Dead or Alive* "Littlest Client" 4-25; *Lawman* "The Journey" 4-26; *Tombstone Territory* "Grave Near Tombstone" 5-22; *Wanted: Dead or Alive* "Estralita" 10-3; *Gunsmoke* "Saludos" 10-31; *Law of the Plainsman* "Desperate Decision" 11-12; *Wanted: Dead or Alive* "No Trail Back" 11-28; *Lawman* "The Press" 11-29; *Texan* "Cowards Don't Die" 11-30; *Have Gun-Will Travel* "The Naked Gun" 12-19; **1960** *Gunsmoke* "Big Tom" 1-9; *Have Gun-Will Travel* "Return to Fort Benjamin" 1-30; *Cheyenne* "Outcast at Cripple Creek" 2-29; *Peter Gunn* "The Long, Long Ride" 3-14; *Gunsmoke* "The Ex-Urbanites" 4-9; *Texan* "Killer's Road" 4-25; *Maverick* "Hadley's Hunters" 9-25; *Laramie* "The Track of the Jackal" 9-27; *Checkmate* "Target...Tycoon" 11-5; *Bonanza* "the Trail Gang" 11-26; *Tales of Wells Fargo* "The Wade Place" 11-28; **1961** *Americans* "The Rebellious Rose" 2-13; *Gunsmoke* "He Learned About Women" 2-24; *Tall Man* "The Last Resource" 3-11; *Rawhide* "Incident of the Running Man" 5-5; *Laramie* "The Fatal Step" 10-24; *Outlaws* "Night Riders" 11-2; *Frontier Circus* "Winter Quarters" 11-23; **1962** *Rawhide* "Incident of the Mountain Men" 1-25; *Maverick* "Epitaph for a Gambler" 2-11; *Broncho* "The Last Letter" 3-5; *Laramie* "Justice in a Hurry" 3-20; *Untouchables* "Arsenal" 6-28; *Untouchables* "The Eddie O'Gara Story" 11-13; *Sam Benedict* "Too Many Strangers" 12-8; **1963** *Wagon Train* "The Johnny Masters Story" 1-16; *Rawhide* "Incident of the Mountain Men" 1-25; *Have Gun-Will Travel* "American Primitive" 2-2; *Dakotas* "Crisis at High Banjo" 2-11; *77 Sunset Strip* "Stranger from the Sea" 3-15; *Laramie* "The Marshals" 4-30; *Sam Benedict* "Twenty Aching Years" 5-15; *Perry Mason* "The Case of the Drowsy Mosquito" 10-17; **1964** *Gunsmoke* "The Bassops" 2-22; *Bonanza* "Return to Honor" 3-22; **1965** *Bonanza* "The Flannel Mouth Gun" 1-31; **1966** *Tarzan* "The Prisoner" 10-7; *Fugitive* "Wine Is a Traitor" 11-1; *Tarzan* "The End of the River" 12-16; **1967** *Monroes* "Killer Cougar" 2-1; *Gunsmoke* "Cattle Barons" 9-18; *Cimarron Strip* episode 12-14; *Guns of Will Sonnett* "The Hero" 12-29; *Tarzan* "Creeping Giants" 12-29; *Wild Wild West* "The Night of the Arrow" 12-29; **1968** *Daniel Boone* "Heroes Welcome" 2-22; *Lancer* "Chase a Wild Horse" 10-8; *Guns of Will Sonnett* "Meeting in a Small Town" 12-6; **1969** *Bonanza* "Old Friends" 12-14; **1970** *Most Deadly Game* "Who Killed Kindness?" 11-7; **1973** *Kung Fu* "An Eye for an Eye" 1-25; **1976** *Starsky and Hutch* "Omaha Tiger" 1-8.

TELEFILMS

1971 *The Desperate Mission* 12-3 NBC; *They Call It Murder* 12-17 NBC.

Adam Williams

A familiar supporting actor, Adam also wrote screenplays. Often cast as a heavy in the numerous western and crime series that he appeared in, Adam continued to appear on television until the late seventies.

His screen career, beginning in 1950, included

roles in *The Big Heat, The Proud and the Profane, Fear Strikes Out, North by Northwest* and *The Horse in the Gray Flannel Suit*; he had a leading role in *Without Warning*, playing a sniper.

GUEST CREDITS

1959 *Rifleman* "The Challenge" 4-7; *Black Saddle* "Client: Frome" 4-25; *Rawhide* "Incident in No Man's Land" 6-12; *Bonanza* "The Hanging Posse" 11-28; *Hawaiian Eye* "The Koa Man" 12-30; **1960** *Black Saddle* "Letter of Death" 1-8; *Twilight Zone* "The Hitchhiker" 1-22; *Detectives* "The Long Jump" 5-6; *Have Gun-Will Travel* "Full Circle" 5-14; *Outlaws* "Starfall" 11-24, 12-1; *Roaring 20's* "The White Carnation" 12-3; *Twilight Zone* "A Most Unusual Camera" 12-16; **1961** *Detectives* "Terror on Ice" 4-7; *Lawman* "The Persecuted" 4-9; *Rifleman* "The Score Is Even" 4-11; **1962** *Gunsmoke* "The Do-Badder" 1-6; *Surfside 6* "The Green Beret" 3-5; *Alfred Hitchcock Presents* "What Frightened You, Fred?" 5-1; *Rawhide* "Gold Fever" 5-4; *Rifleman* "The Executioner" 5-7; *Rifleman* "The Wanted Man" 9-25; *Rifleman* "The Anvil Chorus"12-17; *77 Sunset Strip* "The Snow Job Caper" 12-28; **1964** *Voyage to the Bottom of the Sea* "The Sky Is Falling" 10-19; **1965** *Bonanza* "The Brass Box" 9-26; *Fugitive* "Landscape with Running Figures" 11-23; **1966** *Felony Squad* "Between Two Fires" 11-21; *I*

Spy "Lisa" 12-7; **1967** *Bonanza* "The Prince" 4-2; **1968** *High Chaparral* "Bad Day for a Thirst" 2-18; **1974** *Cannon* "Daddy's Little Girl" 12-18; **1977** *Switch* "The Four Horsemen" 2-13; **1978** *Sword of Justice* "The Skyway Man" 10-19.

TELEFILMS

1976 *Helter Skelter* 4-1, 4-2 CBS; **1977** *The Girl Called Hatter Fox* 10-12 CBS.

Chill Wills

(born July 10, 1903, Seagoville, Texas; died December 15, 1978)

Named Chill because he was born on the hottest day ever recored in his birthplace, he began his acting career with a tent show in West Texas at age 12. He appeared in nearly every vaudeville theater throughout the midlands and south, and did two dozen plays with stock companies.

Moving to California, he was signed for films while doing a singing engagement at a popular nightclub. He made his screen debut in 1935, and eventually appeared in over 300 films. Movie roles included work in *Meet Me in St. Louis, Tulsa, The Sundowners*, an Academy Award Nominated role in *The Alamo, McClintock!* and *The Rounders*. Chill also provided the voice of Francis the Talking Mule in a half-dozen films.

He came to television in a 1958 *Alfred Hitchcock Presents* episode, and later became a regular on *Frontier Circus* (1961-62) and *The Rounders* (1966-67). Many of his TV roles were in western series, but his wonderful versatility made him effective in every role. He died of cancer in 1978; his gravely bass voice and familiar greeting of "Hey cousin" is surely missed by fans everywhere.

GUEST CREDITS

1959 *Trackdown* "The Samaritan" 2-18; *Texan* " 90 "Tomorrow" 3-7; **1962** *Gunsmoke* "Abe Blocker" 11-24; **1963** *Burke's Law* "Who Killed Cable Roberts?" 10-4; **1964** *Burke's Law* "Who Killed Avery "The Eyes of Captain Wylie" 2-23; **1960** *Playhouse*

Chill Wills (center), appears in a dual role in this 1966 episode of *The Rounders*, flanked by Ron Hayes (left) and Patrick Wayne. Inaddition to his series regular role, Wills plays Pack Saddle Charlie in "You Hold Your Temper, I'll Hold My Tongue" (ABC).

Lord?" 3-6; *Route 66* Where There's a Will, There's a Way" 3-6, 3-13; *Rawhide* "Incident at Deadhorse" 4-16, 4-23; **1965** *Burke's Law* "Who Killed the Toy Soldier?" 1-20; **1967** *Gunsmoke* "A Hat"10-16; *Judd, for the Defense* "Confessional" 2-16; **1968** *Tarzan* "End of a Challenge" 2-16; *Gunsmoke* "A Noose for Dobie Price" 3-4; **1970** *Night Gallery* "The Little Black Bag" 12-23; **1971** *Marcus Welby, M.D.* "Another Buckle for Wesley Hill" 1-5; *Men from Shiloh* "The Angus Killer" 2-10; **1972** *Alias Smith and Jones* "The Biggest Game in the West" 2-3; **1974** *Hec Ramsey* "Scar Tissue" 3-10; **1978** *Hallmark Hall of Fame* "Stubby Pringle's Christmas" 12-17.

TELEFILMS
1969 *The Over-the-Hill Gang* 10-7 ABC; **1970** *The Over-the-Hill Gang Rides Again* 11-17 ABC.

Ned Wilson

(died 1983)

A fine television supporting actor of the seventies, Ned's promising career was cut short by his death in 1983 (details unavailable).

GUEST CREDITS

1975 *Harry O* "Mayday" 10-23; *Joe Forrester* "Powder Blue" 11-18; *McMillan and Wife* "Secrets for Sale" 12-7; **1976** *Rookies* "Episode 83" 1-13; *Rockford Files* "A Portrait of Elizabeth" 1-23; *Switch* "Switch-Hitter" 12-7; *Police Story* "The Jar" 12-14, 12-21; *Rockford Files* "Piece Work" 12-17; *Delvecchio* "APB: Santa Claus" 12-26; **1977** *Bionic Woman* "Doomsday Is Tomorrow" 1-19, 1-26; *Police Woman* "The Killer Cowboys" 2-8; *Charlie's Angels* "The Vegas Connection" 2-9; *Kingston: Confidential* "Eight Columns Across the Top" 3-30; **1978** *Switch* "Dangerous Curves" 1-2; *Police Story* "A River of Promises" 1-14; **1981** *Trapper John, M.D.* "Creepy Time Gal" 1-4; *Greatest American Hero* episode 3-18; **1982** *Father Murphy* "Knights of the White Camelia" 2-2.

TELEFILMS

1976 *Eleanor and Franklin* 1-11, 1-12 ABC; *Richie Brockelman: Missing 24 Hours* 10-27 NBC; **1978** *A Question of Love* 11-26 NBC; **1979** *The Billion Dollar Threat* 4-15 ABC; *Salem's Lot* 11-17, 11-24 CBS; **1980** *Enola Gay* 11-23 NBC; **1981** *Jacqueline Bouvier Kennedy* 10-14 ABC; **1982** *Drop-Out Father* 9-27 CBS.

Edward Winter

(born Ventura, Calif.)

Educated at The University of Oregon, Edward had Broadway experience under his belt before his first televison exposure on two soaps: *The Secret Storm* (1969) and *Somerset* (1971). His first significant prime-time role was a series regular slot on a 1973 sitcom, *Adam's Rib*. In December of 1973 he

made the first of 7 hilarious visits to *M*A*S*H* as the goofy Colonel Flagg. During 1977 he became a regular on *The Feather and Father Gang*.

In the fall of 1978 he took the lead role in *Project UFO* during it's second season. During the eighties Ed had three additional series regular roles, on *Empire* (1984), *Hollywood Beat* (1985) and a syndicated version of *9 to 5* (1986-88).

Later eighties guest credits included *Finder of Lost Loves*, *Falcon Crest* (3), *Cagney and Lacey* (2), *Hotel*, *Law and Harry McGraw* and *Jake and the Fat Man*.

GUEST CREDITS

1973 *Mannix* "Climb a Deadly Mountain" 9-30; *New Perry Mason* "The Case of the Furious Father" 11-11; **1974** *Magician* "The Stainless Steel Lady" 1-28; *Marcus Welby, M.D.* "The Outrage" 10-8; **1975** *Barnaby Jones* "The Alpha Bravo War" 10-31; **1976** *Joe Forrester* "Fire Power" 1-6; *City of Angels* "Sudden Silence" 4-13; **1977** *Charlie's Angels* "Angel Baby" 11-16; *Barnaby Jones* "Shadow of Fear" 11-24; *Lou Grant* "Housewarming" 11-29; **1978** *Police Woman* "Sixth Sense" 2-8; *Salvage 1* "Golden Orbit" 3-12, 3-19; *Project UFO* "Sighting 4005: The Medicine Bow Incident" 3-26; **1979** *Little House on the Prairie* "The Odyssey" 3-19; *Lou Grant* "Influence" 9-17; **1980** *Trapper John, M.D.* "If You Can't Stand the Heat" 2-17; **1981** *Lou Grant* "Business" 3-23; *Dallas* "Little Boy Lost" 10-30; *Dallas* "Sweet Smell of Revenge" 11-6; *Greatest American Hero* "Classical Gas" 12-2; **1982** *Trapper John, M.D.* "Angel of Mercy" 1-17; *Magnum, P.I.* "Heal Thyself" 12-16; **1983** *Hart to Hart* "Pounding Harts" 1-18; *A-Team* "Holiday in the Hills" 3-15; *Simon and Simon* "The Skeleton Who Came Out of the Closet" 3-31; *Dynasty* "The Cabin" 4-20; *Dynasty* "The Arrest" 9-28; *Hardcastle and McCormick* "Killer B's" 11-6.

TELEFILMS

1974 *The Disappearance of Flight 412* 10-1 NBC; **1976** *Eleanor and Franklin* 1-11, 1-12 ABC; *The Invasion of Johnson County* 7-31 NBC; *The Feather and Father Gang: Never Con a Killer* 12-6 ABC; **1977** *The Girl in the Empty Grave* 9-20 NBC; *The Gathering* 12-4 ABC; **1979** *Rendevous Hotel* 7-11 CBS; **1980** *Mother and Daughter: The Loving War* 1-25 ABC; *Moviola: The Scarlett O'Hara War* 5-19 NBC; **1981** *Joe Dancer: The Big Black Pill* 1-29 NBC; *Fly Away Home* 9-18 ABC; **1982** *The First Time* 11-8 ABC.

Estelle Winwood

(born Estelle Goodwin, January 24, 1883, England;
died 1984)

A wonderful British character actress, Estelle
made a stage debut in 1899. She came to America in
1916, with her film debut in 1933. A true television
pioneer, she did an experimental TV production in
1940. Fifties television credits included *Lights Out,
Suspense, Kraft Theatre* (2), *Studio One* (2), *Robert
Montgomery Presents* (2), *Climax* (2), *Alfred
Hitchcock Presents* (2) and *Matinee Theater*.

Estelle worked regularly in guest roles throughout the sixties and seventies, including 4 episodes of
Batman and 2 appearances on *Love, American Style*.
She made her last television appearance at the age of
100.

GUEST CREDITS

1960 *Twilight Zone* "Long Live Walter
Jameson" 3-18; *Bourbon Street Beat* "Ferry to
Algiers" 6-6; *Adventures in Paradise* "A Penny a
Day" 4-24; *Thriller* "Dialogues with Death" 12-4;
1964 *Dr. Kildare* "The Last Leaves on the Tree" 10-
15; **1965** *Rogues* "Wherefore Art Thou, Harold?" 3-
21; *The FBI* "The Monster" 9-19; **1966** *Perry Mason*
"The Case of the Final Fade-Out" 5-22; *Man from*
UNCLE "The Her Master's Voice Affair" 4-11; *Girl
from UNCLE* "The Kooky Spooky Affair" 4-11;
1968 *Name of the Game* "The Taker" 10-4; **1969**
Outsider "The Secret of Marino Bay" 1-15; **1970**
Name of the Game "Island of Gold and Precious
Stones" 1-16; **1973** *Banyon* "Time Lapse"1-12;
Barnaby Jones "Murder in the Doll's House" 3-25;
1974 *Cannon* "The Sounds of Silence" 12-4; **1976**
Switch "One of Our Zeppelins Is Missing" 2-10;
Police Story "Monster Manor" 11-30; **1980** *Quincy,
M.E.* "Honor Thy Elders" 1-10.

Michael Witney

(born 1931; died 1983)

Briefly a regular during 1963 on *The Travels of
Jaimie McPheeters*, husky Michael Witney frequently appeared in action roles in his television
guest appearances, from 1965 to 1981. His abbreviated film career began in 1967 and he had a role in
Darling Lili.

Michael was married to famed British model
Twiggy.

GUEST CREDITS

1965 *Fugitive* "The Good Guys and the Bad
Guys" 12-14; **1966** *Tarzan* "A Pride of Assassins" 1-
27; *Tarzan* "The End of the River" 12-16; **1967** *12
O'Clock High* "The Hunters and the Hunted" 1-12;
1968 *Daniel Boone* "The Flaming Rocks" 2-1; *Star
Trek* "A Private Little War" 2-2; *Bonanza* "The
Stronghold" 5-26; **1969** *The FBI* "Moment of Truth"
3-30; *The FBI* "Gamble with Death" 10-19; *The FBI*
"Flight" 10-26; **1971** *Bonanza* "The Prisoners" 10-17;
1972 *Owen Marshall, Counselor at Law* "Libel Is a
Dirty Word" 9-28; *Sixth Sense* "I Did Not Mean to
Say Thee" 11-11; **1973** *Cannon* "The Dead Samari-
tan" 1-10; **1977** *Delvecchio* "Cancelled Contract" 3-
13; **1978** *Kojak* "Mouse" 1-21; *Charlie's Angels*
"Angel on My Mind" 11-22; **1980** *Charlie's Angels*
"Angel's Child" 1-9; **1981** *Charlie's Angels* "Let Our
Angel Live" 6-24.

TELEFILM

1972 *The Catcher* 6-2 NBC.

Kate Woodville

(born 1939, England)

Catherine "Kate" Woodville entered films in 1961 and spent 11 years doing TV guest roles and telefilms. She also did a stint on the soap *Days of Our Lives*.

Kate was married to noted actor Patrick MacNee (1922-).

GUEST CREDITS

1968 *Mission: Impossible* "The Spy" 1-7; **1968** *Star Trek* "For the World Is Hollow and I Have Touched Sky" 11-8; *Mannix* "A View of Nowhere" 12-14; **1970** *Bold Ones: The Doctors* "Dark is the Rainbow-Loud Is the Silence" 3-1; **1971** *Mannix* "What Happened to Sunday?" 1-9; *Psychiatrist* "The Private World of Martin Dalton" 2-10; **1974** *Kung Fu* "The Gunman" 1-3; *Harry O* "Guardian of the Gates" 9-26; **1975** *Kolckak: The Night Stalker* "Primal Scream" 1-17; *Rockford Files* "Say Goodbye to Jennifer" 2-7; **1976** *Rockford Files* "A Portrait of Elizabeth" 1-23; *Ellery Queen* "The Adventure of the Wary Witness" 1-25; **1978** *Little House on the Prairie* "The Man Inside" 10-2; **1979** *Wonder Woman*

"Amazon Hot Wax" 2-1; *Salvage 1* "Mermadon" 4-16.

TELEFILMS

1969 *Fear No Evil* 3-3 NBC; **1970** *The Aquarians* 10-24 NBC; **1974** *The Healers* 5-22

NBC; **1976** *Widow* 1-22 NBC; *The Lindbergh Kidnapping Case* 2-26 NBC; **1978** *Keefer* 3-16 ABC.

Cassie Yates

(born March 2, 1951, Macon, Georgia)

Perky Cassie Yates came to television in guest roles in 1975 and shortly thereafter became a regular on *Rich Man, Poor Man-Book II* (1976-77). After a another dozen guest shots she co-starred in an abbreviated sitcom, *Nobody's Perfect* (1980). She was also a regular on *Detective in the House* (1985).

Later eighties guest work included *Hotel* (2), *Fantasy Island*, *Simon and Simon*, *Murder, She Wrote* (2), *Magnum, P.I.* (2), *Finder of Lost Loves* and *Cagney and Lacey*. During 1987-88 she moved into a highly visible role on *Dynasty*.

GUEST CREDITS

1975 *Marcus Welby, M.D.* "The One Face in the Wind" 12-9; **1976** *Barnaby Jones* "Wipeout" 3-4; *Bionic Woman* "Bionic Beauty" 3-17; *City of Angels* "Say Goodbye to Yesteryear" 5-4; *Streets of San Francisco* "Castle of Fear" 11-11; *Delvecchio* "Red Is the Color of My True Love's Hair" 12-12; **1977** *Barnaby Jones* "Runaway to Terror" 5-5; *Rosetti and Ryan* "Everybody into the Pool" 11-3; *Baretta* "It Goes with the Job" 12-21; **1978** *Quincy, M.E.* "Speed Trap" 10-12; *Sword of Justice* "The Gemini Connection" 10-21; **1979** *Barnaby Jones* "A Short, Happy Life" 3-1; *B. J. and the Bear* "Never Give a Trucker an Even Break" 3-24; *Vegas* "Mixed Blessings" 10-3; *Quincy, M.E.* "Babes" 10-11; **1980** *Tenspeed and Brownshoe* "Savage Says: What Are Friends For?" 3-2; *Vegas* "Deadly Blessing" 12-10; **1981** *Quincy, M.E.* "The Golden Hours" 11-4; **1982** *Trapper John, M.D.* "Getting to Know You" 12-12; **1983** *Simon and Simon* "Betty Grable Flies Again" 12-8; *Knot's Landing* "Denials" 12-15.

TELEFILMS

1977 *Having Babies* 10-28 ABC; **1978** *Who'll Save Our Children?* 12-16 CBS; **1979** *The Seeding of Sarah Burns* 4-7 CBS; **1980** *Father Figure* 10-26 CBS; *Mark, I Love You* 12-10 CBS; **1981** *Of Mice and Men* 11-29 NBC; **1982** *The Gift* 3-16 CBS; **1983** *Listen to Your Heart* 1-4 CBS; *Agatha Christie's "A*

Caribbean Mystery" 10-22 CBS.

Dick York

(born September 4, 1928, Fort Wayne, Indiana; died February 27, 1992)

Dick York lost a lengthy battle with severe pain from a degenerative spinal condition, and emphysema, on February 27, 1992 The back ailment forced his retirement, in 1969, from his highly popular role as Darrin Stephens on *Bewitched*. His final years, aided by his wife Joan, were spent in tireless efforts toward acquiring food, money and clothing for the homeless.

He entered television in 1955 and had numerous roles on live dramas: *Playhouse 90* (4), *Kraft Theatre* (3), *Goodyear Playhouse, Kaiser Aluminum Hour* and *Philco Playhouse*. Dick was an especial favorite on Alfred Hitchcock productions, appearing in 7 of his shows durng 1957-63. *Going My Way* provided his first series regular role, during 1962-63.

Some of his fine dramatic work was forgotten by fans after his huge success on *Bewitched* (1964-69). Continuing syndicated reruns will keep his comedic and dramatic talents before us for many years to come.

GUEST CREDITS

1959 *Playhouse 90* "Made in Japan" 3-5; *Playhouse 90* "Out of the Dust" 5-21; *Alfred Hitchcock Presents* "The Dusty Drawer" 5-31; *Alfred Hitchcock Presents* "The Blessington Method" 11-15; **1960** *Twilight Zone* "The Purple Testament" 2-12; *Millionaire* "Millionaire Sandy Newell" 2-17; *Untouchables* "The White Slavers" 3-10; *Alcoa Theater* "The Glorious Fourth" 4-4; *Alfred Hitchcock Presents* "The Doubtful Doctor" 10-4; *Stageocach West* "Three Wise Men" 12-20; **1961** *Naked City* "Bullets Cost Too Much" 1-4; *Rawhide* "Incident of the Broken Word" 1-20; *June Allyson Show* "School of the Soldier" 1-30; *Twilight Zone* "A Penny for Your Thoughts" 2-3; *Americans* "The War Between the States" 5-1; *Frontier Circus* "The Shaggy Kings" 10-5; *Adventures in Paradise* "The Reluctant Hero" 10-8; *General Electric Theater* "A

Francine brought an enthuiastic quality to all her film and television roles. She made a television debut in 1961 on a sitcom, *Bringing Up Buddy*; there were numerous subsequent sitcom guest shots on shows like *Batman, Gomer Pyle, U.S.M.C., Hazel, Green Acres, I Dream of Jeannie, Bewitched* and *The Odd Couple*.

Slattery's People (1965) provided the only series regular role for Francine, but she had a lengthy stint on the soap *Days of Our Lives* during 1978. Later eighties guest work included *Masquerade, The Love Boat* and *Riptide*.

Dick York (right) is joined by *Bewitched* co-stars Elizabeth Montgomery (left) and Agnes Moorehead as they observe a bit of witchery. These players are deceased, but they have left a legacy of laughter to many generations as the 1964-72 ABC hit series continues to enjoy tremendous popularity in syndication.

GUEST CREDITS

Musket for Jessica" 10-8; *Wagon Train* "The Clementine Jones Story" 10-25; *Outlaws* "Night Riders" 11-2; *Dr. Kildare* "The Lonely Ones" 11-9; *Alfred Hitchcock Presents* "You Can't Be a Little Girl All Your Life" 11-21; **1962** *Thriller* "The Incredible Dr. Markesan" 2-26; *Wagon Train* "The Charlie Shutup Story" 3-7; *Alfred Hitchcock Presents* "The Twelve Hour Caper" 5-29; **1963** *Route 66* "What a Shining Young Man Was Our Gallant Lieutenant" 4-26; *Alfred Hitchcock Hour* "Terror at Northfield" 10-11; *Virginian* "Stopover in a Western Town" 11-27; *Rawhide* "Incident at Confidence Creek" 11-28; **1964** *Wagon Train* "The Michael Malone Story" 1-6; **1983** *Simon and Simon* "Too Much of a Good Thing" 12-1.

Francine York
(born August 26, 1938, Aurora, Minnesota)

1961 *Shirley Temple Theatre* "The Little Mermaid" 3-5; **1962** *Surfside 6* "Portrait of Nicole" 3-26; **1963** *Dick Powell Show* "Luxury Liner" 2-12; **1964** *Slattery's People* "Question: What Became of the White Tortilla?" 10-26; *Burke's Law* "Who Killed Super Sleuth?" 12-16; **1965** *Burke's Law* "Who Killed Rosie Sunset?" 1-27; *Burke's Law* "Who Killed the Rabbit's Husband?" 4-14; *Perry Mason* "The Case of the Wrongful Writ" 5-6; **1967** *Lost in Space* "The Colonists" 3-15; **1968** *Ironside* "Memory of an Ice Cream Stick" 1-11; *Land of the Giants* "Doomsday" 2-15; **1969** *Ironside* "Not with a Whimper, But a Bang" 4-10; **1971** *Mannix* "What Happened to Sunday?" 1-9; *Adam-12* "Log 88- Reason to Run" 4-1; **1972** *Adam-12* "Sub Station" 2-16; *Mission: Impossible* "Break!" 9-16; **1973** *Hec Ramsey* "Mystery of the Yellow Rose" 1-28; **1974** *Kojak* "Slay Ride" 10-13; *Streets of San Francisco* "Bird of Prey" 11-21; **1975** *Petrocelli* "The Sleep of Ransom" 1-15; *Columbo* "The Forgotten Lady" 9-14; *Barbary Coast* "An Iron Clad Plan" 10-31; **1976**

Petrocelli "Falling Star" 1-21; *Bert D'Angelo/Superstar* "Murder in Velvet" 2-21; *Quest* "Prairie Woman" 11-10.

TELEFILMS

1969 *Any Second Now* 2-11 NBC; *I Love a Mystery* 2-27 NBC; **1975** *The Adventures of the Queen* 2-14 CBS; **1976** *Time Travelers* 3-19 ABC; *Flood* 11-24 NBC.

Robert Yuro

(born August 1, 1932, New York City)

Following a 1959 New York stage debut, Robert came to films in 1962. One of Hollywood's busiest guest players from 1964 until 1977, Yuro was typecast early-on as a heavy and played dozens of killers, outlaws and underworld types.

Not a physical type, Bob imparted menace with a baleful glare and a carefully modulated voice that dripped with foreboding. He worked mainly in crime and adventure series but was also highly effective in westerns. In his early career, he played youthful servicemen in two episodes each of *Combat* and *12 O'Clock High*. A member of Quinn Martin's distinguished "stock company", Bob appeared in numerous QM Productions.

Bob has been happily married to actress Rosemary Forsyth for 25 years.

GUEST CREDITS

1964 *Combat* "A Gift of Hope" 12-1; **1965** *12 O'Clock High* "To Those Who Are About to Die" 1-1; *Fugitive* "The End Is But the Beginning" 1-12; **1966** *12 O'Clock High* "Which Way the Wind Blows" 1-24; *Laredo* "Meanwhile, Back at the Reservation" 2-10; *Fugitive* "The Chinese Sunset" 3-1; *Big Valley* "Hazard" 3-9; *Combat* "One at a Time" 3-22; *Laredo* "A Taste of Money" 4-28; **1967** *Laredo* "Scourge of Santa Rosa" 1-20; *Invaders* "the Watchers" 9-19; *Run for Your Life* "The Company of Scoundrels" 10-18; *Mannix* "Beyond the Shadow of a Dream" 11-4; *Virginian* "Paid in Full" 11-22; **1968** *The FBI* "The Messenger" 3-17; *High Chaparral* "A Joyful Noise" 3-24; *Bonanza* "Catch as Catch Can" 10-27; *Mod Squad* "Love" 12-10; **1969** *Mission: Impossible* "The System" 1-26; *The FBI* "Silent Partners" 10-12; *High*

Gunslinger Robert Yuro (left) is confronted by the bluster of Don Knotts in a 1968 Universal film, *The Shakiest Gun in the West*. In the ensuing duel, Yuro bites the dust, but not from Knotts' gun.

Chaparral "Bad Day for Bad Men" 10-17; **1970** *Silent Force* "Wax Jungle" 10-26; **1971** *The FBI* "Eye of the Needle" 1-24; *Mission: Impossible* "Underwater" 11-6; *Night Gallery* "The Diary" 11-10; **1972** *Sixth Sense* "The House That Cried Murder" 2-5; *The FBI* "The Engineer" 10-29; **1973** *Bonanza* "The Marriage of Theodora Duffy" 1-9; *Griff* "Hammerlock" 12-15; **1974** *The FBI* "The Betrayal" 2-3; *Mannix* "The Girl from Nowhere" 2-17; *Get Christie Love!* "Fatal Damage" 11-6; *Kolchak: The Night Stalker* "The Energy Eater" 12-13; **1975** *Streets of San Francisco* "Asylum" 2-20; *Caribe* "School for Killers" 4-7; *Bronk* "Open Contract" 9-21; **1976** *Rockford Files* "Joey Blue Eyes" 1-30; *Harry O* "Hostage" 2-19; **1977** *Barnaby Jones* "A Simple Case of Terror" 2-3; *Most Wanted* "The Tunnel Killer" 2-19; *CHiPs* "High Explosive" 12-9.

TELEFILMS

1970 *The Old Man Who Cried Wolf* 10-13 ABC; **1973** *Toma* 3-21 ABC; **1976** *The Keegans* 5-3 CBS.

Carmen Zapata
(born July 15, 1927, New York City)

Although Carmen Zapata had stage and film experience, she was primarily a seventies/eighties television character actress. She usually appeared as Mexican housekeepers or concerned Hispanic mothers. She was a regular on *The Man and the City* (1971-72) and *Hagen* (1980), and had a starring role on the 1976 sitcom *Viva Valdez*.

Carmen appeared as a regular on the daytime series for children, *Villa Alegre* (1974-79); it was made especially for Spanish-speaking pre-schoolers.

GUEST CREDITS

1970 *Marcus Welby, M.D.* "Daisy in the Shadows" 10-27; *Adam-12* "Log Fifty-Four-Missing Child"10-31; *Silent Force* "In by Nine, Out by Five" 11-23; **1971** *Bold Ones: The Doctors* "A Matter of Priorities" 1-3; *Storefront Lawyers* "First…We Get Rid of the Principal" 1-13; *McMillan and Wife* "Murder by the Barrel" 9-21; **1972** *Adam-12* "The Parole Violator"1-26; *Streets of San Francisco* "Hall of Mirrors" 11-4; *Owen Marshall, Counselor at Law* "Love Child" 11-9; **1973** *Mod Squad* "Death in High Places" 1-25; *Owen Marshall, Counselor at Law* "Sweet Harvest" 10-3; **1974** *Faraday and Company* "A Matter of Image" 1-9; *Kojak* "Hush Now or You'll Die" 9-22; *Nakia* "Pete" 12-21; **1975** *Streets of San Francisco* "False Witness" 1-9; *Kolckak: The Night Stalker* "Demon in Lace" 2-7;

Harry O "Elegy for a Cop" 2-27; *Archer* "Blood Money" 3-13; *Mannix* "Design for Dying" 3-23; **1976** *Blue Knight* "Mariachi" 2-11.

TELEFILMS

1972 *The Couple Takes a Wife* 12-5 ABC; **1973** *The Girls of Huntington House* 2-14 ABC; *My Darling Daughters' Anniversary* 11-7 ABC; **1975** *Winner Take All* 3-3 NBC; *A Home of Our Own* 10-19 CBS; **1976** *Shark Kill* 5-20 NBC; **1978** *Leave Yesterday Behind* 5-14 ABC; *Flying High* 8-28 CBS; **1979** *Like Normal People* 4-13 ABC; **1980** *Homeward Bound* 11-19 CBS; *Children of Divorce* 11-24 NBC; **1982** *Not Just Another Affair* 10-2 CBS.

SPECIAL OFFER

To say thank you for purchasing this book I'd like to make a special offer to you. You obviously enjoy reading and/or researching the wonderful actors of yesteryear. To enhance this enjoyment, I would like to extend to you a special purchase price on my first book *Television Guest Stars* which was published in 1993 by McFarland and Co., Inc.

Television Guest Stars chronicles 678 actors who guest starred in 15 or more TV dramatic series episodes between 1960 and 1979. This 598 page, library bound book includes 515 photographs, a bibliography and an index.

That book's list price is $75.00. However you may purchase it for $63.00 postpaid directly from me. Please send your check or money order to Lakeshore West Publishing Co., P.O. Box 314, Cleveland, OK 74020. Allow three to four weeks for shipping.

A few of the actors chronicled in *Television Guest Stars* are pictured below and on page 385.

Dabney Coleman

Ed Asner

Tom Bosley

Leslie Charleson

Mariette Hartley

Ricardo Montalban

Gavin MacLeod

Wayne Rogers

Telly Savalas

Robert Webber

I am touting my earlier book, *Television Guest Stars*, to you for two reasons. First, a couple of pages of space exists that otherwise would have been blank. Secondly, the publisher of that book has a moderate quantity of them in warehouse space and sales of the 1993 publication have slowed.

When I extend my modest author's discount to you, I receive no royalties. My reason for wanting you to have a discounted copy of *Television Guest Stars* is simply that unsold books are like lost children to an author. Their gathering dust in a warehouse defeats my purpose of providing enjoyment to as many readers as possible.

The publisher, McFarland and Company, Inc., sells primarily to the library trade and to customers who buy directly from their catalogs. They do not actively solicit sales to the general bookstore trade and many of you have never been exposed to that book unless you have seen it in a library.

I will extend the offer until: (1) McFarland's supplies are exhausted or (2) July 1, 1997, whichever comes first.

I am sure that you would be very pleased with the book, its appearance and contents. In addition to the actors pictured on pages 384 and 385, there are chronologies of 668 others. A sampling would include: R. G. Armstrong, Barbara Babcock, Ina Balin, Lloyd Bochner, Joseph Campanella, Anne Francis, Pat Hingle, Diana Hyland, BarBara Luna, Scott Marlowe, Strother Martin, Vera Miles, John Milford, Lois Nettleton, Albert Paulsen, Donnelly Rhodes, Peter Mark Richman, Madlyn Rhue, Tom Skerritt, John Vernon, Jessica Walter, Fritz Weaver and Anthony Zerbe. And there are dozens like Michael Baseleon, Don Eitner, John Lasell and William "Bill" Sargent who appeared in countless guest starring roles but labored in relative obscurity.

And there is a well-written foreward by Scott Marlowe. I am indebted to Scott for offering so many insights into the highs and lows and struggles an actor endures in a quest to continue working over decades. He is typical of so many actors; highly intelligent and totally dedicated to their craft. Our conversations were so enjoyable and covered so many fascinating subjects that it was several years before I ever got around to asking his non-stage name (Ronald DeLeo).

Having the opportunity to meet and talk to many actors has been a fringe benefit to the research necessary to do books on television performers. Almost without exception they have been candid and open and enthuiastic when they know their privacy won't be compromised by giving out phone numbers or addresses. The actors I've enjoyed knowing are just hard-working "supporting players"; some had their days in the sun, but are without the terrible ego problems and blind arrogance of so many of today's younger "stars".

End of editorial, end of story! If interested in the book offer you may follow the instructions on page 384. My thanks to you if you purchased the book you hold in your hands. If not a purchaser, thank you for reading it; if you enjoyed it, my efforts and mission are accomplished.

Jack Ward
June, 1996

Bibliography

Barabas, SuzAnne, and Gabor Barabas. *Gunsmoke: A Complete History*. Jefferson, N. C.: McFarland, N. C., 1990.

Brooks, Tim. *The Complete Directory to Prime Time TV Stars, 1946-Present*. New York: Ballantine, 1970.

Chapman, Peter. *The Players*. New York: Windsor Press, 1994.

Copeland, Mary Ann (contributing ed.). *Soap Opera History*. Lincolnwood, Ill.: Mallard Press, 1991.

Gianakos, Larry James. *Television Drama Series Programming, 1947-1959*. Metuchen, N. J.: Scarecrow Press, 1980.

Gianakos, Larry James. *Televison Drama Series Programming, 1959-1975*. Metuchen, N. J.: Scarecrow Press, 1978.

Gianakos, Larry James. *Television Dramas Series Programming, 1982-84*. Metuchen, N. J.: Scarecrow Press, 1987.

Inman, David. *The TV Encyclopedia*. New York: Putnam Publishing Group, 1991.

Jones, Ken D., Arthur F. McClure, and Alfred E. Twomey. *Character People*. Secaucus, N. J.: Citadel, 1976.

Kaplan, Mike (ed.). *Variety's Who's Who in Show Business*. New York: R.R. Bowker, 1989.

Lentz, Harris M., III. *Science Fiction, Horror and Fantasy Film and Television Credits, Vols. 1 and 2*. Jefferson, N. C.; McFarland, 1983.

Marill, Alvin H. *Movies Made for Television, 1964-84*. New York: Zeotrope, 1984.

Martindale, David. *Television Detective Shows of the 1970s*. Jefferson, N.C.: McFarland, 1991.

McNeil, Alex. *Total Television, 3rd Edition*. New York: Penguin, 1991.

Oliviero, Jeffrey. *Motion Picture Picture Players' Credits*. Jefferson, N.C.: McFarland, 1991.

Parrish, James Robert, and Vincent Terrace. *The Complete Actors' Television Credits, 1948-88, Vols. 1 and 2, 2nd Edition*. Metuchen, N.J.: Scarecrow Press, 1990.

Ragan, David. *Who's Who in Hollywood, 1900-76*. New Rochelle, N.Y.: Arlington House, 1977.

Robertson, Ed. *Maverick: Legend of the West*. Beverly Hills, Calif.: Pomegranate Press, 1994.

White, Patrick J. *The Complete Mission: Impossible Dossier*. New York: Avon, 1991.

PERIODICALS

TV Guide. Radnor, Pa.: Triangle Publications, 1960-1977.